The Life of
SENNA

D1428207

The biography of Ayrton Senna

Ayrton Senna was in many people's opinion the most brilliant Formula One driver who ever raced. His death on Sunday 1st May 1994 was as shocking as it was public. Over 200 million people watched him perish on television, and the knowing realised he was dead as soon as his car came to rest. In this first full account of the life of Ayrton Senna, the author and his collaborators examine each detail of the driving maestro's life – from his earliest days to his first race, his pole positions and his world championships, and finally his death and its aftermath. It is a story that has never been fully or properly told, and it is a story that needed to be told.

The Life of
SENNA

TOM RUBYTHON

FOREWORD BY GERHARD BERGER
PHOTOGRAPHY: KEITH SUTTON

The Life of Senna is published by:
BusinessF1 Books

A biography of Ayrton Senna written by Tom Rubython and
photographed by Keith Sutton.

Proof Edition first published on 1st January 2004
Hardback First Edition published on 1st May 2004
This Softback edition published on 14th October 2006

British Library Cataloguing-in-Publication Data
A CIP record for this book is available from the British Library.
ISBN 0-9546857-3-3
Copyright © 2006 Tom Rubython and Keith Sutton
First edition in softback
The text of this book is set in Bembo 11/14

Printed and bound in Germany by GGP Media GmbH
Additional Research by Caroline Reid and Ania Grzesik
Copy-editing by Paul Jones and Shelley White
Book design by Jo Maxwell
Softback production by Rowena Cremer-Price

BusinessF1 Books

a division of BusinessF1 Magazine
7 Mallow Street London England EC1Y 8RQ

Contents

Contents

Contents

Appendices

"If I ever happen to have an accident that eventually costs me my life, I hope it is in one go. I would not like to be in a wheelchair. I would not like to be in a hospital suffering from whatever injury it was. If I am going to live, I want to live fully. Very intensely, because I am an intense person. It would ruin my life if I had to live partially."

Ayrton Senna
Estoril, Portugal
January, 1994

Acknowledgements

Many individuals in London, Australia, Portugal and Brazil helped to research and write this book, and many asked for anonymity. In three cases, individuals agreed to provide answers through intermediaries. The Senna family had asked many individuals who were involved on the day he died not to comment about the experience and in all cases we respected this wish. Many working journalists gave us access to taped interviews recorded over the years. And we examined almost everything ever written about Ayrton Senna in press archives in London, São Paulo and Lisbon.

Insiders will know that *The Life of Senna* was planned as a book of some 400 pages and ended up being 600 pages, after we uncovered new material and spoke to more and more people. We felt obliged to include everything relevant about his life. By necessity the book is also nearly two years late, three times being postponed and finally fatefully ready on the 10th anniversary of Ayrton Senna's death.

The book started life when I edited *Formula 1 Magazine* after we all realised a short series of articles we had published justified something much worthier of the man who, in my opinion, was clearly the greatest Formula One driver who ever performed on the circuits. I am indebted to current and former colleagues who have helped in this production.

I would especially like to thank my close collaborators, Gerald Donaldson, David Tremayne, Caroline Reid, Peter Collins and Ania Grzesik for their help in researching the nuts and bolts of Ayrton Senna's remarkable life. Also the others whose help in individual chapters was invaluable and include: Josef Leberer, Ralph Firman, Dennis Rushen, Dick Bennetts, Martin Brundle, Peter Goodman, Alan Challis, Peter Warr, Gerhard Berger, the late Tony Rudd, Professor Sid Watkins, Jo Ramirez, Martin Donnelly, Nigel Mansell, Murray Walker, Eddie Baker and Andrew James. I thank Julian Jakobi for casting his eye over crucial chapters and Andrew Frankl for making sure everything was shipshape. The book would not have been possible without Keith Sutton throwing open his vast library of Senna images, especially from the early days. Also his staff for scrutinising proofs.

Rowena Cremer-Price and Jo Maxwell did a remarkable job in organising the production process. And Paul Jones and Shelley White were amazing as they edited every word and read it all again, twice. Luckily they were fans.

The efforts of all were unstinting, although the words that follow – and any errors or omissions – are naturally my responsibility alone.

My Friend and Team-mate
by Gerhard Berger

Ayrton Senna had a concentration level different from all of us. He could find in himself such a high concentration mode and nobody understood how he could do it.

During my three years with Ayrton at McLaren, I was thinking at night how was I going to beat this guy. Usually you always find a weakness in a team-mate and then I would work on this weakness, increase this weakness. But not with him. Ayrton Senna, my friend, was strong in qualifying, unbelievably quick in the racing – consistently quick in lapping, quick in the rain, quick on the quick circuits and quick on the street circuits. Every day I was racing I was thinking, 'Shit, how am I going to beat this guy'.

By nature, he was an extremely hardworking and ambitious fellow. That, and his extraordinary ability, perhaps made him unapproachable for many: a supernatural being whom one couldn't relate to. He taught me a lot about our sport; I taught him to laugh.

We had many great times together, especially at the end of the 1980s. I call them our 'James Bond years', which have formed the basis of one of the chapters of this book. Before the Brazilian Grand Prix, I sometimes went to spend a few days at his beach house in Angra, and in Europe he was sometimes on my boat as we sailed around the islands of Sardinia or Ibiza.

What happened on 1st May 1994 should never have happened. We could and should have done something about Tamburello. After all, we had had plenty of warning. When I had my big accident in 1989, in exactly the same place, before I went into the wall I remember thinking I was going to die. I was disabused of this a few moments later by Professor Sid Watkins, whose efforts to get a tube down my throat to assist my breathing hurt more than the accident.

Afterwards I said to Ayrton – and I remember my exact words – 'we have to change that terrible wall, it's too dangerous.' I wish we had. We certainly had opportunity. The following year after a test session at Imola, Ayrton and I walked to Tamburello. He looked behind the wall and saw there was a river, and he said to me: "Gerhard, we can't change it as there is a river behind it." We looked at each other and said okay, we cannot change it; and I said to Ayrton: "I know we can't do anything but someone is going to die at this corner." Sure enough, he died at exactly the place where we were standing and talking. River or no river, we should have done something.

I last saw him in Bologna hospital. I knew he was dying and there was no chance of him pulling through. Professor Watkins let me into his room for a few moments alone with him, for the last time. I spent a few minutes with him, and then that was that.

In this life you are a little prepared for death. In fact, during my career a lot of my team-mates and friends have died – Michele Alboreto, Elio de Angelis, Roland Ratzenberger, Manfred Winkelhock, Jo Gartner and so on. But of all of them, Ayrton was my closest friend and although it wasn't entirely unexpected, it really hurt.

Afterwards, actually getting back into a car was one of my hardest achievements in motorsport. The soul-searching was very difficult, especially when my daughter came and asked whether it was true that Ayrton was dead. It was tough, but all the drivers in 1994 had to face the same thing. Did we want to do this anymore? Was it crazy? It was a very emotional and difficult time.

My last real memory of Ayrton is of him turning around to smile at me on the grid, as the drivers' names were called out on the loudspeakers and the San Marino crowd cheered. It was the smile of a friend who was pleased to see the people's support and love for me. That is the last thing I remember of him.

Gerhard Berger
San Marino
Italy
Sunday 20th April 2003

Memories of Ayrton
by Keith Sutton

I officially became a pukka freelance photographer in 1980, at the age of 20, just as Ayrton Senna was doing the same thing in race cars. After three years covering motor races around England as a hobby, I took the plunge and would sink or swim on my talents.

Travelling around Europe and England, taking in as many races as I could, was a struggle. Then, at the start of 1981, luck came my way when I met Ayrton Senna da Silva by chance. I first saw Ayrton at Thruxton circuit in England on 8th March 1981. As fate would have it, I was there working for a Brazilian motorsport magazine that wanted photographs of Brazilian drivers racing in England. Otherwise I would probably have paid him no attention at all.

I was shy in those days so I never introduced myself. I just took lots of photographs of him in the paddock, on the track, everywhere. He must have wondered why this photographer he had never seen before was taking so many rolls of film of him at only his second outing in a race car. But I was just doing my job – taking photos of Brazilians. That day he finished third and I thought no more of it, apart from developing the photos and worrying about getting paid for them.

The following weekend I was at a loose end, so I took out a free British Rail promotion ticket I had been given and used it to travel to Brands Hatch circuit, where Ayrton was racing. Recalling it now, I am certain that I only went because of the free ticket and for no other reason. It was pure fate and my life was destined for a change of course. I have no idea what I was thinking of as I embarked on the eight-hour journey that day. The distance between my home in Manchester, in the north of England, and Brands Hatch, south of London, was some 230 miles.

When I arrived in the paddock it was a normal Brands Hatch Sunday, with the sloping paddock packed with transporters and loads of hopeful young drivers. The chances of not seeing someone you knew were very high. But almost as soon as I set foot in the paddock he was in front of me, out of nowhere, as if by magic. He instantly recognised me from Thruxton and came up to me. I have no idea if he had been planning to approach me or it was spontaneous. I never asked him. He had a reputation for being shy but he just marched up and said: "Are you a professional photographer?" They were his first words. There was no 'hello' or 'how are you?', just straight down to business in his very poor English. "Yes, of course," I replied.

"Well, I need photographs, can you help me out?"

"Yes, of course."

"I need the photographs to send to Brazil on a regular basis."

"Yes, of course", I repeated for the third time.

And that was it. From that day on for over three years, I was effectively his personal photographer. Although it seemed perfectly normal at the time, in a few moments, an obscure Brazilian Formula Ford driver had acquired a personal photographer – a luxury even today's Formula One drivers do not have. I am not sure why I agreed but he was special and I guess I sensed that.

That day he went on to win his heat, and win the race. It was very exciting and I was there on the podium to capture the moment. It was late evening, the light was fantastic and I took some memorable black-and-white photographs of him with his then wife Liliane.

It was the start of my relationship with Ayrton. I carried on working with him and taking photographs. I effectively became his PR man as well. I wrote his press releases and answered his fan mail for years. I suggested to him that we send photographs and press releases after each race to all the magazines around the world and the Formula One team managers such as Ron Dennis, Bernie Ecclestone and Ken Tyrrell, letting them know about Ayrton's performances. Headed notepaper was organised for him, with his helmet in full colour, and the bottom of the paper proudly stated: 'For further information, contact Keith Sutton, 17 Ashfield Road, Cheadle, Cheshire'.

I wasn't a journalist or a writer, I just wanted to help him because I saw the talent and thought by helping him it would help me. Occasionally he sent me a cheque for £100 for my troubles. I think it covered the postage and my petrol.

I was only nine months older than him and we both had the same ambitions, although in totally different directions. He wanted to be the best driver in Formula One and I wanted to be the best photographer. We both knew it would take time, so we followed the same apprenticeship. As he competed in Formula Ford 1600, Formula Ford 2000 and Formula Three, I photographed him, moving up the various formulas in tandem until we both arrived in Formula One in 1984.

We used to discuss everything from God to girls. I laugh today when people whisper to me that Ayrton didn't really like girls and that he was gay. I know better. It brings back the days when we travelled to the European races and I shared a room with him and we talked non-stop. Many a time he would quietly ask me if I would go and share a room with his mechanic for the night because he had met a Danish girl or Dutch girl or French girl and wanted to entertain her.

I remember on a return flight to England when he told me he had split up with his wife Liliane, and met another Brazilian girl who was studying in Brussels, Belgium, who he wanted to be with. Many things he told me about his life I can never repeat – they were intimate moments and he trusted me.

At his first Grand Prix, he invited me to Brazil with Toleman and took care of the airfare and my hotel room on Copacabana beach. I couldn't believe it. We had finally got there. He was so happy to go to Brazil, his home country, and I had always wanted to visit after hearing so much about it from him.

I had a great time there but it also marked the moment we went our separate ways. We had both achieved our first ambition: to get to the arena. And then his focused and selfish side, which we would see so many times in the years ahead, came out. He wanted me to end my business and work for him full-time as his personal, private and exclusive photographer. He knew where he was going but so did I. I told him I wanted to form my own agency and couldn't achieve my ambition of becoming Formula One's top photographer just working for him. He understood and accepted my decision, but from that moment on we were never close again. He was such a focused man and emotionless about his work. He just moved on to the next thing and the next photographer.

As I stand photographing the cars at the Imola circuit and remember back to that tragic weekend on Sunday 1st May 1994 the memories start flooding back and I remember the great times we spent together in the early days and what a huge influence he had on so many lives, including my own.

When he won the world championship in 1988, I had never seen him so thrilled, happy and emotional, and we exchanged glances and a few knowing words. I knew what it had taken in the early grinding years of racing round Britain, every weekend in the freezing cold circuits, the sacrifice of his marriage and friends, to get to that point. And as he looked into my eyes, I knew that he knew I knew.

Keith Sutton
Imola Circuit
San Marino, Italy
20th April 2003

A Chance of Fate

But for a simple row of tyres

The basic facts are clear. On Sunday 1st May 1994, Ayrton Senna was leading the San Marino Grand Prix when suddenly his car veered inexplicably off the track at Tamburello curve. His Williams Renault crossed over both the grass and concrete run-off strips before finally impacting the concrete wall. It killed him. It is known for certain that a piece of the Williams' front suspension broke off during the impact with the wall and flew like a bullet to Senna's forehead; it impacted and broke through his helmet, forcing his head back against the car's carbon-fibre backrest and causing multiple fractures to the back of his skull. The piece of suspension was never officially identified.

Italian law necessitated an official investigation into the cause of Senna's fatal crash. The legal system came to a conclusion that simply wasn't credible and the world waited for a proper explanation, but never got one.

This book covers all the possibilities and has its own theories as everyone did. But in reality the theories and explanations are all wrong and in honesty not even relevant. The reason he died was clear: the solid concrete wall was not protected by a tyre wall, as it indisputably should have been. And why it wasn't is one of life's unanswered mysteries.

Ironically, on 9th March 1994, Ayrton Senna was in a position to save his own life. Barely two months before he met his end, at the same place, he stood at the apex of Tamburello corner with Imola circuit director Giorgio Poggi discussing the safety of Tamburello.

Poggi adored Senna and would have done anything he asked. But all Senna wanted was a bump smoothing out that had caused him some trouble in testing. As fate would have it, the two men were filmed by an amateur photographer, and the videotape appeared four years later in the trial of the people the Italian authorities believed were responsible for Senna's death.

The gaping deficiency at Tamburello bend was the lack of tyre wall protection. Whilst Senna and Poggi discussed bumps in the track, they missed the big picture. Senna merely had to say to Poggi: 'Put me a row of tyres along that wall will you Giorgio' and it would have been done. Two or three rows, if he had asked. But he didn't. In that way he was responsible for his own death. He had the means to prevent it.

He also realised, while testing that same day, that he had got it wrong on driver aids. He had campaigned vigorously for a ban on electronic driver aids, such as traction control and active suspension, mainly because his McLaren team, at the time, didn't have them and its main opponent Williams did. Ironically, they were banned the year he arrived at Williams. Stripped of its driver aids, the new Williams was a very difficult car to control.

In fact Senna disliked the new breed of car from the start, and by the time he reached Brazil he was extremely worried. Presaging something terrible, he warned: "The cars are very fast and difficult to drive. It's going to be a season with a lot of accidents and I'll risk saying we'll be lucky if something really serious doesn't happen." As Gerd Kremer of Mercedes-Benz, Senna's close friend, recalls: "The last time I saw Ayrton was in Brazil, at the Grand Prix. It was his birthday and he told me that he was worried. He was afraid something would happen to him. He was frightened for the young drivers, and that there was nothing he could do if something went wrong with his car."

His words were prophetic – by the end of the season, two drivers were dead and one disabled.

Whatever other reasons there were for Senna's death that day – the track, the car, his own driving skills (and no one really knows to this day) – he sealed his fate by not asking for a tyre wall. So when the inevitable loss of control happened, he was unprotected. Ironically, the Friday before the race, Rubens Barrichello's life was saved by tyres when he flew off the circuit and plunged into them. They dissipated the forces of the accident and he miraculously survived intact. No one has ever been able to invent a better way of absorbing impact than used tyres tied together in multiple rows. If a tyre wall is damaged by an accident no more racing is allowed until the tyres are repaired.

Now, Tamburello bend is smothered in tyres, three rows of them. Drivers going off, however fast, will bounce into them and walk away. And tyre protection has mushroomed at every track in the world, saving drivers from death or serious injury every day of the year. But Ayrton Senna had to die to save them.

The FIA insists on three rows of tyres at every danger spot. Two drivers lives have been saved by tyres in living memory, Michael Schumacher at Silverstone in 1999 and Luciano Burti at Spa Francorchamps in 2001.

And that is the deep irony of Ayrton Senna's death: he has saved many other lives since in all categories of racing. So many drivers now hit soft, absorbing rubber than cold, unforgiving, solid concrete. And that is all down to Senna. It is his real legacy to international motor racing.

He has also doubled the popularity of Formula One. And the effect of the publicity and drama that surrounded his death, and the money his memory has raised, have made literally thousands of poor homeless children in São Paulo happy, housed and fed again.

So much good has come out of his death that it begs the question: did it happen for a very good reason? Senna believed in God, not through the often-hypocritical church-going or public displays, but the basic believing. His death, at a similar age as Princess Diana when she died, had a reason and a meaning. He will always be remembered for what he was at that point; he will always be a legend; and his legacy will endure for many hundreds of years.

And before that, he had a life of such pleasure to enjoy, and which he did enjoy, that he would have seen the value he got from God in his life.

Tom Rubython
London
England
28th November 2003

CHAPTER 1

Life: 2:17pm
Sunday 1st May 1994

Thursday 7am to Sunday 2:17pm

Thursday 28th April 1994 was destined to be a busy day for Ayrton Senna. He woke in his villa in Quinta do Lago in the Portuguese Algarve as usual and went for an early morning run around the sand dunes and golf greens. His Portuguese housekeeper, Juraci, was already up doing errands and fussing around him. He hated leaving his Portuguese home. The four-bedroomed, white-walled villa sat in its own grounds set in a dream resort of around 2,000 acres. With golf courses and lakes on one side and a beach on the other, this paradise was still a well-kept secret as far as Senna was concerned. Only people who had been there understood the unique atmosphere and climate. The resort had a five-star hotel, four championship golf courses and many top restaurants and a nightclub.

But most of all Quinta do Lago gave him the anonymity he craved.

The people also spoke his language, Portuguese. It was the only place in the world outside Brazil that he felt at home. André Jordan, the developer of Quinta do Lago, had employed Brazilian architect Júlio Neves to design much of the infrastructure. And over the European winter, when he had been in Brazil, the house was remodelled and redecorated. In 1994, for the first time, he planned to spend the entire European season in Portugal and not return to Brazil at all.

His one servant was Juraci, who was in permanent residence. Her duties were to cook, clean and chauffeur and she did them all admirably.

In fact Senna felt good every time he drove past the rainbow-coloured 'Q' logo statue that rotated slowly inside a fountain at the main entrance to the complex. He felt he was entering a unique environment where nature was in complete harmony with his design for living a Brazilian lifestyle in Europe. His garden was a breathtaking vista of exotic, tropical plants – palms and banana trees, giant hibiscus, vivid yellow mimosa, whole walls of bougainvillea, orange, lemon and avocado trees. The area, legally protected since 1987, was a unique natural habitat for more than 200 resident or migratory birds, including a number of rare and endangered species. The lakes were a rich repository for shellfish and other marine life.

When he wanted he could jet-ski or windsurf on the lakes and run for hours along the nature trails. It made his fitness regime more bearable in the wonderful climate and beautiful surroundings. And when he needed a social life he went to the golf club, where the locals and residents knew him but, more importantly, knew not to bother him. At the restaurants and nightclubs on the complex, the same rules applied. And he regarded the security firm that looked after the site as his own personal one. It was so effective that petty crime in Quinta do Lago was virtually non-existent.

And things were about to get even better. On Saturday afternoon his girlfriend, Adriane Galisteu, a 21-year-old model, was arriving to join him for the whole of the European summer. It had been a month since she had seen him off at the airport in São Paulo, when he left to start his challenge for the 1994 world championship. They had been together for 14 months and she was everything he liked in a woman, good-looking but ethereal rather than beautiful, blonde, small-breasted and long legged but not too tall and with no attitude. In fact her naiveness was refreshing and their sex life was stimulating and compatible. She was also intelligent in an unobvious way, with a perception of things that weren't always clear. She understood the things that mattered. He was really looking forward to Sunday evening, when he would return from Italy and they would be reunited.

He packed a small overnight bag himself for the three nights he was going to spend in a hotel in San Pietro near Bologna, whilst competing in the San Marino Grand Prix. There were no formal dinners or commitments that weekend, so his clothing needs were minimal. As he packed he remarked to Juraci that life couldn't get any better than it was that bright sunny morning in the Algarve. But he was always saying that to the people around him, reminding them all, and not least himself, how lucky they all were to be sharing the life Formula One had given him.

But there was a small irritation in his life that glorious morning. His brother, Leonardo, was staying until Sunday and would be coming with him to Imola. Leonardo was on a mission from his family to try and persuade him to give up Adriane. For all sorts of reasons the family, with the exception of his mother Neyde, who loved what he loved, detested Adriane. They regarded her as little better than a peasant girl, and not good enough for their son, the hero of Brazil. The truth was that it was none of their business, and Senna loved the girl and would probably ask her to marry him when this summer was over. But this family was tight, very tight, and usually everything was everyone's business within a circle of six people – Milton his father, his mother, his sister Viviane, his brother and his sister's husband. Adriane's arrival marked the start of a long period living together when he would not return to Brazil for six months, something he had never done before. This decision had precipitated a family feud, and Leonardo had been dispatched to try and change Ayrton's mind. Over that week, it had led to some rare harsh words between Senna and Leonardo. But Senna would not be moved. He was staying put for the summer, even if it meant seeing far less of them, especially Leonardo, as he knew his brother would not return to Portugal whilst Adriane was around.

Senna spent his time between two tight groups: his family, with whom he congregated in Brazil; and his private circle of friends, which was just as tight as his family group, and with whom he spent time in Europe. Adriane was part of this group which consisted of around a dozen people headed by Antonio Braga, a wealthy Brazilian who also divided his time between Brazil and Portugal. The second group had embraced Adriane, unlike his family, and many would hang around with him at races. He liked having them around. The upcoming race at Imola would be no different.

The family dispute had annoyed him, as it meant that Adriane could not join him at Imola for the weekend when Leonardo was around. If she did there was a danger of a public row and Ayrton Senna did not wash his private family linen in public.

After his run Juraci prepared a light breakfast for him and Leonardo, who was returning to Brazil after the San Marino Grand Prix. She then delivered them to Faro airport, where Captain Owen O'Mahoney was waiting in Senna's own BAe HS125 jet to fly them to Munich for a morning meeting with executives from Audi. Senna had been negotiating to take over the Audi franchise in Brazil. This was a meeting to finalise the terms. A few hours after landing they were ready to take off again this time for Forli airport near Bologna. From Forli the brothers would go by helicopter to Padua and the Carraro bicycle factory. Senna had a new deal with Carraro to manufacture a carbon-fibre bicycle called the Senna that would carry his famous double 'S' logo. It had been planned for some time and was one of many new products under the famous 'double S' Senna brand . He was also to import the Carraro bicycles into Brazil. Annoyingly, the argument about Adriane continued on the aeroplane. As Leonardo got older, he seemed to get more fractious and emotional about things. Senna could not understand why his family was so upset.

After arriving at the factory to formally sign the contract, he would go on to the Sheraton Padova Hotel on the highway from Milan to Venice.

At around 4 o'clock he arrived in Padua and landed his helicopter in the grounds of the Carraro Industria factory. After signing the contract he went with Giovanni Carraro to the hotel for a press conference. It was part of the start of a new life for him as an entrepreneur when he retired from racing. He wanted to talk about it but there were hardly any journalists he recognised at the press conference and naturally all they wanted to talk about was motor racing, not bicycles. Senna told the press conference: "The world championship is just beginning for me in Imola, with a handicap of two races."

Even though the journalists present were not Formula One veterans, they were enthusiastic Italians and wanted to ask him questions about Benetton's supposed traction control. Senna was surprised about their depth of knowledge. He said: "I really can't say much about it," and then said, in a way that revealed both very little and yet a lot: "It's difficult to talk about things one cannot prove."

At around 5:30pm he left the Carraro factory and flew to the Imola circuit. On the way he collected Mike Vogt, marketing director of TAG Heuer. Senna and Vogt, who knew each other from his McLaren days, discussed a new Senna watch the company was developing. Even though Senna had left the McLaren family, of which TAG Heuer was a part, Vogt still wanted to do business with him. He knew he could sell plenty of Senna watches at $2,000 apiece.

At six o'clock the helicopter landed on the infield at Imola. Senna wanted to show his face to the team on the Thursday, when the cars did not run. He also wanted to see the results of a whole programme of aerodynamic modifications that had been planned from the last test session the week before in France. He checked in with his engineer, David Brown, and chatted to Williams' marketing chief Richard West about how the Carraro launch had gone, before getting back into the helicopter for the short flight to Castello, a typically Italian hotel in Castel San Pietro, a spa town about 10 kilometres west of Imola.

The hotel was run by Valentino Tosoni, whom Senna had known since he first started staying there with McLaren in 1988. It was the McLaren team hotel and 1994 was his first year there without McLaren. But he had still booked the same room he occupied every year – room 200, a small suite. Interestingly, Frank Williams was staying in the suite directly below him and Ron Dennis in the one directly above.

That weekend there were seven male friends and colleagues staying with him at Imola, a popular race on the calendar. His brother, Leonardo, Julian Jakobi, his manager, his close friend and neighbour in Portugal, Antonio Braga, Galvao Bueno from TV Globo, Celso Lemos, managing director of the Senna brand licensing company in Brazil, Josef Leberer, his personal physio, and Ubirajara Guimaraes, head of his new import company.

Soon after he checked in Leberer arrived to give him his regular massage.

That evening they all dined together in the hotel. Senna was back in his suite just after 10 o'clock. He picked up the phone and dialled his apartment in São Paulo, where it was just after seven o'clock, to speak to his girlfriend, Adriane. She was packing to prepare to fly out to Portugal the following day and couldn't disguise her excitement on the telephone.

In the morning Senna caught a helicopter to the circuit at 8:30am, ready for the start of practice and qualifying. In-between Japan and Imola, Williams had been testing intensively at the Nogaro circuit in south-west France to find the source of the Williams car's problems. A number of changes were promised for Imola but Senna was sceptical that the modifications would work. The car had been consistently slower than the Benetton despite a much more powerful engine. Both Senna and his team-mate Damon Hill had said openly it was horrible to drive. Hill remembers: "We were always changing the set-up of the car in an attempt to find that perfect combination which would turn the promise of a great car into a reality. But it is difficult to become familiar with a car if it is constantly being changed – it becomes a vicious circle."

It was clear from the difference in Senna's and Hill's times that Senna was driving through the problems. As Hill admits: "Ayrton had enormous reserves of ability and could overcome deficiencies in a chassis."

At just after 9:30am Senna climbed into his car and completed 22 laps, posting a fastest time of 1m 21.598secs, more than a second quicker than his team-mate. Hill was pleasantly surprised by the behaviour of the modified chassis. Senna was not. He thought the team was going in the wrong direction with the car and spent a lot of time with David Brown afterwards.

At 1pm, the first qualifying session began and Senna was soon fastest. But 15 minutes into the start of the session the Jordan of Rubens Barrichello hit the kerb in the middle of the 140mph Variante Bassa chicane. It flew through the air, hitting the tyre barrier before smashing against a debris fence. The crash was horribly violent but the tyres had taken some of the pace out of it as Barrichello bounced around upside down. He put his hands over his helmet and waited for the car to stop. He ended up suspended unconscious in the car. Immediately after the accident nobody dared to believe that he had got away with just a broken nose and bruised ribs.

Senna did not see the accident but Betise Assumpcao, his PR chief, went off to investigate Barrichello's condition. Senna got out of his car and went straight to the medical centre. Finding his way barred he went in through the back and climbed over a fence. Barrichello regained consciousness minutes after the accident and found Senna looking over him. He told Barrichello: "Stay calm. It will be all right." As Barrichello remembers: "The first face I saw was Ayrton's. He had tears in his eyes. I had never seen that with Ayrton before. I just had the impression he felt as if my accident was like one of his own." He shed a few tears, the first of many that weekend.

Once he made sure Barrichello was all right he returned to his cockpit and was back on track at 1:40pm when the qualifying session resumed. Senna bettered his time immediately and just before the close set what was to prove the quickest time of the weekend: a 1m 21.548secs lap at an average of 138.2mph.

In the emotional aftermath of Barrichello's accident, it was a repeat performance of what happened in 1990 when Martin Donnelly crashed. Senna was the only driver to stop at the scene of the enormous accident at the 1990 Spanish Grand Prix when Donnelly's Lotus car disintegrated against the barriers. After that accident he had gone faster than ever, and won yet another, his fiftieth, pole position, but he found such bravery came at an emotional price, as he said: "As a racing driver there are some things you have to go through, to cope with. Sometimes they are not human, yet you go through it. Some of the things are not pleasant but in order to have some of the nice things you have to face them. You leave a lot of things behind when you follow a passion." As one observer put it: "It was an emphatic reminder of Senna's supreme skill and courage."

Damon Hill remembers the shock of Barrichello's accident: "What shook us most was the rate at which the car took off; at one stage it looked as if it was going to smash through the fence and fly into the grandstand. The Jordan, more by luck than anything else, finished on its side, upside down and against the barrier. That was bad enough but the marshals promptly tipped the car over and, as it crashed on to its bottom, could see Barrichello's head thrashing around in the cockpit."

Hill continued: "I was astonished that the marshals did that, particularly in view of the neck and spinal injuries received by JJ Lehto and Jean Alesi during test sessions earlier in the year. Barrichello could have sustained similar injuries. He should have been left as he was or, if there was a risk of fire, then at least the car should have been put down gently."

At the end of the session Senna climbed out of the car and left the pit garage for the motorhome to do some prearranged press interviews. As he walked a few fans shouted to him from the Paddock Club balcony above the Williams transporter. They said: "Now's your chance to show Schumacher who's the champion." He acknowledged them but didn't stop.

Inside the motorhome he greeted the waiting journalists but told them there was a problem with his car and he needed an hour with David Brown. They agreed to wait. In with Brown, Senna produced the usual two-page hand-written A4 list of jobs he believed needed doing on the car. For all the speed, he was clearly not happy with it.

An hour later he joined the journalists and briefed them on the business interests he was building for when he retired. Shadowing him for the weekend was Mark Fogarty of the new *Carweek* magazine, who also had a photographer inside the Williams pit. He said afterwards that Senna was not focused at all: "Usually if Senna agreed to do an interview, he would give it his full attention. This time he just wasn't focused. His answers were halting and he looked glazed, as if he was mentally worn out." When RTL reporter Kai Ebel asked him about Rubens Barrichello he began a sentence three times, but kept losing the thread of his thoughts. He then ominously changed the subject and told the journalists that Imola was a dangerous circuit, that there were a few places that were 'not right as far as safety is concerned'. They asked him why the drivers hadn't done anything about it and he told them: "I am the only world champion left – and I have opened my big mouth too often. Over the years I have learnt that it's better to keep my head down."

His pilot Owen O'Mahoney was also surprised at some of his actions over the weekend. He had often pestered Senna for some signed photos of the two of them together but he had never got around to it. So he was very surprised when Senna called him over as he passed by the Williams garage, fished them out of his briefcase and signed them for him. O'Mahoney says: "The odd thing was that he gave them to me in the middle of practice. It was so out of character for him to think about anything other than racing. It was almost as if he wanted to tie up loose ends."

When the journalists left it was down to work with Brown again and they were together for two hours. It was eight o'clock by the time he left the circuit and returned to San Pietro. Again Josef Leberer arrived in his suite for the regular massage. The two men were great friends and chatted about Barrichello's accident. Senna told him he thought Barrichello was very fortunate not to have more serious injuries. Leberer found Senna more distressed about it than he would have expected.

That night he dined with his brother and friends at the Trattoria Romagnola restaurant but was interrupted throughout by autograph seekers once word got out he was there, albeit in a private alcove at the back.

Afterwards he walked quickly back to the hotel to telephone Adriane before she got on the Varig flight to Lisbon that night. He told her: "I can't wait for you to get here." Adriane said later they had a long discussion about their relationship and she told him she was no longer scared of being his girlfriend, as she had been at the start. Then, according to her, he burst into tears and started recounting the details of Barrichello's accident. She says: "Can you imagine what it is like to receive a phone call from Ayrton Senna when he bursts into tears?" She said the call showed his despair at what had happened. She said of the moment: "I felt absolute panic and kept asking him what happened, what happened." In the end she had to break off the call in order to catch her flight.

The next morning he followed the same routine and at 9:30am was on the track in unofficial practice completing 19 laps, this time with a best of 1m 22.03secs. Both he and Hill agreed the car had been much improved overnight and Senna's work the previous day had paid some dividends.

Soon after the first unofficial practice Rubens Barrichello arrived back at the track from Maggiore hospital, where he had been kept overnight for observation. His front teeth were chipped, his lips cut, his broken nose swollen and his right arm bandaged. He told Senna he was flying back home to England and would watch the race on television. His weekend was over but he told journalists he would be back for the next Grand Prix in Monaco in a fortnight.

At one o'clock the second qualifying session began. In the early minutes

Hill increased his time and dragged the car up to fourth on the grid.

At 1:18pm Formula One's good safety record ran out after eight years. Austrian driver Roland Ratzenberger was competing in his second ever Formula One race for the hopeless Simtek team, which relied on rent-a-drivers to survive. He crashed heavily after his car lost its steering and took off at 314.9kph when the front wing became partially detached. The Simtek car slammed into a concrete retaining wall on the inside of the Villeneuve curve before being thrown back into the middle of the track.

TV cameras caught Ratzenberger's head slumped lifeless on the side of the cockpit. Viewers could clearly see he was unconscious. Bernie Ecclestone was sitting in his motorhome chatting to Lotus team principal Peter Collins when the accident happened. He turned to Collins and said: "This looks bad." Ecclestone grabbed his walkie-talkie and headed off as Collins went back to his garage.

Senna had watched replays of the accident on the monitor in the Williams pit garage. He knew it was bad. He rushed into the pitlane, grabbed a course car and told the driver to take him to the scene of the accident. They drove down past the Tamburello bend to the scene.

Unlike Senna, Hill was on the track when the accident happened and ran past the wrecked car and the debris. He also realised it was bad, as he said: "I could see where the debris had started and, judging by the distance travelled, it was obvious it had been a very big accident. As I went by, I had a strong sense of foreboding about his condition because there was so much destruction. With Barrichello we had been lucky. This time it was clear that poor Roland was not going to be let off so lightly."

The medical team of Professor Sid Watkins, the FIA's medical director, was at the accident 25 seconds after it happened. They cradled Ratzenberger's limp head in their hands and frantically cut his chin strap to remove his helmet. But he was already clinically dead, having suffered massive head injuries. When Watkins arrived he glanced at the driver's pupils and realised the situation was grave. He ordered his men to extricate him and try resuscitation. They were successful in getting his heart going, an ambulance arrived seven minutes later and he was quickly taken to the medical centre before going on to Bologna's Maggiore Hospital by helicopter. The resuscitation team managed to keep his heart beating long enough to get him to the hospital but he was gone.

By the time Senna arrived at the accident scene Ratzenberger was gone in the ambulance so he inspected the wrecked Simtek car. He then got the driver to take him back to the pitlane and immediately marched off to the medical centre for the second time in two days. He went thorough the same scenario – he was not allowed to enter the front way so jumped over the fence at the back. He found Sid Watkins, who took him outside and told him Ratzenberger was clinically dead. Senna was devastated. Watkins said: "Ayrton broke down and cried on my shoulder." The two men were extraordinarily close and Watkins regarded him as family. He realised then that Senna had not been in close proximity to a death before. Watkins was one of Britain's most famous surgeons and was used to it but he was still deeply upset.

Watkins said to him as he was crying on his arm: "Ayrton, why don't you withdraw from racing tomorrow? I don't think you should do it. In fact why don't you give it up altogether? What else do you need to do? You have been world champion three times, you are obviously the quickest driver. Give it up and let's go fishing."

Watkins recalls Senna's response in his book *Life at the Limit*: "Sid there are certain things over which we have no control. I cannot quit. I have to go on." Watkins recalls that those were the last words he ever spoke to him. On his way out Martin Whitaker, then press officer of the FIA, brushed past him. He says: "I asked Senna if he knew what had happened. He didn't reply. He just looked at me and walked away but I won't forget that look."

After leaving the medical centre Senna went straight to the Williams pit garage and signalled to Damon Hill and Patrick Head to join him. He told them Ratzenberger was dead. He said: "From what I witnessed there is no doubt about it." Frank Williams asked him to carry on qualifying but he refused. Afterwards Williams said he had asked him 'more as a matter of form than expectation'.

Then Senna went into the transporter to change out of his racing over-alls. Hill could not decide whether to go out again or not. In the end the decision was made for him by Williams – the team withdrew from the rest of qualifying.

Michael Schumacher was also deeply affected and JJ Lehto was crying. He said: "I drove up here with Roland from Monaco." Heinz-Harald Frentzen, who raced with Ratzenberger in Japan, went straight back to his hotel and said: "I don't want to talk to anyone."

Fifty-seven minutes after the accident, at 2:15pm, Ratzenberger's death was announced at the circuit, although everyone in the paddock already knew. It was the first fatality at an actual Grand Prix since Riccardo Paletti was killed at the Canadian Grand Prix in Montreal in 1982. The last Formula One driver to die had been Elio de Angelis in 1986 during private testing.

After changing out of his overalls, Senna ran the few yards from the transporter to the Williams motorhome, where he found Damon Hill and his wife Georgie with Betise Assumpcao. She remembers: "His spirits were so low. I just stroked his head and talked to him a little, but he was very quiet."

Andrew Longmore, a Times journalist, wrote in an article published later that Senna broke down again in the Williams motorhome and had to be picked off the floor by Damon Hill. His mood was bad enough for Frank Williams to be concerned about his emotional state and he asked Assumpcao to arrange for a meeting with him later that evening.

No one bettered Senna's Friday time so he was on pole for the race the following day but he seemed not to care and told officials he would not attend the obligatory press conference. That should have attracted a fine but in the circumstances the FIA officials declined to punish him, although he was called out of the motorhome in front of the race stewards for illegally commandeering a course car to take him out on the track when Ratzenberger crashed. Senna was in no mood to accept the censure of the FIA and that of the permanent FIA steward, John Corsmit, and a row ensued. Senna stormed off in disgust and the stewards took no action. Corsmit said: "He seemed bothered by lots of other things." Senna was privately disgusted with Corsmit's attitude.

Outside Niki Lauda buttonholed Senna and told him the drivers had to present a united front on safety issues. Lauda told him he planned to hold a meeting at the next race at Monaco in two weeks' time. Senna left the track shortly before 5:30pm and nobody dared go near him. People who saw him said he had an aura of absolute isolation and inapproachability about him after the meeting with Corsmit.

Hill decided to stay at the circuit and eat in the Williams motorhome but found it difficult to think of anything other than the accident. He said at the time: "Look, I'm not going to stop racing; I'm looking forward to the Grand Prix. I enjoy my motor racing just as Roland did. Every second you are alive, you've got to be thankful and derive as much pleasure from it as you can." That night every one of the drivers had the same thoughts and came to the same conclusion.

When Senna arrived back in San Pietro at the Castello, he found the inevitable Italian Saturday night wedding in full swing having taken over the whole hotel. He was so upset that when he was asked to pose for a picture with the bride and groom he uncharacteristically refused.

As soon as he got back to his suite he telephoned Adriane, who by then had arrived at Antonio Braga's house in Sintra near Lisbon and was with his wife Luiza. She asked him how he was and he replied: "It's like shit. Shit, shit, shit," before he started to cry again. Adriane thought he was still upset about Barrichello's accident the day before until he told her about Ratzenberger's death. Then he broke down completely and told her he was not going to race the next day. He said: "I have a really bad feeling about this race, I would rather not drive." Adriane had to catch an 8:30pm flight to Faro that night. When Josef Leberer arrived at his suite for his regular massage he sent him away. Leberer had introduced Senna to Ratzenberger earlier that year during a test in the winter. Senna said he was too upset about Ratzenberger and even more upset by the callous attitude of the race officials. He was furious at the treatment he had received from the stewards. He told Leberer: "How dare they tell me what I could do. I am driving the car and they tell me about safety."

Meanwhile, Senna went out for dinner at the Romagnola. The meal had been planned for Josef Leberer's birthday but few felt like celebrating. Instead he questioned Leberer about Ratzenberger as they were both Austrians. The mood of the evening was very sad, and it was clear that it had stayed in Senna's mind.

When he returned to the hotel he found a message under his door from Frank Williams asking him to pop down to his suite for a chat. He went downstairs and talked to his team principal, who found him a lot calmer than he had been earlier. Leberer offered to do his massage before he went to bed but Senna said he simply wasn't in the mood.

When Adriane finally arrived at Quinta do Lago, after nearly 24 hours of travelling, she made straight for the shower. As she got out the phone rang – it was Senna. He told her he had decided to race after all and when he won he would uncoil an Austrian flag and fly it on his victory lap in honour of Roland Ratzenberger. During the call, his housekeeper Juraci shouted to Adriane to tell him she was preparing his favourite meal of grilled chicken and steamed vegetables for when he returned on Sunday evening. She handed the phone to Juraci, who told him the meal would be waiting for him when he got back. He then said to Adriane: "I want to spend the night awake. We will talk until morning comes. I want to convince you I am the best man in your life." As the conversation got lighter, she laughed and said to him: "But you don't know the others." He said: "I will prove to you I am the best." She said: "If necessary, I will join the queue like any other fan."

Her last words to him were that she had news for him. The news was that she had been training and would be running with him on the first day after the race. During their conversation, Senna said he had changed from being deeply depressed to being happy again. He asked her to come out to Faro airport with Juraci when she picked him up on Sunday evening and told her to be there at 8:30pm. They were the last words they ever spoke.

On Sunday morning Captain O'Mahoney rang Senna at 7:30am in his suite and asked him what time he could pick up his bags at the hotel. It was a wake-up call – something he did every race day morning at that time. Senna got up, threw his things in his bag and went downstairs where a helicopter was waiting to take him to the track. By the time he arrived the sun was shining and a beautiful day was developing. In morning warm-up he was once again faster than the rest of the drivers. He sent a short greeting over the Williams pit radio to Alain Prost, who was at his first Grand Prix of the year and was in the Williams pit. "Hello my friend, I've been missing you," he said.

When he returned to the pits, he told David Brown not to touch the settings on the car – finally he was happy with the set-up.

During the half-hour he was driving, his press spokeswoman Betise Assumpcao had dropped her guard and told journalist Karin Sturm that the race officials were trying to intimidate Senna by censuring him over the commandeering of the safety car. She said: "But it's like that the whole time. That suspended fine because of Irvine – they only did that because they wanted to put him under pressure, because they knew what he wanted to do about a drivers' trade union."

Meanwhile, Hill found practice difficult that morning, especially going past the point where Ratzenberger had crashed. As he remembers: "I could imagine the force of the impact because I was actually travelling at the same speed he had been doing before he went off. Under normal circumstances I wouldn't have given it a second thought because, even though speeds reach 200mph, it is not a part of the circuit where you come close to the limit; it is not a place you worry about. You are relying entirely on the car and, in the light of Roland's accident, it brings it home that sometimes you are just a passenger, putting your faith in the components."

Senna was again fastest in warm-up by nine-tenths of a second. Afterwards he climbed out of the car, changed and wandered into the Williams motorhome, where he spotted Alain Prost sitting at a table.

When he saw Prost he sat down with him for a quick breakfast. The pair talked animatedly for 30 minutes and Senna lobbied him to help with safety improvements. Prost agreed that they would meet before the Monaco

Grand Prix in two weeks' time. He later recalled: "For the first time in ages we had a really normal conversation – we set aside the differences between us." In fact Prost was wholly surprised at Senna's attitude towards him that weekend, as he said afterwards: "I was very surprised as normally he did not even say hello if I crossed his path."

Afterwards Senna recorded a lap for TF1, the French television network, for whom Alain Prost was working. During the recording Senna said: "I would like to say welcome to my old friend, Alain Prost. Tell him we miss him very much."

When he got out of the car he wrote a letter to Roland Ratzenberger's parents and asked Assumpcao to fax it.

At 11am Gerhard Berger called by the Williams motorhome to collect Senna for the drivers' briefing. On the way Senna asked him to bring up a safety point about the pace car on the formation lap. He didn't want to do it himself because he believed there was personal animosity between him and race official John Corsmit.

At the briefing the talk was all of the events of the day before. The drivers stood in silence for a minute in memory of Ratzenberger at Bernie Ecclestone's suggestion. Senna took no direct part in proceedings and sat at the back sobbing.

Then Berger raised the point about the introduction of a pace car during the final parade lap leading to the start. He said that he felt it was nothing more than a gimmick and contributed little else apart from making the cars run far too slowly and therefore less able to put heat into their tyres. Berger said: "Going that slowly increases risk, as everybody's tyres and brakes are too cold at the start." He demanded forcefully that it shouldn't happen in future. The other drivers supported Berger and Senna and the race officials agreed to abandon the idea.

After the briefing Senna chaired a brief discussion about safety with his colleagues, notably Michael Schumacher, Gerhard Berger and Michele Alboreto. They agreed to hold a meeting on safety issues with all drivers in Monte Carlo on the Friday before the next race.

There was no dissent but Hill believes that the talk of a drivers' meeting about safety to take place before Monaco rang alarm bells with the Formula One organisers. He said: "Whenever drivers group together there is the potential for trouble. We were all together in the pre-race drivers' briefing as usual, and we weren't happy."

Then it was on with the show. Senna went to the Paddock Club to talk with Williams' sponsors and their guests for half-an-hour. Team-mate Damon Hill went with him – it was a situation he was very used to and carried out with relish, despite being less than enthusiastic about life that morning.

At midday he ate a light lunch, then shut himself away in the motorhome with his thoughts. Afterwards he picked up his spare overalls from the debrief room and went off to the Ferrari motorhome to see Gerhard Berger. It was the last Frank Williams saw of him.

Half-an-hour before the start, Senna went to the Williams garage. Everybody there said he was different from usual. He paced round the car, examining the tyres, and rested on the rear wing, silent and alone. Betise Assumpcao says: "He usually had a particular way of pulling on his balaclava and helmet, determined and strong as if he was looking forward to the race. That day you could tell just from the way he was putting on his helmet that he didn't want to race. He was not thinking he was going to die, he really thought he would win, but he just wanted to get it over with and go home. He wasn't there, he was miles away."

At 1 o'clock Sid Watkins climbed into his medical car and ordered his driver Mario Casoni to drive round the circuit on his normal inspection lap to make sure the medical intervention cars were in place and the people manning them alert. When he returned to the pits he inspected the medical centre. Everything was perfect. Roland Bruynseraede, the FIA delegate in charge, then did the same.

The cars gradually left the pit garages, did a lap and formed up on the grid. Senna's style was to sit quietly belted up in his car for the 15 minutes or so before the start with his helmet on, preparing mentally for the first corner and playing it in advance over and over in his head what he was going to do. This time he broke his usual routine by taking his helmet off, removing his nomex fireproof balaclava and loosening his seat belts whilst remaining in the car.

On the grid Williams technical director Patrick Head talked briefly with him and there was a hint of a smile as they spoke.

As usual the circuit commentator announced the grid and when he came to Gerhard Berger's name, because he was a Ferrari driver, the San Marino crowd cheered wildly. Senna turned around and smiled at Berger alongside. Berger remembers: "It was the smile of a friend who was pleased to see the people's support and love for me. That is the last thing I remember of him." Josef Leberer was standing by Senna's car as he usually did on the grid ready to hand him his helmet. he gave him a last drink and then Senna put his helmet on for the last time. With the helmet on he checked Senna was happy. The mechanics started the engine and Leberer waited a few moments before running back to the Williams garage to watch the start.

Meanwhile, at Senna's home in Portugal, Adriane and Juraci settled in front of the television to watch the race eating their lunch.

In the medical car four men were belted in their seats waiting to follow hard on the heels of the pack of cars on the opening lap in case of an incident. In the front was Watkins and Casoni. In the back seat, Dr Baccarini had his IV infusions ready, the cervical collar, and the paraphernalia of resuscitation. Next to him was Dr Domenico Salcito, deputy chief medical officer for Imola.

Up in the BBC commentary box Murray Walker made his customary preamble to British TV viewers: "Ayrton Senna in pole position, Michael Schumacher next to him on the grid. So now with just seconds to go the grid is being cleared and you will see the cars going around in less than 30 seconds' time."

At exactly two o'clock the cars pulled away on the pace lap and straddled back to the grid. The procession of Formula One cars went past Watkins' medical car and took their places. The race started bang on time as the lights went red, then four seconds later turned green and the cars streamed into the first turn.

Almost immediately yellow flags were waving everywhere. Pedro Lamy's Lotus had run into the back of JJ Lehto's Benetton, which had stalled on the start line. It was a violent accident similar to that of Riccardo Paletti all those years ago. But this time Lehto survived, albeit hurling bodywork everywhere as a wheel of his car became detached and went into the crowd.

Casoni drove the medical car straight through the debris with wrecked cars on each side. When Sid Watkins observed that the drivers were out of their cars uninjured, he tailed the main pack while others cleared up the mess. He expected a red flag to stop the race while the track was cleared. But it didn't come and instead at 2:03pm the safety car came out while the debris was cleared.

Senna led the cars round with Michael Schumacher, Gerhard Berger and Damon Hill following. The medical car finished its lap uneventfully, and as it reached its permanent position in the chicane, the leading Formula One cars were completing their second lap. The marshals cleared the circuit in less than six minutes and swept up.

At 2:15pm David Brown told Senna over the pit radio that the safety car was about to pull off. Senna acknowledged him in the last words he ever spoke.

When the safety car peeled off Senna put the hammer down. With a fully loaded car he clocked 1m 24.887secs on the sixth lap on full tanks and cold tyres. It was a very good time and only two drivers bettered it by the end of the race – Damon Hill and Michael Schumacher.

Schumacher couldn't keep up that speed and fell behind immediately. The pace worried Sid Watkins – he remembered a premonition, turned to Mario Casoni and said: "There's going to be a fucking awful accident any minute."

At exactly 2:17pm Senna approached the Tamburello curve for the second time after the restart and the seventh time overall. His car veered off the track just after the apex of the bend at a speed of 190mph and slammed sideways into the unprotected concrete wall. As he braked he slowed the car to 130mph on impact. The next moment the red flags were out again and Casoni put his foot to the floor and steered towards Tamburello. Sid Watkins said: "Somehow I knew it was Senna."

At exactly 2:18pm Watkins' Alfa-Romeo pulled up at Tamburello behind the wreck of a blue and white car. Life had suddenly gone wrong for one of the best drivers the world had ever seen. He had driven his last lap.

CHAPTER 2

1960-1980: Early Life

Against all the odds

Ayrton Senna was born on 21st March 1960, the first son of Milton da Silva and Neyde Senna. When he was born they nicknamed him 'Beco'. In Brazil it was very common for a son to have a family nickname. It was also common to combine the names of husband and wife to form his family name, and that is what da Silva and Senna did, to create Ayrton 'Beco' Senna da Silva.

The Senna da Silvas were a prosperous family who lived in Santana, in north São Paulo. They were attended to by servants and enjoyed all the advantages of wealth. But São Paulo had a population of 15 million people, and was very competitive for a young boy dreaming of a big future.

Milton da Silva's father had been wealthy, even though his son had started out lowly. The family business made parts for cars, employing nearly 1,000 staff. It also distributed soft drinks. But the family crown jewels were cattle farms covering over 90,000 acres, on which more than 10,000 cattle were said to roam.

Senna's childhood is not well chronicled, even in Brazil, but it was well ordered and, some say, idyllic. Senna was the second child, arriving two years after sister Viviane, and was followed by younger brother Leonardo. He attended the local Colegio Santana school.

Astonishingly, given what happened later, Senna had a coordination defect. A neurologist diagnosed a motor-coordination problem. He ordered an electroencephalogram to be done, but could find nothing seriously wrong that would warrant medical attention.

However, something was certainly different about him. His mother would have to buy him two ice creams since he invariably dropped one on the ground. He apparently also had difficulty doing even simple things like walking up a flight of stairs.

In addition he was diagnosed as hyperactive and, conversely, introspective. It was obvious early on that he did not make friends easily and preferred his own company. Accounts differ of his academic prowess. Some say he was good in school, others not. But there is plenty of evidence to indicate he was not a diligent student and showed no real sign of being bright in an academic sense.

His one passion, from very early on, was cars. His father was directly involved in the motor industry through his spares business. At three Senna was bought a pedal car, and a year later a go-kart was made for him for his fourth birthday. The machine was powered by a one-horsepower lawn-mower engine with a plastic bucket seat and a crude aerodynamic fairing at the front. The kart never went fast enough for the fairing to be any use, but it was all the young boy ever wanted.

The tiny kart put together by his father was all it took for Senna to discover his passion. Almost overnight his neurological problems were cured and he became a normal young boy.

It was clear that driving cars was what he wanted to do, and any problem that got in the way was solved. Early on his calling had been answered, and his talent discovered. Driving his little kart was an outlet for his energy, and he showed extraordinary application. But his academic career suffered.

He was allowed to enter junior races in the kart and remembered later: "I was then about eight years old and the majority of people there were 15, 18, 20, and the way to decide the grid position was by drawing, so they put papers with the numbers inside a helmet, and as I was the youngest I drew first and I pulled number one so I was on pole position for my first event.

"I was small, light, so my go-kart was the fastest one with the weight advantage I had. I stayed in the front for many laps because people just could not overtake me – they were quicker than me in the corners but on the straight I was going away from them. I was third with three laps to go and the guy behind me, who was always trying to overtake me, touched me and I went off so I didn't finish the race, but it was really good fun."

His father applied the carrot and stick, denying him the pleasures of the car if his homework wasn't done. It worked in a limited way. Young Ayrton loved and respected his father, and wanted to please him.

At the age of seven, his father caught him driving a jeep on one of the farms without permission. Far from punishing him, he was astonished at his skill in controlling the giant vehicle when he could barely reach the pedals. He couldn't reach the clutch and changed gear by listening for the right time in the revs.

His extracurricular driving came to an abrupt halt when, aged eight, he borrowed the family car and was caught by the police for driving under age on São Paulo's public roads. His mother had known all about it and turned a blind eye. Milton berated her for being so foolhardy. Luckily for Ayrton his father was a motor racing fan, and smoothed it over with the police.

Senna's idol was Jim Clark. He was eight years old when he was killed at Hockenheim and he was shattered. He had always idolised Clark and wanted to be him. When he died Jackie Stewart became his new idol.

His father was also a Clark fan, and promised to buy Senna a proper go-kart when he reached his 10th birthday. He was delighted and even then he appreciated the wonderful opportunity his family had given him, as he said: "I had a good opportunity in life to live well and to live healthily and learn a lot. I believe I was led at the key moments in the right direction."

As it got more TV coverage, motorsport began to become popular in Brazil, especially when Emerson Fittipaldi started to make his mark. Fittipaldi, the son of a São Paulo sports journalist, had started his career in karts and, in seemingly no time at all, graduated to Formula One as Jochen Rindt's team-mate at Lotus.

It heartened Senna no end – he knew that if Fittipaldi could do it then so could he. On the other hand, he wondered whether there would only ever be room for one Brazilian driver in Formula One: had Fittipaldi stolen his thunder? He couldn't have been more wrong about that.

He was astonished when Rindt was killed and Fittipaldi took over as team leader, in no time at all becoming world champion.

With his head full of dreams of becoming a second Fittipaldi, he celebrated his 10th birthday by tearing the gift wrapping off a full-sized kart with a 100cc Parilla engine. He had to wait three long years before he was eligible to race it. That didn't stop him driving it.

When Fittipaldi became world champion in 1972, it put Brazil on the motorsport map, and it applied to host a Grand Prix. São Paulo won the bid and the first race was staged at the Interlagos circuit in Senna's home city of São Paulo.

The first race was run in 1973: Senna, who was nearly 13, watched

Brazilian brothers Emerson and Wilson Fittipaldi compete for honours. Emerson won and it seemed that the whole of São Paulo went wild. There was more to celebrate when he claimed a second world championship in 1974, this time for McLaren.

Fittipaldi remembered meeting the young Senna in the mid-1970s when he set up his own team: He said: "When I was testing the Copersucar in 1975 and 1976 at Interlagos, he used to be testing his go-kart on the other track. He would come up and talk to us and I remembered him from then. He was a quiet boy, very shy. A few years later he came with his manager to my office before he went to Europe to race Formula Ford, and we kept in touch from there."

When Senna finally reached the qualifying age to race professional karts, he entered a kart race at the Interlagos kart circuit through Elcio de São Thiago, who ran a kart racing club. It was held on Sunday 1st July 1973. Maurizio Sala was the driver to beat, and Senna beat him first time out. It was obvious straight away he was an outstanding talent. But from that day, it would take 11 years to get into Formula One.

From then on he was dedicated: racing became his life. He tested at Interlagos two or three days a week and learned how to change the engine or the carburettor, and how to set up the chassis. It gave him his feel for mechanical things, which endeared him so much to his teams later – and especially to Honda.

He had found his source of contentment: "I discovered this extraordinary sensation: being first, the fastest, the winner. It is a stronger emotion than mere speed."

Ruebens Carpinelli, then president of the Brazilian national karting commission, spotted his talent early: "His dedication was self-evident. Every time I went to the kart track he was there, training. He was impressive. He was only a boy, ready to talk to anybody about his kart.'

Two weeks after victory on his debut, Senna won the junior category of the São Paulo winter championship. And when the summer season started, he fought his way to the full junior title.

The next year he won the national junior championship, followed in 1976 by the senior championship of São Paulo and victory in the three-hour kart race in his new 100cc kart. This, too, was the season in which he first appeared in the yellow helmet with green and azure bands, the colours of Brazil. The South American title fell to him the following year.

Meanwhile in 1973, his education continued unsuccessfully, as one of 560 students at Colegio Rio Branca. His time there was not memorable, although the school revelled in having him as a pupil when he became famous. Later he attended secondary school and spent his time, by all accounts, drawing pictures of racing cars.

Karting and racing were all he lived for. In certain circles of São Paulo all the talk was of the feud between Maurizio Sala and Senna. Sala and Senna crashed together frequently and Senna was completely fearless on the circuit. He would not give way, but expected others to give way to him. Nothing intimidated him: once he was out in front, getting past was difficult. In the rain, he was the master. It was a dress rehearsal for his battles with Alain Prost still 15 years in the future.

His parents were astonished at his prowess, especially considering his eye-body coordination problems of the past. But these had genuinely disappeared.

In 1990, he said of that time: "At the beginning I was just doing it for the feeling of driving: I liked the feeling of moving the steering wheel, braking, putting on the power, feeling the engine, listening to the engine, feeling the air on my face, the speed. It was something that got to me when I was a kid: it got inside of me then. And it stayed there."

He also discovered girls, and dated his chief rival's sister, Carolina Sala. It was unusual as his personality was as introspective as ever. But it gave him a psychological edge over competitors who could not understand his motivation.

He also established a relationship that was to endure for his whole karting career, with a Spanish kart mechanic called Lucio Pascual Gascon, who was known to everyone simply as 'Tché'. His father introduced him to Tché, who prepared a lot of karts in São Paulo, but Senna established a special relationship with him very quickly, as he did with so many engineers and racing people in the years to come.

Tché, who had been Emerson Fittipaldi's mentor 10 years earlier, prepared Ayrton Senna's racing engines personally and his father paid the bills. Senna spent all his spare time at Tché's workshops, absorbing the rudiments of a knowledge that would make him technically able to converse with his race engineers in Formula One.

South American championship titles followed in 1977, 1978, 1979, 1980 and 1981.

In 1977 Senna went international kart racing, taking him all over South America, and in Uruguay that year he won the South American series. He also met Mauricio Gugelmin, who became one of his best friends.

Tché remembers his young charge as if it were yesterday: "He always came to a race to win it – enemies and competitors didn't exist to him, he was there to win. I used to say 'Keep cool if you can', and he would reply 'No, for me it's first place or nothing!' He was an individualist, always seeking perfection. He never permitted a crooked wheel or other small details, and he always paid attention to his timing to make sure nobody else could outrace him."

In 1978, at the age of 18, Senna was ready for his first trip to Europe, to compete in the world karting championship: that year it was being held at Le Mans. His father contacted the Parilla brothers of Milan-based DAP, Europe's top kart constructor. DAP agreed to run him a kart and his father paid the bill. He amazed his family when he announced he would travel to Italy alone. They were worried as he spoke no English, no French and hardly any Italian.

He set off three weeks before the world championship so he could test in Italy. The works drivers for DAP were English driver Terry Fullerton and Dutchman Peter Koene.

Fullerton also took part in the test session, supervised by Angelo and Achille Parilla. Fullerton, the 1973 world champion, was preparing for the championship at Le Mans. Senna attacked the unfamiliar track and ended the day outpacing him. The Parilla brothers signed him up as their second driver for Le Mans, and after a fortnight's preparation in Italy the team left for France, where they were joined by Tché, dispatched at the family's expense to give expert assistance with the team's engines.

Senna persuaded Fullerton and Koene to help him perfect his driving skills. He won two heats in the world championship before retiring in a third when the engine expired.

He found the competition was a good deal fiercer than in Brazil, and in the three races which constituted the final he came seventh in the first, retired in the second and came sixth in the third, finishing sixth overall in the world championship. *Karting* magazine described the performance as 'sensational'.

In 1979 Senna resolved to return and focus on Europe. That year he won the Brazilian championship again, before returning to Europe for a few races and the world championship at Estoril in Portugal. In a preliminary race at a track called Jesolo he had his first big accident. Going into a fast corner, two inside wheels lifted, he was thrown out of the kart at 50mph into a steel barrier and the flying kart hit him. He was not injured, but suffered shock.

There were three finals. Senna led in the first but finished fifth. In the second he was second before taking the lead after the leader retired, but he was overtaken and finished third. He then won the third race. He was joint winner of the whole event but lost the championship on lap difference.

In 1980 he won his third Brazilian championship and went to Nivelles in Belgium for the world championship, where, aged 19, he came second again. He had failed to win any of the three world championships he had competed in. It was a blow to his confidence and he was less sure of his future than ever.

His father Milton, sensing a weakness in his resolve, took the opportunity to persuade him to join the family firm. He told him his brother and sister had settled down to conventional careers, and so should he. He never dreamed his son had what it took to make it in Formula One, and he didn't want him to waste time on it. Viviane da Silva was a psychologist, while Leonardo was a software writer.

Reluctantly, the young Ayrton enrolled in a business course at São Paulo University. It lasted three months and in November 1980 he headed off to Britain to secure his first drive in a car. There he was told he needed a wife to be successful and, once back in Brazil, asked his long-standing girlfriend to marry him. Surprisingly she agreed and he left for Britain wedded to Liliane Vasconcelos Souza, a girl from a wealthy Brazilian family. Neither of them could speak barely a word of English as they headed for the eastern English county of Norfolk to begin a new life.

CHAPTER 3

The First Year in England

An overnight success in Formula Ford

Fresh from his fourth Brazilian karting championship and second place in the world kart championship at Nivelles, 20-year-old Ayrton Senna decided he wanted to race cars full time. He finally won a struggle with his father, who wanted him to join the family business, stay in Brazil and complete a business studies course he had begun. Senna scrapped the course and in November 1980 arrived in England to sort out a drive for the following season in Formula Ford. It was his only choice if he wanted to start on the ladder to Formula One. Formula Ford had been set up with the aid of the Ford Motor Company in 1967 in a bid to provide a cheap platform for top-class entry-level single-seater racing. Senna could have chosen the German or Italian Formula Ford championships, but he had worked it out that Formula One was British based and that is where he would attract the most attention. The fact that he didn't speak a word of the language and that he had never been to Britain hardly entered into his decision.

Coming to faraway England was a nerve-wracking experience for a young man on his own with an uncertain future. In England he signed his name Ayrton Senna da Silva – because da Silva was such a common Brazilian name he thought it would be more memorable if he included his mother's maiden name Senna as well. He soon realised it was far from memorable, but that was for later.

Having chosen British Formula Ford Senna went for the best – the works Van Diemen team run by Ralph Firman. Van Diemen was a late entrant in

Formula Ford, having first built a car in 1973. It was an overnight success and since then had been consistently the car to beat. Driving for the factory Van Diemen team meant Senna would be automatically among the championship favourites. Since 1973, Firman's team had won four Formula Ford Festivals and five Formula Ford 1600 championships. That year it had won the triple crown of the Festival and the BRSCC and RAC championship titles with another Brazilian, Roberto Moreno, doing the driving.

Senna's November visit was designed to get everything sorted out. He had agreed a £10,000 budget with his father but a top car cost £20,000 to run in those days. Senna believed he could get a works drive and actually get Firman to pay him. He was soon to be disabused of that notion.

Senna had the best possible introduction through Chico Serra, who for two years had been singing his praises to Firman after watching him race karts.

In theory he should have come to Britain a year earlier but his own indecision and the wrangles with his father had prevented that. Senna had been to Europe many times for his karting career but that was for individual races. Car racing needed a full-time commitment that would take him away from home for almost eight months.

Arriving at London-Heathrow in mid-November, he was met at the airport by Serra. He had offered to help smooth the young driver's path and had arranged for Senna to meet Ralph Firman for dinner the following evening. Getting into one of the three Van Diemen works cars required cash and it was not easy. But Firman had already provisionally decided that Senna would be his lead works driver in 1981 and that he would subsidise half of the £20,000 cost of running a single car – an outlay that 20 years later had risen to £200,000. Firman usually charged £30,000 for a season in order to give himself a profit.

He was used to dealing with young Brazilians. He introduced most of them to single-seater racing. Through Serra, Senna asked Firman for a free works drive and a salary. It was an incredible cheek. That was not the way it worked in Formula Ford. All drives were paid for, although some were subsidised if the owners could see talent.

The young Senna also had money in his pocket – £10,000 supplied by his father, the equivalent of £100,000 today.

Over a long dinner with Firman, during which Serra acted as translator, Senna was told he could test drive the following day at Snetterton and if he was good enough he would get the drive for 1981.

The following day Senna's first experience of a real racing car was not a happy one. He took to the track for 10 laps in a Van Diemen-Minister RF80 in front of Firman. The team boss was impressed but not overawed by this new Brazilian's talent. As he recalls: "I'd known about him for two years from his reputation. When he arrived there was this great interest. We knew he would be good." Just how good was not yet clear. Firman, a cautious man, had seen good drivers come to nothing before. But he was impressed enough to give him the drive.

Senna recalled later: "I did not enjoy it very much. I thought it was too difficult to drive the car. But Ralph thought I was good enough to have the factory drive the following year."

Before leaving to go back to Brazil Senna arranged for accommodation in England for the season with Ralph Firman's wife. Serra then dropped him back at Heathrow and that was it. He was a works Formula Ford driver for 1981. When he got back to São Paulo in Brazil, his father Milton da Silva wired Ralph Firman a 10 per cent deposit for his son's season of racing and hoped for the best.

Senna had three short months to prepare for his first season abroad. He was also planning to carry on his karting career. He was a professional karter and drove with big teams on a salary. That was his job and he had no intention of stopping. By that time he was winning virtually every karting race he entered, except the elusive world championship events.

Senna had married Liliane Vasconcelos Souza in February 1981, which meant that the trip to England would also serve as their honeymoon. Souza was the daughter of wealthy parents and part of São Paulo's aristocracy. She was a glamorous blonde with blue eyes and a perfect figure.

When they arrived at Heathrow it was as a couple of starry-eyed Brazilian kids who spoke little English and had no idea of the British way of life. In those days British winters were still fierce and snow covered the ground. It was an unwelcoming sight as they set up their first house together in a small rented bungalow in the village of Eaton, outside Norwich, not far from the Van Diemen factory and the Snetterton circuit. Senna inherited the lease of 29 Rugge Drive from countryman Raul Boesel, who had finished his time in Formula Ford and moved on to Formula Three.

Firman says it was difficult for a young foreign driver racing in Britain for the first time. As he recalls: "We were very close at the time. Like the other foreign drivers, he relied on us, especially my wife, to organise things for him."

As soon as they got there Senna wondered why he needed his wife. He expected immigration officials to turn up at any minute to inspect her – or a representative of the local authority to arrive for a similar inspection. She may not have been essential but at the time she was his biggest asset. She had the appropriate domestic and social charms necessary for the young Brazilian to make his mark.

But Liliane was horrified at her first experience of Britain. It was cold and she had moved from a life of luxury in São Paulo to a very ordinary middle-class life in rural Britain. The central heating thermostat was turned up to the maximum but it was still not enough to keep them warm.

Like her husband, Liliane spoke little English but drew a lot of attention in the paddock. The early races were held in freezing weather until the British summer began to emerge in May. She may have despised her social circumstances but she enjoyed life as best she could in the tedious paddocks of Britain's racetracks. She found herself almost every weekend spending three days at a racetrack with virtually nothing to do. Life as a Formula Ford driver's wife, traipsing around Britain's club racing venues, was very different from the privileged stratum of Brazilian society to which she was accustomed.

It was not what she had signed up for and nothing like she had imagined. Very early on she decided that this would be her first and last season if it was to be her husband's full-time occupation. She loved her husband but he was pursuing a career he loved. To relieve the tedium she started cooking for the whole Formula Ford paddock and often went to races laden with food. Her speciality was Brazilian-recipe banana cakes.

Her husband was having trouble adapting as well, as he said: "Everything was new to me. I didn't know the language, there were new people, new customs, and the weather…" But he was quickly accepted by the Van Diemen mechanics and quickly gained the honour of a nickname, which meant he had earned his place in the team. He was called 'Harry' by those who struggled to pronounce his Brazilian-Portuguese name.

Senna also found himself with some experienced team-mates in the guise of fellow South Americans Enrique Mansilla and Enrique Toledano – it was a good yardstick and they made him feel at home.

His first race was the opening round of the P&O Formula Ford 1600 championship at Brands Hatch on 1st March 1981. He had time only for a minimal amount of testing before this first outing in the previous year's car, the Van Diemen RF80.

Senna's debut was impressive, but not sensational. From a grid position of eighth, he made his way up to fifth by the end of the race, eight seconds behind the winner, Argentine Enrique Mansilla, after 12 short laps. Some in the paddock felt he could have gone faster if he had wanted to, but was slowly getting used to racing so as not to show himself up.

Senna himself was unimpressed. He said at the time: "I didn't enjoy the race because the car was not so good. I had virtually no experience but still finished fifth, which was a bonus for me. It was not in my contract, so I couldn't really complain."

Brands Hatch was the first and last time Senna competed in the P&O championship – after that he concentrated on the two other major Formula Ford 1600 series. In 1981, there were several 1600 series in Britain, the two principal ones being the Townsend Thoresen and RAC championships. The same crowd of drivers competed in each one and there was a great deal of crossover between them. Races would often be held for one championship on the Saturday/Sunday and the other on the Sunday/Bank Holiday Monday at different tracks around the country. It was an intensive programme.

A week after his debut race for the P&O at Brands Hatch, Senna was at Thruxton, competing in the Townsend Thoresen championship. He finished in third place, winning the battle for the final podium spot from the aggressive Enrique Mansilla.

A week later he was back at Brands Hatch, again competing in the Townsend Thoresen championship. Senna arrived at the track determined to be a success. He had been thinking hard about the importance of publicity in pushing forward a young driver's career and the week before had decided to hire someone to do his public relations. Astutely, he decided a photographer would be his best bet.

He had spied a likely candidate in young snapper Keith Sutton, then in only his second year as a professional photographer. He had spotted him the previous weekend at Thruxton but the two men had not spoken. As Sutton remembers: "I was at Thruxton working for a Brazilian motorsport magazine that wanted photographs of Brazilian drivers racing in England. I was shy in those days so I never introduced myself – I just took lots of photographs of him, in the paddock, on the track – he must have wondered why this photographer he had never seen before was taking so many rolls of film of him at only his second event in a racing car.

"For some reason I decided to go down to Brands Hatch the following weekend on the train, using a free British Rail promotion ticket. It was a long way from my home in Cheadle – in fact it took me eight hours' travelling time there and back. I had just arrived in the paddock when Senna approached me after recognising me from Thruxton. He asked me why I had been taking photos of him. 'Are you a professional photographer?' he enquired. 'Yes of course,' was my reply. 'Well I need photographs to send out to Brazil on a regular basis. Can you help me out?' Naturally I agreed." Senna's hiring of Sutton was to have an immediate effect on his career, as the young photographer set out to get Senna noticed as well as photographing his every move. He paid Sutton a few hundred pounds for the work: the young Mancunian had chosen a good weekend to sign up.

It rained all weekend. Brands Hatch in soggy March was not the glamorous motor-racing venue Senna would later inhabit – and race day Sunday 15th March 1981 was even wetter than normal. The scheduled Formula Ford 1600 race went ahead despite the downpour, the spindly little cars running on the short Indy circuit, just around the pits and back, rather than the famous Grand Prix track. Few knew beforehand that this race would make history – they didn't even realise afterwards.

A full lap of the circuit was a little over a mile, and the junior race lasted for just 15 of these short laps. The names of the frontrunners on the spectators' dog-eared race programmes were only slightly more familiar then than they are now – Andy Ackerley, Rick Morris, Alfonso Toledano, Ayerton da Silva. The spelling of the first name, 'Ayerton', was a careless mistake by the organisers, based on the tri-syllabic Brazilian pronunciation that was abandoned in later years.

The grid positions for round two of the Townsend Thoresen championship were to be decided by two qualifying races. Senna went in the second heat, starting from third spot. The track was wet and the Brazilian stormed into the lead, winning by a second after 10 laps and setting the fastest lap on the way. This put him in pole position for the main race.

Owing to rain delays, it was after the scheduled time slot of 4.30pm when the cars lined up on the grid. They shuffled cautiously into their grid spots between the puddles in a three-two-three-two pattern, the young man in car number 31 slotting into pole position. Senna demonstrated the first signs of his wet-weather mastery that day.

The race started and even as the cars pushed off the grid, he was pulling ever so slightly away. By the first corner he already looked invincible. "He just drove away into the distance," remarks then Van Diemen mechanic Malcolm 'Puddy' Pullen. "You could see he was going to be a winner."

The Brazilian took victory by 9.4 seconds from his friend, Mexican racer Alfonso Toledano, pulling away at roughly two-thirds of a second on each 59-second lap. It is probable that if pushed he could have gone even faster;

he did not set the fastest lap as he had done in the heat, but he did not need to go faster.

"It was fantastic," Firman admits. "But I'm a pretty laid-back sort of chap. To me he was just doing his job."

When an emotional Senna cruised into the pitlane after his victory lap he was immediately met by Liliane, who rushed to congratulate her husband with a kiss before he had even climbed out of his car. She had been watching events unfold from the pitwall with the team. Malcolm Pullen had stood beside her during the final lap: "There is no feeling on earth like winning for the first time. As he went over the line Liliane nearly picked me up off the ground. She was ecstatic – I mean she was nearly in tears."

Liliane joined Senna on the podium for the victory celebrations, overjoyed with her husband's success. Evening was drawing in, victory was a novelty and the celebrations were beginning to roll. On the podium, Senna was understandably delighted and with Liliane clinging around his neck he was presented with the reward for his efforts: a laurel wreath, a winner's trophy and a cheque for £70. But the real prize that day was a new-found reputation and a boost to his racing career.

Firman says: "His talent was starting to come through and it did on that particular day. It was his driving force, his total dedication to succeed. That's one of the main reasons he was so successful."

The next two rounds of the Townsend Thoresen championship were both held at Mallory Park, two weekends apart. Once he had tasted victory, Senna did not want to lose but he was unlucky in both. Even so, at the first event he clocked pole position, although the race was overshadowed by an altercation with Mansilla. Senna had lost out to Mansilla at the start but chased him down until, on the last lap, Mansilla edged him onto the grass and Senna had to settle for second best. The Brazilian was furious – there was a scuffle in the pitlane and the pair had to be dragged apart by onlookers. Senna felt he had been denied victory unfairly, and even at that early stage of his career, it rankled him more than anything.

On 21st March 1981 Senna celebrated his 21st birthday, although there was little time for a big party as the focus was on racing. The early season had been frustrating with only one victory. And it was to get worse before it got better.

At the second Mallory Park race, following a tangle with another team-mate Alfonso Toledano, Senna was pipped to victory in the last few corners by the experienced Rick Morris, losing the battle by only a fraction of a second. Snetterton on 3rd May was a different story. Again it was wet and again Senna took pole position. He led all the way, taking a small lead and building it up while the other drivers were taking care in the rain. Observers who had thought he was a good driver before were beginning to see the makings of greatness in the Brazilian novice.

Three weeks later at Oulton Park, Senna entered the first round of the RAC Formula Ford 1600 championship, which was contested by most of the familiar drivers from the Townsend Thoresen event. He won there on the Sunday, then at Mallory in the Townsend Thoresen championship on the Bank Holiday Monday, then again in the Townsend Thoresen championship at Snetterton two weeks later. He seemed unstoppable.

Firman recollects that after his initial caution he was predicting great things for the Brazilian: "At about the middle of that season I was convinced he was going to be world champion in Formula One. There wasn't a flash of light or anything – it was a gradual feeling that this one could go all the way."

But Senna was about to come down to earth with a bump. A fortnight later at the International Trophy meeting at Silverstone in the RAC championship, he was beaten at the last corner by Rick Morris, who executed an audacious overtaking manoeuvre that left Senna speechless. The Brazilian had burst into the lead at the start and looked to have a convincing lead until Morris caught him in the closing laps. A fraught last-lap struggle ensued and as the cars approached the final corner, the Woodcote Chicane, Morris went for the inside line. Senna blocked him, but unperturbed Morris ran around the outside, bumping over the kerbs a fraction inside the penalty line. Morris went home with a tale to tell his grandchildren. Senna was furious.

So furious in fact that in the next race against each other, a Townsend Thoresen round at Oulton Park less than a week later, Senna pushed Morris out of the way for the lead on lap one and won the race. Some years later Morris would complain: "Senna was the first Brazilian I didn't really get on with the way I did with the others." Even halfway through his first season of racing, all the familiar Senna characteristics were there: wet-weather brilliance, determination to succeed, strong anger when he felt he had been cheated, ruthlessness against those who stood in his way.

At Donington Park for the next RAC round in early July, Senna started in second but put in an amazing first lap to get away at the front from the rest of the pack, build up a lead and stay there – something of a dress rehearsal for the time almost 12 years in the future when he would produce the best opening lap in Formula One history at the same track. Firman had noted this as a particular skill in Senna: "He won so much of the time because he did it on the first lap. The lights went out and bang, he was away. In a few more laps the other drivers would be lapping as quickly as he did but by that time it was all over. They'd lost the race."

He should have won the next round at Brands Hatch, but a late excursion onto the gravel meant a damaged water pipe and he slipped back to fourth. On 25th July he won the Townsend Thoresen round at Oulton Park, then on the following day the RAC race at Mallory Park. A week later he took victory in a Townsend Thoresen race at Brands Hatch, and another week later, on 9th August, again in the pouring rain at Snetterton, he claimed his first car-racing championship with victory in the penultimate round of the RAC series. As other drivers skidded off in the storm Senna simply glided on to victory. Another week, and he won at Donington Park in the Townsend Thoresen championship and then wrapped up the title in the penultimate round as well with a victory at Thruxton, much to the delight of Liliane, his parents Milton and Neyde and brother Leonardo, who had travelled all the way from Brazil to watch. It was six wins in a row – in an intense racing career of just six months he had claimed two championships and 13 race victories.

Senna recalled: "After some problems, I won both of the important British championships, the RAC and the Townsend Thoresen. It was a fantastic first season."

Fantastic it was – he had the world at his feet, the best possible start to a career in motor racing and looked as if nothing could stop him. But however glorious things appeared on the surface, there was trouble lurking in the depths.

In mid-September Senna went to the world kart championship in Parma, an event he had never been able to win before. A controversial change in the rules meant he lost out to racers with quicker karts. He finished fourth. After that he returned to Formula Ford for the final round of the Townsend Thoresen series on 27th September 1981. It was a small national club meeting at Brands Hatch. The race was won by Rick Morris, while the runner-up's spot on the podium was snatched by Senna, who had no need to win with the championship already sewn up. There was a particular end-of-season atmosphere on the podium and everyone was looking to the future. After congratulating Morris on the win, circuit commentator Brian Jones turned to the Brazilian and asked him about his options for the following year. Senna simply said: "I am finished with racing. I go back to Brazil."

It was not the expected response – everyone thought Senna would move to either Formula Ford 2000 or even Formula Three for 1982 – there had been no warning signs that he was considering quitting so it came as a complete shock. He had won everything in sight and looked to have an amazing future ahead of him – admittedly lots of people do that in Formula Ford but very few to Senna's level of dominance.

The decision to quit took immediate effect, and Senna and Liliane returned to Brazil almost immediately. He told Sutton he might return for the season finale, the Formula Ford Festival, but he didn't. On 18th October, Firman signed Irish racer Tommy Byrne to take his place: Byrne won.

Most thought that Senna had made a quick, and seemingly final return to Brazil, in order to save his marriage. That was probably true but he never admitted it. He blamed the financial situation and the collapse of the Brazilian economy for his return.

Several years later he explained his decision to quit racing in financial terms: "When I left I was unhappy for a number of reasons. One of the main reasons was that in order to find a sponsor you need good publicity. That is especially important in Brazil because it is so far away. Of all the Brazilians who have come to England I was the first to win two championships in the first year, the RAC and the Townsend Thoresen. I won 13 races out of the 18 I entered. It was a very good result but I couldn't get good press in Brazil and without it I couldn't find a sponsor. I knew that I needed a sponsor before I moved into Formula Three and I tried very, very hard. I was competing for space in the newspapers with Roberto Moreno and Raul Boesel, who were winning in Formula Three, and also Nelson Piquet who was winning the world championship. After all that there was no room for Formula Ford 1600."

Senna had debuted in an age of talented Brazilians. The surge in popularity of motorsport in Brazil had conversely made it more difficult for young drivers to make the break. Senna felt that Moreno and Boesel were getting the better deal, but despite winning three races in the British Formula Three championship, Moreno could only afford to compete in half a season, although he secured a prize test drive with Lotus for his efforts. Boesel's family was wealthy even by the standards of Brazilian racing families. He had also won three British Formula Three rounds – albeit over a full season – and was testing for McLaren. Nelson Piquet took three Formula One wins in 1981 and emerged from the season as world champion. Senna's great Formula Ford achievements just did not have the same cachet, even though he was sending scores of press releases to journalists back home with the help of his young photographer Keith Sutton. Sutton was continually harassing Formula One team principals about his driver. But at the end of the day Piquet was the man in the news and no one was interested in the young man from São Paulo.

On top of that, sponsorship was becoming more difficult to find because Brazil had plunged into recession. Milton da Silva had promised his son a year funded by the family, but no more. He had not really wanted his son to pursue the dangerous, expensive and fickle business of racing.

Another reason for Senna's quick exit was the possible humiliation of not being able to get a drive in 1982 and therefore having to give up his career almost as quickly as it had started.

There was a drive on the horizon in senior Formula Ford 2000 for 1982, even though Senna should have moved straight into Formula Three. His potential new team-owner, Dennis Rushen of Rushen Green Racing, had offered to give him a year in the British and European championships of the Formula Ford 2000 series, the next rung on the ladder, for £10,000. But Senna could not raise the money and his father refused to give him any more.

Milton da Silva saw racing as an expensive hobby and wanted his son to return to Brazil to learn the running of the family farming and building supplies businesses.

Apart from his wife's unhappiness Senna himself had experienced home-sickness, living on a foreign continent, struggling with a language he spoke little of, far away from the life he knew. But for Liliane it was much worse. Her husband had his racing, but she did not like the sport. It made her nervous for his safety. Her English was minimal and the rented bungalow close to Snetterton in Norfolk was a far cry from the luxurious family home in sunny Brazil where she had servants to do the chores. There was little money that did not go on racing; Senna's father was paying for the drive and even the race-winner's prize money was just £70, with decreasing amounts for the rest of the top six and a fund of £100 for the eventual champion. Liliane had little to keep her occupied and she had no friends in England. Few could blame her for wanting to return home.

Those around him felt that Senna might have liked to continue racing, to wait longer to see if sponsorship materialised, but concern from his father and wife persuaded him that a return to Brazil would be better than scrimping and saving far from home for a career that might never take off. There is a very fine line between fame and obscurity. Many young drivers have had successful first racing seasons only to fade from memory when the funds dried up or they found other things to occupy their minds. Ayrton Senna was very, very close to becoming one of them and it is impossible to guess to what extent that might have changed the sport of today.

Senna's desire to race always burned strongly and it is this that made him turn his back on retirement and the happy farm in Brazil. He was determined, in a world where determination could count for more than talent. His peers were not always so dogged. His rival of 1981, Rick Morris, was talented but he decided to buy a house rather than continue to spend his money racing. Senna would not let anything stand in his way. Had he accepted obscurity, he would almost certainly have still been alive today.

But the desire to race that coursed through his veins had not diminished. He had a decision to make: "When I got back to Brazil, my father needed help in some of his businesses, and he wasn't convinced that I wanted to be a professional driver. He thought he could persuade me. I had won 13 races out of the 18 I had started and by September had enough points in both championships to be sure of being champion, but I gave up in the end because he needed me. I came home to help the business. By then I was a bit disappointed with racing. I wanted to be self-sufficient in sponsorship, so I decided to take a break. I stayed at home until February 1982, not thinking about motor racing. I tried to give it up, because it was important to my family. But I realised that I could not give up. So when February came I knew I could not be at home when the season was about to start in Europe."

CHAPTER 4

Return of the Prodigal Son

Indecision as the best-laid plans go wrong

During 1981 Ron Dennis had noticed Ayrton Senna as he dominated Formula Ford. It was Dennis's first season in Formula One in charge of McLaren and he was looking for drivers for the future. He resolved to make Senna an offer if he ever returned to England. But at the time his return was in severe doubt.

When Senna went back to Brazil with his wife Liliane, as far he was concerned that was that. He would bow to his father's wishes and commit to the family business. After all, he was the eldest son: it was his duty.

There was also a nagging doubt as to whether his adventures in Europe would come to anything. He was not sure he had got what it takes to win at the highest level, and that was all he was interested in. If he didn't think he could graduate to Formula One and dominate, he didn't want to waste his time in Europe.

He had already sacrificed competing in the 1981 Formula Ford Festival, which showed his lack of commitment to a motor racing career. He also had qualms about spending his father's money on motor racing. And then there was Liliane. He wanted to make a go of his marriage.

It took five long months for him to realise where his future lay. By the time February came, he was convinced racing had won out and he knew where he had to be. It was not São Paulo.

But he had one major problem – money. He had little sponsorship except for some personal support from Banerj Bank. The 1982 season would cost

£30,000, which meant his father would have to pay.

It was a difficult decision to make. As Senna said later: "When I decided to come over in 1981, it was the first time my father had not supported me completely. He did once I had signed the contract, but it was not quite the same. I also had no sponsors in 1981, and I knew that if I was going to go as a professional then I would have to go by myself, not depending on my family. My motor racing meant everything to me. I had to give it 100 per cent in order to establish myself, and I found I couldn't give that if I was married."

He told Liliane and his father the news. His father accepted it and promised more money. Liliane told him the marriage was over if he went back to England, and he accepted that.

Milton da Silva was no autocrat: he loved his son and only wanted the best for him. He saw that he was unhappy and gave him the choice. He agreed to give him the £30,000 he needed and Senna promised to pay him back as soon as he could.

With the decision made he immediately called Ralph Firman at Van Diemen's factory in England to see about a drive. Senna said: "I phoned Ralph and said 'What about Formula Ford 2000?' He said he could make arrangements for me with a private team and I said 'OK, let's do it'."

By coincidence the private team Firman mentioned was Rushen Green. So in February 1982, Senna returned to England to take up Dennis Rushen on an offer he had made the previous year.

The two men already knew each other well. On 3rd May 1981 Dennis Rushen, owner of the Rushen Green Formula Ford 2000 team, had just seen Senna drive for the very first time, at the Snetterton circuit in Norfolk. He was competing in a works Van Diemen in a Formula Ford 1600 race, the junior Formula Ford series. Rushen remembers: "I wasn't paying that much attention to the race. It had started off dry and I was just walking to my car. I noticed there was this little yellow-and-black car in the lead and then the rain started. The next time they came past me he was in the lead by half a lap!"

Rushen was impressed with the man who would later become his close friend. As he recalls: "When he stopped I went over to meet him. I introduced myself and explained who I was. I was so impressed that I told him if he wanted to race in two-litre the following year, I could do him a good deal. I offered him £10,000."

At the time, a Formula Ford 2000 season could cost as much as £40,000 for a young driver. Rushen's wasn't a serious offer, more a token of how highly he rated the Brazilian. But Senna did not forget it.

Nine months later he signed a late deal to drive for Rushen Green Racing for 1982. In the intervening period he had won two Formula Ford 1600 titles, retired from racing, gone back to Brazil to work for his father, separated from his wife and returned to Britain to continue racing. A lot had happened to the young racer, then just shy of his 22nd birthday.

Senna tried to keep Rushen to his original offer but in the end they agreed that he would pay £30,000 instead of £40,000 for the Pace British and Euroseries Formula Ford 2000 championships.

There is still an apocryphal story circulating that says Rushen was forced by Senna to accept the original offer of £10,000, and it has passed into motor racing folklore. Van Diemen boss Ralph Firman laughs out loud at the story, and Rushen denies it outright. Both insist the real sum was around £30,000 – still a good deal.

Rushen remembers: "History shows that he went back home, but then he got rid of his wife and came back. We had been in contact in the winter through Ralph Firman, who wanted him to return. Very late, just before the start of the season, he said he had decided to come back. He said 'Yeah, I do want to do this after all'. We sat down with Ralph Firman over dinner to discuss the deal. Ayrton suddenly piped up and said 'Dennis said I could have the whole lot for £10,000'. Ralph was stunned. He had remembered our conversation from all those months before. He was quite astute even then. But we couldn't possibly do it for £10,000."

Senna had funding from his father that would cover the year and also sponsorship from Brazilian bank Banerj and Pool jeans. But he had nowhere to live so he phoned fellow Brazilian Mauricio Gugelmin, who was competing in Formula Ford 1600 that year as Senna's replacement at the works Van Diemen team. He had been recommended by Senna, just as Senna had been recommended by Brazilian Chico Serra the year before. Gugelmin was living with his wife Stella at a house in Eaton, Norwich, where they paid £160 a month in rent, and was more than happy to lodge his friend. Stella was more tolerant of racing than Senna's wife Liliane had been, and the couple are still together today. Visitors to the house remember a happy atmosphere.

With the season rapidly approaching, Senna only once got to try out the car, a Van Diemen RF82, before he had to race. The major difference between the 1600 and 2000 Formula Ford cars was that the 2000s had wings and slick tyres. Dennis Rushen recalls Senna's attitude to the innovations: "We went to test at Brands Hatch and he said to me 'Right Dennis, teach me about wings'. So I showed him the wing and he went out and within a few laps he was on the pace. He came back into the pits and said 'Yeah, I understand that now'."

In 1982, Formula Ford 2000 was not the major junior championship in Britain or Europe, although the Euroseries had the advantage of being the support race for four of the Grand Prix events that season. In other words it was good publicity, and by the end of the year Senna had attracted the attention of many past, present and future Formula One team bosses, characters as famous and diverse as Frank Williams, Ron Dennis, Wilson Fittipaldi, Bernie Ecclestone and Eddie Jordan. He was aided by the efforts of Keith Sutton, who was putting out press releases and photographs to all the top people in the sport long before it became common practice for up-and-coming drivers. Senna even received firm offers, but had resisted all attempts by the bosses to put him under their thumbs. He was his own man and wanted – needed – to be in Formula One on his own terms. He had so much faith in his own ability that he did not want to take the first offer that came along, no matter how good it seemed.

Senna had turned down offers from European Formula Two and British Formula Three for that season, including the established Swiss Formula Two team Maurer Motorsport. Formula Ford 2000 was not the only option open to him, and it was not the highest rung on the ladder, but there is little doubt that Senna made the right choice. His team-mate would be Kenny Andrews.

It is not unfair to the drivers to say that the standard of Formula Ford 2000 at that time was lower than in the other two series. From the contestants in the 1982 British and European championships, only one driver besides Senna made it to Formula One: Volker Weidler, a German who never pre-qualified for a Grand Prix in seven attempts. It was a long way from the late-1980s Euroseries heyday, when Michael Schumacher, Mika Häkkinen, David Coulthard, Rubens Barrichello, Heinz-Harald Frentzen and Mika Salo were all competing for honours. The majority of drivers in the European rounds were Scandinavian and Benelux gentlemen racers. In contrast, in the British Formula Three championship, Martin Brundle, Roberto Moreno and Tommy Byrne all made it to the top level, as did the entire championship top 10 and more, including Thierry Boutsen, Stefan Bellof, Stefan Johansson and Alessandro Nannini, from the European Formula Two series. Senna won 77 per cent of the races he competed in that year, and would no doubt have struggled to achieve that in one of the other championships.

To put it into context, 77 per cent was phenomenal. It was to be the highest win-to-start ratios of Senna's career. In Formula One the best he managed was 50 per cent in 1988. Such a performance is not unheard of in the British junior formulas, but it is special all the same. His total for the Pace British Formula Ford 2000 championship alone was 83 per cent, with 15 wins out of 18. All in all, it totted up to 23 wins out of 30 attempts. He finished 26 of the races and his percentage from this total was 88 per cent.

It began at Brands Hatch on 7th March, with the first round of the Pace British Formula Ford 2000 championship. Senna took pole, clocked the fastest lap and won the race by 9.8 seconds. Then, on Saturday 27th March, he took pole, fastest lap and victory at Oulton Park, then the same again over 100 miles away at Silverstone the following day. A week later he was off to Donington Park, and it was the same old whitewash. Senna's mechanic at the time, Swede Petter Dahl, said later: "He had three goals for every race: take pole position, set fastest lap and win." Anything less was failure.

The next race was just a few days after Donington, at Snetterton on Good Friday. It was business as usual, with Senna taking pole and pulling away into the distance as other clumsier drivers got caught in a pile-up way behind him. As he came past the pits and over the debris to begin his second lap, however, he slowed dramatically: first his team-mate Kenny Andrews got past, and then other cars. Senna was soon down in seventh and it looked as if he would be forced to return to the pits. Unknown to his crew, a shard of debris had sliced through his front brake line and he was driving the car with only rear brakes.

Suddenly, though, Senna started to speed up again. One by one he began the painstaking work of picking off the six cars in front of him. He had figured out that by switching his adjustable anti-roll bar to full soft setting and throwing the car around the corners as if it was a kart he could drive almost as fast as normal.

When Andrews saw Senna 15 seconds behind him on the track he was sure he had won the race. But Senna, naturally setting the fastest lap on the way, soon caught his team-mate and made his way past. He won the race by 12.6 seconds.

The Rushen Green team members were naturally perplexed by the incident, although they got a clue to the answer when the Brazilian had some trouble stopping at the end of the race and skidded to a halt about 400 metres after the other cars. When he explained that he had no brakes, they were at first sceptical. Then they examined the car and found that the front brake line was sheared and the front brake discs cold.

Dennis Rushen remembers the race well. As he says: "It was a strange race. I was watching from the pitwall and when I noticed him slow I knew that something was wrong. When he told us what had happened afterwards we all just looked at the car and couldn't believe it. He had no front brakes at all! And he wasn't big-headed about it, he was very matter-of-fact.

"After the race we had a meeting in the truck. Kenny Andrews asked him what he could do to improve and Ayrton told him he should brake later. He said 'I was braking later than you into the corners and I had no brakes'!"

On Easter Monday, Senna went to Silverstone. It was pole position, fastest lap and victory again.

Senna was so far ahead of his competitors it hardly seemed worth his while. Was it easy for him? Once the season was over he said: "In 1981 everything was new. I was driving against people with one, two, three years' experience in Formula Ford. That's a big, big difference, but we still got there. It was the same in 1982. Yes, Calvin Fish was the only one who really put the pressure on me, but at times I think his car was better than mine."

Of course Senna was using the word 'pressure' comparatively. On all but a few occasions the best Fish could manage was second. It would have sounded arrogant if the facts had not backed it up: six races, six pole positions, six fastest laps, six victories.

Senna could even be modest about the whole affair. He said later: "I must say that I had very good equipment and support. You wouldn't believe the effort Ralph Firman put in for me in 1981, and it was the same in 1982 with Dennis Rushen. They both gave me very competitive cars and after that it was down to me."

The following weekend Senna took part in the first round of the EFDA Formula Ford 2000 Euroseries at Zolder in Belgium. There were new European drivers to compete against but he was still the favourite. His reputation had spread and his fellow competitors were eyeing him nervously. They were doubtless even more nervous when he took pole position by a second.

But this time it was not to be. His Ford engine let go on the third lap, before he had even had a chance to set his customary fastest lap, and the race victory went to Dutchman Cor Euser. It was the first time Senna had lost that season. All the same, the offers were flooding in from people who had recognised his talent, although he refused them all, even ex-Daytona 24-hour winner Toine Hezemins, who offered him £50,000 for the chance to promote him. Senna was going to do things his own way.

He put his Euroseries record straight on the familiar territory of Donington two weeks later. It was pole position, fastest lap and victory once again. The following day he was at Mallory Park for the next round of the British championship. He lost out on pole position for the first time that year and had to settle for second, but still took fastest lap and victory.

The next race, on 9th May, was another Euroseries round at Zolder, the support race for the 1982 Belgian Grand Prix. It was a turning point for Senna and for Formula One.

It was the weekend that Gilles Villeneuve was killed. The Ferrari star plunged into the catch fencing in qualifying while desperately trying to beat the time of team-mate Didier Pironi. Villeneuve was a popular man with those who knew him and the fans. He was the biggest legend to die in a Formula One car until almost exactly 12 years later, with Senna's own death at Imola.

The race weekend fell under a shadow. Although the Formula Ford event was a sideshow, a Rushen Green mechanic had seen the aftermath of the crash. It was awkward for the drivers and a major milestone, as many of them, like Senna, were competing at their first Grand Prix.

The event provided a chance for the drivers to be noticed on the international stage, and Senna had the advantage that his fame had gone before him. He was easily the biggest thing in the series. He confided to Rushen that he had been offered contracts by McLaren and Toleman but could not accept them. Both involved a subsidised season in Formula Three followed by an option for Formula One the following year. Senna wanted a firm guarantee that he would get a Formula One drive before he agreed to limit his choices. It took a lot of courage to turn down offers of that calibre, and a great deal of self-belief.

Senna later recalled why he turned down the offer from his future mentor Ron Dennis – one that most Formula Ford drivers would have given anything for. He said: "Ron Dennis was not the first Formula One manager to offer me an opportunity in Formula One. He offered me a Formula Three programme, a test contract in Formula One, good money and nothing to worry about. There was the possibility of a full-time Formula One place with McLaren in 1984. But I was not sure. I did not know Ron. I had read a lot about Formula One and talked to a lot of people but I was a bit worried about it. I preferred to organise my own Formula Three programme and go from there. I did not turn down Ron: I told him that I preferred to make the choice of Formula Three team myself. I felt that I was in a better position to choose than he was, because I knew the people involved. He did not understand that. But it is the reason I did not go with him. And I still believe that decision was correct at the time."

Such a cool attitude certainly did not stem from any lack of excitement at the prospect of Formula One. Senna's first Grand Prix support race was a big day for him and he was looking forward to meeting the stars. The biggest star in Brazil at the time was reigning world champion Nelson Piquet. Rushen recalls: "Ayrton said to me 'I'm going to introduce myself to Nelson Piquet because I want to be like him'. He was so excited, just like a boy, and all I could say was 'Yeah, okay'. But Piquet snubbed him and he took it personally – you do at that age. He was very angry and said 'I'm going to beat him one day'." He did.

Senna predictably took pole for the race. He got away from the rest easily at the start and had soon clocked the fastest lap and was leading by over 13 seconds. Then the unthinkable happened. He spun off.

It was the first time in his single-seater career that he had been put out of the race by his own mistake, and he had done it in front of his most important audience to date. He trudged back to the pits in a foul mood and muttered an apology to his team.

Rushen recalls: "He lost concentration and just fell off the track. He was so far in the lead. It's strange because he did exactly the same thing at Monaco in Formula One in 1988. He did it on a number of occasions. I never did figure it out.

"I think maybe the reason he went off at Zolder was because he was distracted by everything. He'd had the offers from Toleman and McLaren that weekend and I don't know if it went to his head. Then there was the Piquet thing. Also he'd met a girl. He wanted to go and meet her somewhere that evening but I had the only car. I told him if he won he could have the car and I'd make my own way back to the hotel, but if he lost he'd have to drive me all the way back. Of course when he lost I made him keep to the deal and he sulked all the way home."

Rushen and Senna were very good friends even by this early stage of the season. Rushen remembers him as a quiet young man who was often misunderstood. He says: "He was shy and he hated the cold. That was the main thing. He wouldn't get into the car until his gloves and balaclava had been warmed up on the radiator and he really didn't want to get out of bed in the morning. Some journalists wrote that he was arrogant, but he was shy. He only opened up with people he had known a while, his friends. And he really loved his family."

Rushen also has strong memories of Senna's racing skills. He says: "You see a lot of impressive young drivers, but he was the most amazing young lad I'd ever seen. He was way above everyone else. He would go out and do a few practice laps and when he came back in he would say that the left rear needed another pound of pressure. And he would be right.

"He once asked me 'Who do you think's the best? Me, Nelson Piquet or Chico Serra?' I think I said 'It's you'. And he replied 'It must be me. I've got so much more experience'. And he had, because he'd been racing in karts since he was four years old."

Senna's next race was the British round at Oulton Park on 30th May. It was his worst to date: he missed pole, missed the fastest lap and retired with a puncture, although he did win the celebrity challenge in a Sunbeam Talbot later that afternoon. In the next four rounds of the series – Brands Hatch on Bank Holiday Monday 31st May, Mallory Park on 6th June, Brands again the week after that and Oulton Park on 26th June – he seemed to have lost his qualifying sparkle, although he brought home four fastest laps and four victories to make the championship all but his. In-between Brands Hatch and Oulton he went to Hockenheim for the next round of the Euroseries. He qualified on pole, but had a bad start and was caught up in a first-corner pileup initiated by leader Cor Euser.

At this stage of the season Senna had won 12 times in 16 races. He had only lost one round of the British championship and had a commanding lead in the title chase. In the European championship he had finished only one of the races, which he had won, and had clocked two fastest laps, leaving him in fourth. However, with Senna on 24 points – just 10 behind championship leader Jesper Villumsen of Denmark – and 20 points available for a win and two for a fastest lap, he didn't consider his position bad at all.

On the plane out to the Dutch Grand Prix support race at Zandvoort on 3rd July, Senna was sat next to none other than Frank Williams. It was the first time that the pair had met. Senna took the opportunity to introduce himself and tell Williams about his career. He stuck in the team owner's memory enough for him to receive his very first Formula One test for Williams a year later. His list of Formula One team contacts was growing. Keith Sutton had been contacted by Bernie Ecclestone, then running Brabham, and Lotus boss Peter Warr, who had both expressed an interest in the young star. Fellow Brazilian and double world champion Emerson Fittipaldi could not offer him much from his struggling Formula One outfit, but was pleased to introduce him to all the team managers. He had also just done a test with fledgling Formula Three team Jordan.

The Jordan test at Silverstone in late June was Senna's first outing in a Formula Three car. Eddie Jordan had been impressed enough by the Brazilian's talent to give him the test for free. Senna completed 20 laps, came back to the pits to make some adjustments, went out again and within another 10 laps had beaten the pole time set the previous weekend by Jordan driver James Weaver. Jordan was canny enough to keep Senna's adjustments, and the team soon won with the car in that set-up in the European races at Nogaro in France and Jarama in Spain.

At Zandvoort Senna missed first qualifying because of clutch problems, leaving him with just one 30-minute session to get to know the unfamiliar track. It didn't stop him from taking pole. Despite another bad start, he slipped past leader Jaap van Slif Hoat on the second lap and led to the finish. It was a remarkable performance.

The next day Senna had to be back in Norfolk to race in the British championship. The car was loaded onto a truck that took the ferry back to Lowestoft. Dennis Rushen remembers: "We used to do all that stuff back then. It was great fun! We didn't test so much and racing was much better for the learning curve of the young drivers."

Snetterton was Senna's home territory. He could again qualify only second, but when the race started the track was soaking wet. Senna snatched the lead from Calvin Fish on lap five and pulled away into the distance. The rain had stopped and the track was drying out. Frank Bradley, a 37-year-old jellied-eel salesman and Formula Ford enthusiast, had started the race on slick tyres, willing to make a gamble where the up-and-comers could not take the risk. On the water-logged track they were hopeless and he was almost lapped by lap five, but as the track dried he began to work his way back up through the field very, very quickly. He was an experienced Formula Ford racer and knew the track well enough to know that it dried very rapidly. He was third by lap 15 of the 20-lap race with only Fish and Senna ahead of him, 20 seconds up the road.

He caught and passed Fish with two laps to go. On the drier track he was eight seconds faster than the rest. Senna, however, was a different problem. Although the tread had worn almost completely off his tyres and the car was all over the track, Senna was demonstrating superb car control to stay in the lead and somehow fend off Bradley. As they came up to the last lap, he was still there, fighting with the car. Bradley made a daring move at Sear corner. It surprised the Brazilian, who on the dry track had nowhere to go. Senna lost.

It was the first time all season that he had not won a race he had finished, but he took it very well, probably sensing that Bradley was not a major rival and had had a great deal of luck with his gamble on slicks. As Rushen remembers: "He was incredibly gracious. He thought it was great."

The following weekend, at Castle Coombe in the British championship, Senna produced his familiar hat-trick of pole position, fastest lap and win. The result was a very early championship victory with the minimum amount of fuss. Dennis Rushen remembers: "It wasn't that exciting. We all knew he was going to win so it was no big deal."

The next race was not until 1st August. It was another Snetterton affair and although Senna took fastest lap and race victory, it was not without controversy. When Fish tried to take the lead, Senna pushed him onto the dirt. Both drivers were furious, blaming each other, although contemporary accounts concur that Senna was in the wrong. To Fish's annoyance, he was fined £200 but allowed to keep his points. It was an unsavoury foreshadowing of later events in Senna's career and a glimpse of the darker side of his personality.

Next it was Hockenheim and the German Grand Prix support race in the Euroseries, which resulted in another pole, win and fastest lap. The Austrian Grand Prix support race was the following weekend. Senna and Rushen drove there together. Rushen recalls: "We were driving through the mountains on the way to Austria and we passed a waterfall. Ayrton told me to stop the car. I asked why and he said 'I'm going to stand by that waterfall and I want you to take my picture so I can send a copy back to my mum in Brazil'. He was like that."

Rushen counts the race at Austria – another pole-position, fastest-lap, victory clean sweep – as Senna's best of the season. He says: "It was amazing stuff. The old Österreichring was even more frightening than Spa. Ayrton came round after the first lap five seconds in the lead. That really made the Grand Prix guys pay attention." Senna won the race by 24 seconds.

Senna was virtually European champion; the next round of the series, at the Jyllandsring in Denmark, was tense but turned out to be a mere formality. He did his speciality – pole position, fastest lap and win – and was crowned champion.

Rushen has extremely fond memories of that race. As he says: "It was incredible, just a lot of happiness. It was much more important to us than the British title." Senna was moved to tears by his achievement. After the race he got drunk – Rushen believes for the first time – and did wheelies on a motorcycle in the street.

Keith Sutton was also at the race that weekend. Senna had paid for his flight and hotel room because he wanted him to be there. As Senna crossed the line to take the chequered flag as champion, he waved his hands in the air and Sutton took a photograph that still hangs on the wall of Dennis Rushen's office today. The picture is inscribed 'To Dennis, Thanks for making my weekend in Denmark extra special, Keith'.

While all this was happening Senna had not mentioned his wife to anyone, other than that she had decided to stay at home in Brazil and not come to England for the 1982 season. There was speculation that she was pregnant. Senna hated to fail but by August he had admitted to Keith Sutton and other friends that his marriage with Liliane was over. They quietly divorced and she eventually remarried and had two children. She has always refused to speak about her time with the man who became a legend. He also rarely mentioned the marriage, although several years later he reminisced: "I consider it to have been a very precious experience. I don't think of it as a mistake because we didn't have children and we both continued our lives with no ill effects."

Sutton clearly remembers the flight home with Senna. He says: "It was a marvellous weekend which I will never forget. On the return flight to England he told me about how he had split up with his wife and had met a Brazilian girl who studied in Brussels. We also discussed the idea of me being his photographer when he got into Formula One." On the back of Senna's European glory, Formula One seemed a certainty. His new girlfriend's name was Maria and she would become a fixture during his Formula Three season the following year.

From then on, with two championships wrapped up, Senna would be racing for fun and glory. In the British championship he scored another two wins and another two fastest laps at Thruxton and Silverstone on the subsequent two weekends. On 12th September he went to Mondello Park in Ireland for the final round of the Euroseries. He took pole, had a bad start, but retook the lead from local racer Joey Greenan on lap two and went on to set the fastest lap and win the 19m 32.7secs race by 18.5 seconds.

But Senna's season was not complete. He dearly wanted to win the elusive world karting championship, which was being held that year at Kalmar in Sweden on 15th-19th September. But all did not go well. A burst tyre on the first lap of timed practice put him right to the back of the grid for the heats. His performance was nothing short of brilliant — he made up 23 places in the third heat and 22 in the second with smoke pouring out of his engine — but the entry was large and in the final he could only make it to a lowly but well-fought 14th place. He was in such a bad mood that he refused to shake hands with the winners after the race.

His mood had not abated by the time he arrived at Brands Hatch for another British championship Formula Ford 2000 race a week later. He wasted time adjusting his front wing during qualifying and as a result ended up just third on the grid, albeit with an identical time to the first- and second-placed drivers. Had he not spent so much time changing his settings he would have set the time first and been awarded pole. In the race he was sluggish, until several laps in when he began to speed up so significantly that he broke the lap record. By that time, however, Calvin Fish was too far ahead to be beaten and Senna finished second by just 0.08 seconds.

It was a sour end to a spectacular season. As Dennis Rushen recalls: "Because he did the world karts and finished 14th he had a real sulk. I never saw him so cross. And then he only qualified third, which was not good by his standards. I was angry because it was as if halfway through the race he had suddenly decided he wanted to win it. It was the only time we had even a slight falling-out."

So Senna left his glorious Formula Ford career behind under a cloud. He returned to Brazil for a holiday, and when he arrived back in England it was to compete in the televised non-championship Formula Three race at Thruxton in mid-November with West Surrey Racing. He did not forget his friend and mentor Dennis Rushen, though, and the pair remained close throughout Senna's career.

Rushen loves to reminisce about Senna. He remembers: "He was always a very, very good friend. I continued to help him when he went on to Formula Three with Dick Bennetts at West Surrey. The last time I saw him was when he was testing for Williams in Portugal in 1994. He was different. His heart didn't seem to be in it any more. The time I saw him before that was in Brazil, where he told me that he wanted to drive for Ferrari. I still miss him."

That was a long time in the future. At the end of 1982 Senna was still looking for his first Formula One drive, although his dominant Formula Ford performances had drawn a lot of attention from the right circles. In his first two seasons of car racing he had four championships and had taken 34 wins from 47 Formula Ford races. It was a phenomenal achievement. Why he wasn't whisked off to Formula One at that point is an enduring mystery.

CHAPTER 5

The Decisive Year

Formula Three on Ayrton Senna's terms

By the end of 1982 Ayrton Senna had won all he could in Formula Ford. Barely two years after arriving in Britain he had wrung everything he could out of the Formula, winning all the championships – in fact, almost every major prize – that the category had to offer. The ones he didn't win were the ones he hadn't entered.

Nowadays he would probably have gone straight into Formula One. But that was then and this is now. By the traditional route, he still had two years of a traditional apprenticeship to serve. He was certain he would get into Formula One, but still uncertain how he would fare. He already had two offers on the table to finance his Formula Three career, from the McLaren and Toleman Formula One teams. In return for signing long contracts, he would be made 'team slave' as he often put it. Alex Hawkridge, boss of Toleman, and Ron Dennis, team principal of McLaren International, offered to give him the £100,000 necessary to finance a year in Formula Three, plus a salary. But it was the last thing he wanted.

Ron Dennis was very impressed. But to his amazement, Senna turned him down. "Of course Formula One is my goal," Senna said. "But I will tread very warily. I would be foolish to take the first offer to come my way. Better to wait until all the cards are on the table. Perhaps if something very good comes up I will take it before the end of the year. Whatever, I'd like to have something set up early so I can test. That is the key to success."

Formula Three was where he wanted to be in 1983 and the British championship was the finest in the world. By then he had enough money from his father and some Brazilian banks to finance a season. Two Formula Three teams were after his services: the fledgling Eddie Jordan-run team and the dominant entrant West Surrey Racing, run by Dick Bennetts.

Senna had had his first experience of Formula Three at Silverstone in mid-June 1982, testing for Jordan's outfit. Up-and-coming drivers, even of Senna's talent, normally had to pay for a test session in a Formula Three car. But somewhat uncharacteristically, Jordan gave him the test for free.

Racing for Rushen Green in Formula Ford 2000 was taking up most of Senna's time, and he turned up at Silverstone on a Wednesday afternoon after a morning's testing at the Mallory Park circuit 35 miles away.

The Jordan team had been racing at the Silverstone club circuit in the European Formula Three championship a week earlier, and the benchmark for Senna was the 54.2 second pole time set by Jordan driver James Weaver in the morning session. He was already at a disadvantage, as the cooler mornings are generally the best stage to set a time at Silverstone in the summer. Senna did 20 laps in the Ralt Toyota, came in, made some tiny changes to the car, and took only another 10 laps to equal Weaver's time. A further 10 laps and he had become one of a very select group of drivers to break the 54-second barrier on the club circuit. Eddie Jordan was hugely impressed with the way Senna had set up the car. His style was to come out of the car and lock himself away and make two or three pages of notes on what needed to be done by the engineers. This habit never changed throughout his career. So successful were the changes he recommended that the team kept Senna's adjustments on the car, and Weaver won the next two races in the championship.

Senna did not test for Jordan again and never discussed a race drive with Eddie Jordan, despite the team principal's continual attempts to reach him by telephone. He had already made up his mind that Dick Bennetts' West Surrey Racing was the pedigree team in Formula Three and he wanted to be with the best. Eddie Jordan admits today it always niggled him that Senna did not think him good enough to race for. Or even to have negotiations with.

In fact several Formula Three teams were on the look-out for him. Dick Bennetts had first come across the Brazilian in 1981, when he was racing in Formula Ford 1600 with Van Diemen, but it was not until Senna moved on to the more powerful Formula Ford 2000 cars in 1982 that he really began to take notice.

As Bennetts recalls: "I was first introduced to him in 1981 in Formula Ford, but the first time we spoke about 1983 was in mid-1982 when we were running the young Argentine 'Quiqui' Mansilla. We were brought together through Dennis Rushen. We'd followed Ayrton, so he was given a test with that in mind. Eddie Jordan was chasing him as well, but once he had tested our car he said 'That's it, I'll do the race with you'."

Unlike Jordan, West Surrey Racing was a team with a pedigree. Bennetts came to England from New Zealand in 1972, and soon gained experience engineering in Formula Atlantic and Formula 5000. In the mid-1970s he worked for March Engineering's Formula Two team. In 1978, Bennetts moved on to Ron Dennis's Project 4 Racing operation, working at its factory, as the team entered cars in various championships. In 1980 he joined Project 4's Formula Three team, and Stefan Johansson won the championship that year under Bennetts' guidance.

Bennetts joined forces with Mike Cox of West Surrey Engineering in 1981, to run Jonathan Palmer in British Formula Three – and he won the championship. As Mike Cox struggled for cash, West Surrey Racing was born as a separate organisation, and in 1982 Bennetts entered Enrique Mansilla in the British Formula Three championship. He won five races and lost the championship to Tommy Byrne by just three points. But what impressed Senna was the team's reliability record. Bennetts had not had a single car failure in 1982.

Senna had raced against Mansilla in Formula Ford 1600, and reasoned that if any team could get Mansilla that close to the title then that was the team to be with. Bennetts says: "One of the key reasons he chose us or wanted to be with us was that he didn't rate Mansilla. They had raced together in 1981 in Formula Ford and they'd had lots of dust-ups. He said 'If you've finished second in the championship with that guy, you must have a good car'. That was his way of looking at it. We had to really work on Mansilla as a driver and the first third of the year was a disaster. But once we got him to understand and give feedback, we just turned him around and then we won five races. He had the raw speed, but he just didn't understand our car. And his technical feedback wasn't very good."

Bennetts wanted to make sure of Senna so he suggested he entered an end-of-season non-championship Formula Three race at Thruxton. The event, on 13th November 1982, was to be televised, and was the perfect opportunity for Senna to prove himself on a bigger stage.

But it disrupted his plans. He had already bought a plane ticket: he planned to return home after he had won the Formula Ford 2000 championship at the end of September, and skip the last two races. He would then spend a full five months in Brazil. But he badly wanted the West Surrey drive, and by 28th October he was back in cold Britain, to test for West Surrey Racing at Thruxton in preparation for the big event.

On the morning of the 28th, on his 14th lap, he set a time of 1m 13.33secs. It was less than two-10ths of a second off the best Formula Three lap ever recorded at Thruxton, and he was on old tyres. Although he came close later that day, he failed to better the time, and on the following day the weather was damp and the opportunity was lost. It was as if he had got the business of proving his speed out of the way and had decided to concentrate on setting up the car. Another test followed at the Snetterton circuit in Norfolk on 9th November.

Bennetts recalls: "At the very first test he was confident. You get a lot of young blokes who are quite nervous, but he was confident and his feedback was very good. He wasn't fazed by it at all. People said that with our good car and his ability we should definitely win at Thruxton. It's not that easy though." Bennetts was taken aback by the confidence in his new driver. He knew just how difficult winning was in the competitive world of Formula Three.

But it was that easy for Senna. After taking pole with a time of 1m 13.34secs, he clocked the fastest lap of 1m 13.94secs and won by 14.57 seconds over 15 laps from the Swede Bengt Tragardh, Calvin Fish and rally ace Henri Toivonen. Senna had not looked vulnerable at any stage of the weekend. In Dick Bennetts' own words he 'just walked away with it'.

That evening he reached a verbal agreement with Bennetts that he would drive for the team in 1983. Bennetts explains: "At the end of the race he said 'Yeah, I'm happy' and headed off back to Brazil. We didn't see him again until the end of February. We didn't have a contract down but he was very happy with the way the car performed and very happy with us as a team. The contract wasn't signed until two weeks before race one of 1983. We had agreed it with a handshake – it was just a matter of sorting out the sponsorship and all that stuff."

Back in Brazil, Senna's confidence about sponsorship was not misplaced. He needed over £110,000 for a season of Formula Three – serious money after the chicken-feed days of Formula Ford, which had cost his father a total of £40,000 for two seasons.

He negotiated new deals with Brazilian bank Banerj and the Brazilian Pool clothing company, which had given him limited support through Formula Ford 2000. With his father chipping in another £10,000, Senna had about

£70,000. It wasn't enough, but Bennetts found the balance from the Valvoline oil company, anxious to be on the championship-winning car.

Later that year, as Senna realised he would be a Formula One driver in 1984 and probably earning at least $1 million, he would decide he needed professional help. Up to then he and his father had handled everything. But his father had his own business to run and no time to tend to his son's business affairs. As his manager he chose an old family associate called Armando Botelho Texheriro. He didn't need any help with negotiations, just with his contracts and back-office affairs. Armando Botelho would remain with him until he died in 1989.

Senna arrived back in England so late before the beginning of the season that there was scarcely a chance to test. He delayed his return as long as possible, savouring the Brazilian sunshine before what he knew would be another season trudging around chilly England.

Luckily for him, the 1983 Ralt Toyota was an evolution of the 1982 car, rather than a completely new chassis, so the lack of testing was not a hindrance. In any case, Senna considered too much testing counter-productive as he said it dulled his driving edge.

He also made another momentous decision. He dropped the 'da Silva' bit of his name and resorted to just using his mother's maiden name, Senna. Da Silva was not distinctive and a common name in Brazil. It was the equivalent of 'Smith' in Britain.

The 1983 British Formula Three season began on 6th March at Silverstone. After his Thruxton win at the end of 1982 Senna was outright favourite, even though some of his competitors, notably Jordan's Martin Brundle, already had a season in the series behind them. But when Senna spun his car in the first qualifying session and could only manage second on the grid, some doubts began to surface.

Senna was fuming. He believed he had been cheated of pole by Magnum's David Leslie. He suspected the team of cheating and said so. He complained to journalists: "It was not fair. For sure they were not within the rules. Where there are so many limitations, there is no way that you can suddenly find a second of time. And when it came to the race they were one second away again. I don't like being made to look stupid."

But Senna still won the race at Silverstone. Then he won the next round at Thruxton on 13th March, then Silverstone again on 20th March, then Donington Park on 27th March, Thruxton on 4th April, Silverstone on 24th April, Thruxton on 2nd May, Brands Hatch on 8th May and Silverstone for the fourth time on 30th May. In those first nine races, he also took eight pole positions – missing out just that once to Leslie – and seven fastest laps. He had won all nine races. It was unprecedented, and no one had ever seen anything remotely like it before. Nelson Piquet held the record for seven wins in a row in 1978, and he was currently on his way to his second world title. Senna had taken nine in a row so far in 1983, and if the 1982 victory at Thruxton was taken into account that made it 10. It was simply phenomenal.

Senna's admirers were torn between whether the April Thruxton victory, when he suffered from 'flu, or his win at Brands Hatch in the wet in May was the greater achievement. Senna admitted at the time that he thought Brands Hatch the best drive, but Thruxton had given him the most pleasure. He said: "I dropped down to third, but I worked my way through. That was my most enjoyable race because it was good to come in from behind. It also meant that I had to understand how my car was working in relation to those around me." Senna above all relished a challenge, although they were not thick on the ground.

He explained: "No race is easy. There are just too many limiting factors and the cars are evenly matched. Also, I am fighting against experienced and good drivers, especially Martin – he is very good – and Davy Jones. If I make the slightest mistake they will be there."

But Senna had not made the slightest mistake. Away from the track things were also going well. He was still happily living with the Gugelmins at their old bungalow in the Norfolk village of Eaton. And in 1983 he made short trips back home to Brazil during the longer intervals between the races.

Bennetts remembers: "He was very professional for his age. These days we all have data-logging and computers, but Ayrton was so precise with his information you almost didn't need it. He was very dedicated, a very focused person. He pretty much kept himself to himself. He didn't mix too well with many of the other drivers. He chose not to make a lot of noise in a big crowd. There was a different side of him that no one else really saw."

Although he was dominating the Formula Three championship he had a big problem looming. Twenty-three-year-old Martin Brundle was clearly the best of the rest, and for every first place Senna was getting Brundle was taking second in Eddie Jordan's car. Coming up to the halfway mark of the season, Senna had 88 points to Brundle's 54. Brundle had finished second in eight of the races and third in the other. He was clearly Senna's only opposition, if he could have been said to have any opposition. The points system was nine, six, four, three, two, one for the top six, with a point for fastest lap and the best 17 out of 20 results to count – a different system might have put Senna even further ahead, but as it was he had a comfortable lead.

The team was predictably delighted with its driver, but at the same time people were getting edgy with the knowledge that the winning streak must one day come to an end. Bennetts recalls: "I just thought one day the bubble was gonna burst. We'd won the first four in 1981 with Jonathan Palmer and that was pretty good. But when I got nine I thought we had to do 10."

The 10th round on 11th June was the biggest race of the year to date. Silverstone was hosting a combined round of the European and British Formula Three championships, and top-class continental opposition would be present.

The two series raced side by side, and drivers could choose – by the end of qualifying – which championship they wanted their finishing position to count towards. The only real difference between the European and British series was the tyres – the European cars ran on highly-developed Yokohama rubber and the British cars on the slower Avons. Consequently the European runners would be a great deal faster than their British counterparts, although because points were awarded independently for both championships, the full nine points would still go to the highest-placed British runner, regardless of where he finished in the overall order.

Senna and Bennetts deliberated, but in the end the Brazilian typically opted for the European event. He was far ahead of Brundle in the British and didn't need the points – for him it was the chance to prove himself on the international stage. Brundle took the conservative option of competing in the British series, looking towards the possibility of reducing the gap from 32 to 22 points while Senna was otherwise occupied.

The first qualifying session was wet, but the track had dried out in time for the second and Senna had soon set the fastest time. Brundle was languishing in 12th, although he was still by far the fastest of the British runners. It was not, however, where he wanted to be. He wanted to win.

In the closing minutes of qualifying, Brundle took what must have seemed a strange decision at the time. He sacrificed the chance of British points for an opportunity to run with the frontrunners and changed over to Yokohamas. He put the car on pole, less than a 10th of a second ahead of Senna.

Bennetts recalls: "We had such a points lead over Martin that we thought we'd go for an outright win. So quite late on we switched to Yokohamas, but even later than us Eddie Jordan and Martin switched to Yokohamas as well.

They caught us out because they had already raced in Europe with the tyres in 1982. They had a good relationship with Yokohama and knew how the tyres worked better than us, so Martin was quicker. We didn't get the best out of the Yokohamas or weren't given the best or both, I don't know. But we were P2 on the grid and Martin was P1."

At the start, Brundle had the best getaway and Senna struggled to catch him. Against the advice of the Yokohama engineers, he had chosen to run three different compounds of tyre all at once, and now he was paying the price, facing massive understeer. He soon found that he was struggling to hold off regular European runner Johnny Dumfries for second. Senna was determined to catch Brundle and put Dumfries onto the grass rather than let him past. But on the seventh lap, he pushed too far.

Bennetts explains: "He was trying to go quick and he crashed at the Woodcote chicane. He reckoned he got a puncture when he came off Club Corner that lap, and the left rear dropped off the edge of the kerb. When he got to the chicane, he turned in and the car just lost its grip. Whether it was a puncture or him, I don't know. I suppose we're all disappointed when we've won nine out of nine and we start to think 10 out of 10 or 11 out of 11 is possible. None of us like losing, whether it's the driver, the team manager or the engineers. That's our job – we're there to win. It was a bit of a worry, but we still had quite a lead in the championship."

Brundle won the race, but because he had been entered for the European championship, the gap to Senna in the British championship remained unchanged. It could easily have been all over right then – Brundle could have had his moment of glory and that would have been that. But Senna had been defeated, and it meant that next time he would have to push himself a little bit harder to make sure there was no recurrence.

The next race was at Cadwell Park in Lincolnshire, near the seaside town of Cleethorpes. Qualifying took place at 9.30am on race day. In the closing stages of the session, Senna found he was just 0.01 seconds ahead of Brundle, so he went out to set a faster lap.

Bennetts says: "He was on pole, that was the frustrating thing, but there was five minutes left. He said there was just a little bit too much understeer, so we put a bit of front wing on and out he went. Someone timing halfway round the lap said he was another three or four 10ths quicker and would have had pole by a mile, but unfortunately he didn't finish the lap. He came very quickly through the left-hander going up the hill, where the cars become airborne and jump, and he dropped the right rear wheel off the edge of the track.

That makes the left front light, so when he changed from left to right there was no weight on the left front and the car couldn't turn so it just went straight into the marshals' post. We couldn't start the race because the car was written off. Martin was second, and third on the grid was miles away from the both of them. By 2.15 in the afternoon I was sitting in our local pub in Shepperton."

Brundle won and set fastest lap. The gap was down to 24 points.

Two weeks later at Snetterton, Senna qualified in fourth. He and Bennetts could not figure out what the problem was with the car. Dumfries wrote off his car in qualifying, so that moved Senna up a place to third on the grid. At the start, he pushed into second and began to chase after Brundle for the lead, setting the fastest lap. On the penultimate lap, he was almost close enough to make a move, so he tried one. Brundle moved across and Senna ran up over Brundle's right rear and spun in front of Davy Jones before crashing backwards into the tyre wall. Brundle won.

Suddenly Senna's unshakeable lead was beginning to wobble. The gap to Brundle was now just 16 points, 89 to 73.

Bennetts remembers: "He got a bit frustrated. I had to sit him down and tell him it's better to finish second and get six points for second and one for fastest lap than to throw it all away and get one point for fastest lap. It was a bit frustrating when he wouldn't accept second place, when he could have won the championship comfortably instead of putting pressure on himself and us."

The next race was at Silverstone and another big one. The British Grand Prix supporting race on 16th July was the showpiece of the season. All the Formula One team bosses would be there on the look-out for new talent. Senna could not afford another silly mistake. And he did not make one. He notched up victory, pole position and fastest lap and increased his lead to 20 points.

At Donington on 24th July, Senna got pole and fastest lap, but Brundle was quicker off the line and won the race – the lead was back down to 18 points. Two weeks later Senna struggled with the car at Oulton Park and lost pole to Brundle. Brundle led, but in the closing stages the two collided heavily as Senna tried to overtake and both went out of the race. At the instigation of his rivals and the stewards, Senna had his licence endorsed, but took a point for fastest lap and opened out his lead to 19 points. A fortnight later, West Surrey Racing tried to take revenge at Silverstone when Brundle's ride height was found to be too low, but the stewards took no action. Bennetts felt that was the only time in the season when the situation got close to nasty: "The rivalry got a little bit heated. We believed they were fiddling the rules a bit. The ride height of the skirts failed. I wasn't that close to Silverstone and Eddie [Jordan] was based there. But every other time it was just good hard racing."

Senna won but missed fastest lap. Brundle was second, but the gap was now a more comfortable 22 points. At the next round at Oulton Park, Senna crashed heavily while trying to overtake Brundle, who went on to win, pushing the gap between them down to 13 points. At Thruxton, Brundle won and set fastest lap, when Senna's engine gave up after two laps, the first-ever mechanical failure in a race for a car run by West Surrey Racing. The gap was three points. At Silverstone, Senna misjudged the rain in qualifying and was back in fourth place on the grid. He fought back to second place, less than a second behind Brundle, but he lost and Brundle also scored fastest lap.

For the first time in the season, Senna was not leading the championship, and there was only one race left. Brundle had 123 points to Senna's 122 and was the man of the moment. As Bennetts remembers: "We thought we'd have to go out and buy some number two [decals]. The pressure was on. Everything hinged on that last round at Thruxton."

Because of his consistency, Brundle would have to drop points; Senna couldn't. All Senna had to do was win. But over the second half of the season, that had proved far from easy.

However, Dick Bennetts had a trick up his sleeve. He had discovered a very important piece of information that would put West Surrey Racing back on a par with the Jordan-run cars. He recalls: "I possibly didn't get on the case quick enough. We both had Toyota engines, both built by the Novamotor company in Italy, but Martin's were being rebuilt in Italy and ours were being rebuilt in England. And ours didn't get the evolution. The chassis was good but we were losing it in straight-line speed. That meant we were running less downforce at the wing, so we had to fight harder through the corners. That's why accidents happened and Ayrton was getting frustrated because he knew he was as good as he had been before but Martin was challenging him. We were a bit slow on the uptake.

"Before the final round we sent our engine back to Novamotor in Italy as well. Ayrton drove out to Italy with it and spent three or four days with Mr Pedrazani, the boss of Novamotor. Plus Ralt had two chassis modifications and there was one for us and one for Eddie Jordan – Ron Tauranac was being fair. We chose the sidepods and they chose a different front geometry or something. We went to Snetterton for a test prior to the final round, both teams at one end of the pits to the other, and we were flying with this new engine. If we'd had it six or seven races before, we wouldn't have had half the accidents. So in the final round we just left Martin for dead again. With the new engine and the better aerodynamics, we got pole position, fastest lap and the win."

It was a remarkably simple and one-sided end to a thrilling season. Brundle never looked like he could beat Senna that weekend. West Surrey Racing was back at its best.

One of the best innovations of the weekend had been Senna's decision to tape up the oil radiator outlet to enable the engine to heat up more quickly and allow him to run faster in the crucial opening laps. The problem was that by lap six the engine had begun to overheat. Senna, however, had thought of this. He could not reach the tape from the cockpit wearing his seatbelts, so had practised unfastening his seatbelts and reaching out of the car on the straight to remove the tape. Just behind him, Brundle saw the Brazilian reach out of the car and almost lose it at the chicane. But once his seatbelts had been rebuckled he began to pull away again until he crossed the line seven seconds ahead.

Eddie Jordan complained that West Surrey Racing had got the better part of the aerodynamic packages from Ralt, but Bennetts laughs it off. He says: "Ralt made two options – we got one part and he got the other. We didn't ask for that one. We didn't know before we entered which one had the biggest gain. So of course afterwards Eddie would complain that we got the better aerodynamics, but he had the better engine for six, seven, eight races."

Senna was champion, but that was not the end of his Formula Three career. A month later he was entered to compete in the Formula Three Grand Prix at Macao. The event had previously been run for Formula Atlantic cars, and this was the first time the prestigious Formula Three event was being held. Top international competition would be present from all the major Formula Three series in the world.

Senna arrived late to the Portuguese colony because on the Monday he had been testing for Bernie Ecclestone's Brabham Formula One team at Paul Ricard, which had followed shortly on from a test with Toleman. He was a man in demand. On Monday evening he flew back to England with Ecclestone in his Learjet, where he caught a flight out to the Far East the following day. Senna did not arrive in Hong Kong until Wednesday night, after a 13-hour flight.

Bennetts recalls: "He was pretty cool. He'd been racing professionally since he was very young and that helped him a lot. He was going to arrive in Hong Kong and I told him when he got off the plane which way to go to the town. He said 'I know. I came here when I was 16 for the world kart championship'. It was our first time there and we'd arrived four or five days earlier, so we thought we could give him some help on where to go."

As well as regular opponent Martin Brundle and some of the other British runners, Senna would face Colombian Roberto Guerrero, who had already completed two seasons of Formula One, and a host of international competition headed by Gerhard Berger. No one had raced in Macao before and the cars would be shod with the unfamiliar Yokohama tyres that Senna had used once, at the European Formula Three round at Silverstone. Senna, Brundle and Guerrero would officially be competing for the Marlboro-backed Theodore team, though Senna would be run by Bennetts, Brundle by Jordan and Guerrero by the familiar faces who had backed him in the Theodore F1 team.

First qualifying was on Thursday and Senna was suffering from jetlag. He still managed joint second in the order, behind Guerrero and equal with Brundle. It was his first time on a street circuit and he learnt about the dangers the hard way when he clipped the wall and ended his session after just three laps.

On Friday, in second qualifying, he struggled with a damaged gear selector and could only complete another three laps. It gave him pole in 2m 22.02secs, almost a 10th of a second ahead of Guerrero. As Saturday was a free day, he went out on the town with the other drivers that night to celebrate his pole position.

Saturday might have been a free day, but it was not one without work. As Bennetts recalls: "I'd arranged to do a debrief with him on Saturday and he didn't turn up when we'd agreed. I got told later he was out at a nightclub on Friday, apparently drinking just water or orange juice. Then someone else told me that Tommy Byrne had laced his drinks with vodka. So he didn't turn up for the debrief and I had to take all the decisions myself. We'd finished preparing it all by about six on Saturday night so when Ayrton walked up to the workshop I said 'Too late, mate' and that was that."

Senna had found out that jetlag and hangovers don't mix, and had spent most of the day running, trying to clear his head. By the Sunday morning warm-up session, he was still feeling out of sorts and completed just two runs before handing the car back to his mechanics, unusually telling them that everything was perfect and nothing needed to be changed. He was soaked in sweat and went back to the hotel to sleep for two hours before the afternoon's two heats that would decide the champion of Macao.

When he awoke he felt fine. In the first heat Guerrero got ahead at the start, but at the second corner Senna was through in a move that Guerrero didn't believe was possible on cold tyres. In the second heat Senna didn't even have that distraction and he led from lights to flag. He was champion and that night he celebrated with the team at the Lisboa Hotel until the early hours of the morning.

It was the perfect end to a glorious Formula Three career and one which did his Formula One aspirations a great deal of good. Even at that stage, he looked head and shoulders above the rest. Over the years, some of the best drivers in the world have passed through the training school of West Surrey Racing – Mika Häkkinen, Rubens Barrichello, Eddie Irvine, Allan McNish, Pedro de la Rosa, Christian Fittipaldi, Cristiano da Matta and Mauricio Gugelmin among them – but Dick Bennetts remembers Senna as the best. He says: "They weren't big then, they were small. I wasn't into management in those days – if I had been I'd have been a very wealthy man now. You've got to gauge each driver by that year and how tough the competition is, but Ayrton did stand out for sure. To this day I'll say that Ayrton and Mika were the two most raw-talented drivers. Ayrton would stand out above Mika because of his technical feedback and so on, because whereas Mika had a lot of raw talent, Ayrton could tell you more about the car. He was like a mobile computer."

Over the following few years, Bennetts kept in touch with Senna after he had recommended Gugelmin to him for a Formula Three drive in 1985. Senna was very interested in his friend's career and even came to races to offer his support. Bennetts thinks he got to know him better in those days, when he had made the transition to Formula One.

He says: "It came to the crunch and Mauricio was about to win the championship. He was sitting on pole position and Ayrton was looking round all the other cars and saying 'You haven't got enough wing on, you haven't got enough wing on'. We'd done two full days of hard testing and we knew where we were going. And he kept looking at the tyres to make sure they were all right. He was really helpful, but I kept him away from Mauricio because he was panicking about not having enough downforce. But once he got ahead he was gone."

There were also some less tense moments, such as the time in 1985 when Senna was looking for a house in England, where Gugelmin would also stay. Bennetts explains: "Ayrton stayed for quite a while at a mansion down in Esher. When he first moved there, I was his front man to avoid using his name. I had to sort out the agents, go round the houses and say what I thought. He briefed me on what he wanted in the price range. Of course, he's there at 25 in a tracksuit and wants to buy this 40-roomed house and the owner just didn't take him seriously. So I'd go along with the tie on, because they didn't think it could be the blokes in tracksuits. Senna and Gugelmin were both looking round saying 'We like this, we like that'.

"They'd look at the garden and say 'We like this, we can fly our radio-controlled planes'. One woman said 'Is that bloke gonna buy it?' I said yes. 'Has he got the money?' she asked. I said 'Don't worry about the money, believe me'. We never told them who he was. One of them recognised him, but we never mentioned his name. They'd just wander round, prodding things and say 'Ooh, that looks nice' or 'No, I don't like that'. I couldn't keep a straight face some days. That went on for about a month.

"We kept in touch for the first few years. Mauricio told me at Rockingham that he still goes to the Chinese restaurant in Shepperton, the Forum, which they both loved. We used to go there once or twice a year. They used to take the mickey out of each other, about who was the tightest money-wise. Their grasp of the English language was amazing. Ayrton said to Mauricio 'You could swim across the Thames with an Alka Seltzer in your hand and it wouldn't melt because your fist is so tight'. I would just crack up laughing. Where do they pick up all that? But as soon as there was a TV camera around Senna would immediately back off and be quiet. There was his private life and then there was his professional life."

At the West Surrey Racing factory, Bennetts has a display of crash helmets from most of his drivers, and four out of five of his British Formula Three champions. The missing face is Senna. Bennetts remembers sadly his last meeting with the Brazilian. He says: "I last saw him at the McLaren Autosport awards at the end of 1993. I'd arranged to get one of his helmets at the British Grand Prix in 1994. When I heard that he'd died we were racing at Silverstone with another Brazilian driver, Gualter Salles. In those days we had two races and Gualter didn't want to do race two. I had to really sit him down and say 'Look son, it's the only thing you can do'. It was hard. I couldn't believe it. I got calls from all over the world: Brazil, Australia, Europe. I couldn't go to the funeral because we were racing in England at the time."

Bennetts hopes that he will be able to get hold of at least a replica of Senna's famous yellow helmet one day to complete his collection, as a reminder of the Brazilian's time in Formula Three. It was a stunning season, and most of Senna's records remained unbeaten until Jan Magnussen's shatteringly dominant season in 1994. Senna had without a doubt made his mark and there was only one place left for him to go – Formula One.

CHAPTER 6

Senna vs Brundle

When careers collided and divided

The talent was similar but the execution was of a whole different order. To understand what Ayrton Senna did right in his career, it is also necessary to understand what Martin Brundle did wrong.

The history of Formula One is littered with tales of under-achieving drivers who before they reached Formula One matched men who would later go on to become champions, and yet who never managed to make a success of their own careers. A classic modern case is Brundle and Senna.

Brundle challenged Senna strongly during an electrifying year of Formula Three racing in 1983, and there was little to choose between them. But Senna went on to achieve immortality with 41 wins, three world championships and 65 poles, while Brundle only stepped onto the podium a few times before becoming a TV commentator. How did so much change after 1983?

Both men entered Formula One is 1984. Arguably Brundle had the more promising start, securing a berth with the Tyrrell team while Senna joined the miserable Toleman outfit. But whilst Senna clearly saw Toleman as a stepping stone, only Brundle saw Tyrrell as the start of a long-term relationship and his career. It was the first sign of the different judgement skills displayed by both men.

Ken Tyrrell was ecstatic and believed he had secured the more talented driver for the following three years. As he said at the start of the 1984 season: "We believe that signing Martin will help because, as I said to Jackie, I think we've found a new JYS."

Likening any Formula Three driver to triple world champion Jackie Stewart was praise indeed, and for Brundle this was the crest of a very large wave that carried him into Formula One. But it was better even than that for the 24-year-old from King's Lynn. Tyrrell had no reason to think he had signed a lesser star. The previous year, Brundle had run Brazilian Ayrton Senna very close for the British Formula Three title. Winning Formula Three in the 1980s meant almost certain promotion to Formula One without having to graduate through Formula Two (the equivalent to Formula 3000). But so evenly matched were they that both Senna and Brundle were launched into Formula One in 1984. However, there the comparisons ended. The moment he stepped into a racing car, Senna had future world champion stamped all over him.

Senna was different straight away. He had charisma, an inner confidence, intensity and desire that was unsettling to some, but distinctly appealing to those who knew the signs of greatness. He had arrived in Britain in 1981 with his young wife to race Formula Ford. By other people's standards he was successful, but not by his. He was ruthlessly hard on himself and at the end of that Formula Ford season, he announced he was retiring. He returned to Brazil for a cold, hard assessment of his life and ambitions. The conclusion was clear. He needed to wipe the slate of all emotional attachments and distractions and start again.

The new Ayrton Senna returned to Europe, having left his wife, but with continued financial support from loyal Brazilian sponsors, and set out on an intensely focused course to become the greatest racing driver ever. It was do or die. In his confidantes, friends and team members he expected total loyalty and commitment. For him there was nothing else in life, and he would do whatever it took to recruit the necessary people to help him achieve his goal. His natural magnetism, aura and skill attracted believers – they knew what he could do. His mindset had few weaknesses.

By comparison, for Martin Brundle, England was home and there was a job to be done in the family business – there was no need to leave home. His family provided support and stability. He needed to keep working because sponsorship in the UK for British drivers was always tight, and he had to support himself. Of course he wanted to become world champion – it was the reason he raced, but his education and culture were vastly different from Senna's. Ayrton Senna and Martin Brundle had the same ambition, competed for the same rewards, but with different armoury and tools, both psychologically and physically. When their paths crossed in 1983, everything appeared to favour the 23-year-old from São Paulo. He had won all there was to win in Formula Ford 1600 and in Formula Ford 2000 in 1982. His Formula Three debut, at Thruxton's end-of-season non-championship thrash that year, had yielded pole position, fastest lap and a dominant victory.

By contrast Brundle was not feared, rather envied in his first season of Formula Three in 1982. And though he was the pre-season favourite, he got blown away initially by Irishman Tommy Byrne.

"I don't mind admitting that at the start of 1982 I felt under one hell of a lot of pressure," Brundle recalls. "There I was with the plum BP drive and there was everyone else who'd missed out saying: 'Why did he get the drive? He's only a tin-top racer'. I decided I wasn't going to let anyone upset me and I made up my mind to approach the season brimming with confidence."

Byrne was dominant, and Brundle kept clashing with another rising Brit, Dave Scott. He fought up to second in the opening race, but his satisfaction, like his confidence, didn't last long. "Les Thacker of BP called me into his office the following day – I thought to say congratulations. Instead he gave me the biggest bollocking of my life. That came as a real shock, as I thought I'd done quite well." The bollocking appeared to work: by season-end he was the fastest man out there, having won at Oulton Park and Thruxton and set five pole positions. But then came 1983.

The only mistake Senna made in the first nine rounds of the 1983 British Formula Three championship was one quick spin in practice for the first race, at Silverstone. Otherwise his West Surrey Racing Ralt RT3 was dominant. Brundle, in his Eddie Jordan Racing RT3, was his closest challenger, only once being beaten for the runner-up slot. Sometimes he led off the line, but always Senna was in command by the end of the lap. A lesser driver would have collapsed psychologically, but Brundle had done a lot of learning. At times he felt having Senna around was the worst thing that could have happened to his career, but gradually he changed that mindset.

"I did wish to God he wasn't racing against me," he says. "Then I started to realise that without Ayrton I'd simply be the guy who was doing what was expected of him, with my Formula Three experience. I think we've all got to admit that 'the man' is something special, so when I beat him it's going to mean a lot more."

Brundle, for all those consecutive defeats, had no doubt that he would win through. It was that resolve that first began to attract the attention that would eventually catapult him into the big league.

The first cracks in Senna's armour appeared when the British series combined with the European Formula Three championship, at Silverstone in June. Both the West Surrey Racing and Eddie Jordan Racing camps opted to run the European-spec Yokohama tyres, rather than Avons as contenders for the British series. Brundle won the race overall. Senna, blaming a graining tyre, spun twice trying to keep up. A week later, at Cadwell Park in Lincolnshire, Brundle won easily after Senna crashed his Ralt in practice. On home ground at Snetterton in Norfolk, Brundle won again, after Senna crashed trying to pass him with two laps to go. "He was quicker out of Sear but I was on the left-hand side of the road and there was only half a car width to my left. He chose to take it, expecting me to lift off. But I didn't. We touched, and I saw the rivets on the underside of his car as it went skywards! Then he stayed on the gas and tried to t-bone me at the Esses." The incident typified the ruthless determination that would become part of the Senna legend. "People said I looked sheepish afterwards, but that wasn't because I'd had him off – it was because most of the witnesses they drew from the crowd were my mates or relatives. Snetterton really wasn't the place to protest against me. We're all related to each other in Norfolk!"

Brundle went on to win at Donington, where Senna dogged his every move, then the duo clashed at Oulton Park when a rash overtaking move by Senna saw him park on top of Brundle's car. The series exploded into a battle that went down to the last race. At Thruxton Senna beat Brundle, and the title was his. But both had by then attracted the eyes of Formula One team-owners.

The difference between Senna and Brundle was that, from the beginning, Senna had a clear vision of his Grand Prix future, and how to achieve his goal of becoming world champion. Already he was discerning and had total confidence in his ability – and his value. On the other hand, Brundle was pleased to be in with a chance of a Formula One drive, any drive. Ultimately Senna opted for Toleman, which was an interesting choice. The team was not an outright winner, but showed much promise. Senna rightly assessed its potential, and that of learning the business of Formula One in such a team. Joining a leading team would have led to high expectations and pressure. At Toleman, he reasoned, he would exceed expectations. Meanwhile Brundle parlayed persistent pestering of Ken Tyrrell and impressive subsequent tests in both England and Brazil early in 1984 into a full-time Formula One ride with the Tyrrell team.

On their debut in Brazil, Senna qualified the turbo-charged Toleman-Hart 16th. Brundle was 18th, in the normally aspirated Tyrrell-Cosworth. Both outqualified their team-mates. They ran together for a while, but

Senna fell back on lap eight with failing boost pressure and retired. Brundle sped to an excellent fifth place. In South Africa, which greatly favoured the turbos, Senna qualified 13th and finished a heat-exhausted sixth, despite losing his nosecone; Brundle qualified 25th and finished 11th. Kyalami highlighted Senna's physical frailty, as he was dehydrated and engulfed by cramps after the race, and promptly christened 'the wimp' by his team. But his impressive race performance counteracted any negative impressions. Belgium saw Senna qualify 19th and Brundle 22nd but both were upstaged by Brundle's team-mate Stefan Bellof as the German beat Senna to seventh while Brundle lost a wheel. In Imola, to his intense chagrin, Senna failed to qualify after tyre dramas, but Brundle was only 11th with fuel-feed problems as Bellof finished fifth. In France, equipped with Michelin tyres instead of the troublesome Pirellis that Toleman started the year with, Senna qualified 13th but blew a turbo, while Brundle qualified 23rd and finished 12th.

It was in Monaco that Senna's Formula One legend truly began. In qualifying Brundle charged the Armco heavily, inverted his car exiting Tabac and narrowly escaped injury. But on race day it was Senna and Bellof who made the headlines. In appalling conditions they were closing on Alain Prost's leading McLaren when clerk of the course Jacky Ickx stopped the race prematurely. Few doubted that given another few laps Senna would have scored his first Grand Prix victory, though some forgot Bellof was actually catching him. Senna had displayed the first glimpse of brilliance that would set him apart. A turbo in the wet was a difficult animal, so he drove his turbo Toleman like a normally aspirated car, changing up through the gears just before the turbo hit boost. In discussion with the team before the start, he had also reasoned it would be a long time before the rain stopped so he decided to start with a very light fuel load. With Michelin he was also on the right rain tyre.

None of this was good for Brundle, who had not made the race in Monte Carlo. Nor did Canada help. Senna qualified ninth and finished seventh, right behind Nigel Mansell, while Brundle qualified ahead of Bellof, back in 21st, and finished 10th. But the next tracks, Detroit and Dallas, favoured the under-powered Tyrrells.

Senna qualified seventh in Detroit, Brundle 11th, more than a second faster than Bellof. While Senna crashed out of the race, Brundle took an excellent second place behind Nelson Piquet's turbo-charged Brabham-BMW. Launching a determined challenge in the closing laps, he finished less than a second behind. It was a mature, impressive performance. Maybe things were changing.

Then came Dallas, where the career paths diverged dramatically.

Senna continued to impress with his speed in qualifying around the concrete wall-lined circuit. Brundle was learning the new track Friday morning when his Tyrrell suddenly twitched out of control, slamming into one concrete wall before bouncing into another. The front of the chassis was severely damaged – and so were Brundle's legs. His Formula One career would never be the same again.

"That accident spoiled my momentum big time," he says. "I was on crutches for six months and lost my fitness level. I was always compromised after that. I could do some aerobic stuff, but no jogging. For the first couple of years after the shunt my feet didn't work properly. I had some curious offs and incidents because of that. My feet wouldn't do what I wanted them to."

He was lucky compared to Johnny Herbert, who damaged both feet, whereas Brundle suffered worse damage to the left. "The right one is stiff, but the left one barely moves. If I was like Johnny I would have been in serious trouble," he says. "At Le Mans, you know, I can't articulate my right foot enough if the brake is higher than the throttle, but my team-mates prefer uneven pedals. It's little things like that, knock-on effects. When left-foot braking came into Formula One I couldn't do it. I can't even press a road car brake properly sometimes. I'm on or off like a switch, there's no finesse."

In time he recovered, rejoining Tyrrell for full seasons in 1985 and 1986 before switching to Zakspeed's turbo for 1987. In 1988 he turned his back on Formula One to lead Jaguar's sportscar programme, becoming world champion. He returned to Formula One with Brabham in 1989 before leaving again for sportscars in 1990, and rejoined Brabham again for 1991. By then people no longer regarded him as 'The Man Who Nearly Beat Senna'.

By then 1983 was a distant memory, and a story was going around that seemingly offering a logical explanation why Brundle had run Senna so close, when ever since the Brazilian had been head and shoulders above. "Eddie Jordan had a single-drive camshaft update on Martin's Toyota engine whereas Ayrton had an older engine with twin-drive," West Surrey Racing boss Dick Bennetts suggests. "We were a bit off the ball there, until Ayrton got one of the single-drive engines for the final race and won by a country mile."

Brundle smiles at the thought. "It's funny, isn't it? I met up with Ron Tauranac in Monaco this year; his memory is staggering. He told me he had always been meaning to apologise to me since Thruxton 1983, when without thinking he just dished out update kits for the RT3. Dickie and Ayrton got the new sidepods, I got the pushrod front suspension. Ron reckoned the pods were worth more with their greater downforce, and that's why Ayrton had that easy win. I don't remember any big deal about engines, but it rings a bell Ayrton making a fuss, driving there and back to Novamotors in Italy to see his new engine tested on the dyno and then bringing it home with him before Thruxton." Again the Brazilian's desire to win knew no limits.

As Senna's career progressed, his desire to improve never diminished. No stone was left unturned. When he realised his performance could be improved by his physical fitness, and understood the importance of blood oxygen levels, he sought professional advice on how to increase his oxygen intake through prescribed aerobic exercise.

In 1992 Brundle finally managed to re-establish momentum, joining Benetton to partner Michael Schumacher. But even then it took him time to find his feet. "It was a different world, like starting again," he admits. "It was the first time for me in Formula One when every race I had the chance of a podium or maybe even a win, though we had only our normal Benetton Fords against Williams Renaults with full active suspension and bells-and-whistles semi-automatic gearshifting. I had to learn to cope with the pressure."

When he finally got going, he beat Schumacher at Imola, where the German spun chasing him, and should have won in Canada after passing Michael and catching eventual winner Gerhard Berger. Faulty bolts in the differential let him down. He was very quick at Silverstone and revived old memories as he battled with Senna for third place until he was baulked momentarily by Damon Hill (he still finished third when Senna retired). And on the day Schumacher won at Spa, it could easily have been the Englishman who celebrated a maiden win. "My fault, that one," he admits. "I should have pitted for slicks when I knew it was the right time, a lap sooner than I did." With Senna-like instinct Schumacher made the right decision, pitted and won. "That killed the momentum again," says Brundle.

By September it was announced he would drive alongside Prost at Williams, but for reasons he still cannot understand the drive went to Damon Hill instead. His career never recovered, despite spells with Ligier in 1993, McLaren in 1994 with Häkkinen, and later with Rubens Barrichello at Jordan before he finally quit at the end of 1996.

Today, Martin Brundle is a very sharp, streetwise Formula One commentator. Never one of life's whingers, he tells it like it is. Looking back at why his career path ultimately diverged so dramatically from Senna's, he is characteristically tough on himself. "The 1983 season certainly elevated me, and Ayrton and I each had someone of value to beat. That year Eddie and I did 22 races on £87,000. I look back on it now with a mixture of wonderment and frustration. In the same equipment as them I beat Ayrton, Michael and Mika on my day, but that's the crucial bit – on my day. I couldn't deliver all the time. Now when I see all the facilities around David Coulthard, I realise why I never delivered my full potential. It wasn't because of my driving ability. Until I broke my legs, I was back in the office every Monday morning after a race running our car dealerships, laughable when you think about it. But I did manage to give those three guys a run for their money at times, the three guys who dominated my era of Formula One. There's an expression I've heard: 'when the spotlight comes on, some people wilt and others draw energy'. I suppose that I wilted."

Brundle never did that. But what he often needed was to hit rock bottom. He did it in 1983 after being defeated by Senna in those nine consecutive races, and again early in 1992 after a run-in with Jean Alesi during practice at Imola, when he admitted he went back to his hotel room and cried.

"In the big years I seemed to need that," he says. "Some of my best drives were comebacks. In 1989 at Monaco, when I was heading for third and the battery went. Silverstone in the Ross Brawn Jaguar in 1991 when the throttle cable snapped and I lost seven minutes, but lapped Michael and co in their Sauber-Merc three times and Keke in the Peugeot five times and had to be lifted out of the car afterwards. Maybe I was normally too cautious, or just too tight. I don't know. But at the end of the day Ayrton won a lot of world championships, and it's not as if I narrowly missed out on a lot of them, is it?"

CHAPTER 7

A Day of Dreams

Senna's first test in a Formula One car

In July 1983 Ayrton Senna drove a Formula One car for the very first time. It was a Williams. That was poignant, as 11 years later his last drive would also be in a Williams. At the time, no one attached much significance to a day of testing at Donington Park after the 1983 British Grand Prix. It was just another test of another new young driver, witnessed by a dozen or so people.

But it would later come to be a cherished memory for those spectators. Luckily, photographers and television cameras recorded every detail of Tuesday 19th July 1983, the day Ayrton Senna first drove a Formula One car. It was warm and sunny at Donington Park, the Leicestershire track built to Formula One standards but which had never held a Formula One race.

Today, the idea of a test session at Donington is unlikely, but it had been earned by Senna who had won the Formula Three support race for the British Grand Prix a few days before. Being Senna, he had won it from pole and driven the fastest lap on the way. Nowadays, a start-to-finish victory, and a 10th win out of the 13 races of the F3 season so far, would have got him an immediate Formula One drive. In those days it was only enough to earn him a test session all of his own with the world champion team Williams. In today's environment young Senna's name would have been on a Williams contract before he sat in the car. But back then the competition for young drivers was nowhere near as intense. The average age of the Formula One grid in 1983 was 30. By 2001 it was 27.

Despite Senna being an obvious star of the future, the test attracted little attention. Frank Williams was presiding. But he had no idea of the significance. It would later turn out to be a day of ironies. Senna would start his Formula One career in a Williams and end it in a Williams, 11 years apart. Surprisingly, very few people remember much about the day, other than the fact that Senna took a Williams around Donington faster than anyone had before. The test session might never have taken place at all had the young Senna, travelling to Zandvoort to compete in the European Formula Ford 2000 support race to the Dutch Grand Prix the year before, not sat next to Frank Williams on the flight.

Peter Collins, then team manager at Williams, remembers it clearly: "When Frank arrived at the circuit he said to me, 'Oh I sat next to some young Brazilian driver, Ayrton Senna da Silva. Do you know him?' 'Yes,' I said. 'I know him. He's racing here.'"

Senna won the race that weekend and went on to take the European championship, winning six races of the nine races and qualifying on pole eight times.

Frank Williams remembers: "Ayrton was a very pushy and determined young man who was always phoning saying 'come on, let me have a go'. He had won most of the F3 races in 1983 and it was clear that he would probably go a long, long way, but no one really knows these things. Patrick Head and I discussed it and decided to test him. Patrick and I thought even if we couldn't use him for 1984 because of existing contracts extending into that year, it would be interesting to help him in his career and he might remember that later on. That is why we tested him. He was an impressive young man and I was very curious as to how he would go in a 500 horsepower machine. He was very determined and the ferocity of how he pursued Patrick and I for a test was impressive. He was persistent. He knew what he wanted, where to go and how to get it.

"On top of the results that he was piling up almost every weekend he was a very motivated young man but very different to his colleagues of a similar age. He was living in the Reading area at that time, which meant he was only about five or eight miles from my home, so my wife and I took him out for dinner half a dozen times in 1983 to try to make him feel a little bit more at home in that part of the world, and in our conversations, which tend to make my wife a little bit bored because they were only about motor racing, it came across how intense he was about his career."

Eventually Williams grudgingly agreed to the test and a date was set right after the British Grand Prix.

Senna arrived early at the track in his grey Alfa Romeo, along with Brazilian journalist Reginaldo Leme of TV Globo. Leme had worked in Formula One since 1972. He had similarly been a friend of Emerson Fittipaldi and Nelson Piquet at the start of their careers.

It was a circuit Senna knew well, but Donington was not a favourite test track for the Formula One teams. Williams had used it before to test another young driver, Jonathan Palmer, a few weeks before. Palmer was no slouch, a former Formula Three champion who had gone on to win the European Formula Two title in the senior two-litre category – one step below Formula One on the racing ladder. Palmer was sufficiently impressive to get a Grand Prix drive at his home race in Brands Hatch later that year.

Palmer's time was used as a marker to measure Senna's performance by. If Senna couldn't match Palmer's time he knew he had no future in Formula One. He didn't expect it to be a problem and it wasn't.

The Donington track of the early 1980s was only just over a minute long for a Formula One car. It was also the days before proper test teams: and Senna climbed into Keke Rosberg's FW08C chassis number nine, with the world champion's number one on the nose. It was the car Rosberg had driven at Silverstone, well out of the points in 11th.

Frank Williams was late arriving after his Jaguar broke down on the M1 and he had to wait for a lift sent out from the Williams factory. When Williams arrived, he and Senna huddled for 30 minutes before he got in the car. Leme says: "I remember Frank was smiling and they talked about all the different things."

Keith Sutton was also photographing the test. Sutton had driven down from Manchester. He says: "I remember my Mark II Cortina only just made it to Donington over the hills." Sutton was busy sending out press releases to all the magazines. "I remember as a 21-year-old I used to get calls from Bernie Ecclestone, Peter Warr, and Frank Williams asking how good he was. It was amazing."

He remembers how it all happened: "Senna called me and said it was a secret test. I need you to be there to take pictures, so we can get some publicity." The irony was lost on the young Brazilian.

Senna's brother Leonardo and his close friend Alvaro Teixeira also witnessed the test. Senna was clearly nervous about what to expect. It was an emotional moment for him. After he changed into his overalls he walked around the car and said in Portuguese "*chegou o dia*", meaning 'this is the day, the day's arrived, the dream day'. Leme remembers him knocking twice on the car. Then he climbed in as the mechanics helped him buckle up. They had written a note on the steering wheel saying 'Take Care, New Driver'.

Leme remembers: "I looked again and he was crying and I asked him what was wrong. He said that he was praying, that's all." Leme was filming the test for TV Globo, to be shown on television in Brazil, where there was already intense interest in Senna's career. He says now: "We were all expecting success."

They were not to be disappointed, as Senna drove an amazing first lap, and improved on his second, third, fourth, fifth laps. Every lap he went faster. Jonathan Palmer's time was soon within his reach. Palmer's best lap in his test at Donington was 61.7 seconds. Within nine laps Senna had equalled that. In total, he covered around 20 laps that day, setting a new Williams record around Donington of 60.1 seconds.

Senna himself called a halt to the test just as he was poised to be the first man to go around Donington in less than a minute. Williams says: "He stopped at about a 60.1 and said 'I think this engine is going to let go, so I would rather not carry on'. We said 'are you sure?' and he said 'yeah, that was fine for me, thanks very much.'"

Frank Williams remembers: "He drove very few laps – only about 20 and he was immediately very quick. It was clear that driving a Grand Prix car was well within his depth. Jonathan Palmer had done a lot of testing there, and his time was around 61.5 and I think Senna had equalled that by his eighth lap. By the end he had lapped in 60.1 seconds, even though he was a tight fit in Keke's car because Ayrton was tall, slim and Keke was quite broad and short. Obviously the guy was a bit different. It was all pretty easy for him, getting down to our previous best time within 10 laps. I certainly went away impressed." The mechanics were surprised that he beat Palmer's time by 1.4 seconds. Chief mechanic Alan Challis, now production controller at Williams, recalls: "It was a case of getting him familiar with what was in the cockpit and telling him to take his time, as you would with any Formula Three driver. The thing that struck me was how quick he was instantly. Remarkably smooth, confident and quick. He came back into the pits and we told him to slow down a bit. He said he wasn't trying."

Race mechanic Charlie Moody was in charge of preparing the FW08C with his number two Robbie Campbell, who already knew Senna quite well because he had worked previously in Formula One with Brazilian driver Emerson Fittipaldi.

"Of course, we'd seen Ayrton racing in Formula Ford 2000," remembers Campbell. "I used to kid him he had a big engine in the car but, of course he didn't. He was just quick. That day he went round Donington faster than anyone had ever driven a Williams there, and really, he wasn't trying too hard because he didn't fit the car. It was Keke's, and he was a really cramped fit length-wise but was loose laterally because Keke was broader.

"He did some laps, then came in and said to me: 'How many gears does this car have?' I told him it had six. 'OK,' he said. 'I only use five so far.'"

Sutton remembers Senna's speed into the chicane. "He was terrific under braking there. He was getting on the brakes so late and he was using all the road, just touching the entry kerb a couple of times. He just looked as if he had been doing it all his life." Steven Tee, another photographer at the test, recalls: "They couldn't believe how fast he was going. I think they might have done a couple of things to slow him down a bit, because everyone thought he was going too fast. They kept refuelling the car, things like that, to keep it heavy. I think they might have changed the suspension geometry and the wings a couple of times, too, without telling him. Nothing nasty, just little things to see if he noticed. To test him. He did notice. He spotted them all."

The team was certainly impressed, as Peter Collins discovered when they returned to the factory and gave him the news on the test. Collins remembers Alan Challis bubbling: "The bloke's incredible. It was just like the first time we tested Jackie Stewart at BRM." Collins and Challis told Frank Williams he should put him straight into the car and let him race. But it was not to be. For a change, Frank Williams was asleep.

When Senna arrived back at West Surrey Racing, team boss Dick Bennetts remembers: "He never really talked about it. He just said it was good. There was a little smile he used to give, a smile of contentment. He was not one of the loud ones and he didn't talk much about things like that. Once he was testing an F3000 car and had a big accident at Snetterton and didn't even tell me about it. I went to the next race and people were asking me about it and I didn't know." Frank Williams was pleased with the test but not enough to move the earth to give Senna a drive.

Williams explains: "We weren't looking for a driver for the following year. We had Laffite and Rosberg and we were happy with that. Keke was already a world champion and was in his third or fourth season, so Senna didn't compare. Both had a phenomenal ability, but Senna's was untapped. He hadn't found his limit yet. There is no mystery to this. We just look at all the evidence and make a decision. There is never any shining beam of light over one driver: you have to take a little bit of a punt."

Astonishingly, Frank Williams didn't sign him up, and let the next Jackie

Stewart slip through his fingers. A few months later Senna would also get a test with McLaren, which also let him slip away.

Keith Sutton's photos are today cherished memories. He reminisces: "He was pretty sensational that day, I have to tell you, and he impressed a lot of people. I never know why Frank Williams didn't sign him up that day. I think he regretted it and I think that probably is the reason why he signed Jenson Button up because he didn't want to let another one go through. It was a great privilege for me to be there that day and to see him in a Formula One car for the first time." But he didn't get the drive, or indeed any top drive the following season.

Senna's first test was the start of six months of intrigue and prevarication that would never happen today. Following that test in July 1983, arguably the greatest driver ever slipped through the hands of Frank Williams, Ron Dennis, Bernie Ecclestone and Peter Warr in quick succession.

After such a test and a junior career, how he slipped through the Williams team's fingers is a mystery to all. Today, Senna's name would have been on four contracts before anyone would even let him sit in a car. Frank Williams plays the situation down today, but privately will admit it was one of his biggest mistakes.

CHAPTER 8

1984: The Toleman Year

The rookie learns the ropes

At the end of 1983 Ayrton Senna knew he would be driving in Formula One in 1984 – he just wasn't sure for which team. The problem, for Formula One's team principals, was that he was too good to be true. He had dominated the British Formula Three championship but not proved himself that much better than runner-up Martin Brundle, who had run him too close.

It meant the the arrival of Ayrton Senna in Formula One in 1984 would be no simple affair. The complex Brazilian made his debut with the cold, methodical calculation that would eventually see him come to dominate the sport and arguably be its best-ever performer. First he turned down deals with three of the most powerful men in Formula One, and then he signed a contract with a team at the other end of the grid – a contract he knew he was going to break. But that's why Senna was Senna.

Nowadays, a driver with his obvious talent, would have been rushed into the formula straight out of Formula Ford 2000. But then there were lessons to be learned and an apprenticeship to be served. It was totally different to the system that operates today where young drivers are hounded by avaricious managers and signed up to long, lucrative management deals.

Back then even ace Formula Three drivers traditionally did not graduate straight to Formula One; a period in Formula Two – or Formula 3000 as it later became – was deemed necessary. Senna was trying to skip a season.

Only Jackie Stewart had previously managed that, back in 1965, and then Emerson Fittipaldi half a decade later.

It was a year of politics, when all the top drives with the four top teams seemed to be sealed for someone else. It wasn't that he was unwanted; events had merely conspired against him. Then, as now, Formula One seats were highly coveted and depended on a mixture of talent, cash and nationality. Peter Warr at Lotus desperately wanted him to replace Nigel Mansell, with whom he did not get on. But title sponsor Imperial Tobacco owned John Player Special and wanted a British driver, so Mansell kept his seat – as did his Italian partner Elio de Angelis, who had an ongoing contract.

Warr remembers how he was on the brink of signing Senna: "I had Ayrton in my office ready to sign for $50,000 and I told Peter Dyke, the promotions manager of John Player, 'you've got to do this!'. He produced the British newspapers on the Sunday morning which had got headlines 'Mansell Third!' They completely omitted the fact that Elio was pole in the same car. So that was justification for keeping Mansell for the following year."

Williams was also interested, but was not in a position to offer Senna a ride because it still had Jacques Laffite under contract for another year as Keke Rosberg's partner. McLaren had Niki Lauda and John Watson under contract. And then Renault sacked Alain Prost, and Dennis swooped to sign him in place of Watson, so there was no room for Senna at McLaren for 1984. There was a place at Brabham but this was blocked by politics. Nelson Piquet didn't want another talented Brazilian threatening him as he had threatened Niki Lauda all those years ago. He had been there and done that as the aggressor, and didn't want it done to him. In any case, Piquet had recognised Senna as a major new talent to threaten him as Brazil's Formula One hero, and had already taken a dislike to him, Senna remembered that. Piquet had snubbed Senna when he had tried to introduce himself in the Belgian Grand Prix paddock at Zolder in 1982.

But this didn't stop every savvy team principal, except strangely Frank Williams, from arriving at Senna's door, contract in hand – not for a race seat in Formula One, for a year of testing. Peter Warr of Lotus, Ron Dennis of McLaren and Bernie Ecclestone of Brabham all presented lucrative deals for testing in 1984, and long-term contracts that tied him to driving later on their terms, if he made the grade. But none of them had a drive for him that year.

He wanted none of it. For one he didn't want to be tied in the long term, and he wanted to race in 1984. It wasn't arrogance; even at the end of 1983 he wasn't sure he had what it took to succeed at the highest level.

So he accepted a two-year deal with Toleman – the best offer he could get at the time. It was all part of the Brazilian's carefully calculated strategy to turn himself into a world champion.

It wasn't the first time he had turned the big boys down. Ron Dennis had casually offered Senna a fully-funded Formula Three drive and an ongoing commitment to Formula One even while he was still racing in Formula Ford, but Senna was wary of committing himself too soon, especially to a man like Dennis, who had all sorts of strings attached. Even then he generally had confidence in the greatness that was to come, and was not about to let himself be trapped at the crucial stage of his Formula One graduation. He had analysed the fate of other promising drivers who had moved up with the wrong team and found themselves helplessly bogged down by an uncompetitive car.

Dennis was not the only one who had watched Senna on the nursery slopes and seen the fabulous artistry at work. Alex Hawkridge, the managing director of Toleman, had also been monitoring his performance closely. He was one of the first people beyond the club racing world to appreciate the Brazilian's prodigious talent.

Midway through 1982, he too offered to pay Senna's way through Formula Three, and he too was rejected – politely but firmly, as was invariably Senna's way.

There may have been no seats to drive but there were plenty of testing drives that came Senna's way after his Donington trial with Williams.

On a cold day late in November, he tested a McLaren MP4 at Silverstone. It was part of his prize for winning the British Formula Three championship, sponsored at that time by McLaren's major backer, Marlboro. The test was a bit of a showdown between him, Martin Brundle and Stefan Bellof. Regular driver John Watson posted a time first thing in the morning, then left it to the young guns to see how they matched up. Senna went first and almost immediately set a fast time, but the engine blew, even though he drove it all the way back to the pits. Dick Bennetts, his old Formula Three team manager, says: "He didn't earn many brownie points from Ron Dennis for that."

The engine was changed and Brundle and Bellof set similar times in a comparable number of laps. The wily Senna badgered Dennis into giving him another go; he realised perception was everything. He went out and set a time faster than Watson's. Still he didn't get the drive. Herbie Blash, then Brabham's team manager, was watching proceedings and told then team boss Bernie Ecclestone what he had seen.

Then Alex Hawkridge gave Senna a test drive at Silverstone in the 1.5-litre turbo-charged Toleman TG183B, a chunky, angular car designed by Rory Byrne, now one of the architects of Ferrari's world championship dominance.

He used this second chance to go much faster. This ability to influence events in his favour was a key difference that would lead their paths on different trajectories in years to come. Senna was ruthless and cunning, and was hell-bent on gaining the greatest advantage he could muster, regardless of what subterfuge he might have to employ. He had a winner's mentality to the exclusion of all else.

When he arrived for the test on Wednesday 9th November, Senna was surprised by a scepticism among the team that he hadn't encountered in earlier tests. He got into the regular car of Derek Warwick, who had left to drive for Renault and was regarded by Toleman engineers as a real star. Senna wasn't.

The track was damp initially, but gradually the day became crisp and pleasant. Ironically Senna's arch-rival in Formula Three, Martin Brundle, was testing for Ken Tyrrell. Arrows was also out, with Marc Surer driving. The scepticism lasted as long as it took Senna to complete his second flying lap. The stopwatches told the story. Senna lapped the Northamptonshire circuit faster than Derek Warwick had ever managed in a Toleman. At the British Grand Prix in July, Warwick had qualified 10th fastest in 1m 12.528secs. Senna's second lap was 1m 12.46secs, some six-100ths faster than Warwick. The car was identical in specification, except for a new six-speed gearbox and a slightly lower turbo-boost setting. The cooler temperature let the turbo engine breathe better and therefore develop a little more power, and the car had been developed further since July; but against that was the ambient temperature drop and less heat in the tyres, although the track pretty much dried out as the day went on. In all, Senna was probably at a disadvantage and his performance, on used Pirelli 91/99 rubber, was a sensation. From then on, Toleman's engineers forgot all about Warwick and focused on a new hero.

Despite a problem selecting fifth and sixth gears due to a loose bearing, and using less than race boost, Senna worked down to an eventual best of 1m 11.54secs on new race tyres. It would have been good enough for eighth on the grid at the Grand Prix four months earlier. "His attitude?" Alex Hawkridge remembers. "Absolutely no problem. The guy did everything we expected of him, and more. I was very impressed with the ease with which he seemed to do everything. He was in complete control from the word go."

Senna did 72 laps before he began to feel sore. He said on the day: "At first I thought I was comfortable in the car. Now I find I wasn't. Look how blistered my palm is. I found the power very impressive in the short gears, and very smooth in the top ratios, but on these tyres you have to watch the car very, very carefully even in a straight line, so you can't relax for a second."

Brundle impressed Tyrrell too that day, taking its normally aspirated 012 round faster than it had ever gone before: his best time of 1m 13.2secs would have been good enough for 12th on that year's Grand Prix grid.

Bernie Ecclestone arranged for Senna to test a Brabham at Paul Ricard; Brabham had won the drivers' championship with Nelson Piquet at the helm and Ecclestone was keen to find a young charger to motivate the Brazilian. But it was by no means certain that he would sign for Brabham: as he headed for Paul Ricard in the south of France to test the Brabham BMW, there was still a chance Bernie Ecclestone would offer all he wanted. But that dream was shattered when Nelson Piquet went out and set a 1m 5.9secs in the Brabham BT52B. Senna, testing with Mauro Baldi, Pierluigi Martini and Colombian Roberto Guerrero, was two seconds slower. It seemed obvious that Piquet had manipulated the situation with his mechanics.

Piquet also decided he didn't want Senna in the team. "I wouldn't blame him if he didn't," Senna later admitted. In reality he knew he had blown it with Brabham: as expected, Piquet blocked Senna and Ecclestone had little choice but to listen to his established driver. It was a rare mistake. But Senna wanted to race in Formula One in 1984 so he took what he could.

He had cannily kept Toleman on ice, and when Italian Teo Fabi signed for Brabham Senna signed a deal with the Toleman team. He said afterwards: "I promised myself I would not go home until I was absolutely sure I had a Formula One ride or had exhausted every opportunity."

Senna read the Toleman contract over the phone to his Brazilian lawyer. Typically, Senna had objected every so often to the best English legalese that Hawkridge's lawyers had drafted. Hawkridge, who appreciated the irony of a Portuguese-speaking Brazilian taking on the Establishment over English syntax, found himself agreeing with his new driver. Every 'i' had to be dotted and every 't' crossed before Senna was satisfied.

"We went afterwards for a drink in a pub down the road from our headquarters in Brentwood," Hawkridge remembers, "and suddenly Ayrton became a different character. It was as if he switched off from business mode and became this different man. There was no outward sign in his bearing or his manner, but it was as if he just decided that he was done for the day and could start relaxing. He began telling jokes, that was how we knew this steely businessman had taken the rest of the day off."

Senna signed a long-term deal that he had little intention of sticking to. He knew he would get a drive with a top team for 1985; he just didn't know which one. To ensure he would be free there was a clause in the contract that he could buy himself out for £100,000. "I will promise you 100 per cent effort every time I get into the cockpit," he told Hawkridge, "but if I decide that the car is not competitive I will go to another team. And if you try to stop me leaving, I will retire." Retirement was a typically empty Senna threat.

He said: "I knew that the impression I made in my first season in Formula One would be vital. And I did not want to be overcome in any political battles by a senior driver within the team. It was important to me that I went somewhere that I had a degree of control over my destiny, and also where I would be given the space to grow at my own pace." As usual, everything was calculated to the nth degree.

Toleman began the year with the same TG183B that Warwick and Bruno Giacomelli had driven the previous season. Warwick's best results had been two miserable fourth places. The car was reasonable, but its Pirelli tyres were no match for the rival Goodyear and Michelin rubber, and Toleman was being exceedingly brave in developing its own Brian Hart 1.5-litre turbo engine in the face of well-funded engines from Ferrari, BMW, Honda and TAG-Porsche. A new car was on the way.

Senna's debut, fittingly, was in Rio de Janeiro in March. Watched by family, friends and expectant fellow countrymen, he acquitted himself and qualified 16th. He was just ahead of new team-mate Johnny Cecotto on the grid, but tellingly he was more than a second faster. In the race he lasted eight laps before the boost pressure plunged, but next time out in South Africa, where he was again over a second faster than Cecotto in qualifying, he lined up 13th. He fought off heat exhaustion after losing the Toleman's wide nose early in the race, then he ran over debris on the straight while checking his gauges to pinpoint why his turbo boost pressure was fluctuating. This upset the aerodynamics and made the steering extremely heavy, and though he soldiered on to bring the car home sixth and score his first point, he collapsed after the race.

After the race Senna went along to the medical centre, where he met Professor Sid Watkins, the FIA's medical director, for the first time. He marched into the centre and, as Watkins recalls, started acting the prima donna. Senna said he was suffering cramp in his neck and shoulders and that it was causing him severe pain. Watkins remembered: "He did not understand the nature of his problem, and was creating a fuss until I told him in a few short, sharp words that his condition was not mortal, it was simply a problem of physical chemistry. The rational look returned to his eyes and thereafter, he behaved impeccably. He was at heart a gentleman."

In Belgium Senna was uncharacteristically slow, qualifying only 19th, half a second behind Cecotto, but finished seventh after struggling with the TG183B's uncompetitive Pirelli tyres. The malaise carried on to Imola where the unthinkable happened: for the only time in his life Ayrton Senna failed to qualify for a race.

But the circumstances were difficult. Toleman was dissatisfied with Pirelli's performance and was looking for a way to break the contract and sign for Michelin. The team alleged that money was owed by Pirelli, and a financial argument erupted between the two at the race; Senna was caught in the middle. He was instructed not to run on the Friday, which was a handicap on a tricky circuit that he did not know, and then when he did get going on Saturday his Hart 415T engine developed a misfire. It was a disaster, especially as Cecotto qualified only 19th, but it was only a momentary setback.

The storm cloud had a silver lining. Next time out, at the Dijon circuit in France, the new Toleman TG184s appeared, shod with Michelin tyres. Senna qualified 13th, well clear of Cecotto, but retired with turbo failure. Then came Monaco.

This was only Ayrton Senna's sixth Grand Prix, and everyone who saw it still believes that the extraordinary decision by clerk of the course Jacky Ickx, himself one of the greatest rain-masters of all time, to stop it prematurely because of the monsoon conditions cost the Brazilian his first victory.

The race began in poor conditions. Alain Prost led, before being overtaken by Nigel Mansell. When the Briton crashed dramatically, Prost took over again. But Senna was sensational. From 13th on the starting grid he picked his way steadily past vastly more experienced drivers who could not match his pace on the streaming roads of the principality. Ninth on the opening lap, he soon disposed of Lafitte's Williams and Manfred Winkelhock's ATS. From the seventh lap, nobody was watching anyone else. On the 10th lap Senna clobbered the kerb at the chicane, but undaunted he swept by Keke Rosberg's misfiring Williams two laps later. Then Michele Alboreto spun his Ferrari, gifting him another place. Soon he caught René Arnoux's Ferrari, then Lauda's McLaren. After 19 laps only Prost lay ahead. Lap by lap he closed on the Frenchman, who at the time was the yardstick of the sport. It took nothing away from Senna's drive that Stefan Bellof in the Goodyear-shod

Tyrrell was gradually hauling him in. Bedraggled spectators and hardy Formula One hands alike watched spellbound as the chunky white car moved closer and closer to its red-and-white target. The worse the conditions became, the faster Senna and Bellof went. It was only a matter of time for Prost, who was in trouble with his brakes and said later that he had been prepared to concede to Senna in the interests of scoring championship points. By the 31st lap Prost was signalling for the race to be stopped, but Senna kept walking on the water, his best lap 1.2 seconds faster than the McLaren driver's. Just before they crossed the line for the 32nd lap the Toleman edged dramatically ahead, but clerk of the course Ickx had instructed the red flag to be deployed. Round that slowdown lap, Senna waved triumphantly to the appreciative crowd, convinced that he had won his first Grand Prix. But to his intense chagrin he was reminded on his return to the pits that the rules backdated the result one lap from the time the red flag came out. Prost had won after all.

Incensed, Senna screamed in disappointment at officials. Unofficial accusations began to sweep the paddock that they had favoured a French driver, but nothing could be done. The race was over and Prost had won. Senna just had to accept it.

Circumstances never allowed him to get close to a repeat performance that year. He finished seventh in Canada after qualifying an excellent ninth a long way ahead of Cecotto, but crashed in Detroit after qualifying a sensational seventh. In Dallas he was sixth on the grid but retired with driveshaft failure. Elsewhere his luck was also out. At Hockenheim he was lucky to escape unharmed from a crash resulting from rear-wing failure, having qualified ninth; at the Österreichring he started 10th but lost oil pressure; and at Zandvoort he was 13th on the grid but retired with engine failure after 19 laps.

But in between these problems came his second podium, when he turned seventh place on the grid for the British Grand Prix at Brands Hatch into third place, also setting the third-fastest race lap. Cecotto never got a look-in against him, and after the Venezuelan's Formula One career ended with a leg-breaking shunt at Brands Hatch, Toleman ran just one car for Senna until Monza.

Engine-builder Brian Hart still raves about his time working with Senna that season. "The guy just had it all. He was so special. I never worked with anyone like him. It wasn't just that he could come into the pits and tell you what revs he'd been pulling in any gear at any given part of any lap; it wasn't just that his feedback was so clear and precise; he really loved what he was doing. It was everything to him, and he gave it everything he had."

But storm clouds were beginning to gather over the relationship. It was possibly all part of Senna's game plan, and he executed it to a tee. At Dallas he argued bitterly with Hawkridge. A sportscar race had left the track breaking up in places, and the team decreed that there was no point in running in Saturday's practice. Senna disagreed, and went ahead regardless.

It was probably a coincidence that he was in negotiations with Peter Warr of Lotus for 1985. Warr was intent on replacing Mansell. He had had enough of the darling of the late Colin Chapman, who would head off to replace Laffite at Williams. Michelin had also indicated that it was going to pull out of Formula One at the end of the season, and Senna saw little chance of Toleman getting Goodyear tyres. That meant patching things up with Pirelli. Toleman was beginning to look less attractive after all for a second season.

By the time of the Dutch Grand Prix on 26th August, Senna had agreed to join Lotus and drive a Lotus Renault, which he thought would be a better car than the Williams Honda in 1985.

He would partner Elio de Angelis, the well-bred Italian. Senna knew from watching him on the track that he was no slouch. He was fast and smooth, and under-rated. But Senna also knew that in a political fight, the Roman gentleman was merely a tyro. Lotus was a team that he could bend and mould to his own will. But there is no doubt that Senna joined Lotus on the basis of being number two. At least that's what he said: "I don't want to be number one, I'm happy to drive with Elio and learn my trade – you know, make some progress."

Warr didn't think this state of affairs would last for long, as he regarded Senna as the most complete driver to appear on the scene since Jimmy Clark.

The contract with Toleman, which was due to run to the end of 1986, would be terminated when Senna invoked the £100,000 buy-out clause as he had always planned to do.

But long before an announcement, rumours circulated and everyone in the paddock knew that Senna would go to Lotus – in his heart of hearts Hawkridge knew it too. However, Senna slightly miscalculated his timing, and was in breach when the Lotus deal was announced because he hadn't actually invoked the buy-out clause. It was his mistake. Hawkridge was incensed that Team Lotus had issued a press release at Zandvoort saying that of course Senna would complete the season with Toleman.

In revenge, Hawkridge suspended Senna from the Italian Grand Prix at Monza, replacing him with Stefan Johansson. Hawkridge knew the Brazilian would be upset and he was. He went ballistic but Hawkridge was unmoved. If Senna wanted to point to clauses in his contract, then so could he. "Of course he was absolutely, totally right to want to leave us," says Hawkridge. "And I can say that now that time and events have healed some of the rift. He was ruthless in identifying what he wanted and going about getting it, even if it meant going against a contract. That was no barrier to his progress."

Hawkridge acknowledges that there was a degree of vindictiveness in the decision to suspend the young driver: "I wanted to teach him a lesson. I knew that stopping him from racing was what would hurt him most, but I wanted him to leave us knowing that there is a price to pay for everything you do in life. It shook him rigid."

A subdued Senna issued a press statement in Monza, denying Toleman's allegations and defending his actions. He said that he had told Hawkridge of his intentions immediately after the Austrian Grand Prix on 19th August, and that he intended to exercise his buy-out clause. In Italy he added: "I intended to keep quiet about the whole thing and deal with the people who were involved at Toleman. I don't want any more aggravation."

It later emerged that Senna's manager Armando Botelho Texheriro had been in secret contact with Lotus since early July, and the negotiations had been underway for two months. Denis Jenkinson, the top F1 journalist of the time, writing in *Motor Sport* magazine, described Senna's tactics as: "A simple case of bad manners and lack of discipline." Senna simply claimed that he had been indicating since early in the season that he would be moving elsewhere.

Johansson did well, bringing Senna's Toleman home fourth.

Senna returned for Toleman at the Nürburgring and made a point by qualifying 12th (a long way ahead of Johansson, who had mechanical problems) but was eliminated in a first-corner shunt. His relationship with the team ended in Portugal, where he set fastest time on Saturday morning and qualified a sensational third, only a couple of 10ths shy of Piquet and Prost and a second faster than his Swedish team-mate. He drove a hard and very competitive race to third; but on the podium, as runner-up Lauda celebrated his half-point world championship victory over race-winner Prost, Senna's expression was initially one of complete disdain, as if he took no joy from either man's success, or even his own. This was, after all, the man who once said: "I am not designed to finish second, I am designed to win."

So Ayrton Senna moved on, and Toleman slid into a crevasse. In later years Senna would be ambiguous about the real reasons why he left, suggesting that it wasn't lack of faith in the team's technical ability after all. He claimed he would have been happy to stay. Perhaps the simple truth was that he really had foreseen the problems that lay ahead for the team as Michelin withdrew. Pirelli was still angry after the argument at Imola, while Goodyear told Toleman time and again there could be no rubber deal for 1985.

Toleman's subsequent tyre-supply misfortunes paved the way for the sale at the end of the 1985 season to its new sponsor, the Benetton family. From 1986 until the end of 2001, the team would race under the Benetton name.

By then Ayrton Senna was long gone. Breaking his contract might not have been fair or moral, and he had handled it badly. There had indeed been a buy-out clause, but the terms required Senna to inform Toleman of his intention to exercise it before entering into any detailed discussions with other teams. His failure to do so was what really caused the friction with Hawkridge.

However, it had been the right thing to do for his career. Hawkridge knew that too, and concedes the point. "You know," he says, harking wistfully back to bygone days and the most magical year of Toleman's brief life, "we never had a better driver in one of our cars."

At the very end of the year, Senna had a health scare when he developed Bell's palsy, an affliction of the nerve of the facial muscles, probably due to a virus. One side of his face became totally paralysed: he was unable to close his eye and his mouth was drawn to one side. He went to see Sid Watkins at the London Hospital: the professor put him on steroids to try to protect the swelling in the nerve, to preserve the possibility of recovery.

CHAPTER 9

Race of the Champions

The day Senna scalped the greats

As long as drivers have raced in Formula One, there has been speculation as to how the greatest drivers would have compared had they been competing in the same equipment and the same era. Rarely is there a chance to discover the truth. But in May 1984, for the inaugural race at the new Nürburgring track, the world got the opportunity to see 11 past, present and future world champions, plus a further handful of Formula One winners and sportscar aces battle it out in identical Mercedes 190E saloon cars. And it was Ayrton Senna, a Formula One rookie in his first season, who emerged the winner.

Technically, Senna shouldn't even have been allowed to compete: the event was for the cream of motorsport history, and at the time the biggest accolade that Senna had to his name was that he was reigning British Formula Three champion. Many of his rivals had never even heard of him. But he had impressed some of the right people and he was granted the right to take part. It was the biggest chance yet to show his genius.

The 14-mile-long Nürburgring had last been used as a Formula One track in 1976, when Niki Lauda's fiery accident had seen it scrapped from the calendar and the German Grand Prix moved to Hockenheim. Though minus a Formula One licence, some racing did continue at the track, but in May 1982 work began on a new, much shorter and safer circuit, retaining only the start-finish straight of its notorious predecessor. The new track was completed in spring 1984, and it was decided that the best way to open it would be to gather some of motor racing's biggest stars for a race.

It was a big occasion for German motorsport. The track was to hold the first European Grand Prix in October, and the promoters and organisers were keen that it should be seen as a major international circuit from the start. Mercedes eagerly provided a fleet of its new 190E saloon cars for the race, knowing that it could only result in good publicity. The Cosworth-engined 190E 2.3-litre, 16-valve saloon was Mercedes' first foray into high-performance saloon cars in that category, and it wanted to show what it could do.

There was the problem of getting all the stars together in the same place at the same time, but Mercedes had the upper hand. For several years the manufacturer had been running a scheme whereby Formula One drivers could receive discounted Mercedes cars ex-factory: some drivers were indebted to the manufacturer and willing to do something in return.

Mercedes invited every one of the 14 living Formula One world champions. Only five would not drive: Emerson Fittipaldi and Mario Andretti because they were qualifying for the Indianapolis 500 that weekend; Jackie Stewart, because he had promised himself never to race after his retirement and the death of François Cevert in 1973; reigning world champion Nelson Piquet, the only one who declined to enter; and Juan Manuel Fangio, who, aged 72, had increasing health worries and was simply too old. But Fangio turned up for the celebrations at the Nürburgring in his capacity as a global Mercedes ambassador.

Jack Brabham, Phil Hill, John Surtees, Denny Hulme, Niki Lauda, James Hunt, Jody Scheckter, Alan Jones and Keke Rosberg would race, and be joined by Formula One winners Stirling Moss, Carlos Reutemann, John Watson, Alain Prost, Jacques Laffite, and Elio de Angelis, as well as sportscar stars Klaus Ludwig, Manfred Schute and Udo Schutz.

Senna was not part of the original selection. When the race was held on 12th May, he had competed in only three Grand Prix events for Toleman Hart, logging two sixth places and a retirement, and had failed to qualify for what would have been his fourth Grand Prix at San Marino a week earlier. He at least had the kudos of being crowned British and Macao Formula Three champion in the previous year, but that hardly put him on the same level as the rest of the illustrious line-up.

He did, however, have friends in the right places. Senna had struck up a friendship with Gerd Kremer of Mercedes when they had met at a Formula Three race the previous year, and they would remain close until Senna's death a decade later. Kremer also had strong faith in Senna's ability, even when the Brazilian's talent was as yet unproven. Kremer, who at the time was the manufacturer's head of product placement in motorsport, was helping to organise the event: with the absent world champions, he found he had a spare place on the grid.

Kremer remembers: "At the time Ayrton did not have all the success that he expected to have. I was organising the Nürburgring event and the idea was to invite world champions and Nürburgring winners from the past. So actually Ayrton did not qualify, but since I was very successful in organising all the world champions and the Nürburgring winners, I was able to insist that I could invite Ayrton for the event instead of Emerson Fittipaldi, who was busy qualifying for the Indy 500. Ayrton took it quite seriously. He was very excited to have been invited to the opening of the new Nürburgring track. At that time he was a no-name."

Over the years Kremer was one of the few people to see Senna's private side. He recalls: "He was one of the finest people in the world. He cared about people and he was thoughtful. He never forgot birthdays or Christmas. He was not arrogant at all, more introverted. He was a Brazilian from his heart. He always needed to go back home to keep recharging his batteries, and he had a beautiful house out there in the middle of nature. And he was a person who believed in God."

Senna was very, very excited to get the chance to race against some of the world's most famous drivers in equal equipment. While some of his rivals looked on the race as a fun day out, Senna saw it as an opportunity to prove himself against the toughest competition and study exactly what they could do.

The drivers would be flying into Frankfurt airport, and ironically Kremer arranged for Senna to be collected at the airport by Alain Prost, as both would be arriving on the morning of qualifying. As Prost recalls: "It was the first time I met Ayrton. I picked him up at the airport as we arrived 15 minutes apart. On the way to the track, we chatted and he was very pleasant. We spent about half a day together like that. He didn't know any of the other drivers, which was quite funny."

The drivers had the opportunity to sit around and chat and catch up on all the gossip. For the retired stars it was a particularly good opportunity to meet friends from the old days. As John Surtees recalls: "It was a social gathering. Some people had more experience than others in saloon cars and suchlike. It was a good gathering and it was nice, but at the same time disappointing to go back to a circuit of which you had very fond memories and find it changed. I remember seeing that the old Sport Hotel had disappeared. It always had an air about it and you could quite imagine the days of all those famous names from before the war. It was a shame in some ways, but it was progress and the new circuit was one which had a wonderful setting but somehow paled into insignificance. I think from my point of view I'd much rather the race had been on the old circuit. At least I would have remembered the track!"

Qualifying saw Prost take pole position, with Senna lining up beside him on the grid. Of all the drivers they were probably the two with the most to prove and consequently the ones who took it most seriously. Senna was the unknown quantity and Prost was an undoubted future champion, already leading the 1984 title chase by 14 points (he would later lose the championship by half a point to Lauda). After the initial pleasantries, Senna's mood had changed. As Prost remembers: "I took pole and Ayrton was just squeezed out into second and he didn't like it. After that he didn't talk to me any more. At the time I thought it was quite funny."

After a night of partying laid on by Mercedes, the race took place on the following afternoon. The weather had taken a turn for the worse and the drivers spent most of the day huddled in the hospitality lounge, chatting about the past. John Watson remembers the conditions as 'bloody awful' and several drivers complained that the 190E's advanced ABS system didn't work as well on a wet track as it did on dry. But it was perfect Senna weather.

The field was divided between those who saw the 15-lap race as entertainment – principally James Hunt – and those, like Senna and Prost, who took it seriously. When the race began, Prost got off to the better start, with Senna tucking in behind him. But after half a lap, Senna decided he wanted to get past and pushed Prost wide to take the lead. As Prost regained the circuit, he tangled with Elio de Angelis and the pair dropped down to the back of the field. The Frenchman was extremely disgruntled by the episode.

The wet weather, the steely determination of some drivers and the blasé attitude of others was a recipe for chaos. As John Surtees recalls: "Driving standard road saloon cars on a race circuit is never particularly interesting or exciting, but the little cars all performed well. Some people treated it seriously, some didn't. I went about it in a way where I didn't treat it too seriously but I certainly didn't treat it with gay abandon either and I tried to make certain that I didn't smash the car up. That was important. I'd taken part in many celebrity races and they were more like a demolition derby, which unfortunately stops manufacturers doing it."

The attitudes of the other drivers differed greatly. Surtees says: "Carlos

Reutemann had two or three sets of tyres ready for his car and Ayrton was using all the track. I think it was particularly James Hunt who was using half the infield in order to cut corners. Somewhere around the circuit I had a big moment with Jack Brabham which nearly took me out of the race. Alan Jones was another one who went dirt-tracking. Him and a few others were not keeping to the circuit. There was a race going on which was on the circuit and [one] which had a short circuit where they cut out some of the corners."

John Watson was one of the drivers taking the race less seriously than some might have hoped. He explains: "In all fairness, it was not something that most of us saw as a positive career move. It was more of a family affair to thank Mercedes for the driver scheme. It didn't clash with anything so we all turned up. The weather was not particularly brilliant and most of us just took it all as a bit of fun. It wasn't going to make a career and it certainly wouldn't have broken one. But Ayrton for sure was on a mission – not just to win, but to prove that he was an outstanding driver."

Amid the chaos, Senna took a steady lead and managed to impress everyone there, even though many of the other drivers had never heard of him before. Surtees recalls: "The most interesting thing that came out of it for me was actually seeing Ayrton Senna for the first time and thinking 'Ah! There's something special there'. I was so impressed when I saw him, by the way he positioned himself and the way he got it all together, that when I was talking to Ferrari not long after I told him that was the driver he should have."

Jack Brabham chuckles at the memory of the unknown star. He says: "He'd got approval from someone somewhere. That was really the first time the name Senna meant anything to me. He won the race, which was very difficult in the rain, and he won it quite comfortably. At the time I thought this guy's going somewhere. And he did."

Stirling Moss was also impressed, as he says: "From that moment he just continued to rise until he got to where he was only equalled, in my opinion, by Fangio." Watson ran at the better end of the pack for much of the race and remembers how impressed he was with Senna's driving style. He says: "The main memory I have of it all is of Ayrton and how he attacked the circuit and in particular the chicane, which in those days was much quicker than today. He was just launching the car over the kerbs like a stone skimming across the water. He went to a different level. Everyone else was being very careful because the cars belonged to Mercedes. It was, I suppose, his calling card. That was the minimum accepted standard from him on display. He was clearly exceptionally gifted. Everyone else had turned up basically for the beer. It was a fun event, a thank you for Mercedes, a nice weekend in Germany in a nice hotel and nobody got stressed about it – except Ayrton, that is."

Senna was delighted to have won and proved himself against the highest competition. He left a lasting impression on many of his rivals, who had seen him race for the first time, which was probably worth a lot more to his career than the victory. He had arrived.

The finishing order that day was Senna, Lauda, Reutemann, Rosberg, Watson, Hulme, Scheckter, Brabham, Ludwig, Hunt, Surtees, Hill, Schute, Moss, Prost, Schutz, Laffite, Hermann and de Angelis. Alan Jones failed to finish after suffering mechanical problems, probably brought on by his rough treatment of the car.

Senna's win was not popular in all quarters, especially with the top figures at Mercedes who had agreed that the winner's car would be given pride of place in the Mercedes-Benz museum at Stuttgart, where it remains to this day. Gerd Kremer remembers: "Professor Werner Breitschwerdt, who was the chairman of Mercedes at the time, said he would have preferred it if John Watson, Carlos Reutemann or James Hunt had won the race if the car was to go in the museum. I said 'Don't worry about it. One day you will be very proud to have Ayrton Senna's car in your museum'. And now we can say we have a car in our museum that was driven by Ayrton Senna. Sometimes Professor Breitschwerdt and I meet up in Stuttgart and he always tells me that I was right about the car."

CHAPTER 10

1985: Lotus and the first Grand Prix win

The search for perfection

The move to Lotus took Ayrton Senna into the money. His Toleman salary was thought to be around $50,000 but the deal with Lotus took him over the $1 million mark; his income from personal sponsorship doubled that. Suddenly he needed management back-up in Europe, to handle the money and the deals that were being offered to him almost every day. It had all become too much for his existing manager, Brazilian Armando Botelho Texheriro, who had run his affairs on a part time basis.

As he cast around for a manager, it seemed to Senna that every other driver he knew was managed by Mark McCormack's International Management Group, a sports agency based in the United States but with offices all over the world. So he contacted IMG, which put him in touch with an executive at its Monaco office who ran its motorsport division. Julian Jakobi, an Oxford graduate, was a qualified accountant who had joined IMG in 1977. He had earned his spurs managing the interests of tennis players Bjorn Borg and Mats Wilander and golf stars Nick Faldo and Bernhard Langer. He then moved to Monte Carlo to open an IMG office that would concentrate on motor racing, an area which IMG boss Mark McCormack saw as having a promising future. One of McCormack's earliest clients had been Jackie Stewart, and the duo became famous in sports marketing circles when McCormack made Stewart the first driver to earn more than $100,000 a year in 1969. Another positive was that Jakobi already managed Alain Prost. Whilst that would have been a definite turn-off a few years later, Senna saw it as an advantage in 1985.

Jakobi was to become Senna's closest business associate in Europe, and the pair became firm friends over the course of the next nine years.

With the money flowing Senna could afford to move into a better house, and with the help of his former Formula Three boss Dick Bennetts, he found a mansion-like property near Esher in Surrey. He shared the house with his old friend Mauricio Gugelmin, who that season was competing in the British Formula Three championship for Bennetts' West Surrey Racing.

The Lotus team was based in Ketteringham Hall in leafy Norfolk. From Esher, Senna could cruise up there in his Mercedes saloon in less than an-hour-and-a-half, and also be at Heathrow within half-an-hour.

The Lotus team had an illustrious history. Its founder, Colin Chapman had died four years previously and the team had been taken over by Peter Warr, a former Chapman sidekick.

Even if the team did not know it, Lotus's glory days were over. But it was still capable of winning races and had an array of familiar names in its employment. The team was owned by Chapman's widow Hazel and her son Clive. Clive was Chapman's heir, but he admitted he had inherited none of his father's genius and was never in line to run the team. Hazel had called in Peter Warr and let him get on with it. The Lotus car factory was by then entirely separate from the team.

By the time he got to Lotus, Senna was already three years too late. Had Colin Chapman not died in 1982, he and Senna might have reconstituted something like the partnership between the Lotus boss and Jim Clark in the 1960s, when they conquered the world with the best driving and ingenious engineering solutions. Chapman was a bold engineer, willing to take a risk to get an edge. Even after Clark's fatal accident at Hockenheim in 1968, Chapman's cars had carried Graham Hill, Jochen Rindt, Emerson Fittipaldi and Mario Andretti to the world title. But the founder's death took away his company's innovative genius, and neither Peter Warr nor his successors could prevent the gradual decline of the team that had once vied with Ferrari for ultimate supremacy.

Luckily the John Player Special tobacco brand had remained a sponsor and the budget was generous, especially as Renault supplied free engines. But Formula One was moving on and Peter Warr had not noticed. Both McLaren and Williams were moving into new high-tech factories and raising the bar. Warr clung to cosy Ketteringham Hall and Team Lotus gradually lost its way.

But Senna loved driving down to Ketteringham Hall and sitting alone in Colin Chapman's old office, gazing out of the stone bay window and wondering what had gone before. He imagined Jochen Rindt, Graham Hill, Jim Clark, Mario Andretti and Emerson Fittipaldi passing by and chatting in that office with Chapman. The office had been preserved exactly the same as the day he died, and had not been used since except for formal occasions. On the wall was a black-and-white photograph of Chapman, from which he looked down on proceedings. Senna loved that room. He would sit there for hours.

Senna had joined Lotus because he really rated the talent of Gerard Ducarouge, the equivalent of the team's technical director. There was other talent there as well. Nigel Stepney, now a legend for bestowing reliability on Michael Schumacher's Ferrari, was a mechanic; and Lotus veteran Bob Dance was chief mechanic. Pat Symonds, the Renault technical engineer, was also there, in his second year of Formula One.

Senna's team-mate was the charming Italian Elio de Angelis. He was into his fifth season as a Lotus driver, having originally been hired by Chapman.

Senna impressed the Lotus team immediately. Peter Warr was astonished by his technical capacity as he said: "His approach was basically to sit down with the engineers, confirm that things he was expecting to be done to the cars had been done, and talk about the set-up. He would spend a lot of time on tyres and he would work out a programme, in conjunction with the engineers and myself, of what we wanted to try in practice, how we wanted to try it, when we wanted to run full tanks, how many laps we would do on this, that and the other and so on."

Nigel Stepney clearly remembers the first time he met Senna, when the Brazilian visited the Lotus factory over the winter of 1984. He says: "I didn't really have a lot to do with him because I was working on Elio's car and he was in the other one, but you could see when he was in his car he was totally oblivious to everyone else. He could wind himself up into a great intensity. You could watch him standing there or sitting in the car concentrating, and somehow he was completely different to anybody else you could meet."

Pat Symonds remembers expecting a rookie driver who needed guidance. He got a shock: "He was a young guy when he came to us – younger than our drivers had been before but he had an amazing maturity. He was very single-minded, very determined – racing was his career and he was going to be the best. We had obviously worked with a number of drivers over the years and we expected Ayrton, albeit with a very high reputation, to come to us needing training. But that was never the case – the guy was technical from day one."

Renault was not used to a driver becoming so absorbed with an engine. Renault designer Bernard Dudot was greatly impressed: "Ayrton was keenly interested in the engine. Right from the start of his co-operation with us, he spent a lot of time with me and [development engineer] Bruno Mauduit, learning how it worked and what parameters governed its operating temperatures, combustion rates and boost pressures – and also how those parameters interact with one another. That's a lot of data to absorb but he grasped it all. He had real insight into the realities, and he expressed himself easily with the engineers. He got so involved with the engine that it became his own. For us it was fascinating and extremely productive. What he gave us was like a method for constructive improvements to be made to the engine."

Mauduit says: "He was pointing out what was good and what was not, and suggesting what we should set our sights on. We realised he had never been wrong and had always steered us in the right direction. He was very keen on turbos, to such an extent that I checked all of them, with him behind me measuring them. He checked everything and tried to understand it all. The worst thing was meeting him in the hotel at 11pm, when we all wanted to sleep."

But it wasn't all serious business. As Warr recalls: "I have hundreds of nice memories but I think the one that characterises the Team Lotus and Senna relationship was the very first day he came to the factory. He arrived quite proudly in a Mercedes 2.3 16V, which he had been given as a prize for winning a celebrity saloon car race at the Nürburgring the previous year. Team Lotus mechanics are notorious for not letting egos get any bigger than they were, so they put a jack under the car and a block under the differential. When it came to the time for him to leave, of course it had to be the race driver's exit with lots of revs and lots of first gear. But when his foot came off the clutch the wheels turned but the car went nowhere. This was not only a joke but a little bit of a tester to see the nature of the animal we were dealing with. He took it in very good spirit. In Rio de Janeiro a few weeks later, he came into our garage and handed round some sweets. He made sure that Bob Dance got the one that turned his mouth – and his urine – blue. He peed blue for two days. That was the type of guy he was, and I think that even though he was young and at the beginning of his career, he was more than just a racing driver. He was a wonderful person and a terrific human being."

Senna spent most of the 1984/85 winter back in Brazil, where he picked up a viral infection of the inner ear called Bells Palsy. His face was inflamed and he was unable to blink his right eye. The condition eventually passed, but it led him to philosophical reflection. As he explained: "It helps you realise how weak you are. How inadequate you can be. You control yourself more, be careful, give more attention to yourself, your mental and physical condition-everything."

He also took the opportunity to respond to questions about his fitness, concerns which were raised after his collapse in the aftermath of the South African Grand Prix in 1984. He said: "I have had two months without any exercise so I am trying hard to compensate for the enforced lay-off. I am training hard but in the end what I really need is to drive the car. Fortunately the season is starting late. The virus had nothing to do with poor health – anyone could have caught it. But from my experience during the season I realise that I was trying to drive 100 per cent the whole distance just as I had been used to doing in Formula Three and Formula Ford events. Now I don't think that's possible. I don't care how strong or fit the driver, you can't drive flat out for the whole distance."

Senna was determined to make it to the very top, and the transition from a mid-grid outfit like Toleman to a legendary team capable of winning races was an important one. He tested the new Lotus 97T Renault for the first time at the Rio de Janeiro track in early February and was quick from the start. It was the perfect opportunity for him and things looked good for his home race, the first of the season at the Rio circuit. But after qualifying, for the first time in his life, he found himself playing second fiddle to his team-mate. Every other team-mate had been blown off at the first race of a new season. But not Elio de Angelis. Senna could only qualify fourth on the grid, a strong position, but one place and over three-tenths of a second behind de Angelis. It was an eye-opener for him – the game had moved up to a whole different level.

Senna adjusted accordingly and passed de Angelis at the start, but Alain Prost's McLaren TAG passed both of them. Senna was running in third place when his fuel injection failed on lap 49. It was a good debut for his new team, but he had not set the world alight.

Two weeks later the Formula One circus headed to Estoril for the Portuguese Grand Prix. It was a weekend that would show Senna not just the makings of a champion, but the look of a legend.

It rained for most of the weekend. At the start of the first qualifying session on Friday, the track was still damp from an earlier storm. But Lotus judged the weather perfectly and Senna and de Angelis left the pits when the track was at its driest, just minutes before another storm. De Angelis threw in a best of 1m 22.306secs for provisional pole, but seconds later Senna came past the line and set 1m 21.708secs. Then it began to rain.

De Angelis, like everyone else, was astonished. His own time had been sensational – 1.3 seconds better than Niki Lauda's third best time – but Senna made it look ordinary. The usually unflappable Italian demanded that a fresh set of tyres be fitted to his car, but the rain prevented him from setting a quick time. Gerard Ducarouge remembered that he was concerned: "I felt that I shouldn't let him out when the track was slippery like that. Trying to outdo your own team-mate in those conditions is asking for trouble."

De Angelis was still determined when it came to Saturday's qualifying session, when the conditions had improved. While Senna stood in the garage, watching the action on a TV screen, de Angelis failed to pull out more than two-tenths of a second on his Friday time. It was only in the dying minutes of the session, spurred by a 1m 21.42secs from Prost, that Senna decided to make an effort. His 1m 21.007secs was easily good enough for the first pole position of his Formula One career. De Angelis could only look on in sheer wonder.

Come Sunday morning everyone was still wondering what they were going to do about Senna. It was still raining and was predicted to last all day. Brian Hart, who had built the engines for Senna's Toleman the year before, was walking round the paddock telling anyone who would listen that they might as well go home – Senna would win. The winds were strong and warm-up had to be delayed by half-an-hour because the medical helicopter was unable to take off. Senna had earlier complained that his engine was short of power and it was changed for the afternoon's race.

The Brazilian seemed unruffled by the morning's dramas, as Warr recalls: "The build-up to the race itself was not very complicated. We did not have that many problems. Senna was quite relaxed and at ease. I would have thought most racing drivers would have been completely fazed by these terrible conditions, and so my lasting memory was that it did not faze him at all. All he wanted to do was talk about how to set the car up for the wet, how to get the best out of it, how to get the engine running so that it could be as smooth and responsive as it could, and so on."

Just before the race began, the rain fell harder still. While his rivals crawled away from the grid, Senna made a perfect start and flew off the grid in the lead. As 17 of the 26 starters gradually fell by the wayside, Senna glided onwards. After 10 laps he led by 12 seconds. After 20 laps, it was 30 seconds. After 40 laps, 45 seconds. Senna had gesticulated at officials as the conditions worsened to stop the race. When the race ground to a halt after 67 laps, as it passed the two-hour mark, Senna took the chequered flag by 1m 2.978secs from Italian, Michele Alboreto's Ferrari, the only car left on the same lap.

As Senna climbed out of the cockpit he was greeted by an ecstatic Peter Warr, a scene captured forever in an historic black-and-white photograph taken by Steven Tee of the photographic agency LAT. Behind Warr was his mother, Neyde, who had flown out from Brazil to watch the race.

Senna shed a few tears before climbing onto the top step of the podium for the very first time in a Grand Prix, flanked by Michele Alboreto and Patrick Tambay. He dedicated the victory to the team and his family.

"He went out there and just blew everybody else away," says Warr. "It was one of the motor races of all time – not for the closeness of competition, but for exactly the reverse. Anyone who stood there that day and saw him drive away from a field of some of the fiercest competitors that Formula One has seen could not fail to be impressed. There is a lovely story that gives a little insight into his character. At one time he got it wrong. He hadn't made a mistake the whole race but then he got it wrong and was off on the grass – the car went sideways and then swerved back to the tarmac. And with a flick of the steering wheel Senna went off down the road. Jenks [veteran journalist Denis Jenkinson] went up to him and said 'My God, that was unbelievable car control. That was really special'. And Ayrton said 'Don't you believe it. I just lost it – how it came back I don't know'. That demonstrated the honesty of the guy and characterised his entire career."

After the race Senna said: "They all said I made no mistakes, but that's not true. On one occasion I had all four wheels on the grass, totally out of control. But the car came back onto the circuit."

It was a stunning performance by a driver with little over a year of Formula One behind him. Senna later recalled: "One of the best moments of my career was my first victory in Formula One, in Portugal, in the rain. It was also the first pole position of my career and together with my first championship was one of the best, if not the best moment of my career so far. It was a race full of memories, full of excitement. It is something that I am going to keep in my mind for the rest of my life, that's for sure."

But at the time it had not all been pleasant as he recalled: "The race should have been stopped – conditions were dangerous. It was difficult to keep the car in a straight line because I could see nothing in front. Conditions were much harder than in Monaco last year. The rain was torrential and I had a few tricky moments. It was purely by chance that I did not come off the road. I knew I had won, it was just a question of keeping going."

Senna was astonished by the worldwide attention he received after his first victory. His initial reaction was to back away from it, telling his German journalist friend and later his biographer, Karin Sturm: "I come from a relatively sheltered world, from the warmth of my family." But there was nothing he could do about it. Suddenly he was the focus of attention at press conferences and every journalist wanted to interview him. He had done very few interviews before that, and journalists discovered he had a habit of not looking at people directly when he was talking to them. They soon interpreted this as a devil-may-care arrogance. Karin Sturm described it as 'an attempt to protect a very sensitive inner core from the harshness and coldness with which he was confronted in Formula One'.

Suddenly any thoughts of him having to play second fiddle to Elio de Angelis were gone. A process had begun whereby de Angelis would be relegated to number two driver. Nigel Stepney said: "The whole nucleus of the team working for him just happened."

Unsurprisingly he was suddenly championship material and would have taken the title in his second season but for the chronic unreliability of his car. It was fast enough as he reeled off pole at Imola, pole at Monaco, front row in Canada and pole in Detroit. By then de Angelis had decided to leave the team – the first of Senna's many Formula One victims. No one could live with him.

The failure of the officials to stop the race in the face of impossible conditions prompted the drivers to get together at Imola two weeks after Senna's Portuguese victory: almost all of them signed a petition drawn up by Niki Lauda to ask for a review of wet-weather safety procedures.

Regardless of the weather, Senna was on form once again at the San Marino Grand Prix at the Imola track. On Friday he clocked a stunning lap of 1m 27.589secs, over half-a-second better than Alboreto, the second placed man. He shrugged: "It was a very good lap, but not perfect. I may never get it perfect." To prove his point he went even faster on Saturday and took the second pole position of his career with a time of 1m 27.327secs. It was a 60-lap race and Senna led until lap 57, when his car ran out of fuel despite his best conservation efforts. He was classified seventh, while de Angelis won after Prost was disqualified for being underweight when he ran out of fuel on the slow down lap after winning on the road. It was not obvious then, but Senna's driving style was very heavy on fuel. It was the way he controlled the throttle.

Next up was Monaco. Senna took his third pole position in a row, but not without incident, as both Alboreto and Lauda felt that the Brazilian had held them up. They were furious: Lauda refused to accept Senna's apology while Alboreto blocked Senna in return at Rascasse, almost causing the Brazilian to hit the barriers. Despite starting on cold tyres after his tyre blankets short-circuited, he led from the start, as at Imola; but he also retired as at Imola, this time after just 13 laps when his Renault engine blew.

Senna's record for the first four races of 1985 was one win, three mechanical retirements. He could easily have had 31 points and been leading the championship. De Angelis was undoubtedly a star, but after the season's first qualifying session, Senna had kept him firmly in check. It was remarkable for someone with so little experience.

The next race was supposed to be at Spa, but it was postponed in one of the more farcical episodes in Formula One history. Cautious of the notorious Ardennes rain, the organisers laid special tarmac which was supposed to make the track easier to drive in wet conditions. Unfortunately the region was hit by a heatwave, and when the Formula One cars took to the track the tarmac disintegrated. Safety concerns prevailed and the race was postponed until later in the year, and the teams moved on to Montreal.

The Canadian Grand Prix marked a fightback for de Angelis. He took pole, forcing Senna to settle for second, and kept the lead at the start. Senna ran in second for six laps, but then his turbocharger came loose and he had to wait in the pits until the components had cooled so his mechanics could repair the damage. It left him five laps behind and although he clocked the fastest lap he was never going to catch the leaders. "He's really good. I was impressed, but Jesus he takes some risks," said Keke Rosberg after watching the lapped Brazilian tackle the track.

Senna was on pole again at the next race in Detroit – by 1.198 seconds. Lotus's Steve Hallam later recalled: "Jo Ramirez of McLaren said 'okay, which short-cut did he take!'" He needed no lessons in street circuit mastery. Senna complained to Nigel Stepney that his car felt strange after he had run over a manhole cover and on inspection of the underside of the car the mechanics found that two lugs had been lost from the oil tank. As no oil was leaking it was decided to keep this from Senna. Stepney confessed after the race, to which Senna replied: "You should have told me, because I wouldn't have gone over that manhole cover again, I'd have driven another line."

Senna failed to finish, crashing out from fourth place while trying to overtake Alboreto for third – he had led the first seven laps but an enforced pitstop to change blistered tyres meant having to fight his way up from the very back. He admitted the crash was his own fault, though he escaped with nothing more than a jarred hand. To his credit, the same corner had also caught out Prost and Mansell earlier in the race, so he was in good company.

The French Grand Prix at Paul Ricard was a similar story. Senna started second and raced in that position until he was forced to pit on lap nine when his gear selectors jammed. He began to pick his way up the order again, but slid off on his own oil when his engine blew several laps later.

Senna qualified only fourth for the British round at Silverstone, as Rosberg clocked the fastest qualifying lap of all time, but he burst into the lead at the start and stayed there until lap 57 when his engine began to splutter. Prost took the lead and Senna re-passed him almost immediately, only to retire a lap later when his car ran out of fuel.

Senna then qualified fifth on a topsy-turvy grid at the Nürburgring – he battled through to first in the race but was put out with a broken driveshaft.

With nine races of the season gone, Senna had just nine points as a result of his win in Estoril. He had led six races and could well have been leading the championship had the Lotus been more reliable. He seemed to have drawn all the short straws. De Angelis had scored points in all of the first seven races of the season before he was hit by two consecutive retirements.

Senna's luck took an upturn at the Österreichring. Despite qualifying only 14th due to bad weather and a turbo failure, Senna fought his way into second by the end of the race. At Zandvoort, bad weather, a burning car and a fine for taking a short-cut left Senna in only fourth on the grid, but he held off Alboreto to take the final podium place in the race. At Monza – a track he had never raced before due to his contractual disagreement with Toleman in 1984 – he took pole, but he could not repeat his pace in the race and finished third. The succession of races had not been spectacular, but he had at least become a consistent points scorer.

In mid-September Senna skipped off back home to São Paulo for two weeks' rest. In the meantime there was testing at Brands Hatch and Lotus found itself without a driver as de Angelis was ill. So Renault driver Derek Warwick was asked to test for the team. Renault was withdrawing its own works team at the end of the year, and Peter Warr was under pressure from Renault to give him the number two seat at Lotus.

Senna returned from Brazil refreshed, ready for the rescheduled Belgian Grand Prix at Spa. Typically Belgian weather meant the race was held in the rain. Conditions were tailor-made for his second victory and Senna duly won again. He qualified second on the grid, just 0.097 seconds behind Prost. The track suited Senna perfectly, and once again he impressed his team with his technical ability. As Bernard Dudot recalls: "He described to me for three-quarters of an hour a single practice lap, with all his impressions and feelings, but in particular all the technical data, rev-counts, oil pressure, etc. At every point, in every bend, absolutely precisely, going into the bend, in the middle of the bend and at the exit from the bend. Afterwards we compared it with the telemetry data – and it was all exactly right. It was incredible."

Senna led all the way in changeable conditions, excluding pitstops for tyres. He had some worries about an engine misfire but was otherwise untroubled. He had recently been confirmed as the leader of Lotus's attack on the world championship in 1986, at the cost of de Angelis, who had decided to move elsewhere. Up until that point Senna had been officially team number two, although few doubted which of the team's drivers really had the upper hand.

After Spa Senna drove to the Lotus factory for a meeting with Peter Warr to finalise terms for 1986. He took Mauricio Gugelmin with him for company. Senna was concerned that Derek Warwick might be his number two in 1986, and told Warr he didn't want him. Christopher Hilton, Senna's first biographer, recalls Warr patronising Senna and telling him he was by then championship material. Gugelmin told Hilton that Senna and Warr had a row: Senna told him he had always been world championship material and that it was the team that was deficient and had to be brought up to scratch. Warr was astonished at his arrogance and the relationship changed after that. By then Senna was effectively running his team. Warr was a passenger.

Britain had two races that year as the European Grand Prix was held at Brands Hatch, a circuit Senna knew like the back of his hand. The race marked the end of the duel for the championship between Alain Prost's McLaren and Michele Alboreto's Ferrari. It was also the weekend when the grid for the following year fell into place. Rosberg had decided to leave Williams and join McLaren for what many believed would be his final season. It set Piquet off to leave Brabham for Williams, and de Angelis seized the opportunity to take his place at Brabham. Senna decided to stick with Lotus when he could have had any of the three drives mentioned. He would have been better off joining any of them. It was a grievous mistake he repeated a few years later.

But that was not evident by the stunning form he was in as the season drew to a close. He was more familiar with Brands Hatch than any other driver on the track, courtesy of his Formula Ford and Formula Three years. In qualifying on Friday, he set a time of 1m 8.02secs, well over a second faster than Nelson Piquet's Brabham BMW, which managed 1m 9.204secs – second fastest.

Lotus was still innovating even without Chapman, and had introduced tyre warmers to Formula One in 1985. On Saturday, Williams and Brabham decided to follow Lotus's example by pre-heating their tyres. Rosberg and Mansell in the Williams Hondas went faster, so Senna returned to the track and put in a 1m 7.786secs, just to make sure. Then Piquet came out and went faster still: 1m 7.482secs. Piquet's time was surely unbeatable, but Senna decided to have another go. With the qualifying session drawing to a close he struck a time of 1m 7.169secs.

"It was a good lap, but not a perfect one," Senna said afterwards to the astonishment of those present. "We still have a bit of understeer we need to get rid of, and in two places I was not that precise, but the car is the best I've had all year. This is not a place for accidents, you know, but when the car is so safe you can go no more; it offers you the possibility to go more."

John Watson, standing in for Niki Lauda at the McLaren team after the Austrian had injured his wrist, was an eyewitness to Senna's unbelievable qualifying performance. He recalls: "I was out on the circuit and had just completed a qualifying run when I saw a car in my mirrors coming very quickly indeed. It was black with the familiar yellow helmet – it was Senna on a committed lap. I gave him all the space I had and he came through, out of Westfield Bend, down into Dingle Dell Corner. And I just sat there gobsmacked, because I had done what I had done to get wherever it was on the grid and here was a guy in a car that to me was dancing. It was like rain dancing on the pavement. That was a clear signal that my time as a Grand Prix driver was effectively finished. Here was a man who was doing things that I had not even thought of, let alone put into effect."

Senna flew into the lead at the start, but Rosberg would not let him disappear into the distance. The doughty Finn looked for every way past, but Senna blocked and blocked, even though the Williams Honda was clearly the faster car. On lap seven, the ever-resourceful Rosberg made a risky move under braking for Surtees. Senna cut across the corner, slicing the Finn's front tyre, and Rosberg spun across the track, collecting championship-challenger Piquet on the way. Rosberg was not surprised, having witnessed Senna's driving style a few times in the past two years. He said afterwards: "After eight years in Formula One, it seems I need to go back to Formula Three for a month to learn how to drive race cars. You get big eyes when someone starts weaving at 180mph – you're not used to that. I'll admit it, I don't have the balls to start banging off on occasions like that any more."

He had fought off Rosberg, but even Senna was no match for Nigel Mansell in front of his home crowd. The second Williams squeezed through into the lead on lap nine and Senna's problems were compounded when Rosberg, by then repaired, emerged from the pits between them and made sure that his team-mate built up a comfortable lead. Rosberg got his revenge on Senna's earlier move, and later revealed he deliberately slotted himself between the leading Williams and the charging Senna. As he says: "I put myself between Nigel and Senna and made sure that Nigel would win the race."

It worked – by the end Senna was second and Mansell took the first victory of his career to an ecstatic welcome home from the partisan British crowd. That day set the pattern for the next seven years, as Prost also won the championship. The three drivers duelled for all the championships of the following years, with only Piquet disturbing the party. But Rosberg was not impressed with Senna's driving, as he said later to Christopher Hilton: "I think he was dangerous in those days."

Senna spent the weekend after Brands Hatch with Mauricio Gugelmin as he polished off the Marlboro British Formula Three championship at Silverstone that Senna had won in 1983.

Although the Formula One world championship was decided, there was still a season to finish. Next up was the South African Grand Prix, although the country was in the grip of apartheid and for a long time it did not look as if the race would go ahead. Certainly Senna's participation in it was in doubt. There had been calls for sporting isolation of the country, but FISA, ever independent, insisted that the Grand Prix would go ahead. Bernie Ecclestone was also determined the race would take place. FOCA spokesman Mervyn Key said: "Motor racing is comprised of private manufacturing concerns, which is not the same as a national team which can be subjected to government pressure. In Grand Prix racing no one represents a country. The drivers are on contract to teams. Teams have contracts with their sponsors to do 16 races and if they miss one or two of them, sponsors will want some of their money back." And with new rules introduced to cover travel costs for the top 10 teams in the championship, every point counted. If the race was to go ahead, then no one wanted anyone else getting the points. Money won. But there was also strong governmental pressure, notably in France. Under pressure from the French government, the Ligier and Renault teams withdrew from the event. The Finnish and Swedish governments joined forces with the French to urge FISA president Jean-Marie Balestre to hold the race elsewhere. Balestre refused. Prost insisted that he did not want to race in South Africa, but said it was McLaren's decision. Rosberg received a request from the Finnish government asking him not to race. "Finland doesn't pay my bills," Frank Williams replied.

The Brazilian government began to put similar pressures on its drivers. Senna said: "It is necessary to weigh the pros and cons. Things seem to be complicated over there and I don't believe it is safe to race under such adverse conditions. I am personally against the regime. I would not like to go there, but I have a commitment to my team." Brazil had recently banned all sporting and cultural links with South Africa, and there were suggestions that Senna could even have been breaking the law if he raced.

Peter Warr said in response: "I think he is still hoping the race will be called off, but it's not a matter of his making up his mind. We are under contract to race at Kyalami, and he is under contract to us. The team will be taking part in the race and Senna has a contract to drive our car. It's as simple as that."

Prost, who had already wrapped up his first drivers' title at Brands Hatch, was clearly hoping for action similar to that taken in the 1982 drivers' strike, but was unable to muster enough support. He told French newspaper *L'Équipe*: "We either all go to South Africa or we don't go. Without Rosberg, Piquet and Ayrton Senna it would not be a Grand Prix."

In the end the race did go ahead – and only Renault and Ligier boycotted, although Zakspeed and RAM were absent for financial reasons. Many of the cars ran without the decals of sponsors who had decided they did not want to be associated with the event – ironic, since all the teams had insisted they must go to South Africa because the sponsors did not want to miss the race. Perhaps a few years later Senna would have stuck by his principles and defied his team and the governing body, but in 1985 he was still in the early stages of his career and did not have the clout of a world champion. It was too much of a risk.

When it came to it, he qualified fourth, but retired after eight laps with another engine failure. Those eight laps were marked by a battle with de Angelis, which could have easily resulted in both Lotus cars going off the road. The Italian said: "I was so angry that I almost came to blows with him afterwards. And although we later shook hands, that was not the point. I think that was the incident which brought out his true character... I mean, with me it's not a matter of saying whose fault it was, I am just saying that what he did was not right. He is a very strange guy, and he had a strange attitude towards me." It was just as well that de Angelis was leaving.

As for the race, Mansell proved that he was a coming man when he took pole and then dominated the race for his second successive victory.

At the last race of the season – the first to be held in Adelaide – Senna's weekend was overshadowed by a disagreement with Nigel Mansell, the first of many. Since Brands Hatch Senna had recognised him as another serious rival and rather than an older fading star, this was a driver who like himself was from the new Formula One generation. Mansell's domination of Kyalami reinforced that. It all started when Senna claimed that Mansell had blocked him during qualifying on Friday, after which Mansell was on provisional pole with Senna in second. The pair traded fastest times through Saturday, but it was Senna who had the edge by 0.694 seconds. No one else got within two seconds of pole.

It was all set up for a terrific race, which everyone realised could be settled on the first lap. Indeed it was, as Senna and Mansell collided while fighting for the lead. Mansell was eliminated and was furious. "Senna was a total idiot to drive me off the circuit like that at the start," he complained. "He might be quick, he might be good, but he is not a good driver."

To top it off, Senna got embroiled in a row with the other Williams driver, Keke Rosberg. "The problem with Ayrton is that he is very talented and very fast but he is just going too hard," he said. Rosberg had battled with Senna for the lead in the middle stages of the race, but Senna ripped the front aerofoil off his Lotus when he ran into the back of Rosberg. Senna pitted for repairs but another blown Renault engine ended his race and brought an ignominious end to his season, as Rosberg came through to win his last race for Williams.

In only his second year of Formula One, Senna had won two races, taken seven poles and led nine Grand Prix races. He finished fourth in the championship with a total of 38 points. It is difficult to judge how far he might have climbed with better reliability from Lotus and Renault, but certainly he would at least have been challenging for the championship.

Many starring rookies fall by the wayside after a brilliant first year, but after a second season of competing at the highest level, Senna had emphatically arrived. He was no longer just another competitor, he had become a threat and a rival to some of the biggest names in the sport. But as good as he had proved himself to be, he was still searching for the perfect lap and the perfect race.

Thirty-year-old Alain Prost took his first world title in 1985 in the

McLaren TAG. Ironically, with a little bit of reliability Senna could easily have been world champion himself and denied Prost his glory. But Senna had chosen the wrong team and was stuck with his choice for another two years. Prost had chosen correctly – McLaren remained dominant for all the years he was with the team. Senna instead had two wins, two seconds, two thirds, but seven pole positions and 10 front-row starts. His 38 points gave him fourth place in the table, just ahead of his team-mate, who had started the season as number one. Cue de Angelis's departure for Bernie Ecclestone's Brabham BMW team. He did not find Senna an agreeable team-mate.

Senna became the undisputed Lotus team leader, and extended his status to the prerogative of choosing his own team-mate. That he chose to veto Derek Warwick was to cause an unholy row in the first few months of 1986.

Just in case Warr dared to defy him Senna approached the Benetton team about the possibility of a drive for 1986. Benetton was the old Toleman team that Senna had left barely a year before because it was in disarray and had no prospects. Since then it had been taken over by the Benetton clothing company and the new owners had lured Williams team manager, Peter Collins to run it. Collins had secured a supply of BMW turbo engines as used by the Brabham team. Senna sensed Benetton was on the up and wanted some insurance as he was determine in his own mind to leave Lotus if Warr signed Warwick. But Warr blinked first and the insurance did not become necessary. The affair was to earn Senna the enmity of most of the the British press. Ayrton Senna had chosen to cross one of their heroes and it did not go down well at all.

CHAPTER 11

1986: Champion Potential

So near and yet so far with Lotus

After just two seasons in the top flight, the 26-year-old Ayrton Senna was already beginning to exhibit the ruthless streak that later became a fundamental part of his image. In no way was this better illustrated than in his selection of a team-mate for 1986. Senna and Lotus clashed mightily when team principal Peter Warr selected a driver Senna didn't want, and it was the young and still relatively inexperienced Brazilian who won out.

Senna had officially begun his Lotus career as team number two to Elio de Angelis, but when the Brazilian's superiority quickly showed through, it soon became clear that this would not be the case for long. Almost immediately the team began to reform around Senna, pushing de Angelis onto the sidelines. It first became noticeable to de Angelis at a test session at Paul Ricard, a few days after Senna's stunning performance at the Monaco Grand Prix. It was then that he decided he would leave the team the following year.

At the close of the 1985 season, de Angelis spoke at length to the now defunct *Grand Prix International* magazine. He poured his heart out and was honest about how deficient he was compared to the Brazilian: "I was put on one side by Lotus. All they could think about was Senna," he said. "There had been some criticisms of the way I had been driving, because I had been more cautious than Ayrton. But I was leading the world drivers' championship. When I got to the circuit they allowed me on the track just to do three laps. Imagine, on the day that I was leading the world championship, being left to trundle round like some new kid on the team. It was that same night that I made up my mind to leave Lotus. From that moment on, as far as I was concerned Lotus was a chapter in my career that was over. I didn't want to be treated like that ever again.

"I knew from the beginning that it was going to be a difficult year. I knew that he would be a difficult person, of course. I admired his determination and he is very determined – maybe too much. I felt that he found it necessary to show off his ability: even with the success that he had with Toleman the previous year, he was desperate to show that he had something more. Like the Arabs say: 'It is written'. There is something strong inside his mind: sometimes it is good for him, sometimes it is bad. I think he found the ground at Team Lotus to build up his personality, with the help of Peter Warr. Ayrton became a protégé to Peter, almost like a son, his own discovery. But he was very quick, I must say.

"I think Senna had a fortunate year: he should have had more accidents than he did. That kind of driving doesn't always pay off. I've had six years at Lotus, and I think I've been crazy enough with this team. People tend to forget I've gone jumping over the top of other cars and banged wheels with people. I've done all those things. But once you've done it, you quickly realise that your chances of having a big shunt are increasing. As far as motivation is concerned, I have much more now than when I started. Now I know exactly what I want: I'm not doing this just for the pleasure of driving in Formula One. That pleasure is what my Brazilian team-mate was enjoying last year.

"Look at Lauda. People say he isn't quick any more. But when the race starts, he's really fast and he's been world champion three times. Senna has been compared with Gilles Villeneuve, and me with Lauda. I could have done two races in 1985 – Imola and Canada – like Senna did, by taking the lead and staying there, knowing that there was no hope of the fuel lasting. I am unspectacular in the car because I work out the situation. Senna is certainly more spectacular than I am.

"Peter Warr is a very ambitious man and a capable team manager, although perhaps he tries to do too much. It would not be difficult for Lotus to spread the workload more widely, and I don't know why it doesn't do that, because one day this situation could be very dangerous for the team."

Ironically, a year earlier it was Nigel Mansell who left the team because he felt unwelcome due to all the attention that was focused on de Angelis. The pair somehow remained friends, and when Mansell saw how de Angelis was being edged out in the same way that he had been, he even went to Warr to complain. But de Angelis felt that although the two situations were similar there were some crucial differences: "Although we received similar technical and psychological treatment, I think my situation was a little bit worse than Nigel's. He had the advantage of being English, which made things better for him, easier for him to cope with. And sponsor-wise he had an advantage. Right to the end, he seemed to be enjoying his driving, while I must admit that I did not enjoy my last few races for Lotus."

With de Angelis out of the way and Senna given the promise of promotion to team number one in 1986, it was time for Lotus to find Senna a new team-mate. Warr traditionally ran a clear number one/number two driver operation and with Senna firmly ensconced as number one he began the search for a replacement for de Angelis. In reality he didn't have to look far: he had always had his eye on Derek Warwick and there was plenty of pressure from Renault, which had disbanded its works team.

It was no coincidence that between the European and South African Grand Prix races of 1985, Lotus tested Derek Warwick with Renault's permission. The test, although no high-speed running was planned, had confirmed that Warwick would be the ideal replacement for de Angelis. He had five seasons of Formula One under his belt: three with Toleman during a period when the team for the most part was struggling to qualify; and more recently two with Renault, where he had often qualified well, only to be hit by reliability problems in the race. Embarrassed by the better job done by Senna and de Angelis with the customer-engined Lotus in 1985, Renault decided to pull the works team out at the end of the year, leaving Warwick stranded with all the top drives taken. In reality Warwick hadn't tried very hard, as he knew he was a shoe-in for the Lotus seat. He had everything Lotus wanted. It would please Renault and please the sponsors, in particular John Player, which wanted a British driver in the car.

Senna also knew what was about to happen – and it was the last thing he wanted. He knew and liked Derek Warwick and understood first hand that he was quick and had a reputation for getting a team to work well around him. But he had seen how the initial focus on the team's number one driver had given Elio de Angelis a much faster car in 1985, and he wanted that attention for 1986. He knew that Warwick, as a popular Englishman with the ear of Renault, would dilute that. Senna didn't fight battles he knew he couldn't win, and he didn't think he could win the hearts and minds of the team with Warwick around.

Senna pointed out forcibly to Warr that when he had signed to join Lotus in 1984 the contract had clearly stipulated that the team's focus would be on the number one driver. He said that he felt the team would struggle to run a two-car operation and therefore he wanted a team-mate who would be his back-up, someone who would not be a threat and would not be looking to challenge him once he had established himself within the team. Warwick did not fit the bill. At the time, people were talking about him as the next British world champion and Senna did not want any question over who was top dog.

Warwick, after his experience at Renault, was popular with the French engine supplier. Mechanics liked him as he was fast and trouble-free. He was also regarded as a very nice man with an infectious sense of humour and a 'Tom Cruise' smile. But there was only one star at Lotus and that was Senna.

Warr desperately wanted Warwick, and the sponsors wanted Warwick; but Senna stood firm and threatened to walk if he didn't get his way. He also felt the team would be in breach of contract if Warwick was brought in on equal footing. Faced with what he saw as a contractual betrayal, he threatened to leave and began approaching other teams.

Although Senna was bluffing and there were no other drives available, Warr buckled. Faced with even the possibility of losing his star driver, he agreed that Warwick would not be hired. The problem for Warr was that he had gone right down the line with Warwick – he had promised him the drive, issued a contract – all that was left was to sign it.

Senna knew that he had to stop the Warwick bandwagon, and it all depended on sponsor John Player. He began barraging John Player with how bad it would be for the team if Warwick was signed. The tobacco company believed him. Senna won.

Warwick later explained to journalist, Christopher Hilton that he had a contract ready to sign, but when he went to the Lotus headquarters at Ketteringham Hall just before Christmas he was met not by Peter Warr, as he expected, but by the team's real boss, finance director Fred Bushell. Instead of the ceremonial signing he had expected in Colin Chapman's old office, Warwick was ushered into Bushell's office. Bushell was always the man to deliver the bad news at Lotus. Chapman had used him to great effect when he was alive, and Bushell later went to jail for doing Chapman's dirty work. He didn't beat about the bush. He simply told Warwick that he was sorry but Senna did not want him in the team. And that was that.

Warwick was devastated and knew his career had been dealt a fatal blow. There were by that stage no other drives on offer. He later revealed that Senna had met with him and apologised for the situation. Warwick was impressed that he was not afraid to face him: "He apologised to me but said that he believed it was the right decision for him and the team. He stuck to his guns and got absolutely destroyed in the British press, but he still stuck to his guns.

"You have to admire the guy for sticking to what he thought was right. I think it was right for him – I'm sure it was right for him. He was hated by a lot of fans and a lot of the press, but he stuck to his guns and those are the traits of a real champion. I would not have done that to another human being but that's probably why I'm not a great champion."

Warwick turned to sportscar racing and signed with Tom Walkinshaw's works Jaguar team. It was very much second best, and probably spelt the demise of his whole career. Although he later got a drive for the declining Brabham team after Elio de Angelis was killed, he was ruined, going on to drive for Arrows in 1987 as his career petered out.

Peter Warr was totally honest about the situation: "Ayrton said he would leave the team if Warwick or any other established Grand Prix driver was signed. Any team that had Ayrton Senna driving for it would be silly not to recognise that their best chance in the championship was with him. We accepted that a number one and number two situation was likely to give a degree of concentration and effort on his racing programme, and his testing programme was most likely to produce results."

As soon as Warwick was rejected, a torrent of abuse came down on Senna's head from the British press. Partisan journalists tried to change Warr's mind. Senna, back home in Brazil, was oblivious to it all. He hardly knew the ruckus was going on and didn't really care.

Warwick may have had a problem getting a new drive but Warr also had to find a good driver to replace him. Warr, very late in the day, set about finding a replacement. Reigning British Formula Three champion Mauricio Gugelmin was strongly rumoured to have Senna's support for the drive. But two Brazilians was impossible for the British Lotus team. The replacement for Warwick had to be British.

In January it was announced that Senna's team-mate for 1986 would be 25-year-old British aristocrat, Johnny Dumfries, whose real name was John Colom Crichton-Stuart, Earl of Dumfries. He was the son of the Marquess of Bute. Dumfries had a good record in the junior formulas – he had been British Formula Three champion in 1984 – and had just spent a year as Ferrari test driver, but Senna had raced against him before and did not rate him as highly as he did Warwick. Dumfries was naturally very pleased to get the opportunity to drive in Formula One, and recited on cue: "I will do my very best to help Ayrton win the title."

When the campaign to reinstate Warwick failed, the British press and fans were livid and Senna was portrayed as a ruthless Machiavellian villain, frightened into dirty tactics by the sheer speed of good old Warwick. The Brazilian became the journalists' hate figure, and the image stayed with him throughout his career, only wavering in the last years with McLaren when he was the only driver with the skill to regularly take the challenge to the superior Williams machine. Warr concluded the sorry affair by saying: "I was disappointed that we didn't have Warwick. He would have been a very solid number two and produced results for us. It would have been a very good mix."

At the launch of the new 1986 Lotus Renault, Senna expressed his public sadness that Warwick was without a drive, but had no regrets. When questioned by hostile journalists, he said he had signed a contract in 1984 that stipulated the team would concentrate on its leading driver. He told them he had been with Lotus for a year and was in a position to judge the team's strengths and weaknesses.

Senna said: "It was nothing to do with Derek personally, nor with my not wanting to have strong competition within the team." He was totally convinced – with some justification – that Lotus would not be in a position to prepare two cars to an equally high standard, and was afraid that there would be internal struggles for resources if there was a strong English driver in the team. He said: "There were the first signs of something like that happening in 1985 with Elio de Angelis and me. I was convinced that if I was to have a chance of competing for the world championship with Lotus, then the major team effort had to be concentrated on one car. And that doesn't work when you have a team-mate who also has pretensions to be number one."

Senna may not have shown it but he was deeply hurt by the accusations of cowardice. His relationship with the British press never returned to normal.

The 1986 season began in Rio de Janeiro with the Brazilian Grand Prix in late March, and Senna knew that he had to prove himself on the track if he was to put the Warwick controversy behind him. The car to beat was clearly going to be the Williams Honda. It had won the last three races of 1985 and dominated winter testing. But the real story of winter testing – in those days largely held by the Paul Ricard circuit in southern France – was the tragic accident that had befallen Williams team boss Frank Williams. He had left a test session, for a flight from Nice back to London, driving a rented Ford Sierra with team manager Peter Windsor in the passenger seat. Williams always drove a road car too fast and the Ford Sierra was notable for its jelly-like characteristics in fast bends. He lost control, careered down a bank and ended up upside down. Windsor crawled away unharmed, but Williams had broken his neck in a quirk of fate that would leave him severely paralysed but with his brain intact.

Senna was devastated by the news, as Williams had given him his first drive in a Formula One car and had been the first serious Formula One personality he had met after happening to sit next to him on a flight to Belgium.

Williams' wife Ginny nursed him back from almost certain death. The news that he would survive cheered Senna, who was in Brazil waiting for the first race of the season. With Warwick gone, he had been allocated Nigel Stepney as his mechanic. Stepney was to learn a lot that year from a very demanding driver.

To the delight of the crowd, Senna promptly took pole by 0.765 seconds from fellow Brazilian Nelson Piquet, racing the Williams Honda for the first time. The new Williams was clearly the class of the field, and Piquet was seething at being humiliated in front of his home crowd. It was a clear demonstration of who was the new king.

The pole lap had been devastating and Senna had given it everything, as Lotus engineer Steve Hallam recalled: "Ayrton went out on his second set of tyres and he gave everything for that lap. I remember seeing him slumped in the cockpit when he had done it – not slumped so much as hunched. He'd given absolutely everything."

In the race, however, the Williams Honda was clearly superior and Senna could not keep up the advantage, although he still finished second to Piquet. There was drama on the first lap when Nigel Mansell tried to pass him for first and spun off, but Senna's race was otherwise uneventful. He later claimed that he could have caught and passed Piquet for the win, but blamed his inability to do so on the new fuel regulations, which had cut fuel allowance from 220 litres to 195 litres. He commented: "Since rules are approved by all parts, we have no other choice but to accept them. But I must say that the fear of running out of fuel at the dying stage of a race may reduce the excitement for the drivers and even the fans." Fuel consumption was to become an even greater concern for Senna in the latter stages of the season. In 1985 he had run himself out of fuel twice whilst leading the race. This year, with the championship clearly within his grasp, he knew that seconds would count. The smaller amount of fuel would work against him.

The next race was the first Spanish Grand Prix at Jerez. On the new track, Senna took another pole position, this time by over eight-tenths of a second from Piquet, and led without drama for the first 39 laps of the 72-lap race. But then Mansell, who had earlier struggled with a confusing fuel read-out, caught him up, and when Senna got stuck behind a backmarker he shot through into the lead. As the Williams pulled away into the distance it looked as if Senna's chances of victory were over, but there was more drama to come. Mansell was struggling with blistered Goodyears, and his lead was slashed in the closing stages of the race. With just 10 laps to go, Senna passed him for the lead and Mansell made the risky decision to pit for new tyres, which dropped him back behind third-placed Prost.

But the race did not end there. On fresh rubber, Mansell soon caught and passed Prost for second before bearing down on Senna. Senna's tyres were also beginning to trouble him, but somehow he held Mansell off, ducking and weaving to gain every possible advantage. They crossed the finish line almost side by side, but it was Senna who took victory by just 0.014 seconds.

It was, and still is, the second-closest finish in Formula One history, after the 0.01-second gap that separated Peter Gethin and Ronnie Peterson in the 1971 Italian Grand Prix. Someone estimated that 0.014 seconds was the equivalent of just 93cm on the track. It was all smiles on the podium as Senna and Mansell's earlier disagreements were forgotten. "It was a hell of a fight," said Senna. "It was very tiring, both mentally and physically. I have been racing in Formula One for three seasons, but this is the first win I have had to fight for. Physically I was at an end, but because I had won I recovered quickly. Winning is the best medicine to regain strength. In the evening I had fully recovered and drove the race again in my mind. I wanted to enjoy my victory once more."

The win also put Senna in the lead for the championship by six points from Piquet. It was the first time in his career he had topped the table, and although it was only the early stages of the season it was a great feeling.

But Senna was feeling the heat from Mansell. Since his debut victory at Brands Hatch the previous year, Mansell, with better luck, could have won every subsequent race. In the event he had won two out of five. It was a massive career transformation – from mid-fielder to race winner – and had transformed the determined Mansell. He was also driving a vastly superior car, which was not obvious as Senna kept annexing pole position.

Senna took his third pole position in a row at Imola, triggering ripples of disbelief around the Formula One paddock. As Lotus designer Gerard Ducarouge recalls: "I was in trouble. We were making pole position after pole position. I had a good friend at Williams, Patrick Head, who came to me and said 'Gerard, you're cheating!' And he was telling everybody that. I was fed up because we weren't. I went to FISA and said to their people 'You stop the car just before it comes back to our pit and you check it for an hour and make all the measurements you bloody want. Patrick and anybody else who thinks I'm cheating can be there, even though I'm not happy with them seeing all the details of the car'. I was going on and on because I was so upset. I said 'If you want to disqualify something, disqualify the bloody driver because he's just too fast'. Nobody understood that it was not the car that we got these performances from – it was the driver."

In the race, Senna retired with a wheel-bearing failure after 12 laps as Prost came through to win. Surprisingly, at the Monaco Grand Prix his run of pole positions was broken, and after two scrappy qualifying sessions Senna was forced to settle for third as Prost took pole.

That was where he finished in the race, as a result relinquishing the championship lead to Nelson Piquet. It seemed that what the Lotus Renault 98T had initially gained in reliability from its predecessor, it lacked in speed. Also, with fuel allowances reduced, the thirsty Lotus was suffering more than most and Senna was having to drive more cautiously than before. Senna no longer had a team-mate who could spur him on and use experience to develop the car. In four races, Dumfries had just one ninth place to his name and was suffering under the pressure of being wiped away so obviously by Senna. He was also hard on the car, destroying transmissions.

A few days after Monaco, tragedy struck Formula One. On Wednesday 14th May during a well-attended test session at the Paul Ricard circuit in France, Senna's former team-mate Elio de Angelis suffered a rear-wing failure on his Brabham BMW BT55 while entering the 180mph Verrerie curves. His car somersaulted over the catch fencing and came to rest upside-down on the verge, where it burst into flames.

There were fewer marshals at the track as it was a test session, and it took around 10 minutes for a group of drivers, led by Alan Jones, Nigel Mansell and Alain Prost, to run to the burning wreckage to try and help de Angelis. The flames were intense and they could not get close enough to right the car or unfasten de Angelis's seatbelts. Eventually a marshal turned up wearing nothing more than shorts and a T-shirt, carrying a fire extinguisher, but it proved difficult to put out the fire.

There was no helicopter at the track and it was over half-an-hour before one arrived to take de Angelis to hospital in Marseilles. He had gone into cardiac arrest, probably as a result of being deprived of oxygen during the fire, although his burns were comparatively light. He died the following day, aged just 28. The official cause was given as serious head and chest injuries, but several witnesses claimed that the real reason had been the length of time he had spent deprived of air in the upturned car and that his other injuries had been relatively minor.

De Angelis was one of the most popular drivers on the grid, and the circumstances of his death made it all the more difficult to bear. For Senna it was the first time someone he knew well had been killed in a racing accident, someone who had been his team-mate just months earlier, and it affected him deeply, although he continued to race. He explained from the peace of Oporto a few days later: "I race because I enjoy it and because I feel a very strong and special motivation for what I do. That's why I intend to carry on. Elio was a very special driver because he did what he did out of love for the sport, not for any commercial reason. He was well educated, a gentleman, someone who was good to know as a person. I am sure he was not responsible for the accident at Ricard, because he was someone who never went over the limit, who never pushed his luck."

Elio de Angelis was the last man to die in a Formula One car until Roland Ratzenberger's accident on the Saturday of the San Marino Grand Prix on 30th April 1994. As with Ratzenberger and Senna, his death triggered a new wave of safety measures in the sport, and there were changes made to the tracks over the following year. As a result, marshalling and medical standards during testing were improved to match those during a Grand Prix.

When Mansell won the following Belgian Grand Prix at Spa-Francorchamps, he dedicated the victory to his former team-mate. Senna had qualified fourth and raced to second, pushing the winner Mansell hard but unable to catch him. Senna did regain the lead in the drivers' championship from Alain Prost, but it was now looking certain that it would be very close between at least four drivers.

Mansell was off on another winning streak. At the Canadian Grand Prix in Montreal, Senna struggled to control his fuel consumption and finished in a careful fifth. Mansell won and Senna slipped to third in the championship, two points behind Prost and equal with Mansell, who was ahead because he had won twice to Senna's once.

Senna redressed the balance at the US East Grand Prix in Detroit. He was a master of the American street circuit and took pole by half-a-second. As Brazil were playing France in the World Cup quarter-finals, he decided to skip the post-qualifying press conference and rush back to his hotel to watch the match on TV, leaving behind a tape recording of his pole position comments. Brazil lost the match on a penalty shoot-out and five Brazilians were reported dead as a result – four from heart attacks and one shot in a heated argument about the match. It showed how passionate the country was about competition, although Senna seemed unaffected by the defeat. Despite a puncture that forced him into the pits, he won the race by half-a-minute and regained the championship lead by three points from Prost.

Pole position followed at the French Grand Prix on the harshly modified Paul Ricard circuit, but Senna spun off after three laps when he hit oil from Andrea de Cesaris's stricken Minardi as Prost romped home. He slipped to third in the championship behind Prost and Mansell, and solemnly apologised to the team for the misdemeanour. He failed to score again at Brands Hatch when his gearbox went on the blink, and remained third in the championship as Mansell took victory and the championship lead. Hockenheim delivered second place, but a win for Piquet meant that Senna was by then fighting to hold on to second place in the championship. Even that second place had been in doubt, as Senna had had to weave his Lotus from side to side to drain out the last drops of fuel and make it to the finish line.

Some good did come out of Hockenheim for Senna, as Lotus announced it would be switching to Honda power for the 1987 season. Renault was pulling out at the end of the season and so far in 1986 the engine had been thirsty, unreliable and underpowered compared to its rivals. Honda, the choice of Williams, was generally agreed to be the most powerful engine of the current crop. The switch would bring Senna a new team-mate: Japanese driver Satoru Nakajima would replace Dumfries. Williams had frustrated Honda by refusing to give the Japanese driver a race seat, but for Senna the affable Nakajima seemed like an ideal number two. Dumfries, who had yet to score and made it into the points on just two occasions that season, was to be pushed out of Formula One after just a single season at the top level.

Renault received a lot of flack from people who felt it had failed to develop the engine and reduce fuel consumption. Peter Warr dismissed that with remarkable honesty: "People were saying 'The Lotus is a good car, Senna is an up-and-coming driver, but they are handicapped by the Renault engine, which hasn't got the fuel consumption'," he says. "But who knows if the truth wasn't that the engine was absolutely fantastic and very powerful, the chassis wasn't that good and Senna was having to drive it above the level of which it was capable to be competitive – which was why fuel consumption was bad."

Formula One went behind the Iron Curtain for the inaugural Hungarian Grand Prix at the Hungaroring in Budapest. Senna took pole and finished second to Piquet, but his compatriot's victory meant that although Senna moved into second in the standings, he was hanging on to the place by a single point. He was, however, just seven points behind Mansell and with five races remaining it looked as if the championship was still on target.

Then it all went wrong. Senna qualified eighth for the Austrian Grand Prix at the Österreichring after an engine problem forced him to switch to Dumfries's car. The troublesome Renault lasted just 13 laps and Prost won again, as Senna dropped to third in the table behind Mansell and Prost.

The Italian Grand Prix at Monza brought more bad news. Senna qualified just fifth after another blown Renault ruled him out of most of Saturday's session, and he didn't make it past the grid when a transmission failure left him stranded on the line. As Piquet won he slipped to fourth in the championship standings, 13 points behind Mansell with three races to go. With two other better-placed competitors for the crown, the dream was starting to look like an impossibility.

Senna could only hope that all three of his rivals would fail to score well in the remaining three Grand Prix races, and that he would have better-than-usual reliability for the remainder of the season. It was the closest championship battle that had taken place under normal circumstances for years. The 1982 season had been more open, but been marred by a series of tragedies and political upheavals that gave no one an advantage. This was real racing. Sensing a great occasion, Bernie Ecclestone got the four challengers together in the pitlane at the Portuguese Grand Prix for a photo session attended by over 50 photographers. Senna, Prost, Mansell and Piquet were all smiles as they perched on the pitlane wall, arms round each other's shoulders. Ecclestone had sensed the occasion for a unique photograph which today counts as one of the most memorable ever.

Ironically, a few years' later it was almost impossible to get two of them to pose together, let alone all four.

Senna then made clear his intentions by taking pole position, his seventh of the year, by over eight-tenths of a second from Mansell. He knew that if he could win he would still have a slim chance of taking the title; and that if Mansell failed to finish, so much the better. Senna also had the advantage that only the best 11 scores of 16 counted, and as he had already failed to finish five times, every point counted. Prost and Mansell had good reliability records and would be dropping scores. And Estoril was the track where Senna had scored his superb first win 18 months before.

Senna could do nothing, though, when Mansell powered into the lead at the start and began to pull away into the distance. He held on to second strongly, for almost all the race, knowing that it gave him an outside chance of the title and that if Mansell hit trouble, victory for the Brazilian would close the deficit to just four points. But it was not to be. With a single lap remaining, the thirsty Lotus Renault drank the last of its fuel and coasted to a halt with its display still claiming there was enough fuel for 1.4 laps left in the tank. Senna was lucky to be classified fourth, but the loss of three points meant his championship bid was over.

It was a downcast figure that traipsed back to the Lotus pit after bringing his car to rest out on the circuit. As Mansell, Prost and Piquet celebrated side by side on the podium, Senna was left with fourth place, no trophy and no chance of the championship. In the excitement over Mansell's strengthening lead in the standings, the fourth challenger was almost forgotten. Senna went straight to the motorhome and turned his thoughts to 1987.

Pole position in Mexico did nothing to cheer the Brazilian, and a third place in the race with another Renault-prompted non-finish at the final Grand Prix of the season in Adelaide did nothing to quell his disappointment. In a bizarre twist, Prost sauntered on to the title as a blown tyre suddenly and cruelly ended Nigel Mansell's bid. Senna ended the year 17 points behind Prost, 15 behind Mansell and 14 behind Piquet.

Of the 16 races, Senna had taken eight pole positions, winning Spain and the USA East, finishing second in Brazil, Belgium, Germany and Hungary, third in Monaco and Mexico, fourth in Portugal, and fifth in Canada. Fifty-five points was worth only fourth place in the championship in an amazingly competitive season.

He had suffered six non-classifications compared to five for Piquet, four for Mansell and three for Prost, plus several classified results where he had failed to make it to the line. With a more reliable engine with better fuel consumption, the championship might have looked very different, but the record books say that Senna merely finished a distant fourth while the other three battled to the wire.

It was a miserable end to a season that had initially promised so much. Senna's dreams had crumbled. He had taken eight poles, but fell one short of the record nine in a season; he had led the championship, won twice and scored more points than in the previous two years of his Formula One career combined, but ultimately failed to play a starring role in the title's thrilling conclusion. For Senna, 1986 had not been a failure, but it had fallen short of the success he had desired.

At the end of the season, Peter Warr commented that he thought Senna would have been better off with Derek Warwick supporting him. Senna was beginning to think he would not make it with Lotus. But he gave the team one more year, with the Honda engine. Lotus also had a new big-bucks sponsor in the shape of RJ Reynolds, the giant tobacco company which introduced its Camel brand for the first time to Formula One. Imperial Tobacco had withdrawn its John Player Special brand from the Lotus team for the second and last time, and had been replaced by the even bigger bucks of Reynolds. With Honda power and plenty of cash, Senna had a right to think the world championship was winging his way. But Peter Warr was about to blow his career in the biggest possible way. With all the advantages, the Lotus team fluffed it. When the team was wanting a good chassis from Gerard Ducarouge, the reason that Senna was at Lotus, he could not deliver.

In-between Mexico and Adelaide, Ducarouge holidayed with Senna in Mauritius, before the island was fashionable. They were high with hopes for the following season, as Ducarouge remembers: "He was a kid and like all kids he loved to play. He was playing like a kid all the time, making jokes. There were one or two people from TV Globo who were very good friends, and myself, and he was absolutely going crazy for everything, doing sport, flying the little aeroplanes, and the jokes. That was the man that no one had seen. It was great to have that privilege, to follow his real moments. In the car or at the circuit he was a totally different man. But on an island like Mauritius he could say 'Now I'll have fun, now I won't be criticised for what I'm doing, nobody will write silly things in the newspapers about this, deforming the truth'. He was completely free to do what is normal when you are 26 and should be enjoying yourself."

But the fact remained that Senna's two years with Renault engines had been blighted by poor fuel consumption, blamed squarely on the Renault turbo engine, and the French manufacturer was harangued for failing to rectify it. The engines were seemingly the thirstiest on the grid, and this had cost a probable four race wins in 32 races, forcing Senna time and time again to slow down and conserve fuel.

After Senna's death, Peter Warr made a telling observation about the fuel consumption problems. He said the team had found that in 1987, with the Honda engine, Senna's fuel consumption was the worst in the field. Warr believed that he was driving it so fast that its fuel consumption was higher.

He told Senna biographer Christopher Hilton: "It was because he had this throttle control technique – blip-blip-blipping in the corners. The reason we had these suspicions was because he kept coming up as the worst of the Honda drivers on fuel consumption. That was partly because he was going the quickest and partly because he was blipping the throttle." The revelations forced him to adapt his driving style. He would not be caught out again.

CHAPTER 12

1987:
The start of the Honda years

Giving up on Lotus

After a successful 1986, and with a Honda engine firmly fastened in the back of his Lotus, Ayrton Senna was one of the hot favourites to win the world championship title in 1987. It was reasoned that if he had been able to take the fight to Williams Honda while running on a less-favoured Renault engine, with the same power unit in the back the title might soon be his. The threat from McLaren, in particular from Alain Prost, was also expected to be strong, and it looked as if a replay of the close battle of 1986 was on the cards.

For Senna it was the beginning of a six-year relationship with the Japanese manufacturer that would ultimately deliver him three drivers' titles, on the back of 32 victories and 46 pole positions. He would become one of the most popular international celebrities in Japan, and win the affections of Honda's top management in a way that was unmatched by his team-mates and even team principals. It was an extraordinary relationship.

Japan was about to make a mark on Formula One in a big way. Honda had returned to the sport as an engine manufacturer in 1983, after the Honda outfit of the 1960s had been aborted in tragic circumstances. The 1986 constructors' crown for Williams marked Honda's first world title. In 1987, for the first time, all 16 races of the season were to be televised in Japan and the Japanese Grand Prix was set to return to the calendar at the end of the year after a 10-year absence, at the Honda-owned racetrack of Suzuka. Senna's new team-mate, Honda protégé Satoru Nakajima, was the first Japanese driver to compete full-time in Formula One.

Once he had realised that Renault would be quitting the sport, Senna had been instrumental in bringing Honda to Lotus after its three-year exclusive with Williams expired. He later explained: "I very much enjoyed working with Renault. I think it was saddled with limited conditions at that stage, in terms of producing the engines and developments, etc, whereas Honda was unlimited in that respect. But as far as individuals were concerned at Renault, I had a good relationship and a good environment to work in. And the company gave me a lot of success. Of course it's no secret that I particularly wanted to go in the Honda direction at that time, which is what happened eventually. I did it because I believed it could do a better job with what it had available. Not that each individual was better than those at Renault, but as a package... As far as the commitment from the company was concerned, I realised that Honda was much further ahead than anybody, not just Renault. And that commitment is fundamental for success."

Senna had worked his charm to get himself the best possible package, just as he had done on so many previous occasions in his career. Honda clearly saw that Senna was the future and his pursuit of perfection held strongly with the Honda ideals. The gruff down-to-earth Williams approach, with the team's warring drivers, did not fit so easily with the Honda philosophy, and the team firmly wanted to do things its own way. Honda was still seething that Williams had lost the 1986 drivers' title and was adamant that this could have been avoided if team orders, most likely for the good of Piquet, had been imposed. Honda also questioned whether Frank Williams was capable of running the team following his car accident. Williams had recovered well from the accident in early 1986 and was attending all the races, his mental capacity undimmed. But the Japanese, who detested weakness of any kind, whatever its cause, were not convinced. In February 1987, Honda moved out of the Williams factory in Oxfordshire and into a new facility in Langley, Berkshire, from which it would supply both teams. It was a symbolic as well as physical move.

Honda's arrival was not the only major change for Lotus in 1987. After 18 years with the team on and off, Imperial Tobacco pulled its sponsorship after it was taken over by the cost-conscious Hanson conglomerate. There would be no more JPS Lotuses.

Imperial may have publicly blamed escalating costs, but the real reason was that it was unimpressed with Lotus's failure to sign a top-flight British driver.

In a way the loss could be attributed to Senna, but the inclusion of Nakajima in the team had strengthened the Honda relationship and that was ultimately what mattered. A replacement title sponsor was easily found in the shape of another cigarette company, RJ Reynolds, and its Camel brand. The familiar black and gold was replaced with sunny yellow.

There was also technical innovation. Fuel was still limited to 195 litres in order to keep some power control over the turbo engines, and boost pressure was limited to four bar. But the big innovation was suspension. The new Lotus Honda 99T was the first Formula One car with active suspension.

The computer-controlled active suspension was a bold and risky leap forward and true to the team's tradition of invention. It had been a long time coming, and was the biggest car development since ground effects, also introduced by Lotus. But the system was far from perfect. It had been instigated by Colin Chapman before he died and would not be perfected until Williams' refinements in 1992.

In 1987 there were inevitably problems. Originally the system was bulky and unwieldy, but it had great promise – if only it could be made to work consistently. After pre-season tests using cars with both active and conventional suspension systems, Senna was convinced that the active car should be the choice for the following season, and pushed the team towards finalising the details. For Senna it was a supreme technical challenge. He said after he first drove the car with the new suspension: "This is what we've got to have for the whole season, from the start – and nothing else."

But at the start of the year there was some doubt that Senna would even start the season with Lotus, as rumours flew thick and fast. One had Senna dumping Lotus to drive for McLaren. The team didn't have a team-mate for Alain Prost, as 1982 world champion Keke Rosberg had retired at the end of the year. Team principal, Ron Dennis had hung on, hoping Rosberg would change his mind. But he had had a lacklustre 1986 season and been deeply affected by the death of his friend Elio de Angelis. Stefan Johansson, always the most likely choice to replace him, was waiting in the wings. But McLaren never looked like a move that Senna would be willing to make, even though Ron Dennis had made it known that he would be welcome in the team. The TAG turbo engine was fading and just didn't have the legs of the Honda, as 1987 proved.

The Brazilian had gone to great lengths to build Lotus into exactly the team he wanted – carefully selecting his team-mate, encouraging the deal with Honda and showing enthusiasm for the active suspension – and a last-minute leap to McLaren would have wrong-footed him in a team focused on Prost. The power of the Honda engine and the seeming promise of a Ducarouge chassis meant it was not the right time for Senna to make the move and he knew it. But the seeds had unwittingly been sown for 1988.

Meanwhile, Senna put everything he had into developing the new car. His new team-mate, Satoru Nakajima, proved his worth when Lotus tested at Donington with Honda for the first time. Senna brought the car into the pits after a few laps and said: "There's something wrong with it because it's vibrating, it feels like it's going to shake itself to pieces." Nakajima then jumped in, and after two laps returned and said: "There's no problem. That's the way the engines always are." Senna was impressed.

The season began in Brazil, as was tradition, at the Rio de Janeiro track of Jacarepagua. Senna proved wrong those who had doubted the new active suspension when he qualified in third place, and then in the race pushed into the lead by lap eight. The Brazilian crowd went wild when he overtook Piquet for the lead, and showed their shifting allegiance, from the old hero to the new. Four laps later, however, Senna was forced into the pits – he complained of handling problems and eventually rejoined in midfield. He had fought back into second place by the time his oil tank broke in the closing stages. He followed Rio with pole position in Imola and also led a few laps, finishing second to Nigel Mansell's Williams. It seemed that in the Honda-powered battle, Williams had taken the upper hand.

The next race was the Belgian Grand Prix at Spa-Francorchamps. Senna qualified third, behind the two Williams cars, but at the start he leapfrogged them both, although Mansell was right on his tail. As they powered down to the fast Fagnes curve, Mansell made his move and pulled alongside the Lotus, but as he moved left to overtake, Senna drifted to the right. Mansell did not give way and the two cars tangled and spun off the circuit.

Senna was eliminated immediately while Mansell continued at the back of the field for a few laps before he was forced to abandon the car in the pits. He was furious. He stormed down to the Lotus pit, where he pushed Senna against the wall and zipped his overalls up to his nose. Some Lotus mechanics intervened before the confrontation grew nastier and Mansell was led away shouting. When asked what Mansell had wanted, Senna replied with one of the classic all-time Formula One quotes: "When a man holds you round the throat, I do not think that he has come to apologise."

Mansell was fuming. "I turned into the corner and the next thing I knew he was sliding down the inside," he said. "I felt a bump from the rear and I was off, spinning into the sand. I don't think I've ever felt more angry in my life. What he did was totally unnecessary and ridiculously dangerous, and it was about the fourth time he had done it to me in the past three years. When I climbed out, I had only one thought on my mind and that was to get Senna. I found him in the Lotus garage and I can only say he was lucky some bystanders kept us apart after we'd had a bit of a scuffle. There could have been a bit of a mess on the garage floor."

Senna naturally saw the incident a different way. "I couldn't believe what he was trying to do – overtake on the outside at a place like that," he said. "I tried to get out of the way, brake as much as possible, but you can only do so much in a situation like that. I was committed to the corner – there was no way I could stop."

Monte Carlo was Senna's 50th Grand Prix and he put the Mansell controversy behind him to celebrate in style. Everyone was still talking about Spa, but both drivers were determined to let bygones be bygones. "My sights are on the world championship, not on any other driver," Mansell said. "I feel the same about him as I feel about all the other 25 drivers in the world championship. They are all drivers I have to beat. I don't want to think about Senna for even 30 seconds."

The battle was hotting up. Mansell beat Senna to pole by over half-a-second, but Senna was himself more than a second better than next-placed man, Piquet. They were so fast that if the current 107 per cent qualifying rules had applied, then only 16 cars would have made it on to the grid. Everyone was predicting a thrilling race, but the battle failed to materialise. They left the grid in formation, with Senna struggling to match the pace of Mansell, who was pulling away by a few tenths of a second every lap.

But on lap 30, when he was 11 seconds in the lead, Mansell's turbo blew and Senna took the lead. To the chequered flag it was a near-flawless drive to victory for Senna, black-marked only when the back end of the Lotus twitched wide in the closing stages. History was made – it was Senna's first victory in Monte Carlo and the first ever for a car with active suspension.

"It is fantastic to win here," Senna grinned. "It is the most prestigious place to win and I am delighted. My main concern was the tyres and keeping a nice steady pace. Mansell was pushing very hard and I don't know if he could have kept it up all the way anyway. It was easier to win this race than to finish third last year. When Mansell pulled away at the start, I just kept him around eight seconds ahead – I wanted to preserve everything and not push too hard."

Not everyone was impressed by this consummate display of Senna's

Monaco skill. Nelson Piquet, who had finished second, grumbled: "We have the same engines. The main difference must be the suspension."

As the Formula One circus temporarily left Europe, Senna headed back to Brazil for a well-earned rest. But it was not all relaxation. On the weekend after the Monaco Grand Prix he launched his own line of men's sportswear in a Rio de Janeiro nightclub. It was an early sign of his ability to think as a businessman as well as a sports star. "This is just a way of investing part of the money I've made on the track," he said. "Racing is still my life."

The next race in Montreal was cancelled, ostensibly because of a dispute between sponsors, but more plausibly because the addition of the Japanese Grand Prix to the calendar had meant 17 races in the season, and the teams were happy with 16. This meant that the next stop was the US East Grand Prix at Detroit and a street circuit at which Senna had always done well.

Mansell continued his dominance of qualifying by taking top spot by over 1.3 seconds from Senna, although the race seemed to prove the jinx that the only race he had won so far that season was the only one where he had not started from pole position. He led until half distance when a lengthy pitstop ruined his chances and Senna took the lead to cruise to his second victory in a row, waving a Brazilian flag from the cockpit as he took his lap of honour. He again insisted that Mansell was pushing the car too hard to keep up the pace, and revealed that a crucial strategic decision on his own part had enabled him to win without the need for a pitstop. "I made the decision halfway through and decided to go for it. We were supposed to stop. Nobody knew we were going all the way except me."

Victory in Detroit gave Senna the lead in the drivers' championship with 25 points, two ahead of Prost, four ahead of Piquet and 10 ahead of Mansell. It looked as if he could go all the way, especially as the active suspension had proved reliable and successful. But the team still had doubts, as the two wins had come on the slow street tracks of Monte Carlo and Detroit. "We have a lot more to prove on the fast circuits to show we are the best," Senna said tellingly. "I think the championship is just starting."

He qualified third at the French Grand Prix at Paul Ricard and raced to fourth, holding onto the championship lead by a single point as Mansell romped to victory. Mansell was dominating the season and was destined to be on the front row in every race he ran. If his car held together it was clear he would be champion whatever Senna did.

The British Grand Prix at Silverstone marked a watershed for Honda, when the Japanese manufacturer took the first three places in qualifying with

Mansell, Piquet and Senna; and the first four places in the race, with Mansell the victor, Piquet second, Senna third and Nakajima fourth. In the world championship Piquet and Mansell were by then behind him in the standings by just one point. "We could not match them for performance or fuel efficiency," Senna admitted. "I just tried to hang in there." Once again problems with fuel consumption were emerging.

Senna had started to realise that although Lotus could deliver him victories on tracks to which the car was suited, to mount a consistent championship challenge he would have to look elsewhere. He had spoken to Ron Dennis about a move to McLaren before, and so he began to solicit the team boss in earnest. Dennis was used to running a team with two championship material drivers, but the retirement of Keke Rosberg at the end of 1986 had forced him to take on Sweden's Stefan Johansson, who while a good driver was not a great one. Dennis wanted to return to the glory days of the Prost-Lauda, Prost-Rosberg partnerships and the cool perfectionist Senna seemed ideal to fill the gap. Besides his talent Senna had something else very special to offer: Honda. As its relationship with Williams turned sour, Senna knew he could persuade the company to instead supply McLaren alongside Lotus in 1988 and end the Williams deal.

On the weekend of the German Grand Prix at Hockenheim, Senna hinted to Peter Warr that he was intending to leave the team. The decision was compounded by his third-place finish in the race, a lap behind Piquet's winning Williams, and with a car in which the pedals had worn through the floor. Senna lost the championship lead to Piquet as a result. The rivalry between the two very different Brazilians was growing intense. Piquet was used to being the nation's hero, but Senna had just been voted Brazil's favourite sports personality with 17.5 per cent of the vote – Piquet had finished back in fifth with 8.5 per cent.

Senna had yet to sign for McLaren, but he had a verbal agreement with Dennis that he would drive. A couple of days after the German Grand Prix, Warr received a letter from the Brazilian's solicitors informing him that he should look for a new number one driver for 1988. Senna was taking a chance as he had not yet signed his contract with McLaren. "Nothing was signed but all the negotiations had taken place, and I believed in Ron's word on the deal," he said.

Warr immediately realised that Senna had taken the high ground in the round of driver negotiations for 1988 and that Lotus was about to be humbled. If he could not keep his driver he at least wanted to win the PR war. He immediately began scheming to bring the driver market back under his control. "It was quite obvious that Senna thought he would be the first to sit down in the game of musical chairs and that everything else would then follow," said Warr. "I wasn't prepared to wait for him – and run the risk of having to choose from the left-overs at the end of the season."

As Warr pondered his options he realised that Honda loved Nelson Piquet almost as much as it loved Senna, and that Piquet was the key for Lotus in 1988. There was no attraction for Piquet at Williams with the engine gone. Piquet had also heard the engine rumours and was pondering his future. The weekend after the German race, Warr flew out to Nice and then helicoptered into Monte Carlo for discussions with the championship leader. The two men talked long and hard that Saturday night. Warr said: "I hadn't spoken to Nelson before that Saturday but I felt we had to act." It went like clockwork and the following Wednesday Piquet flew to Heathrow to meet with Warr and Fred Bushell. Piquet, sensing that Williams was about to lose its Honda engines a year early, had nothing to lose and everything to gain. He signed a two-year deal to drive for a Honda-engined Lotus team. Warr had effectively stolen Senna's thunder.

On Thursday evening, Senna arrived in Budapest for the Hungarian Grand Prix, completely unaware of the deal with Piquet. He found out when the news was made public the following morning, 20 minutes before qualifying. It looked as if Senna had been pushed out of the team in favour of Piquet, and with the Lotus door closed he had lost a powerful bargaining tool with Dennis. He was furious.

"There is no reason for me to rush to announce my plans," he told assembled reporters. "I am open to suggestions, but I am certainly finished with Lotus. That happened a long time ago. It amazes me that a company as big and famous as Lotus should behave so unprofessionally. They could have called me on Wednesday – the day he signed – to let me know. Instead I found out here on Friday morning."

Senna qualified just sixth, but finished second in the race – to Piquet.

In Austria Senna qualified seventh and after a bad start raced to just fifth. It seemed as if the Lotus title challenge had gone off the rails. Piquet moved 11 points ahead of Senna in the championship and it was looking as if Lotus would have the number one on its car in 1988 after all.

There were no snags in the final negotiations and Senna took his father Milton, who came over to England specially, down to Woking to sign his contract with Ron Dennis. His father was with him because it was a very big deal, involving over $20 million for three years. They left Esher early in the morning, then got delayed at the McLaren factory as they looked around and met all the people. By all accounts Ron Dennis did not offer them any lunch, and they got home late and very hungry. Milton da Silva was an extremely methodical man. He liked his lunch at 12:30, his supper by 7:30, and was in bed by the stroke of 10. If these things didn't happen he got upset.

When they finally arrived home to the Esher house he shared with Mauricio Gugelmin, it was after 11. His father simply made a few sandwiches in the kitchen and took them up to his bedroom. As it happened, Gugelmin, who had been left at home, had decided to play a joke on Milton. He filled up his bed with weightlifting irons he had brought from his gym. Gugelmin remembers: "We only heard a horrible noise and a scream." "Son of a bitch!" yelled Milton in Portuguese. Exhausted, he had apparently collapsed onto his bed.

On 1st September, in an interview with Brazilian newspaper *O Globo*, Senna made it public that he would switch to McLaren for 1988 in a three-year deal. That did not come as a shock, but there was plenty to surprise and anger at Lotus in Senna's vitriolic statement. "I'm in Formula One to be a winner," he said. "My goal is to win while Lotus's is merely to survive. We just couldn't continue together. They knew I was on my way out. I just didn't tell them that my next stop would be the McLaren team, with which I had everything straightened out, as well as with Honda. It's a question of philosophy. Warr does not like to take risks, and he runs Lotus with an iron hand. But when the competition starts, it's each man for himself. The amount of money behind the Formula One circus is so high that no one could care less for anything else. I behave just like any driver in search of winning. Once a new driver comes along, many people want to knock him down. The only reason I'm still racing is because I want to become a world champion." He added: "From a personal point of view I am very happy to work with Alain: two top drivers working together can only make a team stronger."

At Monza the official announcement was made that both Senna and Honda would be joining McLaren in 1988. There had been another year to run on the Williams Honda deal, and the team was left without another top engine manufacturer to turn to. It had refused to take on Satoru Nakajima, and the following season would, as a result, be using the debuting normally-aspirated engine from an English engine-builder called John Judd. It effectively ruled the team out of the championship before it had even started. To soften the blow, Honda paid Williams $24 million in compensation for breaking the contract and agreed to pay for a year's supply of the Judd units. But the team was left in the lurch until it was rescued by a few Renault managers knocking on its motorhome door with the offer of help in 1989.

Senna had turned 27 and was no longer the young rookie with nothing to lose. He knew he should have won at least one world championship between 1985 and 1987 and possibly all three. But in the wrong choice of team he had won none. The hard truth was that Lotus was incapable of taking the championship, and he was sorry he had not recognised that in 1984. He was certain he could take the team and mould it into his own. Now he realised that Formula One was moving and Lotus was stuck in a time warp after Chapman's death. The team did not want to leave its roots behind and enter the new technological data-driven world of Formula One. Its roots were mechanical.

Senna and Dennis had struck a hard bargain. Dennis later revealed: "He was incredibly tough, even in those early days, and in the end we just came to a complete stalemate over the last $500,000. I suggested that we flipped a coin for it but he did not understand what that meant. Having had it explained to him that it was the simplest way to break the deadlock, I then had to draw a picture of a head and a tail to make absolutely sure that there was no doubt as to the interpretation. I wrote down on a piece of paper the rules to this very simple thing but he still did not have a complete command of the English language. I won the toss and he never forgave me for it – I paid a million times over for that. It was only about 10 days later that it suddenly dawned on him that it was not $500,000, but $1.5 million because it was a three-year contract."

Despite that, it still put Senna into the really big pay league. The amount he was paid meant a great deal to Senna, not for material reasons, but as a marker of how much he was worth. As he explained in 1992: "It's all a question of market, of negotiating your deals in an appropriate way. I'm the highest-paid driver today: it's not because of my skin colour, my eyes, my hair or anything, it's because it's worth paying me the money and nobody would pay anything to anyone unless they could get it back somehow." Although the amount of money he was paid for that McLaren contract was never revealed, it was believed to be $7.5 million a year, the going rate at the time, as Formula One drivers' salaries had suddenly exploded and multiplied four times in three years as the world's economies boomed and new sponsorship money, mainly from tobacco companies, poured into the sport.

Piquet won the race, his Williams then fitted with active suspension that seemed not to have the same troubles on fast circuits as Lotus's. Senna had led in the middle of the race, but excessive tyre wear caused him to spin off and he finished second. Mansell finished third after an inexplicable lack of race pace, and several Williams team members hinted in private that they thought Honda was determined that the 1987 world champion would be driving a Honda-powered car in 1988.

Senna was 14 points down in the championship going into the Portuguese Grand Prix, and with Williams looking stronger every race his prospects looked dim. Senna and Mansell both failed to score – Senna had qualified fifth, then suffered a lengthy tyre stop and fought his way back to seventh from the rear of the field; Piquet was third and Prost took victory, claiming a record 28th career win. There were four races to go and Lotus was looking far from the team it had been at the beginning of the season.

Senna kept the championship mathematically alive with a fifth place on heavily worn tyres in Jerez, although his chances were admittedly faint. He had 51 points to Piquet's 70 and Mansell had overtaken him for second place in the standings.

His hopes ended in Mexico. He qualified only seventh, but in the race was battling with Piquet for second when he spun off. He tried to restart the engine, but an unsolicited push from some marshals meant an illegal push-start would have been declared if he had rejoined the race. Senna was furious and got out of the Lotus and punched one of the marshals. He was fined $15,000 as a result.

Shortly after Mexico, FISA president Jean-Marie Balestre announced that active suspension would be illegal from 1st January 1988. It was a blow for Lotus and Williams and for the top teams, which had all secretly been developing their own systems.

The championship was over on the Saturday of the inaugural Japanese Grand Prix, when Nigel Mansell hit a wall and suffered broken bones. Honda got its wish and Piquet was set to take the number one to Lotus for the 1988 season. Senna finished second in the race – the highest runner for Honda on the manufacturer's home ground. At the final race of the season in Adelaide he was again the second driver to cross the line, but on this occasion he was subsequently disqualified for using illegal cooling ducts on his brakes. Second place in the race would have clinched him second place in the championship from Nigel Mansell, but in the end he had to settle for third.

It was Senna's least successful year for Lotus. He drove 16 races, taking only one pole position but winning in Monaco and Detroit, finishing second at Imola, Hungary, Italy and Japan, third in Britain and Germany, fourth in

France, and fifth in Austria and Spain. It was enough to give him 57 points, worth third place in the championship. But it meant little. He wanted the championship, which by then had been denied him three times.

And that was the inglorious conclusion to Senna's Lotus career. He had moulded the team for his own needs, but ultimately it could not deliver what he really wanted – a Formula One world championship – and like Toleman, like his wife Liliane, it had been bluntly discarded when it failed to fit in with his dreams. Senna was heading for McLaren.

CHAPTER 13

1988: The Golden Car

Instant glory and personal happiness

The 1988 season was an important one for Ayrton Senna. It not only heralded a new team but also a new girlfriend – someone many people, including his close friend Gerhard Berger, believe was the real love of his life.

When they met, Xuxa Meneghel was a bigger star than Senna – and earned more money. She had been a well-known figure on Brazilian television since the dawn of the 1980s and had her own top-rated show. Such was her success that she was reckoned to be the 38th best paid entertainer in the world, although she was relatively unknown outside Brazil.

It was Xuxa who spotted Senna first, when she was flicking through a magazine. He was on the verge of becoming really famous when he joined McLaren, and was on the cover. Inside there were pictures of him with animals. She remembers thinking: "Wow, look at his face. He likes animals just like me, and is also famous."

She even discussed him with her manager, Marlene Mattos, but was certain it would come to nothing. "These things don't happen in my life," she said at the time. So she closed the magazine and forgot about it. A week later Senna phoned her dressing room at the TV Globo studios. She was recording her show but he left a message, and she called him back. He said to her: "Hi, most beautiful woman of Brazil." They talked freely straight away and he asked when they could meet. She said her show was filmed Monday to Saturday and she could not get away. He asked her about Sunday but she said she would not have enough time to get to São Paulo from Rio. He told her he would send his plane for her and she agreed. The plane arrived on the tarmac at Rio dead on time, and there was a little note for her from Senna. She took some colleagues back with her on the flight, then went to her house in São Paulo. She called Senna and tried to make excuses, saying she was very tired.

"How long would it take for me to get to your house?" he asked. "Fifteen minutes," she replied. "I'll be there in five minutes," he said. And sure enough, five minutes later a car was outside her house with the wheels spinning and smoke billowing from the exhaust. Xuxa remembers he was really nervous, but then so was she. She says when they touched and shook hands for the first time she felt it was really special – and that her dog Zé fell in love with the Brazilian straight away.

It seemed almost love at first sight for Xuxa and Senna too. That evening they stayed at her house and just talked. They had a lot in common – they both knew fame, had money and were single. He did not stay the night and they did not make love – but it was the night two Brazilian stars got together. It was the start of something long term and they both knew it. As he was leaving he asked if he could see her the next day. She said she was going to see her grandmother. "I would like to meet her," he said. But Xuxa made an excuse. In reality she thought the relationship was moving too fast. When Senna left, her dog made a huge fuss and followed him to his car. He looked at Xuxa and said: "This dog knows what's good for his boss."

Unfortunately circumstances conspired against them. With Senna about to return to Europe for the Formula One season they hardly saw anything of each other that year, except fleeting visits. Xuxa was committed to a very heavy TV schedule, working out of São Paulo for much of the time. Senna did find time to appear as a guest on her show and they saw each other occasionally, but did not sleep together. She knew he had other girlfriends and didn't want that sort of relationship. For the time being it was left in abeyance – the timing was wrong but the seed had been sown.

Joining McLaren was not easy for Senna. Alain Prost was king of the hill, having won the world championship twice already. But Senna had a nice surprise when he arrived. He immediately found two people he was to bond with and who would remain lifelong friends: team manager Jo Ramirez and physio Josef Leberer. The main impact on his life would come from Josef Leberer, an Austrian expert in sports medicine and a top physiotherapist. Senna had never really had contact with a top physiotherapist and nutritionist. All his training was done by Nuno Cobra in Brazil, who he had worked with since starting in Formula One.

Leberer was a protégé of another Austrian, Willy Dungl, who founded the world-famous Dungl Clinic in Gars-am-Kamp in Austria. Dungl was famous in Formula One circles for his work with Niki Lauda in the 1970s. Leberer was his protégé.

Ron Dennis had hired Leberer for the start of the 1988 season to ensure that Senna and Prost were in tip-top condition. Not just keeping them physically fit, but mentally strong as well. Leberer worked well with both Senna and Prost, but quickly drew close to the Brazilian, as did most of the team. He looked after him mentally and physically and stayed close. He quickly devised a new training programme and diet for Senna, and personally cooked as many of his meals as he could, also briefing the housekeepers in his houses in Brazil and Monte Carlo. Senna also instantly bonded with 47-year-old Jo Ramirez, a Mexican Formula One veteran who had already been in Formula One for 27 years. He had worked with the Eagle, Tyrrell, Fittipaldi, Shadow, ATS and Theodore teams, and finally McLaren from 1983.

They helped Senna overcome Prost's dominance within the McLaren team. Prost was not only the biggest man at McLaren but also the biggest man in the paddock. As Ramirez said: "When Ayrton first drove for McLaren, the biggest man in the paddock was Alain Prost. He was the man that Ayrton wanted to emulate – and eventually the man he wanted to beat – so he ended up driving the same car as Prost in the same team."

At the time, most paddock observers had no doubt that Senna would be blown off by Prost in 1988. No one thought he would come in and overpower Prost the way he did and neither did Prost. In fact at the start of the season Prost was totally unconcerned about his new team-mate. "McLaren is the only team that can have two top drivers with equal skills on the material and psychological scales," he said at the time. "I will help him become a member of the team.

"He has never been with a team-mate who drives fast. He has the advantage of his youth and motivation; I have a lot of experience, and I have a say in the matter. Our aim is to build a top-flight team and if we have the best car, we will compete against each other, and for the championship. There are two kinds of contestants: there are your opponents, and there are your team-mates, who are often the most redoubtable because that's the only way to size yourself up, since you're driving the same car."

There was no doubt that Prost was the more experienced of the two. But

Senna was convinced he would prove the faster driver – and he was right. The Brazilian also had a huge advantage through his relationship with Honda, which had been amazed by his grasp of engineering. He was the first driver the company had successfully communicated with. But Prost had already done four years with the team. It was his team. Senna knew his main battle in 1988 would be against his team-mate. However, he was in no doubt about the outcome, as he told friends: "I'm going to blitz him."

In reality Prost never had a chance. Senna knew his own weaknesses as well as his strengths: he was the faster driver and qualifier, but knew that Prost was probably the better race driver, who carefully devised a strategy that would yield good results by the finish.

However, much of the finesse was unnecessary, as Honda took advantage of changes in turbocharger regulations to produce a blindingly fast engine, which blitzed the opposition. It was the last year that turbochargers were allowed and the regulations had been continually tightened over the previous few years. It was not an easy job to develop an engine capable of satisfying the requirements regarding boost pressure (2.5 bar or less) and fuel efficiency (tank capacity of 150 litres or less). But it was a tightrope that Honda's engineers, with Senna's help, negotiated perfectly. John Barnard, the original designer of McLaren's MP4, recalls how they did it: "Honda manipulated the regulations to accommodate the boost level and found a way to circumvent them that masked the boost limit level by putting cunning shapes within the manifold, which effectively put the head of the pop-off valve in a low-pressure area. So although the boost limit was 2.5 bar the engine saw as much as 2.9 bar." It took Ferrari a whole six months to catch up and do the same thing.

The RT168E engine was an immediate winner and the car felt very good out of the box. McLaren had the best engine, the best chassis and the best drivers. The technical team on the 1988 car was technical director Gordon Murray with Steve Nichols, Neil Oatley and Tim Wright.

The new McLaren MP4/4 was so good that Alain Prost – who had driven no shortage of capable cars in his career – declared that it embarrassed him. He said: "It's perfect so it's very difficult to make mistakes in."

With Williams facing a year uncharacteristically out of contention with a normally-aspirated hybrid engine built by an engineer called John Judd instead of a turbocharged Honda, Ferrari was McLaren's only real competition. Williams had had its bank account enriched by Honda to the tune of several million dollars to break its engine supply contract early. Lotus also had the Honda engine but a useless chassis. If the team had been any good, Senna would not have left.

This was to be a golden year for McLaren, one of those rare years when a team has the best chassis and the competition is in disarray. Senna had jumped into the team at precisely the right moment. That golden scenario was reversed just four years later when Senna found himself up against Nigel Mansell and the dominant Renault-engined Williams.

Ferrari had been quick in testing but, as ever, reliability was suspect. Gerhard Berger and Michele Alboreto were two good drivers, but not a patch on Prost and Senna. In addition, team principal Enzo Ferrari was in poor health.

Ironically, the portents for McLaren were not particularly good for the new season. As a result of factory tinkering with the turbocharger, Honda's new V6 turbo engine was late, ready just a week before the season opened. The car made it to Imola for only the last day of a three-day test, after being air-freighted to Bologna.

Senna flew to Europe especially for the test and to open up his Monte Carlo apartment for the new season; he planned to fly back to São Paulo straight after.

On Wednesday 23rd March, Prost climbed into the car and was doing competitive times from his first lap. In the afternoon Senna took over and was a whole two seconds faster. Next came Gerhard Berger's Ferrari, which had already been testing for two days. With barely 500 kilometres done, the car was driven back to the McLaren factory in Woking, crated up again and flown off to Rio.

As a result of circumstance, the opposition was humbled, and the two McLaren team-mates strongly suspected they had a car capable for the first time in history of winning every Grand Prix in a season. Senna even suspected he could win every race, given the chance. And with perfect reliability he may well have done.

Senna was delighted how easy his new car was to drive compared with a Lotus: "I used to cover the palms of my hands because if I didn't I would get these terrible blisters and that would make steering difficult. I don't do that anymore now. My new car is lighter, easier to handle."

Even though the season started at the beginning of April, Prost's and Senna's race cars had done no running at all when they were uncrated in Brazil for the opening race of the season in Rio de Janeiro.

Apart from an upcoming intra-McLaren battle, the early-season pundits had predicted that Nelson Piquet in the Lotus Honda would be a challenger. That proved a joke, but a serious war of words started with Piquet off the track.

The knives were out straight away when Piquet gave an interview with a Rio newspaper on the eve of the race: he was quoted as saying Senna was homosexual and that his well-publicised flings with women were a front. Piquet claimed he had been told this by an ex-girlfriend of Senna's who he was seeing at the time. Senna was incensed and wanted to issue libel proceedings, but was persuaded against it by Philip Morris's John Hogan, who argued that the subsequent publicity would be far worse. Nigel Mansell had experienced similar problems with Piquet in the past so Senna chose to ignore the allegations.

Then the matter took a more serious turn when the Brazilian edition of *Playboy* was published just before the race, with Piquet smearing both Senna and Mansell. He repeated the Senna jibes and called Mansell an uneducated fool with an ugly wife. It caused a minor stir in the local newspapers and some ripples abroad. A former girlfriend of Senna's, 24-year-old model Surama Castro, was quoted as saying: "If that man is gay I would like to have a gay man in my bed every night." Senna had dallied with Castro the previous year after meeting her in Milan.

Press reports after the spat were amusing: "One woman alluded to his mystical allure: 'Although I have never met him somehow I feel a rather extraordinary presence emanates from him which even transcends the physical.' And another wrote of his broad appeal: 'He is the complete man who is incredibly brave, very intelligent, extremely lucid and eloquent, deeply spiritual, a loving part of a family unit and at times a playful child.'"

But the interviews had raised doubts in people's minds about Senna's sexuality on the basis there was no smoke without fire. Until his death, rumours persisted that he was bisexual, though without a shred of evidence to back them up. Senna was aware of the rumours but chose to ignore them. His lack of a regular girlfriend didn't help. He was a bit of a loner and liked his own space. After Maria and Marjorie who followed each other from Formula Three into Formula One, there was a succession of girlfriends that lasted months, mainly in Brazil, including models Virginia Nowicki, Patricia Machado, Christine Ferraciu and Marcella Prado, and actress Carol Alt. None lasted more than six months and few came to races.

If Piquet had timed the publicity to out-psyche and upset his Brazilian rival, it didn't work. Senna took pole in Brazil. But he was immediately warned how different it would have been if Williams still had the Honda. In a hopelessly underpowered Williams but with a brilliant chassis and a brilliant driver at the height of his powers, Nigel Mansell proved he was the best driver that day by squeezing Alain Prost off the front row. Piquet was only fifth, out of contention.

It was a false dawn for Williams. Prost won in what should have been a comfortable one-two, but Senna's gearbox failed on the warm-up lap. He switched to the spare and started from the back of the grid, working his way up to second before a flat battery pushed him back to sixth. However, it all proved academic as the switch of car was subsequently deemed illegal by the race stewards: on lap 31 a marshal stepped out onto the track in front of Senna's car waving a black flag with a board in his other hand that read 'number 12'. Being black-flagged was a rare event in Formula One racing – the equivalent of being sent off in a football match.

Senna was disqualified just as he was getting ready for another charge up the field. There was plenty of anger from Senna and McLaren about the disqualification and the fact that it had been enacted so late in the race. The reality was that Ron Dennis had been arguing with stewards on Senna's behalf. The ruling was harsh and ultimately fair, but the decision about the punishment very, very slow.

Then FISA president Jean-Marie Balestre was adamant the whole thing had been the team principal's fault: "To be stopped like that in the middle of the race is extremely disagreeable but the rules are the same for everybody. The other drivers would not understand if the rule were not applied. It's the law of the sport. The rule is very strict. It's regrettable on a sporting level, but a rule is a rule. This incident shows the regrettable lack of knowledge of the rules on the part of team directors and drivers. If anyone is to blame in this affair it's Ron Dennis."

Senna didn't want Prost running away with the championship early but he knew this was a race he had lost, not one his team-mate had won.

The first race saw Senna build up a good rapport with his new physio Josef Leberer. "I remember the first race," said Leberer, "I think he had an engine failure, anyway he did not finish the race. In the evening, I did cooking for him. I wanted to do everything so good. I was completely tired and suddenly in the evening he called 'hi, Josef what are you doing?' I said, 'you need some food, he shouted, 'no, no, no we go out, I have some friends here, we are going out, do you want to come with us?' Can you imagine how I felt. This is the first race, this guy is a Brazilian hero and he is thinking about me. With his friends he was a different person, so friendly and funny, talking in Portuguese. He said to me: 'I am sorry that we talk Portuguese'. So they talked English with me. It was really relaxed." Leberer soon found he was also a big friend of the family

But it was a chastened Senna who returned to Europe in the second week of April to his Monte Carlo apartment. Home for the past few seasons had been a glass and marble block of flats of the type only found in Monaco called The Houston. It was on the Italian side of the seafront, which stretches down to the Beach Plaza. At the time Monaco living suited him for the tax advantages and the fact that it was close to the Paul Ricard circuit, where most of the testing was done in those days. His first test of the European season was scheduled for Monza on 19th April. He did 42 laps and shunted the car but walked away.

The calendar was very different then and the second race of the season did not come until Sunday 1st May; six years later, that day would be very different. In 1988 Senna led from start to finish to win the San Marino Grand Prix at Imola, with Prost coming home second after fighting back from sixth when his engine almost stalled leaving the grid. They lapped the rest of the field. The win had been a lucky one and just after the finish line Senna pulled up, fresh out of fuel.

Even though it was one win each, Prost still held the advantage. It had not been lost on Senna that every time he won, Prost would probably be there and take second. And every time he made a mistake or retired, Prost would again be there to take the win. He suddenly had the realisation that the best man would not necessarily be world champion.

At Monaco, Senna took pole by 1.427 seconds from Prost. It was possibly the greatest qualifying lap of all time, and Senna later described it in mystic terminology, explaining that he had been in a kind of trance, going faster and faster with each new qualifying lap. The McLarens were two seconds faster than anyone else throughout the weekend.

In his subsequent report of the race in *Motor Sport* magazine, legendary journalist, the late Denis Jenkinson, described the other drivers' objective as not to get lapped by Senna too often.

Leading off the line, and easily in front for 66 laps, the Brazilian had the race in his pocket. In this situation Prost would have simply eased off and controlled the race majestically to the finish. But not Senna. If there was ever a race that indicated and explained so vividly why Senna only won 41 races from 65 pole positions it was Monaco in 1988. He realised he was in the best car at his most successful circuit – probably the closest he would ever get to perfection in Formula One. Throughout the race he tried to push the limits of perfection, and lapsed into a trance similar to the one he had experienced in qualifying.

Shortly before the 67th lap he began to go too quickly for his team's nerves; as he started lap 67, Ron Dennis radioed to him to slow down. But as he obeyed and began his cruise towards the finish, demonstrating some racecraft, of which he was not a great practitioner, Alain Prost pulled one of the legendary strokes for which he was so famous. Sensing Senna was suddenly easing off, Prost put in a very quick lap to pull back six seconds. It took the gap to under 50 seconds and Senna literally panicked that he was losing the race. It was the reaction Prost wanted. He had out-psyched Senna and his reaction was exactly what he thought it would be. On lap 67, distracted by the command from his team principal to slow down, Senna lost the plot, and sped up again as he deftly flicked his McLaren through the left and right of Casino Square down to Mirabeau and round the Loewes hairpin, down towards the seafront close to where he lived. He went into the right-hand corner just before the tunnel and glanced the Armco, which pushed him across the track where his front wheel touched the wall lightly at Portier. Monaco forgives no mistakes and he was out with a bent suspension arm. He climbed angrily from his car, brushing away help from marshals by the cockpit, and leapt the barrier as Prost sped by in the lead. He walked straight back to his apartment in the Houston block overlooking the Mediterranean. Only in Monaco could he make the five-minute walk home from a retirement without passing by the pits to explain. He was deeply upset by his own failure. He refused to talk to anyone and it was only much later that McLaren deduced the reasons behind the crash. An astonished Prost commented: "I was happy to be second and did not expect to win today. I was very surprised when I realised I was in the lead. I could not believe it."

It was devastating because there had been only 11 laps to go to the flag. Prost was second, nearly a minute down the road, and Berger's Ferrari was way down on him. Murray Walker, who was commentating that day, was as amazed as anyone: "It was one of the very, very few mistakes that Senna made through loss of concentration," he said at the time.

Jo Ramirez said: "The moment he saw that Alain was second and could pull back something like six seconds in one lap then he panicked. I remember Ron shouting to him 'stop, stop, slow down, it is only six laps, slow down'. Of course slow down was not in his vocabulary – the next lap he did another fastest lap and then he crashed."

Murray Walker remembers: "He was so upset, appalled and distressed by what had happened that he walked straight back to his apartment, which was not very far from where he had gone off, and completely disappeared for the rest of the day." That was distressing for Walker and his co-commentator James Hunt, who had viewers at the biggest race of the year.

It was up to Ramirez to find out what had happened: "I kept ringing the apartment but the telephone didn't answer," he says. "Finally, at 10pm, the telephone was answered by a Brazilian woman who used to look after the flat. So in Portuguese I said that I knew Ayrton was there, and could I please talk to him. She insisted he was not there but I said I knew he was, he just didn't want to talk to anyone, but that I needed to talk to him. Eventually Ayrton came to the phone and he was still crying. He said: 'I don't know what happened – the steering came off in my hand'."

Alain Prost says: "Ayrton was angry at Monaco when he did not win. But he did not know who to direct his anger at. He was always like that. Sometimes he just wanted to have a fight and his biggest motivation was to fight against me."

Senna thought he had lost the championship that day. He realised that although he could routinely smash Prost in qualifying, and was without doubt significantly faster, Prost had an edge over him in races and could manipulate him – and, like in Monaco, he was helpless to do anything about it. Prost took full advantage of his psychological breakthrough and won again in Mexico; Senna, worried about his fuel consumption, deliberately settled for second.

Astonishingly Senna was only third in the championship after Mexico. He may have annexed pole position for every race, but Prost was running away with the championship and Gerhard Berger was in second. The scores were Prost 33, Berger 18 and Senna only 15.

But at Montreal for the Canadian Grand Prix a fortnight later, it was Senna who won and Prost who had to settle for second. After complaining that pole was on the dirty side of the track, Senna had lost the lead to Prost at the start and had to overtake his team-mate to regain it. Prost was afterwards full of praise for his rival, even admitting he was the quicker driver: "He is the quickest, most professional driver. I don't know if I'm as fast as I was last year or two years ago. But for sure Senna is the quickest. The car is so good this year that we're going to win almost all the races."

Senna was back in the groove and the Monaco disappointment was forgotten. He took a lights-to-flag victory in Detroit at the next race and lapped everyone except Prost. It was the hottest race of the year and Senna had come through with flying colours, at last translating his mastery into successive race wins. Only eight cars completed the whole race distance. It put Senna in second place in the championship with 33 points to Prost's 45.

The car was embarrassingly quick, to the point that it smothered the careers of drivers like Thierry Boutsen, who reached his peak in the wrong year. The McLarens made everyone else's performance academic. In Detroit Boutsen finished a good third for Benetton Ford and said afterwards: "The only problem was that I didn't have a McLaren."

Senna didn't care whether the dominance of the McLaren was having a detrimental effect on the sport. It was his first year in a really competitive car and he was making the most of it. Unlike Boutsen he was peaking and had the best car. Asked by journalists if McLaren's domination was good for the sport, he smiled and said: "I don't really care." He was entirely focused on winning the world championship.

McLaren was already leading the constructors' championship by 78 points to Ferrari's 27. Ferrari team manager Marco Piccinini told the press that the team would be a lot more competitive in the second half of the season. Ron Dennis laughed: "If the second half means the last eight races and Marco is giving us the next three, then we'll take them."

Even more remarkably, Senna had been on pole position for every single race that season. It was unprecedented. Despite that, he was not leading the world championship – and that was also unprecedented. Senna shared the record of six consecutive pole positions with Stirling Moss and Niki Lauda. But he was not destined to break it.

The run came to an end just as his world championship charge hotted up. In France, Senna failed to take pole for the first time that year, as Prost squeezed out every inch in front of his home fans. The Frenchman would have been humiliated if Senna had beaten him to pole at home, and he proved he could still do it, even if a little bit of his motivation after winning two championships had disappeared. In reality he dominated the race – the only time in 1988 he was dominant. After taking an early lead, a fumbled pitstop saw him lose it, and Senna was three seconds ahead. But Prost hauled him in majestically and swooped past for the lead, making Senna look like an amateur. Prost romped home and Senna was second. The Brazilian later said he had gearbox problems, but still praised Prost's driving.

After Paul Ricard the team went straight to Silverstone for testing before the British Grand Prix. Senna used it as a chance to practise his model-aeroplane skills, and between sessions was to be found at the back of the circuit in the desolate, wide-open spaces. In the test session he was one of the slowest drivers there, six seconds adrift of Prost, as he focused on set-up and tyres for the race.

At the Silverstone event in mid-July, it seemed as if Marco Piccinini's predictions may have been correct. For the first time the McLarens were not on the front row. Instead the Ferraris of Gerhard Berger and Michele Alboreto led the qualifying, relegating Senna and Prost to third and fourth. But the session was far from typical, interrupted by rainstorms and a blown engine for Senna to contend with. He also spun the car right round twice in the day, looking to shave off 10ths at Stowe corner. The McLarens were bested by the Ferraris that day. Amazingly, after both his spins, Senna controlled the car, got it pointed in the right direction and carried on as if nothing had happened.

Come race day, the rain poured down and Berger took the lead at the start, but on lap 14 Senna powered past into first, albeit nearly taking out his team-mate, who was on a slow lap en route to retirement. Senna stayed there for the rest of the race, followed home by Nigel Mansell, while Prost, no lover of wet conditions, complained of handling problems and parked his car in the pits from 15th. Despite the victory the team was unhappy, and Ron Dennis said: "Taken as a whole, I don't think we did a very good job this weekend." For any other team at the time a win would have been greeted as a miracle.

It seemed not to matter that McLaren had won its eighth consecutive race, which was another record in a single season.

There was controversy afterwards as Prost admitted he could have carried on despite his clutch problem, but that he thought the conditions were too dangerous. It was a signal for normally pro-Prost French journalists to lay into him, accusing him of being a coward and not as fast as Senna. They implied his performance was disgracing the whole of France. Ron Dennis leapt to Prost's defence, saying he employed the two most professional drivers in the sport and if one or both made the decision to stop because it was dangerous he would support them 100 per cent. The criticism unnerved the team.

As the season wore on, Senna was appreciating all the attention from Josef Leberer. Never had one man made so much difference to his life. First Leberer focused on his back and gave him regular massages. Leberer remembered: " He was so committed and in the evening it was good to relax and 'come down'. I really took a lot of time to look after his back and massage. I think he really appreciated that. The chemistry was good. He was a special person."

At the German Grand Prix at Hockenheim in late July it rained again and qualifying went to form, with Senna on pole and Prost second. But journalists had smelt blood and were baying for it at the delayed post-qualifying press conference. Prost laid into the journalists, slamming their attitudes. Led on by French colleagues, they were baiting Prost, hoping he would crack and give them a story. In the race Senna led all the way with Prost coming in second, nearly 14 seconds behind. Senna had closed to within three championship points of the Frenchman.

In the first week of August at the Hungarian Grand Prix, the scene of so much happiness for Senna, he took the championship lead for the first time, heading a McLaren one-two after a close scrap with his team-mate: just over half a second separated them. He and Prost were equal on 66 points, but after 10 races Senna had six wins to Prost's four. He was very close to equalling Jim Clark's and Alain Prost's joint record of seven wins in a season.

Before Belgium the McLaren team-mates had an important task: to do first tests with the new normally-aspirated V10 Honda engine that was ready for the 1989 season. Turbos were banned for 1989 so Honda had no choice but to build a new engine. Senna had rarely driven a normally-aspirated Formula One car. Prost tried it first in mid-August at Silverstone. On the same day Senna was at Monza testing the regular turbo car. Then they swapped and Prost flew to Italy and Senna to Silverstone. Senna crashed the car heavily first time out and ended the test. He was simply unused to the characteristics of a normally-aspirated car in Formula One. His only experience had been his tests with Williams and McLaren in 1983, an encounter long since forgotten.

It didn't phase him. At the Belgian Grand Prix in Spa in late August, Senna took his fourth victory in a row, from pole to flag, to equal the seven-win record. But of more interest to him than records were the points-scoring per-mutations. With the seven wins altogether and a dropped score points system that favoured the Brazilian, the title was looking good. Prost, who finished second, conceded: "I think it's over. I know it is not over mathematically, but I cannot really hope to win four out of five races. That would be too difficult. I think Ayrton is going to win the world championship and deserves to, for what he has done this year and the last two or three years. He has had a fantastic season and I am not stupid. The pressure will be off me now."

That meant the pressure was on Senna. The claims irritated the Brazilian, who said: "I am happy with the result, but you cannot say I have won the title yet. I am close to it but it is not finished and I will keep on fighting the same way. I have to carry on working. You cannot afford any mistakes when you are racing against someone like Alain. Wait and see. It is not finished yet." McLaren was on course to win every race in a season, a feat never before achieved. The team had already won the constructors' and drivers' championships, it just didn't know which driver was taking the title. But the train was about to temporarily hit the buffers.

In August 1988 Senna was saddened when it was announced Enzo Ferrari had died just before the Hungarian Grand Prix. The Italian Grand Prix was the only event the man known as 'Il Commendatore' ever attended – and then only on the Friday, for qualifying. Senna hardly knew the Ferrari doyen but had hoped to drive for the team before he died. Nigel Mansell was the last driver to be signed personally by Il Commendatore. As a result, the Italian event at Monza was a sombre occasion. It was the first race in Italy since Enzo Ferrari's death, and the Ferrari team was particularly fired up to do well for the departed patriarch.

Despite that, Senna and Prost took their customary places on the front row; the Ferraris of Berger and Alboreto lined up behind them. It was a record 10th pole of the season for Senna, who had beaten Jim Clark's long-standing best of nine. In the middle of the race Prost's Honda failed, but with two laps remaining Senna was still in the lead, pursued by Berger, after leading every lap. It was then that the miracle happened.

Nigel Mansell had caught chickenpox and had been replaced at Williams by Martin Brundle and then 39-year-old French near-rookie Jean-Louis Schlesser. When Senna came up to lap the Frenchman for the second time in the race, Schlesser did not notice him and stuck to his line. Senna went for the gap anyway and collided with the Williams. The second McLaren was out, Berger and Alboreto were handed an astonishing one-two and the crowd was delirious.

Schlesser explained afterwards: "I didn't want to block Ayrton, but then at the last possible moment I had to turn. When I went he was on the kerb inside and then he hit my wing. I feel very sorry for him, but I don't think it was my fault. However, I am going to see him and say sorry."

Berger was delighted to take Ferrari's first home victory since title-winner Jody Scheckter in 1979: "It is the greatest win of my career and I'd like to give it to the old man, to Ferrari. Seeing all those people on the track cheering for me and the team was fantastic. It is one of the best days of my life."

McLaren's loss was ironic after all the testing it had done at Monza.

Two weeks later, in Estoril, Prost won and Senna could only finish sixth. It seemed as if he was beginning to crack and for the first time things had got nasty. Prost had taken pole, but Senna got the better start. As Prost pulled

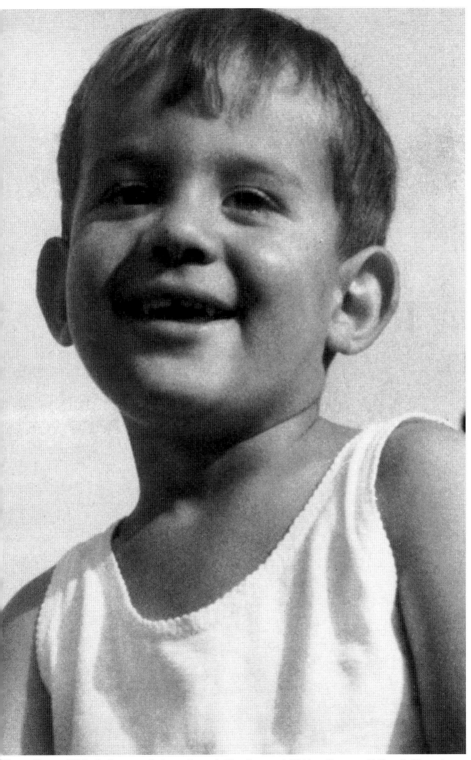

The earliest published photograph Ayrton Senna da Silva, the second child but eldest son of Milton da Silva and Neyde Senna. He was never meant to race cars but to run the family car-components business and cattle ranches. Eventually his father reluctantly agreed to fund his early race-car career. His son paid him back many times over.

The young Ayrton da Silva in São Paulo

Above: Waiting to race in 1979. By then he was winning everything in the Inter category.

Right: The oldest photo of Senna, when he first developed an interest in cars. He even pedalled faster than other children.

Below: A grainy old school photo from the Colegio Rio Branco archive.

Below right: 13-year-old Ayrton with his father Milton at a karting event.

Karting: 1974 to 1982

Above: Ayrton, aged three, makes his first foray into motor racing in a home-made go-kart fitted with a secondhand lawn-mower engine.

Above: Lucio Gascon, known as Tché, was Ayrton's karting mentor, and guided his career.

Left: Senna drives the DAP kart with which he enjoyed great success in 1979, although the karting world championship forever eluded him.

Ayrton debuts in the Formula Ford 1600 category in 1981
The young 21-year-old Ayrton Senna da Silva arrived in Britain with his young wife. In his yellow-and-black Van Diemen RF81 he won most of the races and both the RAC and Townsend Thoresen championships. In a typical scrap he leads Mexican driver Alfonso Toledano in an early round at Mallory Park. **Right:** Ralph Firman, Van Diemen's founder, provided cars for his first two seasons of car racing. Ralph Firman was Senna's team boss and mentor throughout his first year of car racing.

Above: Liliane Vasconcelos Souza became Mrs Liliane da Silva in 1981. The marriage lasted just a year.

Above: Ayrton waits to race with his loyal mechanic Malcolm Pullen.
Liliane watches. She was bored all year.

Ayrton's first car victory ever
Above: He celebrates his first victory with Van Diemen team-mate Alfonso Toledano on 15th March 1981. It was the first of 13 wins in 1981.
Above Left: Ayrton with his mother Neyde and brother Leonardo Senna
Left: He waits on the wet Brands Hatch grid before the start of the first race he won.

Formula Ford 2000 in 1982 with the Rushen Green Racing team

Right: Ayrton Senna takes his Van Diemen round Devil's Elbow at Mallory Park.

Below: On this occasion, on 3rd May, he could only make second on the grid but still sprinted off to win the race. It was the story of the season and no one could get close to him as he dominated the series.

A season of great success in Ford 2000 in 1982

Ayrton Senna da Silva's mentor in 1982 was Dennis Rushen, team principal of Rushen Green Racing. He charged the young Brazilian £30,000 for a season's racing in what was effectively the works Van Diemen team. Rushen and Senna remained close friends until the end of the driver's life. The season was a wrap-up for both the team and the young driver.

A Brazilian also conquers Europe in 1982

At the Jyllandsring in Denmark, Ayrton Senna wrapped up the 1982 Formula Ford 2000 Euroseries title driving the Van Diemen RF81 for Rushen Green. Team owner Robin Green (left) and Dennis Rushen celebrate with Senna.

Race, pole position and championship victory on 22nd August 1982 in Denmark

Ayrton Senna took the race and the trophy on that memorable weekend. He had dominated almost every round featuring the best Europe had to offer.

Middle: Keith Sutton and Ayrton Senna afterwards.

19th June 1983, 21 years ago

Ayrton Senna had a memorable 19th June in 1983 at Cadwell Park when he totalled his Ralt Toyota against the banking and came to rest in the straw bales. Senna was going for pole position but ended up having to sit out the race.

Above: The story of the season, as Senna leads Martin Brundle into Copse Corner at the 1983 British Formula Three Grand Prix support race. But Brundle kept coming second and then got his hands on a more powerful engine.

Dick Bennetts of West Surrey Racing, friend and mentor, in 1983

Despite blandishments from Eddie Jordan and the offer of funding from Ron Dennis's McLaren team and Alex Hawkridge from Toleman, Senna chose Dick Bennetts and did his own thing, as he said: : "I decided he was the best team and he was the best guy to be with. I was right in my choice."

Winning the prestigious Macao Grand Prix at the end of 1983
Still driving for Dick Bennetts, Senna was entered in Macao by Teddy Yip's
Theodore team in Marlboro colours. As usual he won convincingly, against the
best F3 drivers in the world. The victory lap (below) was a moment to savour.

A summer of two halves

Martin Brundle reversed Senna's run of success in the summer of 1983 after a series of accidents for the young Brazilian. This one was on 12th June at Silverstone.

The Brazilian connection

Leonardo da Silva was a frequent visitor to the pit garage of West Surrey Racing in 1983. He listens in on a debrief between his brother and Dick Bennetts.

On top of his chief rival at Oulton Park

Ayrton Senna ended up on top of Martin Brundle's car and neither driver finished the race.

Senna and Brundle

Above: Senna and Martin Brundle, who was racing with Eddie Jordan's F3 team, were in a class of their own in the 1983 British Formula Three championship. Jordan wangled Brundle a faster works Novamotor engine. Then Senna found out.

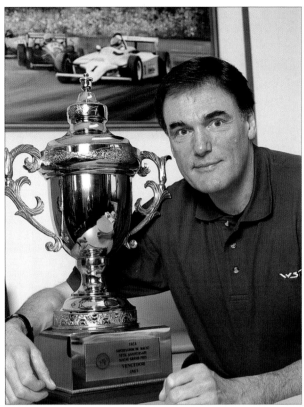

Martin Brundle in 1983
Senna and Brundle were first and second.

Golden memories for Dick Bennetts
Dick Bennetts today with the 1983 Formula Three Macao Grand Prix trophy.

It was arguably the best season of Formula Three ever in 1983
Senna beats Brundle and Allan Berg to the top step of the podium at the Silverstone Prestige Formula Three race. Brundle and Senna occupied the podium for the vast majority of the year.

Tuesday 19th July 1983, Senna's first test in an F1 car
Top right: Senna tests a Formula One car for the first time.
Senna examines the Williams FW08C Ford V8 (right) as Frank Williams
(below) makes detailed notes of Senna's handling analysis. Surprisingly
Williams made little attempt to sign him up to a drive. It was a mistake.

Four F1 tests at the end of 1983

Senna impressed when he first drove the Williams at Donington in July 1983, and then tried the Toleman TG183 Hart at Silverstone in autumn 1983. Finally he had a go in the McLaren, then the Brabham at Paul Ricard in France. He slipped through the top teams' fingers.

Right: Bernie Ecclestone and Gordon Murray oversee the secret test in a Brabham BMW at the Paul Ricard circuit in 1983.

Above: Senna discusses the Williams turbo FW08C with then chief mechanic Alan Challis.

Left: Senna wheels out the McLaren Ford MP4/1 at Silverstone in October 1983, watched by an anxious Martin Brundle, his F3 rival that year.

The first year in Formula One with Toleman

Ayrton Senna's Toleman TG184 Hart heads Elio de Angelis's Lotus Renault at the wet 1984 Monaco Grand Prix. He very nearly won the race in the wet conditions and was incensed when race director Jacky Ickx brought the race to a premature close, and handed the win to Alain Prost.

Below: Senna fights for position with Derek Warwick's Renault at the 1984 British Grand Prix at Brands Hatch, leading a host of illustrious cars and drivers.

Above: Senna in the Toleman Hart TG184.
Not the most competitive of cars.
Left: Senna enjoys a light-hearted moment
while discussing data with Toleman team
manager Peter Gethin in 1984. Senna learnt
all he could from ex-F1 driver Gethin in
that first year.

**On the podium
Above:** Senna followed
Niki Lauda and Derek
Warwick onto the podium
in the 1984 British Grand
Prix. Both drivers had
vastly superior cars, as did
the drivers who finished
behind him.

The first Grand Prix
The Senna da Silva family
share a meal on the eve of
the eldest son's first Grand
Prix in Brazil. It was a
magical moment, in 1984.

Race of Champions in identical Mercedes at the Nürburgring in 1984. Senna was an interloper but still won Senna joined a host of big names to battle it out in Mercedes 190E saloon cars in the race that opened the new Nürburgring in 1984. **Trying out sportscars** Senna was highly inquisitive and wanted to try every form of racing. He shared a Joest Porsche 956 with Stefan Johansson and Henri Pescarolo at the Nürburgring in July 1984.

Senna's first Formula One win

Once he joined Lotus, the first Grand Prix victory was inevitable. It came quickly at the 1985 Portuguese Grand Prix on Sunday 1st April. He took pole and got the jump from de Angelis, Prost and Alboreto at the start.

Another great Monte Carlo performance
Senna took pole at the 1985 Monaco Grand Prix and
led the race for 12 laps before his Renault engine
failed. He was denied victory.

Left: Senna lines up for the 1985 United States
Grand Prix at Detroit in his Lotus Renault 97T,
watched by his race engineer, Steve Hallam. His pole
position at the bumpy street circuit was one of 16 in
his three years with Lotus.

Below: Ayrton Senna chats to his 1985 Lotus
Renault team-mate Elio de Angelis at Monte Carlo.
De Angelis often proved a tricky opponent for the
less-experienced Brazilian. The Italian was killed
testing a Brabham at Paul Ricard the following year:
Senna was devastated by his first brush with death in
Formula One.

Four world champions in 1986 on the pitwall, in one of Formula One's golden years
Ayrton Senna and Nigel Mansell were yet to win championships. But as this picture, taken at Estoril in 1986, got older it grew more historic. From the left: Ayrton Senna, Alain Prost, Nigel Mansell and Nelson Piquet. The unique picture was organised by Bernie Ecclestone for photographers as each driver had a chance of winning the 1986 world championship at that stage.

The top team in 1985 Peter Warr, team principal, Gerard Ducarouge, technical director, Steve Hallam, chief engineer, Ayrton Senna and Lee Gaug of Goodyear watch qualifying unfold.

Below right: Senna took his first-ever F1 pole position in the Lotus Renault at the 1985 Portuguese Grand Prix at Estoril.
Below left: Senna on his way to his eighth pole position in the Lotus Renault at Jacarepaguá, Rio de Janeiro, in 1986.

The Camel Lotus year with Honda in 1987

Senna demonstrates his wet-weather mastery in the Camel Lotus Honda 99T during a wet practice session in the Belgian Grand Prix at Spa-Francorchamps.

Above: Senna receives his first Monaco winner's trophy in 1987 in front of Lotus boss Peter Warr, Princes Rainier and Albert and third-placed Michele Alboreto. It was his first of a record six triumphs in the principality.

Rare moment of accord: Senna and Nelson Piquet were usually bitter rivals throughout their careers

Senna shares a rare joke with Piquet after beating him to victory in the 1987 United States East Grand Prix at Detroit. He disliked Piquet even more than he did Prost.

Senna had to wrestle his Lotus Honda 99T at Monte Carlo in 1987. He was stunning, the car was not.

The sixth Formula One win came at Detroit, a twisty street circuit where he always excelled.

1988 was the golden year for Senna and Ron Dennis

Ayrton Senna won eight times in 1988 in his debut season for Ron Dennis's McLaren Honda team. He took his first world title from team-mate Alain Prost. The pair gave the team a record 15 victories out of 16 races that year.

Top: Senna hits the barriers at Portier during the 1988 Monaco Grand Prix from a commanding lead. Calls from the pits to slow down broke his rhythm and he collided with the Armco, as a result handing victory to Prost. He was very upset afterwards.

Above: Senna salutes the crowd on his victory lap at the 1988 Canadian Grand Prix.

Below: Senna discusses technical data with McLaren designer and engineer Steve Nichols.

Celebrating second place at the Mexican Grand Prix 1988.

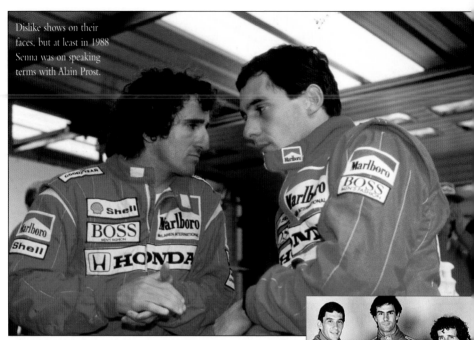

Dislike shows on their faces, but at least in 1988 Senna was on speaking terms with Alain Prost.

Above: Senna, test driver, Emanuele Pirro and Alain Prost at the launch of the 1988 car.
Below: Hostilities between Prost and Senna came to a head when racing got a little too close at the 1988 Portuguese Grand Prix at Estoril. Here Prost leads Senna into the first corner.

Above: Senna takes his first victory for McLaren Honda at the San Marino Grand Prix at Imola in 1988.
Below: Senna receives his trophy from FISA president Jean-Marie Balestre at Imola in 1988, flanked by Piquet and Prost.

Above: Alain Prost was Senna's biggest rival, and that rivalry was accentuated by the two years the pair had to spend as teammates at McLaren Honda in 1988 and 1989.

Right: A victorious Senna leads Prost and Thierry Boutsen to the podium at the 1988 Canadian Grand Prix, guided by race director Roland Bruynseraede and a marshal. After two seasons together, Prost would rarely smile and shake hands when Senna won.

Below: Senna and Prost in anxious discussions with McLaren Honda boss Ron Dennis under the awning at Detroit in 1988. Senna was a master of the street circuit, and took pole and won the race that year. None of the men were as happy as they should have been.

1988: The Golden Car at Monza

Arguably the best Grand Prix car ever raced, the almost invincible McLaren Honda MP4/4 should have won every race of the season. In the event it took 15 out of 16. Gerhard Berger's Ferrari ruined the party.

Ron Dennis keeps the peace in 1989

Ron Dennis gives instructions to Senna and Prost before a press conference. He had a tricky time and many difficult moments in 1989.

Senna and Prost do battle at Hockenheim in 1989.

1989: The year of discord between Senna and Prost
Senna and Prost collide at the Suzuka chicane in 1989, an incident that decided the world championship in the Frenchman's favour.

Below: Senna steers his broken MP4/5 into the pits for repairs. Prost watches on his way back to the garage, aware that his 1989 championship could be resting on the outcome of the stop.

The showdown for the 1989 world championship
Qualifying was a vital time for McLaren Honda during practice at the Japanese Grand Prix in 1989. But for Senna it proved to be a poisoned chalice getting pole, which as usual was not advantageous at Suzuka.

Left: Alain Prost celebrates a controversial 1989 world championship victory in Japan. Senna's disqualification from the race left the Frenchman with an untouchable points lead.

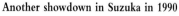

Another showdown in Suzuka in 1990

There was a sense of déjà vu at Suzuka in 1990, when Senna and Prost collided for the second year in succession. Prost's Ferrari leads into the first corner; but Senna determinedly refuses to give up the line; the rivals thunder into the gravel trap locked together; both are eliminated from the race and they trudge back to the pits together, Senna the new world champion. The following year Senna admitted that his actions had been deliberate, to even the ground after the controversies of the previous year.

Senna and Ron Dennis watch the action unfold in 1990
Senna was a lot more comfortable with Gerhard Berger as his team-mate. Senna also found him a faster driver in qualifying than Alain Prost, although Berger could not match Prost's race craft.

1990: The second world championship
Ayrton Senna was baked a cake to mark his 50th pole position at the Spanish Grand Prix at Jerez in 1990. The occasion was marred by Martin Donnelly's heavy crash in qualifying in a Lotus.

Right: Senna and Berger celebrate a one-three for McLaren Honda in the Belgian Grand Prix in 1990.

The story of the 1990 season
Ayrton Senna's McLaren Honda MP4/5B leads Prost's Ferrari at the 1990 Spanish Grand Prix at Jerez de la Frontera.

A lot of talking got done
Senna smiles as he considers his second world championship at a press conference during the Australian Grand Prix weekend. He gave journalists hours of his time at the race, where he philosophised on life, death, God and motor racing in no particular order.

Pierliugi Martini climbs from his Minardi Ford at the scene of Martin Donnelly's crash at the Spanish Grand Prix at Jerez in 1990. The Irishman was extremely lucky to survive the heavy crash.

Martin Donnelly's accident on Friday 28th September 1990 at the Spanish Grand Prix
The remains of Donnelly's Lotus, showing the exposed rubber fuel cell, testify that the accident could have been even worse.

Above right: Senna was visibly upset as he attended the post-qualifying press conference following Donnelly's accident.

The scene that shocked Senna. Martin Donnelly lies motionless on the track with the monocoque seat back panel still strapped to his back. Miraculously he survived under the care of Professor Sid Watkins (above right). Straight away Watkins reassured Senna, telling him Donnelly would survive.

Another wonderful season in 1991 as Ayrton Senna wins his third world championship

Senna and Gerhard Berger enjoy a joke in Portugal in 1991 as they dominated in a less-than-competitive car.

Left and below: Senna and Berger had the most wonderful relationship as team-mates. In Montreal that year Senna, Honda Chief Osamu Gotu and mechanics celebrate 50 Formula One victories for McLaren's engine manufacturer, Honda.

The shine wears off at McLaren in 1992 as Honda doubts grow

Top: As Berger and Senna are interviewed for television at the Canadian Grand Prix at Montreal in 1992 they were looking for the exit, believing Honda would pull out. Senna knew before Ron Dennis and tension grew between the two men, who had achieved so much success.

Above: Senna leads Berger at the 1992 Canadian Grand Prix. Senna's retirement due to electrical problems would hand Berger the victory.

1991 and Nigel Mansell and Williams Renault serve notice on McLaren Honda. The spell was broken

Nigel Mansell and Senna dice into the first corner in Mexico in 1991. Mansell would take the championship fight to the penultimate round.

Right: Senna celebrates his first victory in Brazil in 1991, scarcely able to hold his flag because of the pain from cramps in his arms.

Below: Senna barrel-rolls at Peraltada during qualifying for the 1991 Mexican Grand Prix. He was trapped upside down in his car, but unhurt.

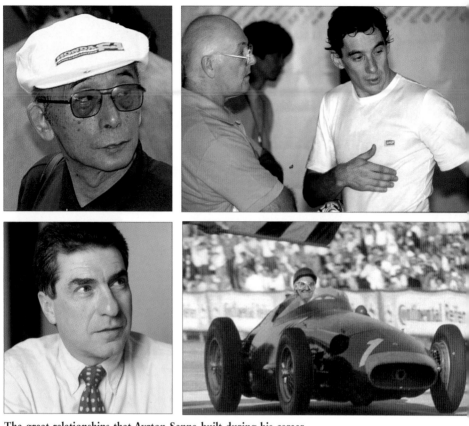

The great relationships that Ayrton Senna built during his career

Top left: Soichiro Honda was very fond of Ayrton Senna and believed he was the finest driver Honda had ever worked with.
Above left: Julian Jakobi's management of Senna's career soon after he entered Formula One made him millions.
Top right: Murray Walker adored Ayrton Senna and handled his death very carefully on live televison on Sunday 1st May 1994.
Above right: Juan Manuel Fangio, five-time world champion, was a huge Ayrton Senna fan. The two men had a serious professional respect for each other. **Below:** Engine genius Osamu Goto created three winning engines for Ayrton Senna: a turbo unit in 1988, a V10 in 1989 and 1990 and a V12 in 1991 and 1992.

out of his slipstream at the end of lap one, the cars were side by side at 190mph with Prost between Senna and the pitwall. Senna seemingly nudged him towards the wall as the pit crews swiftly pulled in their boards. It was that close. Exhibiting some incredible car control, Prost skimmed towards the concrete but still managed to take the lead. The Frenchman said afterwards: "It was dangerous. If he wants the world championship that badly, he can have it. I said I had lost the title in Belgium and I still think that way. But if my car is as perfect as it was today then I have a chance in the next three races. Who knows what can happen."

The Portuguese race marked the start of the enmity that was inevitable once the championship was at stake. Prost was right on that occasion: Senna should have given him the room, but he didn't.

At Jerez Prost won again, while Senna struggled to fourth from pole with a fuel indicator problem. The title was too close to call. Prost was ahead on total points – 84 to 79 – but only the best 11 scores counted. Prost had been the more consistent McLaren driver and as a result his win at Jerez counted for only three points instead of nine, because he had already taken five firsts and six seconds. It meant that Senna needed only to win in Suzuka to put the championship beyond Prost's reach. The situation was unprecedented as the teams headed for Japan.

With the championship so close between two drivers in the same team, things took a comic turn as Jean-Marie Balestre, president of governing body FISA, got involved. He wrote a letter to Honda's president, Tadashi Kume, telling him how important it was to make sure that both drivers had equal equipment for the final two races of the year. The strong implication of Balestre's letter was that Honda had been favouring Senna and giving Prost inferior specification engines in 1988, which was why Senna had proved the faster driver. It was a partisan move, Balestre and Prost both being French, and highly provocative.

It was designed to spook Senna and upset Honda. It worked and Honda was furious. But Balestre, for all his bumbling, had hit a nerve. It was something a lot of people had been thinking, if not openly talking about. Senna had blasted Prost away so comprehensively in qualifying all season that it seemed obvious to a French eye what was going on. Only at the French Grand Prix at Paul Ricard had Prost seemed on equal terms, and then he blasted Senna away. The implication of that was obvious as well. The publicity advantage of Prost winning his home race for Honda in France was far higher than Senna winning.

As well as his letter, Balestre was also privately briefing journalists – including Brazilians – about the situation.

It certainly irked Tadashi Kume, who was moved to respond to Jean-Marie Balestre in an open letter. It was pinned up on the press room noticeboard at Suzuka. The letter reassured Formula One fans that Honda would supply equal equipment for the last two races of the season and not favour one driver. It also reiterated that Honda had been supplying equal equipment for the whole year. Kume's letter vented its anger on Balestre in the most condescending way possible. The last paragraph read: "Finally I would like to express my sincere gratitude to you for consistently performing your important role as president of FISA." The deep irony of that comment was completely lost on Balestre.

Everyone sensed Senna would be champion at Suzuka. His old Formula Ford 2000 entrants Dennis Rushen and Robin Green decided to make the trip to be there when it happened.

It set the scene for the world championship showdown. As expected, Senna took pole. But it turned out to be to his disadvantage, as it was situated on the dirty side of the track. Qualifying was interesting as it was interspersed with damp conditions. Prost had continuing niggling problems with his car and the outcome was no surprise.

Senna later told his first biographer, Christopher Hilton, how he felt at the beginning of a race: "You must think of everything in the enormous turmoil at the start of a race. It is a totally unreal moment, it is like a dream, like entering another world."

The pressure got to Senna and at the start he stalled as the other cars rushed past his stranded McLaren. His hands shot up from the cockpit warning the cars behind him. He knew he could get the car going and was desperate not to be hit from behind, which he knew would end his chances. He dipped the clutch and the car started rolling forward. In the days before sophisticated electronic transmission, drivers changed gears just like in a road car and he managed to get the car going on the slightly downhill track, but by that time he was back in 14th place and Prost was pulling away into the distance. The rest was pure driving mastery, as he clawed his way back to the head of the field.

By the end of the first lap he was in eighth. In three successive laps on a damp track he passed Alessandro Nannini, Thierry Boutsen and Michele Alboreto. On lap 10 he took Gerhard Berger, and on lap 19 Ivan Capelli's Adrian Newey-designed March Judd suffered electrical failure while battling for the lead: Senna was in second. Luckily for him Prost was having his own gearbox problems, probably similar to what had caused Senna to stall on the grid. On lap 27 he passed Prost for the lead but drama was still to come. In the latter stages of the race it began to rain again and he pointed to the sky each time he passed the pits, trying to have the race stopped by officials, just as Prost had done when he had been catching the Frenchman at Monaco in 1984.

On the last corner he raised his fist and as he crossed the line both fists went in the air. Hundreds of Brazilian flags waved in the grandstand as Senna banged his fists on the steering wheel all the way round his parade lap. He was crying in his helmet in this only private moment before he faced the press and the congratulations.

He had won his first world championship at the age of 28. As he crossed the line he looked upwards, thanking God. Later he told journalists that he had seen God at the moment he became champion.

As the new world champion watched replays of his move on Prost, after the race, he had tears in his eyes. "I still can't believe it's all over," he said. "I love to win. That is why I joined McLaren and Honda. I wanted to be in a winning car. The fact that Alain Prost was in the team made no difference to me." Some people scoffed when he claimed he had seen God as he crossed the finish line, but for Senna it had been a moving experience. It was clear in the press room later that most of the journalists had been rooting for Prost and were disappointed to see Senna win.

Afterwards Senna made time for the friends who had got him there: Robin Green and Dennis Rushen, Keith Sutton and Reginaldo Leme of TV Globo. His friends got the best interviews and the best pictures.

The Suzuka result made the season finale in Adelaide, Australia academic: Prost took victory with Senna second. But the irony of the season's rankings was not lost on him or Prost: under today's points scoring system, Prost would have triumphed by 10 points. But that was then. In 1988 the governing body was playing by Senna's rules and he didn't care how he had won. He had won. Senna finished the championship three points ahead of his rival. McLaren finished the constructors' championship on 199 points. Its nearest rival Ferrari only scored 65. That was the scale of the domination.

Years later, Senna said the McLaren Honda MP4/4 was by far the best car he ever drove in his career: "To be successful, you must have everything. And apart from all the organisational structure, a good engine and a good car, that is what McLaren gave me. The best car I drove in my career, by far, was in 1988. That McLaren was a fantastic car, with a beautiful Honda V6 turbo engine." It was a year when McLaren Honda rewrote the record books in the world of Formula One racing with an unprecedented 15 victories out of 16 races. It was also the last season for turbocharged engines.

Senna handed a lot of the credit to Ron Dennis for his championship win. He said: "Ron Dennis is a super person to organise a racing team, because he has a wide span of knowledge, he knows the drivers and the engineers, and he has very good organising power."

Almost immediately Senna returned to Brazil to celebrate his championship with his own people. He was also keen to reacquaint himself with Xuxa Meneghel. He knew that now he was champion, everything would be different in his life.

CHAPTER 14

1989: Losing the Battle

Winning Xuxa but not the Championship

The relationship started in earnest with Xuxa Meneghel on the first day of 1989, deep in the Brazilian summer. They had arranged their schedules to spend time together – Senna would get home to São Paulo as often as possible – but it was always going to be difficult. However they resolved at the beginning in January to spend a whole year together come what may, and they did. But the careers kept clashing and they both knew it was not to be, although it took a long time to really dawn on them.

To facilitate the relationship and to give him a private place, he bought a beach house in the Brazilian resort of Angra. Prior to Angra he had never really had a home of his own in Brazil, relying on his parents. At 29 it was finally time for him to leave the nest.

His long spell with his parents had had other beneficial effects. His essentially quiet and reserved nature, together with his keen intelligence and conservative upbringing, meant that he was never tempted by the sex, drugs and rock and roll excesses of many Brazilian celebrities who couldn't handle sudden fame.

He was immensely grateful to his parents and never tired of saying so. Right up to his death, he still called them Mummy and Daddy when speaking to them in English: "I think I am very fortunate because my father and mother gave me the fundamental feelings that I have until today. Together with that I have a wonderful sister, a special brother, and we always live very close to each other, always thinking as a group, as a whole, always being positive about things. We always had a healthy life, we always had everything we wanted in life."

He was deeply attached to all his relatives. When Viviane's children arrived later, he treated them as his own. Whenever he was in Europe he remained in constant touch with his family. He telephoned them daily to keep them posted on what he was doing.

But when he came home after the 1988 season he was an overnight hero as world champion. Suddenly he had supplanted Nelson Piquet as the country's top sportsman. The dangers of excess were apparent. He had girls throwing themselves at him and all the temptations he could imagine.

He was also richer than he had ever been. The Lotus years had been relatively poorly paid. His 1988 salary for McLaren was around the $8 million mark. He is said to have earned as much again from external sponsorship. Because he had been born into affluence and was accustomed to it, he was never tempted to fritter away his money on a decadent lifestyle.

Senna used his money to create for himself his version of the good life; typically, it was sophisticated, comprehensive and imaginative. "Money has never been my motivating factor," Senna once said. "I don't need racing for any material reason. I only need Formula One for the pleasure it gives me."

Senna always believed he was better than any other driver on the tracks, and he wanted paying accordingly. Right from the very early days, when he had asked Ralph Firman for a salary in 1981, he had done his own negotiations and always started them by asking for the earth. It was a simple technique that always worked.

Because of his brilliance behind the wheel of a racing car, and his personal charisma, he kept his sponsors in the limelight more than any other driver. Such was his drawing power that his car inevitably logged much more TV time in front of the cameras than anyone else. In 1988 the world was booming and so was Formula One. It was nothing like the 1997/1998 boom, but there was more money around from sponsors than had ever been seen before. Formula One was also relatively cheap in the era before sophisticated electronics. It was possible for a top team to go racing for around $16 million a year plus drivers' retainers.

Senna was also canny about his own image rights and personal sponsors. As drivers' salaries went up, team-owners resisted letting drivers have personal patches on overalls. None more so than Ron Dennis, who liked his cars and his drivers to look a certain way. Senna however kept his undergarment rights and was allowed to put his personal sponsor Banco Nacional, the Brazilian national bank, prominently on his helmet, overalls and cap. It was an enormous concession for Ron Dennis to make. But it was also important for Senna: the bank paid him a rumoured $3 million a year to sport its logo on his cap and driving suit.

He used up $3 million of his new wealth buying Angra, which quickly became his favourite place to be and the place he really regarded as home. It was a five-bedroomed beach house on a 14,000 square metre plot located on the Atlantic coast at Angra dos Reis, 200 kilometres south of Rio de Janeiro. He said: "Here, I manage to switch off, maybe not one 100 per cent, but almost."

As he wiled away the inter-season months, enjoying the Brazilian summer at his new house, he was worried about 1989. It was to be the first year of normally-aspirated engines and there was no guarantee Honda's new 3.5 litre V10 engine – developed to satisfy the regulations specifying a maximum displacement of 3500cc, with no more than 12 cylinders – would be any good.

But all the signs were that it would be. He and Prost had been testing the new engine since August of the previous year: it had proved only marginally slower than the turbo cars and way ahead of the times the best normally-aspirated cars were doing. But competitors such as Ferrari and Renault had not yet showed their hand.

The new engine delivered output of 650 horsepower and he hoped that would be enough. He was under no illusions that 1989 would be the cakewalk 1988 had been.

When he got back to Europe to test the new car and engine, which together formed the MP4/5, he found it much harder to drive and nowhere near as sweet as the obsolete MP4/4.

Honda's new V10 concept was 'the power of a V12 engine with the lightness of a V8'. Senna said he noticed most of the difference switching from turbo to normally aspirated. He said: "It's a different technique to drive. Mainly it's an engine with more bottom and mid-range power and torque. The top end not so much, similar to a turbo engine of one year ago. But it's a 10-cylinder engine, so the car is built differently around the engine, and the handling and driveability are different, so the driving technique has to be different in order to get the best out of it."

The main opposition was to be the John Barnard-designed Ferrari, with a very strong driver pairing of Gerhard Berger and Nigel Mansell, and the Williams Renaults, bristling with electronic devices and a clearly strong

Renault engine. McLaren Honda still had the edge but in 1989 it was not as big an edge.

As always, the season opened in Rio. There were none of the Piquet problems that had dogged Senna in 1988. Piquet was emphatically shown the door: with the same engine, Senna had demolished him. Piquet barely featured at all in the 1989 season. He was left completely humiliated as Honda took away his Lotus team engines and the team was forced to buy second-rate powerplants from John Judd – the engines Williams had used the year before. It was effectively the end of Piquet as a force and the end of Lotus.

To all intents and purposes, it seemed to the casual observer like a rerun of 1988 as the race started with Senna in pole position. But Prost was back in sixth, 1.3 seconds behind, and Senna looked around to find the Williams Renault of Riccardo Patrese beside him on the first row. Only Senna knew how much harder getting on pole had been. As well as the Williams, the Ferraris were also mixing it with the McLarens. The start was a disaster for Senna as Patrese, he and Berger wrestled for the lead at the first corner. In the *mêlée* Senna lost his nosecone and had to pit, losing a whole lap in the process. Otherwise his car ran perfectly as he finished 11th, and Nigel Mansell romped to a totally unexpected victory in his first outing for Ferrari. Mansell had been so sure his Ferrari would not finish that he had booked a flight home before the end of the race. Afterwards Gerhard Berger, who was forced to retire, was not happy about it and said he would not be intimidated by Senna's driving tactics. Berger said: "Senna chopped twice across me to make me back off, but he should not do that with me. Never in my life will I back off in that situation." Prost finished second with no clutch.

As Senna got wealthier with his near-$20 million-a-year income from driving and sponsorship, his attention was turned to what he could do for the poor of São Paulo. His focus was on children, and he was giving away around $2 million a year.

Josef Leberer remembers: "We were driving through São Paulo and I had to ask him, 'you are a wealthy guy, you see these poor areas, what do you think about it?'. He was such a good person. And you could see that it went deep into his heart because he said, 'this is a big problem in Brazil and sometimes it is difficult with the corruption, but I would like to do something already'. He was supplying children in hospitals but he was never talking, he said 'I don't like to talk about it, I like to do it'. I remember I thought I was really proud to have the chance to meet someone like him."

At Imola for the San Marino Grand Prix, the story returned to normal after extensive testing at Imola, as Senna and Prost qualified first and second – 1.6 seconds ahead of Mansell's Ferrari in third. Before the race, Senna and Prost hatched a secret plan. Senna put it to Prost that they should not race until Tosa, and thus avoid an accident like the one at Brazil, on a track that both of them knew to be dangerous. Thinking of the good of the team, Prost agreed.

Senna had the better getaway and Prost slotted into second, as arranged. But the race was stopped following a horrific accident on the third lap. Gerhard Berger's Ferrari flew straight off the track at Tamburello, where it hit the wall and burst into flames. Berger thought his number was up and was knocked unconscious by the sheer violence of the accident. He was pulled intact from the wreckage by marshals, suffering only minor burns, broken ribs, a fractured shoulder, concussion and shock.

At the second start, Prost took the lead, but Senna seemingly broke the accord and overtook him at Tosa on the first lap; it stayed like that until the end. By then Prost was 40 seconds behind in second. A team statement later blamed the deficit on his tyres going off early.

Prost was absolutely furious and seething as he took his helmet off. Journalists and the team, unaware of the accord, were bemused. He told them an accord had been breached. The hacks had no idea what he was talking about. Prost stormed straight off to the McLaren motorhome, where he told Ron Dennis what he thought of Senna and the damage he was doing to team morale. When Dennis would not immediately take his side, Prost grew even angrier and immediately left the circuit for the airport in a helicopter. He refused point blank to go to the post-race press conference and was fined $5,000.

When Dennis tackled Senna afterwards, he had plenty of excuses ready. Firstly he told him that the accord only counted towards the first start not a restart, that Prost had broken similar agreements on several occasions in 1988 and that the accord had lasted only until Tosa.

Dennis wasn't at all convinced and ordered Senna to apologise. Senna explained to journalists afterwards: "He got the jump early, then I got the slipstream immediately, and I was in the slipstream all the way until the first corner, and I got much more speed than him. So that is the truth."

The following week McLaren was due to test at Pembrey, a little circuit near Llanelli in Wales. Pembrey was a very low speed circuit with the characteristics of the Monte Carlo circuit, the next race. It was chosen for privacy and it was here Dennis brought his drivers together and Senna duly apologised. Afterwards Ron Dennis simply said: "The problem is resolved." To make things quite clear, he added in a statement: "They had agreed [Senna and Prost] that whoever made the best start, would exit the first corner ahead. Alain made the better start but Ayrton took the corner., which was not consistent with the agreement they had made. A subsequent discussion between them at Pembrey resulted in an apology from Ayrton."

But the problem wasn't resolved, far from it. Senna later spoke to writer Gerald Donaldson off the record, in an interview not published until after his death. Senna told Donaldson that Prost's problems at Imola had not been caused by tyres – that had simply been an excuse from the team. He said: "His mistake was spinning off, with no car problems. Although it was stated that there was a tyre problem, there was no tyre problem. So putting everything together there was an unhappy situation for him, and he tried to blame it all on the start.

"At Pembrey I was quiet, I was doing my work. I kept everything to me, but I'm going to say exactly what happened. There was the threat of him stopping racing. As far as I was concerned I had nothing to do with it. I had something on my mind, and I did what I thought was correct in that situation."

In the few days between the race and the testing at Pembrey, Dennis spent hours on the phone to Senna urging him to apologise to Prost, who was apparently making dire threats to Dennis that he would either retire instantly or leave the team. With big sponsorships and commitments riding on the season, Prost had panicked Dennis and the team principal went into overdrive, pressuring Senna to apologise.

It was reminiscent of his rescue mission 12 years later when he had to prevent star car designer Adrian Newey from leaving for Jaguar. Senna confirmed this: "I had a lot of pressure from Ron in order to accommodate the situation, to give, let's say, some room for somebody to take the blame. And that's what I did. Yes, I apologised. I realised how bad he felt in his mind, at Pembrey. Personally, I felt bad, because I don't like to see anybody fucked in the head. And I realised he was completely fucked in the head. I was not responsible for it. I did not feel I was responsible in a bad way. But it happened to be that I was involved. At that time, we discussed about the thing itself. He had a view, and I had the view I told you. And Ron was trying to put things in a way in order to accommodate [Prost], because he was so fucked in the head, he was not in a position to accept anything. And if anybody had to do something, it was Ron, who tried very hard – and did a good job to convince me to change my mind. And I actually changed my mind.

"After a big discussion, I said, 'Okay, so I changed my mind, okay, I made a mistake.' But to accept that I made my mistake, I had to change completely my knowledge of how an overtaking manoeuvre is done. You know, my concept of an overtaking manoeuvre is when you start to come along, and then you finally overtake. And in my concept, I got to the overtaking manoeuvre before the braking point. And I had to change. So I accepted that I did the final overtaking under braking. But I changed my concept completely. I was moved by the bad feeling I had in my heart to see some-body fucked in the head like he was. And due to some pressure from Ron, [who was] trying to make me see the magnitude of the problem: maybe he would stop, and how bad this would be, not only for him but also for the team, and for the rest of the season."

Senna asked Donaldson to check his version of the facts with Ron Dennis. Before he could do that the situation got much, much worse. Prost revealed full details, seemingly on the record, of what had happened, which up to then had largely remained secret. The whole story soon appeared in French sports daily *L'Équipe*.

Senna then responded at length, on the record, to Prost's version of events. He told the press he had not apologised to Prost of his own volition. Ron Dennis was back to square one. But Prost's threat of retirement had gone, and he never mentioned it again.

But the revelations to *L'Équipe* marked the start of serious hostilities between the two drivers that would endure until May 1994. Before this spat the relationship had been relatively peaceful, and might have remained so had Senna not appeared to have broken the accord he himself had suggested. Senna made it worse by continually making it quite clear to anyone who listened that Ron Dennis had forced him to apologise.

Senna again stated: "It was stupid because it meant I had changed my opin-ion on the concept of our accord and I have never changed my opinion. I said sorry for the good of the team, to calm things down, because I was compelled to. I wiped away a tear because at that moment it was harming me."

Prost was incensed when he heard this. He fumed afterwards: "As far as Senna is concerned, I want nothing more to do with him. I have always tried to keep relationships good in the team, but I will no longer do that to Senna. What I appreciate more than anything is honesty. He has not been honest. Ron Dennis has put him under a lot of pressure to get him to tell the truth and Ayrton was very upset. He even cried. It was incredible."

On balance, Senna had broken his accord with Prost. It appeared much later that he had always expected to be ahead at the first corner and had therefore given it no thought. But Prost's superior race thinking ensured he made a better start. Senna genuinely believed he was in the right, though as he did with so many track clashes later in his career. He was never able to give the other side any benefit of any doubt. There is little doubt he did suffer from a problem some people have, in that they recall a different version of events after an incident and from then on believe their version to be 100 per cent true.

But Prost had also been wrong by speaking to the press about it.

The situation between the team-mates was irreparable.

At Monaco, Senna was totally dominant in qualifying. If anyone asked him about Prost, he said: "I don't want to hear any more talk about that guy." He also walked away with the race, winning by almost a minute from Prost to reverse the disappointment of 1988.

In Mexico, Prost attempted a reconciliation, but Senna blanked him completely and did his talking on the track, taking the 33rd pole position of his career. Prost lagged Senna's winning car by almost a minute, but on this occasion there were another three cars between them.

Observers believed Prost had cracked and five-time world champion Juan Manuel Fangio advised him to retire. The Argentine said: "I had 10 very good years. Jackie Stewart had 10 years and you will have had 10 years after this one. Now is the time for you to think about other things in life and in the future. There are lots of other things in life apart from motor racing." Prost did not agree.

For Senna, with two wins on the trot, the 1989 world championship seemed a foregone conclusion. But typically, Prost had scored points in all four rounds.

The United States Grand Prix was held in Phoenix, in early June, in 38°C of heat. It was a momentous occasion as Senna scored his 34th pole position, beating Jim Clark's record. Senna had never seen Clark race but was well aware of his reputation, as he said: "I feel rather light-headed." In the race Senna retired due to electrical problems while leading, and Prost scooped his first victory of the season.

Reinvigorated, Prost followed that up with pole again, upping his game in front of so many French-speaking Canadians that it felt like his home race. Senna was completely eclipsed by the Frenchman in qualifying, as he had been at Paul Ricard the year before. But in a wet race the following day he was completely back to form.

The Williams Renaults had a clear advantage over the McLarens in the wet and Prost was out of it anyway as he suffered a suspension failure on lap two. Senna battled bravely against superior opposition, pitting in and out for wet and dry tyres to find an advantage. He had it won with three laps to go when his engine expired and let the two Williams through for the team's first victory since 1987.

For the French Grand Prix at Paul Ricard, Alan Prost once again raised his game in front of his countrymen and got pole. Senna was to suffer his second mechanical retirement in a row and did not even complete one lap as the drivetrain failed on the restart. Prost won again.

But the main action for once was not on the track, as Prost announced at the race that he would be leaving McLaren at the end of the year, citing preferential treatment for Senna from McLaren and Honda. Prost did not say where he was going, but most seemed to think he would take Fangio's advice and retire.

That was not the end of it. In an astonishing mea culpa, Ron Dennis admitted that he believed Senna had been running with a superior engine since he joined the team. Dennis's explanation, however, was gobbledegook: "I have not said anything about this before, but I feel we should say that there have been results from the engines which have made us query their performances. Fuel consumption, for example, has been different from one engine to the other. We and Honda have worked very hard on these differences since they became apparent after the Brazilian Grand Prix. It is something which is very difficult to understand from the theoretical and mechanical point of view as the engines are exactly the same. It has been of great concern to us all. We, McLaren, the team and Honda are working to understand them. I can say that any differences such as these are not planned."

Prost's announcement focused all speculation on his future but did nothing to clear the air in the team. Dennis was anxious to retain his star driver line-up and hoped he could persuade Prost to stay.

Senna may have been getting Honda's development engines, but that was hardly surprising. Senna had a brilliant relationship with the Japanese whilst Prost did not have one at all. Senna's engines were not reliable, however, as Silverstone was to prove. He placed his car as usual on pole, but was out after a few laps as Prost cruised to victory.

But when the car held together and he had no problems, Senna would inevitably win. At Hockenheim however, during the German Grand Prix, there was bad news from Brazil: Senna's manager, Armando Botelho Texheriro, had passed away from cancer in São Paulo. Ron Dennis knew how much Botelho meant to Senna and didn't want him stressed on the eve of an important race. He gathered the Brazilian journalists and asked them to keep it secret until after the race. They agreed.

Senna won the race ahead of Prost. When the press conferences had been concluded, Dennis took Senna to one side and told him about the death of his manager. Dennis had been right. Senna's grief was palpable and it led to ludicrous rumours in the press room that he was planning to retire.

In Hungary, McLaren was beaten out of sight by Nigel Mansell's Ferrari. Senna finished second while Prost could only manage fourth.

At the Belgian Grand Prix a fortnight later it was back to normal as Senna won from Prost at a soaked Spa: Prost's championship lead had been whittled down to just 11 points. But the Spa event was more significant as Prost had intense secret negotiations with Ferrari about signing a three-year contact to drive for the team from 1990. When the Italian team agreed to pay him $12 million a year, he signed. That Ron Dennis could not persuade him to stay at McLaren Honda was no surprise, after all that had happened.

After the Belgian Grand Prix, in an interview with French magazine *Auto Hebdo*, Senna revealed how difficult the situation had become: "I speak to his mechanic and he speaks to mine but between us, it's finished. I adopted this attitude and I will maintain it. Because it's me who will not talk to him, not the other way round. I never wanted to betray our agreement at Imola and I never thought for a second it was dishonest. Prost undoubtedly interpreted the manoeuvre differently, that I will admit. What I found out of all proportion was his reaction after the race. He lost fair and square. Even if he had led at the first bend, I would have beaten him. I was faster that day, that's all. What was I supposed to do? Lift my foot off the accelerator on the straight because I was going faster than him? Are we racing or aren't we?"

On the eve of the Italian Grand Prix at Monza, Prost announced what everyone by then knew: he would drive for Ferrari for three years starting in 1990, alongside Nigel Mansell. At Monza, he thus immediately became the new hero of the tifosi. But he also let himself off his self-imposed leash, having developed a grudge against Ron Dennis as well as Senna. Prost felt Dennis had taken Senna's side and was favouring him.

He immediately began to heap criticism upon Dennis, whom he said had offered him money not to drive the following season. He told the French press: "Ron Dennis proves the regard he holds for me in doing everything to stop me driving against McLaren. It's flattering. In 1988, I had the chance to say no to Senna's arrival. But I thought the team would need a driver of his ability when I stopped. I was had. It's a lesson, that's all. There's no point in having thoughts like 'I would definitely have been world champion twice more'." Prost even suggested that Honda could be aiding Senna by deliberately slowing his engine via satellite from Japan.

In 1990 Senna refuted this version of events when his original biographer, Christopher Hilton, sent him a pre-publication manuscript and he scribbled in the margin: "One year earlier that McLaren having Honda, both Ron and Prost even went to Japan to convince Honda to come to McLaren and yet Honda came to Lotus. As for 1988 I initiated the work towards Honda and Prost would not have had Honda in 1988 if Senna was not part of the team. OK." It seemed more plausible than Prost's explanation, but maybe Prost was unaware how close Senna and Honda were.

Prost also attacked his own team at the track. Having given his opinion on Honda he stated the Senna's car preparation was favoured by the team itself. This was too much for Ron Dennis, who called one of his motorhome press conferences to state unequivocally that the team gave both drivers absolutely equal treatment, but, he admitted, he could not speak for Honda.

Senna duly took pole while Prost qualified only fourth, and led all the way until lap 44 when a blown Honda handed victory to Prost. It was yet another mechanical failure for Senna in a season full littered with them. The Italian fans went wild. On the podium, Dennis still disgusted by Prost's remarks threw the constructors winning trophy down at his feet. The crowd began to shout "cup, cup, cup." Prost inexplicably took it and lowered the trophy into the crowd, and someone ran away with it. Prost's contract stated that all winner's trophies belonged to the team – the originals are extremely valuable. But it was not the money that angered Dennis. He owned a complete set of trophies for every race McLaren had ever won, and they were proudly displayed at the Woking factory.

Italy 1989 remains to this day the only gap in the collection. Dennis is a very ordered man and Prost's act struck right at his heart. From that day the relationship was over. The win left Senna trailing by 20 points in the championship. Prost simply kept on berating McLaren and Dennis, seemingly without limit. Discipline had broken down between employer and employee. Dennis decided to strike back and threatened to suspend Prost from the team for breach of contract. When it became clear that he faced the sack from the team, Prost backed down. Even Ferrari's team manager Franco Lini was aghast at the situation. He said: "He should not say these things. He is a double world champion. He should be above it all. The Italians like to see a man proud and strong, not complaining and whining."

Lini saw a much-increased value from having the current world champion driving for the team the following year, and he had realised that Ron Dennis could simply resolve the championship in favour of Senna by sacking Prost. There was little doubt that Dennis could legitimately do this in the wake of Prost's attacks and the breach of contract by giving the trophy away.

FISA's French president Jean-Marie Balestre, however, sided with Prost, telling French radio: "The proof is that Senna was gaining more than a second each lap. I was furious. Until recent months, we have had a fantastic battle between Prost and Senna. It's clear that if Senna's car shows its superiority in the next four Grands Prix, considerable damage would be done to the value of the world championship."

By Portugal there had been a showdown between Dennis and Prost, and by all accounts the French driver had come close to being fired. He suddenly realised that he was in a dangerous position and reached a compromise with Dennis. McLaren issued a statement: "As a result of the consequences of the press statements at the Italian Grand Prix, Alain Prost, Honda and McLaren have had extensive discussions and wish to put on record their intentions of creating the best possible working environment for the driver and the team for the remainder of the season. Honda and McLaren have again reassured Alain, to his satisfaction, of their commitment to equality and will continue their policy regardless of Alain's move to another team for the 1990 season.

"Alain deeply regrets the adverse publicity and the resulting embarrassment that has been caused by his actions. Honda and McLaren have accepted that these resulted from Alain's perception of his treatment by the team and were not made with malicious intent. He has agreed that in future any doubts that he might have had about the parity of performance of his car will be discussed with the relevant engineers prior to comments being made to the press. The team also expresses its disdain and dissatisfaction over the inaccurate, unqualified and damaging statements made by third parties subsequent to Monza."

The statement marked the end of an extraordinary situation and it was a massive climbdown by Alain Prost, who had clearly had to make concessions simply to keep his drive for the remainder of the season.

Dennis breathed a sigh of relief at the Portuguese Grand Prix in Estoril, as the focus switched to a conflict between Senna and Ferrari's Nigel Mansell.

A collision with Mansell in rather unusual circumstances put Senna out of the race, handing victory to Gerhard Berger's Ferrari and second place to Prost, and putting the world championship almost beyond Senna's reach.

Mansell's Ferrari had been black-flagged for a pitlane infringement, but the Englishman stayed out on the track, later saying that he could not see the flags. Senna was closing on race leader Berger when Mansell flew past him into a corner. In response, to hold his position, Senna perhaps unwisely steered across the Ferrari: the pair collided and ended up in the gravel. Mansell was subsequently handed a $50,000 fine and a one-race ban.

Senna fumed: "Why did Nigel stay out after he was disqualified? Everyone could see from the television transmission what happened. I really don't want to comment. You can't get far like that, it's a kind of suicide. Mansell risked someone else's life. If there had been a barrier I could have ended up dead. That's why I say this is serious. Mansell's ban from one race, seen from this point of view, is very far from being the just punishment."

Mansell retorted: "Senna cut me. He saw perfectly well I was starting to overtake, he even turned his head slightly towards me." Mansell was furious and threatened to quit the sport if his punishment was not revoked. Suddenly the championship seemed over. The clash with Mansell meant that Senna needed at least two wins and a second place from the three remaining races to take the championship, but he had not given in: "I can still win the championship and I believe I still will." In Spain it looked as if he still might. He won the race while Prost finished third, but now needed to win both the remaining races to take the crown, a difficult but not impossible task.

With the championship as good as sewn up and the prospect of being sacked by McLaren having receded, Alain Prost returned to the attack and threw caution to the wind. Before the Japanese Grand Prix in Suzuka, Prost openly attacked Senna in the French press. "He's a man who just lives for and thinks about competition," he said. "He has abandoned everything else, every human relationship. He feels sustained by God and he is capable of taking every risk because he thinks he is immortal. In the Formula One world he lives completely apart, he is not at all appreciated, except by our team for the risks he takes. With his way of approaching competition, I don't think he can continue for a long time, which is a pity because he's an exceptional driver."

At Suzuka, Senna replied by blitzing Prost for pole by 1.730 seconds, over two seconds ahead of his next nearest rival Gerhard Berger. It was unheard of. But to Senna's fury he found that pole position would still not be moved away from the dirty side of the track. There was a huge row which concluded with the status quo, which was no good to Senna. He could not believe it and began to wonder why he had bothered to make such an effort. It was one of the tracks in the world where pole didn't mean pole. But he was still fired up for the race: "Tomorrow I will drive as fast as I can to win the race, whatever it takes. I have nothing to lose. Therefore I have to go for the maximum, I have to win. It's the best way, it's the way I like to race: I never liked to race for points, or having to sit there for second or third place, even if that was enough to win a championship. I always loved the challenge of having to win. Although the pressure is high and stressing, it's a kind of challenge that stimulates me and gives me something extra."

Consequently Prost got the jump at the start and, for most of the race, Senna could not catch him. But in the closing stages, desperate for victory, he began to close. On lap 46, he was close enough to have a go at the final chicane, but as he dived down the inside, Prost planted himself firmly on the line. The pair of McLarens sidled down the escape road locked together and came to a halt.

Prost got out immediately and began to survey the damage. But Senna was not finished yet and with a push from the marshals he managed to get the car going and steered it out of the escape road, minus a front wing. He came into the pits a lap later, passing Prost on foot, and regained the track behind the Benetton Ford of Alessandro Nannini, which had taken the lead since the collision. With just two laps to go, Senna repeated the move on Nannini that he had tried on Prost, only this time it was successful. Senna took the chequered flag, believing he had won the race.

Senna explained what had happened in some detail: "My car was damaged. When I saw the nose damaged, I thought it was finished. Like I said, I disconnected my radio, but we had to push the car out of the way. My car was in a dangerous place, and it is the duty of the driver to put the car in a safe place. That is one of the rules: you can have assistance from the marshals, under your direction, to move the car to a safe place. That is what I did. If in the process of doing that, according to the rules, if you are able to restart you are able to do so without any infringement of the rules.

"Then suddenly, when I was going down the escape road, I have enough momentum to try to restart. So I put the ignition on and I bump-start, and the engine restarted. So when the engine re-started I was already down the escape road. It was only after they pushed me a lot that I had that situation; I am almost between the tyres when the engine starts. So I go down the escape road and rejoin the circuit, after the gravel, because here it is all gravel or sand, and I cannot go here. So I have to just go around the sand and rejoin the circuit at the safest place.

· "I saw the wing under the car, and suddenly halfway round the lap the wing comes off. I am coming to the pits and I know that for sure my mechanics are waiting there to try to fix it, if they can. And they were able to fix it, so I was able to go back."

But the race win didn't stand. He was immediately disqualified and not allowed to go on the podium. Dangerous driving for cutting out the chicane was cited as the reason. The disqualification meant Prost was champion. Senna saw the hand of Jean-Marie Balestre behind the disqualification.

Senna was understandably livid and completely astonished at the turn of events that had handed Prost the title. The team declared it would immediately appeal. He said: "The results as they stand provisionally do not reflect the truth of the race in either the sporting sense or in the sense of the regulations. I see this result as temporary. It's a pity that we had to appeal in abnormal situations like this, it's absurd but it is the only way when we have a problem like this. We must fight with all our available resources. Now the matter is out of my hands. What I have done is done and is correct. From now this matter will be in the hands of lawyers, people who understand the theoretical side. But as for the practical side it was obvious that I won the race on the track. The taste of victory was taken away, I couldn't go onto the podium and celebrate with the crowd in the grandstands, probably my biggest fan club outside Brazil, and with my mechanics. I would say that it is a shame for the sport. As to our defence, I do not want to comment as it will be prepared very carefully on the basis of the regulations and on fact. I do not want to say any more on the matter. As to the incident, that was the only place where I could overtake, and somebody who should not have been there just closed the door and that was that."

McLaren Team Principal, Ron Dennis called a press conference and showed reruns of helicopter videos overhead which showed the opposite to what Balestre said he had seen. Because McLaren immediately filed its appeal, Prost's championship was not confirmed. The celebrating had to stop.

Prost had been celebrating in the McLaren pit garage when he heard that his championship had become provisional as the team had appealed against the result. He was cynical about it as he said: "You know Ayrton's problem?" he scoffed. "He can't accept not winning and because of that he can't accept someone resisting his overtaking manoeuvres. Too many times he tries to intimidate someone out of his way."

Ron Dennis left it to McLaren director Creighton Brown to comment: "It is our duty to try and win every race. Both drivers understand this, and understand why we are appealing. It is purely to do with the race result and has nothing to do with the world championship."

Prost sounded a little smug when he said: "It was my corner. I wanted to win the race and prove myself a winner and it is sad that I could not do that. I felt very comfortable in the race and I was in control. I was allowing him to close up on me when I wanted to, to further wear his tyres at the front. I said this morning that I would not open the door for him any more and he should accept that. He has no right to think he can pass me because he wanted to. I'm upset at winning after this sort of altercation again. He has had a lot of bad luck this year. But winning my third title is not going to change my life."

At the track on Sunday evening, Balestre told reporters he had seen a video of the accident and was convinced Senna was in the wrong.

Just over a week after the race, Prost was confirmed as world champion at a meeting of the world council in Paris. The disqualification would stand, and Senna was accused of endangering other drivers. He was fined $100,000 and given a six-month ban, suspended for six-months. Balestre complained: "You don't have the right when you are a great driver to have a stupid accident which destroys the sporting spectacle. It is very clear – and the film of the race proves it – that it was excessive speed which caused the accident. I do not accept drivers who try to win at any price. That's what I have against Senna. I feel responsible for the safety of the drivers – in a way, they are my children. We have made great strides in security standards in the last five years. The courses are much safer but the international federation does not want our improved image tarnished by inconsiderate or unsafe driving, even if I know there are many admirers of Senna and the acrobats, those tight-rope walkers of the track who are above the norm."

It was a cruel blow to Senna. He had gone to the meeting to explain why it had been necessary for him to cut the chicane and had been punished for another matter entirely. When Ron Dennis objected to Senna's treatment and hinted at further procedures to upturn the appeal decision, Balestre threatened to exclude him from the following year's championship if there was any hint of legal action from the team. Prost said: "This title has been the most difficult to win psychologically, since I was in a position of inferiority at McLaren. It is a personal victory but it is also a victory over my team." The Brazilian public was furious. Senna sensed a conspiracy and said later: "They wanted to disqualify me for whatever reason they could, for whatever argument they could say." He had a point.

After all the drama, the final race at Adelaide was inevitably a letdown. In a rain-affected race, Senna tangled with Brundle and appeared to drive straight into the back of his car while he was lapping him, putting himself out of the race and ending an explosive year.

Before the race, Senna gave a long, often rambling and emotional press conference He said: "I have had difficult times the last few days but I believe through hard times a person's real personality comes out and your strengths become stronger than ever. I thought about stopping, going home and not coming to Australia. What happened in Suzuka was unfair, unrealistic and took place because the people who had the power decided to do so.

"Afterwards you wonder why you should do this on and on when you're not being fairly treated. But racing is in my blood and I know that the situation we face only motivates me deep inside to fight against it and to prove what I'm doing has values. I'll do here exactly the same I've done all my life and drive the way I feel is right. If I have my licence taken away then probably the values that keep me going in Formula One will go with it, and I will not be in Formula One any more.

"But I refuse to walk away from a fight. That is my nature. I will fight to the end whatever happens, whatever the cost so that for once we can bring justice to our sport." He added for good measure: "I am a professional, but I am also a human being, and the values I have in my life are stronger than many other peoples desires to influence, or destroy those values."

His year also ended dramatically, emotionally. After almost a year together, he and Xuxa realised their lives made a relationship impossible. There was just one problem: both were deeply in love. Senna's family also loved Xuxa and urged him to marry her. There were rumours that he did propose. But Xuxa was not sure that Senna was being faithful to her.

Tensions reached a height over New Year and, deciding she wanted to be alone, she fled to New York. Senna tried to convince her to stay in São Paulo with him for the holidays. She was unmoved, but when she arrived in New York, and opened her bags, her apartment was full of little notes from him. She later recalled it was 'very beautiful'. When she arrived at the place she was going to stay, there nothing there and it was practically unfurnished. There was no television, no sofa, nothing in the kitchen.

Someone went to buy her the basics, including a TV. Well after his death, Xuxa recalled that she expected them to be delivered three hours later. But one hours 40 minutes later she heard a knock on the door, and thought something was wrong. "When I opened the door, I found it was Ayrton and had a large TV with him and a message in his hand. It read: 'I'm in New York, because there is someone who I love there, and who loves me.'

It was a great start to their 1990, but it was not destined to endure.

CHAPTER 15

1990: Senna vs Prost

The Confrontation Year

yrton Senna's dreamy start of the year with Xuxa Meneghel in New York was not a reflection of the turmoil in the rest of his life. When he returned to São Paulo from New York a serious row was brewing in Europe, which would put his career in jeopardy.

It all stemmed from the events at the Japanese Grand Prix in 1989, though trivial in themselves, and centred around how he had rejoined the race after colliding with Prost. Senna felt strongly that FISA president Jean-Marie Balestre had disqualified him from the race unjustly, finagling the situation to give Prost the championship.

As if the disqualification and lost championship were not enough punishment, at the appeal in Paris Balestre had also fined Senna an additional $100,000 and handed him a six-month suspended ban.

In those days the governing body had the right, if an appeal was made against a stewards' decision, to impose further penalties. It was legally barmy of course, but the FISA under Balestre's leadership was run under wild west rules. That he was partisan to Prost, a Frenchman, seemed obvious to Senna.

At the beginning of 1990, then, it looked uncertain that Senna would be racing at all in 1990. It was a game of brinkmanship between him and Balestre, which neither side could be certain of winning. It was all about who needed who the most.

For his part, Senna was determined to face off Balestre and not pay the fine. Balestre stated firmly that if it was not paid Senna would not be issued with a FISA superlicence to compete. Neither side looked like giving way.

On 10th January, with Senna away from Europe in São Paulo, Balestre upped the stakes at a news conference in Paris and dropped a bombshell. On top of the six-month suspended ban and the fine he had already received, Balestre declared that if Senna did not publicly apologise for suggesting FISA had favoured Prost to win the title, he would be refused a superlicence. Balestre said that, at a FISA meeting in December, it had been proved beyond doubt to Senna and his lawyer that he had not intervened. For Senna, already hit with a disqualification, a suspended ban, a fine and a lost world championship – as a result of a small collision that had turned out nicely for Prost – it was another bitter pill to swallow and only went to confirm his fears of a French conspiracy. Balestre accused Senna of arrogance and pointed out that he had yet to pay the $100,000 fine. Senna believed that Balestre was totally in Prost's pocket and that the governing body had been morally corrupted. Both men were resolute and would not be moved.

But caught in the middle were the McLaren team and Honda, who had a heavy investment riding on Senna appearing in 1990. The simple answer for them was to pay the fine and accept the punishment and go racing. The apology, however, threw that plan into disarray. Ron Dennis was sure he could simply pay the fine and the problem would go away.

Balestre gave Senna a deadline of 15th February – when the final entry list was drawn up – to apologise and pay the fine. Over the following month debate raged on in newspapers around the world. When Balestre appeared at the Monte Carlo Rally in January, he expressed his view that he now suspected a conspiracy against him. In reality Balestre held all the cards. But just as in the FISA/FOCA battle of 1980, he miscalculated his own position and believed his hand was weak. He appeared to believe that certain elements within Formula One were out to get him and that Senna was merely the instrument. As a defence, he extended the hand of contrition towards Senna. He said: "Senna has been used as an instrument. He has been sent into the front line by others. I appreciate Senna's present attitude. Discretion is more effective than explosion. I think several of you had no mercy for a Formula One driver in snatching statements from him which do not always reflect his deeper thoughts."

Balestre started a process of back-tracking, believing his own personal position at FISA was under threat. He claimed that FISA had been misinterpreted by the press and that there had been no demand for an apology. Balestre's exact words had been: "The World Council will not give a superlicence to Ayrton

Senna in 1990 until he makes a public statement taking back statements which are both false and detrimental to FISA." Technically it wasn't a demand for an apology, rather for a retraction of Senna's earlier remarks, but no one who had heard Balestre was in any doubt as to the words' meaning.

Few shared Balestre's views and believed the battle to be Senna against Prost again, but this time with the Frenchman hiding behind Balestre, who was fighting the battle for him.

It didn't look as if Senna would to give in, so at the end of January Balestre turned up the heat and rejected the McLaren's team application to enter the 1990 world championship 'until a solution has been found to the Senna case.' Balestre explained: "He has been sanctioned by race commissioners, then he has accused and insulted sports authorities, saying the world championship had been manipulated, that Alain Prost was a false world champion. Senna is not alone. He has a team manager, Ron Dennis. And we think he is under the bad influence of McLaren's team manager."

Dennis was furious and aghast that he could be considered Senna's puppet. But Dennis had bigger responsibilities: he relented and paid the Brazilian's fine. McLaren Honda would be in the championship in 1990, but with only two weeks to go until the deadline, the outcome was still in doubt. Rumours spread. People were saying that Senna had not even bothered to apply for a licence. Others were saying that McLaren planned to announce another driver in his place, then withdraw him at the beginning of the season to let Senna take his place as the replacement driver. The Brazilian president's 13-year-old son even asked the French prime minister to intercede.

When the 15th February deadline came, Ron Dennis announced Gerhard Berger and Jonathan Palmer would be the team's provisional drivers. A FISA statement read: "Ayrton Senna had until 15th February at midnight to put himself right with FISA, in order for FISA to accept his application for a superlicence. After long talks with Senna and Ron Dennis these last days and hours, FISA, despite its patience and understanding, regrets to conclude that Ayrton Senna is in an irregular situation. FISA is obliged to refuse his application for a superlicence."

Ten minutes later Balestre received a phone call from Dennis and within hours a new statement was issued, granting Senna entry and attaching a statement from Senna: "During the meeting of the FISA world council which took place on 7th December 1989, I listened to statements and testimonies from various people, and from these statements one must conclude that they provide proof that no pressure group or the president of the FISA influenced the decisions regarding the results of the 1989 Formula One world championship." It was a bland statement without an apology, but it proved enough for Balestre.

On paper Balestre had won the stand-off, but it was a hollow victory tinged with bitterness that had damaged both sides, particularly Senna. The whole saga had left him thoroughly depressed, and his motivation sapped. He felt his status within Formula One had been damaged, and for the first time in his life he was not looking forward to the start of a season. He thought the process would affect his driving, and revealed that he left the final decision of what to do to the team. As he explained at the time: "I asked myself about continuing to race. I was perfectly calm and I discussed the matter with Honda and McLaren. I said to them that I was only a driver and that McLaren and Honda would continue after me. I said I did not want to compromise their efforts and those of the people who work to run the cars. I asked Nobuhiko Kawamoto and Ron Dennis to decide in my place. I said I would completely respect their wishes, that I was ready to retire or fight on as they thought fit."

It was not over. Balestre held a press conference to put his side of the settlement. He almost suggested that the dispute was really a war between Brazil and France, in which peace had not totally broken out. He said: "There is no turning back on FISA's decision to grant Senna a superlicence. As with all other drivers on the start list, he is sure to start, in principle. But there is a legal safety device in case a driver is tempted to breach the FISA rules in the meantime." That confirmed Senna's entry, but then he went on to warn the team that it would be given no leeway during the season: "I have no trust left in my counterparts after realising they were not keeping their promises. If there is the slightest problem, it won't be approved. I don't mind if it causes a revolution in Brazil. In every conflict we have been through, my only desire has been for rules to be respected. People like Ron Dennis have been misled in thinking that FISA would back down because we needed them. If people in São Paulo think that the Senna controversy will make FISA more lenient about their circuit's inclusion, they're wrong."

Balestre actually held back Senna's superlicence until the eve of the year's first race, scheduled to be the United States Grand Prix in Phoenix, Arizona. McLaren was so concerned about the situation that it cancelled the public launch of the MP4/5B and held a sponsors-only event.

Finally, as the teams reached Phoenix, the politics were forgotten and people started thinking about the racing again. The 1990 season was set to be

even harder than 1989 for Senna. He faced a stronger Williams Renault team
and a very strong Ferrari team, with Nigel Mansell and Alain Prost in tandem.

Sensing that 1990 would be his toughest challenge yet, Senna had embarked
on a physical fitness regime in Angra over the winter. His personal trainer
Nuno Cobra, who had helped ever since he entered Formula One in 1984,
was engaged full time. Together they significantly upped his capacity for
the start of 1990, as Cobra remembers: "In 1984, we had a skinny, highly
motivated young guy, and it was right here that everything began. At first he
had a tough time doing 10 laps, but he gradually became an athletic
performer who could run 40 or 50 laps with incredible endurance, but he was
not an athlete. He transformed himself drastically."

By the time the season started, Senna could easily manage 50 laps of a
400-metre track. Senna was in no doubt that his vastly improved fitness
levels would help him: "It is not simply stronger muscles but it is really the
power and strength you get physically and mentally. I have tried to learn
about myself, learning how to get better overall."

Cobra recalls with amazement how he could 30 or 40 laps and each would
be within a second or two of the others. He said: "I witnessed all that and I
couldn't believe my eyes, because his rhythm was fabulous. Every single day
he had to win in one way or another. Life was throbbing within him and
either he bettered his record by one-10th of a second, or his heart rate
dropped or, again, he improved his post-effort recovery time. Never once did
he exceed his limit, although he did constantly push them back in this solitary exercising along this track, on which, he told me, he had worn out the
soles of dozens of tennis shoes." Senna confirmed he had been running up
to 20 kilometres a day during the winter.

The fitness programme was all part of Senna's seemingly maniacal bid to
find his own limits. He knew that even at 30 he had not peaked physically
or in the car, as he said at the start of the season: "On a given day with a given
circumstance you think you have a limit and you then go for this and then
you touch this limit. As soon as you touch this limit something happens
and you suddenly can go a little bit further. With your mind power,
determination, instincts and experience you can fly very high."

To reinforce his fitness regime Senna also acquired a proper home in
Europe, on the Algarve in Portugal, close to Faro airport. It was impossible
to train properly on the streets of Monaco, and Portugal, with its temperate
climate, was perfect. He sold his lavish apartment in the Houston block in
Monte Carlo, buying a smaller one there for tax reasons to maintain a

residence and for the Monaco race.

But on arriving in America from São Paulo, it was a subdued 30-year-old Ayrton Senna who turned up in the pitlane ready to practise. He told journalists close to him that his motivation had gone and that he was thoroughly disillusioned with Prost, Balestre and FISA.

Alain Prost, feeling that he had won the war and humbled Senna, offered to shake hands, but Senna refused, saying that he didn't believe the Frenchman was sincere. He told people 1989 had been a nightmare, the worst year of his life. And he didn't consider it past either. There were still scores to settle and issues unresolved. Ron Dennis did not share Senna's opinion and was surprisingly sanguine about the end of the Prost era in his team, which had lasted six years. He told journalists: "The period in which Ayrton and Alain drove together was a challenge that I gladly accepted because the benefits of having them both together in the same team vastly outweighed the disadvantages."

One issue that had been resolved was team-mates. No longer was Prost in the same garage or the same motorhome. His new team-mate was Gerhard Berger, who had become free when Prost signed for Ferrari and was snapped up by Ron Dennis. Berger was the same age as Senna and they were alike in their outlook on life. Although they were always regarded as firm friends, their competitive drivers' nature kept them from being really close. But it was the start of a period that became known as the 'James Bond years', as Senna and Berger bonded.

Berger joined McLaren and went into 1990 believing he could match Senna on the track. But he was soon disabused of that notion. In qualifying Berger would be much closer to Senna than Prost had been, but he soon recognised that the man deserved his reputation. Berger found Senna brought a level of focus to the job he had never experienced with other team-mates. In fact Berger was stunned by his commitment. Berger said: "A lot of the drivers don't know how hard he works." Ron Dennis confirmed it: "Because he is hard on himself it's easy to accept that he is hard on the team, but we are not there to have fun, this is a very difficult and demanding occupation."

Berger also had his own problems to overcome. He was the tallest driver on the grid and the McLaren monocoque was built around Senna's smaller frame. For 1990, Berger was continually struggling with a cockpit that was too small despite the efforts of BBC commentator James Hunt, the retired world champion, to bring the problem to Ron Dennis's attention. During

1990 Hunt watched Berger struggle, knowing what it meant from his own experience with McLaren in the mid-1970s. Hunt was also lanky and he had inherited a McLaren car built around the considerably smaller Emerson Fittipaldi in 1976.

Ron Dennis seemed unconcerned, and in the confines of a modern carbon-fibre monocoque there was little he could do about it until the following season.

The opening race of the season, the USA Grand Prix in Phoenix, would not pass without drama. It started with a strange qualifying session which saw Gerhard Berger get pole and Senna a lowly fifth. It was a wake-up call for Senna that his team-mate was fast and that Ferrari had got its semi-automatic transmission sorted. The Williams Renault was also very close and bristling with innovative electronics his McLaren Honda didn't have.

McLaren was working on its own versions of these innovations, but they were still two years away from being introduced. With the success of the Honda car, McLaren had missed a trick technologically. Luckily, in 1990 it didn't matter – even to the extent that Neil Oatley, the McLaren designer, saw no reason to pen a brand new car and simply modified the previous year's chassis, which became the MP4/5B.

The first Grand Prix of the year turned into a surprising qualifying session, as a number of factors intervened. A rain storm had put paid to most of Saturday's qualifying session, so it was Friday's times that counted. And as Friday had been the first day of the new season, it was a mixed result. The Tyrrell team was enjoying a renaissance with new French star Alesi in the driving seat. Tyrrell had an unexpected advantage of Pirelli tyres, which were working well on the rough street circuit. Pirelli was also a major factor as the Minardi and Dallara teams did well.

As a result, Senna was also outqualified by Pierluigi Martini's Minardi and Andrea de Cesaris's Dallara, as well as pole-sitter Berger and Alesi's Tyrrell. Alesi swept into the lead at the start and it took 35 laps for Senna to get past. But the 25-year-old French-Sicilian retook the lead at the very next corner. Senna overtook Alesi a lap later, but it had been a spectacular battle. Alesi said: "For me it was a dream come true to race with Ayrton. Two years ago he was my hero when I was in Formula Three, so for me it was incredible to fight with him." Alesi's comments were a clear sign that Senna had completed the transition from next big thing to established star.

The Ferrari challenge stuttered to a halt: Prost had suffered an oil leak on lap 21 and Mansell's engine blew up on lap 49. The Ferraris had been well off the pace and people were beginning to say that the biggest challenge to Senna's title hopes was Berger, or even Balestre.

The FISA president had not gone quietly away. Before the next race in Brazil, FISA held a summit meeting to discuss Balestre's arguments with Senna and with the organisers of the Le Mans 24 Hours, which had seen the famous race temporarily struck off the international calendar. The outcome was a whitewash and a FISA statement declared 'total confidence' in its president. This did nothing for his image in Brazil, however, and when the feisty Balestre, perhaps unwisely, turned up unexpectedly at the race he was surrounded by bodyguards following death threats. Spectators at the Interlagos track, which he had threatened to remove from the calendar due to 'sub-standard' facilities, shouted abuse, threw coins at him and made a variety of interesting uncomplimentary hand signals.

Once again victory on home ground eluded Senna. He took pole and led for over half the race but a collision with Satoru Nakajima's Tyrrell, as he was lapping the Japanese driver, sent him in for a new nosecone. Prost was handed his 40th career victory and first win for Ferrari in only his second outing with the Prancing Horse. The writing was already on the wall.

Prost was so overcome with emotion at winning his first race for Ferrari that he cried openly on the podium. Before the next race at Imola, rumours spread that Senna had signed for Ferrari for the following year. Both Senna and Ferrari team manager Cesare Fiorio denied that there had been any contact, but there were suggestions it was Fiorio who had approached the Brazilian. Whatever, it certainly would have done no harm in Senna's ongoing negotiations with McLaren – his three-year contract came to an end at the close of that season – and in the Machiavellian boiling pot at Maranello it probably scared Prost and Mansell, who were fighting desperately with each other for supremacy in the team. Senna felt sorry for Mansell.

Senna was forced to spend quite some time denying the Ferrari rumours, but not his eventual desire to drive for the Italian team: "Any driver who has been in F1 for some time has always a dream to drive for Ferrari, because it is the team with the greatest prestige in F1. I could have moved to Ferrari now, or two years ago. For sure it's going to happen in the future. When? That's only a question of time."

At a press conference he was challenged on his denials, but he was adamant he had never said the words the journalists were quoting back to him: "At no moment did I ever say I would 'love to drive for Ferrari next year'. Then I saw things written in the press that I was trying to open a door in Ferrari and so on. I can categorically say that I have not done that and I am not doing it. And if I was to do that, I would not do it in public. I was close to doing a deal with them many years ago but a deal never came together."

The categorical denials ended the rumours.

Senna was also upset about other things. As he prepared to leave São Paulo for the beginning of the European season, he and Xuxa Meneghel had virtually agreed to go their separate ways. He wanted someone to join him at the track, and she wanted someone to fit around her schedule.

In the 18 months they had been together, Xuxa had dominated his thoughts. He was in love with her, no doubt, as she was with him, but the logistics made them call it a day, leaving them free to pursue other relationships. They agreed it was an impossible relationship. But she would remain his official girlfriend until late 1992. She said: "We were pretty much the same. But I knew that the logistics of one career centred in Brazil and one in Europe made life impossible. I wanted a person like him, and I thought everything he did was a lot, but he was choking me. He gave me so much more then I ever expected, but I needed time. I thought we would meet later. I tried to talk to him at various times, but didn't. It was meant to be for another life." Senna said: "Only one time in my life, I thought about having a family, with children and it was with her, with Xuxa."

Certainly the Senna family believed she was the one for him. They had adopted her a surrogate daughter-in-law and that relationship was maintained. She had made a deep impression on them and they were rooting for her. They accepted their son's assurances that it would have to wait until after retirement. His sister Viviane said: "I'm sure that if Ayrton ended his career he would go back to Xuxa."

That may have been true, but it was back to the drawing board, as he said about his continuing quest for the perfect woman to marry: "She has to be very, very understanding as I'm not an easy person to live with. I'm not easy on myself and I don't like people who are not demanding of themselves. She also has to be extremely intelligent. It is no good having a 'yes' woman with no intelligence with which to command respect. I'm very romantic and I think real success in life is building up a two-way relationship with another person. Real love, true love, is being at peace with your partner and feeling easy with her. Attraction based on physical beauty only last a few hours a day."

Back in Europe to continue the season, Senna took pole at the San Marino Grand Prix at Imola and led, but a puncture after just four laps scuppered his chances. Prost finished fourth. At Monte Carlo, despite a loss of power in the closing laps, Senna took pole and victory – by just a second from Alesi, while Prost's gearbox failed when he was running second. Senna led every lap.

It was pole and victory in Montreal, and Prost finished fifth. Senna, his depressions fully shaken off, said: "Having won three races out of five, having led five races out of five is something that shows you've got potential." Early-season predictions were being borne out and Berger was proving his closest rival: Senna had 31 points to Prost's 14, but Berger was on his tail with 23. It was a flash in the pan, though, as Berger would never come closer.

Mexico City looked as if it would be more of the same. Prost qualified 13th and was 15th at the first corner as Senna charged into the lead from third on the grid. Senna led the first 61 of the 69 laps until a dramatic puncture put him out of the race. As a result, Prost led home Mansell to a Ferrari one-two. Senna's championship lead over Prost was cut from 17 to eight points. The real challenger had put his marker down.

As Senna established his supremacy over new team-mate Berger, they found they got along like a house on fire. It was a first for Senna to have a genuine relationship with a team-mate. In fact Senna found Berger a breath of fresh air after his tribulations with Prost. He said: "We work together. Together, we do a similar job. We have similar feelings, common feelings, similar points of view about different things."

But he criticised Berger's initial approach: "When he started, he was not used to working that hard. He was a spoiled driver coming from Ferrari at that time, and then he found the McLaren environment a completely different one. He soon realised that if he wanted to compete and improve himself he had to work hard with engineers and the personnel. I think he had a very open mind, then, to look around how the engineers worked, how the team and mechanics and everyone. He changed a lot, I think, and he has improved a lot. You can see the results, you can see the performance. He has definitely improved a lot, he is really competitive."

At Paul Ricard, Prost had the honour of taking Ferrari's 100th Formula One victory while a slow tyre change left Senna in third. The championship gap was cut to three points. Prost won at Silverstone, with Senna in third, but the race was overshadowed by Mansell's shock decision to retire at the end of the season after months of trouble at Ferrari. Almost unnoticed, Prost took the championship lead by two points.

Senna was not surprised about Mansell's troubles with Prost, and even less surprised when Mansell's retirement plans proved short-lived.

Senna fought back at Hockenheim, taking pole and victory as Prost finished only fourth, regaining the championship lead by four points. At the Hungaroring, Thierry Boutsen, amid rumours that he would be out of a Williams drive in favour of Senna for 1991, took pole and led every single lap – try as he might, Senna could not find a way past. He finished second and Prost retired with gearbox failure. Senna went 10 points in front and grinned: "I never remember in the past two years being 10 points ahead in the championship at this stage of the season, after the Hungarian Grand Prix. It is a totally different kind of championship this year and we are driving different cars. I thought Ferrari would be very strong here, but this is a beautiful result for me to be second and take six points."

The rumour mill ground to a halt in the week preceding the Belgian Grand Prix, when Prost first announced that he would be exercising his option to stay with Ferrari for 1991 and Senna then revealed he had signed a new McLaren contract for 1991, worth just under $16 million, with an optional second year. Ron Dennis admitted the negotiations had been bruising: "He is a hard and totally inflexible negotiator who will use all the methods at his disposal to maximise his position."

Frank Williams told the press that talks between him and Senna had been 'just about planes'. Williams was not yet in the $16 million-a-year class. But it appeared Senna had opted consciously to stay at McLaren, feeling the McLaren-Honda combination gave him the best chance of a championship in 1991. He was right about that, but it proved a terrible mistake in the long term as he lost his chance of joining Williams Renault, which would prove to have the fastest car for the next seven years. It almost certainly cost him two world championships. Within two years he would also be begging Williams to give him a drive. Senna's decision left the way open for Frank Williams to persuade Nigel Mansell out of retirement on a two-year contract worth $12 million a year.

Senna took pole and victory again at Spa, ahead of Prost, and they finished in the same order at Monza, for Senna to pull out a lead of 16 points, with four races remaining.

Up to then it had been a quiet, incident-free year between Prost and Senna, and believing he had the upper hand, Senna felt magnanimous. In fact Senna believed he was in the best car and the championship was in the bag. With that in mind he began to show Prost a conciliatory hand. Remarkably, the pair shook hands and declared their feud over. Prost generously said: "I will enjoy our fight for the title, whoever wins it, much more if we can understand each other. We are both professionals and what happened last year really doesn't matter any more. If we both accept it that way, it will be much better." Senna continued in the same vein: "We are true professionals. What matters now is this year. I don't want to think about what happened last year any more. Not that it was not important then, but now we are here. If he is ready in his heart to prepare to accept this fact I'll accept to shake his hand. We have to race this championship. It will be a tough battle and I hope we can do it better if we are on better terms." It was a total about face with the old rivalries and tensions forgotten. But the shallowness of the public statements would be shown by the shortness of the calm.

Senna admitted to journalists that he had not forgotten, and had not forgiven either. The truce would last precisely until the next incident, which wasn't long coming.

In Estoril, Mansell won ahead of Senna, then Prost, allowing the Brazilian to increase his title lead to 18 points. Under the best-of-11 scoring system, to win the title Prost would have to win all three of the remaining races and hope that Senna could not score more than a few points. It seemed impossible, but Senna was cautious. "As far as the championship is concerned I will wait until it is mathematically beyond doubt before thinking seriously about it," he said.

Friday's qualifying session for the Spanish Grand Prix at Jerez was marred by a horrifying accident that befell Martin Donnelly. The Irishman's Lotus was torn apart after hitting a barrier at high speed. It was the latest in a spate of injuries in the 1990 season and Senna was deeply affected by it. It was his first serious brush with tragedy in Formula One. He and Pierluigi Martini were the only drivers to stop at the scene, where Donnelly's horribly twisted body lay in the middle of the Jerez track. Most people were sure the Lotus driver, whose car was demolished, could not have survived; yet Senna felt compelled to stand there, watching rescue crews work over Donnelly. He said: "I went to the place where he was lying on the track. When I saw the immediate consequences of the accident it was very difficult to cope and maintain my mental balance. I thought about not running anymore in qualifying. I had some minutes on my own in the motorhome. They were special moments which helped me gather myself. But afterwards I didn't know how fast I could go. Or how slow."

Of course he went faster than ever, and won yet another pole position, but he found such bravery came at an emotional price. "As a racing driver there are some things you have to go through, to cope with. Sometimes they are not human, yet you go through it and do them just because of the feelings that you get by driving, that you don't get in another profession. Some of the things are not pleasant, but in order to have some of the nice things you have to face them. You leave a lot of things behind when you follow a passion."

One thing Senna never left behind was his essential humanity and his natural concern for his fellow man. His compassion extended to other drivers who suffered, and he was notably sensitive to the plight of peers who might be in trouble. He was one of the few drivers to visit Martin Donnelly (who eventually recovered, though he never raced again) in hospital. The pole position was the 50th of his career. But on Sunday Prost won, while Senna retired with a holed radiator. Senna now had 78 points to Prost's 69, and from the next race they would both have to drop scores. Senna stood to lose four points once scores were dropped, while Prost's lowest score was just two. When it all panned out, all Senna had to do to win the title in the next race was to finish ahead of Prost, whereas all Prost had to do to keep his championship alive was to win. But the next race was at Suzuka, theatre of previous showdowns.

Senna travelled to Japan with Mauricio Gugelmin and Gerhard Berger. Gugelmin was there to see his friend win the world championship for the second time. During a trip on the famous Japanese 'bullet train', there were plenty of high jinks. Senna decided to gain revenge for previous practical jokes at his expense, and put up Gugelmin to fill Berger's shoes with shaving foam.

Berger would later attempt to take his revenge. An hour before the race started, he asked Josef Leberer to prepare a glass of freshly squeezed orange juice and offer it to Gugelmin before the race. Berger crushed four sleeping pills and mixed them into the orange, the idea being to knock out Gugelmin so he would miss the race. A suspicious Gugelmin didn't drink it. He said: "Can you imagine it? The cars roaring by at the track and I snoring in the cabin."

It provided some light relief. As soon as they arrived at the track, Senna was thrust into a series of press conference and media interviews. Senna denied that he was affected by arriving at the scene of his 1989 championship-deciding collision with Prost a year earlier. They were, after all, friends now – they had shaken hands to prove it – and there had since been no more trouble between them. "I have not thought about last year or the collision," Senna said. "It is in the past. I thought I was the winner but it is gone and it is just an experience now." Forty-eight hours later, he had an entirely different opinion.

His first task was to establish which side of the track would be pole. The pole-position saga was into its third year. Senna said on the eve of the race: "Myself and Gerhard went to officials to change pole position place because at the wrong place, it was in the wrong place there. And the officials said 'Yes, that's no problem, we will put pole position on the outside.'"

Reassured, he went out to get pole. Despite losing half an hour of qualifying time on Friday after he spun out on the circuit, he managed to take it by just 0.232 seconds from Prost.

He believed that it had been agreed that pole position would this year be moved to the more favourable side of the track, as he had wanted in 1989; but once he had secured the top spot, officials gave him the bad news. He was incensed and even Prost thought the decision was wrong. Inevitably Balestre got the blame. He said: "I did the fantastic job to be on pole. It was important to be on pole for the race. Then what happened? Balestre gave an order. We told them 'we agreed before the race meeting, and you know that the pole position should be on the left side.' It was an order from Balestre, because I know from inside. And this is really shit, you know. And I tell myself 'OK, you try to work clean, you try to do your job properly; and you get fucked all the time by stupid people. If on Sunday, at the start, because I'm in the wrong place, Prost jumps the start and beats me off the line, at the first corner I'm going for it. And he had better not turn in ahead of me, because he is not going to make it."

And that is exactly how it happened.

As the lights went out Prost, starting from the cleaner side of the track, got the jump on Senna on pole. As the field rushed down to the sweeping 150mph first corner, Prost moved onto the racing line in front of Senna. Senna did not yield and went for the inside line. Prost naturally shut the door, but Senna kept coming. The pair touched at speed and spun wildly into the gravel trap where their cars were beached in a cloud of dust. Both drivers were out of the race on the spot. Senna was world champion.

To most observers it looked deliberate, an act of blatant revenge by Senna for the injustice he felt he had been done at Suzuka a year earlier. But he denied it – he even blamed Prost – although a year later he would have some very different views on the incident.

Prost was immediately on the attack: "He did it on purpose because he saw that if I made a good start, that my car was better, so he had no chance to win the race. So he pushed me out. This makes him champion. That is very good for him, but it is more than unsporting. It is disgusting. I have no problems with losing the championship. I have lost many. But not this way. It is so bad from the sporting point of view. I hate it and I hate this kind of situation. He has completely destroyed everything again. I hope that every-one can see he has not been honest. I never expected what he did – I thought he was one of the human race and fair on the track. But he was not.

He just did not brake and he did it on purpose. I am not prepared to fight against irresponsible people who are not afraid to die."

Senna was immediately on the defensive: "The first corner was always going to be critical, especially after the officials decided the pole could not be moved to the outside as I wanted. We had officially requested it on Wednesday as we had earlier in the year in Mexico, Germany and Portugal. But the offer was refused. If pole had been on the outside I am sure there would not have been the accident. I went for the inside and he did not open the door and I could not avoid making touch and we both went off. He knows I always go for a gap. I cannot be responsible for his actions. He closed the door, not me. As usual, he has his points of view. But he has tried to destroy me and he will not. I know what I can do and I don't give a damn what he [Prost] says."

The drivers' respective team bosses were inevitably unanimous in their support of their own drivers. Ferrari team manager Cesare Fiorio said: "It is a scandal they didn't stop the race. It should never have been allowed to go on. Prost was in front and had the right to turn in. I am very surprised the world champion did something like that." Ron Dennis, meanwhile, shrugged and smiled and said: "It is rough justice, but the accident would never have happened if the officials had moved the pole over to the other side of the track."

Later in the evening, Senna was more introspective and appeared to genuinely regret what had happened: "I really wished it didn't happen but it's just that it happened exactly as it had to happen. He took the start; he went on the jump on me, and I went for the first corner. He turned in and I hit him. And we were both off, and it was a shit end to the championship. It was not good for me, it was not good for Formula One. It was the result of the wrong decisions, and partiality from the people that were inside then, making some decisions. I won the championship, and so what? It was really a bad example for everyone: This was the most exciting championship as far as I am concerned, because it's not only one team dominating. It was really a hell of a championship."

Prost got hold of the helicopter video coverage that he said proved he had acted correctly.

At the press conference after the championship was won, Senna found that journalists that covered Formula One were again hostile to him and the majority would have much preferred to see Prost triumph.

One asked him why he was always such a miserable SOB. He replied: "I never smile much, because that's my way to be. But I am very happy inside. You people don't know me at all. And not knowing me, you cannot have the right feelings for it. I think I give a lot of my dedication to my profession. I work very hard, with the technicians. And we all won this championship together, step by step, race after race. And not in one race. We didn't win the championship here, we won the championship throughout the season, making the right decisions and the right choices at critical moments. That's why you win a championship. And not like last year."

The reaction in France and Italy was explosive. Balestre, who had watched the race on television in Paris, complained: "It is a scandal that a world championship should be decided on such a collision and I leave everyone to be their own judge of who is to blame. I am sure all motor racing fans throughout the world will feel as frustrated as I do after such an appalling end to the world championship. I am the FISA president, not a judge. Last year, race stewards disqualified Senna because he cut short in a chicane. This time, they told me on the telephone that there were no elements to allow Senna's disqualification. In any case, I do think that Senna deserved this world title for his achievements since the beginning of the season. But I regret he did not win it in style."

Even the French sports minister, Roger Bambuck, intervened: "The world championship has not been worthy of the investments placed in it and Balestre may if he wishes, and I wouldn't criticise him if he does, not award any title this year. I am not entitled to prompt FISA to do it. FISA is an independent body. But if Balestre does it, it will be appreciated." There was even some scaremongering at Ferrari. Cesare Romiti, managing director of Fiat, which owned Ferrari, declared: "Ferrari would be forced to take some drastic and painful decisions, perhaps even to abandon Formula One. We are not prepared to put in so much capital and man hours building better cars just to see them shunted off the track at the first bend."

Adelaide, the final race of the season, was the 500th world championship Grand Prix and was supposed to be a special occasion, but it was completely overshadowed by what had happened at Suzuka. No one could talk about anything else. Prost was still bitter: "He is bad for the sport. If it ever came to the point where I had to do the same things to win the world championship, I would have to think about whether to stay in the sport." "In the end, he makes me laugh," retorted Senna.

During race weekend Senna had a huge public row with former world champion, Jackie Stewart on a live show on Australia's Channel 9. Stewart believed the incident with Prost in Suzuka had been Senna's fault. They vigorously disagreed and at the end Senna told Stewart he would never appear on television with him again.

For the race Senna took pole, but the grudge match everyone had been expecting failed to materialise. In the race, Senna spun out while Prost finished third. Most of the action occurred off track, where Prost refused to attend press conferences, the drivers' briefing and the celebratory photograph of past world champions. The photograph was a one-off opportunity with so many champions present, including Juan Manuel Fangio, Denny Hulme and James Hunt, plus Senna himself. It was an opportunity missed: a few years later they were all dead. The organisers threatened draconian punishments for the Frenchman. Senna must have smiled to himself at how the situation had been reversed since 1989.

But he knew it had been another hard season. The McLaren Honda was gradually seeing its dominance whittled away, but his will to compete had increased after the opening race at Phoenix, where he admitted he had been very low and uncertain what the future held. He said: "At the end of last year I had a tremendously hard time in my mind. Psychologically I was hurt. I went to Phoenix with no desire to race, and I found myself racing just by my instincts. I still won the race in such conditions. After that, to go to Brazil it made me feel better to discover the right feelings for racing. With such a warm crowd in Brazil, I found my heart again in racing. I was able to fight back to eventually win the championship. So in that aspect it was a championship that was won more by inner strength than anything. I am young and full of life and full of time to race, and I love my racing so much. In 1990 I have raced on many occasions with my heart, and some occasions with my mind, and on other occasions with the best combination of the two. To be champion under those circumstances is very rewarding."

His career was certainly becoming very rewarding and he bought his second home in Brazil, which he intended to be a family ranch. The property would take three-and-a-half years to complete the plans he had for it – to make lakes and go-kart tracks and turn it into a rural playground. Rather than his own home, he intended this to be a family home which they could all share. The 200-hectare cattle ranch was called Fazenda Dois Lagos, at Tatui, some 120 kilometres outside São Paulo.

It was a paradise where he would recuperate rather than go to for pleasure, like the beach house at Angra. As well as a home it would remain a proper working farm, with 50 pigs and 50 cattle, and fields full of vegetables growing. When it was complete, he would be able to enjoy go-kart races with his nephews on the private circuit, tennis and long sleeps in the 10 bedrooms that would all be rearranged to have views of the lake and access to the central jacuzzi he planned. The renovations he planned were budgeted to cost $3.16 million.

Behind the purchase of the farm was his unfulfilled dream of settling down with the wife of his choice and starting a family. Over the years he constantly spoke to journalists about his quest for the perfect woman, and how he had never found her. He said: "When one makes a non-stop trip around the world for professional reasons, it is absolutely necessary to be able to return to one's roots, stay in touch and avoid losing oneself."

The farm was also what he called his 'reference point' for his family. He explained: "The members of my family are my life: they are my point of reference. It's always important to come back to a reference point when you go all over the world. Otherwise you may lose your way."

He continued: "I wouldn't be here as a racing driver, with so much success, if I didn't have a good family, special people around me throughout my life, that really led me in the right direction. People who share with me the very good moments, but also the very bad moments. It is very important for me to have that side of my life separate from the racing, because racing is really difficult to put together. My biggest problem in motor racing is having to be away from Brazil, where I have my family and friends. If you have the right conditions, you can have a very nice life in Brazil, and I like my home in São Paulo very much."

Senna looked ahead to his planned new paradise, to when his niece and nephew would be old enough to enjoy them: "I think at the right moment I will find the right woman and I will make a new family, an extension of my own family, and I will have my own children. Right now I have my nephew, I have my niece, and I enjoy being with them very much, to share a lot of my time with them when I am in Brazil. I love them, and of course they love me, we have fun and we share a good time. We are all children, aren't we. The difference between the man and the children is only the toys. As you grow up you start to have more things to think, more things to worry about and you lose it. So it is important when you have the opportunity to have the place to go back a little bit like a child, so you can recycle your mind a little bit. Just slow down and enjoy life, like children do. They do not think about tomorrow, they do not think about next year or next month, they think about right now. They just see a game and they try to play that game right now. It doesn't matter an hour ahead, they do not think an hour ahead, so they enjoy completely life and its full potential."

The farm would also give him the safe opportunity to indulge in his favourite weekend pastime, flying his miniature model aeroplanes.

He enjoyed this with such a passion that seemed often to transcend even physical sport, and sometimes even driving, as he said: "It takes your mind completely away from anything else because it absorbs your mind, your concentration, so it is relaxing in a way to forget any racing cars or interviews or things like this."

He used to indulge his passion with an old Brazilian school friend called Celso di Santi. Santi recalled that Senna had extremely precise reflexes. He said: "In order to fly [safely], the aeromodelist must have extremely precise reflexes. He has to be exacting, very meticulous and an extremely careful individual. All these virtues, if they may be called that, were possessed by Ayrton"

Santi said that even with many months of inactivity whilst he was in Europe, Senna could return to Brazil and immediately on his very first flight perform manoeuvres: "He flew with consummate perfection, something that is not common."

Santi recalls how they used to perform manoeuvres with two planes and once they clashed in the sky. As he recalled: " His plane struck mine aloft. The wing dropped off and my plane plummeted like a missile. But my plane's propeller had sheared off a bit of one of his plane's wings and part of its fuselage. Yet he succeeded in landing his half-twisted aircraft. This was something that made him happy."

His ongoing relationship with Santi reflected the shyness of his nature. Hardly any of his friends in Brazil were new friends. They were all from his childhood, before he was famous. Despite the shyness of his nature he was like a kid, especially when he hung around with old friends. He spent a lot of time making jokes and kidding people. Santi remembers him as amusing and fun to be with.

Alfredo Popesco was another old friend from his youth. He remembers that fame never changed Senna. He said: "He remained always the same person, a humble and sincere friend, at a time when he was already a three-time world champion, if he saw us eating pizza he would park his Honda NSX and stroll over to nibble things out of our plates, the way he always had. He was the friend who had gone abroad for a while and had come home from his trip. He was eager to join us in everything that we did to follow our routine, to dine out in a restaurant or enjoy some other leisure activities. He had no bodyguards and made no show of being a celebrity."

At the end of 1990 Senna invested in a 16-storey office building located in the Edificio Vari suburb of São Paulo. It marked the start of his serious business ambitions. The office would take 18 months to refurbish and have a helicopter deck installed on the roof. It would be occupied by Ayrton Senna Promotions Ltd and other companies in his empire, which were run day to day by his cousin Fabio Machedo. He also bought a 17th-floor apartment for his brother Leonardo and him to share in São Paulo. It was mainly occupied by Leonardo but also by Senna when staying in the city overnight.

He proudly showed off his new office block to journalists: "It is my new office, it is going to be my new office and the top of it is especially being built for the helicopter we have three levels of the building just for our activities." In the end his activities took over seven floors. Ironically all his business ideas were coming to fruition in the spring of 1994 and that year his companies would earn $4 million profit aside from his racing activities.

Around this time he also conceived the Senna official logo: a stylised double 's' in a distinctive maroon colour. The logo had another purpose: as a trademark enforcer for Senna-endorsed products. It was inspired by the esses section of corners at his home circuit of Interlagos in São Paulo. Senna could see how personal drivers' merchandise was starting to develop, especially in the American NASCAR saloon car series. He wanted his own mark and what became known as the Senna 's' would be skilfully promoted by him from 1991 onwards.

Whenever he could he turned down his overalls to his waist which revealed a t-shirt with the distinctive logo perfectly displayed. Later Michael Schumacher would prove, with far less flair and skill than Senna brought to the design of merchandise, that he was right. Even so after his death Senna t-shirts were sold in the hundreds of thousands around the world for premium prices, earning millions for his foundation.

He returned to Europe just one more time in 1990, to attend the FISA season awards ceremony in Paris. It proved especially emotional as Honda's patriarch, Soichiro Honda, became the second individual, after Enzo Ferrari, to receive a special FISA award. The old man and the young man were immensely close, and Soichiro Honda whispered in Senna's ear at the ceremony: "We'll make the best engine for next year again." The old man brought tears to Senna's eyes.

CHAPTER 16

Afternoon of a Hero

Witnessing tragedy for the first time

Although it may be argued that he made dirty-driving manoeuvres legitimate fare in Formula One, and inspired Michael Schumacher in the belief that winning was all that counted, there was always much to admire in Ayrton Senna, both as a driver and as a man. Never were these two aspects of his charismatic character more visible than one weekend in Spain in 1990, when Martin Donnelly hovered on the edge of life after his Lotus crashed heavily after suspension failure. In the aftermath of the accident, the cruel edge of the sport was met with unflinching heroism and, courtesy of Senna, a dark weekend was lifted by the sheer power of the human spirit.

In September 1990 Ayrton Senna came close to tragedy for the first time in his Formula One career. It was 13:52 on Friday 28th September. Martin Donnelly's Formula One career ended in the time it took his Lamborghini V12-engined Lotus 102 to disintegrate after it ran into the barriers. Spectators at the last right-hand corner of the Circuito Jerez de la Frontera in Spain's sherry region, just before the left-hand hairpin that ends the lap, are afforded a view of the preceding unnamed right-hander.

Jean Alesi, driving Ken Tyrrell's 019, had been setting the pace with times in the high 1m 19secs. Spectators became aware of one of the garish yellow Camel-sponsored Lotuses doing something it should not. Viewing at that spot is akin to being at the entry to the pits at Magny-Cours where, if you are looking back down the pitwall, you can be tricked into thinking a car is heading straight for the barriers when in fact it is entering the pitlane.

But this time it was no optical illusion. Onlookers just had time to register there was no run-off area, where the barrier curved slightly out of view on the entry to the corner, when the Lotus disappeared in a cloud of fragments.

Those who were there hold the memory of the absolute silence that suddenly stilled the scream of the Lamborghini V12 engine. As the dust cleared, it became apparent that it was Martin Donnelly who was lying in the middle of the track. Spectators did not believe that the orange-and-blue-helmeted figure could possibly have survived.

Journalist David Tremayne was one of those standing at the corner. He said later it was the most horrible thing he had ever witnessed. That momentary lack of noise was quickly replaced by bedlam as spectators began screaming at the sight. TV monitors captured Donnelly's inert form, the remains of his seat strapped to him like a skydiver's parachute that had failed to open. Nobody could remember the last time a Formula One driver had been thrown from his car but, beyond the engine and gearbox assembly, there was no car. The Lotus had disintegrated into little pieces. Ironically, that complete deformation probably saved his life.

Minardi driver Pierluigi Martini brought his car to rest on the track in front of Donnelly's body as a form of protection. The Ulsterman's team-mate Derek Warwick rushed to the scene and organised the marshals. Donnelly was lucky. The era of Professor Sid Watkins and his team had begun and the medics were quickly on the scene.

Ayrton Senna was in the McLaren garage at the time of the accident and appreciated immediately how serious it was. Senna rushed out there, having felt a compulsive need to attend. Part of him saw a fellow driver in distress, another part felt an intense need to learn more about such situations. Perhaps yet another part felt the need to face up to them. He lacked knowledge of them, therefore he needed to learn. Impassively, Senna watched Watkins tend to Donnelly who, astonishingly, was alive against all the odds of surviving the most violent non-fatal accident of modern-day Formula One.

Donnelly had sustained serious leg fractures and concussion and would be in a coma for weeks. But as Senna leaned over him momentarily, he had shown signs of recognising the Brazilian before lapsing into unconsciousness. Senna realised there was at least hope. Warwick, meantime, returned to the Lotus pit to tell Donnelly's fiancée, Diane McWhirter, that he was alive and hopefully going to be okay. Warwick admits now he was lying: "At the time it was complete bullshit," he admits, "but I knew I had to keep her spirits up. As it turned out I was right, but when I left the scene I didn't reckon Martin had a chance."

As is the way of Formula One, as doctors tended to Donnelly in the medical centre, qualifying resumed. Once stable, Donnelly was airlifted by helicopter to Seville's Virgen del Rioco Hospital, 70 kilometres to the north of the circuit. Meanwhile, most drivers made only token efforts in the remaining eight minutes of the session, shaken by severity of the accident and a sudden realisation of the circuit's manifest dangers.

But not Senna. He had seen the carnage first hand and he was astonishingly frank about his feelings. Such moments were what made him so charismatic. "It was a very sad moment for all of us," he said when the session had ended. "I went to the place where he was on the ground. When I saw the consequences of such an incident, I went away for some private moments by myself. It was very, very difficult to cope and to maintain a balance. I thought about not running any more that day, but I had to understand it, absorb it and to go forward from that. I had some quiet moments in the motorhome and I was able to go through some very special moments there, to see inside myself. I gathered my thoughts and went back out. I did an incredible time. It was my tribute to Donnelly. But no one understood."

Senna had climbed back into his McLaren Honda and lapped in 1m 18.900secs, almost a second faster than anyone else. In fact the lap was so fast, the time almost remained good enough for pole position the following day. Some felt it was a callous thing to have done, but it was far from that. It took cold, raw courage to do that. Senna was never admired more than that day.

Afterwards he retreated to one of the McLaren trucks and just sat inside, holding his head in his hands. He stayed like that for many minutes before finally taking off his famous yellow helmet. Then he went to the medical centre again, to see Donnelly. "I don't remember any of that, of course," Donnelly says today, his lilting Irish voice still rendered a throaty whisper by the accident that he would not have survived only a handful of years earlier. "I don't remember recognising Ayrton when I was on the track, or in the medical centre. In fact I don't remember the accident at all. All I could ever remember was sunbathing in Portugal a few days before Di and I went to Spain, and getting sunburnt. But the Prof told me Ayrton took an extraordinarily keen interest in my welfare and in all the procedures the medics went through. A lot of others did too, of course, but Ayrton was in constant touch with the Prof. I was touched when I found out about it all later. Ayrton was quite a guy like that."

The following day in final qualifying Senna produced another astonishing lap to take pole position. The shadow of Donnelly's accident had created an indelible air of tension and Senna's pole-position press conference was one of those magic, spellbinding affairs that only he could ever create. Watching him baring his soul was both humbling and uplifting. You listened, then left the room feeling you had been in the presence of true greatness.

He went faster than ever, and won pole position as he said: "Yesterday was an amazing lap for me," he said quietly, thinking through every word. "Unbelievable for me under the circumstances. No matter how I try to express my feelings, nobody can know and understand what I felt. Inside me. In the car. The way that I drove. It is something I am not able to express."

Senna rarely swore in public, but that afternoon he had been incensed by mutual blocking actions of Nelson Piquet and Olivier Grouillard, who were behaving as if Donnelly's accident counted for nothing. "I saw the two cars fucking about, and it was totally unacceptable. If you are on a quick lap and somebody doesn't see you, you have to control your feelings. Sure the instincts sometimes tell you to hit the brakes. But you yourself know that there could be somebody coming on you at 200kph more than you are going, and in blind corners this could be fatal. It is really sad, we have seen yesterday what an accident can cause us. If I had hit either car today I could have taken off. That would have been totally unacceptable. It is really crazy."

Donnelly recovered, but only ever drove a Formula One car once more. Senna never gave up his interest in the medical side of the sport and had frequent discussions with Sid Watkins, with whom he forged a close personal friendship. When Erik Comas crashed his Ligier at Spa in 1992, it was Senna who stopped his car to render assistance. "We'd talked about what to do for a driver in such circumstances," Watkins recalls, "but only once or twice. Yet when I arrived at the scene Ayrton had done everything we had discussed, and he had done it perfectly."

But why had he done what he did that Friday in Jerez? Had he believed that Donnelly was dead, and tried to prove something to himself? Had he gone out and attacked Jerez to show that a mere track could not break the human spirit?

Later that season, Senna gathered together a group of journalists in his hotel room in Adelaide and tried to put his thoughts into words. It was an enthralling moment, as raw emotion stripped away all cynicism and overrode whatever personal antagonism had risen from time to time towards a man who was so driven by his passion and self-belief. For a long time he sat immobile in an armchair, saying nothing. Reliving the day. Marshalling his thoughts. Long before he spoke, his eyes welled up with tears. At last, when he did speak, his voice was just a whisper. You had to crane forward to be sure of hearing every word.

"For myself," he began. "I did it because anything like that can happen to any of us. I didn't see anything and I didn't know how bad it was. I knew it was something bad, but people just go crazy and say all kinds of stupid things. I wanted to go to see for myself. I felt the need to know – if it was bad, how bad it was. The best way is to see for yourself and not to listen to other people. There was nothing I could do at that moment, but if I was there maybe there would be something I could do."

There was another, longer pause. The tears were now threatening to run down his cheeks as he pondered the question of whether he needed to be brave to do what he had done, to confront racing's demons and then to overcome them so forcefully. "As a racing driver there are some things you have to go through, to cope with," he replied finally.

Whatever the personal tests were that Ayrton Senna put himself through that afternoon in Spain, he came through them with the honour and dignity that impressed the most vehement of his detractors.

CHAPTER 17

The Feud with Prost

Six years of continual conflict

It was probably Ayrton Senna's long-standing feud with Alain Prost that was most responsible for creating his negative image in the media. While Prost manipulated the media, Senna was constantly at war with it.

The feud started in a small way when Senna debuted in Formula One in 1984. That year the Monaco Grand Prix was held in the rain. Behind the wheel of his under-powered Toleman, Senna found himself in second place with the fastest car on the track. He was poised to overtake race leader Alain Prost in his McLaren when race director Jacky Ickx stopped the race and 'caused' Prost to win. Prost accidentally became Senna's *bête noire*.

The Lotus years were quiet ones and the feud did not build up until Senna replaced Stefan Johansson as Prost's team-mate in 1988. Prost had been used to running with inferior number-two drivers and Rosberg openly admitted he could not get near him. When Senna finally arrived after Rosberg retired, the Finn did not expect him to bother Prost. Rosberg was absolutely stunned when Senna was faster. And so was Prost.

When the animosity developed, Prost was supposed to fit into the 'decent bloke' category, and journalists assumed Senna was at fault. Typically, Senna's side of the story was always different: "I have worked with Gerhard Berger, Michael Andretti, Elio de Angelis, Johnny Dumfries, Satoru Nakajima and Alain Prost, so I think it is necessary for everybody who looks into this particular matter to consider the reality: as far as team-mates are concerned, I have always got on very well with all of them except one. The only driver I have ever had problems with as a team-mate is Prost."

The chemistry between Senna and Prost was a volatile brew of contradictions, and melding their characters into a productive force was a delicate business – as McLaren team principal Ron Dennis discovered. He says handling Senna and Prost required a combination of disciplines ranging from ego manager to tightrope walker, juggler to marriage counsellor. As he explains: "The relationship between any two human beings is a very complicated thing, like in a marriage, and the drivers' relationship is very, very complicated. But the negative aspects of having two such drivers can be turned to produce a motivating force. However, as in any finely-tuned situation, you walk a tightrope between falling off into failure and successfully getting to the other side.

"The challenge was to try to understand their negative differences, try to isolate them, then turn them into positives. I'm not a marriage counsellor but I think guidance and support are the words to use when it comes to handling drivers. I had to support and guide them through racing problems and human problems."

The conflict was perhaps inevitable, and their feud continued far beyond their tenure as team-mates. The tension between Senna and Prost initially stemmed from real, or imagined, preferential treatment of one driver over another. In 1988 when Senna joined McLaren, where Prost had ruled for four years, it was obvious that Senna was the faster driver, but less obvious that he was the better driver.

The slower driver needed to salvage his bruised ego and began to find fault with his equipment. McLaren provided both drivers with identical cars but when Senna became faster, Prost began insinuating that Honda was giving the Brazilian better engines. By the time Prost left McLaren, because of the personality clash with his team-mate, he was openly accusing the team of favouring Senna – and perhaps he was right.

Soichiro Honda, the founder of the great car company, had developed a great relationship with Ayrton Senna from the days they had started working together in 1987 with Lotus. Senna was the first driver Honda was compatible with, and who gave the company the best and most reliable technical feedback. He was the driver who visited Honda in Japan and tended to its needs. The company had no relationship with Prost, who was not good at that sort of thing. In fact Prost's one big weakness was his inability to foster corporate relationships in the long term. So if there was a better engine Senna got it. After all, he had brought the fantastic Honda engine with him. The team was at its peak and, with equal equipment at their disposal and the freedom for each driver to use it to his best advantage, the stage was set for a major confrontation.

Prior to their coming together at McLaren, Prost had won 26 races and claimed the 1985 and 1986 driving titles with the team. Senna, five years younger than Prost, had won six races with Lotus and was obviously destined for greatness.

Both men hated to lose. As Keke Rosberg once famously said: "Show me a good loser and I'll show you a loser – period." And since each man's team-mate represented an impediment to winning – or, worse still, had the potential to turn the other into a loser – it was vital for both Prost and Senna to take immediate steps to gain the upper hand at McLaren.

From a cautious mutual respect in its early stages, the relationship between Prost and Senna rapidly deteriorated into a mutual dislike that ultimately became what can only be called silent hatred. As Senna explained himself: "On the path to the summit, there isn't room for two." Prost said: "Nothing else was important. He just wanted to beat me and to beat me in a bad way sometimes. When I thought I was committed 100 per cent or just 99 per cent to Formula One, because the one per cent missing was maybe my family or my children, a different way of life, you know he was committed 110 per cent."

In 1988 the two were interviewed together in the McLaren motorhome and asked which of them would win the championship. Prost said: "Can we be equal?" Senna replied: "No there can only be one winner." Prost thought it was all very funny but Senna took it deadly seriously.

The war started, and came to a serious head at the 13th round, the Portuguese Grand Prix. Senna seemed to swerve deliberately in front of Prost, squeezing him so close to the Estoril pitwall that several signalling crews ducked for cover. Prost, who had been leading Senna at the time, and in fact went on to win, was livid.

Even Ron Dennis could not fix this one: from then on it was open warfare. Dennis tried by constantly throwing the two men together. For instance, he made them travel in the same helicopter to races. It had no effect and they did not talk to each other, merely stepping from the helicopter stony-faced and walking apart, to the bemusement of onlookers.

Senna ultimately won the 1988 world crown and Prost was second: as McLaren partners in 1988, they garnered a total of 15 victories. But Prost's belief that his Brazilian team-mate was a dangerously disturbed madman grew when Senna revealed that he had found religion. When Senna announced that he believed in God, the press ridiculed him and Prost used it against him. "Ayrton has a small problem," he said. "He thinks he can't kill himself because he believes in God, and I think that's very dangerous for the other drivers."

Journalists, sensing a colourful story, reported that Senna thought he was invincible because God was his co-pilot. "It's unreal to say those things," Senna responded angrily. "Of course I can get hurt or killed in a racing car, as anybody can, and this feeling, this knowledge, is absolutely necessary for self-preservation."

But 1988 was nothing compared to what was brewing for 1989. The season got off to a flying start at the San Marino Grand Prix when Senna, who went on to win the race, overtook Prost at the start. The disgusted Frenchman said the manoeuvre represented a sneaky breach of a previous agreement, instigated by Senna, that whoever was in the lead going into the first corner should be allowed to maintain it to avoid unnecessary risks. The basis of the first dispute was that Prost accused Senna of not respecting a 'non-aggression pact'.

After the Imola race, Senna and Prost traded what Japanese newspapers cutely called 'honour-injuring remarks'.

Senna won the race but Ron Dennis made him apologise to Prost. Senna admitted: "At that moment, the emotion made me cry. I said sorry, but I thought it was unfair. The world of Formula One has bent me like no person ever could for the rest of my life."

The war lasted six years, with constant sniping to favoured journalists. Senna said once: "Prost is a coward." Prost responded: "He takes himself for a mystic, he thinks that nothing can happen to him. That he's invulnerable. It's a philosophy that puts the other drivers in jeopardy."

Although Prost let Senna by on that occasion, his open-door policy was definitely not in effect in the championship-deciding Japanese Grand Prix.

Prost set the stage for the events in the race, saying: "A lot of times last year and this, I opened the door and if I did not open the door we would have crashed. This time I will not open the door."

Prost had the advantage because if both went out he would be crowned world champion. Senna, for all his intelligence, seemed not to have grasped this simple fact. When the two McLarens collided at the Suzuka chicane, Prost walked away from his car (which was later found to be undamaged) and although Senna recovered and went on to win the race, he was later disqualified (for missing part of the circuit) and Prost was declared world champion.

It happened the next year, too, and again at Suzuka where Prost, by then with Ferrari, once more closed the door on Senna and the Brazilian again used his McLaren as a battering ram to open it. The incident, in the first corner on the first lap, put both the McLaren and the Ferrari out of the Japanese Grand Prix but Senna's lead over Prost in the standings meant the 1990 championship went to the Brazilian. "I am at peace with myself," he said afterwards, while the incensed Prost insisted his actions were 'deliberate, unsporting and intimidating'.

Senna retorted: "I never caused the accident in Suzuka. It was never my responsibility and you should see that from the video, not my own words. The way the whole affair has been treated is like I have total responsibility. I was blamed for everything, I was treated like a criminal! So of course I thought about stopping. Many things have gone through my mind, but I am a professional, and the values I have in my life are stronger than to be influenced by other people."

British TV commentator Murray Walker, for one, didn't buy it: "There is no doubt at all that in 1990, if he did not drive into Prost, he had certainly made his mind up, as he subsequently admitted at that famous press conference. He had decided before the race, because in his view he was on the wrong side of the track. He believed that he should have been on the left-hand side, and because of the circumstances Prost was there. Senna bitterly resented that and said to himself before the race, as he subsequently admitted, 'I am going to go for it and if Prost turns in on me that's his hard luck'."

Occasionally the storm abated, and they would shake hands. Then it worsened still further. After the 1990 clash there was an attempt at reconciliation, as Senna said: "What happened between us in the past hasn't been in any way pleasant, either for us or for anybody else. It has been a bad time for everybody. I don't think we were ready to try to make friends a year ago. Now I have to try to believe that it will work. It may not work, because only time will tell: for him, for me, and so on. But you cannot say no, to yourself or anyone. You have to try under the conditions, under the circumstances. And I think we will try. We want to try and we will try. But only time will tell whether we can succeed."

Senna was right. The truce did not last long but he had tried, as he said: "I always try not to criticise him, or react to criticism from him. That doesn't build anything, it is just destructive. What we have to be very aware of is words. We can build a lot, but we can also destroy a lot. I prefer to build than to destroy. So it is not necessary to go into details about any particular case or anything. It is just my philosophy of how to behave."

A year later, after he had won the 1991 world championship, Senna gave his version of what had happened the year before at Suzuka. "It was a sad championship, but that was a result of the 1989 championship. Remember, I won that race and it was taken away. I was so frustrated that I promised myself that I would go for it in the first corner. Regardless of the consequences, I would go for it. He [Senna by this time never used Prost's name] just had to let me through. I didn't care if we crashed. He took a chance, he turned, and we crashed. But what happened was a result of 1989. It was built up. It was unavoidable. It had to happen. I did contribute to it, yes. But it was not my responsibility."

There was more trouble in the German Grand Prix in 1991. Prost poured all his venom out on Senna in a television interview, in which he accused him of deliberately weaving and brake-testing him. After the German Grand Prix, Prost made one of the most dangerous statements any Formula One driver has ever made: "He drove across me, braking in a strange way and weaving. If I find him doing the same thing again I will push him off, that's for sure." The inflammatory remarks later resulted in Prost being handed a suspended one-race ban. Senna took the threat calmly and spoke considerable truth when he said of his rival: "I think everybody knows Prost by now. He is always complaining about the car or the team or the circuit or the other drivers. It's never his fault."

Senna was dismissive of Prost's post-Hockenheim threat. He pointed to the fact that Patrese had got by him easily after two laps and was faster. He said Prost just could not get by: "We could have touched then at 300kph and if we had there would have been a big impact. He could have caused it. It was a desperate move by him."

Prost concluded by saying: "Now that my championship chances are over, I shall do my best to help Nigel and Williams Renault to win the title."

That was the end of the battles on the track. Prost retired for a season in 1992 and came back in 1993 with Williams. That started another off-track feud that simmered for two years during 1992 and 1993 over a drive at the dominant Williams Renault team. Senna basically wished to be Prost's team-mate in 1993 in the best car. Prost would have none of it – it was reportedly written into his contract that Senna could not be his team-mate.

The precedent of a top driver refusing a team-mate was forgotten by the media after Senna moved to Team Lotus and in 1986 would not allow Derek Warwick to join the team. His reasoning was that Lotus was not up to the task of providing two equally competitive cars for two top drivers and the sport's insiders agreed with him. But the British media did not and since Warwick was a 'thoroughly decent bloke', Senna was called everything from a coward unwilling to face competition to a ruthless manipulator of other people's lives.

Mercifully, Prost and Senna eventually grew tired of fighting and after the Frenchman retired at the end of the 1993 season they finally shook hands and resolved to try and forget their differences.

The last time they met on the track was in the 1993 Australian Grand Prix at Adelaide. It was a momentous event for Prost who, with Williams, had already clinched his fourth world championship and made his decision to retire from the sport; and for Senna, who would the following year replace Prost at Williams after six seasons with McLaren.

At Adelaide Senna scored his 41st and last Formula One victory, a record second only to that of the man who stood beside him on the victory podium. Prost finished second in his final Grand Prix, thus retiring with 51 wins – the most successful of all Formula One drivers by that criterion. Then another kind of history was made as the two protagonists, who had dominated the sport for so long, gave in to their emotions. Their deeply-felt sense of occasion moved them to overcome their mutual animosity and stage a dramatic and emotional post-race reconciliation.

Prost extended a hand of friendship to Senna, a gesture that seemed to sweep away all those years of bitterness. A misty-eyed Senna hauled Prost up onto the top step of the podium to share the limelight, and embraced him warmly. Their peace pact was sealed with champagne, which they playfully showered over each other before discussing their feelings.

Senna was asked what he really thought of his rival now that their celebrated feud was relegated to racing history. "I think our attitude on the podium speaks for itself," he replied. "It reflected my feelings and, I believe, his feelings too."

And did Prost think they could ever become close friends? "I think only life will tell that. If you want to speak about the future you must also speak about the past and we don't want to do that. It's best that we remember only the good times we had."

Gerhard Berger, Senna's team-mate at McLaren, has his own clear-cut ideas about why the Senna-Prost relationship was so full of conflict. "If you have someone like Ayrton or Schumacher as your team-mate then there are different ways you can handle it. At that time Ayrton was clearly the best and everyone knew that. Alain was in the same car and knew he didn't have a chance of beating Ayrton in speed terms, so he realised quite quickly that pace couldn't compensate. At that point he had the chance to say 'Okay, I'll find my own level and work at that, and get the team working with me as well'. But he refused to accept the situation so it all became political – he found fault with everything, and didn't hesitate to allocate blame. It caused a lot of aggravation and that was a problem for Ayrton, as he knew he was the best and that Alain was simply finding fault. It was clear there was going to be a big explosion."

Tragically, Senna's future was short-lived and few felt worse about that than Prost. Just prior to the ill-fated 1994 San Marino Grand Prix at Imola, Prost, who at the time was a member of the media, met Senna privately and they agreed to formally end their long-standing animosity. Prost recalled: "We had the warmest conversation I can ever remember. For the first time I felt he really wanted to be friends." Senna gave a message on live TV for the man he called a 'Formula One pensioner': "I miss you Alain". Two hours before he died, Ayrton said to the TV cameras: "Greetings to my friend Alain. I miss you, you know."

A few hours later, Alain Prost was one of millions of people who wept when Ayrton Senna was killed.

Senna once said: "All it takes to change people's view of a subject is to listen to the other side. Only then do you get the complete story." And now, as investigations proceed into the full extent of his remarkable life and achievements, Ayrton Senna is being praised more highly than he ever was when he was alive. When it is finally realised how truly extraordinary he was as a man and a driver, he will surely be accorded the full honour that sadly was missing during his lifetime. Perhaps this will be Senna's most important legacy to Formula One: by his remarkable example, to have created a greater awareness and understanding of genius so that it can be more easily recognised and appreciated, should anyone of such stature ever come along in the future of the sport.

Ron Dennis is sanguine about the feud as it fades in the memory. He says he learnt a lot from it. It was one of the main reasons why Dennis kept the reasonably amicable partnership between Mika Häkkinen and David Coulthard intact for so long – because of his experience with the most notorious of all team-mate feuds: the one between Senna and Prost.

History showed that Senna gave Prost full credit for his achievements. On television he was asked to rate the world's best-ever drivers. He rated Prost the third best: "I would say Fangio was number one. Unfortunately I come from a different time, so I didn't have a chance to see him really driving. For me he is the undisputed number one. In the 1980s and 1990s... Niki Lauda was another outstanding driver. And Alain Prost is the next one. The four championships he has achieved are real, they are reality. No one can dispute that."

CHAPTER 18

1991: Title by Default

A World Championship to forget

Ayrton Senna left the 1990 season behind him a world championship richer, but with his reputation in tatters. His standing with journalists was at its lowest and there was no love lost on either side. The press corps that follows Formula One around includes roughly 300 journalists and most were horrified at Senna's actions at the first corner at Suzuka, when he rammed Alain Prost's Ferrari off the track to take the title. It shocked even his most ardent supporters.

It was the unpleasant flipside of his single-minded determination to succeed – no one really knew how far he would go in pursuit of perfection. Forcing rivals to run wide and disobeying gentlemen's agreements was one thing; deliberately causing a potentially dangerous high-speed accident was another. Senna had made the transition from rogue to villain, and with the defence of his crown at stake in 1991, it looked as if things weren't going to improve.

Senna was out of contract at the beginning of 1991 and was unwilling to sign a new three-year deal with Ron Dennis. He realised that 1991 was going to be a tough year. Although McLaren had walked to victory against no opposition in 1988 and 1989, he had had to work immensely hard in 1990 and expected more of the same in 1991. He said: "It was a consequence of being too successful. McLaren had won so much, particularly with Honda – it is hard enough to get to the top, but even harder to stay there."

He sensed correctly that the three-year McLaren Honda dominance was coming to an end and that a period of Williams Renault supremacy was in the offing. If it was going to be a hard season he wanted paying plenty. And he wanted to be ready to make a hasty exit to Williams whenever the time came. He also sensed that Honda was not as keen as it had been and might not be around for much longer. He realised McLaren would suffer if Honda withdrew. But at the time it was still the top contender, so tortuous negotiations started with Ron Dennis for a new contract and lasted several weeks. Senna wanted $20 million and Dennis wanted to pay him nearer $12 million, the same as Frank Williams was paying Nigel Mansell for his return to the team from Ferrari. Dennis sensed that Senna had nowhere else to go and that for the moment he had the best car.

Senna was still sensitive to the trick that Dennis had pulled on him when they could not agree on the finances of his first contract in 1988. Then Dennis had suggested they toss for the extra $500,000 that separated them. Dennis had given Senna the impression that the actual amount they were tossing for was $1.5 million because it was a three-year deal but that was not the case. Senna didn't like being caught out like that and it rankled.

He did not altogether trust Dennis and was determined to make him pay this time. In the end they settled on $15 million for a one-year deal. Senna would partner Gerhard Berger for a second year. He found Berger put him under huge pressure in qualifying and he liked that, as his Austrian team-mate kept him honest but rarely bettered him. Senna thought Berger a far faster driver than Prost but without the killer instinct that he and the Frenchman both possessed in spades. There was another key difference between him and Berger. If offered $1 million or a Grand Prix victory, Berger would inevitably take the money. Senna would not.

McLaren team chief Ron Dennis admitted he was bruised by the negoti-ations with Senna. "He is a hard and totally inflexible negotiator who will use all the methods at his disposal to maximise his position," he said. It was a careful choice of words.

In fact Senna was much more concerned about the technical situation. He realised that McLaren Honda's dominance of 1988, 1989 and even 1990 was gone. He resolved to be a lot harder with the team to make up the difference and seize a third championship. Honda duly delivered with the new engine. And Senna was very hard with McLaren and Honda engineers in technical meetings. As he admitted: "I was giving my personal opinion, my honest feelings, face to face, objectively. And they couldn't disagree with many of the things because Gerhard had similar feelings, similar expressions. Therefore they understood, they realised. But they also needed some help from us, to get the message all the way through the system, not only to the test teams or the development teams at the race circuits but also the development teams back at the factories who did not come to the race circuit – they needed to get the message as well so that the whole group could pull strongly in one direction. There are two ways you can send a message – one that is frustrating and demotivating and the other being positive about it. I believe we did it the right way because we got everyone together, more than ever. And the results show it."

The new McLaren MP4/6 made its first appearance on 27th February – just 12 days before the first race of the season. Ron Dennis blamed a 'technical restructuring' at the team for the delay but it was more likely due to hold-ups with the engine. Honda had produced a new V12 engine for 1991 to counter what it saw as an upcoming challenge from Renault's new V10. The old V10 was palmed off for the Tyrrell team to use.

There was clear tension in the air at the launch.

When Senna took to the track at Estoril, he realised the car was a good one, although he had his doubts about the new Honda V12 engine. Honda engineers countered that the engine wasn't suited to the Portuguese track and would run much better in Phoenix, the venue for the first race of the season.

If Senna was worried about 1991, his concerns were not lessened when he saw the new Williams Honda FW14. It was bristling with innovation and electronics that made the McLaren seem agricultural in comparison. The combination of veteran technical director Patrick Head and young designer Adrian Newey had produced a concept that was totally new, between the aerodynamics, the transmission and the engine. If it worked, Senna knew it would put the team well ahead of everyone else. The McLaren strategy was different. It was a more conventional concept of a racing car: the transmission, the aerodynamics, the suspension, the chassis, everything. Only the engine was new and innovative.

Whatever Senna's worries, they seemed to be unfounded at the United States Grand Prix. Despite complaining of gearbox and balance problems in the race, he had a dominant weekend, taking pole position by well over a second and winning by more than 16 seconds from Alain Prost's Ferrari. The threat from Ferrari, Williams Renault and his McLaren team-mate Gerhard Berger had failed to materialise and for Senna it all seemed too easy. Notably the Williams duo of Nigel Mansell and Riccardo Patrese were among several retirements, as the team struggled to get to grips with its revolutionary new semi-automatic gearbox.

The race marked Senna's 27th Grand Prix victory, equalling Jackie Stewart's record for the second-highest number of wins in the history of Formula One.

The next race was in Brazil. In seven attempts, Senna had never won on home soil but he had come tantalisingly close. In his favour, after a long stay in Rio, the race had returned to the Autodromo Carlos Pace at Interlagos in his native city of São Paulo.

The Thursday preceding the race was Senna's 31st birthday and celebrations resulted in a cream cake fight breaking out in the McLaren garage between him and Gerhard Berger, with Ron Dennis watching. On Saturday he inevitably took pole, although he left his fast lap until the closing minutes of the session. The crowd was ecstatic. Come race day he started well and immediately began to pull away from the Williams Renaults of Nigel Mansell and Riccardo Patrese. Until lap 50 of the 71-lap race he looked invincible.

But on lap 50 he lost fourth gear and was faced with the problem of having to shift directly from third to fifth. Soon he also experienced trouble with the other gears as they started to jump out of position and he was forced to steer with his left hand while he held the gearstick in place with his right.

Mansell was rapidly homing in on the Brazilian and Senna's problems showed no sign of abating. Then to his good fortune, Mansell spun on lap 60 after experiencing gearbox problems of his own. Patrese was 40 seconds behind with 11 laps left, so if Senna could keep the car in its current condition he would be able to make it safely home.

But the race was far from over. With seven laps to go the gearbox almost failed completely. Senna's lap times began to plummet and he started to lose six or seven seconds a lap. With his arm already aching from holding the gearstick in place, he found the only gear that was functional – sixth – and stayed there. Although he ran the risk of stalling if the revs dropped too low in the slow corners, he dared not risk changing gear.

Unknown to Senna, Patrese was also having problems with his semi-automatic gearbox. The Brazilian managed to bring down the times so that he was losing only a couple of seconds a lap to the Italian, but he knew he was still not safe and the car could give up at any moment, denying him his much-wanted home victory. With three laps to go it began to rain and it became all the more difficult to control the car. Senna could see Patrese in his mirrors. Ever the religious man, he said a prayer and hoped for the best.

He did not want to be cheated of his home victory now.

The engine died just after Senna took the chequered flag. He was in immense pain from cramp induced by the extreme effort of controlling the car and he could not climb out of the cockpit. All the same he was elated and the fans went wild. Eventually Wilson Fittipaldi helped him from the car and he was greeted by his family, friends and team. On the podium, he looked close to collapse but he savoured the victory. When he tried to hold the winner's trophy aloft he could not manage it and had to be helped by Ron Dennis.

At the post-race press conference, Senna was overwhelmed as he said: "I finished the race with nothing left at all. Physically I was exhausted but God gave me this race and I am very happy." Even following this great drive his detractors voiced their views, but to little avail. To some, his declaration that God had helped him to victory was awkward and embarrassing, even arrogant, but Senna had very deeply-rooted beliefs. Nelson Piquet even doubted that Senna's achievement was possible, but in-car television footage proved him wrong. It was one of Senna's greatest triumphs, as his 28th victory moved him into territory thus far only charted by Prost.

The next race was the San Marino Grand Prix at Imola. On a wet week-end Senna took victory and the 55th pole position of his career. He suffered oil pressure problems in the closing stages of the race and was running with a dry set-up early on, but he still looked unbeatable. Even better for him, it seemed that the predicted Ferrari threat would not materialise.

After running him close in 1990 against the odds, the political Prost was in full flow against the political Ferrari. Prost had already disposed of Nigel Mansell and the continuing in-fighting was disturbing the team's efforts as Prost attempted to oust team manager Cesare Fiorio. At Imola the Frenchman had embarrassingly spun out of the race on the warm-up lap. His team-mate Jean Alesi had also spun out on lap two. Williams Renault was struggling as well: the team's only finish had been Patrese's second place in Brazil.

Things were never going to be difficult for Senna at the next race – at Monte Carlo, his best track. It was another pole position and another victory, this time by over 18 seconds from Mansell, who finished his first race of the season. The only other man on the same lap was Alesi.

No one had ever won the first four races of the season before and to cap it off, Senna had also clocked four pole positions. With 10 points awarded for a win for the first time, he was leading the championship by 29 points from Alain Prost. He had also led all but nine laps of the season. On the downside, he had suffered mechanical problems in three of the races, but they were nothing compared to the problems that had beset Williams and Ferrari. It was also a tribute to the new Honda V12 engine that it managed the unheard-of feat of four opening victories.

The next race was the Canadian Grand Prix at Montreal. To the surprise of everyone, Senna was off the pace all weekend. He qualified in third place behind the Williams Renaults, bringing to an end his run of seven straight top qualifying spots. In the race he was running no higher than third when electrical problems on lap 25 caused his display unit to fail and he was out. It was the first time since the Australian Grand Prix in November 1987 that he had gone through a race weekend without topping any session or leading any laps.

To Senna's favour, neither Ferrari finished and the biggest threat to his championship challenge was defused when race-leader Nigel Mansell mysteriously coasted to a halt on the final lap and Riccardo Patrese managed only third as he struggled with his gearbox. Senna's championship lead was still a healthy 24 points over Nelson Piquet in a Benetton, who had been the lucky winner in Canada, and he was 29 points over Prost, 30 over Patrese and 33 over Mansell. Canada, however, had proved that he was not invincible and with the increasing pace of the Williams Renaults it had become clear that the battle for the championship was going to be a lot tougher from then on.

Mexico was next and Senna flew straight off home to São Paulo. He spent a glorious week and a half at his beach house at the resort of Angra dos Reis. It was his paradise, where he could indulge in every form of water sports or simply fly off in his helicopter to a deserted beach for the day.

On the following Monday he was indulging in his love of jet-skiing with friends from São Paulo who were staying with him at the house when he fell off the jetski and cut his head open. Luckily he was not knocked out and was able to return to the shore unaided. He was rushed off to the local hospital with a towel around his head. The gash required 10 stitches straight across the back of his head. Being Brazil the news got out – there was much speculation about the accident, the upcoming Mexican Grand Prix and his race fitness.

Senna was remarkably unperturbed by the accident. It was speculated he would not race, but he did not consider such a prospect. At São Paulo airport he joked with Brazilian journalists: "Everything is well. I was playing with some friends and I fell off my jet-ski. If I win as many points on Sunday as I have stitches I will be doing very well." The journalists questioned whether he should be indulging in such dangerous extra-curricular activities during the Formula One season, with so much at stake. He replied: "Driving in the São Paulo traffic is more dangerous."

One side-effect of the accident was a modified helmet. He would be wearing a special helmet with space carved out to avoid putting pressure on the wound. But the accident had dulled his senses and whether he should have been racing at all was a moot point.

In Friday qualifying, Senna suffered his second big accident in five days when he spun in the closing minutes of preliminary qualifying on the exit of the notorious 130mph Peraltada turn. He skidded across the track into the tyre barriers backwards, with the wheels off the track and the car flying through the air in reverse, as caught dramatically by photographers. The McLaren was flipped over and he was trapped in the cockpit until marshals arrived and helped him out.

It was a big shunt, but Senna was not flustered. What did disturb him was that he finished the day only third, unable to match the pace of Williams. It was the same story on Saturday, and Senna had to settle for best of the rest and third on the grid as Patrese and Mansell again monopolised the front row.

There was no change for the race: Senna was forced to follow Patrese and Mansell home, 56 seconds behind. Ominously there was now no sign of the gearbox problems that had plagued Williams in the early stages of the season, and with the reliability issue sorted out, the car's outright pace was showing through. Senna still led the championship by 24 points from Patrese. It was Williams' first win of the season and a firm message to the rest of the field that the car with the revolutionary but complex electronics, designed by ace young designer Adrian Newey, was coming together.

None of this was lost on Senna – he saw it as a sea change reflecting the fact that the first four straight wins had been a fluke. He was in a reflective mood following the race: "It was tough for anyone to match Riccardo and Nigel here today. I tried my best but I could not overtake them – it was just not possible. The two Williams were much faster than us the whole week-end. They demonstrated how much superior they are. At one stage I was able to maintain the same pace as Nigel but I could not overtake him, even when he had engine problems. Realising my engine was on the limit with its temperature, I eased off and decided the best thing was to try and finish on the podium and take four points towards the championship. I hope this will gain us some time to help Honda and McLaren make improvements to the engine and chassis. We need these corrections. Williams showed here what it can achieve. I have said for some time that the championship is still open and this proves it."

Once again Senna implied that the Honda V12 was lacking power. Reports surfaced that the power had begun to lag in comparison to the Renault V10 that Williams was using and Senna had demanded revisions. He was not looking forward to the return to Europe and the run of high-speed tracks that was coming up, including Silverstone, Hockenheim, Spa and Monza. He hammered the Honda engineers in meetings and told them he was relying on them to win the championship. They scuttled off back to Japan to redesign the engine.

But first came the inaugural French Grand Prix at the new track of Magny-Cours. No one was happy about the new track and in qualifying Senna could again only manage third behind Patrese and Prost but ahead of Mansell. However, it was Mansell who had the better race, bringing his Williams home for his first win of the season, followed by Prost, with Senna over half a minute behind in third. Senna still had a lead in the championship of 25 points, but now Mansell was in second.

The next race was Mansell's home Grand Prix at Silverstone. He traditionally flew in front of his fans, whereas Senna did not perform well at the circuit and had won there just once, aided by a downpour of rain in 1988. Silverstone produced a thrilling qualifying battle; Senna took provisional pole with 10 minutes of the session to go, but in the dying moments Mansell slashed his time by six-10ths of a second. In the face of it, Senna was magnanimous. He said: "I did my best but Nigel really deserves to be on pole."

The new Honda engine appeared for the first time at Silverstone. But McLaren told no one. Senna said much later: "We tested it at Silverstone, and I raced it at Silverstone. Gerhard and I both had the engine available – I chose to race, he didn't, because the performance was very similar between the two engines. It was a completely new thing and we had to develop it in order to go further."

At the start Mansell made a bad getaway as Senna out-psyched him and took the lead. However, the Williams driver had caught Senna by the time they reached the Hangar Straight and he powered through at Stowe. The crowd was as vociferous as when Senna had won in Brazil. From then on Mansell never lost the lead. Senna was comfortable in second place, but on the final lap he ran out of fuel and saw his six points transformed into three for fourth and a lead of 18 points in the championship.

Famously Mansell stopped on his slowing-down lap to pick up Senna and give him a lift back to the pits on the back of his Williams. He recalls: "Ayrton got a lot of flack at Silverstone because we were closing up in the standings. When he broke down I thought it would be good camaraderie to give him a lift. What is amazing is that some journalists actually criticised me for it, because they said he could look at the dials on my steering wheel and find out the secrets of the car. I had never heard anything so ridiculous." Nor had Senna, who wished he had thought of it afterwards. He was similarly generous towards Mansell and it seemed that their past disagreements had been put behind them. Senna said: "What happened? It was just incredible. Mansell simply flew past me and I could do nothing. He drove so well and was so quick. It was a great victory for him."

Senna blamed the team for miscalculating the fuel consumption, but it was to prove much more fundamental than that. McLaren simply didn't make that sort of mistake.

A few days later, Senna had his third big accident of the year, when he suffered a 150mph crash at Hockenheim in testing for the German Grand Prix. Driving behind him, Patrese saw the McLaren ride over a kerb and somersault five metres into the air. Senna was rushed to the medical centre, where he was treated for whiplash and bruising before being moved on to the hospital at Mannheim, where he stayed overnight. His friend and countryman Mauricio Gugelmin accompanied him there, and Senna told him that he believed a punctured tyre had caused the crash and he felt very lucky not to have been more seriously hurt.

When Senna was released from hospital the following day he was scathing about the track's safety standards. He said: "I was very, very lucky. I noticed about 500 metres before the first chicane that the left rear tyre had lost air. Then, shortly after, it just exploded. I remember my helmet pounding on the asphalt many times." He said that the kerbs at that point of the track were too high and should be removed. He added that he would certainly race in the Grand Prix the following weekend.

The German Grand Prix marked Senna's first real disagreement that season with Alain Prost. Prost was not featuring in the championship and was heading for a major dust-up with his team, who by that stage disliked the imperious little Frenchman. Equally, Prost disliked the unpredictable Italian drama queens, as he called them.

As Mansell ran away with the lead, Senna and Prost battled it out for second place until Prost hit a cone whilst attempting to outbrake the Brazilian and was forced to retire. The general opinion was that Senna had been hard but fair. But the drama was not over; Senna ran out of fuel on the last lap for the second race in a row. The championship lead was down to just eight points.

As Senna raged at Ron Dennis and his team for their seeming incompetence for letting him run out of fuel in two consecutive races and endangering the championship, Prost raged at Senna. The Frenchman complained: "He did everything to stop me passing him. He weaved, braked early and then drove across me. If other drivers can be fined for minor things, then he should be fined too. Now that my championship chances are over, I shall do my best to help Nigel and Williams Renault win the title. What he did is unfair. And I shall have no problems in Hungary in driving against him. If he does it again, I shall push him off the track. I will show that I can be aggressive too. If he gets in my way again like that at Hungary I shall just have to push him off."

Senna was dismissive: "He is always complaining. Patrese got by me easily after two laps and he was faster than me. Prost just could not get by. We could have touched then at 300kph and if we had there would have been a big impact. He could have caused it. It was a desperate move by him."

The events of Hockenheim had clearly left Senna in a very bad mood and he was no longer as willing to be generous to his rivals. As Mansell recalls: "After that round Ayrton came to me and said: 'This is the last that you will win this year. We have a new engine and we will have 50bhp extra from the next race'. Of course I didn't take him seriously, but lo and behold next time around the team had this new engine developed by the Honda guys at Wako in Japan. There was a little bit of gamesmanship going on there."

What no one knew was that Senna already had the new engine: that was what had caused him to run out of fuel twice, as it was consuming more than its predecessor. Senna said later: "The engine management system had some wrong calibrations. As a result the expectation of fuel consumption at a given race was wrong. The read out was wrong and so we ran out of fuel – totally unexpectedly, and a big mistake. It was not a small difference, it was a big difference that caught us out, because we always have a margin to play with. But it was so big, the inaccuracy, that it caught us up. And it cost us six points in two races. Can you imagine? Six points in two races."

On Monday 5th August Soichiro Honda, Senna's patriarch and a legend in Japan, died. Senna was deeply upset and immediately donned a black armband – a tradition in Japan in deference to a fallen leader.

The Prost scuffle ran over into the next round at the Hungaroring. Prost's remarks had created a lot of attention in the press and FISA was angry at his accusations. Both drivers had been given formal warnings after Hockenheim and Prost had received a suspended one-race ban for his anti-FISA comments. The pair were called together for a meeting in the neutral territory of the Williams motorhome and emerged after 90 minutes to publicly shake hands.

FISA had clearly made big threats to Prost. He said: "I think we fixed all the problems. First I thought he wanted to push me off the track – it really looked like that to me – but when I saw the video I realised it was purely my mistake. It was a stupid situation that was exaggerated by a certain element of the press. When I admit my mistakes it's not because of FISA's reaction. For the sport it's much better if the two of us can sort out our relationship. When you have the kind of relationship we have, you must be objective and honest. I made some mistakes in the past. In fact, I made them quite often. If I am totally honest I can't call him a friend yet. But you never know. Anything can happen."

Senna was well behaved. He said: "It's not peace yet, it's just a beginning. We have had too many personal problems in the past. We have tried to overcome them, to improve the situation. Above all, it's important to enjoy this job instead of having negative, destructive emotions."

Senna won the Hungarian round and took pole position that weekend. Mansell was second, although by the narrowest of margins. The new Honda engine was doing its job well. Senna dedicated his victory to Soichiro Honda.

Reflecting on Honda, Senna said he still felt the advantage of 1988 had disappeared and he had his own reasons for this, as he explained to journalists after the race. "I believe that Honda has established such a domination in Formula One over the past few years that it has been difficult for the team to motivate its own people to continue working at the same level. That is a normal thing to happen, with some of the people involved losing a little bit of motivation. And as a consequence, we have the difficulties we have right now. But it was recognised some time ago, and a huge effort has been made to change the situation. Honda brought up a new specification of engine, which is completely new as far as all internal parts are concerned – something you can [normally] only have from one season to another. And it did it within 30 days. We still don't have [exactly the specification of engine that] we need, but the Honda engineers have shown that they are trying very hard."

In mid-August, Bertrand Gachot, Jordan's young rent-a-driver, was charged with assaulting a London taxi driver with CS gas and went to prison. Jordan hired a young unknown called Michael Schumacher for the Belgian Grand Prix at Spa, who immediately impressed and then signed for Benetton the race after. It was an insignificant sideshow at the time, hardly noticed by Senna. But a future rival had arrived. For Senna, armed with the new Honda engine, the Belgian Grand Prix was an easy run after Mansell's engine failed. The gap was then 22 points. But Mansell won in Italy, where a late pitstop relegated Senna to second and reduced the deficit to 18 points again.

There was a surprise at Estoril in Portugal when Dennis and Senna announced they would race together again in 1992. They had signed a new one-year contract and Senna had received a $3 million rise to re-sign, taking his pay up to $18 million. He knew he had nowhere else to go and took advantage of Dennis's propensity to have his drivers signed well in advance. He and Gerhard Berger would be teamed together for a third year. McLaren boss Ron Dennis explained: "The negotiations went very smoothly. I am delighted with the outcome."

But before that, Senna received the most audacious offer of his career when Eddie Jordan also got in on the act. He had entered his own team in 1991 for the first time and achieved moderate success – he had certainly not disgraced himself. Halfway through 1991 he could see the McLaren-Honda relationship was faltering, and that Senna would have liked out of it if there was a good exit. He approached him with a bizarre idea – and probably the most audacious offer ever made in motor racing. The Irishman looked Senna square in the eyes and said: "I want you to drive for me. But I'll pay you nothing."

Senna listened because the Irishman had given him his first test drive in a Formula Three car in 1982 and provided stern competition that year after he had signed for another team. Senna had helped him when he entered Formula One and smoothed his path with Bernie Ecclestone. The relationship remained cordial. Jordan couldn't hope to match Senna's $15 million retainer with McLaren – more than his whole budget. But Senna could sell his own advertising space on his car and overalls, which was potentially worth millions, and would also get equity in the team, maybe as much as 50 per cent. It would become his own team. Jordan says: "I thought the idea would appeal to him. Ayrton would have been seen as the one who turned the team, his team, into a winner. You can only fantasise about what might have happened, but together we could have won races."

Senna, his career at a crossroads, apparently gave the offer serious thought. But he was well aware of what had happened to the career of fellow Brazilian Emerson Fittipaldi in 1976 when he had gone off to join his brother's Copersucar Fittipaldi team on a similar deal. It had been a disaster – it had ruined Fittipaldi's career and probably prevented him winning two more world championships to add to the two he already had. Having thought about it he told Jordan: "Don't wait for me."

Sealing his deal with McLaren was the impetus he needed, because at Estoril the championship swung decisively back in Senna's favour. Mansell lost a wheel straight after his pitstop and was black-flagged because his mechanics consequently fitted new rubber while his car was stranded in mid-pitlane. Senna could manage only second behind Patrese, but it was enough to give him a 24-point lead in the championship and leave him needing just seven points from the last three races to take the crown.

Senna was hoping to have the title wrapped up at the following round, the first to be held at Barcelona's Circuit de Catalunya. Mansell had injured his ankle in a football friendly against the press on Friday evening, and spent much of the weekend with ice packs pressed onto his leg. It could have given Senna a major advantage, but it did not turn out that way. A blown engine meant Senna qualified just third, but he rushed past Mansell at the start of the race, with Berger taking the lead. Mansell hunted Senna down. The pair had had a row in the drivers' briefing, refereed by FISA president Jean-Marie Balestre, when Senna accused Mansell of aggressive tactics at the start in Estoril, so pride as well as the championship was at stake. On lap five, Mansell pulled alongside Senna on the long straight and the pair rushed to turn one wheel to wheel. It was Senna who gave in, and Mansell famously surged into second place.

A poor tyre choice resulted in a spin for Senna on lap 13 and he could finish only fifth as Mansell powered to victory and closed the championship gap to 16 points. Senna's sullen mood of the latter part of the season worsened and he confronted Mansell after the race to complain about the overtaking move that everyone else had seen as a moment of genius. Mansell recalls: "Ayrton could intimidate anyone on the track. At Barcelona he came up to me and said 'beep beep effing beep you're mad'. He thought the move had been dangerous and he wanted to intimidate me. I think that weekend he finally got the message that he couldn't intimidate or harass me like he wanted to. From then on it was a bit more pleasant and he was always fair."

Senna only had to finish second in the penultimate round to take the championship. But the race was at Suzuka, where the championship had been decided in the previous two years with collisions between Senna and Prost. With the Mansell situation the way it was, it seemed likely there might be more controversy there in 1991.

Senna did little to quell the gossip when he remarked: "I have tried to avoid accidents, but sometimes that is a stupid way to go on and I may have to be a bit tougher in the last two races. There is always the chance of another accident. It is time for Mansell to think about the situation as well. We are both hard racers and I will make my contribution, but he has to make his too. Something would have happened in Portugal if I had taken a harder view. He would not have gone through the first corner. I will drive my own race in Suzuka and I will do what I want."

Mansell responded: "Senna has a 16-point advantage going into the last two races so I can't understand his attitude. We have had some great, clean races and this should be no different." Since Spain, Jean-Marie Balestre had been replaced as president of FISA by Max Mosley, a move that delighted Senna given his chequered past with the Frenchman. Mosley was inevitably drawn into the row but he insisted there would be no trouble. He said: "They are two of the finest drivers in the world and both about 30 years old or more. They are grown-ups and they know exactly what they are doing. It is not for me as an amateur, in the driving sense, to advise them or tell them about the consequences of their driving. They know that far better than me."

In Japan, Berger took pole with Senna and Mansell separated by just two-100ths of a second in second and third respectively. Mansell commented: "It will be tough – that goes without question. I'll be really surprised if Ayrton does anything silly because all the world will be watching."

At the start, Berger pulled into the lead while Senna remained in second with Mansell – who needed to win – boxed in behind him. Mansell pursued the Brazilian until lap 10 when he pushed too hard and spun out of the race. At the age of 32, Senna became the youngest-ever triple world champion in the history of Formula One.

When he saw Mansell's championship challenge end in a cloud of dust, Senna's immediate reaction was to drop the conservative drive-for-points approach and go racing to win again, even though Ron Dennis told him over the radio to take it easy and remember the constructors' championship battle between Williams and McLaren. Senna explained afterwards: "Once Nigel was out I said OK, now we go for it. I want to drive hard. I want to give a show for all the fans. The atmosphere in Suzuka was unbelievable. Everyone had been waiting for this race all over the world."

Over the radio Dennis asked him to give the victory to Berger, who was second. He could hardly refuse but first decided to put on a show, leading Berger for the final laps before handing the win to his Austrian team-mate almost on the line. Throughout the season Berger had made many valuable contributions on Senna's behalf, several times sacrificing his own perform-ance in favour of Senna's championship cause. Now Senna rewarded him, giving Berger his first win in a McLaren.

Afterwards Senna admitted he found it difficult and, for a moment, almost decided against it (even though he had told Dennis by radio he would). "It meant I would have to back off for the first time in my career for a race that I had fought for so long. How can you have a better way to win the championship than by winning the race? So it was tough. But Gerhard and I work really well together, we have great respect for each other and he has helped me in the past on many occasions. It was my turn to help him. Sure, it was tough and it hurt in my heart. But that pain is nothing compared to the feeling I have with the third title. Now we're going to go for it next year, and do it again!"

Some people, although not Berger himself, thought that the unsubtle move was ungracious and disingenuous and compared it unfavourably to the 1955 British Grand Prix when even Stirling Moss was uncertain whether or not his team-mate Juan Manuel Fangio had allowed him to win. But this was a different era, and in a more ruthless and competitive age Senna had done the honourable thing.

Senna's celebration of his third world championship was, at first, a very pri-vate one. Although he was surrounded by well-wishers, no one saw the depth of emotion he was feeling behind the mask of his famous yellow helmet. As he climbed out of his McLaren Honda Berger hugged and congratulated him, happy for his good friend and thankful for the victory. Ron Dennis ran up to Senna and he, too, hugged him, shook his hand and yelled his congratulations. Akimasa Yasuoka, the Honda team leader, did likewise and all the McLaren personnel joined in. Even Mansell patted him on the back and raised the new world champion's arm aloft in a fine gesture of sportsmanship.

Still Senna kept his helmet on, not wishing the world to see the tears in his eyes and the conflicting emotions he felt. Certainly there was a feeling of supreme satisfaction at the success, which came despite more adversity and competition than he had previously encountered in his career. But he was also overcome with feelings of frustration and anger at what he felt were past injustices. In this regard he felt his third title was a kind of revenge and the pent-up resentments from seasons past were shortly to boil over.

Senna went through the prize-giving formalities with dignity and aplomb. Close observers might have noticed an occasional glimmer of emotion as the Brazilian national anthem was played, but Senna was all smiles as he playfully engaged in the ritual champagne-spraying on the podium. And he was able to laugh heartily when Ron Dennis sneaked up from behind and poured a bucket of cold water over him.

But when he entered the post-race press conference, Senna was ready to speak his mind. At first he spoke softly, reviewing the season and comparing his latest triumph to those in the past. "This year I had a lot of excitement, a lot of pressure, a lot of stress. It's been the most competitive world championship I have ever been in because we fought with different cars, different engines, different drivers – not just inside the same team. Therefore it was really tough.

"We started the year well, then we had a tough time from the fourth race onwards. Because we won those first four races it was difficult to convince the team, Honda and Shell that we needed to work harder to catch Williams. So we stopped progressing and I ran out of fuel on two occasions. Then everyone finally understood and bit by bit we slowly got closer to Williams Renault and put pressure on the team. We won a couple of races at the critical part of the championship, in Hungary and Belgium, scoring the right results even when we could not compete with Williams on an equal basis. It wasn't until the last few races that we caught up to Williams and here we were able to do a one-two finish again, which is fantastic. So it has been a memorable championship – not only for me, but I think for Formula One over the past few years.

"Fortunately we were able to have a clean championship, without politicians, without people playing games. It was a technical and a sporting championship this year, and I hope it will be an example not only for myself but for everyone competing in Formula One now and in the future."

Then Senna began to reveal his inner feelings about what had transpired at Suzuka in the past. He said it had also been a memorable occasion when he clinched the 1988 championship at the Japanese circuit. And the next year was memorable, too, but for all the wrong reasons. Senna lost the title to Prost when he was disqualified for what was called an illegal re-entry to the circuit, following his controversial collision with Prost at the chicane.

Of this decision Senna said: "I was robbed, badly, by the system – and that I will never forget." On the occasion of the 1990 championship, also decided by a collision with Prost but this time in Senna's favour, instead of elation he felt bitterness: "It was a sad championship, but this was a result of the 1989 championship, a result of the politics that we had in 1989 and 1990."

As he began to elaborate it became clear that the villain in Senna's eyes was Balestre. He saw his departure as an opportunity to finally speak his mind. And he certainly did that, frequently lapsing into earthy English expletives as he gave vent to his anger. At one point during his vitriolic outburst Berger joked that 'you should hope that Balestre doesn't come back next year!'

The last time Senna had been outspoken in his criticism of FISA, following his loss of the 1989 championship, Balestre demanded an apology or said he would take Senna's racing licence away from him. Senna now said that his so-called apology to FISA was theatre perpetrated by Balestre, who faked an apology from Senna in a press release that was quoted around the world. "Now," said Senna, "I think we must all say what we feel is right and what we feel is wrong. We are in a modern world and we are racing professionals. There is a lot of money and image involved here, yet we are not allowed to say what we feel. Because if you say what you feel you get penalised, disqualified, fined, banned or lose your licence. Is that a fair way of working? It is not." In the tirade that followed, Senna indirectly blamed the ex-president for causing the first-corner accident with Prost. Before qualifying started, Senna said everyone agreed that pole position should be moved to the outside so as to give the pole-sitter the best line into the first corner. Senna then won pole position and hoped this advantage would enable him to get far enough ahead to prevent a replay of what had happened between him and Prost in 1989. "Remember, I won that race and it was taken away. I was prevented from going to the podium by Balestre. Then last year after qualifying, Balestre gave the order to not change pole position. And I found myself on the wrong side of the track.

"I was so frustrated that I promised myself that if, after the start, I lost first place, I would go for it in the first corner. Regardless of the consequences, I would go for it, and Prost would not turn in the first corner ahead of me.

That's what happened. And it was a result of the politicians making stupid and bad decisions.

"I was determined to get to the corner first and I was not prepared to let the guy turn in front of me – because if I was near enough to make that corner, he couldn't turn in front of me. He just had to let me through. I didn't care if we crashed. He took a chance, he turned, and we crashed. But what happened was a result of 1989. It was built up. It was unavoidable. It had to happen. I did contribute to it, yes. But it was not my responsibility." Opinion was sharply divided as to whether or not this was a confession of guilt or an admission of absolute commitment.

Balestre and FISA were understandably furious with the outburst that had tainted Senna's victory and made it another controversial conclusion to the title battle. A few days later the governing body forced Senna to make an awkward apology to Balestre. He issued a statement which read: "I now feel that my remarks concerning the former FISA president were inappropriate and that the language used was not in good taste. What I said was that I had decided, in the event of both drivers going for the same piece of road, that I would not be the one who gave way. All racing drivers do this occasionally. At no time did I deliberately collide with Alain." But the apology could not revoke what he had said and there were clear inconsistencies between his apology and his original outburst. Dennis insisted it had been Senna's decision to apologise, but few believed him.

The final race in Adelaide was a downpour and was halted after just 14 laps with Senna receiving half points for victory, enough to clinch the constructors' title for McLaren. Mansell crashed heavily in the rain and suffered concussion. The final championship standing was 96 points to Senna and 72 to Mansell, which barely illustrated how close things had come in the middle of the season. Had Williams sorted out its reliability problems earlier in the season, it could well have been a very different story.

When Senna attended FISA's annual prize-giving in early December he publicly made his peace with Balestre. The pair embraced and Senna presented the outgoing president with one of his racing helmets, a gift which clearly moved Balestre, who congratulated Senna on his championship. Senna told the audience: "It is time to clear up any misunderstandings. We have had our differences at different times, in different places and it is difficult sometimes in these situations, but I want to put all that behind us. I sincerely hope all our problems are now in the past and I mean this in a very sincere and sporting way."

Despite the apology, Senna had done little to improve his reputation in the year since his second Suzuka crash with Prost. In some ways he had sullied it further with the admission that the collision had been deliberate and pre-meditated. With his third world title he had joined an exclusive group – only Juan Manuel Fangio, Jack Brabham, Jackie Stewart, Niki Lauda, Nelson Piquet and Alain Prost had previously matched the feat – but controversies on and off the track had tainted the triumph. There were two Sennas: the introspective philosopher who valued his family and God above all else; and the ruthless champion who many thought had changed the face of Formula One for the worse. The truth was a complex amalgamation of the two.

As he reflected at the end of the season, he knew that he, not McLaren, had won the world championship. But, as he enjoyed the Brazilian summer at Angra, he wasn't at all confident about 1992.

CHAPTER 19

1992: Sensational in Monte Carlo

But little other glory

After Ayrton Senna's third championship, with his annual sponsorship income starting to approach $40 million and the prospect of heavy licensing income opening up, he finally persuaded his manager Julian Jakobi to split with Mark McCormack's IMG company, which also managed Alain Prost, and set up on his own as his own full-time manager.

Jakobi set up a Senna licensing operation in London and his own company called FJ Associates, with offices just off London's Baker Street. Senna and Jakobi started discussing ideas for after he retired. One was setting up their own Formula One team. But it was a decision for later. In 1992 he wasn't about to make the same mistake as Emerson Fittipaldi had when he set up his own disastrous team with his brother at the peak of his powers.

Meanwhile Senna was delighted he had separated his own commercial affairs and put some distance between him and Prost. Prost stayed at IMG and remained friendly with Jakobi.

As the 1992 Formula One season approached, the world was expecting Senna, as the reigning world champion, to be the dominant force all over again. Williams Renault had been strong up to the middle of 1991, but towards the end of the season McLaren Honda had regained its form to give Senna the title.

However, behind the scenes McLaren and Senna were struggling. Senna said to journalists in Brazil at the end of 1991: "I wouldn't like to do it, the same job again, that I did this year. Last year, when it was also very tough, I said 'no way can it be harder than that'. But this year it was even harder. And we did it – because once you are in it, there is no way out, if you are really committed. You have a commitment with everyone that is part of your team." Unfortunately that commitment was not enough in 1992.

The new MP4/7A had major problems with speed and reliability and the team had decided it would be best to leave it at home until the European season began. Williams, on the other hand, seemed to have solved all its reliability worries and would be running a revolutionary computer-controlled active suspension system in 1992, alongside the powerful Renault engine. The active suspension was rumoured to be capable of a second-a-lap advantage over its rivals, although some had questioned its reliability and Nigel Mansell remained cautious. He said: "I am looking forward to this season more than ever before. My commitment is stronger. If I didn't believe I could win the title, I would not be around. I will go to the limit racing against Ayrton as I demonstrated in some of the races last year. As always, the favourites will be McLaren, Honda and Senna. It is astonishing they have not tested much this winter, which probably means they have something up their sleeves and are confident of coming straight out and doing the business."

But McLaren did not have something up its sleeve, and the lack of testing was symptomatic of the team's technical struggles. The Honda V12 did not have the outright superiority of its predecessors, although it was still the best engine on the grid. But the McLaren car had fallen badly behind the Williams and it would be another year before it caught up again. Rumours had begun that the Japanese manufacturer would be pulling the plug on its Formula One programme at the end of the season.

The rumours were true – early in 1992 the Honda board of directors decided to pull out of Formula One. When he knew the decision Soichiro Honda telephoned Senna straight away and told him. The relationship between the two men was immensely close. Senna knew McLaren would be stuffed without a works engine for 1993.

McLaren team principal Ron Dennis was not told until later and Senna was certainly not about to tell him. But he did confide in his team-mate Gerhard Berger and told him to jump ship. Berger contacted his friends at Ferrari, as he knew a seat was available there for 1993. Senna began talking to Williams, which unbeknown to him was also talking seriously to Prost, who had no drive for 1992 after being sacked from Ferrari as a result of his politicking. The McLaren drivers both decided it was time they made their exits, as it was clear a down period would begin without the Honda engine. As Berger says:

"Ayrton went to Williams in 1994, but in fact the move had started much earlier. When he found out that Honda was going to withdraw, he warned me things were about to change. He had much better information from Japan than Ron himself – Ayrton was always the first to know what Honda was doing." Berger did the deal to move to Ferrari for a rumoured $12 million. Senna confided it was his ambition to drive for Ferrari one day but not yet. He asked Berger to let him know when he thought the time was right. Senna had already decided his next team was Williams.

When Senna was looking for a way out he made it very clear to Josef Leberer, who was by then a very close friend, that he would have to move too. Leberer was privy to Senna's secrets and he shared everything with him. Leberer remembers: "Whenever he had a telephone call, I never had to leave the room. He used to say 'no, don't worry, I trust you'. It was really nice." Senna told him: "We don't have to talk about it now our friendship, but I just wanted to say it, if I move or change, it is clear that you are coming with me. I would like you to stay with me as long as I am in Formula One."

Although he knew his McLaren would be inferior to the Williams that year, it was still a shock to Senna to see Nigel Mansell romp away with the first five races of the season. In doing so he beat the record that Senna himself had set the previous year when he won the first four rounds. To make matters worse, Mansell simply looked invincible. The Williams Renault FW14B was just too fast for the opposition and Mansell was also too fast for his team-mate Riccardo Patrese.

As a result of Williams' dominance, McLaren was forced to take drastic action. The team had planned to use the MP4/6B, a revised version of the previous year's car, for the first three races of 1992. The MP4/7A was due to make its debut at the Spanish Grand Prix, the fourth race of the season, and the team had planned to use the four-week break between Brazil and Spain to test the final package and make any necessary adjustments. But in a desperate attempt to challenge Williams, McLaren brought the MP4/7A in a race early, for Senna's home race in Brazil. This lost the team vital testing time and neither Senna nor his team-mate finished the race – Berger retiring with an engine failure after four laps and Senna suffering an electrical failure after 17 laps.

It was the engine that was the real problem. With Honda about to quit, engine development was as good as finished. Senna felt the RA121E had not been developed enough during the off-season. The development unit, the RA121E/B, was incredibly thirsty and had an added weight handicap of 60lb.

The car was underdeveloped, the engine was underdeveloped – and heavy and thirsty to boot. The McLaren package was simply too technically inferior to the Williams Renault FW14Bs to seriously challenge for wins. Monaco was the first race of the season when the engine developed horse-power comparable to that of its 1991 sister unit.

But Ayrton Senna was a racer through and through and never stopped trying. He had only once failed to make the top three on the grid, in Mexico after crashing heavily in the Friday session. He had retired from three of the five races so far, but had made the podium both times he had been able to finish. His third place in Imola was well deserved, but not an easy feat. He drove so hard to get on the podium that he was wracked with crippling torso cramps, which left him slumped in the cockpit for 20 minutes after the race.

The sixth race of the season was the 50th Monaco Grand Prix, and it was important for Senna. He had scored four wins on the street circuit and was racing for the Graham Hill trophy, awarded to anyone who could equal or beat Hill's record five wins in Monte Carlo. But Mansell, leading the world championship by 26 points from Patrese and 42 from Senna, had never won Monaco, the most prestigious race on the calendar. In the back of his mind he believed he could win every race that season, so dominant was his car. He had peaked at just the right time.

Thus Mansell and Senna arrived in Monaco, two drivers equally determined to win. But few believed Senna could beat Mansell. Williams and Mansell were in such great form that Senna only had a chance if something went wrong. And that didn't look likely, as Williams Renault had 90 per cent reliability in the first five races, four of which were one-two finishes, with Mansell's team-mate Riccardo Patrese retiring once.

As Monaco loomed on the horizon, Senna's morale was low. The Monte Carlo circuit was one of his favourites, but the car's handling was unpredic-table – potentially disastrous for a circuit like Monaco with 20 turns.

In the first qualifying session on Thursday, Mansell was on excellent form and soon topped the timesheets with an impressive 1m 21.535secs. A suppressed yawn rippled around the paddock. The Williams-Mansell domination was a tired storyline. Then Senna hit the track, and astonishingly bettered Mansell's time by 0.004 seconds: a minuscule amount, but enough to earn him a round of applause in the pressroom, where journalists had perked up at the hint of change that Senna's lap had brought. Determined to stay at the top of the timesheets, Mansell went out again, pushing his car over the limit and consequently spinning off, ruining his tyres. While Mansell was in the pits,

Senna went faster with a time of 1m 21.467secs, a further 0.064 seconds quicker. Once new tyres were fitted to Mansell's car, he asserted his authority, recording a startling 1m 20.714secs, 0.753 seconds faster than Senna's best time. The Brazilian was aghast. Even his most determined drive around his favourite circuit was not enough.

McLaren took advantage of the rest-day Friday to fit a lighter engine specifically for the second and final qualifying session on Saturday afternoon. So determined was the Brazilian to get pole position, he pushed the car beyond its limits and paid the price. He lost control on the exit from Casino Square, and as he came down through Mirabeau, the rear of the car twitched under braking and spun, causing the rear wing to fall off as he passed through the tunnel.

He turned to the spare car for the rest of the session, and bettered Thursday's time, but could not match the Williams' times. After trading provisional pole position, Nigel Mansell and his team-mate occupied the first row of the grid, with Senna relegated to third, 1.113 seconds off the pole pace. Mansell's pole lap of 1m 19.496secs was nearly a second faster than Senna's 1991 pole time, the first-ever lap of Monte Carlo completed in under 1m 20secs and over 150kph.

"We can't do anything with the Williams here," Senna said after qualifying. "I must be patient during the race and hope that something happens to Nigel."

Race day dawned sunny and warm, a stark contrast to the previous year's dire conditions. Patrese was fastest in the morning warm-up, but Mansell was still favourite to win. Senna knew that he would be pushed to get on the podium with the car the way it was. He was seated on the grid next to Ferrari's young hotshot Jean Alesi, whilst McLaren team-mate Gerhard Berger and another young new talent, Michael Schumacher, driving the promising Benetton Ford, made up the third row of the grid.

Mansell's start was faultless; Patrese's less so. He had the slight disadvantage of starting off line on the dirty side of the track and failed to accelerate on line immediately, allowing Senna a chance. Although a row behind, Senna had the benefit of the racing line and the clean track. As the cars approached the first corner, the sharp right-hander Ste Devote, he made his move. He dipped past the Williams and up the inside of the corner, which meant Patrese could either yield or push for the racing line and take them both out. Patrese chose to yield and Senna swept past the Italian.

"If Riccardo had been ahead of me out of that corner, I doubt I would have ever got past him," Senna said after the race. "It was the only chance I had to make up a place. Monaco is the hardest place to overtake in the world. I went for it at the last moment because if I had given Riccardo any indication that I was going to try and pass him, he would have closed the door. I got into second, but the problem then was to stop the car before I hit Nigel, because I was coming up so quickly that I thought he might not have seen me! But it worked out OK and it was a good manoeuvre."

Once in second place, Senna started to challenge Mansell, but he soon realised that his charge was fruitless, as Mansell edged away by a second a lap. By lap four Senna was four seconds behind, eight seconds behind six laps later and 20 seconds behind by lap 20. Patrese hassled him only one second behind, but despite being in a superior car, he could not get past the Monte Carlo maestro. All he could do was harry him into a mistake and that was unlikely. With Senna's driving skills the Brazilian soon eased away, but made no progress on Mansell's Williams in the ever-growing distance.

"I knew there was no way I could beat him," Senna admitted. "It was impossible with the superiority of his car – we were in no position to challenge Williams for a win. But you never know in Monaco. So I tried to push hard enough so that I was in a position where I would benefit if anything happened to Mansell. Already in the early stages of the race, I was planning for the later stages." Senna always had a Plan A and a Plan B strategy for every race. Plan A – getting past Mansell at the start – hadn't worked, so he settled for Plan B – conserving his tyres and brakes should he be given an opportunity to get in front. There was no point in chasing the Williams.

Senna drove consistently hard, but not on the limit. He kept Patrese at bay, but Mansell stayed a constant 20 seconds in front. On lap 60, Senna's race nearly ended. Michele Alboreto lost control and spun on the narrow downhill section between Mirabeau and Loews. Senna had to slow to a halt to avoid ploughing into the Footwork. "I just managed to stop with wheels locked, maybe about half a metre from his car," he recalled. It delayed his charge and Mansell gained another 10 seconds, to lead the race by 30 seconds. "I sat there thinking it just can't be true, now I've perhaps lost any chance, even if Mansell gets a problem, I am so far behind… it wasn't easy after that to fight on fully, to put the last ounce of effort into driving again. But I did." The race continued uneventfully, with only 12 of the original 26 starters left on the track. With six laps until the end of the race, Mansell stormed through the tunnel for the 71st time. As he did, he lost the back end of the Williams, and slid sideways across the track. He radioed his pit crew, informing them that he had a puncture in his left rear tyre and to prepare him another set of tyres. He drove to the pits at a reduced pace, but the Williams team, which had already packed away half the equipment, was caught off guard, completely unprepared for an unscheduled stop. His tyres were changed, but the stop was tardy and the new tyres that were fitted weren't heated properly.

After seeing Mansell's spin, followed by the frantic behaviour of the Williams pit crew, McLaren radioed Senna that now was his chance. They quickly calculated that Senna could get ahead if he started charging immediately. As Mansell pitted, Senna was entering the tunnel. He had to make his way round the rest of the track and get past Mansell during the pitstop. Mansell was crawling to the pits, and had a 10-15 second stop ahead of him, plus the time it took to drive the pitlane. Senna knew he could do it. He duly produced a blistering lap time. As he passed the pit straight, the McLaren personnel on the pitwall had their eyes firmly locked on the Williams, still in its bay on the pitlane. For the first time in 1992, something other than a Williams was leading a race. "I could see Ayrton go by and I knew I had lost it," Mansell said afterwards.

He rejoined on lap 72, with Senna leading by 5.1 seconds. Furious that he had lost the lead, Mansell proceeded to break the lap record twice in as many laps, with the final time standing at 1m 21.598secs at 91.234mph. Within three laps of Mansell leaving the pits, Senna's lead had been reduced to 2.1 seconds. Senna was driving on worn tyres that caused his car to slide every time he put the power down. Mansell's car was superior and the new rubber had by then warmed up to optimum temperature. Senna was tired, but he never gave up.

"I was always at the absolute limit," he explained afterwards. "At the technical limit, the car's limit and also my own human limit." Mansell attacked Senna's lead super-aggressively. But having seized the initiative, the Brazilian was not going to relinquish it. Mansell tried to squeeze through, but Senna kept his cool. As Mansell remembers: "Sometimes I saw three cars in front of me. I was driving very hard, but he did – from his point of view – what he had to do... we were both way over the limit."

With any other driver Mansell would have got past, even at Monaco. But this was a battle between the two finest drivers in the world at that point in history. Mansell had the faster car but Senna had track advantage. He knew where Mansell would try his hardest to regain the lead – at the chicane on the harbour front. It was there a year earlier that Mansell had taken second place from Alain Prost, and Senna knew Mansell would be planning an action replay. As they came to the chicane on lap 76, they came upon JJ Lehto's Dallara. Lehto pulled out of the way but the fractional delay to Senna was enough for

Mansell to sense his chance. But Senna kept his cool and stuck firmly to the racing line, leaving Mansell ducking and diving behind.

For the next two laps Mansell tried his hardest, darting across the track to find a way back into the lead. Around Loews hairpin on the last lap, Mansell pushed so hard he locked up, tyres smoking. Going into the final set of corners at Rascasse, Mansell made a last-gasp lunge down the inside and when that failed made another move around the outside. It was a brave attempt but he had to go too wide to clear the McLaren and his chance was lost.

"For the last five or six laps, I had nothing left to give," said Senna afterwards. "I knew Nigel would catch me on fresh tyres, that he would try everything and that I was in for a major war in the last three laps. It was exciting but very difficult because he was several seconds faster than me and I had no grip to put the power down. It was like being on ice. On the straights it was like a drag race, with wheelspin in third and fourth gear. Fortunately I only had three or four laps that way. But I gave it everything."

Senna attributed the power through the tunnel to the downforce and rear wing on the McLaren chassis, and Williams later countered that it was down to Honda horsepower. But it was neither. It was Senna's management of the track, the car and engine, and his superior driving skill. He was not just in control of himself and the car; he was controlling Mansell, his Williams and the entire race. His McLaren team-mate Gerhard Berger summed up Senna's performance perfectly: "Nobody but Senna could have won this race under these circumstances. Anybody else would have made a mistake."

Senna won the race just 0.215 seconds ahead of Mansell, elated but exhausted after the gruelling seven-lap chase. He got out of the car, took off his helmet and rubbed his face and hair, as if to try and wake up. His face was flushed from exertion, and sweat beaded on his forehead. Mansell, not as fit as his Brazilian rival, suffered chronic fatigue after the race. He staggered out of the car, bug-eyed from his failed attempts to pass Senna. He had to be steadied on the podium, and after the formalities were over, he collapsed on the ground clutching his bottle of champagne, totally worn out.

Ironically, Mansell hadn't had a puncture at all. A crooked, vibrating brake disc caused a wheel nut to loosen, which caused the wheel to wobble. Instead of a slow four-tyre change, the real problem could have been solved with a three-second burst from a wheel gun. "That is Monte Carlo," said Nigel ruefully. "Ayrton was fantastic. He did nothing wrong at all and I have no complaints." Mansell knew Senna had scored a popular win and broken the Williams dominance. His victory breathed fresh life into the stale 1992 season.

It was a triumph for Senna to savour and he lingered at the post-race press conference for nearly an hour, where the media congratulated him for breaking Mansell's run and winning the Hill trophy. "Monaco is the most important Grand Prix of all," he told them. "That's why it is so great to have equalled Hill's record here. For me, it is one of the greatest things that can be achieved in motor racing."

His victory in Monte Carlo in 1992 was the highlight of his 41 race wins. It was a victory against the odds and stopped Nigel Mansell establishing a new world record of six consecutive Grand Prix victories in one season. Unfortunately for Senna, Monte Carlo was about as good as it was going to get that season. Although Senna took pole, his team-mate Berger scooped the following round in Canada when Mansell, Senna and Patrese failed to finish, and then Mansell won the next three rounds in a row. Senna won the next, in Hungary, but Mansell's second place was enough to clinch both championships, with as many as five races of the season left to go.

Senna was demoralised and highly unsatisfied with his team's efforts. To make matters worse, Mansell had overtaken him as the premier figure in Formula One. When British police flagged down a speeding Porsche on the M25 and posed the question, 'Who do you think you are? Nigel Mansell?', the car's Brazilian driver replied wearily and truthfully: 'No, actually I'm Ayrton Senna'."

Naturally there were rumours that Senna would be leaving McLaren and even Formula One. At the British Grand Prix in July, Senna explained: "I will stop if I don't find a competitive car. There is no reason to risk my life for third place. The only pleasure I get from Formula One is being competitive. I cannot turn my back on McLaren because it has helped me take the title, but I want a team that can give me technical and organisational guarantees."

It was a warning to McLaren – and a sign of Senna's absolute commitment As well as Mansell, he had a new adversary to contend with in the form of Michael Schumacher. The 23-year-old German had burst onto the scene at the previous year's Belgian Grand Prix, making an impressive debut for Jordan. So impressive, in fact, that he was snatched away by Benetton in time for the following round in Italy. He remained with Benetton for the 1992 season, and while the team was usually not as fast as McLaren it had the greater reliability. This meant that with Mansell beyond reach, Senna and Schumacher would be fighting Patrese for second place in the championship.

In Schumacher, Senna had found an adversary who refused to be intimidated. The German accused Senna of blocking him in Brazil and on the first lap in France the pair collided, putting Senna out of the race. A few days later everything came to a head in pre-race testing for the German Grand Prix at Hockenheim. Senna, still mindful of his heavy testing at the track the previous year, accused Schumacher of blocking him. He grabbed Schumacher by the throat and Schumacher in turn tried to push him off – the pair had to be separated by McLaren mechanics before things became more serious. Schumacher shrugged off the incident and said: "He only massaged my neck. I was on my last lap and saw him in the mirror. I thought he would drive slowly. So I kept the line and drove completely normally into the pits. We have made up the quarrel. There is nothing more to say." But Senna refused to comment on whether the pair had reached reconciliation.

Schumacher won his first-ever race at the Belgian Grand Prix in late August by beating the field on the track in the wet. Senna, long renowned for working wet-weather miracles, could manage only fifth.

Reports surfaced that Senna had signed for Ferrari for the following season, but the Brazilian revealed he had rejected the offer. He also let it be known that he had offered to drive for Williams in 1993 for nothing. Whether he was serious no one knew, but it was probably designed to unsettle Prost's deal with Williams for that season, which by then was public knowledge.

The upcoming Italian Grand Prix was to prove momentous for its announcements. On the Friday, Honda finally announced it was withdrawing from Formula One at the end of the season. Then Frank Williams revealed that Alain Prost would be coming out of retirement to drive for the team in 1993. As a result, a disgruntled Mansell announced he would be heading to IndyCars. Senna would have loved to drive for Williams, but the arrival of Prost put paid to any hopes of that. Prost refused to have Senna in the team. His contract reputedly contained a 'no Senna' clause, although this was not yet public knowledge.

The two announcements were a double blow for Senna. His own team was scuppered and his escape route closed off on the same weekend. Faced with a choice between him or Prost, Williams had chosen Prost under pressure from Renault, which wanted a French world champion.

Venting his anger, he ran away with the race that weekend, taking only his third win of the season against the Williams steamroller after both Williams had retired.

In Portugal Senna learned about the 'no Senna' clause in Prost's Williams contract for 1993. He again offered to drive for Williams Renault for nothing, in order, he said, 'to show how strongly I want to get this car…' Finally realising the real opportunity of signing Senna for 1993, Williams tried to persuade Prost to drop the clause. Prost said to Williams, knowing he had the full backing of Renault: "If you get Senna, then I go." Renault desperately wanted a French world champion.

Senna was angry at Prost's refusal to have him in the same team. At the next race in Portugal he complained: "I think if Prost, who is already a three-time world champion, wants to be called the sole champion and maybe win another championship, he should be sporting. The way he is doing it, he is behaving like a coward. If he wants to be sporting he must be prepared to race anybody, under any conditions, on equal terms. The way he wants to win a championship, everything has been laid out for him before the start. It is like going for a 100-metre sprint and you are allowed to have running shoes while everyone else has to use lead shoes. That is the way he wants to race. It is not racing. And it is bad for all of us. We had two fantastic world championships last year and this year. And we had two very bad ones in 1989 and 1990. They were a consequence of unbelievable politics going on and bad behaviour by some people. I think now we are coming back to the same situation again."

Prost retaliated: "We have had all this in the past. He wants to manipulate everyone and to have his own way. He has done it before and he wants to do it again. I am sure we will face each other on the track again next year and it will be very important for the international federation to be strong."

Senna meanwhile had the fight for second place in the championship on his hands. A win for Patrese at the Japanese Grand Prix and a non-finish for Senna and Schumacher left it wide open as they entered the final round at Adelaide.

During the two weeks between the last two races of the 1992 season, in Japan and Australia, Senna was very pensive, undecided and a little bit unsure of himself. He really seemed not to know what he really wanted to do in 1993. Sometimes he looked almost desperately for explanations to justify carrying on with McLaren. At Spa in Belgium, he had said he was 99 per cent certain that he would leave McLaren and have a year off.

He told his great friend, the journalist Karin Sturm: "We can't know why many things happen the way they do. Perhaps for some reason I simply shouldn't drive next year, it's predestined. Such things are not always necessarily in our hands..."

Many of those who knew him best believed that to take a year off, as Prost did in 1992, and then come back, was impossible for him. If he went, then he went for good because in that time he would find something else to do that would give him 100 per cent fulfilment. "I don't know," he said after long reflection, "I really don't know, everything is possible."

On the other hand, would he last without racing at all? He, of all people, who believed racing was in a way like a drug, "sometimes on which one becomes dependent - and it's been proved that the human body in certain stress situations produce drug-like substances such as adrenalin…"

Here too, there was the same uncertainty and the unspoken plea: Please don't press me. I really don't know the answers myself.

Adelaide was the last race of the season, the farewell race of Nigel Mansell, the new world champion, who was leaving for the American IndyCar series. The two of them fought bitterly for the lead once again, until their last appearance together ended with a collision. On lap 19 of the 81-lap race, Senna came up behind leader Mansell and the pair collided on the slow 50mph. Mansell was livid, but the stewards and even the Williams team agreed that the crash had not been Senna's fault.

"Because Mansell braked 50 metres too early and caught me by surprise, I was so close behind him that I couldn't help driving into him," said Senna, who, after dropping out, watched the remainder of the race on the screen in the McLaren garage, keeping his fingers crossed for his team-mate Gerhard Berger. He was delighted when Berger won his last race for the team.

But there was no farewell between him and Mansell. He was annoyed by the collision and a little with his team for ditching him for Prost. In that he had a commonality of interest with Senna. Senna was disappointed Mansell had gone without a handshake of goodbye: "I would have liked to have said farewell to him with a handshake after so many years together in Formula One." Mansell left the track, seemingly turning his back on Formula One for good, without saying a word to Senna. The pair would never meet again.

As a result of the collision and Schumacher's second-place finish, Senna was forced into fourth place in the championship, behind Patrese and Schumacher, even though he had three victories to their one apiece. Reliability had been the issue: Senna had only finished half of the 16 races that season, a terrible record. It was an ignominious end to a far-from-illustrious season for Senna and his patience was beginning to wear thin.

When he got back to Brazil Senna resumed an affair he had had with a Brazilian model called Marcella Praddo. He had last seen her in 1985, when he first started driving for Lotus. He soon realised why it hadn't lasted then, and after a month it was over, as he played the field again. At the end of 1992 the world had got out in Brazil that his relationship with Xuxa Meneghel was well and truly over and the pair were not even seeing each other occasionally. That winter, it seemed that every single girl in Brazil was making a play for him. He enjoyed himself immensely, virtually entertaining a different girl every weekend at his beach house in Angra. His racing life may have been in chaos but his personal life couldn't have been better. And it was scheduled to get even better still come the New Year.

As he relaxed at Angra, he had plenty to think about that winter. First, he had no drive for 1993, although the McLaren was his for the taking; second, the team had no engine; and third, a new young rival had appeared who was fast and threatening and was certain to give him trouble in the future. Lastly, his old rival Alain Prost would be driving the fastest car and would be untouchable. In actual fact it was to turn out nowhere nearly as badly as Senna imagined. But he had no way of knowing that then. His mission for 1993 was to secure himself a Williams drive for 1994.

Meanwhile, Ron Dennis was doing all he could to solve his engine problem so as to make sure he could offer Senna a competitive package in 1993 and possibly beyond. The key to that was securing a Renault deal.

As soon as he knew Honda was leaving, he made a beeline for Renault and the head of Renault Sport, Patrick Faure. Dennis knew Renault would let out a second supply of engines at some point and he wanted them. But Frank Williams and Patrick Head got in his way. Twice they had seen Dennis snatch away valuable contracts they had in the past, and this time they were ready for him. Dennis, as hard as he tried, found his way blocked at Renault. The engines would be supplied to Williams for five years, under an exclusive basis. The exclusivity could not be broken. And it is believed that the contract also contained a 'no McLaren' clause. Frank Williams had learnt his lesson and Dennis was paying the price of previous plunders.

But in the course of his travels in France, Dennis began a relationship with car-maker Peugeot, which wanted to enter Formula One. It was a relationship that would bear fruit for 1994 but not solve his 1993 problem. For that he increasingly realised he would have to speak to Cosworth Engineering, the Formula One engine-maker based in Northampton, England. Cosworth had a budget again from Ford and was in a strong phase. But another barrier was up there as well in the shape of Flavio Briatore, the team principal of Benetton. Briatore did not have an exclusivity clause but he had a deal whereby, if Cosworth supplied a second team, it had to be two specifications of engine backwards. As the latest specification engines would have pneumatic valves, then they would be a long way from what Benetton had. In the end Dennis settled for that, and it would be announced in the New Year. In truth Senna had nowhere else to go in 1993, although 1994 would prove another story.

CHAPTER 20

The James Bond Years

Three golden seasons with Gerhard

Gerhard Berger labels the three years 1990 to 1992 as 'the James Bond years' – a period he and Senna spent together as team-mates at McLaren when money, success and girls littered every corner of their lives. It is a moment in time he says will never be repeated, when life was a big game and the world was at their feet.

And what a game it was. The two wealthy young racing drivers lived a life few can comprehend. Not only did they have incredible amounts of money – both earned in excess of $12 million a year from salary and sponsorships – but they were adored around the world and were heroes to 100 million people.

Berger readily admits: "We certainly had a good life. Ayrton had a great house in Angra and I had a nice yacht, jet and helicopter. I remember on one occasion when I went to visit him in Brazil, we decided to take the helicopter to go swimming. We landed on the beach, causing complete chaos as no one could see a thing – they all had sand in their eyes; then we calmly got out, went swimming and returned to the helicopter. On the one side you could say we were being childish.

"We had everything that it was possible to have materially – planes, helicopters, fantastic houses and we had fantastic careers. It's only afterwards, sitting here today, that I realise just how fantastic it really was. We lived the kind of life you only see in a James Bond film, but even in the James Bond films there is always a tragedy and unfortunately, Ayrton had the role of the tragic hero."

Gerhard Berger and Ayrton Senna hit it off from day one. They met in 1983, while competing in international Formula Three, and instantly became friends. They had a lot in common – both had wealthy self-made business-men as fathers – and both were struggling to make it into Formula One. It was a friendship that endured right up until 1st May 1994 when, 15 minutes before the flag went up on the San Marino Grand Prix, they exchanged grins for the last time. The James Bond years may have been over but the memories remained. Understandably, ever since that fateful day, competing at Imola has held dark memories for Berger. And not only because that is where he lost his best friend. The infamous circuit was the scene of a similar accident five years before, on 23rd April 1989 – one in which Berger himself was lucky to escape with his life.

He remembers the details of his own accident as if it were yesterday, despite the fact that it is now 13 years ago. He admits that when it happened, his whole life rushed before him and he was convinced that he was not going to survive.

At the time he was team-mates with Nigel Mansell and had started fifth on the grid. Ferrari was on a high. Against all expectations it had won the first race of the season in Brazil and had high hopes on home turf. Mansell and Berger were the darlings of the crowd.

As Berger says: "Perhaps the strangest thing about my time with Ayrton is the fact that I had my big accident in exactly the same place as he had his, the Tamburello curve at Imola." Berger can't quite come to terms with the deep irony of this, and the astonishing coincidences that led to a series of events involving him, Senna and Tamburello that defy explanation.

At the start of that 1989 Grand Prix, Senna and Prost were followed by Mansell in third and Berger in fifth. The accident happened during the fourth lap, when Berger's Ferrari went straight on at the Tamburello, crashing into the wall at around 160mph. The impact destroyed the car, which bounced down the wall for 100 metres before bursting into flames. It took 20 long seconds to put out the fire – a surprise considering fires had virtually been eradicated from Formula One by then.

By all accounts it was a smaller accident than Senna's, far less violent. But even though he survived the impact, it was still a miracle that he then survived the flames – a fact not lost on the Austrian.

As he lost control of the car, Berger remembers thinking that he was going to die. "Just before I hit the wall I remember thinking 'oh shit Gerhard, this is not going to work out, you're not going to survive'. So I put my hands across my chest and braced myself for the impact," he says.

Berger was unconscious when Sid Watkins found him. "The next thing I knew I woke up and there was Professor Watkins sitting on my chest trying to get a tube down my throat. It really hurt, so I knew I was still alive."

He had a broken rib, chemical burns to his body from the fuel spillage and second-degree burns to his hands. In a scene very reminiscent of Senna's crash five years later, the race was stopped while Berger was tended to and airlifted to hospital. He says: "The next day Ayrton phoned me to see how I was and I said to him 'Ayrton, we have to change that fucking wall, it's too dangerous'."

Berger's burns meant he missed the Monaco Grand Prix but recovered in time for the Mexican race a month later on 28th May.

When they returned to test at Imola the following year, Senna and Berger walked out to the Tamburello corner. As Berger remembers: "Ayrton and I walked to the Tamburello to see what could be done. Ayrton looked behind the wall and saw there was a river and he said to me: 'Gerhard, we can't change it because there is a river behind it.' We looked at each other and agreed that there was nothing we could do to change it. I said to Ayrton: 'I know we can't do anything but someone is going to die at this corner.' Sure enough he died at exactly the place where we were standing and talking."

Berger and Senna first met in 1983 when Berger was having difficulties with his Formula Three car at Silverstone. Senna was dominating the British series, but both were competing in a European Championship round at the Northamptonshire venue and using different tyres from the Avons that were mandatory for the British Championship. Berger says: "I had the worst of set-ups at Silverstone, so I went to talk to Dick Bennetts (co-owner of West Surrey Racing, Senna's Formula Three entrant) and Ayrton was sitting with him. I asked them which gears I needed and which springs, and Ayrton just looked at me as if to say 'who is this guy who just pops round the corner and starts asking me what his set-up should be?' At that time we didn't have a clue how the future would turn out but there was a good empathy between us and we knew we liked each other."

They were not particularly friendly at this point. But Senna's highly competitive nature was intrigued by Berger's more open approach.

They met again later that year at the prestigious Macau GP for Formula Three cars. At the time, neither driver had much idea of his true destiny, but Senna was already headed for Formula One with Toleman. Berger says: Ayrton won the race and I came third, but they gave me the quickest lap. I thought there must be some mistake, as I was convinced Ayrton had run the fastest lap, but they gave it to me so I forgot about the controversy and just accepted it. That evening there was a party and it was there that I met Ayrton for the first time. He said to me 'look, I have the quickest lap'. But all the official reports were out so there was no point in arguing. I just said to him 'you have it but it's mine!' Then we had our first chat and we had a laugh and got on very well. I think that a friendship had already started without us even knowing."

In 1987 Senna took more serious notice of Berger when he moved to Ferrari from Benetton. At the time, Senna was struggling at Lotus and clearly envious that Berger had snagged a top drive. "Ayrton suddenly realised there was another competitor he needed to get rid of, so he started being very friendly, questioning me on how things worked at Ferrari so he could glean all the information he could," says Berger. "That was his way – the moment he realised that someone or something could take away what he wanted, he would focus fully on that person or thing to fathom out how it worked."

It was then that the friendship really began to develop. There is a myth that Berger taught Senna to laugh and Senna taught Berger to race, but the truth is a little more complex than that. As Berger admits: "Ayrton had a big advantage in that he already had a lot of race experience as he had started racing at four, whereas I was 21. He worked hard but I didn't see him working harder than other top drivers – he just had a special talent for concentration. He was fully concentrated the whole time – he recognised his weak points and worked on them until they had been corrected. He really did have an unbelievable understanding of the whole show – the politics, the fights on the circuit, analysing technical data and driving lines. He understood the whole game."

Senna's mastery of Formula One was never in question. But he didn't have the same strengths in all areas of his life. As Berger admits, the Brazilian was never worldly-wise. "As Ayrton had started racing so young, he never did anything else, whereas I had a lot of experience of real life and had already been through the discos and nightlife era. I had to bring something to the friendship that he hadn't experienced and that was it. But it isn't true I taught him to have fun - there is no one better than a Brazilian to know what to do in a disco – they are born to it. He just had to be led there and then he would get on with it."

Because Berger has never spoken about Senna and the friendship they shared, he has allowed the many myths that have evolved over the years to go unanswered.

He says now: "In life, and above all in the world of motor racing, everyone plays a role. Senna played the role of the 200 per cent committed racing driver and I played the role of funny boy, but the truth was we were both committed to racing and we both had fun in our private lives. It was clear to both of us that we had a racing career ahead of us, and we had to concentrate on that."

In 1990 Berger left Ferrari and became Senna's team-mate at McLaren Honda when Alain Prost left to take his place at Ferrari. Senna had had an unhappy time with Prost and Berger proved to be a breath of fresh air, creating arguably the friendliest set-up between team-mates in the history of Formula One.

It marked the start of three years of happiness for both men. It was also the first real test of their relationship, as Senna was clearly the faster driver in identical cars. In the previous two years he had vanquished Alain Prost, often qualifying over a second faster. Suddenly he had a team-mate who was pushing him hard and qualifying within two-10ths of a second most of the time.

Berger remembers: "If you put all the qualifying times together then maybe I was closest to Ayrton. I saw his talent and experience, and I knew I couldn't regularly beat him so I just did my best, and got as close as possible. But I didn't fight him or let silliness destroy a good friendship. Maybe I did it differently from Alain.

"Obviously Ayrton was the dominant factor at McLaren – he was world champion, the best driver in the world, he had an unbelievable personality, and everyone was behind him, supporting him. But he never made me feel less because of that. Except at critical moments like when he was going for the world championship, I always had the feeling that the team was as happy if I won as if Ayrton won. Maybe that was because of the way I approached the situation."

Berger has his own clear-cut ideas about why the Senna-Prost relationship was so full of conflict. "If you have someone like Ayrton or Schumacher as your team-mate then there are different ways you can handle it. At that time Ayrton was clearly the best and everyone knew that. Alain was in the same car and knew he didn't have a chance of beating Ayrton in speed terms, so he realised quite quickly that pace couldn't compensate. At that point he had the chance to say 'okay, I'll find my own level and work at that, and get the team working with me as well'. But he refused to accept the situation so it all became political – he found fault with everything, and didn't hesitate to allocate blame. It caused a lot of aggravation and that was a problem for

Ayrton, as he knew he was the best and that Alain was simply finding fault. It was clear there was going to be a big explosion."

Not that everything was always smooth between Senna and Berger. Berger soon realised that his team-mate would use any method possible to maintain his advantage and would be completely ruthless in achieving his ambitions. He learnt this to his cost when he brought his Ferrari race engineer, Giorgio Ascanelli, with him to McLaren.

Ascanelli is regarded as a brilliant engineer, a technical genius who can grasp and solve a problem before the driver has even had time to step out of his car. Berger agrees: "Giorgio was my race engineer at Ferrari and he was the best. But I underestimated his importance – all I had to do was say three words to him when I came back to the pits and he would know exactly what I needed to go quicker. When I went to McLaren it all became more difficult – they didn't understand as well, so I knew I had to get Giorgio to switch teams too. I finally managed to persuade him to move to McLaren and then Ron Dennis told me he was going to be working with Ayrton.

"That just summed up Ayrton. He realised that I was about to gain an advantage and corrected it before it had a chance to happen. It was my fault – I simply didn't fight hard enough. Giorgio and Ayrton started working together and although they had a few problems initially, they soon became an unbeatable combination."

Early in 1992 the Honda board of directors decided to pull out of Formula One. Soichiro Honda told Ayrton Senna before McLaren team principal Ron Dennis. And Senna told Berger. They both decided it was time they made their exits, as it was clear a down period would begin at McLaren without the Honda engine. As Berger says: "We agreed it was time to jump ship but we had different objectives. For me money was very important but Ayrton wanted to increase his success, so he was looking for the best technical option. At the time it was clearly Williams. Technical prowess wasn't my motivating factor – I wanted to go back to Ferrari because I enjoyed being with the team and although it was bad technically at the time, that was a challenge to me as I knew that sooner or later it would come good again. I decided I would go back for the right amount of money and I got it so I went back. Ayrton and I spoke about it and I said 'okay, I'll go there and have a look, maybe I can move a few things, get things going and in a year or two you can come too'. In the meantime he aimed for Williams. Unfortunately his negotiations with Frank stumbled and so he had to stay at McLaren for another year. If he had joined me at

Ferrari, I have no doubt that he would have enjoyed the same level of success as Michael Schumacher has had."

Senna had already initiated a long dialogue with Frank Williams in order to secure a drive with the team. The only problem was his hated rival Prost had got there first. Berger says: "Ayrton told me he was going to drive for Williams – that he had fixed everything with Frank and the deal was going ahead. Then everything turned around and he said he was never going to work for Williams. Two months later he was back on the trail again. He said he had to try and drive for Williams because it was the only car that would allow him to win everything in the future. During this time there were continuous negotiations and it was clear that Ayrton was going to end up at Williams sooner or later. Ron tried everything to hold onto him but he didn't have the right technical package, he only had money and Ayrton wanted world championships so it was clear that he was going to go eventually."

Senna had a traumatic time with Ron Dennis over his departure. Berger says the Brazilian's relationship with Dennis was ruptured: "Those kind of negotiations always destroy a little of the relationship and especially with Ron, who is very protective of his team. He always believes he has the best and can never accept otherwise, but everyone loved Ayrton as he did such a lot for the team, and after the negotiations were completed, the relationship with Ron was quietly put back in place."

Before that Senna had no choice but to stay put and sign a provisional agreement with Ron Dennis for 1993. It led to a famous incident on a short helicopter trip when Berger tossed Senna's briefcase out of the door mid-flight. He confirms that this unlikely story is actually true: "Just after he had re-signed for McLaren we were staying at the Villa d'Este on Lake Como for the Italian Grand Prix at Monza in 1992," says Berger. "That morning, just before we boarded the helicopter, Ayrton told me he had just agreed another year with McLaren. So when we were airborne I decided to throw his briefcase out of the helicopter – it was all part of the game at the time."

The seven years Berger and Senna were friends has provided the Austrian with a collection of incredible memories that means he will inevitably one day write his own book about his time with his Formula One team-mate. But that is not for now – as he says, not enough time has passed yet.

At times Berger frightened Senna off the track. In 1992 Senna said: "He's dangerous sometimes because you never know to what level he will play games. From that point of view he's a difficult man, but on the other hand he has a good character and we have got along very well all those years."

Berger has many special memories of Senna the driver. And surprisingly says his best performances came in his three races for Williams. "The most impressive times he put in were with Williams," he says. "At the time it wasn't really a car for putting on pole position but that didn't bother Ayrton – he did it anyway. He was very special in qualifying.

"I remember one qualifying session with him at Imola when we were both driving for McLaren. I was quickest, then he was quickest, so I went quicker and then he went out again and went even quicker – we just drove against each other. Then we started to look at each other before the other one went out and after a while he undid his seatbelt, came over to me and said 'hey, it's becoming dangerous now' and I said 'yeah, let's go and do another round'. He was able to rise to every challenge that was presented to him."

Berger sees lots of similarities between Senna and Schumacher: "Ayrton and Michael are very similar in the way they approach things. When I talk to Michael he reminds me a lot of Ayrton, the way he analyses things and the wide view he has of everything. I don't see anyone else in Formula One at the moment who is similar to Michael," he says. "I had a very sensitive feeling for the technical side, for what had to be changed on the car, but these guys have a much better understanding of what to focus on. They don't try and fix 10 things at the same time, they pick two and fix them 100 per cent, and that's what really makes the difference. You can go for all 10 problems and fix them all one by one and go faster, but what really makes the difference is identifying the two or three problems that, when fixed, will really make you go quicker. Michael will recognise that difference – just as Ayrton used to. The car can be understeering, jumping, or whatever, but they immediately know which is the one factor that needs to be changed to make it go two–10ths of a second quicker. Most drivers don't have that talent."

Berger's last memory of Ayrton is of him turning around to smile at him on the grid as the drivers' names were called out and the San Marino crowd cheered. "It was the smile of a friend who was pleased to see the people's support and love for me. That is the last thing I remember of him," he says.

"After the accident some people were saying there was no problem, he was out of the car, and others were saying there was a big problem, but at the time I didn't realise how bad it was. I had to stop the race after six or seven laps and come into the pits. Another driver – I don't remember who – came up to me and told me Ayrton was in a bad way, that he was in hospital in Bologna and very critical. Then immediately after that, suddenly there was a mechanic flying through the air in front of me – the result of another accident – this time in the Lotus pits when Michele Alboreto lost a rear wheel during his pitstop. I was just sitting thinking 'shit, what is happening now?'

"Sid Watkins was at the hospital with Ayrton and he told me it was very, very, very critical and basically there was no chance of him pulling through. Then they let me into his room and that was the last time I saw him. I spent a few minutes with him and then that was that. In this life you are a little prepared for death – in fact during my career a lot of my team-mates and friends have died – Michele Alboreto, Elio de Angelis, Manfred Winkelhock, Jo Gartner. But of all of them, Ayrton was my closest friend and although it wasn't entirely unexpected, it really hurt."

After he had said his final goodbyes to the man who had shared his life, Berger flew straight home to Austria and shut himself away in his house. "I didn't talk to anyone for two days. I watched the telephone filling up with messages but I didn't feel like talking to anyone about it as nothing could change things. I just wanted to spend some time alone before flying to Brazil for the funeral." He and Johnny Herbert were the only two Formula One drivers to go to both Senna's and Ratzenberger's funerals.

Berger has had plenty of time to mull over the cause of that tragic accident, and come to his own conclusions. "For me it wasn't an accident due to a lack of concentration, or a driver error, which you simply can't have on a dry circuit at this corner. I don't know what it was but for me it was a technical problem. Everyone has questioned Ayrton's concentration and whether he was distracted by Roland Ratzenberger's death the day before, but Ayrton was the master of concentration and once he was at the start he would have put away everything and concentrated on the race ahead. A professional racing driver can concentrate even in difficult times because he knows if he doesn't it could cost him his life."

Berger believes Senna was the best of the best: "Ayrton was a very special person. He had a very special way of presenting himself, of making his show, but he also had a big heart and looked after people around him. He loved Brazil – he was full-on Brazilian and very Latin. From time to time in the world you have someone really special, Enzo Ferrari was someone very special, but not just from the world of motor racing, it could be a president or a leader, or just an ordinary person with special qualities. For me Ayrton was one of these special people. In terms of performance Schumacher is as good as Ayrton, but from a human aspect Ayrton was one in a million. He was indeed a great and very special man. I miss him as a colleague but most of all as a very great friend, and he will never be forgotten."

CHAPTER 21

1993: The Split with McLaren

A year of pleasure and complication

As 1992 ended and 1993 began, Ayrton Senna had plenty of time to relax, rest and review his life. At the end of 1992 he became a free agent and was out of contract with McLaren, which meant he had no sponsor commitments for the team and, more importantly, no testing to do. Senna hated testing – he thought it largely a waste of time. He also believed that endless grinding around the track dulled his driving edge. He preferred to leave it to others. In fact he often found test sessions were just thinly-disguised promotional events for McLaren sponsors, with him roped in.

Not being tied to a team meant that for almost four months he was able to indulge himself in the pursuit of pleasure and for the first few weeks of 1993, following the Christmas holiday period, he had few cares in the world. Only as January closed did a cloud descend over him, as he wondered if he had overplayed his hand with Ron Dennis.

When he returned to Brazil from Australia he had initially been depressed. He was badly disappointed that he had been beaten to the Williams drive by Alain Prost, and realised he should have made a different, more strategic decision at the end of 1990 when his contract with McLaren expired.

That winter his mood swung between giving up for 1993 – avoiding another frustrating year with no chance of winning or challenging Prost – and beating him with an inferior car. He doubted the wisdom of handing Prost the world championship without a fight. But no one would have been surprised if he had taken a year's sabbatical, as Prost had done in 1992 before joining Williams. At the 1992 Silverstone race, when he realised that Prost had outfoxed him, he said: "I'd rather have a year off, like Prost this year." In fact that is what most people expected him to do. All except him. In his heart of hearts, he knew he never could.

Being out of contract is a double-edged sword. It gives maximum flexibility, but the money is neither flowing nor guaranteed. However, that winter Senna refused to let concerns over money mar his time off. He decided to put it out of his mind and focus on his farm at Tatui.

The rebuilding and development of the farm was completely finished by early 1993. The work had taken several years, having started when Senna first took it over in 1989-1990. The end result was a total transformation – from a pretty mundane farm to something quite spectacular.

When the builders eventually left, it was clear that Tatui had been turned into a proper small estate in the old style. Although the original farming continued, the principal object of the estate was as a pleasure palace for Senna and his family.

The work to create this rural paradise had included some major projects, among them the joining of two lakes to create one huge water feature. Senna said: "There were originally two lakes, one higher than the other. We decided to join them to make one big lake of over a kilometre in length. The water is natural spring water, it is completely clean." Once the work was complete, he then had the new lake stocked with over 100,000 fish so the family could enjoy some superb fishing.

Work on the main house took almost three-and-a-half years to complete. The main object was to ensure that the living rooms and 10 bedrooms all faced the lake so there were waterside views from all the main windows. As a finishing touch Senna added a boathouse and moved hundreds of trees around. He said: "Everything is facing the lake so there is always a view of the water. There is a tennis court right in front, and a boathouse on the left. We have tried to preserve the original trees so that the atmosphere and the environment remain as untouched as possible." The house also had a magnificent swimming pool in front of the lake, and a world-class go-kart track down one side.

When Senna had finished he was like an artist surveying a canvas. It was clear to the Brazilian TV crews and journalists who visited that he loved his farm. As he told them: "Being close to nature is wonderful. It really helps me relax."

He had also built 10 new houses on the estate for his farm workers. He explained that he wanted the people who worked for him to have a good way of life. He personally supervised their design and construction: "It is nice to see new things done properly, with the right shape, right design and right style," he said.

Senna got a lot of pleasure out of spending his vast fortune but his wealth troubled his conscience. He soothed it by giving away around $4 million a year to the poor of São Paulo. He said: "Brazil has lots of problems, lots of difficulties, but I try to focus on the good things it has to offer. It is a paradise – you can have peace, be close to nature, and enjoy life in your spare time. There is a beautiful ocean and beautiful vegetation – this is where I recharge my batteries before going back to my racing car, and once you experience that it is difficult to live without it. It is a way of finding your equilibrium. Whenever it is possible I like to get away from big cities and be close to nature, either by the sea or in the country."

Senna never had any doubt about the purpose of his farm at Tatui. It was not only for him but for his sister Viviane and her three children, his mother Neyde, father Milton and brother Leonardo. They were his family and they were sacred to him. In fact he told them that the farm was not his but theirs, and they were to treat it as their own without reference to him at all. He created it so perfectly to pay them back. He knew his father would enjoy the fishing; his mother the farm; his sister the tennis; his brother and nieces the swimming pool; and his nephew the go-kart track. He would enjoy watching them enjoy it. He was also desperate for them to be together as much as possible, and the farm was another way of ensuring that happened. Even today people do not appreciate how close he was to his family and what an incredibly tight bunch they were. As he said: "I am very fortunate because my father and mother gave me the fundamental feelings that I have today."

But as January 1993 drew to a close, his focus was back on racing and the forthcoming season. And the game of poker with Ron Dennis began.

There was no precedent for the situation he found himself in. He had made the decision to leave the team in early 1992. As he said: "It is a decision I made. It was within myself. I didn't share it with anyone. But I knew I had to move. I had to do something else. It was the right thing for me, and I feel confident I have made the right decision." But making the decision and actually leaving were two different things.

It was only because of his enormous clout as the best driver in the world that he knew he could get away with behaving as he did at McLaren. The team looked up to him, as Josef Leberer confirmed: "He was very hard on himself and he was very hard to the others and he was hard to himself as well, and that is why they respected him so much."

But Senna had increasing disrespect for his team principal, Ron Dennis. There had been frequent clashes with Dennis, minor in nature, but clashes nonetheless. He realised he had been with Dennis too long – they were simply too familiar with each other, and familiarity had bred contempt. Dennis annoyed him intensely in early February as they began to have discussions about salary if he did return to drive. Dennis had by then sensed Senna had nowhere else to go in 1993; his only rival was a sabbatical. As he had done to Niki Lauda in 1985, when he had sensed he had nowhere to go after his championship year (and later with Damon Hill in 1997 and Mika Häkkinen in 2001), he made an insulting lowball offer. He offered $5 million, plus performance bonuses. Senna told him he wanted a minimum of $15 million, which was $1 million less than he had earned in 1992. But Dennis was under pressure as well. His lowball offer was a bluff. He was being pushed by Marlboro boss John Hogan to sign Senna.

The negotiations with Dennis made Senna realise he had made a huge mistake in 1990 when he had missed the opportunity to drive with Williams in 1991. Then he had decided his future lay with McLaren and Honda. But now Honda was gone, and McLaren faced an uncertain future as a non-works engine team. The 1992 season had been terrible and his McLaren Honda MP4/7A had not come close to the mighty Williams Renault FW14B driven by Nigel Mansell and Riccardo Patrese. In 1992 Senna had won just three races and taken only one pole position – by his standards it was a disaster, almost a return to the Lotus years of 1985-1987. But he knew he only had himself to blame and that he had to make the best of it.

As he pondered his options at the beginning of 1993, he realised he had not spoken to Ron Dennis seriously since the final race of the season at Adelaide, when he had left without staying for McLaren's traditional Sunday night party at the Adelaide Hilton. Before he left he had dangled a carrot in front of Dennis – if he could sort out a reasonable engine deal over the winter months, Senna would test the car in January or February and decide what to do then. As a three-time world champion, he was confident he could afford to keep his options open and leave things late, because there would always be someone wanting to offer him a drive. Some people still believed he would choose to take a year off, but most knew he would find it impossible to live without racing for that long.

Speculation was wild. In the press, Senna was linked with all the top teams. The Italians were convinced that he would be heading to Ferrari, despite the contracts of Jean Alesi and Gerhard Berger, already in place for the following season. Prost's public spat with FISA led to rumours that the Frenchman would have his licence revoked and Senna would get the Williams drive after all.

He was aided by the fact that the entry list for the 1993 championship turned out to be a shambles, not only because of the Senna-McLaren wrangling. Williams Renault initially forgot to submit its entry form and its participation had to be agreed on by every other team before it could go ahead. Williams' number-one driver, Alain Prost, fresh out of retirement, was also in doubt after he launched an astonishing assault on FISA in the French press over the winter.

Even when McLaren announced a Ford engine deal at the beginning of December, it did nothing to quell the rumours. McLaren would only be a customer team, and it was expected that the engines would lack the power of the works units supplied to Benetton. Benetton would get the latest engine with pneumatic valves instead of springs. Senna's would have springs and be 15-30 horsepower down.

With that in mind Senna could see no reason to commit himself early to McLaren, and the Williams situation was promising enough to wait. Prost had got himself into a real mess when Max Mosley had taken over from Jean-Marie Balestre as FISA president at the end of 1991. Now the boot was on the other foot and Mosley had taken offence to some remarks Prost had made about FISA. FISA was no longer under Prost's influence as it had been in the Balestre days, and Mosley had refused him and the team an entry. It was unsure at that stage whether the Williams team's problems would even be resolved, although it was unthinkable they would not. Whilst that situation was fluid, Senna preferred to wait and see if Prost was ejected from Formula One.

Meanwhile Ron Dennis was playing his own game. He had lured Mika Häkkinen from Lotus as test driver for 1993, and already had Mario Andretti's son Michael signed as number two. If Senna didn't drive, then Häkkinen would.

It seemed as if McLaren had made Senna's decision for him on 10th February, when the FISA entry list revealed that McLaren had named Michael Andretti and Mika Häkkinen as its drivers for the coming season, leaving Senna out in the cold.

Dennis had taken the psychological advantage, and Senna's office was by all accounts thrown into a state of confusion. His five years with McLaren had earned him $60 million, and another $60 million from his outside sponsors and businesses. He had spent some of it buying a 16-storey office building in the Edificio Vari suburb of São Paulo. His business empire, under the umbrella of Ayrton Senna Promotions, occupied the top seven floors. He appointed his father, his younger brother Leonardo and his cousin Fabio Machedo to run the business day-to-day so that he could focus on his racing.

The attraction of the building was that he could have a pad on the roof to land his $1.2 million helicopter, which he flew himself. He had also bought a new HS125 jet at a cost of $7.9 million, which was kept in Europe. In addition he was funding the development of various new businesses, making sizeable charitable donations, and having to maintain no fewer than five homes. It had created huge overheads, which meant Senna needed to drive in 1993 to keep things ticking over. If he didn't he would have to return a lot of money to sponsors, and cashflow would dry up. He would not be poor but he would be poorer, and would have to stop doing some of the things he had planned.

The announcement of McLaren's drivers, without Senna's name on the entry sheet, literally panicked him into action. He was at his beach house in Angra when he got the news from his cousin Fabio Machedo at the Senna offices in São Paulo. Suddenly he was not sure if he held a strong hand or not. The telephone lines between Angra, São Paulo and Woking were sizzling after several long telephone calls between Senna and Dennis. The next day Senna's name was officially added to the team entry, taking advantage of a new rule which said a team could nominate three drivers for two places, something that had clearly gone unnoticed by Senna's advisers.

Although Dennis held the advantage, knowing Senna wanted to race, under renewed pressure from Hogan, and irked by FISA's 10th February announcement, he also knew he would have to pay him the going rate. Senna finally agreed to drive for McLaren in 1993, although only on a race-by-race basis. He told Dennis he would test the new McLaren Ford MP4/8 at the end of February, and if it was competitive he would drive at the first race of the season in South Africa.

Even from his weakened position, Senna had got Dennis to agree to pay him a salary of $1 million to race at the Kyalami circuit. Dennis was sanguine about the situation. He knew that Senna would find the McLaren Ford a much better proposition than he thought. The new engine had prompted a new design and it featured all the latest electronic gizmos – including active suspension – that McLaren had got right first time out and which Dennis believed was better than the Williams version. This was no surprise, given its huge in-house electronics expertise and resources.

Dennis was realistic enough to see that Senna's loyalty owed everything to McLaren's ability to supply him with equipment capable of winning. But underneath he resented Senna's apparent willingness to desert McLaren so quickly when things were not going so well. When asked about the Senna situation, he always paused and chose his words carefully, as if he was still wrestling with the reasons for the effective disintegration of their relationship. "The relationship, obviously, has been a good one," said Dennis, a faraway look in his eyes. "We've achieved a lot of good results together. But like all relationships, when things aren't going the way you want them to, they become strained. And it's at times like that, by desire, you hope you come closer together. But in reality – and this really applies to all people in Formula One, who are very competitive people – you tend to pull apart. You're committed individuals who are focused on the tasks of winning and achieving, and when you're not doing that you build up in yourself a range of reasons, based on logic, and then look to the situation to identify and apportion blame. Of course, if you are a proven world champion who has won lots of races, it's quite obvious that why you're not winning now is because you've not got the right equipment. And of course Ayrton hasn't."

Dennis's handling of the situation was deft. Rather than issuing fruitless denials and glossed-over press releases, he admitted the Ford engines had inferior power, and that the team was trailing the frontrunners in aerodynamics and other parts of the package. He also admitted the car was not reliable enough, as he said: "To overcome the disadvantages our cars have to be pushed harder, which puts greater stress on the components and creates problems of unreliability. All these things make for a frustrating time which, as a team, we have to bear... and share."

The only criticism Dennis was prepared to make of Senna was his reluctance to share the bad times along with the good. At the time Dennis wasn't to know that the bad times were set to last four years. He knew (but Senna didn't) that he would have works Peugeot engines for 1994 and thought the team would immediately bounce back. Dennis saw Senna's reluctance to share the burden, and help get McLaren back on course, as a deficiency and suggested it was an unreasonable attitude. He said: "His main weakness is not being tolerant of uncompetitiveness, which is always going to exist in a racing team. You're just not going to get it right every year. And if you are not winning, obviously you are not doing your job, you are not fulfilling the fundamental objective of the team. For us, and specifically for me, it is extremely painful to be uncompetitive. It is that pain which pushes us in our desire to be competitive. But there is no magic in it, and it takes time."

All in all, Senna could not complain about Dennis's treatment of him in public, and the first test of the new McLaren Ford MP4/8 went better than Senna could have expected. He found himself happy to race it.

Just a week after he had first driven the new McLaren Ford, Senna stepped off the overnight flight from London to Johannesburg on the Wednesday morning before the South African Grand Prix. "I feel tired," he admitted. "But I am pleased to have made my decision and happy to be racing this weekend. It has all happened quickly. There has not been much time. But the car is reasonably good and I am sure it will be competitive. I would not be here otherwise, would I?"

A press conference scheduled for the following day was promised to reveal everything. It didn't. Senna said he wanted to fight for the championship and praised the MP4/8. Dennis said he was considering running a three-car team at some races that season.

At first it looked as if the Williams team's total domination of the previous season was no more. Prost took pole, but Senna was just 0.088 seconds behind, the pair of them one-and-a-half seconds ahead of the rest. At the start, Senna took the lead when Prost almost stalled. He bravely held the Frenchman off until lap 23, when Prost forced his way through in the clearly faster car. It was a good hard fight, but the rivals were set to have their first falling-out of the year on the very first weekend of Prost's return to racing. In the final laps, a sudden storm passed over the circuit and Prost gesticulated wildly for the race to be stopped early, later explaining he believed that 'for safety reasons they should have stopped the race – it could have been very dangerous'. It reminded some people of Monaco in 1984, when Prost had urged for the race to be stopped in the rain and Senna had lost out as a result. Senna shrugged: "I agree on safety reasons but not for competition. You have the choice to stop if you want. Or you can carry on."

Prost had returned to racing in the best car and had won the first race convincingly, but his off-track relationships were still causing him grief. In the week after Kyalami he was called to Paris to face the FISA world council over his anti-FISA stance. Most people expected he would be hit by a multiple-race ban – some even suggested that Senna would take advantage of his race-by-race contract to jump into the FW15C and replace him. But Prost, perhaps sensing Senna's invisible hand on his shoulder, was full of righteous rhetoric to support his case. Playing the martyr, he said:"After being in motor racing for 20 years, in Formula One for 12 and winning 44 Grand Prix races and three world titles, I think I have the right to express my opinions." On the day, he capitulated and told the world his remarks had been misinterpreted and he had never criticised FISA. Max Mosley let him off.

With his last chance of joining Williams gone, Senna announced on the Wednesday before the Brazilian Grand Prix that he would be driving in his home event. "This is the same agreement we had for the South African Grand Prix and after the race we will talk about the rest of the season, which is our objective," he said. On race day, the weather was changeable. Prost spun off and Senna took his second home victory, to the crowd's delight. He hugged Juan Manuel Fangio on the podium. The weekend also marked Senna's first meeting with Adriane Galisteu, the 19-year-old blonde model who was working as a Shell publicity girl at the event. She remained his girlfriend for the rest of his life – a real love affair that was the most serious and public relationship he ever had.

Senna won the wet one-off European Grand Prix at Donington two weeks later. But no one expected the performance he put in to do it. He overtook four cars on the first lap over 2.5 miles of track – a lap that has gone down in history as one of the greatest ever. Murray Walker, commentating for the BBC, said:"If I take one lap of all the Grand Prix events that I have seen over the years to my grave with me, it is the first lap of the European Grand Prix at Donington." Senna simply said after the race: "It was great, we lapped everybody, we could have won the race with one lap over everybody. It did not happen in the end because we just slowed down but it could have been that way – I don't remember a Grand Prix that was won in such style. It was one of those days when everything came together. The team and the circumstances on the circuit, the pitstops, the information, the strategy – together they created an incredible, fascinating result."

Against all odds, Senna had won two out of the first three races of the season and was heading the championship by 26 points to Prost's 14. At the post-race press conference, the Frenchman, who had finished a lap down in third, grumbled: "I had gearbox problems, clutch problems and the tyre pressures were not correct. We took something off the wing too, which was not the right decision." Senna smiled:"Maybe you should change cars with me."

After the race, Senna insisted that the championship was by no means within his reach and blamed Ford for his McLaren's shortcomings. He said: "You only have to look at the stopwatch, under normal conditions, to see how much ahead Williams is. Part of it is the engine – and I think the situation with Ford is ridiculous. Its only chance to win Grand Prix races is with McLaren. Benetton may win a race, but only if Williams and McLaren are out. So, as it is, Benetton is stopping Ford from giving us a better engine, which is available. It is only a matter of fitting it in the back of our car. This is a ridiculous situation.

"Benetton is damaging Ford by doing this and taking away some better results for McLaren. Ford now has two Grand Prix victories and is leading the championship after three races with a car that is still well underdeveloped, with an engine that is well recognised as being at least half a second down on the other specification Ford engine. It is an absurd situation. I feel really frustrated about it and I just hope that someone at Ford picks this thing up and puts it right, straight away."

Senna flew straight home to São Paulo from Heathrow after the race and missed the eulogies to him in the Monday morning newspapers in Europe. Back in Brazil, someone brought him a selection from Britain and Italy. He was delighted: it was virtually his first good press for years in Europe. He said: "I didn't read what was in the papers in Europe after Donington because I flew straight back to Brazil but there it was very nice."

Unfortunately the honeymoon period didn't last long. Senna threatened not to race at Imola if the situation with Ford was not resolved, and at first it seemed as if Ford had taken notice, actually supplying the team with some of the latest spec engines. As Ford's contracted factory team, however, Benetton had other ideas. Flavio Briatore refused to let McLaren use the latest development engine and told it to keep the Series V. McLaren fitted the Series VII pneumatic valve engine for the San Marino Grand Prix just in case Ford persuaded Flavio Briatore to change his mind, but Benetton stood its ground and on the Thursday evening before the race, it was removed. "If Senna doesn't want to drive then he should stop," said Briatore. "Who needs him now anyway?" Senna had to wait until Silverstone in July to get his hands on a series VII with pneumatic valves. And by then Benetton had a series IX.

Senna was still in São Paulo on Thursday evening and taking up Briatore's suggestion was a real option for him. After each of the year's early races, he had returned home to Brazil to spend time with his new girlfriend Adriane. He had fallen deeply in love and wanted to spend as much time as possible with her. As Mika Häkkinen got ready to drive his first race for McLaren, Senna left his own decision until the Thursday before the race. He was on the phone constantly to the Ford people in Brazil and the top brass in Detroit, urging them to give him the engine to do the job. The lure of racing proved too strong. He decided to race. Adriane drove him to São Paulo for the flight to Rome. The 13-hour overnight flight landed just two hours before practice was due to begin. Imola was almost 200 miles away. But Captain O'Mahoney was ready on the tarmac with Senna's HS125 to fly him to Bologna, where a helicopter then dropped him at the track. He arrived in the garage just three minutes before the first practice session began. He promptly spun into the barriers at Tosa on his first run, although the team blamed problems with the active suspension. Asked why he had decided to race, he explained: "In the end I'd only be doing a favour to Benetton by not driving. By digging its heels in it would have achieved what it wanted – it would have eliminated me as an opponent."

It rained for the race, but a hydraulic failure put paid to Senna's chances and Prost won to close the title race to two points. Ron Dennis even offered Benetton technical assistance to secure the engines, but to no avail. He commented: "I have a strong view. My competition is not Benetton. Benetton's competition is not McLaren. It is Williams. Therefore if we can be stronger together then to me it is logical to be together. I am willing to explore anything that can improve either of our performances and close the gap on Williams. I don't know about Benetton, but I am here to win and that is who we've got to beat." It was not the most complimentary offer he could have made the other Ford team, even if it was true.

Straight after the race Senna headed off to meet Adriane at his beach resort in Angra. He then flew on to Spain for the Barcelona race: Prost won, with Senna in second, and the Frenchman took the lead in the championship.

Meanwhile, unpleasant pressure was building between Senna and Dennis, who was aware that negotiations were progressing between Senna and Frank Williams for 1994. Marlboro's John Hogan also got wind of it, and of Williams' sponsorship by the rival Rothmans brand for the following year. The pressure from there rescinded. On the Saturday afternoon at Barcelona, Senna left the circuit just after 4pm instead of staying on to work with his engineers until 7pm as he usually did.

Amazingly, between Barcelona and the German Grand Prix, Dennis continued to pay Senna $1 million a race, but there was uncertainty about whether he would continue to do so. He said: "I can only see what develops."

Come Monaco, Senna had more or less decided he would race for McLaren for the rest of the year. He opened up his house in Portugal and brought Adriane to a race for the first time. It was an entirely appropriate location to publicly announce their romance. Adriane was so sure he was going to win she had even bought a ballgown to attend the victory ball.

Senna didn't let her down – he retook the championship lead in Monaco, when almost inevitably he clocked his record sixth victory in the principality. Despite being in pain after a brush with the barriers on the Thursday before the race, it was a powerful victory, aided by a 10-second penalty imposed on Prost for jumping the start, who then compounded it by stalling his Williams in the pits. Afterwards he celebrated with the other members of the team to thank them for his win. He said: "When I win a race and when I am on pole and establish a quick lap, I try to pass on to the rest of the team the feelings that I am going through so that they can feel part of it. The hours that the mechanics and engineers put into preparing a racing machine – going through the night, no holidays for 12 months of the year – can only be justified if they experience some of the thrill that I get. And the only way to do that is to share my feelings with them."

It seemed unthinkable, but after Monaco it was three wins apiece and Senna was leading the championship by 42 points to Prost's 37.

It didn't last, but Senna had never believed it would, no matter how much others were tipping him for a fourth title. He was disconsolate in Montreal when he qualified back in eighth and the Williams Renaults looked ever more dominant. It was his lowest qualifying spot since August 1986. He raced to fifth after a lap and a half, and second by lap 30, but an alternator failure ruled him out with just eight laps to go.

Before the French Grand Prix, everything was on a knife-edge. Senna had been applying his own pressure everywhere. He told Marlboro he would commit for the season if the money was right. But Ron Dennis wouldn't budge and threatened that Mika Häkkinen would drive at Magny-Cours if Senna didn't sign the contract on his terms. By then Dennis had sussed that Senna desperately wanted to race and believed he had the advantage.

Senna responded by not entering the Magny-Cours circuit as he usually did on the Thursday before a race.

He told his friend, journalist Karin Sturm: "If I get into the car tomorrow morning then it is for the rest of the season, otherwise no more for this year."

It was all down to money, and in the end it seemed that Marlboro may have broken the deadlock and paid the difference between Dennis's $5 million and the $15 million Senna wanted. On Friday morning, one hour before the start of practice, Dennis and Senna finally agreed a deal. The contract was signed a week later at Silverstone, and after that he agreed to start testing again for the team, something he had not done all year.

But by then Alain Prost was virtually untouchable. Victories at Magny-Cours, Silverstone and Hockenheim followed for the Frenchman, while Senna was only fourth in Magny-Cours; had to settle for fifth after he ran out of fuel on the last lap at Silverstone; and at Hockenheim, a track that favoured powerful engines, he was fourth. Senna was floundering 27 points behind in the championship.

He knew that his contract antics had accelerated the team's summer crisis. As he said: "The fact that half of the year, when I had no contract, I never did any testing certainly didn't help. But that's how things were. And anyway, we could never really have posed a threat to Williams."

The summer was also a rocky ride politically. As well as his ongoing contract negotiations with Frank Williams, there were a number of disagreements over the rules. An unspecified majority of cars were found to have had illegal fuel at the Canadian, French and British Grand Prix races, and were threatened with expulsion. That was not all. Plans by FISA to outlaw expensive active-suspension and traction-control systems mid-season almost amounted to the withdrawal of Williams and McLaren, whose cars were not designed to race without them. The ban was brought in, but McLaren, Williams and Footwork successfully appealed after risking disqualification by racing with the banned technology. On the safety front, Derek Warwick crashed his Footwork in wet practice at Hockenheim; and, in rare agreement, Senna and Prost campaigned for increased safety at Hockenheim in the wet. Prost won the race, despite being hit by a 10-second penalty when he cut a chicane to avoid Martin Brundle's Ligier Renault, which was blocking the track.

Prost seemed content with his points cushion and did not push the car as hard as he would have done in closer circumstances. As a result his team-mate Damon Hill took a hat-trick of wins in the next three races at the Hungaroring, Spa and Monza. Senna suffered throttle failure at the Hungaroring, got fourth at Spa and collided first with Hill and then with Brundle at Monza, while Prost took a third place and two mechanical failures. Senna was nearly involved in a major accident at Spa, when Alex Zanardi crashed his Lotus heavily at Eau Rouge and Senna spun through the debris, missing the stranded Italian by mere feet. Williams wrapped up the constructors' championship at the same race and its number-two driver, Damon Hill, overtook Senna as Prost's principal challenger.

There was another strange event in early September when a Brazilian model Marcella Praddo, with whom Senna had had a romance in 1985 and then another brief dalliance at the end of December 1992, gave birth to a daughter who she named Victoria and whose father, she said, was Ayrton Senna. This only became public after Senna's death. Senna knew he couldn't be the father as the dates did not match. It took a DNA test after his death to prove he was telling the truth.

With a 23-point lead from Hill and 28 points from Senna, Prost could clinch the title in Estoril. Senna and Ron Dennis were spotted having a blazing row in the McLaren motorhome, but no one outside the team knew the exact subject.

Dennis was feeling the strain. Earlier in the weekend he had said: "I want to win each and every race. I know it sounds trite, but I really do. I don't feel discomfort in saying that I want to win them all. In fact, I want to finish first and second. When we're not, I'm bad news to live with. And that's at 46. I handle it better than I did when I was 36, and I've had the experience of success. But the pain of failure is such an incentive to succeed that you don't need anyone barbing you or motivating you. I am just a terrible loser. When I say that, I don't mean in a sporting sense. I may be able to go and have a drink and feel relaxed, but the pain is there all the time. It's the eyes opening on Monday morning when the first thing that comes into your brain is 'was there a Grand Prix the day before?' and the second thing is 'where did we finish?' If it is anywhere other than first, the next thing is more pain." Senna felt much the same way.

There had been changes at McLaren since Monza. Despite scoring his first podium of the year at the track, Michael Andretti was out, to be replaced by the team's test driver, Mika Häkkinen. The son of Italian-American 1978 world champion Mario had struggled in his first season of Formula One and scored just seven points – including the four from his third place at Monza – and had reached a mutual agreement with McLaren to allow him to return to racing in America. There had been questions over his commitment, as he had still been living permanently in Miami and flew out to races and test sessions when required. To give him his due, the MP4/8 was not the best car in which to begin a Formula One career and he had the worst possible team-mate. Also, the man he was replaced by was himself a future double world champion, so Andretti was up against the very best. Even so, seven points was a far-from-impressive tally and several drivers in weaker cars had scored better.

Senna got a wake-up call during Saturday practice in Estoril when new boy Häkkinen outqualified him by 0.048 seconds, taking third to Senna's fourth. Senna had only been outqualified by his team-mate on 17 occasions in his Formula One career – the last by Gerhard Berger at the Mexican Grand Prix in March 1992 – and to have been beaten out of the blue by a young upstart at such a critical point in the season put him in a foul mood. He was dismissive of Häkkinen's ability, which the Finn thought was funny as he had just outqualified him. As Häkkinen recalls: "I went quicker than Ayrton and he didn't like things like that. He could not understand how it could happen and he couldn't accept it. He couldn't understand that there were a couple of corners where this Häkkinen had been quicker. In the end, we joked about it, but that was later."

The race was won by another young star, Michael Schumacher, which handed Prost the title through his second place. Senna's engine had failed after 19 laps while he was running in second. It was easier to bear than the occasion of Prost's controversial last world championship in 1989, not just because this time there was no collision and Prost's victory had been inevitable, but because in the eyes of the world Prost had had by far the best car and had not even had to try, while Senna had proved himself by far the best driver on the track in inferior equipment.

Prost immediately announced his retirement from racing. Everyone knew what that meant, and within days it was announced that Senna would be heading to Williams Renault in 1994. Prost could never have accepted another season as Senna's team-mate, especially considering the Brazilian's form.

With the championship already decided, the Formula One circus arrived at Suzuka for the penultimate round of the 1993 championship in relaxed mood. Senna was no stranger to Suzuka – he also had his Williams deal signed and sealed for 1994 and knew he was at last free of Prost. The race was memorable not because Senna won but because of a remarkable fight with new rookie driver, Irishman Eddie Irvine.

At Suzuka Senna got a tremendous reception from the fans. His reputation had been growing in Japan and he was arguably the country's favourite international sportsman. But the attention in Suzuka was close to getting out of hand and he was continually jostled by fans even within the confines of the paddock. It seemed every single Japanese wanted a piece of him. It bothered him: "Sometimes you just want to be yourself, be on your own to concentrate on something, but you have people following you the entire time – and sometimes they even bump into you, which feels like a real invasion. You cannot move along and you cannot turn around because you are surrounded and that is not so good sometimes. Success brings that, and if you are not successful then you don't have that – it is part of it and you just have to learn how to cope with it."

In qualifying Senna finally got the place on the grid he had always coveted – second, which he regarded as pole. He beat Häkkinen in qualifying by 0.042 seconds, second place to third. It was an uncomfortably close margin at a track considered to be one of Senna's best, but it was a relief all the same. Eddie Irvine qualified eighth in his Jordan.

Senna won the race ahead of Prost with Häkkinen in third, but there was trouble for Senna with another young driver – Eddie Irvine. Senna, Suzuka and controversy seemed to go hand-in-hand.

Senna had been holding off Prost for the lead on a damp track when they came up to lap the battle for fifth between Hill and recently-acquired Jordan Hart driver Eddie Irvine. Senna picked off Irvine with some difficulty, but was not so quick to catch the Williams of Prost, and Irvine decided to unlap himself. Senna eventually won the race but was furious and had not calmed down by the time of the post-race press conference. Once the interviews were over he met up with Gerhard Berger, who encouraged him to drink a few glasses of schnapps. Several drinks later he set off to the Jordan hospitality area to give Irvine a piece of his mind. Realising his frame of mind and sensing trouble, McLaren's PR chief Norman Howell and Senna's race engineer, Giorgio Ascanelli, followed him.

Irvine was sitting alone. Jordan's Ian Phillips, number-one driver Rubens Barrichello and some other team members were also hanging around. As it happened, Irvine and the rest of the team were re-running the incident on a monitor when Senna walked in.

Senna couldn't remember what Irvine looked like so asked for him by name. Irvine raised his hand and Senna walked over to the table, where a heated exchange ensued. Unfortunately for Senna, a journalist sitting nearby switched his tape recorder on and recorded everything. A transcript of the row was plastered all over the British and Italian newspapers the following morning.

"I overtook you!" Senna raged. "And you went three times off the road in front of me, at the same place, like a fucking idiot, where there was oil. And you were throwing stones and all things in front of me for three laps. When I took you, you realised I was ahead of you. And when I came up behind Hill, because he was on slicks and in difficulties, you should have stayed behind me. You took a very big risk to put me out of the race."

"Did I touch you? Did I touch you once?" Irvine asked nonchalantly.

Senna replied: "No, but you were that much from touching me, and I happened to be the fucking leader. I happened to be the fucking leader!"

Irvine shrugged. "A miss is as good as a mile."

The argument continued, with Senna venting his fury and Irvine refusing to be drawn. At one point he even agreed with everything Senna said, winding the Brazilian up further. "You're not racing!" Senna spat. "You're driving like a fucking idiot. You're not a racing driver, you're a fucking idiot!"

"You were in the wrong place at the wrong time," Irvine piped up. "I was battling with Hill."

Senna replied: "Who is supposed to have the call? You, or the leader of the race who comes through to lap you?"

"The leader of the race," Irvine admitted. "But you were too slow, and I had to overtake you to try to get at Hill."

Senna thought he had won the argument. "Really? How did I lap you if I was too slow?"

"Rain," Irvine explained. "Because on slicks you were quicker than me, on wets you weren't."

"Really? Really?" Senna replied. "How did I overtake you on wets?"

"Huh?"

"How come I overtook you on wets?" Senna demanded.

"I can't remember that," Irvine replied. "I don't actually remember the race."

Senna was in no mood for jokes. He punched Irvine on the side of the head, causing the Irishman to fall off the edge of the table where he had been perched. Howell and Ascanelli dragged the Brazilian out of the Jordan motorhome, while he shouted expletives at Irvine, who muttered from the floor that he would claim for injury from Senna's insurers. Senna shouted back: "You've got to learn to respect where you're going wrong."

As news of the incident spread in the pressroom, Senna was vilified, especially by some sections of the British press, who had not forgiven him for falling out with Nigel Mansell a few years earlier. Irvine played the innocent victim: "He is totally out of control, completely and utterly. He hit me across the head and I fell down," he said. There was even talk of the Brazilian losing his superlicence as a result. With just a single Grand Prix to his name, Irvine was a stranger to the sport and people had yet to recognise the psychological games he would play to good effect on other drivers in later years, and which had caught out Senna and consequently himself at Suzuka.

Damon Hill was unsympathetic. "The era of one driver saying 'after you' to another is long gone and that is as much due to Senna as anyone else. He started being very aggressive when he came in and everyone else has copied him. It has been the same for everyone since 1984. We all know that in

Formula One you have to be very aggressive, just like Ayrton, if you want to succeed."

Senna had also had a more minor disagreement with Prost after the race. The Frenchman had pointed out that it could be their last time on the podium together and that they should shake hands. Senna had completely ignored him. Perhaps he had decided there would be one further podium meeting.

The Australian Grand Prix at Adelaide was Prost's final race. It was also Senna's final race for McLaren. Senna was in the middle of a holiday with Adriane and looking forward to an event where the McLaren Ford would be competitive around the street circuit. He duly took pole. Once upon a time that had not been unusual, but Williams Renault had been so strong that it had enjoyed a run of 24 consecutive poles since Senna's last front-of-grid spot at the Canadian Grand Prix in June 1992. With electronic driver aids due to be banned the following season, everyone was saying it was the end of an era, but no one could have guessed it would mark Senna's final victory.

It was fitting that on Prost's big occasion, Senna stole the show, because it had always been like that between them. The Brazilian led through all but pitstops and as a result McLaren broke Ferrari's all-time record of 103 victories. Between them Prost and Senna had scored 65, well over half the total. On the podium, Senna surprised everyone, including Prost, by giving his old rival a farewell hug and telling him he would miss him. Perhaps even Senna realised that Senna without Prost was not the same show as Senna and Prost together.

Senna was moved by the occasion: "I had to keep my feelings very much under control because in those moments emotions were taking over. I had to win this race, that is why I had to keep my emotions under control." Prost said: "It was very difficult for me before the start. I kept thinking it was the last time I was putting on my gloves and the last time I was doing everything. It was very difficult to keep my concentration, but the motivation was there. It was not easy in the car. Altogether, it was very strange for me. I feel tired now."

With victory in Adelaide, Senna took second place in the championship with five wins and 73 points to Prost's seven wins and 99 points. He finished ahead of Hill, with his Williams Renault, and ahead of Schumacher and Riccardo Patrese, with their superior Benetton Fords.

After the race, Jo Ramirez presented Senna with a framed montage of his greatest moments with McLaren. At the bottom there was a message from Ron Dennis that read: "Dear Ayrton, The best in anything is expensive. Occasionally though, you get value for money. Not all the time, but most of the time. Thanks for all the results and the good times shared. Have a nice holiday in Didcot. From one friend to another. Ron Dennis."

That evening Senna and Adriane went to a Tina Turner concert organised to coincide with the end of the Grand Prix weekend. It was held within the circuit after the race to encourage people to stay on and ease the severe traffic congestion. Team personnel had a special VIP area to the right of the stage. Suddenly Tina Turner struck up her trademark number, 'Simply the Best'. She walked stage left and beckoned to Senna to join her, holding his hand as he came forward and brought him onto the stage. She told him how wonderfully he had performed that day and how the song was for him. It didn't seem like Prost's occasion to celebrate his retirement and fourth world championship.

But Senna had not forgotten his rival. Now the Frenchman was retired and no longer a threat, a thaw had set in: "We both love motor racing. We are both world champions and despite the difficult times we've had in the past, today is the end of an era," he said. "When we were both on the podium we had the opportunity to wish each other well. It is a good way to end. Next year there will be a little bit of emptiness."

Ron Dennis was extremely sad about Senna leaving the team. He realised he was the best the team had ever had. But by season end he felt some bitterness at the way in which he was leaving. The five victories he scored during the year in many ways made it even worse. Dennis liked to win as much as Senna. He said: "This year, most of the time, I think Ayrton has done an extremely good job, and the results have reflected that, both in qualifying and racing. Some of the time, and understandably so, he possibly struggles with the motivation to give 100 per cent. But I accept that. It happens only rarely, and does not last very long. But that is normal. I find it difficult, too. So does anybody who is accustomed to winning and is no longer doing so."

Dennis also thought the lack of a really competitive team-mate had blunted his edge somewhat that season: "Ayrton's strengths – his commitment, focus and skills – are obvious and there for all to see. I think that over the years, by and large he has been able to maintain his own standards. I also think if there is a higher level to be reached it can only be reached when he is racing against another driver with the same equipment. That's when he's prepared to dig deeper and try harder. Obviously at the moment that's not the case." Dennis also thought Senna would miss McLaren, which had effectively become his team: "The environment he is in is very important to him. It's possible that if he's not part of the McLaren team he might find himself in a situation he won't like, because he's possibly forgotten the styles and cultures of the other teams he has driven for. I think McLaren is a company that's focused on winning, We've done that fairly consistently, and there is an inevitability about the fact that we'll do it again. The same cannot be said for many other teams. One of the things that I can never understand is how so many of the teams that have never won a Grand Prix can accept their situation and how others seem happy to rest on their laurels. That's not the way we think. We will win again, no mistake about it."

Dennis's underlying bitterness at losing Senna showed in his final comment: "It is a criticism I level at virtually any driver – when they win it's them that's winning and when they lose it's the team that's losing. I think it's just something that spirals out of the character profile that you have to have to be a world champion. But it's still a disappointment. You get flayed in the press when you're failing and you don't even get the recognition when you're succeeding. But that is motor racing and you have to live with it."

Senna was sanguine: "I know there have been some negative comments from him, which are very sad and unfortunate because we worked together for six years and we won three championships together. I have good memories despite whatever happens now or in the future. I think respect must always stand. I know he has been saying some bad things to the press [about me] and I really feel sorry about that. I feel sad in a way because I developed for the team... as much as they did for me... I also did a lot for the team. I worked well for everybody. I have no problems with anybody in the team. We did our maximum under all the circumstances, even when we didn't have a competitive car. For me, to say the sad things he said about me is very unfortunate. I think he will regret it."

The final months of the year were spent solely with Adriane, as Senna prepared for what he believed would be a certain title with Williams Renault in 1994. Contractually he couldn't drive his new car until 1st January 1994, and that suited him fine. As he said: "I have one regret – that I do not have enough time to devote to my private life." Since he had discovered Adriane, Ayrton had finally found the balance. Before her he had been seen with a succession of Brazilian beauties on his arm, mainly TV personalities. At one point he had even said he had been cured of marriage, as Brazilian gossip columnists raked over his previous acquaintances as stories of his romance with Adriane appeared almost daily. He was linked among others with Australian model Elle MacPherson, American actress Carol Alt and former top model Lauren Hutton, a woman nearly twice his age. One columnist avidly described the reason women found Senna so attractive. The article said that women saw in his warm brown bedroom eyes great tenderness as well as sexual passion, and many of them tried to put their feelings into words in love letters to the man of their dreams. It was typical of the hyperbole of the time. But for him, for the first time in his life, he had found someone he wanted to be faithful to.

At the end of 1993, friends were saying in Brazilian newspapers that he was close to proposing to Adriane. If he was he wasn't saying, and he certainly never did. But he did say that winter: "She carries my happiness," as he took his nephew Bruno karting on his private track at Tatui, and joined his two nieces, Bianca and Paula, in the swimming pool afterwards.

Adriane then joined them and all five took Senna's two dogs, Kinda the Schnauzer and mongrel Samanta, for an evening walk.

The two dogs told a story in themselves. They had just turned up on Senna's farm one day by fate. As he said: "They just came to me. I didn't go and buy them or programme it. It just happened. I love them and everything I have, everything that is part of my life, I love."

As for the children he said: "This is my apprenticeship for becoming a father." And he didn't mind if Adriane heard either.

Some time during his last long Brazilian summer, Senna told friends he had seriously considered retiring from competition to live permanently in Tatui. His helicopter pad in São Paulo made it possible for him to travel to his offices every day, and return mid-afternoon. He had the perfect life and he knew it. Formula One somehow interfered with that life. Little did he know how it would unravel in 1994.

CHAPTER 22

The Best Lap Ever Driven

Senna's finest two minutes

Although much else in the field of superlatives in Formula One is constantly in dispute, the question of the greatest lap in history is not in doubt. It happened one miserable Sunday in the English Midlands. As Sunday 11th April 1993 dawned, rain was teeming down in desolate Leicestershire.

At 6am or thereabouts, Ayrton Senna rose from his bed and looked out of the window to survey the countryside from his suite in the opulent Stapleford Park Hotel in Melton Mowbray, Leicestershire. Stapleford Park was a haven, created by an unlikely founder, American pizza restaurant entrepreneur Bob Payton. But it had no appeal that Sunday morning for Ayrton Senna. He was focused on how to get out to the Donington Park racetrack, where the European Grand Prix was being held that day.

At once he decided to drive to the track and not risk using TAG's helicopter, just in case it couldn't land at Donington.

Not only was it raining but there was a deep mist hanging over the countryside. The fog was so bad Senna wondered whether the race would even take place. The rules require that a medical helicopter needs to be able to fly before a race can begin, but despite the poor weather, flights were not disrupted into and out of the track.

The Donington Park circuit sits right alongside East Midlands airport. Senna had toyed with the idea of commuting right into Donington from Faro airport near his home in Portugal. He was glad he hadn't taken this option. His HS125 jet was sitting on the East Midlands tarmac ready to fly to Portugal and new girlfriend Adriane. He wished she was here with him, but he knew that she would be bored in greyest middle England with nothing to do.

The night before he'd had dinner with Ron Dennis, Mansour Ojjeh, pop singer Mike Rutherford of Mike and the Mechanics, plus Mario and Michael Andretti and communications magnate and IndyCar team owner Bruce McCaw. It had been a good night. He liked the company and Ron and Mansour, despite occasional strains, adored him. Ayrton Senna was accompanied for this race by his friend Galvao Bueno, a commentator for the Brazilian television station TV Globo. As ever, TV Globo was covering virtually every last detail of Senna's life.

Bueno was in another hotel and Senna would meet him at the track. His thoughts went back to Bueno and he gave him a quick call to make sure he was up. Bueno and another TV Globo man, Reginaldo Leme, had been very important to Senna's career. Bueno had come to the fore after Senna had fallen out with Leme, just as the driver had fallen out with many people as he became more successful. Senna regretted it but it was the way of the world. His friends and helpers from the early days expected everything to be the same when he became world champion – and it wasn't. Bueno was a newer friend and he understood the pressures.

Public relations and publicity had always been of huge interest to Senna. Right from the early days he had employed PR people to send out press releases when no one had even heard of him. By 1993 he was more organised, with his own full-time PR staff headed by Brazilian Betise Assumpção, who followed him from race to race. In addition, Brazilian newspapers paid him obscene amounts of money to write columns that he probably would have contributed for nothing if pushed. The irony of others paying him to promote himself was not lost on him.

As it was he always kept a TV Globo man at hand to attend to his PR needs. In the old days it had been Leme, now it was Bueno. It was extraordinary how Senna could manipulate people and situations to get what he wanted. The result of this access and manipulation was many misconceptions about the Brazilian that he never cared to correct. They were, he reasoned, part of the myth and the legend that would be so important to him when he retired.

One of the biggest misconceptions concerned his mastery in the rain. The truth was he hated the rain and he thought driving a Formula One car on anything but a bone-dry track was extremely dangerous. But everyone thought he loved driving in the rain and prayed for it. However, his advantage was that others hated it even more.

Senna liked to sleep with the curtains open on the eve of a race so he could see the weather as soon as he woke up. When he saw the rain on the hotel window he bounded out of bed. He knew he could win.

The McLaren Ford was not the fastest car – it did not even have a works engine. The Renault-powered Williams and the works Ford-powered Benettons were both faster with their high-revving pneumatic valve-operated engines. Renault had pioneered the process of replacing steel springs with pneumatic operation in the 1980s, allowing engines an extra 1,500rpm. Three of the four cars with this type of engine were ahead of him on the grid.

As he watched the rain, his race strategy was already forming in his mind. To win, he had to be ahead at the end of the first lap; from fourth on the grid. As was his habit, Senna used the quiet of the morning to plan how he would get in front. One of Senna's mystical talents was that he could record in his mind how he wanted to drive a lap, and replay it later and hone it to perfection before he even got in the car. He sat down on the bed and drove the lap in his head, this time on a very wet track.

Another of his talents was going into what he called 'spiritual mode'. He could turn off from reality and sink into an inner consciousness. That way he could achieve great things in a race car while not really conscious. And when he woke up he knew he would win the race, reliability allowing. He didn't expect anyone else to understand it: that was just the way it was. He left the hotel at 7am and drove to the track in 30 minutes in his hire car with his physio, Josef Leberer. At the track Leberer prepared him a breakfast of his usual muesli and coffee, then supervised Senna's normal race morning stretching and aerobic exercises.

Weather conditions in the warm-up session were damp but the morning was otherwise uneventful. As the cars edged round to take their places on the grid at 1.30pm, the rain was getting worse.

Donington is a tight track and not only did Senna not like the rain, he didn't like the circuit, on which he had first driven a Formula One car exactly 10 years before. He may not have liked either but he excelled at exploiting them, especially the wet conditions.

There were two plans in his subconscious. One was taking the lead from the start, which would render 'plan B' unnecessary. 'Plan B' entailed him being fourth or fifth after the start, which he thought the most likely. In the back of his mind was the fact that, in the dry, the Williams Renault cars would be two seconds a lap faster. And that was the reason he needed to be in front at the end of lap one – so he could build that cushion in case the weather improved. Senna peered up the grid at the cars ahead of him. He knew Alain Prost, on pole, hated racing in the rain, a loathing that probably dated back to his involvement in the accident that seriously injured Didier Pironi at Hockenheim in 1982. Prost had been only 11th quickest in the warm-up; Senna knew that when the chance came he would be easy meat.

The Brazilian also knew that Williams number two Damon Hill would be keen to get his first victory at his home Grand Prix. Although the same age as Senna, Hill was driving only his fifth Formula One race and he had lucked into the best car on the grid. In third was Formula One's newest star, Michael Schumacher. To beat the German it would be imperative to get the upper hand early as his car could rev 1,500rpm higher. Senna's plan was to pounce on his opponents before they got into a rhythm and control the race from the front, being the only man with a clear track and clear vision.

He doubted whether any of the drivers in front would have a serious plan for this race, bar keeping their cars on the track. But that was their way. The Senna way was different. It was what made him the greatest of his time. The parade lap revealed the challenge the drivers were to face. The undulating circuit was waterlogged in the dips and slippery on the crests. It would be all too easy to make a mistake and end up in the gravel. As Senna slotted his car on to fourth on the grid the atmosphere was tense.

As the lights changed to green the field was obliterated in a cloud of spray. Spectators could see nothing and only TV viewers had any real idea what was going on.

Prost was the one man unaffected by the spray and took off into the lead with Hill sticking to his tail, probably following pre-arranged team orders. Senna was blocked by Schumacher and it was Karl Wendlinger's Sauber that went past both of them into Redgate Corner to take third. No one had expected that.

Senna was totally out of position and found himself alongside team-mate Michael Andretti, in danger of dropping to sixth. Somehow he held on, and as the cars screamed into the treacherous right-hander at Redgate he moved clear of his team-mate and on to Schumacher's tail. As they exited the corner Senna got the power down better and moved alongside. Schumacher employed his usual tactics and squeezed him, forcing him to put a wheel off the track. Undeterred, Senna blasted past. One down, three to go.

Wendlinger was next. As they went through Hollywood and into the daunting high-speed downhill sweepers of the Craner Curves, Senna and Wendlinger were side by side, Senna on the inside. Neither man gave way as they dived through the curves, but at the bottom was the Old Hairpin and everyone knew that only one car could go through that at a time. Senna was still on the inside, so Wendlinger had to give way.

The Sauber driver said afterwards: "I saw him in the mirrors and I could see the way he was driving. I knew his reputation in the wet and I knew precisely what he was going to do. I decided I'd better leave some room. I didn't want to go out of the race there and then." Still half a lap remaining and only another two cars to go. Hill was the Brazilian's next target. Senna said afterwards: "I had to put the car on the wet side to overtake and I knew I couldn't delay." He caught Hill as they headed under Starkey's Bridge and up the rise, but the Englishman managed to stay ahead there and as they went through McLeans. However, after the short straight and into the right-hander at Coppice, Senna went for the inside.

Hill recalls it clearly: "I made a bad start. I actually thought I could get ahead of Alain into Redgate and I was a bit peeved to be behind him. I couldn't really see and my concern was to stick with him and hopefully we'd pull away. You can't see what's going on behind you: you see there's a car behind, and you might just make it out as a red car or a white car or something, but you don't know which until it's alongside. I might have fought the corner but it was very early in the race for a risk like that. When he got past me I thought: 'For God's sake, Ayrton!' Then I thought, 'Hold him up, Alain. Make sure you don't let him get ahead'."

As Senna accelerated out and down the main straight, behind him Wendlinger and Andretti collided in the spray. Prost was now only a ball of spray ahead. Senna began to close the gap rapidly. He knew that given an equal car he could lap much faster than the Frenchman on pure driving skill. And in the wet, the balance was firmly in the Brazilian's favour.

Prost was ahead as they went through the Esses on to the new Melbourne Loop – but Senna had planned his move. As they raced down the short straight to the Melbourne Hairpin he dived for the inside line. Prost was forced to decide: give way or collide with the McLaren. Senna knew the answer before he made the move. He took the lead. He exited Goddards and crossed the start-finish line once again, this time 0.698 seconds in front.

The crowd rose to their feet. Most had not seen much of the lap and were astonished to find the Brazilian out in front – especially those on the entrance to Redgate who had last seen him battling not to fall back to sixth. The tens of millions watching on TV had seen the finest and most exciting lap they would ever witness.

Millions of Brazilians went berserk; the rest of the world was silent in awe. On the pitwall Ian Harrison, the plain-speaking Williams team manager for Prost and Hill that day, looked around in astonishment and frustration. "Why are we bothering?" The race had been won after only 1m 35.843secs. There would never be a greater lap in the history of Formula One.

In the post-race press conference Prost blamed various problems during the race for his poor performance. Senna simply asked him if he wanted to swap cars. Prost was embarrassed into silence.

CHAPTER 23

The Secret IndyCar Test

Senna sizzles in the desert

yrton Senna did not sign a contract to drive for McLaren in 1993, until well into the mid-season. The simple reason was that he didn't want to drive for the team. The loss of the works Honda engine meant 1993 would confine him to also-ran status in another year of Williams dominance, this time with his arch-enemy Alain Prost. But all options were closed to him in Formula One and it was McLaren or nothing. The latter was a real option – in fact he thought about taking a year off. He also thought of switching to Indianapolis-type racing in the American CART series, a move Nigel Mansell had already announced for 1993. It was a serious option.

Senna's good friend, two-time world champion Emerson Fittipaldi, had retired from Formula One and taken up IndyCar racing with great success. He drove for the Roger Penske-owned team and had been trying to persuade Senna to test an IndyCar for several years.

Fittipaldi had a special place in Ayrton Senna's story. It was he who had first introduced Senna to Formula One in the early 1980s, and introduced him to the famous team principals as an up-and-coming star.

When the pair met up in São Paulo at the beginning of December 1992, he put the idea to him again. Senna decided to take up his offer and Fittipaldi immediately picked up the phone to his team boss Roger Penske to make the necessary arrangements.

Penske was not just any CART team. Since the championship had been instituted in 1979, Penske drivers had taken the title on six occasions and the team had a reputation as the best. In 1992 Fittipaldi had taken four victories in the car, and was one of the favourites for the 1993 title. Penske also had historically close links to McLaren, aided by the Marlboro title sponsorship that both cars carried. For Senna, it was the perfect opportunity.

The Brazilian was adamant that the test should be kept a secret, away from media attention, quashing any theories that it was for publicity reasons alone, to pressure Ron Dennis into paying him more in 1993. Before the cars arrived in Arizona, the only people who were told of the plans were those essential in setting the test up.

Besides Senna, Fittipaldi and Roger Penske, also officially in on the secret were Marlboro sponsorship chief John Hogan, Penske team manager Chuck Sprague in the US and Penske managing director Nick Goozée at the English factory in Poole, Dorset. There was also a mysterious nameless Senna ally at McLaren, probably Jo Ramirez, who arranged for his equipment to be sent to Poole.

Goozée recalls: "Emerson spoke to Ayrton and between them they agreed the best time to go through with the test. Emerson called me and told me that it was going to go ahead. We knew that there would be a lot of media interest in it, so we made sure it was a secret – we didn't even tell people within the team. Emerson told me Ayrton would get in touch, which he did. He called to say that his helmet and everything was on its way to me and he was looking forward to driving a Penske. I had Ayrton's helmet on my desk for a day before it was shipped to the test. Inside the visor was a note from someone at McLaren saying 'Please don't do it Ayrton!' so the secret was less than it was supposed to be!"

The test in Phoenix was arranged for Sunday 20th December, to coincide with the first shakedown of Penske's 1993 challenger. The team would be testing across town on the city's oval track for three days before Senna's test, prior to moving on to Firebird West to give the new car its first run.

Phoenix, Arizona has its own place in motorsport history. It was around the city's street circuit that Jean Alesi boldly re-overtook Ayrton Senna for the lead in the 1990 United States Grand Prix, and where in 1991 Mika Häkkinen and Jordan Grand Prix made their Formula One debuts. The city's international oval hosted the first-ever round of the CART championship in 1979. The slow and twisting Firebird West track is not so well remembered, and was then mainly used for smaller events.

Emerson Fittipaldi flew out from Brazil with Senna to Arizona. As he recalls: "We arranged to go out there for four days. Roger didn't want him to drive on the oval, so he watched my testing at the oval then he went to test for himself at the road course."

Goozée says: "The team didn't know he was going to be testing until he turned up. He didn't appear until the end of the test and always maintained it was to give him the specific opportunity to drive an IndyCar. Obviously everyone was surprised to see him. There weren't many people about, but there were a couple of photographers. Over the next week there were pictures in the worldwide motorsport media of him sitting in the car."

The test was less secret than intended. Among the Penske team personnel, rumours had already begun to spread that Senna would be coming to test the car before he arrived at the track. Nigel Beresford, Penske's head of engineering, remembers: "When we were testing at the oval we heard rumours that he would go out to the oval to test – which I thought was an extremely bad idea because there's so little room for error. So we knew there was something going on. After the test some freelance journalists phoned us up because they were annoyed that we hadn't tipped them off. It definitely created some interest."

Senna, in the company of John Hogan of Marlboro, quietly watched Fittipaldi drive the one-mile oval before the team headed to the road course on the other side of town for the following day. It was arranged that Fittipaldi would first take out the 1992 chassis, the Penske Chevrolet PC21, before Senna himself got his first taste of Indy racing.

Nigel Beresford explains: "Firebird West is a small Mickey Mouse track out in the desert just to the south-east of Phoenix, and is nothing like as grandiose as its name implies. Normally when we've built a new car we take it out there to give it the first run. As I recall it was a pretty nice day – at that time of year Arizona is typically nice and sunny and warm without any of the really high temperatures you get in the summer. The weather in the northern half of the United States is so unpredictable in the winter that the only sensible places to go and test in December are in California, Florida and Arizona. Besides Emerson, our other two drivers were also present: Paul Tracy and Rick Mears, who had just stunned us all by completely unexpectedly announcing his retirement at the Penske Racing Christmas party 10 days earlier."

It went unsaid among the team, but the departure of the three-time CART champion Mears had left a space to fill. To some observers, the timing of Senna's test seemed more than coincidental.

At 11am Fittipaldi took to the track in the PC21 as Senna looked on. After spinning on cold tyres on his out-lap, he soon began to set respectable times, and after coming in for new tyres, clocked a best lap of 49.7 seconds. At 12.55pm, it was over to Senna.

Beresford says: "It was everything you wanted it to be. He was very charismatic and had an aura about him. He just got in the car and set off around the track. He set off very slowly, learning the track and getting acclimatised to the different seating position and cockpit of the car. He wasn't very comfortable using a conventional gearshift again – most Formula One cars by this time were running steering-wheel mounted paddles so it had been a while since he'd had to change gear in that way. He'd never driven a car with a sequential manual shift either. He kept losing his way in the gearbox so would slow down, shift back down into first gear and then start off again. He couldn't tell what gear he was in, and his ear wasn't tuned to the engine so he couldn't tell what revs he was pulling. We left the same tyres on as Emerson had used and after 15 laps on the same – by now well used – tyres, he bettered Fittipaldi's time by 0.2 seconds, which was pretty amazing."

After the first 16 laps, Senna returned to the pits to give his opinion of the car to the team. Beresford says: "The first thing he said when he came into the pits was that he didn't know what gear he was in and he hadn't calibrated his hearing so he didn't know when he should shift. Ayrton was very complimentary about the engine response and driveability. He said that he could really feel the extra weight of the car in comparison to his Formula One car, and he sensed that it had a higher polar moment so it didn't change direction as easily. He also noted that the car did not move around much in comparison with a Formula One car – it didn't squat much on power and felt more stable. The car was tempting him to run harder through the one fast corner at Firebird, but he didn't want to push it. He was taking it easy because he didn't want to run before he could walk."

Senna confided his excitement at driving the car to his friend and fellow Brazilian Fittipaldi. He says: "He liked the Penske very much. To my surprise, he said the suspension was quite stiff because he thought it would be softer than in a Formula One car. I could tell he was nervous to be on a new track and in a new car, but he was very enthusiastic about the whole thing. He was enjoying himself and he was very comfortable with the car. When he came into the garage after the first run his eyes were shining like a little boy with a new toy."

He may have enjoyed the experience but perhaps he wasn't being completely truthful with Fittipaldi. He later told his girlfriend Adriane Galisteu that he had not much liked driving the car after Formula One but had found it interesting.

For his second run, Senna wanted to try something different with the car, so the team softened off the rear springs and rear anti-roll bar to induce understeer. Then he returned to the track for a second time, which Beresford's run sheets illustrated to be of a greater consistent speed than the first tentative attempt:

Chassis PC21-04	Lap 17	OUT
	Lap 18	57.48secs
	Lap 19	53.79secs
	Lap 20	51.16secs
	Lap 21	50.20secs
	Lap 22	49.14secs
	Lap 23	49.24secs
	Lap 24	53.83secs
	Lap 25	49.12secs
	Lap 26	61.76secs
	Lap 27	49.25secs
	Lap 28	IN

In a total of just 28 laps on the track he had blitzed Fittipaldi's time by over half a second. And that was it. After just 28 stunning laps he returned to the pits and handed the car back to the team. Beresford says: "He came back into the pits and said, Thank you very much, I've learned what I needed to know'. Then he got out of the car and that was that."

Fittipaldi says: "He enjoyed it a lot. He said he was quite impressed with the acceleration. He was not happy with the first run – he had some problems with the seat and everything – but on the second run he was very, very quick."

Senna returned to Brazil for Christmas, leaving the motor racing world to try and predict where he would race in 1993 as news of the secret test broke. Beresford says: "It would have been stepping backwards for him to come to IndyCars. There was a lot of publicity at the time about Mansell's switch to CART, and it seemed that Senna was interested in finding out what the cars were like. I think he was considering life after Formula One. It might also have been a bargaining tool as he had not properly signed with McLaren for the following year. His run in the car predated Mansell's first run in an IndyCar by a few days, so there were some in the press who interpreted it as a means of stealing some of Mansell's thunder, although I didn't take that very seriously."

By early January, many people were convinced that Senna would dump Formula One in favour of CART in 1993. Nigel Mansell, embarking on his own IndyCar career, was questioned by journalists about Senna so many times that there was a distinct note of irritation in his voice at his own first test, when he said: "I don't care what Senna is doing. He is not part of my life any more and he can do what he likes. I am concentrating on my new job here with my new team and that's all there is to it."

Towards the end of the month, speculation had grown so intense that newspapers were reporting that Senna was 'widely expected' to be heading to the States. However, the situation was thrown into further confusion on 27th January when Penske announced Fittipaldi and Tracy as its drivers for 1993. There was no mention of Senna, who kept a low profile, although his spokesman Charles Marzanasco reported that he was still undecided over his options for 1993.

It seemed as if McLaren had made his decision for him on 10th February, when the team announced Michael Andretti and Mika Häkkinen as its drivers for the coming season. Ron Dennis had taken the psychological advantage and Senna had his decision made for him. Immediately after the McLaren anouncement he knew what he wanted and agreed to drive for the team in 1993. He ruled out the possibility of driving in America. To others it seemed that the Penske test and the idea of driving in CART in 1993 had been nothing more than a clever ruse to kick McLaren into line, but Emerson Fittipaldi thinks there was more to it than that.

As he says: "He wanted to drive for Roger in 1993 in the Indianapolis 500. That was partly because Nigel was there. He was extremely enthusiastic about the possibility of driving Indianapolis and a few months after the test he called Roger to check if there was still a drive available. It was possible because he was only driving for McLaren on a race-by-race basis. But Roger didn't want to have three cars in the race. For me it would have been a dream to start against Nigel and Ayrton in the same race. It would have been a fantastic experience."

Had eventual 1993 Indy 500 winner Fittipaldi's dream come true, Senna would have lined up on the grid for one of the greatest Indy 500s ever. He would have joined not just Fittipaldi and Mansell, but also Nelson Piquet, Mario Andretti and a host of other CART and Formula One stars.

But it was not to be, although many of those involved still fondly think of what might have been. Nigel Beresford says: "I've still got all the run sheets. I usually just throw them away, but I wouldn't sling those out with the history they've got attached to them. It's funny to remember it now. We were there on this Mickey Mouse track next to a main road out in the desert and the greatest driver in the world was driving round this overgrown go-kart track with people in pick-up trucks leaning over the fence, very probably not aware of what they were seeing. It was very strange."

CHAPTER 24

Senna's Polar Passion

A colossus in qualifying

Ayrton Senna didn't live long enough to hold many outright Formula One driving records. He won neither the most world championships nor the most races. But one record he did hold was for the most pole positions from the 161 starts he made. He achieved pole in 40 per cent of his starts, clocking up a total of 65. It is such an exceptional record, few think it will ever be broken. Michael Schumacher is the next best, but he is way behind with 37. Senna holds many of the qualifying records: the most pole positions, the most successive pole positions (eight), the most pole positions at the same circuit (eight at Imola). His team-mates never ever came close enough to the legendary Brazilian to offer him a real challenge, and he qualified behind his team-mates only 18 times out of 161 races.

Senna believed that he had never ever driven a perfect lap, as he said: "A fast lap requires a high level of sensitivity between body and mind. It is the combination of the two that gives the performance. But I have never done a perfect lap, because I know, in looking back, that there was always room for improvement. It doesn't matter whether it's one-10th, or a hundredth, or a few 10ths: you always find room for it. On 90 per cent of occasions you go faster on your second set of tyres than on your first, because of the information in your mind from the first run. It doesn't matter if the first one was already very fast. If you use properly the information, and apply all the things I described before, 99 per cent sure, you will go faster than before."

His first pole position came at Estoril in 1985 and was one of his finest moments, as he still recalled years later: "I always wanted to be in pole position for a Grand Prix. And when I got it, at Estoril in 1985, it was an amazing feeling. Then I just keep trying the same." He said every pole gave him a personal pleasure.

The spine-tingling spectacle of Ayrton Senna on a qualifying lap provided some of the most thrilling moments in the history of motorsport. There has never been a faster driver over a single lap, nor has anyone felt or thought so deeply. His passion for pole position was palpable. No other driver put more into it, nor has anyone ever been able to explain it as well as the brilliant Brazilian, for whom the pursuit of pole was also an intellectual exercise.

So great was Senna's depth of feeling, his pure passion for pole, that just listening to him speak about his qualifying experiences was mesmerising. When he talked about his most memorable lap, the one that left the most indelible impression on his exceptional mind, his eyes shone with a faraway look and his voice quivered with intensity.

McLaren team member Tyler Alexander was by Senna's side for most of those pole attempts, as he recalls: "Senna always wanted to be quicker, not necessarily because somebody else had gone faster – just because he wanted to be quicker every time he went out. In the garage we began to notice the thing he did with his belts just before he went out to go quicker than ever – usually on the last or second-to-last run. After one of the guys did up his belts, Senna would reach down and give them an extra pull to somehow make himself smaller in the car. We picked up on that and it became something we would all just stand back and watch. Our guy would pull the lap straps as tight as possible. Senna would tug at them a couple of times and by the third or fourth pull: whoops – watch out, here we go. Everyone thought he was going to get pole – and he certainly went out with the intention of getting it – but he still had to do it. He never said 'I'm going to go out and get on pole', it was just 'this is what I've got to do and I'm going to go and try to do it'."

Former Team Lotus mechanics Kenny Szymanski and Clive Hicks remember the days when Senna would sit in an armchair, mentally driving the Monte Carlo circuit using an invisible steering wheel, gear lever, brake, clutch and throttle. Senna admitted he was mesmerised by getting pole at every race, to the point of obsession, as he said: "It was Monte Carlo '88, the last qualifying session. I was already on pole and I was going faster and faster.

One lap after the other, quicker and quicker and quicker. I was, at one stage, just on pole, then by half a second and then by one second – and yet I kept going. Suddenly I was nearly two seconds faster than anybody else, including my team-mate with the same car. And I suddenly realised that I was no longer driving the car consciously."

Senna was qualifying for his third race in his first season with McLaren Honda, where Alain Prost ruled supreme. The Brazilian had won the 1987 Monaco Grand Prix (with Lotus) but prior to that Prost had won this most supreme test of driving skill three years in succession. Now, uppermost in Senna's mind, on the circuit where overtaking is near impossible, was the need to outqualify his French team-mate. To accomplish this, Senna summoned all his considerable powers, then found even more, as he revealed: "When I am competing against the watch and against other competitors, the feeling of expectation, of getting it done, doing the best and being the best, gives me a kind of power that in some moments when I am driving actually detaches me completely from anything else as I am doing it… corner after corner, lap after lap. This is what happened in Monte Carlo."

Senna was astonishingly fast in Monte Carlo that day in 1988. Almost stupefyingly fast – 1.427 seconds quicker than Prost, who was second on the grid – that even Prost was moved to say: "Fantastic! There's no other word for it." The Frenchman suspected Senna's exceptional performance was rooted in their rivalry, that Senna's need to prove himself quickest was similar to the way Prost had felt a few years earlier when he took extra risks to beat the then established star in the McLaren team, Niki Lauda. "In those circumstances," says Prost, "you take chances like you never will again." But Senna took those chances, again and again, to establish his record of 65 poles.

Senna admitted he had gone too far that day in Monaco. He was already on pole by a considerable margin yet, as if in the grip of a superior force, he was unable to apply the mental brakes. Amazingly it was done on race tyres and not special qualifying rubber. Qualifying was over two days then, and there were no lap restrictions as now. He said: "In qualifying, we used race tyres, not qualifying tyres, so I could do many laps."

As he sped ever quicker through the principality's treacherous guardrail-lined streets, where the tiniest error could mean disaster, Senna was taken on a wild ride through a surrealistic tunnel into the great unknown. In his description of what followed, Senna struggled to contain an other-worldly experience within physical parameters that could be understood. "I was kind of driving by instinct," he said, "only I was in a different dimension. It was like I was in a tunnel, not only the tunnel under the hotel, but the whole circuit for me was a tunnel. I was just going and going and going and going – more and more and more and more. I was way over the limit, but still I was able to find even more."

It was like a dream sequence, with the driver somehow detached from the act of physically handling the car and becoming a passenger along for the ride. It was a dream that at first brought euphoria as if Senna was intoxicated by the exuberance of his own velocity. Then, abruptly, the dangerous reality of his perilous situation took on a nightmarish quality that snapped him out of his trance-like state: "Suddenly, something just kicked me. I kind of woke up and I realised that I was in a different atmosphere than you normally are. Immediately my reaction was to back off, slow down. I drove back slowly to the pits and I didn't want to go out any more that day."

Since he devoted so much of himself to understanding every facet of driving fast, this experience humbled Senna. He had pushed too far, lost control and broken through a barrier of comprehension. He was lost, confused and worried by feelings of uncomfortable vulnerability he had previously not known. "It frightened me because I realised I was well beyond my conscious understanding. It happens rarely but I keep these experiences very much alive in me because it is something that is important for self-preservation."

Senna was never the reckless, unthinking madman that some of his critics – including Prost – claimed made him a danger to himself and to his peers. He was fully aware of the perils of his profession and while he chose to meet them head-on he was not afraid to admit he was fearful of them: "The danger of getting hurt or getting killed is there because any racing driver lives very close to it all the time. It is important to know what fear is because it will keep you more switched on, more alert. On many occasions it will determine your limits."

Yet the phenomenon of probing his limits fascinated Senna and he found ways to use even the fear factor to extend the boundaries of possibility. His constant philosophical inquiries into the relationship between thought and deed in a racing car had much to do with his seemingly superhuman speed. The danger factor that added an extra dimension to those watching one of his breathtaking qualifying laps was also an attraction to the man behind the wheel, as he confessed: "Because we are in a close relationship with the experience of fear and danger, we learn how to live with it better than other people. In the process of learning to live with it you have extraordinary feelings and emotions when you get near to an accident. There is the feeling of 'Oh! I have just almost gone over the limit'. It is fascinating and even attractive in a way. But it is a challenge for you to control it and not to exceed those things. So the feeling of living in that narrow band, of overdoing it and being too easy, is very small. The challenge to stay within that band is very much a motivation."

Senna's quest to fully explore the 'narrow band' resulted in personal revelations that were a source of ever-greater inspiration. Since his insights gained from yet more speed were never-ending his motivation never peaked, as he once explained: "The motivating factor is the discoveries that I keep having every time I am driving. When I push, I go and find something else. I go again and I find something more. That is perhaps the most fascinating motivating factor for me. You are like an explorer finding a different world. You have this desire to go into places you have never been before. The situation is extremely absorbing. And perhaps, because I have experienced on many occasions the feeling of finding new things – even if I thought 'OK, that is my maximum' – then suddenly I find something extra. It is the challenge of doing better all the time. That process is something almost non-stop, in terms of excitement and motivation."

While Senna never stopped extending the frontiers of speed, the deep thought that matched – sometimes exceeded – the intense physical effort he put into his driving left Senna exhausted. "I do try very hard to understand everything and anything that happens around me. Sometimes I think I know some of the reasons why I do the things the way I do in the car. And sometimes I think I don't know why. There are some moments that seem to be only the natural instinct that is in me. Whether I have been born with it or whether this feeling has grown in me more than other people, I don't know. But it is inside me and it takes over with a great amount of space and intensity. And it takes a lot of energy. At the end of every session in the car I feel very tired because I just give everything I have. It drains me completely."

In Brazil in 1991, in front of his home crowd in São Paulo, yet another scintillating qualifying lap secured Senna the 54th pole of his career. He then sped to victory in the race and passed Jackie Stewart on the all-time list of Formula One winners. Senna's 28th win, which at the time was second to Prost's record of 44, meant he had won exactly one quarter of the Formula One races he had entered. Yet it was the pole lap that weekend that Senna remembered most: "My heart was going hard, but my mind was cool. The perception and the reaction to such a lap is so great and it happens instantly. It is a mixture of natural instinct, macho bravery and all the technicalities it takes to do it. A billion things go through your mind and body. It all happens so amazingly fast, it is like a mystical feeling that is focused on an inner point so far away your eyes cannot see and your mind cannot project."

Laps such as this produced the maximum sensual involvement that Senna sought. In the profusion of stimuli he encountered on an all-out lap there were occasions when he reached a state of hypersensitivity that enabled him to separate and better enjoy many of the factors that contribute to the sheer visceral thrill he got from pure speed: "There are times when your sensitivity is higher, when your ability to feel the experience and react to the things you feel in the car is almost infinite. You can sense the car touching the track, you can smell the brakes. You can hear very clearly the engine's sound. You can feel very well the vibrations that are happening around your body, from the steering wheel or the chassis, or the turbulence from the air that touches part of your body. They are all happening at the same moment, and yet you can separate each of them in such a clear way that makes everything so fantastic and so challenging to fully understand and react to."

At Suzuka in October 1989 Senna attempted to explain how he got pole position: "The prefect lap is achieved when the driving becomes automatic because your brain controls the throttle, it knows your braking ability, your gear-change points. It depends on your eyesight before a corner, on your judgment of your speed into a corner. Sometimes you're not even looking at the rev counter when you change a gear, but using only your feeling, your ear, which tells you how to be on the right revs. This is vital, because in a high-speed corner, if you look at your revs, for a split second you will not be as committed to your driving as you should. So your ear then plays an important part of it. It's not easy to I think it is a matter of putting in everything that I have and everything that I am still finding that I can have."

Senna said his experiences in the car sharpened his senses and heightened the emotions that gave him so much satisfaction: "Life would be very boring without feelings, without emotions. And there are some feelings that only drivers can experience. It is a fortunate and unique position to be in, but it is stressful at the same time. Either getting pole, winning, or breaking a record, losing, going through a corner at a speed that a few seconds before you didn't think you could, either failing, feeling lucky, feeling anger, enthusiasm, stress or pain – only we can experience the deep levels of such feelings.

Nobody else can, considering that in our profession we deal with ego a lot, with danger, with our health, continuously, second after second, not just day after day or month after month or year after year. Our life goes by in seconds, even milliseconds."

Ever conscious of the ticking clock, Senna also thought about when his time might run out. Before the 1994 season began he had this to say: "If I am going to live, I want to live fully and very intensely because I am an intense person. It would ruin my life if I had to live partially. So my fear is that I might get badly hurt. I would not want to be in a wheelchair. I would not like to be in a hospital suffering from whatever injury it was. If I ever happen to have an accident that eventually costs my life, I hope it happens in one instant."

But the last word goes to the witness of most of Senna's poles, Tyler Alexander: "There was this old saying going around then that Alain Prost was the best Formula One driver around. The only problem was that Ayrton Senna was quicker."

CHAPTER 25

Senna's Quest to Win

The groundwork of victory

Winning was no accident for Ayrton Senna – it's what his whole life was about right to the end. In his last Grand Prix in Imola on 1st May 1994, he was leading the field from pole position when he died.

Many of Ayrton Senna's 41 Grand Prix victories amounted to comprehensive driving lessons that remain textbook examples of how to win at the pinnacle of motorsport. Only death stopped him challenging Alain Prost's 51-win record and possibly putting it beyond the reach of Michael Schumacher or any other successor.

To win was what he desired more than anything else. That he was more successful at getting pole than he was at winning was a mystery to him, as it was to others. He once said: "You either commit yourself as a professional racing driver who is designed to win races, or you come second, third, fourth or fifth. I am not designed to come second or less. I race to win. As long as I feel it is possible. Sometimes you get it wrong, sure. It is impossible to get it right all the time. But I race to win because I am designed to win."

And that was probably the problem – he tried too hard to win and wore out the car or went off trying when he should have held for second and possibly inherited victory.

Senna's designs on the art of winning, his detailed planning to parlay his superlative natural talent into ultimate success, were unsurpassed. Michael Schumacher has become the dominant driver of his era by emulating Senna's pioneering pursuit of excellence. But prior to Senna, none of the sport's other superstars worked as hard at winning. Sir Frank Williams only employed him for a short time but it was long enough to realise what distinguished Senna from the team's other greatest winners, Nigel Mansell and Alain Prost. "Ayrton was the most committed of all. What was outstanding about him was his mental application. He had an air of invincibility around him. He put his entire body and mind into winning."

The Brazilian's ceaseless search for perfection involved extensive investigations into every aspect of driving, beginning with such fundamentals as the correct seating position in the cockpit and placement of the hands on the steering wheel. He believed in the classic 'quarter-past-nine' position, with his hands exactly opposite each other on the wheel. However, his distinctive cornering technique was at odds with conventional wisdom, involving quick stabbing applications of the throttle throughout the turn. From the entry, around the apex and through the exit of the corner, Senna controlled the rear of the car with the throttle and the front with the steering wheel. But it was his way of gaining control of races that most set him apart from his peers.

For Senna the race began on the formation lap, during which he deliberately worked at intimidating his rivals. While everyone else used the formation lap to warm up their tyres by weaving from side to side, Senna employed not so subtle forms of psychological warfare. By pretending to squeeze a following car out of position in a corner, feinting overtaking a car in front, or weaving ominously near a car that might venture alongside, he forcefully demonstrated his intentions and ambitions for the race. He called this aggressive behaviour 'a sort of declaration of war' and felt that such tactics would make it easier to later 'swallow up' the opposition. Senna considered the start and opening laps to be the most important parts of the race and believed they must be approached with great determination. "A driver must not wait for things to happen – on the contrary, he must act first, creating a situation that may be to his advantage," he once said. He thought deeply about the start, visualising a perfect getaway but allowing himself different alternatives 'so as not to be demoralised if things didn't work out as imagined'.

More often than not it was his scintillating starts and devastating opening laps that demoralised his peers. The prime example of getting the jump on his rivals was his breathtaking first lap in the rain at the 1993 European Grand Prix at Donington, when he overtook every car in front of him and never looked back en route to one of his most memorable victories. Though he was capable of winning by the kind of stealth and cunning often used by his arch rival Prost, Senna's competitive fires burned so fiercely that he favoured winning by fighting hard, preferably by annihilation. His essential philosophy was straightforward. Since the whole point of racing was to finish ahead of everyone else, he believed that if a driver was behind someone his goal should be to overtake them, and if he was ahead then he should do everything in his power to avoid being overtaken. It was contrary to Senna's mindset to simply sit where he was and wait for the chequered flag. For him the race was a battle from start to finish.

Unrivalled as an overtaker, Senna had an extensive repertoire of manoeuvres he employed to suit individual circumstances. While a surprise attack might sometimes work, he believed that a successful overtaking move more often came 'after you have studied your opponent and discovered his weaknesses'. In order to identify such flaws he advocated staying behind for a few laps before pouncing. "The driver behind must actively create chances for overtaking and pressurise his opponent into a mistake. This is the real fascination of Formula One racing."

As much as he concentrated on continually perfecting his driving skills, Senna worked at developing a winning mindset that everyone acknowledged was on a different plane. Gerhard Berger – team-mate, friend and now BMW's director of motorsport – thinks the Brazilian's secret weapon was his mentality, especially his unwavering single-mindedness, his steadfast self-belief and his absolute determination not to be beaten. When they were together at McLaren, and Williams had the technological advantage, Berger might set the third fastest time in a practice session behind the two Williams cars and then be content with that because, after all, the Williams cars were better than the McLarens. But as Berger says: "For Ayrton, Williams didn't exist. The only thing that existed was himself – and he had to be first. That thinking gave him the ability to create a power."

While most drivers tailored their performance expectations according to their car's capabilities, Senna refused to be beaten by mechanical limitations. "It is simply in your mind – believing you can do it," he said. "First of all, you've got to have the knowledge; you've got to have the experience, the basic feelings for doing it. After that it's only a question of believing you can do it, and committing yourself to it, before you actually achieve it. It's like knowing what's going to happen before it happens. Like believing things you cannot see and feeling things you are not touching. That is the key, the power."

Senna's relentless quest for ever more speed and his predilection for pushing himself harder and harder were seen by critics as potentially fatal flaws in his make-up. Often condemned for what was regarded as excessive risk-taking, he defended himself against charges that his conviction that he had a divine right to win made him dangerous.

On the contrary, Senna insisted he thought carefully about the role of fear and used it to manage the risk factor. "I always think about risk before I get in the car, especially if the circuit is one of the more dangerous ones," he said. "I must think about this because the more calculating you can be, the less can go wrong because of an unexpected situation. There is the possibility that you could also make a mistake because your judgement might go wrong on that day. At the same time, you should not have too much fear or you cannot commit yourself."

Undoubtedly, Senna thought more deeply about his profession than any of his rivals, including Alain 'The Professor' Prost, who was renowned as a thinking driver. Throughout his career, which paralleled the increasing takeover of technology in the sport, the engineers who worked most closely with him marvelled that his mind was more than a match for any computer. When Senna was at Lotus, the team's technical director, Gerard Ducarouge, said: "With Ayrton we don't need telemetry." Nigel Stepney, now at Ferrari, also worked with him at Team Lotus, where he recalls: "Senna's precision was unbelievable. On a debrief he could spend five or 10 minutes telling you about one lap – every bump, every entry, every apex, every exit, every line he'd taken through every corner. I think he wore Ducarouge down with his memory power and explanations of what he'd done."

Senna's insistence on lengthy debriefing sessions was legendary and his determination fully to understand the technical aspects of making a car go quickly meant he was often the last driver to leave the circuit. He would sit for hours analysing the data amassed by the engine and chassis telemetry, working out ways to improve the performance of the car and maximise its potential. Steve Hallam, formerly with Lotus and now with McLaren, considers it a privilege to have engineered cars for Senna, whose understanding of how a Formula One car actually worked was unmatched. "He was able to extract the maximum from all those parameters that go towards fulfilling a car's performance. In other words he would get the maximum from the brakes, the tyres, the engine, from every single part. He would consider each of them separately to find his limit and where he could extend it. Then he would combine them and channel his skills into well-defined periods of time. For a pole lap or an entire race."

Senna once tried to describe how he put everything together to help achieve those unbeatably quick laps. When his mind was in gear it seemed he could anticipate the physical act of driving to the point where it was as if he was operating on automatic pilot. "It is always my objective to concentrate on the task, taking into account everything within me: my personality, my training, both my weak and my strong points," he said. "I can then get to a level where I am driving ahead of the next corner. I am a split second ahead entering a corner, halfway through a corner, exiting a corner – just before braking, just before changing gear, just before putting down the power. I can almost predict what I'm going to face and correct it before it happens. And that takes a lot of concentration as well as instant reactions. It means a lot of tension goes through the body, because it's like electricity. Every movement is instant and has to be 100 per cent precise, or as close to 100 per cent precision as possible.

"In this way the driving becomes automatic because your brain controls the throttle. It knows your braking ability, your gear change points. It depends on your eyesight before a corner".

On one of his really quick laps Senna was a sight never to be forgotten. One of the most eloquent descriptions of him at speed is given by John Watson, who was driving a McLaren in the 1985 European Grand Prix at Brands Hatch where Senna, in his second season in Formula One, finished second in the race after starting from pole. Watson had just completed his own qualifying lap when he saw Senna's familiar yellow and green helmet coming up behind him at a phenomenal speed. He moved over to let the flying Lotus Renault past and this is what he saw: "I witnessed visibly and audibly something I had not seen anyone do before in a racing car. It was as if he had four hands and legs. He was braking, changing down, steering, pumping the throttle, and the car appeared to be on that knife-edge between being in and out of control. All of this at absolutely awesome speed. It was a master controlling a machine. I saw something very special that day: a little glimpse of genius."

With the same genius for pure speed that secured a record 65 pole positions, Senna won 41 of his 161 Grand Prix races. Only very seldom did he back off and simply cruise to a victory. It was against his nature to go anything much less than flat out, an aspect of his character that was dramatically driven home to him in a lesson he never forgot. Because he was so intensely self-critical and analytical about his driving, any mistake he made caused him great mental anguish, and none more so than the one that cost him victory in the 1988 Monaco Grand Prix. Having won there the year before, with Lotus, Senna was then with McLaren, where his intense rivalry with team-mate Alain Prost was in its early stages. After beating Prost to pole by an astonishing 1.427 seconds, Senna was determined to destroy his team-mate in the race. By lap 54 he was nearly a minute ahead of Prost, who, after getting past slower traffic, reeled off a succession of fast laps. When Senna retaliated with even quicker laps, worried McLaren boss Ron Dennis ordered them to slow down and hold their positions for the good of the team. A few laps later – while leading Prost by 46 seconds – Senna crashed. The accident happened at Portier, the right-hander that brings the cars out to the tunnel beside the Mediterranean. There sat the abandoned McLaren, and when Prost cruised over the finish line to score an easy win. It was one victory less.

After the accident he in his flat he wept until he fell asleep, so disconsolate and embarrassed at making such an elementary error. Ramirez remembers: "That's how intense the guy was. That's how much it meant to him. I've never known anyone with Ayrton's will to win."

There was another element to Senna's emotional state at the time that no one else knew about. It was only after he clinched the 1988 championship that Senna spoke about the spiritual transformation he had experienced at Monaco. "Monaco was the turning point in the championship," he said at the time. "The mistake I made woke me up psychologically and mentally and I changed a lot after that. It gave me the strength, the power and the cool mind to fight in critical situations. That was when I took the biggest step in my career as a racing driver, as a professional and as a man. I have to say that it brought me closer to God than I've ever been and that has changed my life completely. I am a better human being now than I was before. I am better in everything I am and everything I do. The accident was not just a driving mistake. It was the consequence of a struggle inside me, which paralysed me and made me vulnerable. I had an opening to God and another to the devil. The accident was a signal that God was there, waiting to give me a hand. I just had to tell him what I wanted."

Senna said that from then on God spoke to him and answered his prayers through passages in the Bible. When he sought guidance and protection, the Bible would open at references to courage, determination and strength. On hearing about the depth of his religious conviction some people ridiculed Senna, and others, Prost included, worried that he might take even greater risks and endanger himself and others because he thought God would protect him. Senna was stung by such criticisms and eventually refused to discuss the religious aspect of his life, apart from with close confidants.

Nonetheless, with or without divine intervention, following that single error in 1988 the fact remains that Senna won the following five Monaco Grand Prix events in a row.

Ramirez was particularly close to Senna and still finds it difficult to mention his name. Of all the 35 victories Senna won for McLaren, the one Ramirez remembers most is the 1993 Australian Grand Prix, in Adelaide. It was Senna's last race with McLaren before his move to Williams. As usual, Ramirez was beside Senna's car on the starting grid, helping him do up his seatbelts, when Senna confessed he felt very strange. Ramirez says: " I said to Ayrton 'You just win this for us and we'll love you forever'. He grabbed my arm, squeezed it really hard, and his eyes filled up. Mine did too."

Ramirez was worried that the emotional moment might adversely affect Senna's performance – but it didn't. He won the race to give McLaren a record 104 Grand Prix victories, one more than Ferrari at the time. Sadly, it was also destined to be the 41st and final victory of Senna's career.

It was later that night, that Tina Turner sang to him 'Simply the Best'. Jo Ramirez says he has that moment on video but has never been able to watch it.

CHAPTER 26

The Last Love Story

So close to happiness

In Ayrton Senna's 34 years on earth he only ever had three serious women in his life. There were lots of less serious ones but they were rarely seen in public and never really partners. The three were his teenage sweetheart and then wife Liliane, between 1975 and 1981; Xuxa Meneghel, a very famous (and rich) Brazilian TV presenter, between 1988 and 1992; and finally Adriane Galisteu, from 1993 to 1994 – the last and the most special. Close friends expected them eventually to marry.

It was a love story that started on 15th March 1993, at 4 o'clock, when Adriane, a 19-year-old Brazilian model went to the offices of the Elite model agency in São Paulo for an audition. It was nothing special and Adriane almost turned it down as a job beneath her. Shell wanted hospitality hostesses for the 1993 Brazilian Grand Prix, and was ready to pay modelling rates for four days' work. The oil company wanted the best: the best worked for Elite, and the oil giant was ready to pay.

The audition almost ended in tears when two Shell executives asked Adriane to model a swimsuit. She misunderstood and said she was walking out. She only calmed down when they told her the uniform for the job had the same cut as a swimsuit, which was why it was necessary. Three directors of Shell turned out personally at the audition to approve the girls. The hospitality arrangements at the annual Brazilian Grand Prix were very important. Big deals would be hatched there and everything had to be perfect.

Adriane passed the audition and got the job. She and nine other girls were offered $1,000 each for the weekend's work.

Formula One was not entirely strange to Adriane. On a break from a photo-shoot in Portugal in 1990, she had watched Nigel Mansell win the Portuguese Grand Prix at Estoril.

The proceedings for the Brazilian Grand Prix weekend kicked off on the Thursday following the audition with a press conference, but Adriane wasn't there. She had a modelling job and refused to break the agreement. To her, the work for Shell was just another job, albeit hostessing rather than posing for a camera, which she had done since the age of 12. As she says: "It never crossed my mind that during that weekend I would find the love of my life."

Adriane was on her way to becoming a top model in Brazil. She was always busy, admittedly not earning a fortune, but always in demand. Already she had been abroad half-a-dozen times on assignments, and was still only 19 years old.

By 5am on Friday 19th March, she was out of bed and in a taxi waiting to take her – still yawning – to the Elite model agency's offices in the middle of São Paulo. She met the other nine girls and headed off to the circuit in a specially hired bus before the circuit traffic built up. Adriane was learning quickly that a downside of being a member of the inner circle of the Formula One circus was that the mornings were always very early. She remembers: "At the circuit we were quickly told how Formula One operates so that we wouldn't just stand there with our pretty faces and bodies. They introduced us to the jargon of the circuit: pitwall, cockpit, pitlane, etc."

Friday went, Saturday came and Adriane barely knew why she had even bothered to go home in-between, so relentless was the pace of the event.

Whispers went around the hospitality suite that Ayrton Senna, having qualified third for McLaren, would be arriving. Senna was a hero in his homeland and it was well known that he was single again. He had finally split up with his long-standing girlfriend Xuxa the year before and there were already rumours that the Shell models had caught his attention. Even the experienced models got excited and rushed to the bathroom, crowding around the mirror. Adriane, however, was non-plussed. She wasn't a Formula One fan and Senna held the least interest for her. That was until she saw him.

He arrived in a frenzy, surrounded by fans and photographers. All Adriane could see was his blue cap. She was immediately impressed with the way he managed to greet everyone personally and take the whole scene in. He made a short speech and looked over at Adriane. None of the girls could tell who had caught his eye. She remembers: "I felt he looked at me. But was it me or Nara who was just behind me? Or was it just an empty gaze?" By then she was very interested.

Ten Shell guests were allocated to each girl and Adriane visited the pit garage with her guests. But she didn't see Senna. Then, on Sunday, as she was walking through the pitlane with some more guests, a man called Jacir approached her and said: "I am Ayrton Senna's personal assistant. He has asked me to get your phone number." She gave him her home number and Elite's office number. Then Antonio Braga came up and asked her for her fax number. He hinted at Senna's interest in her. Braga, who was a banker and lived in Portugal, was attending the race as Senna's guest. It was the start of a lifetime friendship between Adriane and Braga, his wife Luiza and their daughters, Joanna and Maria.

Jacir, meanwhile, had also asked half-a-dozen other girls for their phone numbers. Later that day, before the race, Senna went to the hospitality suite again. Shell was a very important McLaren sponsor. He made another speech and told the assembled guests: "I can win." The girls were all lined up right in front of him in a protective cordon as he spoke. Adriane got her first close-up look at him. This time his gaze caught hers and he gave her a smile. She admits that she was hooked on him from that moment, but was determined not to show it.

In the race, after Alain Prost retired, Senna stormed to victory at his home Grand Prix. It meant a celebration party that night at the Limelight Club in the middle of São Paulo. Adriane went along reluctantly and feigned tiredness, making out she was exhausted after her hectic three days. In truth she was frightened by what was happening to her. She says: "As if it was an invented Cinderella story he arrived when the clock struck 12." For some reason she had not expected him to attend, and had dressed down in jeans and a black top, with a red silk scarf.

She resolved to say hello to Senna and leave. She found him in a padded banquette with his 27-year-old brother, Leonardo, talking to Brazilian footballer Pelé. The younger Senna was also popular with women and the table was surrounded by at least a dozen girls, dressed to the nines, crowding out the three men. As it happened because she was dressed down and, had made no effort, she stood out. She shook his hand and said she was just leaving. But Senna pulled her towards him and persuaded her to stay for a drink. She was scared and retreated to her role as Shell's representative. He grabbed her hand as she babbled some PR-speak. Looking back, it was comical, as Adriane remembers: "I said, 'You were great. I am here on behalf of Shell'. He wouldn't let go of my hand. Only briefly, to get a glass of champagne which he handed to me." But Adriane had never drunk alcohol and asked for a regular Coca-Cola.

From this point accounts of that night vary. Adriane insists she left immediately afterwards whilst others insist they remember her dancing the night away with Senna. But it appeared that the eye-witnesses mistook Adriane for another blonde model with whom Senna did indeed dance the night away.

Adriane says she turned to him and said: "I have to go, you have my phone number." She simply wasn't prepared to stay and compete with all the other girls. It wasn't her style. By then she wanted him quite badly and knew that walking away was a risk. But walk away she did.

Jacir followed her at Senna's behest and invited her to a barbecue that the driver was holding at his beach house in Angra a few days later. It was a going-away party before Senna returned to Europe for the European season. Adriane didn't give Jacir an answer and rushed off home.

Back at home, her mother's maid woke her early the next day and told her Ayrton Senna was on the phone. Annoyed, she went to the phone thinking it was Jacir. She rasped 'So?' into the phone, in the best sarcastic manner she could manage. To her intense surprise, it was Senna himself, virtually cooing down the phone. She says: "The sweet and calm voice in which he answered me back was like a cold shower cooling me down."

He had rung to invite her to his barbecue. Continuing her 'hard to get' stance, she was non-committal and told him she had to rush for an audition. He asked her to call him when she had finished and gave her his direct phone number.

She admits that she melted from that moment on, and couldn't resist calling him back as soon as she got the chance, as it happens, from a call box. Senna took her call and was very interested in the TV commercial she had been shooting – and which, ironically, starred his great track rival Nelson Piquet. Still attempting to play hard to get, when Senna mentioned the barbecue again, she changed the subject. She asked him his star sign. "Aries," he replied. "Me too," she said.

She told him she was unsure of the barbecue because she didn't know him. He replied that everyone knew him. To get to know him better, he invited her to dinner with his friends at a famous restaurant called The Place in São

Paulo. But later that evening she heard other girls had been invited and furious she upped the stakes dramatically, and stood him up. Nevertheless, just in case he called the next day, she packed a small weekend bag and put it in the boot of her car ready to go to Angra.

Senna had indeed invited one of the other girls from Shell, named Daniela, to dinner. Daniela was a blue-eyed blonde from southern Brazil.

The following morning he dropped her off at the Elite model agency where Adriane was waiting to go on a job. Inside Daniela referred to Senna as her new boyfriend and left no one in any doubt as to what had happened the night before.

Adriane was insanely jealous and decided she had probably overplayed her hand and that she had nothing to lose by calling him. When she did he asked her to Angra again and, amazingly, she told him she was still thinking about it. She admits now that she was desperate to say yes.

What happened next was that Adriane found herself in Senna's 17th-floor apartment in São Paulo, in circumstances she admits she couldn't control. He had invited her over and she had gone straight away. She remembers he was wearing cream-coloured slacks and no shirt. When she arrived he was doing grass slides across the two-inch-thick shagpile carpet in the cavernous apartment he shared with his brother Leonardo.

When they had finished they sat on different sofas, silent and shy. He finally said: "I am pleased to meet you. My name is Ayrton Senna da Silva. I am 33 years old and I do not have a girlfriend."

She asked him about Daniela and he pretended he couldn't remember who she was. He admitted he had got drunk the night before.

They talked for an hour-and-a-half. Then she got her bag from her car in the basement car park and jumped into his black Honda NSX to go to his offices in the suburb of Santana, where his helicopter was waiting on the roof. As she had suspected also waiting on the roof were Daniela and another model who had also worked for Shell at the Grand Prix, plus Senna's personal photographer Norio Koike. Senna had hedged his bets and Daniela was as shocked to see Adriane as Adriane was to see her.

It was Adriane's first trip in a helicopter and once the girls' shock of finding each other on the trip subsided the atmosphere was good as they all looked forward to a weekend at the sea.

They were greeted at Angra by housekeepers Maria and Matesus, along with Senna's dog Quinda. She also found out that Senna was called 'Beco' by his Brazilian friends.

Adriane discovered Angra was a paradise on earth and was Senna's private playground. It had a wonderful pool and was situated directly on the beach. The waves came right up to the bedroom windows. By day the resort was swamped in sunlight, by night it was bathed in moonlight.

Senna's brother Leonardo and his assistant Jacir were also there.

On the first evening, Senna and Adriane danced the night away in his private discotheque and afterwards he showed her to her own room. They did not even kiss. She says: "I felt that each minute the temperature between us kept rising. He sat by my side. There was something special in his smiling tanned face. It was clear he found it very difficult to take the first step. And I felt, for the first time, the warmth of the proximity – real and spontaneous. Between us there was something special: a long talk, a look, a touch. He tried to kiss me. I backed up – not yet."

Daniela and the other girl were forgotten but it seemed to take forever for any real intimacy to develop. In the end, they did kiss. For Adriane, it was immediate love and she felt as though her world had stopped turning. Then they fell asleep in each other's arms. She remembers the details of that first kiss: "Standing, he kissed me. The first kiss. A real kiss. And then one more, another one, and another one. Kisses, kisses and more kisses. It seemed like the night had stopped around us – everything stopped, the night, time, the noises, the sea, the wind. Kisses and caresses. But nothing more than that."

The next day brought renewed embarrassment and Adriane kept her distance. Saturday was a perfect day with perfect weather and they took his speedboat out. Everything was recorded by Norio Koike, who clicked his camera seemingly non-stop.

The intimacy problem was eventually solved by the arrival of more guests, which meant Adriane had to vacate her own room and share. He took her up to his immaculate bedroom and said: "This is my room. Now it is also yours. Make yourself at home." She didn't demur. It was there that she was first introduced to Senna's eccentricities. In his vast wardrobes she counted 40 pairs of tennis trainers and hundreds of pairs of shoes. There were also endless belts. He appeared obsessed with belts. He also had enough clothes to change twice a day without washing anything for a year. And this was just one of his four homes. He said to her: "I am a bit fanatical about clothes." She nodded in agreement. She told him she was obsessed with creams and perfumes. Then he showed her to the bathroom and his own creams and perfumes, which rivalled hers.

She remembers her feelings that day: "To me sharing his bedroom didn't necessarily mean that we'd have sex. I adored his paradise and I wanted to make sure that I would be coming back there as a friend or a girlfriend."

That night she donned what she called "armoured pyjamas" and they fell asleep. Until he woke her up and asked if he had to marry her to have sex. Then he started caressing her feet, her weak point. He told her: "You are the first woman in three years to provoke desire in me. I don't feel like kissing your feet, I want to kiss your entire body."

It finally happened, and then she fell into blissful sleep. When she woke he was gone. She looked out of the window and discovered him whistling on the pier, deep in thought. Then in the middle of that afternoon he took her in his helicopter to Angra airport for the short flight back to São Paulo. She was scheduled for a fashion show the next morning. After that, they were inseparable, staying at his apartment in São Paulo, or the family farm at Tatui, his parents' home. She would return to Angra many times over the next 12 months. As the relationship developed he she her if she would join him at the Monaco Grand Prix. Monaco was very social and he liked to have a girlfriend with him at the race, especially as he believed he would win again for the sixth time in 1993 and would need a partner for the winners ball thrown by Prince Rainier.

So on 17th May Adriane got ready to go to Europe. It would be the first time she would be publicly at his side. She was the Shell grid girl transported to be the girlfriend of the fastest driver alive, at the most glamorous place on earth. On arriving in the principality, they went straight to Senna's small Monaco apartment to be greeted by his Monte Carlo housekeeper Isabel, who was Portuguese. He only stayed there for a week a year, for the race. He had sold the big apartment he used when Monaco was his permanent home, before moving to the Algarve in Portugal two years before. But for tax purposes he listed Monte Carlo as his home.

Senna walked Adriane around the Monte Carlo track, introducing her to the intricacies of driving a Formula One car. He also took her to the casino, where they quickly lost the $300 they had changed into chips.

Adriane had brought three evening gowns to prepare for the annual post-race ball, where she also sensed her new boyfriend would take the laurels. After all, he had won Monaco five times previously and his car was ideally suited to the tight circuit.

She was hampered at the ball by only being able to converse in Portuguese as her English was very limited. She was introduced to Betise Assumpção, Senna's press secretary, who was Brazilian herself.

Senna hardly let go of her all weekend in Monaco. Wherever they went they attracted the intense attention of photographers and fans. But on Thursday when the racing proper began, she noticed a sudden change in him. At night he changed into his pyjamas and took the bible to read as he went to sleep. It was a different man to the one she normally shared her life with.

During practice, when Senna had a small accident and hit the guardrail, Adriane quickly ran down to the track from the apartment – but it was nothing. On the Sunday she watched the race from the commentary box of Brazilian broadcaster TV Globo alongside Senna's friends, Galvao Bueno and Reginaldo Leme.

When he won, she ran from the box to be with him and cried as the Brazilian national anthem was played. In the evening, they dressed up and went to the sporting club to collect his prize. Few journalists knew who she was and hundreds of picture captions on Monday morning, in newspapers all over the world, would call her 'the mysterious Brazilian blonde'.

The couple sat on the top table at the sporting club. When Adriane turned around she saw she was sat next to Prince Albert of Monaco on one side, while on her other side were Michael Douglas, Richard Gere, Cindy Crawford and Princess Caroline. As Adriane ignored the champagne, Senna joined her in drinking Coca-Cola. Afterwards they went to Jimmyz', the most famous nightclub in the world and a symbol of hedonism in Monte Carlo. As they sat at their table next to the dance floor, Adriane was astonished by the enormous number of girls who threw themselves at her boyfriend, some quite brazenly.

When they got home and drifted into sleep, Adriane thought to herself: "Is it a dream? Is it true?"

After Monaco, they flew from Nice to London in Senna's HS125 jet flown by Captain O'Mahoney. It was Adriane's first visit. On 26th May, they flew home to Brazil after an extraordinary nine days. They only returned so quickly because Adriane had bookings and relied on her income as a model to live.

She remembers now: "Looking back, I realise it was a good combination: our first trip abroad had been the best trip of all trips. It's because later things got complicated on the tracks, problems arose in McLaren, victories became less frequent and tensions built up."

Back in Brazil, as he left every fortnight for a race, she befriended his brother Leonardo. The young man confided in her and asked her whether he should marry his long-standing girlfriend. Later this relationship would sour and Leonardo perceived that Adriane was driving a wedge between Senna and his family.

That summer she accompanied Senna to Europe whenever she could and stayed at his Algarve house. On one trip his mother and sister joined them, and with Adriane jetted off on shopping trips to Europe's capitals. The shopping almost got out of hand. When Senna met up with them in Paris in mid-July he went to their hotel rooms and found they had 38 pieces of luggage between four of them. Later that relationship would also sour for the same reasons.

Adriane's second Grand Prix of 1993 was to be Hungary, where they would stay at the new Kempinski Hotel in Budapest on the banks of the Danube. It was special for her as she had never been and she had Hungarian ancestry. Her maternal grandparents, Alexander and Agnes, had migrated from Hungary to Brazil during World War II.

Hungary marked a low spot in his relations with Ron Dennis and he asked Adriane to teach him Hungarian swear words to use if the need arose.

In the evenings they forgot his troubles and walked by the side of the Danube. They shared the visit with Senna's close friends, Christian and Birgit Schues and their two young children. Adriane stayed in Budapest for much of the time Senna was at the track.

On race day, Senna retired from the Grand Prix and they were to attend the post-race party at the Gundel restaurant staged by the race organisers. There, now-famous pictures were taken of them being serenaded by a violinist. It was another magical evening. Adriane says now: "It was a photo of two people in love. We were in love." Hungarian-born publisher, Andrew Frankl was at the Philip Morris-sponsored party. He was a long-time friend of Senna's from his days as publisher of *Truck* magazine; and had met him at the Toleman team when it was owned by the eponymous transport company. He says: "Ayrton was in tremendous form, clearly much in love, holding hands with Adriane. It was so obvious. I was convinced they would marry."

In the middle of August, back in Brazil, Senna bought Adriane a new car, a silver Fiat Uno. He called it 'her present for August'. She immediately phoned his mother, who said: "Come and take me for a drive."

All summer it was the same pattern, as Senna returned to Brazil after every race to spend time with Adriane at Angra. Looking back now, she thinks it was someone telling him time was running out and he had to make the most if it.

On one occasion, he returned from Belgium and was angry at coming fourth. When she picked him up from the airport in her Fiat he asked for the keys, saying: "Where is the key to the tin of sardines?" He took the wheel, pursued by waiting photographers keen to have photos of him with the mystery Brazilian blonde. Reporters still did not know her name and the love story was the talk of Brazil. It was getting her plenty of work – her picture was on billboards advertising jeans all over São Paulo.

On 3rd September they boarded a flight to stay at his house in the Algarve and later proceeded to the Portuguese Grand Prix in Estoril. But first it was to Monza and Italy. They flew into Lisbon, where Captain O'Mahoney collected them in the HS125 to fly on to Faro before going to Lake Como for the Italian Grand Prix, the penultimate race of the European season.

Tennis ace Monica Seles was there to cheer her favourite driver, but Senna retired halfway through and drove straight back to the hotel with not a word to Adriane. He ordered room service, choosing for her without asking what she wanted. When crowds began cheering his name in the car park he snapped out of his bad mood. He said to her: "But I lost – these Italians are crazy." She told him: "They're crazy for you." Sensing his mood, she added: "Are you finding it too hard having me around?" He said: "I promise you that when we leave Italy I will leave the frown behind." That night she went to the hotel bathroom and wrote on the mirror in lipstick: 'Good Morning! Smile'.

The next two weeks were spent in the Algarve. Senna trained hard – the Portuguese Grand Prix was like his home race and he wanted to do well. But this year it was even more important. Inside his briefcase was a fax copy of a signed option with Williams to drive for 1994, replacing Alain Prost, who was retiring.

He was very moody during that period. The fax machine in the Algarve house whirred continually with draft contracts and notes from his manager, Julian Jakobi, in England. Adriane remembers one phone call with Frank Williams in England lasting a staggering five hours and 40 minutes. He couldn't sleep until the negotiations were over: when the document with Frank Williams' signature on it was faxed through, he signed it and faxed it straight back.

When they left for Estoril and the race she packed up ready to fly home immediately after the race without him. She would next meet him in Tokyo on the Monday after the Japanese race. The last two Grand Prix events of the year, in Japan and Australia, were a fortnight apart and they decided to take a holiday in-between, joking it would be a honeymoon rehearsal.

Senna sensed he was in for a change of luck and indeed he did win both of the last races.

A fortnight later Adriane started the 28-hour flight from Brazil to Japan and she was picked up at Tokyo's Narita airport by photographer Norio Koike. She found Senna in his hotel cursing an Irish driver, Eddie Irvine, then a rookie. Earlier he had had a bust-up with Irvine who, he made clear, he didn't like. Senna had ended up hitting him.

Adriane and Senna flew to Bora Bora in Tahiti for an idyllic week before the race in Adelaide. But then Senna fell ill after four days and spent the last two in bed. As they flew to Australia, his strength returned. At the airport he bought a dozen belts. and she knew he was well again.

But help was at hand as Josef Leberer restored him to full fitness with some long massages and he was soon back on top form winning the race.

After two days off in Sydney, they flew back to São Paulo for five months of hedonism. It was a glorious routine, splitting their time between the family farm in Tatui, his São Paulo apartment and the beach house in Angra. It started off with six unbroken weeks in Brazil. Adriane remembers: "Beco and I came back from Europe, and were living together at the apartment in Rua Paraguai, sharing the same friends, going out to dinner, we were a typical boyfriend and girlfriend – although there was no wedding ring, there were intimacies like sleeping together in his parents' house. I felt he liked to show me off a bit." At the beginning of December they flew to Europe for a go-kart race at Bercy in France. Belgian driver Bertrand Gachot, a former Grand Prix regular and a friend of Senna's, recalls: "I saw them at Bercy a lot and he was very much in love with her. They didn't separate for one minute and it was really nice to see."

Gachot had a serious soft spot for Senna. When he was jailed for an assault on a London taxi driver in mid-1991, Senna was the only driver who came forward as a character witness, writing a letter of support to the English judge who jailed him.

From Bercy, they flew to Heathrow and on to the Williams factory in Berkshire for a seat fitting. It was his first visit there and the staff were sworn to secrecy. His move had not been declared but Williams wanted to make another splashy announcement for maximum publicity. Frank Williams greeted them personally. Adriane noted that the close relationship with Frank Williams was totally different from Senna's relationship with McLaren team principal Ron Dennis. He had told her Ron was 'moody' which he found increasingly difficult to cope with. He said Frank was a 'real team manager', stressing 'manager'. But he added that although the relationship between him and Dennis had cooled, he loved the McLaren team to the extent that he felt it was his real family and that he would return one day if circumstances were different. In her book Adriane notes that in 1994 she observed, while standing in the pit garage, that Dennis seemed to take a perverse pleasure every time Senna retired that year. For certain relations between them were strained, which Senna told her was a shame after so much success.

But that was all in the past, as Senna took her hand and toured the Williams factory, introducing himself and her to the Williams people – his new home for at least the next three years. His actions were a clear sign she was a fixture in his life and would be a part of his new life at Williams.

From Heathrow again, it was straight back to Brazil, and Christmas with the da Silva family at Tatui. But Adriane decided at the last minute that she must return to her mother and 80-year-old grandmother, who was very ill, and she left on Christmas Eve. She borrowed Senna's mother's Volkswagen car to drive back to São Paulo.

The official Christmas celebrations with Senna's parents lasted until 17th January and, in-between, Senna took a quick trip to Europe, testing the new car and tying up business deals in Germany. He already had one eye on life after Formula One and wanted to create a business to challenge him when he anticipated retiring, at the turn of the century. He wanted to import the best European goods to Brazil. After he returned to Brazil on 24th January, they went straight to Angra. Their happiness was interrupted when Adriane's grandmother died on 26th January 1994. Otherwise it was an uninterrupted six weeks before his home race opened the season. There would be one more testing trip to Europe before that, but without Adriane.

During the holiday and that period before the first race, they talked deeply. He discussed his past girlfriends with her. She says: "It was done in an atmosphere of passion and confidences. He talked to me about his past love relationships as if to put them behind him."

She says of that time they had together: "I felt I had been given a present by the gods." Senna also asked her about her ex's. And he spoke of claims that were currently being made in the Brazilian press about an illegitimate daughter called Vitoria, who he was supposed to have fathered by a girl called Marcella Praddo. Senna admitted he had spent the previous New Year's Eve with Marcella but that the baby could not possibly be his. (Later proved by DNA tests after he died). They spoke as the waves lapped their bedroom windows. The idyll was only disturbed when Senna had an accident on his jet-ski, and almost stopped breathing after he hit the water very badly. But it was only a momentary panic. Resuscitated, he recovered by laying perfectly still for a week.

Senna went to Europe again, for a pre-arranged testing and visit to Germany, at the beginning of March and returned to Brazil on the 11th. They then went back to Angra. The sojourn was only interrupted by the return to São Paulo for the Brazilian Grand Prix, the biggest sporting event of the year in Brazil.

But shortly after the dreamy days at Angra, a problem arose that threatened the very existence of the relationship. Adriane was becoming famous as Senna's girlfriend and he warned her about being exploited by the media for that fame. From being a mystery blonde, in Brazil she was already a celebrity in her own right. She didn't see trouble coming and his words of warning fell on deaf, 20-year-old ears.

She received the chance of a big photo-shoot with a Brazilian weekly magazine called *Caras,* the Brazilian equivalent of *Hello!* magazine. It was a swimwear shoot on Camburi beach. Adriane asked Senna's permission and, when he realised the photographer would be Fabio Cabral, he agreed she should do it.

Senna initially approved of the individual photos he was shown on 21st March, as he and Adriane celebrated his 34th birthday, before the magazine was published. She also showed them to his mother, who thought they were beautiful. But when the magazine was published, two days later, the photos had been arranged in a provocative fashion over a 12-page feature and on the cover. Senna thought it was cheap, and exploited their relationship. It didn't help that the magazine was published in the same week as the Brazilian Grand Prix. The magazine's editor believed he was introducing properly the beautiful girlfriend of the national hero. Senna thought differently and was incensed. As Adriane looked at the magazine, she remembers her inner thoughts: "I felt a shiver down my spine. The article was beautiful. The text was perfect. But I kept asking myself, should I have done it?"

That night in the Rua Paraguai apartment, Senna exploded: "You look like this, I think a commoner. How could you let them do this?" He threw the magazine against the wall of the apartment he shared with his brother.

Adriane remembers: "I didn't move. Any argument would have been in vain. Dozens of times I had seen him like that, but never as a victim. I never thought it would be me."

She told him she was a model. That was what she did and she needed the work and the money. He shot back: "You must understand that you are not the same person any more, Adriane. Now you are my girlfriend. You don't have to show the world you have a beautiful body, this other side of Adriane Galisteu." She knew she was in real trouble as he had never called her Adriane before. He had always known her as 'Dri'. She said: "I am not forcing you to understand, I am very happy about my choices."

She remembers it as if it was yesterday: "I wanted to cry, but I tried not to. I proposed the end of our relationship, but my heart was the size of a pea and cried 'no, no'. Suddenly, I noticed tears were rolling down his face. I understood that he was telling me 'Yes, it's over, goodbye…' I told him: 'We have had a wonderful time. We've never had a fight like this. I'm really shocked with what happened here today. You showed me an Ayrton that I couldn't recognise'."

When she asked him what he specifically didn't like, he said: "All this shit, especially the photos." She admitted to him she had been wrong, and apologised. All that night the argument continued. In the morning, he said to her: "I never doubted your character, I only said I didn't like what happened." As they parted, he admitted he was also jealous, a trait not usually part of his character, as he said: "You should show your beautiful body only to me." She shot back: "I am jealous myself." He asked her to buy the copyright of the photos from the magazine so he could keep them himself.

He later admitted he had been irritated by the photographer's 'boldness'. He said: "I am experienced by the banana skins people place in the way of famous and respected people. But you are just a girl and you must be careful not to hurt yourself."

The Brazilian Grand Prix came and went. Senna got pole position, but retired after a spin, and his new great rival, Michael Schumacher, won. The following Tuesday he had hired an aircraft hangar in which he would announce to the Brazilian motor trade that he was introducing the German Audi range of cars into Brazil. It was the culmination of his winter trips to Germany.

For the evening reception, Adriane accompanied him dressed to the nines. Senna announced he would also have deals with Ducati motorcycles and Mont Blanc pens for Brazil. These would be the first of many products he would import to Brazil for his new business life, when he planned to effect a seamless change from top racing driver to top businessman. He had seen the demoralising effect of retirement on drivers and he did not intend that to happen to him.

Afterwards Adriane had the uncomfortable job of apologising to Milton and Neyde da Silva for the *Caras* photos. They were also upset. But after a heart-to-heart discussion, she thought they had put it behind them.

However, there were other matters rankling the family, matters that were not discussed. Over the winter weeks at Angra, Senna and Adriane had hatched a plan whereby she would join him in Portugal at his Algarve house for the whole of the European Grand Prix season and they would stay there permanently for five months, and not return to Brazil. His usual style had been to return home after every other race for a week. It bothered the family immensely, but they could say nothing, and do nothing. It created an unseen rift between them and Adriane and that would erupt in the week before the San Marino Grand Prix culminating in Leonardo being sent to Europe to persuade him to give Adriane up.

Senna's decision not to come home for five months was received very badly by the family and was squarely blamed on Adriane's influence and it particularly upset his sister, Viviane, and brother, Leonardo. In truth, it had been Senna's decision and Adriane had gone along with it as his wish. He wanted an uninterrupted summer with her in the Algarve. The family were having to learn the lesson that their famous son was at last ready to flee the nest and settle down with the love of his life. They didn't take it well. But Adriane knew none of this at the time.

On 3rd April 1994, Adriane saw Senna for the last time. He was going to Japan and she was staying on for a month in São Paulo to take an intensive English language course. If she was to settle in Europe for half the year, she would have to be able to speak English.

She drove Senna to the airport in her silver Fiat Uno for his flight. He would not return to Brazil until the end of September. She would leave Brazil four weeks later and move into his house in Portugal and they would live together. It was clearly the prelude for something big. She felt he had nearly proposed several times and she expected to come back to Brazil as his fiancée.

Adriane says now of 3rd April: "It was a very special day and I didn't know why at the time. Before he went we had a long afternoon of love. We got to the airport early and we stayed in the car and talked, hugged and kissed. He said to me 'I'll keep an eye on you little girl'. He said goodbye, and gave me a long kiss in the car." She recalls his words the last time they were at Angra together: "One day I will marry you and one day I will work for Ferrari. I will end my career there and end my life with you."

He told her he planned to leave Williams two years hence, when he believed the team would peak, and move to Ferrari, which he believed would then have its act together after the return of Luca di Montezemolo as boss. He told her: "Even if the Ferrari is as slow as a Volkswagen Beetle, I still want to be driving it on my last start, my last lap, my last race. Ferrari is the myth of Formula One. The tradition, the soul, the passion."

And that was it. She would never see him again. She threw herself full-time into the English course, which occupied all her time – as well as packing for five months away. Senna went to Japan but retired from the Pacific Grand Prix as his rival for the championship, Michael Schumacher, won again. He later told Adriane, as he told everyone close to him, that he thought Schumacher's Benetton was running banned electronic aids from time to time. Time differences and a heavy sponsor commitment meant he missed speaking to her on her birthday and did not get through until 6am the following day, desperately apologising for waking her so early. She understood the pressures on him in Brazil, as she had witnessed them herself the previous year. By 21st April, Senna was back at the Algarve house. She was cramming English lessons into the evenings as well. Later that day, she faxed him her first love-letter in English. She carried on with the lessons right up to her Varig flight to Lisbon on Friday 29th April.

CHAPTER 27

The Invincible Philosopher

The bodywork was his second skin

Ayrton Senna always realised he had an odd personality but thought it a consequence of being the best driver in the world. As he said: "I have applied my personality in motor racing so many times – it's one of my qualities. Sometimes it has cost me a race or a good result but it is my personality and that's what I am."

Senna said that before the start of a race, he would concentrate so hard that he felt as though the bodywork of the car became a second skin. "This carbon-fibre incarnation could sometimes prompt acts of folly," he said. "In 1988, at Monte Carlo, I was in pole position. But I was on a cloud. Pointlessly, I stepped up the chase again, only to wake up and realise that the others weren't going too slowly – I was going too fast. I'd let the intensity of the emotion get the better of me, and I'd overstepped my limits."

Years later Senna revealed that in 1989 at the Spanish Grand Prix, he was weighed down by too much pressure. He says he won without really savouring the victory. So the next morning he got hold of a Fiat Panda and went back to the circuit. He explained: "During the Grand Prix I felt no joy. I said to myself 'You can't leave here without enjoying yourself'. So I went back on the track. There was no one there. It felt good. I savoured it."

That his whole life was focused around motor racing was never a doubt in Senna's mind. He admitted it controlled him rather than him controlling it: "Everything in my life is aimed at the point when I sit in my car on the grid. It's a focused situation, where you want to search deeper and deeper inside in order to find the next step. This situation takes you to a different world. You have this desire to go into places where you have never been before. It is something that is very lonely in a way, because once you get in a car, on a circuit, it is you and the car, nothing else. That situation is extremely absorbing. Perhaps it's because I have experienced, on many occasions, the feeling of finding new things. Even if I thought 'OK, that is my maximum', suddenly I found something extra. That process is almost non-stop in terms of excitement and motivation."

Senna saw it as an asset even when it cost him a race win, as it did many times. Although most motor racing commentators attest to the fact that he rarely made a mistake, close examination of his record does not back it up. It also comes back to the fact he scored a third more poles than race wins. When his record is properly examined, not only in races but practice and qualifying, it is clear that Senna made plenty of mistakes, mostly going faster than he should have been. But he was always unrepentant: "The main thing is to be yourself and not allow people to disturb you and change you. You have got to be yourself, even though many times you make a mistake due to your own personality. You learn, and you must learn through your mistakes and get better.

"I believe if you have the ability to focus strongly on something then you have the ability to gain from it. It's been like that all my life – it's always been a question of improving. There is no end, as you go through you just keep finding more and more, it's fascinating. We are made of emotions and we are all looking for emotions – it's just a question of finding a way to experience them."

The Brazilian hated making mistakes and admitted they got to him afterwards. The most public was Monaco in 1988. He once said: "Those things can get to you if you're not careful because you really see how fragile you are - you have no power, you are just there. You can be gone in a fraction of a second so you realise suddenly you are nobody and your life can have a sudden end."

He claimed he had always confronted problems and never run away from them: "You are faced with some unexpected situations and you have to face them – it is part of your life and you either face it or you just drop it and don't do it any more. I happen to like what I do so much, I can't drop it."

Jackie Stewart believed this absolutely and says he often saw an imprisoned look in Senna's eyes. "I never thought he looked like he was getting the degree of pleasure he deserved because he worked as hard as any man could work at mastering his art. I've seen a lot of other people who while doing that have also had a quality of life and an appreciation of life that might have been fuller than Ayrton gave himself the privilege of having. I think that's what made the difference because in all the great drivers they've all been given a gift from God. Some have manicured and massaged that gift to the highest level of their potential. Ayrton did it more recognisably through sheer hard work and it would almost seem aggravation to him. He had his ego factor, which everybody has but it looked like it wasn't a pleasure. He was sometimes what I would call a rushed driver. He didn't look as though he had the same time in the cockpit as Jim Clark to do things. Everything was more hurried, more abrupt, more nervous. I don't think his reactions were faster − or braver. It's just that he drove right on the limit. And I believe he went closer to the limit than a lot of other people would. He survived them all but I was always waiting for the accident. Not the kind of accident that happened at Imola. I was waiting for the type of accident where he would use too much of the kerb and the thing would flick on him."

That comment strikes right at the heart of what Senna was. He believed in his ultimate superiority over any man and any machine. He believed it was his divine right to win in Formula One from 1988 onwards and when he didn't he always looked for the answer. It was his inquisitiveness that stood him apart from other men. And it made him one of the most unpredictable men alive. No one ever knew where they stood when he was around. He said in 1990: "The newest machine in the world will never match the human being. Therefore, really, what we are all looking for is how we function, how we operate: why this, why that? There is a logical way of looking at it, there is the spiritual way of looking at it − through religion, through God, and it's a process with no end."

Senna rethought the process of life more often than any other driver of his era and possibly ever in Formula One. He was constantly not only trying to learn about his cars but also about himself. He called it a 'non-stop process'. But he admitted there were many things about the way he behaved and how he could drive faster than others that he simply didn't understand. He didn't understand why he could never accept coming second and why he won far less races than he won pole for. He said: "There are so many things to which you just cannot find the answers."

His religion gave him some of the answers he craved. He read the Bible primarily to find answers and in religion found a new way of life. He said in 1989, after he lost the championship that year to Alain Prost: "I still want lots of answers but I think I have a new road where I am finding those answers slowly. I believe there are many things about which you're not aware, human qualities that were given to you by God. If you get to understand just a little bit, it makes so much more sense: it makes things so much more peaceful to understand the difficulties – particularly – and to better enjoy the good moments. Unfortunately, I had not experienced that before: I wish I had."

In Montreal in 1991, Senna told journalists: "Winning is like a drug. Do I think I am totally addicted? Maybe, I don't know the meaning correctly in English, but I am totally dependent at this moment on winning." It was that philosophy that made him what he was – the good and the bad. He was like a drug addict who would commit any crime to get his fix. It was the single thing that drove everything he did.

Ayrton Senna was a hugely contrasting and complex man. One minute absorbed and lost in the Bible, the next ruthlessly disposing of fellow competitors on the race track, sometimes to the extreme unpopularity of the journalists who observed his every move. Only his vast talent and intelligence excused his behaviour on many occasions. Senna's formidable intellect was one of the secrets of his speed. His career was a triumph of mind over matter and his philosophy of life and words of wisdom are among his most important legacies. Senna believed there was some truth in the old saying that the ideal would be to have two lives because in the first life you would learn how to live and then you would use that experience to live the second life to the full. But, typically, that wasn't enough for Senna. He said: "You need a third life and a fourth because you wouldn't ever get to the bottom of it." His wisdom went far beyond his years, and he managed to pack more into his short lifetime than most people achieve in a longer life. He was able to do this because he applied his exceptional intelligence to thinking about the whole business of living, not just racing.

However, his passion for his sport was so all-consuming that it was inevitable that his greatest insights about life would come from racing. With Formula One as the catalyst his powers of reasoning were honed and the framework created for the development of his personal philosophy. His superior intellect was ideally suited to the fast-paced world of Formula One, where quick-thinking is a way of life, and his racing experiences sharpened his senses and accelerated his intellectual development.

He once said: "One thing that happens in our lives as racing drivers is that we do a lot of things in a short period of time. So we have to live our lives very intensely. And by living very intensely, everything happens so fast. The difficulty is doing it right all the time. With so much pressure and stress it's quite easy to get it wrong. That is the major challenge. To do it properly, do it right, positively, constructively. You don't always manage it but in the end the aim is really to do the best you can all the time. Because then you are at peace."

Senna said that as a young boy he didn't even know who he was, a knowing observation that in itself reveals the concern for self-understanding which went on throughout his life. For Senna, his relentless quest to explore himself, to push his personal limits and discover how far he could go was key to becoming one of the greatest racing drivers in history. Beyond that, his search to find himself was a prime reason for living, a motivational force that went far beyond his fundamental need to win races. "I think I am a complex person," he said, "because I am never convinced that 'this is it'. I don't sit and wait for things to happen. I'm always searching for more, particularly within myself. In this area it is infinite. Because where do you stop? You don't know what capability you have in your mind. What you read, what you can learn about - we only use a fraction of our capabilities, our competence. So this research is fascinating. It's a continuous feeling that 'there's more, there's more'.

Wherever and whenever he found more, Senna, like a true explorer, became excited by his discovery, especially if the revelation came behind the wheel of a Formula One car. "This situation takes you to a different world," he said. "You have this desire to go into places where you have never been before. It is the challenge of doing better all the time."

When a racing driver continually pushes himself he is also exposing himself to greater danger. It is the nature of drivers to take one of three approaches to this most difficult of dilemmas. The easiest way, and the most common, is to slow down, to never exceed the personal limits of safety they feel comfortable with. Obviously that would never work for Senna, a man who once said: "The motivating factor is the discoveries that I keep having every time I am driving. When I push, I go and find something more. I go again and I find something more. That is perhaps the most fascinating motivating factor for me."

The second way drivers handle the danger factor is to virtually ignore it. They do this either through having a lack of imagination (or deliberately repressing it) about what might happen to them in a big accident, or refusing to believe they could ever be seriously injured or killed in a racing car. Unfortunately, drivers who are ignorant of danger or believe they are invincible tend not to last long.

Like most thinking drivers Senna was fully aware of the dangers and he was not afraid to admit he was fearful of them. Typically he used this as a way to improve his driving. "The danger of getting hurt or getting killed is there because any racing driver lives very close to it all the time. It's important to know what fear is because it will keep you more switched on, more alert. On many occasions it will determine your limits."

But just as he went faster than nearly anyone else, perhaps in order to be able to get his mind in gear to be able to do that, he went further than anyone else when dealing with the fear factor. He was fascinated by it and chose to meet it head on.

"Because we are in a close relationship with the experience of fear and danger we learn how to live with it better than other people. In the process of learning to live with it you have extraordinary feelings and emotions when you come near an accident. There is the feeling of almost going over the limit. It's fascinating and even attractive in a way. But it's a challenge to control it and not exceed it. The feeling of living in that narrow band, of overdoing it, is very small. The challenge to stay within that band is very much a motivation."

Senna had a highly developed sense of personal values, which he attributed to his parents giving him the proper upbringing and to his religion. "I can put my hand on the Bible and say that everything I have done, everything I have said and everything I believe has been done in the straight way of life. This is the honest way, the professional way, the sporting way. It respects people and it respects their way of life."

When others contravened his personal code of conduct, or committed what he felt was an injustice – to himself or others – Senna was never afraid to speak out. After Roberto Moreno was unceremoniously fired by Benetton to make way for Michael Schumacher in 1991, Senna was the only driver to speak out against what he considered was a morally corrupt and ethically incorrect act by Benetton.

As much as he devoted his life to racing Senna thought his sport paled in comparison to the plight of the poor and the oppressed people and the environmental problems of the world. "Formula One is nothing compared to those things," he said. "People have to have a chance, a basic chance at least, for education, nutrition, medical care. If this does not begin to happen then there is little hope for the future and little wonder that the problems become greater and that violence arises. Unfortunately, I am not blessed with the powers to solve the problems. But it touches me deeply and worries me considerably."

Though he refused to talk about it publicly, he spent millions of dollars of his own money to help the poor children in Brazil. In the last year of his life he spent over $5 million developing his 'Senninha' (little Senna) project and publishing comic books detailing the adventures of the crusading cartoon character, patterned on himself and dedicated to fraternity, good sportsmanship and the defeat of wickedness.

As for such problems as drugs he thought he could contribute on another level: by setting an example. "The best way to help, if you are in a position that gives you credibility, is to do your own activity in a way that is consistent with good values. In other words, I don't need drugs to be successful. I don't need drugs to go fast. I don't need drugs to have feelings or happiness or emotions."

Experiencing the full range of emotions was one of the major satisfactions Senna found in racing. "Life would be very boring without feelings, without emotions. And there are some feelings that only we can experience. It's a fortunate and unique position to be in, but it's stressful at the same time. Either winning, or breaking a record, losing, going through a corner at a speed that a few seconds before you didn't think you could, failing, feeling luck, feeling anger, enthusiasm, stress or pain – only we can experience the feeling and the level of it. Nobody else can, considering that in our profession we deal with ego a lot, with danger, with our health, continuously, second after second, not just day after day or month after month or year after year. Our life goes by in seconds or milliseconds."

Because he thought so deeply about his profession, Senna was able to find in it greater rewards than most drivers. But his profound commitment also brought him more than his share of despair. While he found driving immensely stimulating he also acknowledged that there was a negative side to this essentially solitary pursuit. "Once you get in a car on a circuit, it is you and the car, nothing else. It is very lonely in a way."

Just as he was in a class by himself in the car, Senna's superior intellect set him apart from others out of it. It was lonely at the top and sometimes his sense of isolation made him feel vulnerable so he turned to others for help and strength. His family in Brazil was a great source of inspiration and comfort. He was closest to his father Milton and his brother Leonardo but once described his sister Viviane and his mother Neyde as his two best friends. He had faith in the family unit as a way of life, loved children – 'they are the honest ones' - and wanted to have his own, probably with his last girl-friend Adriane Galisteu, because he 'needed someone to share his life'.

But Senna also sought, and found, inner peace and spiritual nourishment through his belief in a superior being. "Psychologically or physically you can be the strongest man in the world but, especially in my profession, you cannot do it on your own. It's such a fight all the time, such a stress, such a tension, there are moments when you need help. You've got to have the source of power. And the only source of power that is with you all the time is God."

His relationship with journalists was far from good. His original confidants, Brazilian Reginaldo Leme and photographer Keith Sutton, worked closely with Senna in the early days but later became disillusioned. Both men gave him everything early in his career when he was an unknown and then found themselves frozen out when they would not bend to his will once he was famous and successful. He often ranted at the press when they failed to take his side and it was something that dwelled on his mind. He often took it too seriously and thought about it too deeply, especially when he tried to explain to a group of journalists the problem: "I really want it to be properly understood, because... it means automatically that this is going to go through, and flow through, the system – which is where you guys are responsible – in order that it gets to the other end. And that is one of the small contributions that, from time to time, I feel I can give, and that I feel strongly about. And I feel really unhappy, or frustrated, when I see that it doesn't get through, or if it gets through, it gets completely wrong. Sometimes I am angry with myself, not necessarily with you guys ... with myself, because I see afterwards that the way I did it wasn't right, I made a mistake the way I put it, because I wasn't clear enough, or ... the way it was passed to you guys gave you an opportunity to interpret it the wrong way. So it's not only your responsibility to have got it wrong there. I am also responsible because I should have done different, to get you to understand what I was trying to say."

Because he was such a deep thinker he found it hard to answer a question simply. They were always long answers but usually worth listening to.

He found the continual demands on his time very stressful but didn't shirk his duties. As he said: "It's not just being a racing driver that is stressful, the stress comes from... yesterday, when I arrived at the circuit, and I was there at 11.30am. And before 2.30pm I could not sit with my engineers to talk about racing, talk about my racing car... I couldn't, because I had to attend to a certain amount of requests. There was no end. And I couldn't cope, I couldn't fulfil the need, no matter how hard I tried... I got out after three hours of work, not only tired and totally down, with no energy, but also frustrated because I felt that I couldn't cooperate the way I would like and would wish... with everyone. And yet it wasn't over, because at 4pm I was in a press conference. And after the press conference was over, a number of people were still around me. And today I am here, for a half-hour interview, and I don't know how long we have been here. And no matter how long we remain here, there is still so much. I tell you, it takes a helluva lot out of me to do that."

CHAPTER 28

Fear, Death, God and Racing

One man's beliefs and motivations

Ayrton Senna feared very little in life – just two things in fact: God, and life itself. He wasn't afraid of death but he was afraid of serious injury and incapacitation. In Adelaide he once said, and repeated a slightly different way in Estoril six months later, that he could never accept not living a full life, the sort of life he already lived. Now the words he used are haunting and worth repeating again: "If I am going to live, I want to live fully, very intensely, because I am an intense person. It would ruin my life if I had to live partially. So my fear is that I might get badly hurt. I would not want to be in a wheelchair. I would not like to be in hospital suffering from whatever injury it was. If I ever happen to have an accident that eventually costs my life, I hope it happens in one instant."

After the kind of accident he suffered at Imola on Sunday 1st May 1994, inevitably he would have preferred the fate he got. He always made that clear.

Senna did feel fear, but always on the day before he got in a Formula One car, as he admitted: "I always think about risk the day before I get in the car, especially if the circuit is one of the more dangerous ones. I must think about it because I am exposing myself to a certain risk. The more calculating you can be, the less can go wrong because of an unexpected situation." Despite those fears, come race or practice day Senna's mind was clear and the fear gone. It was the way he prepped for a race.

Although, apart from Elio de Angelis's death in testing in 1986, he did not experience death at a race track until, ironically, the very last weekend of his life, he knew the dangers and often used to talk about them. Above all he was aware of the charmed life he led – something denied to most other people. He said: "I don't really know the meaning of fear in English, but the way I see it, the danger of getting hurt or getting killed is there because any racing driver lives very close to it all the time. It is because we are in a close relationship with that experience, consistently, that we learn how to live with it better than other people."

The Brazilian had an incurable fascination with accidents that caused injury. In the few times a driver was injured during his time in Formula One, Senna was always close to the action. It might have been considered morbid behaviour by those unfamiliar with his personality. But he thought that by being there and learning what had happened he could understand the process of an accident - and how to survive it. This particular characteristic was never more apparent than during his last weekend at Imola, when there were two serious accidents. One where the driver – Rubens Barrichello – went to hospital and the only serious consequence was him missing the race; the other where the consequence was rather more severe and the driver, this time Roland Ratzenberger, effectively died in his car. Senna was immediately on the case visiting the site of Ratzenberger's accident in the pace car (and getting into trouble for it) and was right by Barrichello's side when he regained consciousness after flying into a barrier and being hospitalised. For him it was more a learning process than human concern.

The faster he drove the nearer he was to having an accident and he was more aware of that than any other driver: "You have extraordinary feelings and emotions when you get near an accident. If you know why you are doing it, and how you are doing it, then you feel fine. You know the limits – you have it in your hands. It's fascinating in a way – even attractive. But it's a challenge to control it and not exceed those limits. The feeling of living in that band, which I think is very narrow, is a real challenge – and maintaining it very much a motivation."

Senna was always adamant that the fear was gone once he stepped into a racing car – any he had existed entirely outside the cockpit. As he said: "You should have no fear because if you have fear, you cannot commit yourself. It's important to know what fear is because it will keep you more switched on, keep you more alert. On many occasions it will determine your limits." When Senna got frightened he was always stopped, as he was at Monaco in 1988.

The Brazilian admitted he often reached the extreme limits in his driving, as he undoubtedly did on 1st May 1994. Whatever went wrong with the car, and no one will ever know what really happened, he might have been able to save the situation if he had not been driving on the absolute limit. But as he said: "We live in extremes: we tend to go to extremes. It is attractive to go to those extremes, particularly with strong emotions, because it becomes a challenge to bring the emotion back to the centre. By going to the extremes, and then being able to bring it back to the centre, you get the performance. It's important to have the feeling of fear, in a way, because it keeps part of you in an area where you can hold yourself in equilibrium."

Senna rarely hurt himself in an accident. Twice in 1991 he was mildly hurt but until 1st May 1994 he had never drawn his own blood in a Formula One car. He had suffered far more serious accidents on his jet-skis than he ever did in a car. Again he was always aware of what danger he was in but believed he was basically in charge: "Once you sit in a racing car, you know you are taking risks, and you know you are exposing yourself to the possibility of having an accident. Of course you never think you are going to have a bad accident or get injured. But you always have it in the back of your mind. And in most cases it determines the limits you establish for yourself... how fast you go in a corner or over a full lap... in a qualifying lap or during a test. And that is a very important feeling to have, because in a way it helps you stay together and not overshoot in many situations. It is self-preservation but without disturbing your concentration and commitment to driving."

In 1988, when Senna won his first world championship, it had a dramatic effect on him. He started talking a lot about God to journalists whereas he had hardly mentioned religion before. He found God as he found success – the inference was that God had given him the world championship and he did not think much of himself until he had won it. It was as if he changed from that day on. He tried to explain it: "I believe we should choose the right moments to talk about such things very carefully. And we shouldn't let it flow completely naturally all the time. There are times when you should hold back a little bit because it won't do any good. What you try to do may go completely the other way if you do not choose the right moment."

It was very hard to understand what he meant but he grew increasingly eloquent as he got older - and started talking about it in greater detail. In one press conference in 1988 he rambled for a good half-hour about his beliefs and what they signified: "In life, people believe in many different Gods. All over the world there are different ways of praying to, or believing in, a superior power. My belief is that there is only one God, and he is the king of kings – the most powerful of them all. In the world generally there is the good power and the bad power; good things and negative things. All that we see, all that is part of the world – the sky, the sun, the moon – has been created by this God. He controls everything: the bad things only happen if he allows them to happen. His reasons and his desires, his objectives, can only be understood by him. We do not have the ability to understand his objectives for us. He knows what goes on in our hearts and minds before we can feel it. And he is the only one who is able to know. I have always been religious, because of my family, but I was what I would call a superficially religious person. However, over the past year-and-a-half, two years, I have started to devote more of my time to my psychological side, my spiritual side, and tried to learn more about this way of life. I have been fortunate enough to have some good people close to me that know a lot more than I do, to give me the help to start at the right place, and learn the right way. As I've been doing it, I have had, on different occasions, situations that have proved [his existence] to me. I was fortunate enough to see things... I wouldn't have believed it if it was just by theory or discussion. I needed the proof to believe in the first place. And I was fortunate enough to have the proof in different situations, on different occasions, of happiness and frustrations, disappointments, doubts and confidence. I had signals that showed me his desire and his power, more than anything his power, to control anything and everything. Of course, talking is fine. Some people, I'm sure, will know what I'm talking about because they have also experienced it. Some won't because they've never had the experience, and they will not believe. What is important to me is to give people the facts that I have been through, let's say the experience I have been through. I'm not doing anything more than relating the experience that I have had so far, as facts. That has changed my life, progressively, and it is still changing my life. I am today a different person, a much better person, and I know tomorrow I will be even better."

It was apparent that he swaged his religious commitments by reading the Bible as he was not a churchgoer. His devotion to God was totally on his own terms – he belonged to no specific religion and had nothing to do with any church. He said explaining: "I share my beliefs with people who have the same feelings as I have, people who see things the same way I see them. These people know a lot more than I do. I have started to learn, to have help from these people, so I can progress and improve."

Senna craved understanding and found it in the pages of the Bible, as he admitted: "The best thing I have ever read is the Bible – it's the best book, the all-time best-seller. There you can find all the explanations and all the answers you are looking for. I don't think a lifetime is enough to read it all properly."

Prayer became ever more important to him right up to the end of his life. As he said: "When things are difficult for me to understand, I try to pray and try to talk to him [God] to ask him to show me my way of life, give me some sign, some light, some understanding. And reading the Bible, I swear to you, many times I got the answers to questions that I could not understand or accept. Opening the Bible, he [God] is immediately there, talking to me about what I am asking, giving me the understanding. That is the beauty of this way of life, to be able to have such a contact. Reading the Bible, he talks to you. It's even stronger than if someone is standing in front of you and talking to you. That has happened not once but many times with me. Psychologically you can be the strongest man in the world, or physically, but on your own you cannot do it, especially in my profession where it's such a fight all the time, such a stress, such a tension – there are moments when you cannot do it by yourself, you've got to have the source of power. And the only source of power that will be with you all the time is him."

After the race in Monte Carlo in 1988, when Senna crashed out of the lead dramatically, he claims he met God. He called it part of the learning experience: "I am learning about it. The more you learn, the more you want to learn, the more you experience it, the more you want to experience it. It's more than power, it's peace: an equilibrium in which your mind and body go into a different level of living. It's natural that you want more – you want to go deeper and live more of this life. So today I face so many frustrating and difficult moments, and yet I find the power and the strength to carry on fighting. I know on some occasions that I would not be able to do it, physically or mentally, just by myself. And if I am doing it, and finding the power and the strength, it's because someone is behind me, and ahead of me, and on my left and my right. I can feel it – and it is a beautiful experience to be able to live this way."

Senna almost became an evangelist because he was so passionate about his beliefs and thought that everyone could reach out to what he had: "It is something that is available to all of us, not just me. It is just a question of asking for it, and of opening our minds and our hearts for him [God]. He is there all the time just waiting for us to say."

He was also reconciled to the fact that it was not always positive and admitted that he had doubts when that happened: "When you have a hard time, you suddenly have doubts. But his [God's] reasons, on many occasions, are only his reasons. Only he [God] knows why things should happen, even if they seem like a bad thing. But in the future it will be a good thing for us. Our understanding is so short, so small, compared to his, that on many occasions we cannot understand. That is where faith is everything. I finally found that in my life, that is what gives me strength to go through the nice times and the difficult times. This year on many occasions I was winning a race when suddenly, boom, something went wrong. I am sure in different years I would get out of the car mad, completely upset, and talk a lot and criticise. I did the opposite this year. I was disappointed, of course, but I had equilibrium and I was at peace. I was able to accept it in a constructive way. I was able to give the people who work with me part of the power that I had to keep whole and look to the future. And that is something I was not able to do a few years ago. What's the difference? The difference between a few years ago and now is that I have finally found him [God], and I have him, like I said before, all around me."

After 1988 Senna appeared to have referred to God in everything he did. He said: "I had not experienced that before: I wish I had found it before [1988]. That's the proof to me. I know my character. I know the way I am, the way I behave. And suddenly I start to find the way I am behaving strange because it's not me. I am much more aggressive and much more pushy when something goes wrong. But suddenly I accept things when they go wrong – I am disappointed but I rationalise it and accept it and look at it as something that will count positively some time in my future even if I cannot understand it in my small mind. That makes all the difference in life."

Somehow Senna always seemed ready for death. As he said: "The day it arrives, it will arrive. It could be today or 50 years later. The only sure thing is that it will arrive."

CHAPTER 29

1994: The Williams Year

A brief shining moment

After a decade of waiting, Frank Williams and Ayrton Senna finally got together at the close of the 1993 season. It was a partnership that had been rumoured on so many occasions that it seemed inevitable – the deal had often come very close but failed to materialise. And it was somewhat precarious right until team principal Frank Williams inked his signature on an option letter before the Portuguese Grand Prix in 1993.

Since providing Senna with a Formula One car to drive at a test session at Donington in July 1983, Frank Williams had been waiting for Ayrton Senna to join his team and Senna had been waiting to join Williams.

As McLaren went into decline and Williams went into the ascendancy, the three-time champion had been looking to move to the team. It was a well-suited and well-timed alliance.

Senna had always had an excellent relationship with Frank Williams and both were passionate about their racing. Williams was also a fan of Senna, and it was almost inexplicable the Brazilian hadn't joined the team first in 1984 and then again in 1985. The next chance came in 1988, but then Williams itself was down on its luck. Frank Williams said then: "I find Ayrton a fascinating character. For me, what sets him apart is his mental application, his ability to focus his mind on one thing. I've had experience of preparation for meetings and negotiations, and believe me, you've got to be ready. It's verbal terrorism – you can feel the bullets. Maybe if we ever did get together, we'd last three months, then kill each other." The words, heard now, are haunting.

The negotiations lasted almost two years. Having made his feeling so plain in 1992 and 1993 that he wanted to join the team, and having declared midway though 1992 that he would drive for the team for nothing in 1993, he had little room for negotiation when it came to his salary for 1994. Prost had earned a rumoured $14 million the previous year, by far and away the most money Williams had ever paid a driver. In fact the hefty pay packet had caused the split with Nigel Mansell in 1992 and was the reason he went to America in 1993 to race in IndyCar. Faced with paying Prost $14 million and Mansell his same salary again for 1993 – $12 million, almost 40 per cent of the team's income – Frank Williams' crude solution was to offer Mansell a new contract worth only $6 million. It was a crass decision guaranteed to upset the team's most successful driver ever, and it did. He stormed out in disgust and turned down a last-minute offer to keep him for 1993 and restore his $12 million retainer. But the situation helped ease Senna into the team for 1994.

As a result of all this, Williams was in an excellent position to negotiate when Senna came calling. The outline of a deal was agreed halfway through the season, as it became clear that Prost was going to win the world championship. If Frank Williams had needed any proof of how good Senna was, he had given it to him that season. Driving a McLaren with a Ford Cosworth engine and a 100 horsepower deficit, he had on occasions run Prost ragged when given half a chance and had won five races.

Frank Williams recalls how anxious Senna was to join the team in mid-1992: "A possibility for Ayrton to join us re-emerged towards the end of 1992, primarily led by him. Ayrton very much wanted to get in the car for 1993 and he just never left me alone. He was very persistent, very tough-minded, and occasionally I was frightened to go home because the phone would never stop ringing. He knew I was there so I would have to answer. I would get half-an-hour's conversation, mainly on his side, of why we should put him in the car." The reality was that Alain Prost had completely blocked Senna out of the picture for 1993. But 1994 was different and a deal was done, regardless of what Prost thought about it.

Senna was in a very poor negotiating position when it came to sitting down with Williams to thrash out terms. He ended up agreeing a retainer of about half the sum he had received the previous year from McLaren. Frank Williams agreed to pay him around $8 million but Senna would have rights to sell a lot of space on his overalls, and retain his cap and tee-shirt rights. Finally, at the beginning of September 1993, after discussions that had gone on all year, Senna and Williams signed a letter of intent for 1994.

When Senna decided to move to Williams, he kept his earlier promise and asked physio, Josef Leberer to go as well. He didn't actually have to ask. Although Leberer had loyalty to the team, it was clear now that his chief loyalty was to Senna. Senna said to him: "You want to change with me, now change your colours?" Leberer says: "It was clear that I was going for him, even though there was such a close relationship with the team. I could not leave him alone. That is how it was."

When Frank Williams informed Alain Prost that Senna would be his team-mate for 1994, Prost was incensed. The 'no-Senna' clause had apparently only extended to 1993. Prost was effectively pushed into retirement by Senna's arrival at the team. The Frenchman decided to depart midway through his own two-year contract, with the prospect of a car good enough to enable him to equal Juan Manuel Fangio's record five world titles on the cards in 1994. It seemed an uneasy separation. He announced his retirement two weeks later at the Portuguese Grand Prix at Estoril. A few days after that Senna revealed to journalists that he would be leaving McLaren without saying where he was going, as if the whole world did not already know.

Prost equally made clear that his retirement was final and inferred how hurt he was by Williams when he said: "The sport has given me a lot, but I decided that the game wasn't worth it any more. I have taken too many blows. I will not drive for Williams or anyone else. That goes for Formula One and all the other formulas. There will be no comeback."

Astonishingly, rumours began that Senna was disappointed with Prost's decision and wanted him back, because Prost had always been the mark against which he measured himself, and without him the challenge was no longer of the same level.

It was all made official when a two-year contract was announced on Monday 11th October 1993 at the team's factory in Didcot, before the final two races of the season in Japan and Australia. Senna was by this time back in Brazil with his new girlfriend Adriane Galisteu, preparing for the last two races of the year. He appeared at the press conference on a special satellite link from São Paulo. Senna was clearly delighted to have at last got his hands on the equipment thought to be the class of the field, and said: "I am really looking forward to driving a Williams Renault in what I consider the beginning of a new era in motor racing for me. It is like a dream come true. I have been close to completing a deal with Frank many times now and am delighted it has finally happened. I've been waiting impatiently for this. I need it for motivation."

An equally satisfied Frank Williams said somewhat disingenuously: "In 1994 we need a team to defend the championships we have won this year. Alain Prost's retirement left us in a dilemma. He is a driver of immense talent who contributed so much to the team both in and out of the car this year. Therefore his most appropriate replacement could only be Ayrton Senna. I have always admired him and his record speaks for itself."

After the announcement Prost was depressed and Senna enthused. It showed in the results – Senna won the last two races of the season in Japan and Australia.

Senna and his girlfriend Adriane spent a few days in Sydney before returning to Brazil. He had never been happier. By the beginning of December he was back in Europe, in Paris for the Bercy kart race, a charity event organised by paraplegic former Formula One driver Philippe Streiff.

The Bercy event was fraught with problems between sponsor Elf and the Shell oil company. Senna was contracted to appear in his McLaren overalls until 31st December. Elf, which would sponsor him in 1994, did not like it; and Shell did not appreciate him carrying an Elf decal on his kart. Senna took a lot of trouble personally to smooth out the differences between the sponsors so that he could compete at Bercy. Finally the two oil giants agreed that he could drive in a neutral white kart.

During these two days in Paris, he was relaxed in a way that had rarely been seen in public. With Adriane always at his side, he laughed that he had one of the special karts they would be driving sent to Brazil so that he could practice. "But unfortunately it arrived so late that I hardly had any time."

In the grand finale, he was dogged by bad luck: he was lying second and gunning for the lead when his kart developed a mechanical fault. He was out of the race. But he was able to joke about it: "Better here than next year in the Williams," he said.

On 8th December he was back in Paris to face the music at an FIA hearing following his fracas with Eddie Irvine at the Japanese Grand Prix. After a three-hour hearing, he was given a two-race ban, suspended for six months. It could have been a lot worse. FISA president Max Mosley commented: "Senna recognised and admitted that he had hit [Irvine]. He was honest and fair, responsible and reasonable and we all felt a great sympathy for him. But what happened cannot be allowed in the sport and there had to be a penalty. Irvine's attitude was extremely provocative and difficult. But Senna also opened discussions in a very heated way." Senna refused to comment on the incident but sources reported that he was 'very upset' by the penalty.

He then flew to London's Heathrow airport in his plane and helicoptered down to the Williams factory for a seat fitting for 1994. It was his first visit to the factory and Frank Williams held a little party in his office for him and Adriane. However, the visit was kept secret. Williams wanted to hold back all publicity for the official launch of the car in January.

Only the barest skeleton of the carbon fibre chassis was ready and Senna offered his opinions on the size and comfort of the cockpit, so any necessary changes could be made over the next six weeks; Adriane sat huddled on a tyre in the corner, shivering.

In mid-December, Senna returned to Brazil where he would spend Christmas and New Year before he returned to Europe on Monday 17th January to prepare for the first of the pre-season tests. As the new car was not yet ready he would be testing the FW15D, a transitional version of the previous year's chassis.

The following evening Senna attended a reception at the Palacio Hotel in Estoril, organised to present the team's 1994 challenge to the press. The mood was buoyant. Frank Williams again expressed his delight at Senna driving for the team. He said: "I have been an admirer of Ayrton for a long time. This gives me very great personal satisfaction. But I am fearful he will think too highly of Williams, so I hope he will not be too disappointed." Senna was not expecting to be disappointed, as he explained: "It's all going to be a bit of a guessing game this year but I suppose I have to say that if I can be as happy at the end of the season as I have felt in the past few weeks it will have been a great year for me."

Everyone present felt that 1994 was going to be his year. A fourth world championship was within his grasp. The combination of Senna and Williams was the best driver in the best car, so what could go wrong? Although firmly convinced that this would be his great year, Senna knew there could be problems ahead even before he had driven the new Williams, shorn of electronic aids, as he said: "With the new rules, the ban on electronic aids, the cards are certain to be reshuffled. Williams will certainly be more affected than others; everything will be much closer between the leaders. I don't see myself as the only favourite this year."

On the Wednesday, Renault revealed its new RS6 engine and the four-day Estoril test began. Senna had a near trouble-free four days, marred only by a couple of spins, and was very pleased with the old car and the new engine. When the teams packed up on Sunday he was fastest with a time of 1m 22.253secs. His nearest rival was his new team-mate, Damon Hill, with a time of 1m 22.662secs; the nearest non-Williams runner was the Ferrari of Gerhard Berger, almost a second behind Hill with a time of 1m 23.631secs. Michael Schumacher and the Benetton team were not present.

The launch of the new car was another month away, because there were more changes to incorporate than in the past few years. Formula One was entering a new era. Driver aids, such as traction control and active suspension, had been banned at the end of 1993, after the top teams had spent massive amounts of money perfecting their systems. The ruling was supposed to cut costs and close the performance gap, but in fact it raised questions about how the new rule could be policed. Refuelling was to return to the sport, raising concerns about safety.

Out went the Kyalami and Donington Park races, and in came Aida, an unpopular Japanese track but one with great paddock facilities. Alain Prost, Riccardo Patrese and Derek Warwick had recently retired, and Heinz-Harald Frentzen, Olivier Panis and Jos Verstappen were about to make their debuts. Also on the grid were Michael Schumacher, Jean Alesi, Rubens Barrichello, Johnny Herbert, Eddie Irvine and Mika Häkkinen. The 1990s had well and truly arrived.

So where did this leave Senna? Unlike Piquet, Prost and Mansell, he would be making the transition to the new era. Approaching his 34th birthday at a time when drivers often raced on into their early 40s, it seemed that he still had time on his side and some people believed that his best was yet to come. He approved of the ban on driver aids, and he didn't think Aida was all that bad when he first visited the track, although he disliked the concept of refuelling. One thing was clear: with the sudden departure of Prost, Piquet and Mansell, he was now the dominant driver. In fact someone pointed out to him that in 1994 he would be the only world champion racing. Consequently he was the only real star in Formula One, and there was a lot of pressure. Although he had had run-ins with Schumacher and Irvine, he had a good rapport with Barrichello, Alesi and Frentzen. He could certainly bridge the gap.

Another characteristic of the new era was the increase in commercialism. There had been a rise in corporate interest in the sport ever since the late 1960s, but in the early- to mid-1990s it moved into overdrive. A driver was no longer just a driver, but also a marketing tool. A computer game called Ayrton Senna's Super Monaco Grand Prix had sold 800,000 copies. There were Senna sweatshirts, Senna mountain bikes, Senna watches, Senna pens, Senna magazines and Senna motorcycles. He had designed his own Senna logo in the shape of a double 'S'. And he was not the only one. The Michael Schumacher Collection had just been launched, and in following years would provide the German's fans with everything from caps and tee-shirts to teddy bears, aftershave and toilet seats.

He had also created his own cartoon character based on himself. The character of Senninha (little Senna) was created by Brazilians Rogério & Ridaut. Rogério had previously worked with commercial designs, while Ridaut was a comic-book creator. They both liked Formula One, and both loved Ayrton Senna. So they decided to create a comic, which would be a copy of Senna, a little Senna: Senninha was born. They didn't have the money to publish it, so they decided to go to the only man who could help them. They went to his office in Brazil in 1992 and arranged a meeting to talk about the project. When they met, Senna realised the two were very talented and loved their ideas. He always wanted to do something for children, but didn't really know what. It had to be educational, it had to be fun – children needed to love it so it had to be exciting. Senninha was the best way to express Senna's feelings towards children. They would learn ethical values in life through Senninha, and have fun reading it. Brazil immediately loved it – it was something of Senna, their hero. He decided to give the first edition of Senninha free to every schoolchild, and it took off in early 1994. He said, as if needing to justify it: "Wealthy men can't live in an island that is encircled by poverty. We all breathe the same air. We must give a chance to everyone, at least a basic chance."

Senna was fully engaged in commercialism of his own in late 1993 and early 1994. He was casting around for a career after motor racing and started to set up business in Brazil.

The first few months of 1994 were spent pursuing those interests and getting the deal together. In between he spent time with Adriane at his Angra beach house and they had a whole month together from late January to the third week of February. In between he was finalising commercial arrangements, with car-maker Audi and the Mont Blanc luxury goods brand, to officially handle their products in Brazil.

In the last week of February, Senna flew to Europe primarily to test the new Williams car and attend a series of business meetings, setting up more commercial deals for him to import European products into Brazil. It was the start of a business empire that would sustain him after retirement, a milestone he figured was now probably only four years away. As he told friends, he had no intention of playing second fiddle to Michael

Schumacher, who was clearly emerging as his chief rival. He reckoned on two years with Williams and his last two or three years with Ferrari.

It was not until 24th February that the new FW16 was finally ready, long after some of the other cars, notably the Benetton Ford B194, had been launched. With the new chassis launched just four weeks before the first race in Brazil, Senna was faced with a hectic test schedule. It was a cold and misty Thursday at Silverstone, and after the covers came off Senna took the car for a 15-lap shakedown test. In public he praised the team's efforts, but he privately admitted to his girlfriend Adriane: "I feel I have arrived here two years too late. The car drives funny." He continued: "I went through a lot to finally be able to sit in that car. But I feel it's going to be hard. Either I haven't adapted myself to the car yet or it's the car that doesn't suit me."

Senna had perhaps naively expected to sit down in the Williams Renault and find the perfect car, as he had done in 1988 with McLaren Honda, and to romp away with the championship. But what he found was a car stripped of all its electronic aids. Without the aids he thought the car potentially dangerous: "It's a stupidity to change the rules. Formula One will regress." Senna told people that he thought the sophisticated electronics system were a big aid to safety. He was also unhappy with the regulations that forced cars to refuel during a race. He thought unnecessarily dangerous and destabilising.

He also wanted to adapt the Williams team to be more like McLaren he had got used to working with his Italian engineer, Giorgio Ascanelli who had not been able to join him at Williams. He said: "I will start making changes slowly. It's a new team, strange faces. I want to change things gradually."

Senna knew timing was everything and he was worried. But sustaining him was the simple lack of competition. Schumacher and Benetton were the only rivals and he felt they would still have an inferior car. He was amazed that chief rivals Prost, Piquet and Mansell had simply disappeared. A generation change had happened without him realising, and he was the man who belonged to neither.

The first week's testing in England was followed by a trip to France, and Senna was more upbeat as he headed to the Paul Ricard track in the south of the country. He was happy to joke about the first time he had visited the French track, just over a decade earlier, when he had been a young hopeful trying out a Brabham Formula One car. He told his pilot Captain O'Mahoney on the way: "When I arrived by train in Marseille from Milan and was standing there at the station, I didn't know how to get to my hotel or the track. Today my jet is standing by. That's not bad progress, is it?"

After the first tests of the new car, Senna had not liked the cramped cockpit (an Adrian Newey design trait) or the position of the steering wheel. After Paul Ricard, he asked for changes to be made to make more room in the cockpit and raise the steering wheel. This was done by cutting away a small portion of the top of the cockpit that formed part of the monocoque and producing a new piece of bodywork. It also necessitated lengthening the steering column and changing its shape.

The modification was necessary because Senna did not like the steering wheel mounted so low, as Nigel Mansell had driven with and Alain Prost had also liked. The lower steering had also enabled a lower cockpit height, which was better aerodynamically.

Senna did not have a chance to test the modifications, which would be ready for the first race of the season in Brazil.

He was due to fly to Brazil on 13th March to incorporate all his promotional activities, but before that he participated in the major test finale of the pre-season: at Imola, the venue for the San Marino Grand Prix on Sunday 1st May.

The Imola test ran from Tuesday 8th to Friday 11th March, with all the major players present. During the test, the drivers noticed a bump on the track at Tamburello that was causing the cars to jump. Senna and Minardi driver Pierluigi Martini went out to the corner and had a meeting with circuit director Giorgio Poggi. The event was filmed by a fan and the film shown at the trial investigating Senna's death three years later. It was one of many impromptu safety meetings held at Tamburello corner, often with Gerhard Berger. They always came to the same conclusion: that the corner was dangerous; there was very little that could be done but the agreed changes were made. There was still a slight bump in the track, but the situation had been vastly improved and Martini believed the bump would only present problems for a car that was already struggling. At the time it was a minor and routine incident. Surprisingly no one suggested that a few rows of tyres against the concrete wall might not be a bad idea.

The surprise of the test was that in the closing minutes of the very last day, Senna's fastest time was beaten by Schumacher. The 25-year-old German slashed Senna's best of 1m 21.2secs down to a straight 1m 21secs. Besides being the last pre-season test, it was the first to pit the FW16 against the opposition, and people were beginning to suggest that they had left it all too late. Senna was unruffled. He said: "The times here are not decisive. This is the end of the winter world championship. The real thing will be seen in

Interlagos." But there was no disguising that the young Schumacher and his Benetton had won the winter world championship.

Senna later let slip to Brazilian journalists that the Williams team had been trying to disguise the car's true potential: he said it had never run with less than 60 litres of fuel, and its fast laps had been timed from a starting point elsewhere on the track – and from there Senna was the fastest.

Everything was not as rosy as Senna made it appear, however. Both he and team-mate Damon Hill had noticed difficulties with the car. It struggled, especially in low-speed corners, was highly sensitive and twitchy, and the cockpit was cramped and uncomfortable. Hill complained: "You don't have to be very far out with the settings and suddenly the car is not competitive. That's good and bad. Good, because it's working straight away. But bad in some ways because you can be out of bed very easily."

All the same, in the eyes of most people, Senna was still the clear title favourite. His biggest challengers were supposed to be his team-mate Hill, McLaren with its new Peugeot engine, and Ferrari. Not everyone took the testing pace of Schumacher's Benetton seriously or believed the driver aid ban would shake up things so much as to wrong-foot the mighty Williams Renaults.

But Senna, the man who had campaigned for a ban on electronic driver aids, was about to find himself wrong-footed. When he had been at McLaren, which didn't have them, he had been a vigorous opponent. Now at Williams, he could see he had got it wrong. In fact Senna disliked the new breed of car from the start, and by the time he reached Brazil he was extremely worried. He ominously reported: "The cars are very fast and difficult to drive. It's going to be a season with a lot of accidents and I'll risk saying we'll be lucky if something really serious doesn't happen."

Schumacher had no idea how bad the Williams was or how good his car was, and he was also downbeat: "Hopefully we can push the Williams. Sometimes to stay close, sometimes to win a race, but, as for the championship, I think we are one more step away from that. They have the best package, but there will nevertheless be races where they don't find the right set-up and we might find the right set-up and it will be very close. We will fight together and then, by strategies or stuff, we will win races. But too many bad things would need to happen to other teams for us to really have a chance to win the championship. Drivers like Senna or Hill, a team like Williams, they don't make mistakes."

In the absence of the 1993 world champion, Alain Prost, Williams would be running numbers 0 and 2 on its cars as 1993 constructors' champion. Against the tradition that the more experienced and illustrious driver took the lower number, Senna would race with number 2 while Damon Hill kept his 0 from the previous year. Senna refused to drive a car labelled zero.

On 11th March he returned to Brazil to spend the two weeks before the Interlagos season-opener with Adriane. After that, he would leave for a whole season in Europe and not return to Brazil until it ended. It was the first time he had done that, and Adriane would arrive in Europe in late April May to spend the season with him.

Once out in Brazil, alongside his press and business commitments, Senna was with family friends and Adriane. There was discord when photographs of Adriane were published in a magazine called *Caras*; Senna thought them unbecoming. But that was a storm in a teacup, reflecting the fact that he really cared for her and that something more serious was afoot in his life than even Formula One. The six-month trip to Europe was a trial run: if it didn't work she would return to Brazil, and if it did they would probably be married.

Senna was also nervous about his first big business venture. He had won the exclusive concession to import German Audi cars into Brazil, and had invited 2,000 guests to a launch on the Tuesday after the Grand Prix. There were hundreds of small details to attend to that week.

On the Monday before the Brazilian Grand Prix he celebrated his 34th birthday with a group of friends. Among them was Gerd Kremer of Mercedes-Benz. He recalls: "The last time I saw him was in Brazil, at the Grand Prix. It was his birthday and he told me that he was worried. He was afraid something would happen to him. He was frightened for the young drivers and that there was nothing he could do if something went wrong with his car."

The Brazilian Grand Prix also brought its own pressures. Senna was Brazil's absolute hero. Only footballer Pelé came close, and he was retired. The pressure on Senna at his home race was enormous. The fans demanded victory and to Senna even second place would be a pitiful reward for their support. An added pressure was that it was the first race of the season – a leap into the unknown for the teams and drivers, and not least Senna, with his growing concerns about the competence of his car.

In the face of all this, Senna still wrestled the car onto pole, the 63rd of his career, with a best time of 1m 15.962secs, 0.328 seconds faster than Schumacher and 1.423 seconds quicker than the next nearest contender, Jean Alesi. Senna topped the timesheets in every practice and qualifying session of the weekend. But he knew what he had needed to do to achieve it. Driving 100 per cent all the time was dangerous, and he told his close friends so. The proof was Hill's position on the grid – nowhere. Just like the latter years at McLaren, Senna found himself carrying the team. He had made an expensive change of team for nothing.

The race was a different story. Senna made by far the best start, and pulled away into the distance as Schumacher got trapped behind Alesi's Ferrari. Two laps later, Schumacher was through and began the seemingly impossible task of chasing down Senna. The cars pitted simultaneously on lap 21, with Senna still in front, but the Benetton pit crew were exceptionally quick and Schumacher regained the track in the lead. Once in the clear air he began to pull away and it was all Senna could do to keep him in view.

After the second round of stops, Schumacher was still out front, but Senna had not given in. In six laps he had reduced the deficit from 9.2 seconds to just five seconds. He was not going to win but that didn't stop him trying. Then his weakness – the reason he had scored 30 per cent more pole positions than race wins – prevailed. Instead of settling down for second, he pushed and pushed and pushed too much. As he rounded the third-gear Cotavelo corner on lap 56, he half-spun and stalled the engine in the middle of the track, for all the world a beginner's error. As Senna unfastened his seatbelts, the crowd began to go home.

Schumacher won. Senna offered no excuses for the spin. He said: "There was nothing wrong with the car. It was my fault. I was pushing too hard. For me it's the most disappointing when I can't give anything back to my fans here, who love me so much. It was obviously my mistake, but I needed to win. A second place in Brazil would have meant nothing to me." Second would in fact have meant six points and less pressure. But his comments summed up the way he drove – a weakness that would simply increase the pressure until that fateful day at Imola.

Damon Hill was no happier with the car, reporting: "I would describe it as virtually undriveable in the slow corners. And in the quick ones, it threatened to turf you off the track at any moment. It is unpredictable."

Even overlooking Senna's mistake, however. Benetton had still run rings around Williams in the race, in clever pitwork and outright pace. It came as a surprise to many, who before the season began had believed the Williams-Senna combination was an undoubted super-team. Schumacher, assisted by rising engineer Ross Brawn and experienced designer Rory Byrne, was forging his own super-team.

But even for those who rated Schumacher's talent, the leap made by the Benetton chassis since 1993 seemed unthinkable. At this early stage in the season, the first accusations began that Benetton was running banned driver aids, including traction control. Senna heard the rumours and was disturbed by them.

He stayed in Brazil for another week after the Grand Prix. The Audi concession launch went well. For a shy man Senna stepped confidently up to the microphone in front of his 2,000 guests and delivered a speech with the coolness of a professional speaker. It surprised his father Milton just how good he was. He was clearly enjoying his new challenge as a businessman. He was as natural at it as he was at driving. A few days later, he said his goodbyes to his family and Adriane and headed back to Europe for essential FW16 testing.

Three hard days at Jerez were never going to solve all the problems, and a few days later Senna was on the long-haul flight to Japan for the Pacific Grand Prix at Aida, with the memory of Interlagos still fresh in his mind.

On the Thursday of the Grand Prix, Senna was spotted chatting openly to Schumacher in the paddock. It was unusual as the pair had never been particularly friendly. When questioned about the meeting later, Schumacher revealed: "He wanted to congratulate me on my win in Brazil, as he had not seen me since and we said some nice things. That is all there was to it." There was probably more to it, and some observers noted that Senna was probably trying to find out all he could about the new opposition.

One of the major news stories at Aida came from remarks in the Italian press by Nicola Larini – standing in for Jean Alesi, who had injured his neck – who implied Ferrari had some kind of traction-control system on its cars. Harsh punishments had been promised for any team found cheating that season, but after an investigation the FIA decided there was no need for sanctions. In reality, at that stage the FIA had little idea of how to police the new regulations. It was all new territory.

In Japan, Senna was convinced that Benetton was using the banned traction control. He wrestled his car again to pole – the 64th of his career – although qualifying did not pass without incident. His time came from the Friday session and luckily for him the Saturday times were slower in the higher temperatures because he spun during his first run, a move mirrored by Damon Hill. A frustrated Senna said: "I really don't know what happened. It's odd that it happened the same for both of us. But I really don't understand because the car had one of the best positions at that point of the corner throughout the weekend. It was disappointing and frustrating because it looks silly and stupid. I feel very unhappy about it... with myself. But it was better it happened today and not tomorrow."

Senna did not like being made to look stupid, especially when there seemed to be no real reason for it. It was reminiscent of his Formula Three career when he had been struggling against Martin Brundle, unable to understand why the Englishman was suddenly quicker than he was and not knowing that Brundle had received engine improvements he had not had himself. He had crashed on several occasions in the second half of the season then. Dick Bennetts, his Formula Three team boss, said: "If we'd had the same engine rebuild six or seven races before we wouldn't have had half the accidents that we did."

Amazingly Senna was hopeful for the race. But it was misplaced. He didn't make it past the first corner, having starting sluggishly, and Schumacher flew past him into the lead. The German braked earlier for the first corner than Senna expected: when Senna braked, the fast-starting Mika Häkkinen ran into the back of him, punting Senna into a spin that resulted in him being t-boned by Larini's Ferrari.

Senna was furious with Häkkinen, his former team-mate. "It was very irresponsible driving and shouldn't be allowed," he burst out. After his accident he spent several laps standing at the side of the track watching Schumacher and the other cars pass. Some thought he was listening for traction control. Schumacher won the race, and with it had claimed a maximum 20 points to Senna's none.

Before the season had begun, people were predicting that the best Schumacher could hope for after two races would be an eight-point deficit to Senna. Claims that in 1994 Senna could score 10 or 11 wins and beat Prost's all-time record were beginning to look shaky. Some less kind commentators suggested that Senna had cracked. But he could not comment on how bad the car was publicly out of deference to Williams and Renault. Once again the pundits had got it wrong, but it all piled on extra pressure for Imola.

After watching the Benetton for lap after lap Senna was sure it had traction control. He had also been surprised how quickly the car had come off the line, and believed it was using the banned launch control as well.

Peter Collins, the Lotus team principal, went to see Frank Williams after the race. While he was waiting, he bumped into Senna. Collins remembers it well: "I said to Ayrton that the Benetton was behaving like a car that had traction control. Ayrton, suddenly animated that I had reflected exactly what he was thinking, said to me: 'I am sure they are. I have followed it a number of times and I am sure they are'."

Senna told Collins he was determined to beat him whatever. Collins says: "He saw himself as being on a crusade of integrity and honour." The conversation ended as Collins went off to converse with Frank Williams: he was convinced that Senna was resolved to do something about it.

Senna arrived back in England on the Tuesday after the race and attended the post-race briefing at the Didcot factory. Williams staffers were surprised. On the following day he flew to Paris where he kicked off a football friendly between Brazil and Paris St Germain. From there he returned to his home at Quinta do Largo in Portugal before he was due at the French track of Nogaro on Monday 25th April, for a quick shakedown test of the reportedly improved FW16. He went from there to Munich, where on Tuesday he had meetings concerning his Audi car importing business in Brazil. On Wednesday 27th April, his pilot Captain O'Mahoney was waiting in Munich to fly him back home and then on to Bologna for his date with destiny at the San Marino Grand Prix.

CHAPTER 30

Death: 2:18pm Sunday 1st May 1994

The final accounting

The first time 200 million TV viewers realised that Ayrton Senna had failed to complete lap seven of the San Marino Grand Prix was when Michael Schumacher's Benetton Ford swept into their screens at the exit of Tamburello. They could just see a cloud of dust in the background, as his Williams Renault rebounded off the Tamburello concrete wall and came to rest in the middle of the run-off area.

Murray Walker was commentating on British television: "Well, we are right with Michael Schumacher now, and Senna, my goodness, I just saw it punch off to the right, what on earth happened there I don't know." Walker's shock and surprise was down to Senna being out of his third race in succession with no points on the board. He had no reason to worry about Senna's safety; he had seen many, many accidents worse than this.

But one man felt immediate concern. Brazilian commentator Galvao Bueno, in the TV Globo cabin, had Senna's friend Antonio Braga by his side. He was the first to realise the accident was probably fatal. He and Braga simply looked at each other. They knew it was very bad. Bueno was more knowledgeable than most TV journalists, simply because he was one of Senna's best friends and had total access. Reginaldo Leme was also in the commentary box with them.

Bueno made no attempt to play down the situation. He said to millions of

Brazilians: "Ayrton has hit [the wall] badly. It's serious, it's very serious." Bueno quickly worked out Senna's crash speed. He told Braga: "You know, when you hit a wall at 130mph, already the deceleration is lethal." In truth, drivers should never survive accidents of this nature, but in reality they do most of the time and, not only that, walk away uninjured. But this was not one of those times.

Murray Walker is no less knowledgeable but not in Bueno's technical way. The BBC was showing continuous re-runs to avoid events on the ground.

But before the marshals could get to Senna and the first medical car had reached the scene, his head moved forward in the cockpit and unknowing viewers were encouraged that the champion was intact. Another man, sitting thousands of miles away in Balcarce, Argentina, knew different. Five-time, world champion, 82-year-old Juan Manuel Fangio knew the outcome when he saw the spasm, the sign of a massive head injury. He switched off his television. He said later: "I knew he was dead."

It soon became apparent that in describing the split-second before the car hit the wall, Bueno had been spot on. Senna had managed to slow the car by 60 mph before it hit the wall, and the impact speed was estimated at 130 mph. The right-hand front of the car took the full brunt of the impact: a wheel flew off and was trapped between the chassis and the wall, as the suspension crumpled and the Williams catapulted back onto the track. The monocoque was split by the force of the impact, but otherwise intact.

Marshals were quickly on the scene, but were frozen in their tracks by what they saw.

As a helicopter with an overhead camera was soon hovering, pictures of the car were being transmitted live to an avid audience. BBC television and Murray Walker sensitively switched to its pitlane camera, but other broadcasters did not and stayed glued to the scene. It was starting to become very unpleasant.

Senna's girlfriend Adriane Galisteu was at Senna's home in Portugal, watching the race on television. When his car hit the wall, she remembers a selfish thought went through her mind: "Oh that's good! He'll be home sooner." She waited for him to throw off his gloves, undo the steering wheel and leap from the cockpit. It didn't occur to her for a second that he wouldn't. Even in the 18 months she had known him, this had happened a few times, always with the same outcome.

Captain O'Mahoney, who had moved Senna's plane to Bologna for a quick departure, was also watching the race on television in the executive jet centre. He got ready to leave early when he saw the crash. But when his boss didn't get out of his car he quickly sat down again.

Josef Leberer was in the Williams garage. He remembered: "I said c'mon, c'mon, move, move, get out of the car, boy." Suddenly a heavy feeling enveloped Leberer, who knew something was very wrong.

The Portuguese TV commentators gave Adriane no cause for concern and there was nothing that suggested to her that the accident was anything out of the ordinary, certainly no more serious than other crashes he had survived. She remembered: "I jumped up from the sofa, holding the plate on which I was having my lunch." But that soon changed. She grew more anxious as he stayed in the car. She shouted out to Senna's Portuguese housekeeper, Juraci: "What are they waiting for?" She said: "He must have broken his arms or a leg." She screamed at the TV: "Get out of the car, get out!" After a few minutes when he had not moved, she recalled: "I was motionless and I started to sob."

As Professor Sid Watkins approached Tamburello in his medical car, he somehow knew it was Senna who had crashed. Watkins found him slumped in the Williams. The doctor from the first intervention car was already with him and cradling his head, aware from the condition of his helmet and seeping blood that he had suffered a massive head injury. The two men looked at each other, unsure of what they would see when they got the helmet off. Watkins frantically cut the chin strap and lifted the helmet off gently, whilst others supported his neck. Blood poured out. His forehead was a mess and, more worryingly, blood and brain matter was seeping from his nose.

Watkins appraised him. Senna's eyes were closed and he was deeply unconscious. Instinctively Watkins forced a tube into his mouth to obtain effective airflow. Watkins shouted for blood – his team already knew Senna's blood type: B+.

By then the other race cars had stopped going around and the crowd was silent. Senna looked serene as Watkins did what he had to, and raised his eyelids. He remembered: "It was clear from his pupils that he had had a massive brain injury. I knew from seeing the extent of his injury that he could not survive." The medics lifted him out of the car. The blood was still flowing. They lay him on the ground, as marshals held up sheets to shield him from view. Watkins said: "As we did he sighed and, though I am totally agnostic, I felt his soul departed at that moment."

There was only one photographer at Tamburello that afternoon. Angelo Orsi, a close friend of Senna's and the picture editor of *Autosprint*, the Italian racing magazine, leapt over the wall when the car came to rest and started snapping. He took close-ups of Senna in the car and after his helmet was removed, and then when he was being treated on the ground, before marshals blocked his view. Galvao Bueno was watching Orsi on television, and said: "He aimed and shot, without even seeing exactly what he was getting."

Adriane Galisteu was watching anxiously on television. She looked at his feet for signs of life, for she understood what she called the language of feet. She saw no movement. His feet told her he was dead, but she put that thought completely from her mind. By then the housekeeper was a screaming wreck, and Senna's close neighbours had started to arrive at the house to see if there was anything they could do. Although people at the circuit were calm, on television viewers had seen everything. The sharpereyed had seen blood seeping from the car like oil; it carried on as Senna lay on the ground, staining the track red. It was not obvious unless you knew what to look for. Later it would be revealed that Senna had suffered a burst temporal artery and lost 4.5 litres of blood.

In the TV Globo cabin, Bueno could not see what Watkins could, but he was reading the body language of Watkins and the doctors: "At the moment of the disaster, by the way it happened and by the way he was rescued, I knew that it was extremely serious, but I had to continue to commentate on the race until the end. Bueno had already had a difficult time on Friday when the young Brazilian driver Rubens Barrichello was taken to hospital.

Frank Williams was watching in the Williams pit; Alain Prost was alongside him. They anxiously scanned the monitors. Williams had experienced death at the track when his driver Piers Courage lost his life in 1970; 24 years on, the same emotions stirred.

Roaming around the garden at Quinta do Lago, Senna's dog also seemed to sense that his master was in trouble and began barking loudly. The neighbours' dogs started to bark. Neyde da Silva called Adriane from the farm at Tatui for information. Adriane had none. After that the telephone never stopped, as neighbours congregated at the house. The peaceful retreat had suddenly turned to bedlam.

Dr Pezzi, one of the trackside medics, got on with intubating Senna and, under Watkins' supervision, the team inserted several IV infusions into the inert form. They had to clear the respiratory passages; stem the blood flow and replace lost blood; and immobilise the cervical area. After that was done Senna had a faint pulse. Watkins followed procedure and decided Senna should go straight to Maggiore Hospital for urgent treatment in intensive care conditions, although he knew it would be fruitless. He radioed for the medical helicopter and asked Dr Giovanni Gordini, the intensive care anaesthetist in charge of the circuit's medical centre, to accompany Senna to Maggiore.

The helicopter quickly arrived but Watkins decided not to accompany Senna as he realised that there was nothing he could do. As medics loaded Senna into the helicopter at around 2:35pm, he took a call on his personal radio from Martin Whitaker, the FIA's press supremo, who was with Bernie Ecclestone in his grey motorhome parked by the paddock gates. Ecclestone wanted information. With Whitaker and Ecclestone was Leonardo da Silva.

Senna was still alive, and Watkins told Whitaker the problem was his head. Over the crackly radio, Whitaker mistakenly misheard him as saying he was dead. This would cause much unhappiness later. Whitaker whispered to Bernie Ecclestone who was eating an apple. Ecclestone saw no point in hiding the truth from Leonardo and told him his brother was dead. He said: "I'm sorry, he's dead, but we'll only announce it after the end of the race." Whilst he was doing this Ecclestone was coping with his own personal grief, and he calmly tossed the apple core over his shoulder. Ecclestone knew that, of all people, he had to remain calm. He was already thinking ahead to what Senna's death would mean, sub-consciously making plans and weighing up every possibility. Leonardo mistook his calmness as indifference and disrespect for his brother, and was astonished that plans were going ahead to restart the race with his brother dead. He was almost beside himself with grief, and although it was quickly established what Watkins had really said, the damage was done: Senna's brother lost control. Ecclestone told Whitaker to fetch Josef Leberer immediately to help Leonardo with his grief. The younger brother was distraught. His last words to his brother had not been friendly and they were still arguing about Adriane that morning.

Meanwhile, as the helicopter ascended, Watkins picked up Senna's helmet. But as he looked around, he couldn't find either his own gloves or Senna's. Neither pair was ever seen again. As he looked for them, another drama was happening in the air. The 20-minute helicopter ride was barely three minutes old when Senna's heart stopped. Dr Gordini worked on him frantically, and finally got it going again.

Adriane watched Senna's motionless body being loaded into the helicopter. Someone pointed out the red stain on the ground after he been moved. It startled her. A neighbour tried to reassure her, saying it was a new kind of fire extinguisher foam. She believed it at the time, thinking to herself: "Nobody ever thought Ayrton Senna would die in a racing car. Neither had I."

Meanwhile, Sid Watkins was driven at speed back to the circuit's medical centre. He quickly told the centre's Dr Servadei details of Senna's condition, so that he could brief Maggiore hospital by telephone for Senna's arrival. In reality he knew there was nothing they would be able to do, other than going through the motions. Watkins doubted Senna could last long, even with the help of a life-support machine. Like Ecclestone, Senna had been a close personal friend, and Watkins was having to deal with his own personal grief at the same time as organising Senna's care. Watkins turned round and saw that Josef Leberer had come into the medical centre. They didn't need to exchange words. Leberer remembered: "I saw Professor Watkins and he just looked in my eyes and then I knew it was going to be a very serious thing. He didn't say anything." After the silence, Watkins briefed him. At that moment Whitaker finally tracked down Leberer and a message arrived for him to go urgently to Bernie Ecclestone's motorhome.

Leberer found Senna's brother Leonardo in a high state of distress. Leberer said: "I had to calm his brother down." At that point, Leonardo thought his brother was dead after the misheard radio conversation. Leberer told him he was in a serious state but still alive and they should get to Maggiore as soon as possible. Leonardo calmed down enough to phone his parents in Brazil from the motorhome telephone. Meanwhile, Ecclestone arranged for his helicopter to take them to the hospital. They left immediately with Julian Jakobi following.

Ecclestone went off to confer with Max Mosley, the FIA president. Afterwards he toured the pitlane, assuring everyone that everything was being done for Senna. What he was sure of was that the race would restart and run to a conclusion. It always did. That was the way of Formula One. Like Frank Williams, emotions from 1970 were flooding over Ecclestone. Months after Williams had lost Piers Courage, he had lost Jochen Rindt who he had managed. But no one could sense his turmoil. Ecclestone was doing what he had always done for Formula One: creating stability in a very unstable environment.

With Leonardo on his way to Maggiore, Antonio Braga called his wife Luiza, who was in their house in Sintra near Lisbon with their teenage daughters Joanna and Maria. He told her to phone Adriane and tell her to get to Bologna as soon as possible. Braga knew that Senna was dying but thought there would be time for her to say goodbye. He told Luiza to charter her a plane from Faro to bring her to Bologna. Braga went back to the TV Globo cabin.

Luiza, who had also been following events on television, called Quinta do Lago. She told Adriane it was extremely serious: "Braga called me from

Imola. It's extremely serious. You have to go there immediately." Adriane replied: "Luiza, come with me. Don't leave me alone."

Luiza agreed to accompany her there: she would charter a jet in Lisbon and pick Adriane up at Faro. She told her she would be there at around 5pm. The flight to Faro would only take half-an-hour, but renting a jet at short notice on a Sunday proved difficult and it would take three-and-a-half hours for Luiza Braga to hire the plane and fly to Faro.

After putting the phone down, Braga discussed with Galvao Bueno what they should do. They agreed to leave for the hospital straight after the race. Braga called Senna's father Milton, who was following the race on television with his wife Neyde. He told them it was serious and to stand by to come to Bologna.

Meanwhile the drivers had no idea what had happened, other than that Senna had had an accident. As they formed up on the grid for the restart, people were saying there was no problem, that he was out of the car; others were saying there was a big problem. Gerhard Berger remembered: "At the time I didn't realise how bad it was. I didn't see his accident as I was in the car behind him but you get a feeling from the atmosphere, and there was a strange atmosphere."

Like Ecclestone, Watkins calmly went about his business. He replenished his medical bag from the stores in the medical centre and walked back to his car to await the restart.

Prior to that, just before 3 o'clock, the wreckage of Senna's car was brought to the parc fermé and put in the steward's garage, under the care of Fabrizio Nosco. Patrick Head was aware of how serious the accident was, as he and Frank Williams had been briefed by Bernie Ecclestone. The gravity was confirmed when the car had not been brought straight back to the Williams garage. Head was anxious to see the telemetry and sent two of his mechanics to the garage to fetch the black boxes. Nosco, a technical commissioner, politely refused them entry. He told them that, under FISA rules, no one could touch the car. They went away and returned with FISA's technical delegate, Charlie Whiting, who ordered Nosco to remove the boxes and hand them to the mechanics. Nosco said: "Whiting told me to open up the garage and that he had permission from John Corsmit, the FIA security chief that day. He told me to remove the black boxes.

"The Renault engine box was situated behind the cockpit. I removed it with a pair of large pliers. The Williams chassis box was behind the radiator near the back wheel, on the right wing of the car. I have seen thousands of these devices and removed them for checks. The two boxes were intact, even though they had some scratches. The Williams device looked to have survived the crash."

Back at the Williams garage, engineer Marco Spiga tried to retrieve the data. But power had been lost to the box and wiped the memory. Although the box was basically intact, the connectors had been badly damaged in the accident. Spiga said: "The Williams box was totally unreadable when we got it back." They had more luck with the Renault box, and the data was transferred to a diskette.

At 2:55pm, 37 minutes after Senna's crash, the race was restarted. Five minutes later, the helicopter carrying Senna landed in front of Maggiore hospital. Doctors rushed out and wheeled him straight into intensive care for a brain scan that would only confirm the diagnosis made at the track. At 3:10pm his heart stopped again. The doctors were able to restart it, before putting him in a clean room on a life-support machine.

In Brazil, the streets of the major cities were quiet on that Sunday morning, as the whole country woke from its slumbers as the news spread and huddled in front of television sets, hanging on Galvao Bueno's every word. Bueno was well aware that, since the accident, probably half of the Brazilian population had woken up and was watching his broadcast and listening to his words. He also knew that Milton and Neyde da Silva and Senna's sister Viviane would be watching. He found it a terrible responsibility: "They were all listening to me, hoping I would say some good news. Reginaldo and Antonio, who was like a father to Ayrton, kept looking at me speechless, having the same worry. Through my earphones I was constantly being pushed forward by our manager, and also from our studios in Brazil they kept asking me to go on. At least three times I left the cabin to catch some breath. And because I had this great friendship with Ayrton, people started coming to our cabin, Rubinho's [Barrichello's] manager, Christian's [Fittipaldi's] girlfriend, everybody apparently expecting something to hope for." But TV Globo had the best sources of information, and a reporter at the studio had given two bulletins on Senna's condition, warning that his brain damage was severe.

The later it got, the streets of Rio de Janeiro and São Paulo stayed eerily deserted at around 8am local time. As Senna struggled for life, and TV Globo commentators predicted the worst, millions of Brazilians held their breath, not quite believing what they were witnessing on live television.

Meanwhile, Berger led the restarted race for the first 11 laps before pitting with a suspension problem. Berger remembered: "I was just thinking 'shit, what is happening now?'"

On lap 41 a wheel had flown off Michele Alboreto's Minardi car at the pit exit and flown into a crowd of Lotus mechanics. It hadn't been fastened properly at a pitstop. Alboreto was almost glad. He jumped out of his car, dumped his helmet in the pit garage and ran to the medical centre to talk to the Italian doctors. They told him the full truth of what had happened to Senna. After a brief discussion in Italian, Alboreto walked glumly back to the Ferrari garage to speak to his old team-mate Berger, who by then had got out of his car, having retired from the restarted race on lap 14. Alboreto told him: "It's very bad with Ayrton, he's in hospital in Bologna and very critical." Berger said: "Why are all these things happening?"

Ten minutes before the end of the race, Bueno realised that it would take them too long to get to the hospital by car with all the race traffic. He told Braga to go and find a helicopter. Braga went off and found Jo Ramirez, the McLaren team manager, who organised it. Brazilian driver Christian Fittipaldi sent a note to his broadcast cabin asking him if he could accompany them to the hospital. Bueno sent a message back to be ready.

For Sid Watkins, the next two hours were terrible, as he watched the cars go by. It seemed interminable. But he breathed a sigh of relief as the race finally ended at 4:20pm with no further incident. Michael Schumacher, Senna's natural successor, inevitably won. He and the other drivers on the podium, Nicola Larini and Mika Häkkinen, had little idea of Senna's condition but their faces revealed that they feared the worse.

As soon as the race was over, Bueno threw off his headphones and left the studio back in Brazil to carry on. By this time Bueno knew Senna was dying and he wanted to be there when he did; not out of any professional duty, as he wanted no part in the reporting of his friend's demise, but out of personal duty. He rushed straight to the Arrows motorhome. Fittipaldi was half-dressed and pleaded for Bueno to wait. Bueno told him to come to the McLaren motorhome, where there was a crowd of people surrounding Antonio Braga, including Gerhard Berger, Ron Dennis and Jo Ramirez. Berger was recommending that Braga call a neurosurgeon he knew in Paris who had once saved Jean Alesi from brain damage after an accident. Berger said that he could organise a jet to bring the doctor from Paris. Braga told him to get on with it. Bueno waited impatiently for Fittipaldi to arrive.

Sid Watkins ran back to the medical centre and found Lotus team principal Peter Collins waiting for him, looking for news about Senna. Collins and

Watkins were close friends; the professor was closer to Collins than to any other team principal. Collins had come to find out about Senna, but he pretended concern over his mechanics, whom he already knew were alright. When Watkins told Collins his mechanics would be fine, Collins asked him if Senna was in a bad way and Watkins simply said 'yes'. When he asked him if there was any hope, he shook his head and simply said 'no'. Collins was the first of the Formula One fraternity to find out the truth that all the others feared.

Bologna's chief medical officer Dr Maria Theresa Fiandri had been called out to Maggiore hospital, and she took charge. She was interviewed by a local reporter who had been tipped off. She told him that surgery was out of the question.

Half-an-hour later, several dozen reporters and some TV crews had arrived. At 4:30pm, Dr Fiandri read out a clinical bulletin. She said Ayrton Senna had brain damage, with haemorrhaged shock and was in a deep coma. She told the reporters there would be another bulletin at 6 o'clock.

The Italian police, tipped off that the accident was probably fatal, had arrived shortly before the end of the race and taken away Senna's helmet.

When Sid Watkins had finished at the medical centre, he knew his place was at the hospital. He quickly changed, leaving his overalls strewn on the floor, and ran to the medical helicopter, which had returned from Maggiore. With Dr Servadei for company, he took off straight for the hospital. He also wanted to get away from the gloom that had fallen over Imola. It was a terrible place to be at that moment.

Bueno, fed up with waiting, told his friends to meet him at the helicopter pad. He rushed back to Arrows to collect Fittipaldi. He ran into Jose Pinto of the Portuguese TV company, threw him the keys to his hire car, and told him to give them to Reginaldo Leme, with instructions to meet him at Maggiore.

As he rushed to the helicopter pad with Fittipaldi, he phoned a TV Globo reporter at the hospital who told him Senna would not last long. After a wait, the helicopter arrived and Braga, Berger, Fittipaldi and Bueno took off for Maggiore. The trip was made in absolute silence. These were four men as close to Senna as it was possible to be. The tragedy that had unfolded that afternoon defied any meaningful words.

The cramped Imola media centre, as word of Senna's condition circulated, was enveloped by a shroud of dread. He would never race again, at best, and most were under no illusion that he would be dead before midnight.

Top journalist David Tremayne had been tipped off by Collins and was starting to write an obituary for the next day's edition of the London *Independent*. Other British journalists with national newspaper contracts followed suit. Many of them hadn't much cared for Senna when he was alive, but the enormity of his imminent passing weighed heavily.

When Sid Watkins arrived at Maggiore, he conferred with the doctors who had been treating Senna. They had ordered an immediate brain scan. It merely confirmed that Senna had no chance of surviving the accident. Watkins was told Senna had multiple fractures of the base of the skull where his head had smashed into the carbon-fibre headrest of the monocoque. What had likely happened was that the right front wheel had shot up after impact like a catapult and violated the cockpit area where Senna was sitting. It impacted the right frontal area of his helmet, and the violence of the wheel's impact pushed his head back against the headrest, causing the fatal skull fractures. A piece of upright attached to the wheel had partially penetrated his helmet and made a big indent in his forehead. In addition, it appeared that a jagged piece of the upright assembly had penetrated the helmet visor just above his right eye. Any one of the three injuries would probably have killed him. The combination of them all made it certain. Only Senna's extremely high level of fitness meant he had momentarily survived. He suffered brain death on impact but the lack of any physical injury to the rest of his body meant that his heart and lungs continued to function. The neurosurgeon who examined Senna said that the circumstances did not call for surgery because the wound was generalised in the cranium. But an X-ray of the damage to his skull and brain indicated he would not last long, even with a machine maintaining his vital functions. Watkins looked at the monitors of blood pressure, respiration and heart rate: the end was near.

Although their helicopter had left before Watkins', finally Leonardo arrived with Josef Leberer. Then Julian Jakobi turned up. He had hitched a lift to the hospital with a Brazilian journalist, who knew the way after a trip the previous Friday to visit Barrichello.

Dr Servadei and Dr Gordini together with Watkins immediately took Leonardo, Leberer and Jakobi into a small room, next to Senna's. He told them that the end was near, that the situation was hopeless. Leonardo was in a hopeless condition himself, unable to absorb the news, but Jakobi and Leberer accepted the news stoically, and supported him. Like Watkins and Ecclestone, Jakobi also had to be strong whilst coping with intense personal grief. Leberer wanted to go in and see Senna whilst Jakobi comforted Leonardo. The doctors warned him that Senna did not look good because of his head injuries. But

Leberer went in to see his friend for the last time. In the room, the life-support systems were noisy. Leberer saw his friend's massive head injuries. He said: "I knew every part of his body. I was there because I wanted to see him there. We were more than six years together. We were friends and I did not have a problem to go there, even if there was a big injury."

As Watkins was talking to Leonardo, Galvao Bueno's helicopter was landing in front of Maggiore hospital. Hospital staff recognised Gerhard Berger and the group was quickly ushered through to the intensive-care unit. The four men were led into the little room where Professor Watkins told them bluntly that Senna was already dead but that his heart was still beating. Berger remembered: "Sid Watkins told me it was very, very, very critical and basically there was no chance of getting him through." Bueno remembered: "Sid Watkins said, 'He is dead. He is brain dead, his heart stopped, we managed to make it go again, and he is kept alive with machines, but the Italian law requires us to wait 12 hours and take another ECG. Only after this can we disconnect him.' I asked him: 'But Dr Sid, will we have to wait suffering for 12 hours?' He answered that he did not believe that even with support Ayrton's heart would hold on for these 12 hours."

Watkins suggested they all went in to see him before that happened. Berger went first, with Josef Leberer supporting him. Berger sat down by his bed with all his memories of the man who had shared his career and also been a big part of his life outside the sport. He quietly spoke to Senna's lifeless form. After spending a few intimate minutes in the bleak hospital room he quietly say his final goodbyes and kissed his friend on the cheek. He said: "I spent a few minutes with him and then that was that."

Then, in turn, the others went in to say goodbye.

By now Senna's family had gathered at the family farm in Tatui. Viviane Senna's husband Flavio Lalli was fulfilling the same role as Ecclestone, Watkins and Jakobi, and had taken charge of a distraught family. Watkins was handed a phone with Lalli on the line. He told Lalli what he had told Leonardo, Jakobi, Bueno, Berger, Braga and Fittipaldi, that the situation was truly hopeless and that Senna would soon die. The family were on the verge of a decision to catch a chartered jet straight to Bologna. Watkins told him it would be inap-propriate as there was nothing they could do. Watkins remembered: "They accepted the tragic news with dignity, and took my advice to remain in Brazil."

After Berger went into Senna's room, Watkins decided to leave, unable to take any more. He was used to death, but this was unlike anything he had experienced. Watkins had borne the brunt of the tragedy. It had fallen to him to tell Senna's family that he was effectively dead. Even he could only take so much. Although Senna was still technically alive there was nothing more he could do. It was just a question of waiting for the inevitable, which Watkins' experience told him would be within the hour. For him, his friend was already dead. He took the chance of a lift back to his hotel. Watkins needed some time on his own to come to terms with the day's events. When he got to his room, a man who had seen death many times discovered his own vulnerability as the television replayed the accident incessantly.

Like Watkins, Berger needed some solitude. He took a helicopter to the airport, then his plane home to Austria. At the airport, in the evening dusk, he saw Senna's plane waiting forlornly for an owner that would never return. Berger broke down, overpowered by the silhouette.

In Portugal, Luiza Braga tried frantically to book a plane, as friends helped Adriane pack enough clothes for three days. She knew there was little hope, but told herself she would be by his bedside, waiting for him to recover. It was the only possible thought, and it kept her going.

As she waited, a neighbour told her she had heard he had recovered consciousness. Adriane's own mother phoned from São Paulo and asked what was happening. Adriane told her she hoped Senna would recover and that it was not as serious as was thought. Her no-nonsense mother immediately disabused her of that and made her face reality. TV Globo was delivering far more accurate information to Brazilian viewers than the more reserved European television channels, which were waiting for an official bulletin and shying away from the reality. Adriane's mother told her the truth: that only a miracle could save him. After putting the phone down from her mother, Adriane felt her emotions going out of control. Her friends gave her a tranquilliser pill. She phoned Neyde da Silva at home in Brazil and tried to calm Neyde down, telling her she had heard her son had recovered consciousness. Neyde told her the family would catch a plane to Bologna at 2:30pm (local time).

Even as they spoke, at Maggiore hospital electrical brain tests confirmed that Senna was brain dead and being kept alive only by artificial means. Senior doctors conferred about the press bulletin promised for 6 o'clock. They did not want to raise any false hopes, nor could they say he was dead, because he wasn't. By law, the machine could not be turned off. They compromised with an announcement saying Senna was clinically dead.

At 6:05pm Dr Fiandri, her voice shaking at the gravity of her announcement, told reporters that Senna was clinically dead. He was still connected, she said, to the equipment maintaining his heartbeat. The news led the early-evening news programmes. In Britain an hour behind Europe, the news bulletins waited for a more final verdict.

Josef Leberer returned to Imola to fetch his car. A doctor gave him a lift.

Neyde da Silva, calling from Brazil, told her son Leonardo to ask the hospital to arrange for a priest to visit her eldest son. The priest arrived, went into Senna's room at 6:15pm, and gave him the last rites. At 6:37pm Senna's heart stopped again and Dr Fiandri decided not to try and restart it. Keeping a man who was effectively dead artificially alive was ethically doubtful. She said enough was enough. At 6:40pm, Dr Fiandri pronounced Ayrton Senna dead, but said the official time of death would be 2:17pm, when he had impacted the wall and his brain had stopped working.

Oblivious to this, Juraci drove Adriane to Faro airport. When the chartered plane arrived, around 6:30pm, Adriane was waiting desperately on the tarmac. As soon as the door opened, she scrambled on board and into Luiza Braga's arms. The pilot told them it would be a three-hour flight. On board, Luiza told Adriane that her boyfriend was as strong as an ox and that she had heard nothing more from her husband at the circuit, other that it was very serious. But even as they spoke, Senna was already dead.

The captain taxied to the edge of the runway, and waited for clearance to take off. As he waited, a message was relayed to the plane. The pilot immediately taxied back to the terminal building, without a word to his passengers. The message was that Ayrton Senna had passed away, but the captain didn't want to be the one to break the news to them. He finally told them there was an urgent call for Luiza back at the control tower. He said: "I don't have authorisation from the tower. There is a call for Luiza and Adriane."

Adriane shook with fear about what the call might reveal.

Luiza rushed off as soon as the plane door opened. Adriane stepped from the plane and was overwhelmed at the silence in the terminal, the silent people there, betraying the news she didn't want to hear. Adriane followed Luiza to the control tower. "I shook all over, from head to toe," she remembered. She waited in silence alone. Luiza Braga was pale when she returned. She took Adriane's hand. "Adriane," she said, but Adriane interrupted her and said: "Luiza, only don't tell me he has died." She replied the only way she could: "He's died."

The two women hugged each other for comfort. They spent 40 minutes in the control tower, sobbing and trying to come to terms with the devastating news. They did not know what to do, and were driven back to Senna's house at Quinto da Lago. The pilot waited at Faro for instructions. When they returned they found the whole house in mourning. Juraci, the housekeeper, who had regarded Senna as her son, was screaming. Adriane made for their bedroom and lay motionless on the bed for two hours. She remembers: "I naively thought I would see him arrive that night, even earlier than expected, with that beautiful smile of his, ready for a reunion after almost a month."

When Josef Leberer returned to the paddock from the hospital he found it a desolate place. Everyone was trying to come to terms with what had happened. By that time his death had been announced. He remembered: "It seemed like everybody was waiting and asking, 'what's happened, what's happened, what's happened?'. I had to tell them."

Leberer had to cope with two grieving teams. Not only his own but also McLaren. Ron and Lisa Dennis and Mansour and Cathy Ojjeh huddled around him for news. He found Frank Williams and Patrick Head in a state of disbelief. After finally getting Senna to drive for them after all these years they couldn't believe he was gone so quickly.

He couldn't cope with too much of it and drove his car back to the hotel.

Meanwhile, Luiza Braga spoke to her husband at the hospital who told her there was no point going to Bologna and to pack some bags and prepare to return to Brazil for the funeral. Braga told his wife to take Adriane to their home in Sintra with one of the cars Senna kept at the villa. He said he would join them as soon as he had got Leonardo back to Brazil and made the arrangements to have Senna's returned to Brazil. He told her to instruct the pilot of the chartered jet, waiting at Bologna, to go. Luiza explained the plan to Adriane, who agreed: "I gathered all I had brought from Brazil," she remembered. "The big suitcase, everything. The three pieces of luggage that I had just unpacked, less than 24 hours before, with all I would need to spend the next five months of the European season by his side. The season that ended before it began." Before leaving, she took a T-shirt and shorts of Senna's she had worn that morning to go running.

Then she walked around the house and gardens for the last time. The garden and lawns were bathed in moonlight, as they only can be in the Algarve. She walked by the swimming pool and then went into his study and checked for messages on his fax. She gazed at his photographs on his desk for the last time and his trophies. She stopped by his powerful Swiss stereo player and wondered what was the last music he had listened to. She pressed the eject button and out came a Phil Collins album. She slipped it into her pocket, as she remembered: "I wanted to know what had been the last CD he had listened to in life. That was one thing that I had the right to share with him. After that I walked in tears around the house."

At around 10 o'clock, the two women left for the two-hour drive to Sintra. They were silent, thinking about what had been a terrible end to a terrible day. Just after midnight, Adriane pulled into the drive of the Braga home, where Senna had stayed many times and he had his own room. Adriane went straight to bed, but not in his room. That would have been too much to bear.

Back at the track, the lights in the media centre burned brightly as 200 journalists prepared 200 obituaries. The pit garage, containing Senna's shattered car, was now guarded by armed police.

At the hospital it was revealed that nurses had discovered a small furled Austrian flag hidden in the sleeve of Senna's race overalls. Journalists concluded he had intended to fly it from his cockpit on the parade lap, and dedicate what would have been his 42nd Grand Prix victory to the memory of Roland Ratzenberger.

Around midnight, Angelo Orsi was back in the developing room at his office. The pictures were not pleasant. He was doubtful any magazine would publish them. Representatives of the Senna family told him immediately they that did not want anyone to even see them. Orsi respected their wishes. The pictures have never been seen, except by the family and Senna's girlfriend Adriane. Today they are believed to be still in a safe in the *Autosprint* offices. Both the magazine and Orsi have turned down significant offers, believed to be well over $100,000, for the rights to them. Orsi's decision earned everlasting respect from Galvao Bueno, who had tipped off the Senna family about their existence: "He is the only person who's got pictures of Ayrton's face, developed and stashed in a safe. He has already turned down fortunes for them, he won't sell, he won't give. His superiors at the magazine understood his action, even with the fabulous offers from agencies, and I find it very dignified."

There is much more Galvao Bueno would like to say about the events of Sunday 1st May 1994, but he agreed with Milton and Neyde da Silva that he would never discuss it. He confided to friends he mentioned the events to: "I shouldn't be talking about this, I have an agreement with his family."

In America, five hours behind Europe, Nigel Mansell was interviewed on the NBC nightly news: "I thought he was bulletproof," he said. "It hurts, it hurts big time."

CHAPTER 31

Anatomy of an Accident

The ingredients of tragedy

The computer on board Ayrton Senna's Williams FW16, registered the start of a new lap at 2:17pm and began to record the last 14.4 seconds of his life in a racing car on lap seven of the San Marino Grand Prix at Imola on Sunday 1st May 1994. He crossed the line in the lead. The car fed data back to the pit garage computer every time it passed the pits, and a burst of digitised information was caught by the tiny radio dishes on the wall in front of the Williams pit. It was instantly relayed to the computer screens of the data engineers in the rear of the garage. It told the story of Ayrton Senna's sixth and final lap of his Grand Prix career.

Sensors had recorded a very fast lap – in fact the third-fastest lap that would be recorded in the race as he attempted to put space between him and his closest rival, Michael Schumacher in second place. The data captured showed the behaviour of the most significant components of the car during the preceding minute-and-a-half of lap six: the temperatures, speeds, pressures, measures, wear rates, steering and hydraulics. Crucially, the steering angle was being measured by a potentiometer placed on top of the steering column, just behind the dashboard. Any steering-wheel movement was registered by the sensor. A pressure sensor mounted on the hydraulic steering system was measuring the performance of the power steering.

On board the car were two data-recording black boxes one belonging to the team and one belonging the engine-maker, Renault. They were unrelated systems which would collect data for the whole race as a back-up to the telemetry. The data recording was primarily to collect information to make the cars go faster, but it also provided data to assess the causes of an accident, in much the same way as an aircraft's black box.

As Senna approached Tamburello bend, the onboard computer was recording hundreds of pieces of data every second and sending it to the black boxes, as well as storing and compressing it for the burst to the pits.

At 9.1 seconds into the lap, Senna's foot was flat to the floor as he entered Tamburello. Beyond it was a small area of grass, then a smaller area of tarmac, then a wall. If something went wrong, a driver was in a lot of trouble with nowhere to go. A 1994 Formula One car had the ability to corner at almost unbelievable speed, on sticky slick tyres, dominated by sophisticated aerodynamics. The car's bottom ran millimetres from the surface of the road. In 1993, sophisticated active-ride systems had kept the cars stable, along with other electronic aids such as traction control. In 1994, these aids were banned and it all had to be done mechanically. In hindsight it was highly dangerous to ban the electronic aids without introducing other measures to combat bottoming.

At close to 200mph, 11 seconds into lap seven, Senna's car was on the very edge, and the aerodynamics were so efficient that it was almost being crushed into the tarmac by nearly four times its own weight in downforce. It generated huge grip, enabling the Tamburello bend to be taken flat out. In fact, the car was set up in such a way that the bend was safer taken flat out. Anything else could have been simply dangerous. Some people say that the worst thing a driver could have done in 1994 was lift off. It could throw the aerodynamics out of kilter, and on the limit the car could not be guaranteed to steer properly. Sensors on board indicated a force of 3.62G at Tamburello. If something went wrong now, the car could literally fly off the road.

But at that exact moment something did go wrong. At 12.6 seconds into the lap, 1.6 seconds before impact, something had reduced the ride height of the Williams. Television viewers saw an intermittent flash of sparks from Senna's car. This was normal behaviour for a car in 1994. Whatever happened, it appeared to cause Senna's car to scrape along the track, with could have caused a huge loss of grip and much-reduced downforce.

The telemetry showed that Ayrton Senna had lifted off the throttle momentarily. The back of the car appeared to step out. With lightning reactions, reacting exactly as would be expected, Senna appeared to steer into the slide. The car gripped and turned it to the right – whether or not this was under Senna's control is debatable. But then it went wrong. The telemetry shows the brakes were hard on, with the driver appearing to try and keep the car on the track. But other forces had taken over: other than trying to slow the car by urgently downshifting the gears, he was a passenger. In any case, his focus was keeping the car on the track and winning the race, not saving his life. But Tamburello was the one unforgiving part of the Imola circuit, where there was the least road and no tyre wall.

Because the accident took less than two seconds from start to finish, few saw him leave the track and did not notice the accident until he had bounced off the wall and was coming to a halt. He went into the concrete wall at a 45-degree angle and the car immediately ricocheted back on to the run-off area. All in all it had taken 1.8 seconds from leaving the track to coming to rest. His head twitched and there was a pause as everyone, including the marshals, froze. It transpired a wheel had become trapped between the chassis and the wall before catapulting up and hitting the Brazilian in the head, forcing it back hard against the carbon-fibre headrest. At the same time, part of the suspension block on one of the wheels snapped off and broke through his visor, hitting his forehead like a bullet. The FOCA TV onboard camera caught the whole incident, bar the last 0.9 seconds of impact.

The day after the accident, Williams technical director Patrick Head was besieged by journalists anxious to know what had caused Senna to go off. He told them that the telemetry the team had been able to retrieve from the Renault box showed only what Senna had done: "We have checked the telemetry. He slightly lifted his foot just at that dip in the place where the tarmac changes. That caused a loss of grip from the car."

But what caused him to lift off is the enduring question that has perplexed every investigator. Plenty of people claim to know the answer – a trial court in Bologna, numerous documentary programme-makers, newspaper investigative teams, the Williams team, eminent scientists and everyone who inhabited the Formula One paddock in 1994. Did his car pick up a piece of debris from an earlier accident and get trapped in, or affect, the suspension, causing it to fail? Did the steering column break? Did the power steering fail? Did the car bottom on low tyre pressures, and cause Senna to back off and lower the car momentarily onto its flat bottom and suspension mounts, after which it slid into the wall? Was Senna holding his breath to heighten his senses for a quick lap and black out? And, of course, there's the conspiracy theory. Were mysterious eastern European forces at work, interfering with his electronics with a telemetric beam? There is also the question of Senna's helmet. It was a special lightweight model, but was it legal? Many people thought not, but it wasn't a contributor to the accident.

The Bologna court investigators were adamant that the steering column had broken. The authors of this book believe the power steering probably failed. Patrick Head and the Williams team believe the car, bottomed and slid off. Most journalists believe the car picked up track debris which affected the car's suspension. Others believe it was simply a momentary reaction by the driver, who believed he sensed a problem and instinctively lifted off the throttle and destabilised the car. Undoubtedly Ayrton Senna's competitiveness contributed to his own death. His actions right up to when he hit the wall indicate he was not trying to avoid a fatal accident but trying to keep his car on the track to win the race.

In truth, no one knows what really happened.

What most people do agree on was that the accident was not caused by driver error. Although Senna backed off the throttle, something caused him to. The late Michele Alboreto, a very close friend of Senna's and a key witness at the Bologna trial, remembered: "It's a very dangerous corner, if something did go wrong on the car it was the wall, very close and at a very high speed. But I am sure because I know, I had the same accident as Ayrton did, that the only way you can go out at this corner is if you have a mechanical failure."

There was also confusion later about exactly what Head had meant when he told journalists that Senna had taken his foot off the throttle. Many assumed he was calling the cause driver error. It caused a frenzy. The Williams PR team went into overdrive and later denied that Head said Senna had made a mistake. Head had not of course said why he lifted, because he did not know.

The Williams team has always believed that the tyres were not warmed up, and that the consequently lower tyre pressures affected the ride height, causing instability that prompted Senna to lift the throttle thereby combining to create catastrophic instability. That the lifting of the throttle caused aerodynamic instability is undeniable.

The lower tyre temperatures were caused by the safety car leading the cars around slowly. The safety car at Imola was a modified Opel estate car. It could not go anywhere near fast enough for Formula One cars. The procedure had desperately worried Senna already in 1994 and he wanted it stopped. The safety car was a new innovation and had only been used once before in 1994, in dry conditions. In Imola, an accident at the start had brought the safety car out for the second time. The cars lined up behind and travelled at a much lower speed, lowering the tyre pressures and consequently the ride height. The car was unable to generate grip it needed, as the downforce would theoretically have been severely decreased.

But that theory is partially discounted by the fast lap Senna drove on lap six and the fact that by then he had used up 20 kilos of fuel and the car must have been riding substantially higher than at the start.

A British television documentary of the accident, 'Going Critical', first aired on 25th September 2001, concluded that the car bottoming out caused the accident rather than any steering problem. The programme investigators came to this conclusion by some new analysis of the telemetry and the onboard camera footage. It told them that Senna was still applying torsional force to the steering column of his FW16 when he went off at Tamburello. The programme-makers appeared to have been given help by the Williams team, and the programme fitted the team's own conclusion that the car bottomed out and started to slide on the suspension mounts. The telemetry shows that Senna reacted within a 10th of a second, and began to compensate with the steering at the moment when the car regained grip. Unfortunately, only the front wheels gained grip and this snapped the car hard right and into the wall.

What this programme had to offer in terms of insight and factual reporting, however, was far from clear. But its hypothesis was as credible as the Bologna prosecutors'.

It was the Italian magazine *Autosprint* that first raised the suspicion, presumably tipped off by Bologna court investigators, one week after the accident, that the steering column had broken. According to the Italians the fracture occurred, or was beginning to occur, in the few seconds before the Williams ran off the road.

If the steering column had broken as the prosecution alleged, then the characteristics of the accident would have been very different, because Senna did appear to have some control of the car right up to the impact with the wall.

The breakage theory would have been easier to prove or dismiss if the memory for detail of the people first at the scene had been better. None of the doctors or marshals could remember having removed the steering wheel, but photographs of the car after the accident indicate that the wheel was not removed from the column by releasing the catch, which allows the driver to get in and out of the cramped cockpit. The steering column was undoubtedly broken at the accident.

At the subsequent trial, the prosecution's case rested on the fact that Williams had modified the steering column in the middle of March before the season started. After the initial tests of the new Williams Renault FW16, Senna wanted more room in the cockpit and figured this could be done by lengthening the steering column by about 12mm. The modifications were ready by the first race of the season in Brazil.

But the modifications had been done in such a way that did no credit to the Williams factory. The modifications were described in legal documents as 'badly designed and badly implemented'. Formula One experts who have seen the pictures, post crash, agree with this statement. It is a stinging condemnation of the capabilities of the Williams engineers who did the modifications. The way the steering column was altered also caused plenty of trauma at the Williams factory.

In 1994 the modification of the steering column was the direct responsibility of young Williams engineers Alan Young and Gavin Fisher, who maintained that it wasn't a rush job, but was planned and executed at the factory according to internal procedures; they stated firmly that they did not believe the modifications were the cause of the accident. But even influential Williams insiders admit the way the work was done was a problem for the team.

The way the modifications were done certainly caused chief designer Adrian Newey much anguish. Years later he told *F1 Racing* magazine: "I asked myself quite sincerely whether I should carry on. A driver had just died at the wheel of a car designed by me. I went through a really bad time. And then I did decide to carry on, but the pain is still there. I was just getting to know him when he left us. It was awful. We'll never know whether the accident was down to design error or something else altogether."

But the steering column modification was an easy place to pin the blame for legal prosecutors. If the charge against Newey, Patrick Head and Frank Williams at the trial had been one of bad workmanship, a guilty verdict would have undoubtedly ensued. But the broken steering column almost certainly did not cause the accident, so it was always irrelevant.

Although it did not cause the accident, it was easy for the Italian prosecutors to make a case against the team based on it. The personal trauma was heavy. Frank Williams admitted the team awaited the outcome of the trial with great trepidation. He said: "It could take many months, even years. God forbid that it should go on so long. "That accident has affected everyone here. It was a tragedy which left us all in the depths of despair. Make no mistake about that. Patrick said to me just the other day that many of our people are still badly marked by the loss of Ayrton. We've got very many things to occupy our minds just now, but losing the man who drives your car is significant and the people who make the car feel it most."

The problem for Williams was that the bad workmanship had coloured the minds of the Italian prosecutors. No one could ever say whether the steering broke before or after the accident. It was impossible. The telemetry clearly said it didn't, but it was not infallible. It all steered the court's spotlight away from other, likely causes of the accident.

If the steering was to blame it was far more likely a power steering failure. This was Patrick Head's first theory, later discounted by the telemetry and the reason he ordered Damon Hill to turn off the power steering on the grid of the restart. If the power steering had failed, one would have expected the hydraulic pressure to fall to zero. But the telemetry showed the hydraulic pressure first rising abnormally and then falling abnormally in the seconds before the accident. No one ever explained why.

Williams was using power steering for the first time in 1994 and it had been very troublesome. Imola was its third race. Getting it right was very difficult – some Formula One teams only got around to installing power steering in the 2001 season, and it was still causing problems then.

Further credence is given to the power-steering failure theory by widespread allegations that, at the time of the crash, people in the Williams garage heard Head, who was standing in front of the TV monitors when Senna started to go straight on, shouting the words 'steering power'. Head is an incredibly quick-witted engineer, they say, and he followed that up by asking people around him, just after the impact: "What happened to the steering?"

No one in the Williams garage that afternoon has ever discussed publicly what happened in the minutes during and after the accident. Jabby Crombac, the veteran journalist, was in the garage but would not even speak to friends about events.

Although no one from Williams was ever allowed to examine the FW16 chassis until it was returned to the factory in early 2002, Patrick Head had full access from the start to the Renault telemetry that survived the accident. He contends strongly that power-steering failure did not match that data, believing that the accident was caused by lower tyre pressures – either by a deflating tyre after Senna ran over some debris, or by a tyre that had cooled after the safety car went out. The glitch in that theory is that on the sixth lap of the race, as the safety car withdrew, Senna recorded the third-fastest lap of the race. Hardly the work of a driver whose car is any less than perfect. But that doesn't discount the theory either. Senna was such a great driver that he could simply drive around such problems.

The debris theory, which claims Senna picked up a piece of track debris from a Benetton car involved in the startline accident has been well argued, mostly by journalists. On the eve of the opening of the Bologna trial, the London *Sunday Times* published a new photograph of a small piece of blue bodywork on the track, with Senna's car about to run over it on the way to Tamburello on lap seven. The debris could have damaged the car or become attached to it, altering its aerodynamics. But no one can say for sure that it did.

Patrick Head has discounted a suspension breakage or debris-induced interference. He said that with an aerodynamic load at that speed of some 2,600kg (plus the weight of the car), of which some 65 per cent would have been on the right-hand side on a left curve, the car would have crashed and dragged along the ground far more violently, if that had happened.

French TV reporter Jean-Louis Moncet studied the view from the camera in Michael Schumacher's Benetton, which was around 10 metres behind Senna's car on lap seven. Moncet maintains a small piece of bodywork could be seen dangling from underneath the Williams momentarily, and flew off immediately after.

The quality of the viewed footage varied. Only FOCA Television, which operated the onboard cameras, had the original and it chose not to get involved unless compelled by the authorities. There was a great deal of compelling going on when Bologna police arrived to arrest Alan Woollard, then the FOCA camera operator, at the following year's race. If Bernie Ecclestone hadn't been on hand to sort it out, Woollard would have been carted off.

Karl Wendlinger, who was driving a Sauber in the race, described that year's breed of car: "The aerodynamics don't work any more if a speck of dust gets on the wing." Former Lotus designer and Senna's close friend, Gérard Ducarouge, who he drove for in the mid-1980s, said: "If only a small part of the front wing breaks on a Tamburello bend at those speeds, with a G-force of 4.5, you instantly lose 500 kilos of downforce. That is a fundamental problem with modern racing cars."

Other drivers' comments seem to sum up what probably happened: some momentary aerodynamic instability that Senna detected caused him to lift his right foot; that error, caused by responding to the sophisticated aerodynamics, caused the accident. Like all fatal accidents in Formula One, it was a combination of events that made the tragedy happen, coming together at once in an unlikely scenario. Tamburello was simply the worst place in the world for it to happen.

Driver error in whatever form, regardless of the emotion it sparks, is still a credible theory, as well as the debate as to what exactly driver error is in a situation like this. There are many who support the Williams team theory that the aerodynamic balance of the car changed quickly in the corner and Senna lost partial control after his instincts told him to come off the throttle. If obeying this instinct is regarded as a driver mistake, then the accident was due to driver error. But this is an explanation no current or former Formula One driver who was around in 1994 can even begin to accept. Gerhard Berger said: "This is not a place where you get driver error. The bend is flat out, you can't do anything wrong." Former world champion and Williams team member Keke Rosberg agrees: "You can drive through there with your eyes closed. It's not a corner."

Gerald Donaldson, a well-known Formula One journalist who has written extensively about the accident, said: "If you ease your foot from the accelerator, there is a shift of weight forwards, as a result of which the car momentarily has more downforce at the front, and when something happens in that situation the tail is more likely to break away, but the car does not veer to the right on a left-hand bend."

Honda engineers who worked for a long time with Senna are convinced that if he eased his foot from the accelerator it was because he noticed that something was wrong with the car. "He could feel the slightest thing," said Osamu Goto. "He was always like a living sensor."

One of the most unlikely theories is that Senna blacked out before Tamburello. Close friends say that one of his techniques to get a quick lap was to try and hold his breath for a lap on the basis that lack of oxygen can heighten perceptions. But the telemetry and rubber strips laid down on the tarmac proved that Senna braked hard and changed gear at least twice before impact from start to end of the accident. If Senna had been incapacitated, none of this would have been possible.

Honda engineers also believe that the violent bouncing of the Williams that had occurred several times during the previous lap – which is constantly mentioned and was put forward as a possible cause of the accident by Michael Schumacher, who was driving close behind Senna – was probably normal, something that had clearly been calculated, Schumacher said: "Otherwise, Ayrton would have reacted, even if for example tyre damage was developing… Or if, because of the long time held up behind the pace-car, or perhaps because of a wrong tyre pressure, the car had sat differently. He was so sensitised to such things. He must have been suddenly surprised by something."

There were internal doubts at Williams that, during the week before Imola, under pressure from Benetton's successes in the first two races of that year, there was perhaps a little too much experimentation and improvisation going on at the same time. For Imola, the front end of the Williams had been completely remodelled aerodynamically. It was just another ingredient of tragedy.

And of course the circuit had its faults. The car failures would have been irrelevant if the circuit had been able to contain the car safely. There is little doubt that by 21st century standards, the 1994 Imola track was unsafe. But Senna had recognised the dangers of Tamburello, twice inspected that corner in the previous two years and had ample opportunity to put things right. Equally Jean-Marie Balestre and Max Mosley of FISA, now the FIA, had seen three huge dangerous accidents, involving Nelson Piquet in 1987, Gerhard Berger in 1989 and Michele Alboreto in 1991 in private testing. These drivers were lucky not to lose their lives but absolutely nothing was done about Tamburello. In their own ways, the drivers, the circuit managers and the governing body all contributed to Senna's death.

It was also unwise to have less than 10 metres of asphalt and grass as a safety zone, and concrete walls at a 200 mph bend? A three-deep bank of tyres, even unsecured, would have saved Senna's life. It has never been debated properly why the tyres weren't there. Mainly because the people who would have been doing the debating were the people culpable for the tyres not being there, including the dead driver himself.

Some drivers even ridiculously argue that a tyre wall would have been dangerous in itself because they would have caused the car to rebound directly in the track, possibly into other cars. This is a fatuous argument that would see all crash barriers on Europe's motorways removed as well.

The argument that one wouldn't have expected an accident there because it was not a critical bend, as put forward by Ferrari driver Nicola Larini after Roland Ratzenberger's accident, might have been valid for the Villeneuve bend, but surely not for Tamburello, after the horrific crashes that had occurred there. The circuit had been given a clean bill of health by Roland Bruynseraede, the FIA's head of safety.

The best theory is that everyone had been lulled into a false sense of security by the advent of the immensely strong carbon-fibre chassis introduced into Formula One by John Barnard, technical director of McLaren at the start of the 1980s. Since then, years of good luck in Formula One had

The great battle of Monaco in 1992

The most entertaining race of 1992 was Ayrton Senna's great battle around the streets of the principality with Nigel Mansell. When Mansell had to pit for tyres near the end he lost the lead, and no matter how he tried he could not get it back. It broke his sequence of race victories. Senna was superb that day against a vastly superior car and engine.

The end of the feud in 1993
Senna salutes Alain Prost on the occasion of the Brazilian's last victory and the Frenchman's retirement at Adelaide in 1993.

Left: Senna exits the first chicane in Adelaide in 1993 in his final race for McLaren, which he won.

Below: McLaren team coordinator Jo Ramirez presents a parting gift as Senna prepares to leave McLaren at the end of 1993. Ramirez and Senna were extremely close friends.

European Grand Prix, Donington Park, April 1993. The best lap ever driven in a Formula One car
After passing Michael Schumacher when exiting the first corner, Senna picks off the Sauber of Karl Wendlinger before hunting down the Williams Renaults of Damon Hill and Alain Prost on the first lap of the 1993 European Grand Prix.
Below: Senna passes Hill to take second place, and begins his pursuit of Prost.

Above: Senna waves a Brazilian flag to celebrate victory at Donington.

Right: Senna shows off his Donington trophy with circuit boss Tom Wheatcroft.

The final farewell after six glorious years
Ron Dennis embraces Ayrton Senna on the occasion of one of the last of the Brazilian's victories for the team, in Japan, 1993. All the old acrimony was forgotten. Dennis was convinced he would return before the end of his career.

Right: Senna proudly holds his trophy aloft after victory in his home race at Brazil in 1993 – one of five that year against the odds.

Winning at Monaco in 1983.

Ayrton Senna in his trademark helmet.
Examples now fetch in excess of US$50,000.

Left: Emerson Fittipaldi checks that everything is running smoothly as Senna prepares to drive an IndyCar for the first time at the Firebird West circuit in Phoenix in December 1992. It had been Fittipaldi's idea for his friend to test his Penske Chevrolet that winter.
Below Left: Senna describes his IndyCar experiences to regular Penske driver Paul Tracy and his team engineers. After just two runs in the car he was able to provide a very detailed comparison between the Penske and his Formula One McLaren.

Above and right: Senna takes the Penske Chevrolet PC21 out onto the twisty Firebird track in Phoenix, Arizona. Despite limited running, he set a better time than Penske's star driver Emerson Fittipaldi in the car that day, and would have liked to have raced in the Indianapolis 500. Privately he told friends that he had never really been interested in American car racing but was glad of the opportunity to try the car out.

The IndyCar test session in December 1992

Above: Fellow Brazilian world champions, Senna and
Emerson Fittipaldi, were firm friends – they met when
Senna used to visit the Interlagos track to watch Formula
One testing in the 1970s. He introduced Ayrton Senna
to Penske team owner Roger Penske (left).

Right: Senna tries out the Penske's cockpit for size as
Emerson Fittipaldi looks over him and Paul Tracy
perches on his rear wheel.

Below: Senna went about his only IndyCar test in a
methodical way, gleaning as much technical knowledge
from the car as he was able.

Ayrton Senna sprays the champagne
after his Belgian victory in 1991. It
was one of his favourite photographs,
printed all over the world.

Seven world champions who won 19 world championships between them, pictured in 1990
Seven world champions are photographed in Adelaide at the Australian Grand Prix in 1991. From top left: James Hunt (1976), Jackie Stewart (1969, 1971 and 1973), Denny Hulme (1967) Nelson Piquet (1981, 1983 and 1987), Juan Manuel Fangio (1951, 1954, 1955, 1956 and 1957), Ayrton Senna (1988, 1990 and 1991) and Jack Brabham (1959, 1960 and 1966). Since that photo was taken, Hunt, Hulme, Fangio and Senna have died.

Helicoptering around Brazil in 1993 and 1994

Ayrton Senna used his own helicopter to ease his passage between work and play in Brazil through the European winter and the Brazilian summer. During late 1993 and early 1994, he was marshalling the first phase of a new business empire that he intended to keep him busy after he retired from Formula One.

Ayrton Senna's favourite place was his family farm at Tatui in Dois Lagos

In 1993 Ayrton Senna spent more time at the family farm in Brazil than at any time in his life. He was sharing his time with Adriane Galisteu, his new girlfriend. In his own helicopter, which he piloted himself, he flicked quickly from the farm to his beach house at Angra on the coastal and to the roof of his apartment and office building in São Paulo. Tatui was a working farm with cattle and pigs.

The paradise of Tatui

Although his parents and family spent most time at Tatui Dois Lagos, it was Ayrton Senna's paradise, with a lake, a beautiful swimming pool and a superb go-karting track where he raced his nieces and nephews. It was a place the whole da Silva family could relax together in comfort without getting in each other's way. It was a private place and when he relaxed with friends he took them to his Angra beach house. Tatui was for family.

The official girlfriend Xuxa Meneghel was close to Ayrton Senna between 1988 and 1992

Xuxa Meneghel was Ayrton Senna's girlfriend on and off for four years. She had a very successful career as a TV presenter with TV Globo and rarely accompanied him to races because of her schedule. The da Silva family adored Xuxa and she was the official widow at his funeral in São Paulo in 1994.

The pursuit of leisure
Ayrton Senna enjoyed himself with Adriane Galisteu at his two homes in Brazil: Angra, on the beach, and Tatui (below left), the family cattle farm at Dois Lagos.

The Lotus years were Marjorie's
Above: His first serious girlfriend after his marriage fell apart was Marjorie Andrade, who accompanied him duing some of the the Lotus years.

The F3 years were Maria's
Below: The Brazilian student was studying in Belgium. They met shortly after his marriage to Liliane ended.

Happy days with Adriane Galisteu in 1993

Left: Senna laughs with his last love Adriane Galisteu outside the McLaren motorhome during the 1993 season. Adriane was an important presence throughout the last year of Senna's life and accompanied him to many races around the world.

Right: Adriane was a model, from an underprivileged background very different from Senna's own.

Below: Senna with Adriane in Adelaide for the Australian Grand Prix in 1993. It was a very happy time for him, with Adriane and a Williams Renault contract in his pocket.

Below: Senna and Adriane at an official photo shoot beside the pool at his Brazilian ranch in Tatui. They also had a beach home at Angra dos Reis.

Above: Senna had a passion for flying his helicopter and Adriane Galisteu would often accompany him on flights.

Left: Senna and Adriane at the traditional Philip Morris Marlboro party in Budapest in 1993.

Two people at peace with the world and each other
Ayrton Senna with his last love Adriane Galisteu, at sunset on the farm called Tatui. It was one of their favourite places. Friends were convinced they would have married after the European season in 1994.

The all-too-brief months of driving and testing for Williams Renault
Above: Senna checks times at Imola. Driving the new Williams, he realised he was in for a more difficult season than he had thought.

Left: Ayrton Senna is besieged by the press at the first Grand Prix of the year.

Below: Senna opted to take the number-two designation at his new team, whilst Damon Hill's car was numbered zero, as it had been the previous season. Alain Prost had retired. Senna takes his 65th and final pole position at Imola in 1994.

Winter testing at Estoril in January 1994
Above: An instant rapport was built up between Frank Williams and Ayrton Senna. It was as if two destinies had collided by design.

Right: Ayrton Senna and Patrick Head immediately knew there was a problem with the new Williams Renault.

Below: Ayrton Senna and Damon Hill launch the Rothmans Williams Renault package at Estoril in January 1994.

On the eve of Senna's first drive of the Williams car in Estoril Senna and Frank Williams at a press luncheon
in Estoril, prior to Senna's first outing on the track as a Williams Renault driver in January 1994. It was the second occasion
that Senna had driven a Williams, following his first-ever Formula One test in 1983.

Above: Ayrton Senna explains the workings of a Formula One steering wheel to the Mayor of São Paulo and his family and
guests, during the 1994 Brazilian Grand Prix weekend.

The start of a new partnership Ayrton Senna inherited race engineer David Brown from Nigel Mansell and Alain Prost, who had both won world championships with him. Senna found Brown as delightful as both Mansell and Prost had. The relationship was destined to be all too short-lived.

Right: Senna made it look all too easy and few knew just how bad the car was. Damon Hill, his teammate, did. He was not on the pace at all.

1994 Brazilian Grand Prix Ayrton Senna takes the lead at the start in Brazil, negotiating the esses that bear his name.

Above: Senna was so quick at Interlagos, in the 1994 Brazilian Grand Prix, that he lapped his team-mate Damon Hill. The Brazilian, however, tried to pursue race leader Michael Schumacher more quickly than his car would allow, and he spun out of the race in the closing stages.

Right: Senna gets out of his car on the grid at the start of the Pacific Grand Prix in Aida.

Inset: Senna is tipped into a spin by Mika Häkkinen's McLaren at the start in Aida and is promptly t-boned by Nicola Larini's Ferrari. **Main picture:** Senna walks away from the Aida first-corner accident, pursued by an apologetic Larini.

A weekend of trouble from start to finish
Rubens Barrichello suffers an impact at the Variante
Bassa on the Friday of the 1994 San Marino Grand Prix.
His car flipped over before coming to rest. He was
extremely lucky to survive an accident which appeared
far worse than Senna's fatal smash two days later.

Right: Senna with Barrichello before the accident.
Next time they met, he was lying on a hospital trolley.
Also with Schumacher (below) after Ratzenberger's
accident and (below right) with Gerhard Berger.

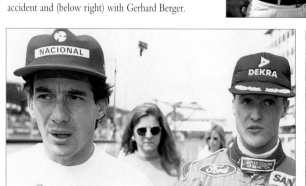

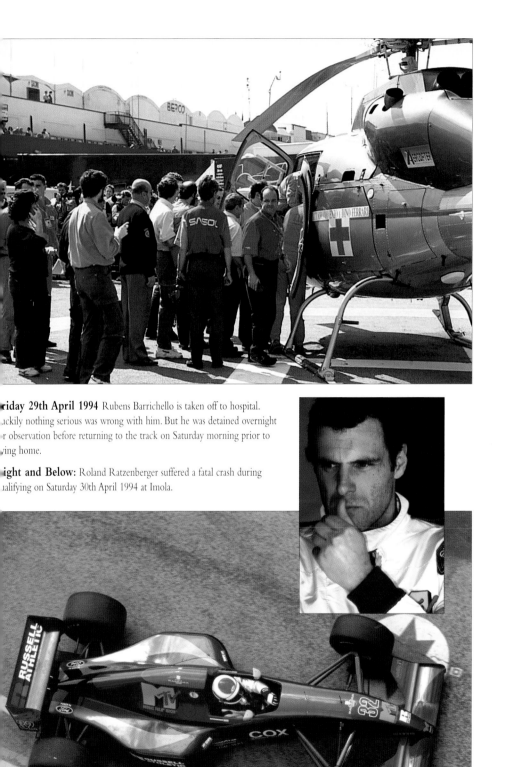

Friday 29th April 1994 Rubens Barrichello is taken off to hospital. Luckily nothing serious was wrong with him. But he was detained overnight for observation before returning to the track on Saturday morning prior to flying home.

Right and Below: Roland Ratzenberger suffered a fatal crash during qualifying on Saturday 30th April 1994 at Imola.

The last moments of life

The famous picture of Ayrton Senna contemplating life in the Williams garage before the race. He had under 30 minutes to live. He managed less than seven laps of the race before he was gone.

Above: In the highly-charged aftermath of the accident, Leonardo Senna, Ayrton's younger brother, blamed everyone for his death.

Below: Alain Prost was with Frank Williams in the Williams pit garage when the accident happened.

Above: Senna leads the field behind the safety car at Imola, an episode which some people believe may have been a factor in causing his crash.

Left: A faulty steering system has also been cited as a cause of Senna's crash. This was unlikely.

Below left: Senna's car rebounds violently from the wall at Tamburello. It was an exceptionally violent impact, bringing the car to a quick stop in a small piece of ground. The accident was so violent that the carbon-fibre chassis split. The in-car camera cut out before impact.

Left: Senna's steering wheel with the remains of the steering column attached.

Above right: Senna is attended by the medical team beside the car.

Above left: The final seconds – Senna enters Tamburello for the last time.

Above right: The shattered remains of the cockpit of Senna's Williams Renault FW16 and the helmet, which took the force of the impact.

Immediate aftermath At 2:17pm, the remains of Senna's wrecked Williams lie in the Tamburello run-off area after the race is called to a halt. The steering wheel is hanging loosely over the right side of the car and the monocoque is fractured in the region of the dash bulkhead. The non-structural cockpit cowling has been removed to allow Senna to be lifted from the car.

Left: Flavio Briatore, Mika Häkkinen and Michael Schumacher prepare to go on the podium, uncertain of the extent of Senna's injuries but having heard the rumours.

Left: Marshals remove the destroyed Williams Renault from the scene of the accident. It would later be impounded by the Italian authorities to be used as evidence in the manslaughter trial, after Senna's death was announced.

Right: Damon and Georgie Hill talk with Bernie Ecclestone in the Imola paddock. Initial reports of Senna's condition were conflicting and most of the drivers did not realise how serious the accident had been until the end of the race.

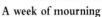

A week of mourning

All over the world, magazines cleared their pages to report the tragedy. The world's most famous magazine, *Paris Match*, put the tragedy on its cover.

The day after Monday 2nd May 1994. Flowers and a Brazilian flag are left at the spot where Senna's car hit the wall at Tamburello.

Right: Ayrton Senna's fans weep outside the Imola circuit on the morning of Monday 2nd May 1994.

Funeral in São Paulo

The funeral was the most extraordinary affair, with São Paulo virtually at a standstill for the day. It was attended by drivers past and present, including his old foe Alain Prost.

Ayrton Senna's final resting place.

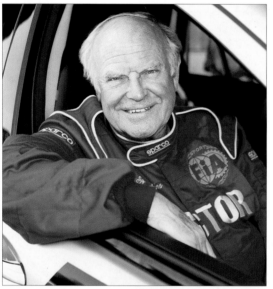

The men left with Ayrton Senna's legacy

The death of Ayrton Senna affected the world of Formula One more than any other event in its history. Bernie Ecclestone, president of the FOM, Max Mosley, president of the FIA, and Professor Sid Watkins, the FIA's medical supremo, moved quickly to change the cars and circuits to make Formula One safer. Since then, no driver has been killed or even seriously injured in a Formula One car, as it becomes one of the safest sports in the world despite the obvious dangers of competing.

Below: A minute of silence on the Monaco grid two weeks later. From left: Mika Häkkinen, Bertrand Gachot, Andrea de Cesaris, Martin Brundle, Mark Blundell, Michael Schumacher, Johnny Herbert, JJ Lehto, Christian Fittipaldi, Rubens Barrichello, Gianni Morbidelli, Olivier Beretta, Pierluigi Martini, Olivier Panis (behind Martini), Eric Comas, Eric Bernard, Jean Alesi and Gerhard Berger, Niki Lauda.

The Court of Appeal Inside the Third Appeal Court of Bologna during the appeal trial over Senna's death, in November 1999. The prosecutor calls on the court to confirm the original requested sentences, which the judge had ignored. **Inset:** Peter Goodman, Williams's British lawyer, who co-ordinated the team's defence at the Senna trial in Italy, after Senna's death.

Below and left: Adrian Newey, Patrick Head and Frank Williams were accused of culpable homicide – manslaughter – in the Italian courts following the events at Imola in 1994. Convictions were never a prospect, but the affair cost the Williams team some $4 million in legal fees.

The Ayrton Senna Foundation

The work that Ayrton Senna started with his comic character 'Senninha', to bring hope to the poor children of São Paulo, continues through the Ayrton Senna Foundation.

Right: Ayrton Senna wears a T-shirt showing 'Senninha', little Senna, a cartoon hero who delights the children of Brazil. He spent $5 million developing the character and sent a free copy of his new comic to every schoolchild in São Paulo.

The Ayrton Senna Foundation:
Frank Williams attending the unveiling of the Ayrton Senna monument at Imola.

Viviane Senna's good works Viviane at the São Paulo office from which she runs the Senna Foundation. The charity carries out a lot of work among the poor children of São Paulo.
Below: Viviane Senna visits the 1999 Brazilian GP with Gerald de Bar, manager of the Paddock Club.

Ayrton Senna 21st March 1960 – 1st May 1994

witnessed many accidents but not a single death, since Elio de Angelis was killed in testing in 1986.

There is also a theory that Senna contributed to his own death by wearing a special lightweight helmet to reduce the g-forces drivers suffer. Some even went as far as to say it was illegal, and that the outer skin was as flimsy to touch as cardboard and could easily be indented. Certainly the company that fitted the radio sets into the helmets doubted its legality. The anonymous technician who did the job said the helmet could be indented easily and was unlike anything else he had ever seen. This was never documented, never the subject of the trial, and never examined by the FIA. No one felt able to go there, understandably. Some bearing on this can be taken from the indecent speed in which the helmet was destroyed, on the orders of the Senna family, when it was released by the Italian authorities in 2002.

That it was as light as possible is not in doubt. A heavier helmet would have undoubtedly contributed to Senna's survival, but it is unlikely to have ultimately saved his life.

And of course there was the inevitable conspiracy theory. In 1994 stories were going around that mysterious eastern European gangs and mafia operations were trying to manipulate the outcome of the 1994 championship. Presumably these people were financed by gambling syndicates who had made bets on the outcome. They had apparently schemed to enable Michael Schumacher to win the championship instead of the overwhelming favourite, Senna. With sophisticated telemetry in its infancy, the gangs were using sophisticated machinery to aim bursts of data at cars to momentarily disable the electronics and cause a car to crash. The bursts of data were supposedly aimed at Senna's car at Tamburello, and caused the power steering to lock, causing the accident.

There is no doubt that team principals had been warned about the possibility in 1994, and advised to electronically shield their systems against illegal interference. Peter Collins, then Lotus team principal, admits he was warned and did instigate modifications to the Lotus electronics system but didn't take the threats seriously. He admits his attitude was coloured by the fact that Lotus wasn't a championship contender and he doubted anyone would want to interfere with its electronics, so he thought no more of it. That theory remained only a topic of light conversation in the Formula One paddock; but now all the cars are heavily protected against outside interference, so it was not as outlandish as it seemed.

One area that left no doubt was the official autopsy. It was comprehensive.

In fact the most controversial finding of all the investigations was not the cause of the accident but the fact that Senna had died instantly on impact with the wall. This had huge implications for the race organisers, as Italian law required the race to be cancelled in such circumstances. But the official and actual times of death were over four hours apart, and a subject of huge disagreement in the medical profession. It appears that in reality Senna was kept artificially alive by the extraordinary medical expertise available to Formula One. Short of a stake through the heart, it is now more or less impossible for drivers to die at the circuit. Fire, once the leading cause of driver death, is now almost extinct in Formula One.

Maggiore hospital doctors are adamant that Senna was still breathing on arrival in Bologna. Professor Watkins is adamant he had a pulse when he was put into the helicopter at the circuit, and doctors have vividly recalled the need to restart his heart during the helicopter trip.

But it is clear that, by any normal standards, he was dead on impact with the wall and 200 million TV viewers saw his last spasm of life in the cockpit. Sid Watkins and his team supported his life as he lay on the ground at the circuit; apart from his head, his body was untouched. But had he remained alive, the brain damage would have left him severely handicapped and totally incapacitated, and Senna would never have wanted that. Accidents such as Senna's are almost always fatal, with the few survivors suffering terrible irreversible brain damage. This is due to the effects on the brain of sudden deceleration, which causes structural damage to the brain tissues. Estimates of the forces involved in the accident suggest a rate of deceleration equivalent to a 30-metre vertical drop, landing headfirst.

Medical personnel attending anyone with severe head injuries, such as Senna's, and believing the heart is still beating, have a three-step procedure. The first is to ensure that the respiratory passages remain free, so that the patient can breathe, usually by means of an emergency tracheotomy. This was performed on Senna immediately. The second is to stem the loss of blood and replace it. Senna lost a lot of blood, which was replaced with intravenous fluid. The third is immobilising the cervical area. This was done as he was lifted from the car and on to the ground.

After that is done, the urgent need is to reach the intensive-care department of a major hospital with the best facilities. It is for that reason that Sid Watkins ordered that Senna be removed straight to Maggiore hospital and not to the circuit's albeit well-equipped medical centre.

The autopsy found that the impact of the 130 mph crash caused multiple injuries at the base of the cranium, resulting in respiratory insufficiency. There was crushing of the brain as it was forced against the wall of the cranium, causing diffuse bruising and oedema , increasing the intra-cranial pressure and causing brain death. The rupture of the artery, caused blood loss and obstruction in the respiratory passages and the consequent heart failure.

With that sort of terminal injury, the ethics of applying the best medical talent to bringing someone back to life and not allowing them simply to pass on are highly questionable. But at a racetrack with the best talent and the best facilities available, it is the natural thing for doctors to do.

Professor Pinto da Costa, a Portugese expert, noted: "From the ethical viewpoint, the procedure used for Ayrton's body was wrong. It involved dysthanasia, which means that a person has been kept alive improperly after biological death has taken place due to brain injuries so serious that the patient would never have been able to remain alive without mechanical means of support. There would have been no prospect of normal life and relationships. Whether or not Ayrton was removed from the car while his heart was beating, or whether his supply of blood had halted or was still flowing, is irrelevant to the determination of when he died. The autopsy showed that the crash caused multiple fractures at the base of the cranium, crushing the forehead, rupturing the artery and obstructing the respiratory passages. It is possible to resuscitate a dead person immediately after the heart stops through cardio-respiratory processes. The procedure is known as putting the patient on the machine. From the medical-legal viewpoint, in Ayrton's case, there is a subtle point: resuscitation measures were implemented. From the ethical point of view this might well be condemned because the measures were not intended to be of strictly medical benefit to the patient but rather because they suited the commercial interest of the organisation. Resuscitation did in fact take place, with the tracheotomy performed, while the activity of the heart was restored with the assistance of cardio-respiratory devices. The attitude in question was certainly controversial. Any physician would know there was no possibility whatsoever of successfully restoring life in the condition in which Senna had been found."

Another expert, Professor Jose Pratas Vital, a neurosurgeon and medical supremo at the old Portuguese Grand Prix, has a different view: "The people who conducted the autopsy stated that, on the evidence of his injuries, Senna was dead. They could not say that. He had injuries which lead to his death, but at that point the heart may still have been functioning."

Because a great driver, possibly the greatest driver, died on Sunday 1st May 1994, endless resources, time and effort have been put into establishing the cause. Unfortunately, as in most crashes involving a Formula One car, the definitive answer has never been found.

CHAPTER 32

Funeral in São Paulo

The long goodbye

The Formula One circus left Imola on Sunday evening and Monday morning in a daze. For some, in the coming week there were two funerals ahead. When Gerhard Berger reached his home in Austria at around 9pm on Sunday 1st May, he shut himself away. He was alone in the house and spoke to no one, as he remembered: "I didn't talk to anyone for two days. I watched the telephone filling up with messages but I didn't feel like talking to anyone about it as nothing could change things. I just wanted to spend some time alone. I stayed out of conversations for a few days and then flew to Brazil for his funeral."

Alain Prost wanted to attend the funeral but he was not sure whether he should. He was desperately sad, but also pleased he had ended the feud with Senna before he died. He remembered: "Ayrton and I had such a history for so long that I didn't really know how the Brazilian people would perceive it: would they be upset if I went, upset if I didn't go, or what?" Prost flew back to Paris on the evening of the accident and Jean-Luc Lagardère, the chairman of Matra, called him to ask about the accident. Lagardère's wife was Brazilian and Prost asked him what he should do. Lagardère told him the Brazilian people would be upset if he didn't go.

Julian Jakobi waited until Monday to fly back to London. He packed a change of clothing and then flew straight out to Brazil for the funeral. He was clear about his role in the coming days: "Because I wasn't family, but I had to keep the family going. So one kept going, really, on adrenalin and everything else."

Josef Leberer had driven home to Austria that morning. He planned to return with Senna's coffin to São Paulo but was unsure of the arrangements, and waited at home for news.

Antonio Braga stayed in Bologna to make the arrangements to return Senna's body to São Paulo. The Bologna authorities refused to release the body immediately, insisting on a full autopsy. Leonardo da Silva was put on the first flight back to São Paulo to be with his family. His grief was unbounded, made worse by the fact that his brother had gone to his grave with the two on bad terms over Adriane.

Adriane Galisteu woke up on Monday morning in a daze. She had slept very little. When she opened her eyes, she was unsure whether she had had a terrible dream. She hoped and prayed it had been a dream. Her future hung in the balance. She soon realised it was the worst kind of reality.

On Monday Senna's body had been moved to Bologna's mortuary in accordance with Italian law. The mortuary was surrounded by fans. The body of Roland Ratzenberger was also there, awaiting its own autopsy.

The Braga house in Sintra, Portugal was also surrounded by reporters, anxious to interview Adriane. Pictures from outside the house were being broadcast back to Brazil. The whole world's media was interested in the story, as the enormity of what had happened sank in. With the immediate family incommunicado, the focus was all on the beautiful 21-year-old blonde model, who, as far as the media were concerned, was effectively Senna's widow.

When Braga rang the house from Bologna, Adriane told him she wanted to come and see Senna's body. She told him she felt a desperate need for firm evidence, seen with her own eyes that he was dead.

Braga advised her against it, and thought it unlikely that she would even be admitted. She took his advice, believing she would be able to see him for the last time in São Paulo before the funeral. In Brazil it was traditional for the coffin to be left open, or at least to have a glass top. What she didn't know was that the indent to Senna's head and the wound caused by the sharp piece of suspension that had penetrated the helmet were disfiguring. Cosmetic experts were to despair in trying to make his face good enough. The coffin would stay closed.

With the bedlam outside the house, Braga advised his wife Luiza that the best option was to stage a makeshift press conference in the house for the media and then they would go away. Adriane agreed to do it. But during the press conference Adriane was asked some ghoulish questions, especially from

Brazilian journalists who had heard about the rift with the da Silva family and were unsure of her status now her boyfriend was dead. One female journalist asked her if she had a return ticket to São Paulo and who would be paying for her ticket. Adriane felt like she was being victimised by a hostile media looking for exclusive stories on the drama of Senna's death. She was in no state to withstand that.

Not so Miriam Dutra, who worked for TV Globo and had been dispatched urgently to cover the story. Dutra was very sympathetic to Adriane, who was clearly in great distress. Afterwards Adriane asked Dutra if she could have all the footage of the crash that TV Globo had. She wanted to see everything she could about the accident.

Monday came and went for dazed Adriane, and she was sedated to help her sleep that night. The sedatives had little effect, as Adriane was still stunned from events.

Meanwhile Antonio Braga and Galvao Bueno were desperately trying to organise the return of Senna's body to São Paulo. Naturally the family wanted it returned to Brazil as soon as possible. They thought this would be relatively simple until the Italian authorities told them the autopsy, would not take place until Tuesday. The body would be released that evening.

On Tuesday morning, Miriam Dutra collected the footage of the race on VHS videotape and the following day sent it by messenger to Adriane Galisteu in Sintra. Adriane sat on the sofa and watched it over and over, accompanied by the Braga children, Luiza and Joanna. They were obsessed with finding the reason for his crash.

Adriane also telephoned Angelo Orsi, the Italian photographer who had taken pictures of Senna after the accident. Adriane felt a desperate need for some physical proof he was dead. Orsi got permission from the family to send her some photographs.

The autopsies of Senna and Ratzenberger both took place, as planned, on Tuesday morning. It was straightforward. The causes of death were no more complicated than in any road accident victim.

By lunchtime the bodies had been authorised for removal. Braga and Bueno worked feverishly on the arrangements to get Senna's body home that day. They had two options: a direct flight with the Italian Air Force, or via Paris with Varig. The Italians were quite happy to fly the coffin straight back to São Paulo.

In the end Senna's parents would decide.

Back in Sintra, Adriane was feeling a cool wind from the Senna family in

São Paulo. On both Monday and Tuesday she had tried to telephone Senna's parents. She was told by the family's maid that both were under sedation and could not be disturbed. After a while this annoyed her, and she wondered what she had done, especially as she had shared her grief with Neyde on the Sunday. On Tuesday afternoon she got through to Viviane's husband Flavio Lalli, who told her it was a very difficult situation at the family house and that he was having difficulty talking to his own wife, who was shattered to the point of speechlessness. Lalli told her it was impossible for anyone to have any sort of conversation with either Milton or Neyde da Silva. They had taken the news worse than anyone else. The parents remained sedated and virtually silent, almost unaware of what was going on around them.

The Italian Air Force's offer was turned down as the family wished his coffin to return home in a Brazilian plane. In particular Varig, the national airline was very keen to do the job as Senna had always flown the carrier to travel home. It was important to the airline that his last flight would be with it. The only flight available was Varig, flight RG723 direct from Paris to São Paulo, leaving shortly before midnight on Tuesday.

Braga contacted the Italian Air Force and asked them to fly the mahogany coffin to the French capital to meet flight RG723. They readily agreed. The coffin left the mortuary at Maggiore hospital at around 2pm in a Mercedes hearse, with a police escort. Galvao Bueno, Celso Lemos and Betise Assumpção followed on behind, with Senna's personal belongings, retrieved from his plane and the Williams motorhome.

Word had got around and most of the route to the airfield was lined with Italians saying their farewells. There was an enormous sense of guilt amongst ordinary people that Senna had died in Italy.

At the airport, the Mercedes was allowed to draw right up to the Italian DC9. An honour guard of two lines of Italian policemen stood to attention as Senna's coffin was loaded on the plane. Brazil's ambassador to Italy, Orland Carbonara, saw the plane off to Paris.

The DC9 took off at around 5pm for the two-hour flight to Paris. On the way Braga, Bueno and Assumpção discussed how often they had flown home with him after a race.

They were all concerned about the 11-hour flight home on Varig, and were determined that the coffin would fly home in the passenger compartment and not in the cargo section, as was normal.

Two hours later, right on time, the Italian DC9 landed in Paris and Senna's body was taken to a special part of the terminal to await the Varig flight.

There were few formalities. By then Antonio Braga was on his way to Lisbon, ready to join his wife and Adriane for the flight to São Paulo for the funeral.

Meanwhile there was some confusion in Paris. The head of Varig's Paris office had assured Braga that they would remove seats to accommodate the coffin in the passenger cabin. He told them that there were only two people booked in first class and 12 in business class. Therefore he said the easiest thing to do was to move the 12 to first class as there were 16 seats leaving the whole business class section free for Senna's coffin and his four companions on the flight.

With this arranged, they awaited the flight. However, when the McDonnell-Douglas MD-11 arrived, the captain, a pilot called Gomes Pinto, told them the coffin would have to travel in the cargo hold because of IATA regulations. There was an argument and Bueno phoned back to the family in Brazil, who contacted Varig's head office. Varig faxed the captain and literally ordered him to let the coffin travel in the passenger section. Bueno recalls: "The captain tried everything to stop us. First he told us it could not be done because of IATA rules. Then he demanded an okay from the family."

There was friction between Pinto and Bueno but he finally relented and six seats had to be removed to accommodate the coffin and it was covered by the Brazilian flag. By then, Josef Leberer had also joined them, flying in from his home in Austria.

Meanwhile Braga had arrived in Lisbon and immediately gathered up Luiza and Adriane for the flight back to Brazil. There were no direct flights: they boarded a plane from Lisbon to Rio de Janeiro, which would continue on to São Paulo at around midnight on Tuesday 2nd May and would arrive at about the same time as the coffin. Adriane sat motionless with Antonio and Luiza Braga. The stewards were well aware of who they were and provided them with every comfort.

Senna's flight home was almost silent, and broken only by prayer. The window curtains were closed and Leberer remembers: "It was something that I will never forget. We were there for 11 hours with the coffin, with the Brazilian flag and a rose on it, but you know that the soul is gone." The co-pilot joined them all for some prayers around the coffin.

When the plane reached Brazilian airspace 10 hours later, a detachment of Brazilian Air Force fighter planes formed an escort. Dawn was breaking as the MD11 descended into São Paulo and as the pilot prepared to land, the fighters departed for their bases. The landing in half light, as the sun came up, was surreal. It was an unforgettable experience and something Senna had done many times in life as he came home, exhausted after yet another race.

Eleven hours after leaving Paris, Captain Gomes Pinto touched the plane down at 6:15am at Guaralhos airport. The first class and economy passengers disembarked immediately. The plane was greeted by São Paulo's mayor, Paulo Salim Maluf, and state governor Luiz Antonio Fleury.

At the same time, the Bragas and Adriane had reached Rio De Janeiro for a 20-minute stopover. The rest of the passengers disembarked, but the three of them were allowed to stay on board. Less than a week before, Adriane had flown to Portugal full of hope for the future. Now she returned to great uncertainty. She was also unsure of the family's reaction. She had not spoken to anyone since Senna's death other than Flavio Lalli, Viviane's husband, who had treated her coolly.

Whilst the plane was being cleaned and refuelled in Rio, she changed into a black suit so she could go straight to the building where the coffin was to be kept until Senna was buried the following day. The plane landed in São Paulo just 20 minutes after the Varig flight carrying Senna.

Waiting were a million citizens, who had got up early to line the six-lane motorway through the suburbs from the airport to welcome their hero home for the last time. Most were under 25.

Brazil's President Franco had already declared three days of national mourning, including a day off for schoolchildren. The Brazilian flag was flown at half-mast on all government buildings across the country.

It took 30 minutes more to unload Senna's coffin. An electric lift carried it down to soldiers from the Polícia da Aeronáutica, who carried Senna's body to the fire engine, where it was draped in the Brazilian flag. The fire engine would carry the coffin into the city centre to lie in state.

At 6:45am the fire engine moved off, preceded by 17 police motorbikes. The policemen were wearing white leather suits and led a motorcade on the 20-mile journey into the city. On the rear of the fire engine, four cadets from the Military Police academy sat on each side of the coffin, facing fore and aft, mounting guard; five more were on the ledge at the rear of the engine. In addition, 2,500 policemen lined the route.

The policemen were to keep the crowds back, but they couldn't stop the cars. The roads were kept open as swarms of vehicles crowded the procession, getting as close as possible to the moving coffin, even on the wrong side of the carriageway, in their desperation to see the last glimpse of the coffin holding Senna's mortal remains. Many cars had been adorned with swathes of black material on the aerials, and pictures of Senna taped to the windows. It would take the fire-engine three hours to reach its destination, as police and television helicopters clattered overhead.

As it neared the end, the procession slowed and an honour guard of 33 mounted cavalry, carrying lances, joined the procession. The horses escorted the fire-engine as it crawled between São Paulo's streets. By now there were huge crowds welcoming their hero home. On both sides of the road they were at least 20 deep.

The fire engine was followed by thousands on foot, and on bicycles and motorcycles. Office workers from tower blocks showered the coffin with ticker tape, confetti and flowers. Banners and graffiti covered all available space on tunnels and bridges: 'Obrigado Senna' (thank you Senna), 'Senna não morreu, porque os deuses não morrem' (Senna isn't dead, because gods don't die). And 'Obrigado, Senna por fazer nossos domingos felizes' (thank you for making our Sundays so happy). They all shouted "Ole, ole, ole, Senna, Senna, Senna." All of the Brazilian TV channels were broadcasting the event continuously.

Tension was also high. Brazilian newspapers were reporting that the real time of Senna's death was 2:17pm and that he died at the trackside. They were saying that he was brought artificially back to life and that the race should never have been re-started. Much of it was being stoked up by Leonardo da Silva, who wasn't thinking straight, blinded by the tragedy that had befallen his family.

The coffin finally reached the state legislative assembly, where it would lie in state. The 1950s building was set in Ibirapuera Park, south of central São Paulo.

Already 20,000 people were waiting in a queue to file past the coffin and pay their respects. Before that could start, the family held a 20-minute service conducted by a pastor Sabatini Lali. An old helmet of Senna's was placed on top of the coffin.

After the ceremony, two soldiers with pikes and four with rifles, with their weapons reversed by tradition for a fallen hero, took up guard.

The people of São Paulo began to file past one side of the catafalque, and the other side was roped off for VIPs. The VIPs, could come and go as they pleased via a rear door. Beyond the special roped-off area was a private room. Entry to both areas was by a special badge, with either a plain 'F' on it for family or 'A' for friends. The 'F' and 'A' badges were given to around 500 people who would also attend the funeral.

A special area and access was given to the media. A raised platform, with some chairs, had been constructed. It was crammed with TV crews and photographers, who used their regular FIA accreditation to gain entry.

Adriane arrived and was bitterly disappointed when she discovered the coffin was closed. She said: "I couldn't understand, I couldn't believe, I couldn't accept it. I thought the coffin would have a glass lid or something that would allow me to see him for the last time. But it was completely sealed. I felt terrible disappointment, a shiver down my spine."

Adriane quickly became the centre of attention, as she flitted in and out. She was protected from the crowds by municipal minders. She needed them, as 8,000 people were passing through the room every hour; that would continue for 24 hours.

Although relations were strained, Adriane greeted Senna's family cordially. But otherwise she kept her distance. They all had their private grief to contain. Of the family, Neyde and Viviane, his mother and sister, were in the worst shape. Leonardo simply paced the room and Milton kept his distance, stoically observing the scene, as was his way.

Senna's Brazilian personal trainer, Nuno Cobra, was distraught and his tears simply overflowed in the most public display of grief in the private area. Afterwards his face was distorted temporarily from crying and his eyes had swelled up. He was being comforted by Josef Leberer. Cobra could simply not believe that Senna would not be returning to Brazil as normal in November to continue his intensive training sessions. Senna was Cobra's whole life, and that life was gone.

In the special room people chatted quietly, including world champions Emerson Fittipaldi, Alain Prost and Jackie Stewart. Derek Warwick turned up. He was not expected but felt he had to come. There was a poignant moment when Neyde da Silva approached him. She told him through an interpreter: "You know Derek, Ayrton always had a special place in his heart for you."

When the current Brazilian drivers Rubens Barrichello and Christian Fittipaldi turned up, the crowd cheered.

Outside a huge display of floral tributes was starting to build up. There were wreaths from almost every racing organisation and from famous individuals. Some were exotic affairs. The most impressive were two huge white crosses from TAG Group and the McLaren team. The wreaths formed an avenue of flowers, together with random bunches from ordinary fans which started to form a carpet of flowers.

That morning in another room, Senna's brother Leonardo held a press conference on behalf of his family. He said the family was furious that the race had been restarted when it was clear Senna had died when his car impacted the wall. He said: "The motorsport authorities are only interested in money."

He condemned the governing body FIA. He said it knew the dangers the drivers were facing at Imola's Tamburello corner and that a narrow strip of grass and 20 metres of tarmac was insufficient to separate the track from solid concrete wall. He said: "If they'd taken the correct precautions, my brother would be alive today." There was some merit in what he said, although it conveniently forget his brother had inspected the facilities many times and agreed that all that could be done at Tamburello had been done.

Leonardo had whipped up a frenzy of anti-FIA, anti-Ecclestone and anti-Mosley fervour. He was almost irrational in his hatred. Leonardo blamed the authorities outright for his brother's death, and said that Ecclestone or Mosley would not be welcome at the funeral. Mosley decided not to come but Ecclestone wished to say goodbye to his friend.

All through that evening, night and morning, mourners filed past the coffin. Ron Dennis, surrounded by bodyguards in dark suits, arrived and sat for 40 silent minutes reflecting on his six years with Senna at McLaren and three world championships.

Senna's family came in and out. Adriane kept vigil all night and did not sleep. She remembers: "I walked around and felt I was being looked at, watched. I didn't care. I felt like jumping into the coffin and screaming." Friends urged her to rest overnight in preparation for the funeral, but she refused. She did, however, take a shower at the Bragas' nearby hotel.

At dawn on Thursday, Frank Williams arrived to pay his respects and spoke to Adriane what words he could.

At 10 o'clock the next morning a 21-gun salute, fired by the 2nd Artillery Brigade, rang out over Ibirapuera Park. It marked the end of the public viewing; over 200,000 people had filed past to pay their respects.

It was time for the coffin to leave. Rose petals were strewn over it, and military cadets took it from the catafalque to a waiting fire engine for the final 10-mile journey to Senna's resting place, the Morumbi cemetery.

Birgit Sauer, the wife of the head of Volkswagen Brazil, arrived to accompany Adriane to the funeral. They had holidayed together in the past and struck up a friendship. They were now united in grief.

Adriane and Birgit got into a minibus, which followed the fire engine carrying the coffin. Gerhard Berger, Christian Fittipaldi and Alain Prost, amongst others, also got in. The bus's curtains were drawn to protect passengers' privacy.

The streets were lined with ordinary Brazilians, mostly in tears and screaming. In the four days since his death, no one had come to terms with it. The day of the funeral seemed to spark emotions even more extreme. A young boy ran with the bus all the way from the building to the cemetery. Two hundred thousand people lined the route, as the rest of Brazil watched it live on television. When the fire engine passed the crowd, clapping broke out all along the route.

Seven planes of the Brazilian Air Force aerobatic display team, in diamond formation, laid smoke trails as the cortege crawled up the hill to Morumbi, high above the city. The last half mile was a steeply winding road.

The Cemitério de Morumbi is a huge round park, with discreet headstones laid into the grass, horizontal and well spaced. Behind the high walls, overlooked by private apartment blocks, waited VIP guests and hundreds of people from the world of motor racing. Many of the racing people had all flown in and assembled that morning at the Intercontinental Hotel, where coaches waited to take them to Morumbi. Others helicoptered in. The helicopters landed behind a small clump of trees. Armed Brazilian soldiers in grey combat uniforms and black baseball caps were responsible for their security.

A rope-lined pathway of light green carpet led to the open grave, where tarpaulins, covered by green plastic grass, protected the edges of the freshly dug hole. When Senna's coffin reached the cemetery it was unloaded and the official mourners followed behind as it was pushed up the hill on a green metal trolley to the grave side. Drivers pushing the trolley and escorting it were Gerhard Berger, Alain Prost and Michele Alboreto, Jackie Stewart, Damon Hill, Emerson, Wilson and Christian Fittipaldi, Rubens Barrichello, Mauricio Gugelmin, Maurizio Sandro Sala, Roberto Moreno and Raul Boesel, Pedro Lamy, Derek Warwick, Johnny Herbert, Thierry Boutsen and Hans Stuck Jr. Six television helicopters flew overhead broadcasting live pictures across Brazil.

As the trolley pulled to a halt, the 2nd Guards Battalion of the South-Eastern Military Command stood at the ready and three volleys of salute from the guards' automatic weapons resounded. In between each volley, the clicking camera shutters echoed round, and the empty brass shells fell to the ground.

At the graveside a white canopy helped protect family and friends from the sun. In front some temporary chairs had been arranged. At the front was the family: Milton and Neyde da Silva, Leonardo da Silva, Viviane Lalli and her husband Flavio and their three children Bruno, Bianca and Paula. In the second row, Adriane Galisteu and Xuxa Meneghel. When Adriane took her place in the second row, Xuxa immediately got up and moved to another seat; perhaps insensitively, the seating plan had the two women sitting together. Xuxa was the family's official widow, and arrived and left with them. It reflected the coolness they all felt towards Adriane, which was only thawed a little by Neyde da Silva.

The service was conducted by the pastor Sabatini Lali who had presided over the earlier service. After he had finished, Viviane rose to speak. She said: "Brazil is going through a very bad time. No one feels like helping anyone any more. People just live for themselves. My brother had a mission, and our family is in deep emotion today because we didn't realise it had made him so greatly loved. I saw how the ordinary people showed their feelings. Some of them were shoeless; others dressed in silk. He united them, even through his death. I think that my brother is not down there but up in the heavens." Finally Viviane threw up her right arm, in imitation of her brother's victory salute. "Valeu Senna!" she cried. And the 500 mourners responded: "Valeu Senna!"

Her address was in danger of being drowned out by the clatter of helicopters overhead. As she finished, the aerobatic team traced a big heart and a giant S in white smoke against the deep blue sky.

Adriane looked at her boyfriend's coffin for the last time, and she said in silence: "I love you, but you left me. I miss you. From now on my life will be a misery." The ceremony had lasted for 30 minutes in bright sunlight, under a perfect blue sky.

After the service, the coffin was lowered and covered with earth. Workmen arranged the flowers carefully around the grave, making sure the wreaths did not cover the plaque set into the freshly laid turf. The plaque, in Brazilian tradition, read 'Ayrton Senna da Silva 21.3.1960 – 1.5.94. Nada pode me separar do amor de Deus.' In translation: "Nothing can separate me from the love of God."

Then the family stood up in front of the small canopied area and all the mourners filed by to pay their respects.

The mourners were in no hurry to leave, but gradually withdrew to their helicopters and coaches. Pointedly, Xuxa Meneghel left in an official family limousine. Adriane Galisteu appeared to attempt to join a family limousine and was turned away. Later she denied that she had, and said she was simply saying goodbye to the family. Whatever happened, afterwards, Adriane was not welcome at the family reception, and left in the bus she arrived in to join the Bragas at their farm.

The apparent rejection appeared cruel, but reflected the majority of the family's view of Adriane and the reason why Leonardo's last conversation with his brother had been adversarial. It later became clear that Leonardo's mission in Imola had been to appeal to his brother to give up Adriane. It was the reason she had not attended the race.

After everyone had gone, vans arrived to unload the flowers from Ibirapuera Park. By 1:30pm they were all laid out, apart from one late-arriving floral tribute from the American singer Tina Turner.

Alain Prost, the reigning world champion, was the last to leave. He was a magnet for TV cameras and radio microphones, and he obliged all requests to talk about Senna's accident. He said: "I was shocked. He was the kind of guy you really think it won't happen to. He was the master of his job. For sure, something happened with the car. Motor racing is always dangerous, but we must minimise the risks wherever possible. I think it's time for changing a lot of things. It's not a question of rules. It's a question of philosophy, of whether you have respect for drivers."

He talked about how he and Senna had become reconciled and were enjoying a growing warmth towards each other, culminating in an embrace at Imola on the eve of the crash. He continued: "For 10 years it was Prost and Senna. Now it's just Prost. Half of my career has gone today."

The funeral had attracted over 400 regular members of the Formula One community. Many had not known Senna very well at all, and some had never even met him. And some who had known him very well did not come.

Three significant figures had elected not to come. Nigel Mansell was in the middle of the Indianapolis 500 race programme, a serious event in America. Instead Mansell sent a letter to the family. He wrote that he fought many races with Ayrton, lost most of the fights, but even when he won he knew that he had had the honour to defeat the best driver of all time. He also wrote that he knew that Ayrton had the habit of anonymously helping needy organisations and people. Therefore, if Ayrton's family was thinking about starting a foundation or something like it, they should please not consider the amount but the feeling – and he enclosed a cheque for $5,000 to kick the fund off. His $5,000 was the start of the Ayrton Senna Foundation.

The current world championship leader, Michael Schumacher, did not go because he simply did not care for funerals. He said: "I can't do something like that in public, in front of everyone. I went to his grave two years later, before the Brazilian Grand Prix. But on my own. Only my wife was with me."

Nelson Piquet was not a friend of Senna's in life, and refused in his death to attend his funeral, hypocritically. He said: "I've never liked going to funerals and I didn't want to act like Prost did, pretending he was Senna's friend when they had actually spent all their lives fighting with each other."

Neither did Max Mosley, president of FISA, attend. He had been the subject of much criticism in Brazil for allowing the race to be restarted after Senna's accident. The da Silva family thought it an outrage and a massive show of disrespect. The family simply did not realise that the race always went on in Formula One, regardless. After all, death had been absent from the sport for so long.

Bernie Ecclestone was also missing from the funeral service but was holed up in the Intercontinental hotel. The family had asked him not to attend. Later in the day he visited the grave. Ecclestone was very close to Senna, who had stayed with him at his London home many times. Ecclestone's two young daughters Petra and Tamara regarded Senna as an uncle. Ecclestone later met with the state governor, Luiz Antonio Fleury, to brief him on what had happened in Imola. A year later there was a rapprochement with the family after emotions had cooled.

As the day wound down, Josef Leberer summed it up, saying he didn't believe his friend would have been afraid of death. He said: "I remember a test in Hockenheim once and he says to me, 'Isn't it, Josef, that we have a fantastic life. Haven't we a good life?' I said to him, 'Are you afraid that this is going to stop one day. He replied: 'No, because I have such a good life now so whatever comes, comes.'"

The da Silva family went back to their farm at Tatui to rebuild their shattered lives. The Bragas and Adriane went to the Braga farm in Campinas. On Friday she got a surprise when Neyde Da Saliva arrived. She wanted to talk to the people who had spent time with her son. Of the family, Adriane got on best with Neyde. After chatting, Neyde arranged to meet her at Senna's apartment at Rua Paraguai, where they had lived together, so that Adriane could collect her things. Adriane had a lot of stuff there. She had lived with Senna for a year, and for the last month alone whilst he was in Europe.

Galvao Bueno spent four days thinking a lot about his career and whether he could carry on now Senna was dead. He decided to carry on because of the young Brazilian drivers Rubens Barrichello and Christian Fittipaldi.

Josef Leberer also had to decide whether he wanted to continue. He stayed with Williams to look after Damon Hill until the end of the season, then rejoined McLaren.

Alain Prost was relieved that he had taken the decision to come to Brazil. The big question was whether Prost would come out of retirement and take Senna's seat at Williams. He firmly discounted that: "Out of respect for him, I would never, never, never take the seat in his car."

Prost remains a favourite of the Senna family. On Friday of that week, Milton and Neyde invited him to join them at the family farm in Tatui. Strangely they found the presence of their son's greatest track rival reassuring. Over the weekend, Prost and Milton da Silva talked about his son's last weekend and his life. Prost told his father that he believed he and his son would have become good friends once they had retired. The reasons for acrimony between them did not exist outside competition in a race car. Prost said: "I think it's not impossible that in time we might have become friends. We shared an awful lot, after all, and one thing never changed – even when our relationship was at its worst – was our great respect for each other as drivers. I don't think either of us worried too much about anyone else. And there were those times we did have fun together, you know."

Gerhard Berger and Johnny Herbert were soon gone from Brazil. They were due to attend the funeral of Roland Ratzenberger, the forgotten victim of the Imola weekend. Berger had his own demons to confront; he was unsure whether he ever wanted to race again.

Derek Warwick simply went home. His career was over, ended by the man he had come to mourn. Afterwards Neyde da Silva wrote him a letter. It was all so unexpected but Warwick says, trying to explain: "I think he knew what he did to me and my career but still felt it was done for the right reasons. I don't know whether he was awkward with it or whether he just knew he had to squash something in order to survive himself. With hindsight I don't bear him any malice for that. I'm actually more angry with myself for not being tougher in certain situations. But you know, I am my character and I'm proud of what I am – but that went against me at the end of the day."

Julian Jakobi had to pick up the pieces of Senna's growing business empire. $47 million had been committed to investment in the future. There were a lot of decisions to make. His three-year contract with Williams would be paid out in full by insurers. Also his personal sponsorships would be covered. After the business was concluded Jakobi finally had time for his personal grief. He had been stunned by the funeral and had no idea his driver had been so revered by his people. He said: "I remember watching John F Kennedy's funeral in Washington in 1963, and even Winston Churchill's when I was a young boy. I'd never seen anything like this. The Senna funeral in Brazil was just quite something. You wouldn't want to be part of it because of what happened, but on the other hand, being there, it kind of put everything into perspective. Here was a guy from Brazil, which has a fledgling motor industry, who could take on and beat the industrialised world. Here was somebody, rather like Pelé, who was a world figure, who was universally respected. And, during the nine years that I worked for him, I didn't understand, being based here in Europe, just how much he was revered in Brazil."

But it was Adriane Galisteu who had the most pieces to pick up. She was the person closest to Senna at the end of his life, and was left with nothing. Despite the opposition of Senna's family, it was thought they would eventually marry. It is possible Senna had already told his family what his intentions were, and that was the reason for the friction between him and Leonardo on that last weekend.

For nearly two weeks Adriane recuperated with the Bragas on the farm. Betise Assumpção came for a visit. They talked non stop about Senna's life. It seemed to make things easier to bear.

Ten days later Adriane went to collect her things from Senna's flat. It was her first visit to São Paulo since the funeral. She found had grown scared of going out, and cowered in the car during the journey. She remembered: "The sight of the city scared me."

At the apartment Neyde da Silva was waiting. Adriane said: "I took the elevator and went up. The door was half open. Everything looked the same – and at the same time it was so different. There was no sign of us there. Everything was in its place. There was no life there anymore. His mother and I sat on the sofa and talked for about 40 minutes."

Afterwards she threw her things in four large suitcases. She asked Neyde if she could keep his toothbrush."

When the time came to leave, both women cried and cried.

Outside it was raining.

CHAPTER 33

The Trial

The worst country to die in a race car

When a racing driver is killed in Italy there is always the threat of a trial, but only if a prosecutor can find someone to blame. It is the nature of the country. Italy is the one place that Formula One team-owners fear going to because of the legal ramifications if anything happens to their drivers. From a legal point of view the San Marino Grand Prix was the worst place for Ayrton Senna to meet his end.

It gave zealous state prosecutor Maurizio Passarini a chance to make life hell for the Williams team, the FIA and Imola circuit officials for over five years as he found plenty of people to blame for the death of Ayrton Senna.

When 39-year-old Passarini lost, he was still not content and appealed against the decision. If he had been successful, he could have destroyed motor racing in Italy, perhaps for ever. That was an outcome the country, home of Ferrari, was not prepared to accept and therefore the verdict was a fudge. But not before a legal circus had left Formula One bemused and confused.

Passarini's zealousness and sometimes poor judgement saw him accuse honest men of being liars and lost any hope of finding the reason for the accident which took the great champion took to his grave. A few men may have known what it was, but any admission could have labelled them guilty of manslaughter in Passarini's unusual court.

His actions certainly put pressure on Williams, Renault and FOCA TV personnel who endured serious trauma in court including being branded liars by the prosecution. In end it didn't change anything. Peter Goodman,

Williams' English lawyer who masterminded the team's defence, said of Passarini: "He did do some things which annoyed us but, as far as I know, he did nothing that was not permissible under the legal system in which he was operating." And that was the problem for the defendants in that the rules were very different to English law. At virtually every hearing there was detailed comment in newspapers and on television, some of it hysterical and clearly by English standards prejudicial. Goodman said: "There was a great deal of television in Italy both before and during the trial which left the whole of Italy apparently convinced that the English team had killed the great Ayrton Senna and were getting away with it by means of an Anglo Saxon conspiracy."

The Williams lawyers always contended that the car hit a series of four bumps in Tamburello one after the other in a random pattern never done before and never repeated since in a freak incident that had a million to one chance of happening. They maintained it caused the car to go down on its suspension and sledge, understeering off the track out of Senna's control.

In the opinion of many, Passarini lost credibility because of tricks. He had not allowed either Patrick Head or Adrian Newey of Williams to examine the wreck of the car from the moment of the accident to the date of the trial. He had also interviewed Adrian Newey and FIA circuit director Roland Bruynseraede as witnesses, without warning them they could be charged. It was a disregard of the law and abuse of power, and took away the atmosphere of a balanced court room and a realisation that there would be little fairness in the trial from the prosecution.

It took two years for six people to be charged with 'culpable homicide'. Three members of the Williams team were singled out as being responsible – team principal Frank Williams, technical director Patrick Head and the car's designer Adrian Newey. By the time of the trial Newey had decided to go and work for the McLaren team and had been placed on gardening leave by Williams. It made life difficult for the Williams defence as Newey had engaged a separate lawyer to defend himself against the charges. Three others faced different charges for the same offence: Roland Bruynseraede, the FIA circuit director at the 1994 San Marino Grand Prix; Giorgio Poggi, the director of the Imola circuit; and Federico Bendinelli, head of Sagis SpA, the company that operated the Imola track.

All in all, five lawyers represented the six men and not only did they have to disprove the charges, it was the nature of the legal situation that they also were obliged to shift the blame among themselves. Initially the lawyers for

Williams, Head and Newey were forced to blame the circuit for the death as part of their defence, and the lawyers for Poggi and Bendinelli needed to blame the car. This suited Maurizio Passarini but seriously handicapped the defence. By the middle of the proceedings Peter Goodman had persuaded all the defendants' lawyers to work together, much to the annoyance of Passarini.

The FIA itself was also effectively on trial through its representative, Roland Bruynseraede. A guilty verdict for him would have been a guilty verdict for the FIA. It would almost certainly have meant the FIA would have withdrawn its endorsement of any motor racing in Italy, making the whole country a motorsport backwater. No one wanted that. Formula One needed Italy almost as much as Italy needed Formula One. The country was a crucial part of the commercial and sporting jigsaw. No one could foresee what would happen without it. As FIA president Max Mosley explained: "The difficulty is that in Italy a small degree of blame in someone's death is still a criminal offence – that means involving either a gross degree of negligence or some deliberate act that was likely to lead to the death, but not serious enough to lead to a charge of murder. The problem is that although culpable homicide in Italy is seen as a relatively small thing, when it is reported in other countries – particularly in countries where an English-style legal system prevails – it is like manslaughter, which nobody wants to be accused of, and it becomes front-page news. So I think there is a feeling now in Formula One that it is not even a question of whether the accused are acquitted or not. Nobody wants to be put on trial for what is really an honest sporting mistake. A lot of people find it very difficult that such a thing can result in criminal prosecution. So the whole situation is under discussion at the moment, irrespective of the outcome of the trial."

Mosley and the FIA were powerless to prevent the trial going ahead – they simply had to go along with the Italian legal process and hope that good sense would prevail; as it had in; all the other fatal accidents in Italy over the years. "Clearly one cannot have a situation where any perfectly ordinary person pursuing a sport in an honest and decent way can expose themselves to criminal proceedings," said Mosley. "They cannot be blamed for anything on moral grounds. It is absurd to think that any of them would deliberately do anything to jeopardise the life of a racing driver."

By the end of the trial, sensing the hypocrisy of the situation, the defendants more-or-less combined their defences and fought as a team. In fact the stakes were high for all the defendants. For Patrick Head and Adrian Newey it was the first time a driver had died in one of their cars. Patrick Head could not comprehend a guilty verdict on his record, as he said: "The charge is quite serious, you know. It is a criminal charge, not under civil law, and we obviously have to defend ourselves to the maximum. If we don't believe it is the case, we have to put full effort into proving to the judge that it is not an appropriate charge. It is certainly not something I want to have on my record." Eventually, Head found the best form of defence was not to expose himself to the trial.

There was another danger for the Williams team; if the team members were found guilty, it could have caused other legal problems for the company. In that unlikely event the Senna family were considering their own negligence suit – as rumoured – a guilty verdict would have given them all the ammunition they needed. But it was also rumoured that the Senna family had long settled its position with the Williams team.

The Senna family had appointed a lawyer to represent them but he didn't turn up every day. The lawyer was merely acting as an observer for Milton and Neyde da Silva, and their daughter Viviane. The family had no real interest in the trial because, as Viviane Lalli said: "It won't bring him back to us."

Although Williams was represented in court by Italian lawyers, the team retained English solicitor, Peter Goodman, then of Schilling & Lom and now of Pictons, to run its defence. Goodman had long-standing links with the Williams team and Patrick Head and Frank Williams. He also had close links with the Senna organisation, folllowing the lengthy negotiation of Senna's contract with Williams in 1993 and became a business associate of Senna's manager, Julian Jakobi, in 1999. Goodman took no direct part in the trial, but had a watching brief: to make decisions on the spot for the team. He hired the Italian lawyers, necessary as much of the trial was conducted in Italian. Goodman had interviewed most of the witnesses and prepared them for trial. He probably knew more about the case than anyone, and attended every day of the proceedings. In one year he made 90 international flights in connection with the case. He said: "It may sound naive, but the Williams approach was always to establish the truth rather than necessarily clear themselves."

The trial provoked the most emotion in Frank Williams. Ayrton Senna was the second driver he had lost in his career as a team-owner. The first was Piers Courage on a windy Sunday in June 1970, in the sand dunes of Zandvoort. Then there had been no legal ramifications. It was simply a racing accident, no more no less, to the Dutch police authorities. Like Senna's death, it had been an awful experience for Williams. Courage was burned to death in his crashed car and that weekend, Frank Williams was so distraught that he refused to even look at the charred wreckage. He asked Jackie Stewart to arrange disposal of it.

Italian law is so absurd when it comes to motor racing that a possible defence would have been just to ignore the trial and let the court make a decision, safe in the knowledge that no penalty would be forthcoming, because the two Grand Prix events held in Italy are simply too important to the country. But that was not an option that Williams, Head or the FIA was prepared to take. All the defendants knew they had to beat the charge for all sorts of reasons. And ultimately they all decided individually that whatever it took to do so was justified morally. In this trial they were the good guys; the defendants and Passarini and his technical experts, the bad guys. Surprisingly, when Frank Williams had first met the then 36-year-old Passarini he found him very pleasant, as he said: "He's a very serious, straightforward magistrate. He's a very honest and open individual who is intent on finding out all the facts before he makes his decision and he won't be rushed." Williams clearly believed at that stage there would be an investigation and the matter would be dropped.

There had been plenty of Formula One precedents for trouble with the Italian authorities, and all had involved the late Colin Chapman and his Lotus team. Three times Chapman had run their gauntlet. Three times he had faced them and won by avoiding them, using every trick he knew. When Wolfgang von Trips was killed in 1961, Jim Clark of Lotus was involved in the accident and deemed the cause. His car was impounded and, although he was cleared of blame, both driver and team were very wary of visiting Italy again. In 1970 Jochen Rindt was killed in practice for the Italian Grand Prix at Monza and charges were threatened. Chapman was scared of being arrested if he returned to Italy, which caused the team principal to enter the cars under a different name for the 1971 Italian Grand Prix. But as it turned out the Italian prosecutors could find no negligence for the accident and there were never any charges, although the authorities impounded the wrecked Lotus for 20 years.

In 1978 Ronnie Peterson, also driving for Lotus, died a few days after an accident at the start of the Italian Grand Prix at Monza. However, Peterson officially died of an embolism in hospital – it was therefore not classified as a motor-racing death and the Italian authorities took no action. In those three cases sanity prevailed but then there was no Maurizio Passarini. The state prosecutor possibly saw the Senna trial as an opportunity for fame, and to put Imola and himself on the map.

The defendants had had plenty of notice of the trial. In 1996, two years after the accident, Passarini finally brought charges against six people. His case was simple enough. He contended that a sub-standard modification had been made to the steering column of Senna's Williams. The column then suffered from metal fatigue brought about by poor workmanship. This suspect modification finally led to a total failure of Senna's steering column as he entered the Tamburello curve at over 190mph. Passarini said that Senna was unable to steer due to a useless steering wheel and unable to brake sufficiently due to the design of the track surfaces, the track edge acting like a launching ramp. Even Senna's skills could not save him from what proved to be a fatal impact with the Tamburello wall.

The nature of the charge was ludicrous, stemming from a lack of understanding of the way Formula One cars are built, modified and prepared for racing. No one denied that the steering column had broken but it was also clearly impossible to know whether it had happened before or after the accident. Passarini said it happened before, Patrick Head said it happened afterwards; and each man claimed he could prove it. In reality neither could, as the trial made clear. But Passarini came close. The weakness in the Williams argument was the presence of metal fatigue and some experts' dim view of the way it had modified the steering column. Other technical directors privately criticised the way the modification had been executed, from pictures of the crash. The professional reputations of Head and Newey were probably saved by the fact that, ultimately, Passarini didn't make his case and chose the wrong grounds for his charges. He may have been right about the steering column but it was unlikely that it broke before the crash, as the video pictures of Senna's cockpit immediately before the accident appeared to show.

Some believe that if it was steering, it was probably the power steering that failed. Many believe that it was a power-steering failure that caused the steering to lock solid in the Tamburello corner.

To press his case, Passarini had gathered together an impressive technical team to help him. It was headed by Mauro Forghieri, the former technical director of Ferrari, and included Enrico Lorenzini, a professor of engineering at Bologna University; Tommaso Carletti, a former Ferrari race engineer; Alberto Bucchi, a professor at Bologna University and an expert in road construction systems; Francesco Bomparole, a representative of the state road contractor; Roberto Nosetto, former president of the Imola circuit; Dr Rafaele Dal Monte, a professor of science and sports; and Emmanuelle Pirro, a former Formula One driver. Passarini's mistake was that the panel was

all-Italian and therefore lacked international credibility.The team had had the
run of the 900-year-old Bologna University's facilities and an Italian military
aerospace laboratory to carry out its investigation and prepare its report.

The trial of the men, effectively accused of causing the death of Ayrton
Senna through negligence, began on 20th February 1997 in a seedy
ballroom, hastily converted from a Saturday night dance venue at the social
centre in Imola, a stone's throw from where the great champion had died
almost three years before. The local courthouse was not big enough. It was
not a full charge of murder the six defendants faced, but one of culpable
homicide, or manslaughter in English parlance. The penalty under Italian law
for manslaughter varies from six months to five years imprisonment, but
there were precedents indicating the penalty could be a fine, as had
happened in other such motor racing death prosecutions. But no one was
really worried by the penalty. It was the cost to personal and corporate
reputations that a guilty verdict would ensue.

The opening day of the trial was marked by a lone man standing in silence
at the entrance to the makeshift courtroom holding a placard with a picture
of Ayrton Senna and the words 'tell us the truth' underneath.

As in any motor-racing event involving Formula One, a collection of the
world's media turned up, bristling with cameras. Judge Antonio Costanzo
swiftly ordered them out of the court room. He decided that two fixed
television cameras would film events, except where witnesses objected.

Surprisingly this was a trial where the defendants, and it seems witnesses
too, were not obliged to turn up. Only one defendant put in an appearance
on the opening day – Federico Bendinelli, director of the company that runs
the Imola circuit. But he had only to walk to the courtroom from his office.
He had the most to lose. If the defendants were convicted no one would
come to race at his circuit any more. A conviction would merely inconven-
ience the other defendants. His livelihood was on the line.

Bendinelli told reporters outside the circuit the obvious dangers for Italy of
a successful prosecution. He said that in Italy criminal investigations are obligatory and added that no one should be held responsible for the accident:"The
risk exists that all races in Italian territory will be banned if we are convicted."

The lawyer representing the Senna family told the court they had decided
not to stand as civil plaintiffs.

It had taken Maurizio Passarini over two years to prepare his evidence,
which ran to more than 3,000 pages. Considering the basic simplicity of the
prosecution's case, the size of its document was astounding. In a

nutshell, Passarini claimed the accident was caused by a modified steering column failure, which caused the driver to lose control of the car. The case against Williams, Head and Newey was simply that the car's steering column snapped. The three race officials were charged with not ensuring that the circuit's safety requirements were met.

Passarini asked for a large-screen TV so he could show second by second the last minute of Ayrton Senna's life. He said he would show video footage coupled to the Williams telemetry recovered from the team's databank. "Each split second we will know what Senna was doing – hitting gas, braking, turning wheels or changing gears," he said.

Only three hours of work would get done that day, dealing with preliminaries. The highlight was a challenge to the state prosecutor, Maurizio Passarini, from lawyers representing Frank Williams and Patrick Head that evidence from tests on the wrecked car should be thrown out because the defendants were not present during the appraisals.

Two more sets of lawyers argued that the case against Newey and Bruynseraede should be thrown out as they had not been told early enough that they were defendants. Newey's lawyer Luigi Stortoni argued that his client had been improperly questioned by state prosecutor Passarini in order to obtain evidence. He argued that Passarini had interviewed Newey as a witness, not as a defendant, and had not warned him he could face prosecution. He said: "This is a scandal. It should not happen in a civilised country." That was the view of almost everyone in the court.

Filippo Sgubbi, Bruynseraede's lawyer, claimed that his client had given evidence under similar circumstances. But Francesco Pintor, the assistant prosecutor, maintained: "All rules and regulations were strictly adhered to."

Oreste Dominioni, the principal lawyer for Frank Williams and Patrick Head, said: "We are absolutely sure the car was in good order. The steering column broke after and not before the crash."

Passarini said he planned to call as witnesses Damon Hill, Bernie Ecclestone and Michael Schumacher, and said the witnesses would testify in the last week of April when the people concerned were due to attend the San Marino Grand Prix. Around 40 other witnesses were also expected to give evidence, including Nelson Piquet, Gerhard Berger and Riccardo Patrese.

The opening day's evidence, once absorbed by journalists, sparked a frenzy of newspaper articles about the cause of Senna's crash. There was speculation that Damon Hill's sister car had been modified similarly. On the Sunday the *News of the World*, a British tabloid newspaper, claimed that the steering columns on the Williams Renaults of Hill and Senna were altered two months before the San Marino Grand Prix, in the same way on the same day. The *News of the World* article quoted Professor Adolpho Melchionda, a mechanical engineer and member of the court's investigative team, as saying: "When you saw through an essential part of the machinery, you alter the crystalline structure of the metal involved. This can work but on the other hand may not work. To say that it was a job well done because Hill had no problems is short-sighted. We believe that the evidence will show that he was driving a potential death trap and was lucky nothing happened to him. The cause of Senna's crash was the work done on the rod. The recent pictures which were released showing the scrap [of bodywork] on the track have nothing to do with it at all."

Melchionda was referring to a picture taken by Paul Henri Cahier first published by the British *Sunday Times* the weekend before the trial began. The newspaper said the photograph explained the riddle of Ayrton Senna's death. Taken 700 metres from the Tamburello bend, it showed Senna's Williams running over a tiny scrap of blue bodywork assumed to be from the Benetton of JJ Lehto. Having solved the riddle, the newspaper also came up with a theory that Senna may have been holding his breath for an entire lap after the race was restarted and simply passed out at the Tamburello and lost control of the car. The alternative theory destroyed the article's credibility.

The article, by respected journalist Peter Windsor, alleged Senna used to do this and got a faster lap as a result. But the likelihood of an intelligent man like Ayrton Senna wanting – or being able - to suspend his breathing for as long as 90 seconds just wasn't credible.

In the *News of the World*, Adrian Newey's lawyer Luigi Stortoni confirmed the same work had been done on both Williams cars: "Work was done on the steering rod. The same work was done on Hill's car. The diameters of the two pieces of pole were different. But to demonstrate that the job was done well, it has to be shown how Damon Hill had no trouble with his car. We are convinced that the welding was not the cause. The work was done in March, and both Hill and Senna had raced two Grand Prix events with the modified cars and there wasn't any problem. On the third, Senna crashed. I don't know how many times, if ever, Hill raced the modified car after that. And Newey certainly did not carry out the work."

Williams and Head's lawyer Oreste Dominioni told the *News of the World*: "Yes, Damon Hill had the same modifications made to his car as Ayrton Senna. And I think he believes the job was well done. It was well done."

The *Sunday Times* and *News of the World* articles, from Rupert Murdoch's newspaper group, generated worldwide interest and the photos were reprinted and examined in more detail in *F1 Racing* magazine in April 1997. It prompted Imola circuit boss and defendant Federico Bendinelli to issue a statement saying that the photo published in the *Sunday Times* had been part of the investigation records since the beginning.

The Senna trial was odd because it was not scheduled as one long hearing, rather as a series of mini-hearings lasting one or two days. It would eventually take nearly 40 days, and last almost a year.

After a gap of seven days the trial resumed on 28th February. Straight away Judge Costanzo rejected the challenges from the two defence lawyers for Williams, Head and Newey. There was a new challenge on territorial jurisdiction from Newey's lawyer, stating the trial should be moved to Bologna, where Senna was declared dead in hospital; this too was rejected. With that and some other legal posturing, the trial was adjourned for another week to 5th March. With the lack of progress and two seemingly wasted opening days, it was an unusual way to conduct a trial.

On 5th March the prosecution was finally able to present its case. State prosecutor Maurizio Passarini laid his cards on the table and said that faulty engineering by the Williams team and a defect in the track were responsible for Ayrton Senna's death. None of the accused was present to hear Passarini state: "A modification to the steering column which had been poorly executed caused it to break." He claimed the car left the track because the asphalt surface was not on the same level as the trackside. "There was an angle with the side of the track," he said.

Williams' and Head's lead lawyer Oreste Dominioni immediately rejected the accusation that the car was at fault, claiming that the state of the track was to blame and that investigators had failed to properly test its surface. He said: "They should have determined whether the characteristics of the course were such as to make the car lose stability and leave the track." Dominioni called for a new technical investigation of the circuit.

The move against the track was promptly countered by a group of lawyers representing Poggi, Bendinelli and Bruynseraede, who said that ample checks had been carried out on the Imola circuit. Dominioni's intervention set the mood of the trial and defendant against defendant. To prove their clients' innocence, the lawyers would have to blame each other. In reality it only aided the prosecution – a unified legal strategy between all the defendants would have been far more effective and much better for the image of Formula One.

Passarini said his case was that the steering column of Senna's Williams car had been badly designed and was not strong enough to withstand metal fatigue. He said: "The steering column had been cut and a new element – which was not of the same quality metal or of the same diameter, being 18mm instead of 22mm – was welded in. It was where the new element had been welded in that the column broke. When Senna had a steering wheel dangling in his hands, he was doing 192mph. He braked and hit the wall at between 130mph and 136mph. If the track had been completely flat, he would have been more able to brake and his speed could have been reduced to 105mph. Senna paid the price of these circumstances." The weakness in his argument was that the video footage did not back him up.

Dominioni denied that modifications to the steering column had been done 'fast and furiously' before the Imola race, and also pointed out that the steering column was identical to that used by Damon Hill in the other Williams car that season. He said he would be able to demonstrate that the steering column had broken after the crash, not before.

Roberto Landi, the lawyer for Bendinelli and Sagis, denied there had been anything wrong with the track to cause the accident. He declared: "All the world's circuits are like Imola."

Adrian Newey's lawyer demanded a new forensic examination of the steering column on the grounds that Newey had not been able to appoint his own expert to attend the original tests, as he had not been warned he was under investigation and might face charges.

Passarini, who spoke for over an hour and a half, also said he wanted to counter suggestions that he was waging a vendetta against motor racing by pointing out that no prosecution had resulted from Roland Ratzenberger's fatal accident the day before Senna was killed.

Passarini said that Ratzenberger's accident occurred because of damage to the car sustained when it left the track, rather than because of design or construction errors – and that only in the case of Senna had the investigations demonstrated a case of manslaughter.

He proceeded to admit various pieces of evidence, including a film taken by a camera on Senna's car, analysis by consultants and a digital reconstruction of the accident using television pictures taken from several angles. He said he also wanted to use as evidence records regarding crashes on the same bend by drivers in previous years: Nelson Piquet in 1987, Gerhard Berger in 1989, Michele Alboreto in 1991 and Riccardo Patrese in 1992.

In addition Passarini wanted to refer to television pictures showing cars grounding on the corner and sending up showers of sparks. Finally he wanted to admit film showing an object thrown into the air by the wheels of either Senna's car or Schumacher's close behind.

Referring to the *Sunday Times* article, Passarini said: "I wish to clarify that I do not attribute any causal significance to the small object on the track." Passarini also laid several other rumours to rest: Senna had not taken any drugs, did not make a driving error and did not pass out. He said the telemetry told him 'Senna desperately tried to stop the car until the end'.

Dominioni said he would be calling as a witness Massimo Angelini, who was driving the safety car around the circuit before the race restarted.

Judge Costanzo put off his reply to Williams' lawyers, led by Dominioni, who had asked for a new expert investigation of the Imola circuit.

A week later, on 11th March, the defence presented its case through five sets of lawyers – but not before Passarini had made some more damning allegations, irrelevant to the case being tried, against the Williams team's engineering prowess. He told the court that a metal plate was welded onto the rear suspension after it was damaged during winter testing at the Paul Ricard circuit at Le Castellet in France. He explained: "I mention that not to say that the rear suspension was the cause of the accident but to note that, despite the fact that these are very sophisticated vehicles, when a problem occurs it is patched up with a metal plate."

Among the early witnesses was Mario Casoni, the driver of the medical car that day at Imola. He said: "I noticed the abnormal state of Senna's steering column, which had been uprooted and was dangling from the cockpit."

Williams' lawyer Oreste Dominioni pounced: in 1994, he asserted, Casoni had said the column was lying on the ground. Casoni replied that he had made a mistake in his statement given to a police officer at the time.

Dominioni had a difficult job. He had many ways of defending his client and one of them was to continually try and defer blame onto the track and therefore to Federico Bendinelli, managing director of Sagis, which operates the Imola circuit. Dominioni pointed to the track-surface problems, saying they had not been fully investigated. But seemingly unknown to Dominioni, Bendinelli's lawyer Roberto Landi produced an amateur video shot at Imola on 9th March 1994 when the Williams team was testing prior to the Grand Prix. The video, taken by a fan, showed Senna talking with track director Giorgio Poggi, apparently discussing track conditions on the Tamburello curve. Another witness, police inspector Stefano Stefanini, head of Bologna's traffic accident unit, said Senna was complaining about dips in the asphalt, which were taken care of the following day by track workers. Other witnesses confirmed what the video showed. At that point Senna had the ability to save his own life. If he had asked for a row of tyres to be placed against the wall it would have been done without question. The reason he did not – and neither did anyone else – at arguably the most dangerous bend of any track in the world is an enduring mystery.

Passarini also took the trouble to prevent the defending lawyers citing the condition of the tyres as a possible reason for the accident. He asked Stefanini about Senna's lap times before the accident. Indicating that Senna was driving absolutely on the limit to put some time between him and Schumacher in second place, Stefanini told the court that Senna, with a fully-fuelled car, had posted a time of 1m 24.887secs on the sixth lap of the restarted race. "That was a very good time," he said. "Only two drivers bettered it – Damon Hill and Michael Schumacher – and that was at the end of the race."

Traffic police commissioner Marcello Gentili was asked about the car's trajectory and signs of braking prior to impact, to ascertain whether problems with the tarmac could have caused the accident. Gentili said there was a 21cm angle between the track and the trackside and there were intermittent signs of braking.

Two doctors who pulled Senna from the wreckage testified that they did not encounter any obstacles, or have to remove the steering wheel, in pulling his body out of the car. This led them to suppose that the steering column was already broken.

The trial resumed the next day with Passarini calling Pierluigi Martini to testify as a former Formula One driver knowledgeable of both the Imola circuit and the Tamburello curve. Martini said: "A driver like Ayrton Senna didn't go off the track at that point unless there was a problem. A lot of things can happen during a race, but in this particular case I don't know what the problem could have been. Drivers took the curve at 300kph and there was a small dip in the middle of the track which disturbed the cars. The bump effect was perfectly normal and is common to every racing circuit in the world.

"I was at Imola with Senna and others weeks before the race when we noticed a small bump in the Tamburello bend. The circuit officials were very efficient and had the asphalt smoothed out, which was the only thing they could do. The cars still touched the ground and were disturbed so you just had to hold your line." He continued: "The repairs had only slightly improved the situation. Senna had complained to me three weeks before

Imola at Aida [Japan], that his car was nervous and the cockpit narrow. But Tamburello could have only created problems for a car that had problems. The people at Imola did everything they could to give us drivers what we asked for."

Martini felt he could not say that the Tamburello bump had caused Senna to veer off the track. There was only one line into Tamburello and the bump could not be avoided without leaving the track. He added that Senna's fast lap time indicated that his tyres were fully warmed up.

Eight course officials who were present at the Imola race were then asked by Passarini whether they had been aware of anything lying in the path of Senna's car, and whether they believed his Williams Renault had left the Tamburello curve in a straight line.

All felt that Senna's car went off in a straight line towards the wall and all said there had been nothing in his way.

The trial then adjourned for the customary week's break until 17th March. When it resumed, crucial evidence was heard concerning the recovery of the car's two black boxes. The first, belonging to Williams, was designed to record data from the chassis and gearbox; the second, belonging to Renault, stored information on the V10 engine.

The wrecked chassis was initially brought back to the parc fermé and locked in the stewards' garage, before being impounded by the Italian authorities after Senna's death was announced. Imola circuit engineer Fabrizio Nosco testified that he had removed both black boxes from Senna's Williams after the crash, having obtained permission from FIA race director Charlie Whiting. The black boxes were then handed over to the two Williams mechanics, who had arrived in the garage with Whiting, and they took them away. They were not handed over to the authorities, as they should have been under Italian law, although at that stage no one knew Senna was dead, or even seriously injured. Nosco stated: "Apart from a few scratches, both were intact." This vital evidence was refuted by almost everyone else who saw the boxes. Williams witnesses were adamant that once the power was removed the data, being RAM, was lost. Peter Goodman, Williams' lawyer said: "The blow was so significant that it caused the chassis to split. The box was severely damaged in the impact."

Bernard Duffort, a Renault engine-electronics expert, was the first to see both boxes. He claimed that the Williams box showed signs of impact and had been damaged. When examined it contained no data. Duffort said the data from the Renault box was transferred onto a computer disk on the day of the crash and a copy handed to the Italian authorities on 18th May 1994, along with the data recorder. By that time, however, the recorder's information had mysteriously been wiped from its hard disk. Duffort said that tests done on the recorder in Paris shortly after the accident, on an engine test bench, had erased its data. Taken at face value, it was all scarcely believable, as the looks on the faces of the prosecutor and the judge reflected. The defending lawyers were embarrassed. But perhaps it wasn't explained well enough. Renault engineers maintained its black box was merely a recording device and once the data had been downloaded to a floppy disk the recorder was totally irrelevant. A lot of people didn't believe it but it was undoubtedly true. Peter Goodman said after the trial: "People didn't understand that the box is simply a recording instrument. There was no interest in the box which was a standard instrument and undamaged. The interest was in the data and this was removed from the [Renault] box in the usual way and put onto a computer disk. The box was then reused. Nothing was mysteriously wiped from its hard disk."

The day's star witness was Italian Michele Alboreto, who had survived a violent crash at Tamburello himself in 1991 when driving in Formula One. He testified that he believed Senna's fatal crash was caused by a mechanical failure in the car, not a track defect. This opinion, he added, was formed from his many years' experience of Imola and other tracks round the world.

The Italian gave his verdict after viewing a video of the crash, replayed in the courtroom, and in particular pictures from a camera on board Michael Schumacher's car, which was close behind Senna's. Film was also shown of previous crashes at Tamburello involving Gerhard Berger, Nelson Piquet, Riccardo Patrese and Alboreto himself.

Outside the courtroom he told reporters: "Senna's shift to the right makes me think it was a mechanical failure. The situation at Imola was not exceptional – we've raced in much worse conditions than those. I hope this trial helps us understand what really happened to Senna, because it still isn't clear. Mechanical failures are frequent, given the nature of the races and the fact that people always aim for the limit. But no engineer can ignore safety." He went on to describe as 'minor' the bumps on the track surface just before the curve, which had been the subject of Williams' lawyer Oreste Dominioni's questions to him, and said they could not have forced Senna's car off the circuit.

The following day, 18th March, had as its star witness FIA race director Charlie Whiting. Initially he was questioned about the modification Williams had admitted making to the steering column. Passarini asked him if he had known about it. In his testimony Whiting said that Senna's car had been modified without permission before the race, but that the modification would have been reported at the next regular check. Whiting said that he had approved Senna's car in February and again in March.

His evidence conflicted with that of the Williams witnesses, who claimed the team had already informed the FIA and could prove it. But after looking at photographs of minor changes to the chassis, Whiting told the court: "I don't remember this on Senna's car."

When asked to explain why he had allowed the black boxes to be removed from the car by the team before it was handed over to officials, Whiting replied that he had done so because of the overriding need to make sure the other Williams car might not suffer the same strange loss of control that had apparently affected Senna's.

He confirmed that he had authorised the Williams engineers to remove the two black boxes immediately after the accident, but that it had been damaged in the crash and the recorder was blank. The problem apparently was that the separate battery that powered the databanks had become disconnected, wiping all the memory.

Whiting's statement contradicted Fabrizio Nosco's testimony the previous day that both black boxes were intact when he removed them from Senna's car. Electronics expert Marco Spiga was called and disputed Whiting's claim: he felt the data should have been available. He said it had taken a month for Williams and Renault to hand over the boxes to the investigators, and when they had received them both were blank. He told the court: "The Williams box was totally unreadable when we got it back."

The confused Passarini asked for a further investigation of the data recorder, and all the parties involved were summoned to an examination of the unit at the engineering department of Bologna University on 24th March.

After the subject of the black boxes had been exhausted, the findings of the autopsy on Senna were read out by pathologist Corrado Cipolla. He said Senna's injuries were caused by a massive blow above the right eyebrow. He affirmed that Senna had not died from the impact of the crash but from a blow to the head by a blunt object. He showed a photograph of a part from the front suspension. He said the blow crushed the front part of Senna's brain, killing him instantly, although his heart and lungs continued to work, assisted by a life-support machine, which was eventually turned off. He therefore gave the official time of death as 2.17pm, although 'cardiac death' occurred at 6.40pm.

Other experts said Senna's blood indicated perfect health and a total absence of banned substances, and that his helmet complied with specifications. This testimony appeared to lay to rest rumours that Senna had been taking performance-enhancing drugs and had a light, illegal helmet to save on weight.

The court resumed again on 2nd April when the subject returned to the black boxes. Maurizio Passarini called on electronics expert Marco Spiga to demonstrate how the external sockets of the data recorder worked. These were the sockets reportedly damaged in the crash. New pin connectors were supplied by Williams expert Giorgio Stirano. However, it emerged that a data card was needed to transmit the information to a computer and this was not supplied. Maurizio Passarini said: "Why are we only told today that we need a card? Williams has never told us this before. Why wasn't it made available?" Giorgio Stirano replied: "Because we were only asked for the pin connectors." The judge took a dim view of the state prosecutor's much-vaunted technical advisers not be able to work that out before the trial.

Edda Gandossi, a lawyer acting for Williams, said: "It would be pointless to try and cast any suspicion or inferences regarding the behaviour of the Williams engineers. This has always been polite and courteous." The day was therefore a write-off and the trial adjourned until 15th April.

Goodman subsequently explained the day's events by saying that, after weeks of listening to ridiculous theories, and what he saw as defamatory accusations, he had decided to use the moment as an opportunity to illustrate that the prosecutor's team of experts, however illustrious, were not familiar with modern racing cars. The Williams engineers co-operated by supplying the lead that Marco Spiga had requested, knowing full well that the lead would not help him prove his theory. The intention was to discredit him publicly and also, by implication, the technical expertise of the prosecutor's team of experts. This was important to Goodman as the trial was about to move into quite complex technical areas.

When the 15th of April dawned there was a surprise, as the two principal defendants, Patrick Head and Adrian Newey, appeared for the first time and spent the day as observers, very interested in evidence that was due to be given regarding the steering column. Passarini called Tommaso Carletti, an ex-Ferrari race engineer, who said: "There are three possible causes of the break: poor quality work, the quick movement of the steering column and a too small diameter of the joins between the three sections of the column."

Mauro Forghieri, ex-technical director for Ferrari, said: "I believe that

Ayrton Senna turned his steering wheel firmly to the left shortly before the crash. If he had not done so he would have crashed immediately. Senna would have realised the steering on his Williams Renault was functioning abnormally and after twice easing off the accelerator, he began to brake."

Enrico Lorenzini, professor of engineering at Bologna University, also gave technical evidence for the prosecution. The following day the defence put its case regarding the steering. Two Williams engineers, Giorgio Stirano and Diego Milen, said that Senna had had a problem with oversteer as his car went over a bump on the asphalt surface of the Imola track. The bump was located just a few yards from where Senna's car began to veer off the bend at Tamburello.

The Williams engineers said the oversteer sent the car towards the inside of the track and Senna countered by steering away. However, his car bumped again and skidded to the right, nine degrees off the ideal line. They said Senna, at this point, decided to keep his line and tried desperately to brake. There was no doubt that right up to the impact his main concern was keeping the car in the race, not avoiding the impact.

Peter Goodman, the Williams lead lawyer firmly contends by this stage of the proceedings the expert committee members had changed their own minds about the snapping of the steering column. He said: "The new theory was that the steering column had already been substantially damaged by metal fatigue and that Senna realised this."

After the hearing, Stirano and Milen told reporters there was no blame to be attached to the track or the driver: there had been an ordinary problem which destiny had made fatal. They said they reached their conclusions after examining the telemetry readings from Senna's Williams and videotapes.

Their view directly opposed that of members of the expert committee – Forghieri, Carletti and Lorenzini - who claimed that Senna's steering column was already 60-70 per cent damaged by metal fatigue and simply stopped responding after the car hit the second bump in the track. It appeared to be a change of mind by the prosecution that the steering had indeed broken. Forghieri told the court: "Senna realised that if he had tried to steer the car in a way to spin it round, the steering would have snapped." It was a valid assumption to make and Forghieri was a powerful witness in Italy. Outside Italy he was regarded as an emotional man who enjoyed drama. The court room in Imola had become his latest stage. Lawyer Robert Landi, acting for race organiser Federico Bendinelli, said the bumps on the track were no different from those drivers had to contend with on other circuits around the world.

Outside the courtroom Adrian Newey spoke for the first time, telling reporters: "Ayrton Senna's accident was down to fate. My defence lawyers will give my opinion on what happened on 1st May." Patrick Head was asked by reporters how he was coping with the stress of the trial and a difficult season with his number-one driver Jacques Villeneuve competing with Ferrari's Michael Schumacher head to head for the world championship. He said: "The only way to deal with it is to put things into compartments. When I am working on our defence, my mind is on that. And when I am working with the other engineers on problems connected with the current FW19 car and its development programme, I have to make sure my mind is concentrated on that. But it is not an ideal situation."

In the last week of April Bernie Ecclestone was due to testify, but the hearing was postponed and then delayed again by a lawyers' strike.

When the trial finally resumed again on 14th May it opened with Maurizio Passarini accusing the Formula One Constructors' Association (FOCA) of withholding evidence. Bernie Ecclestone did not arrive – instead three FOCA TV personnel appeared. The court was told Ecclestone would not attend in person but would give his evidence by means of written questions and answers, via official channels, and known as an international 'rogatoire'.

The FOCA staffers at Imola on Sunday 1st May were Alan Woollard, the director; Eddie Baker, the production manager; and Andy James, the engineer. All appeared as witnesses. It is believed that a deal had been done beforehand that guaranteed the three men would not be arrested. In 1995 at the San Marino Grand Prix, Italian police had tried to arrest Alan Woollard in an attempt to force FOCA to reveal more tapes, which Passarini believed existed. FOCA had initially been very reluctant to release any on-board footage. In the end it had been forced to by the persistence of Brazilian journalist Roberto Cabrini of TV Globo, who knew it existed.

All three men told the court it was pure coincidence that the videotape was changed just prior to the fatal crash. They all said that the tape from the camera on Senna's car was turned off at almost the precise moment his Williams Renault left the track, 0.9 seconds prior to impact with the wall at the Tamburello curve. It was the moment when one camera cut and another was waiting to cut in.

Passarini told the court there were 1.4 seconds of indistinct pictures and greyish lines which were apparent on the tape when the view switched from Senna's camera to Berger's. It was at the onset of this period that the accident occurred. The explanation given for this interference was it was the pause between camera switches. At the time, FOCA TV supplied in-car footage to the national television networks before the advent of its own digital TV network. It also owned the copyright to other filming at the circuit. Thirteen cars out of the 26 were carrying in-car cameras at the race, and four could be viewed and recorded at any one time. Transmissions from three of these could be chosen to be relayed to the network broadcaster. The restrictions lay in the system. The signal was sent from the cars up to a permanent helicopter in the sky and then relayed down to FOCA's equipment at the track. There were only four channels. Therefore only four of the 13 cameras could be used at any one time and Woollard switched the signal between them. As fate would have it he cut Senna's at the split second before the accident.

FOCA had eventually handed the tape over to TV Globo and it was broadcast. But the version of the tape it handed over to Cabrini ended 12.8 seconds into the fatal lap – or at least the record states that.

Information taken from Senna's on-board computer confirmed the crash had occurred 14.2 seconds into the lap, so there was a period of 1.4 seconds before the impact with the wall at Tamburello. The tape FOCA TV sent to the Italian authorities ends 0.9 seconds before impact, the court records that 0.5 seconds of new footage remains unexplained.

The decision to switch the camera shot coming from Senna's car to that of Japanese driver Ukyo Katayama was taken approximately 10 seconds before, as Senna was leading the race and there was nothing of interest ahead of him.

But in fact, Passarini said, the next shot on the tape was from Gerhard Berger's car, not Katayama's, and it too showed an empty track. "What, if I might say so, is the point of the shots if they have not been tampered with?" he asked.

According to the court records the three FOCA witnesses all said that wrong button was pressed, thus mistakenly selecting pictures from the camera on Berger's car and creating the interference, which explains the 1.4 seconds of indistinct pictures between the last shot from Senna's camera and the first from Katayama's. FOCA executives Andy James and Eddie Baker dispute this and have restated that it was the pause in the changeover.

Passarini's claim that the videotape was supplied to the Williams team 15 days after the accident, but only received by the court on 9th September, was met with the reply that the request had been interpreted as being for pictures of the impact, which did not exist. Passarini didn't believe a word of it. It was also revealed that better quality tape could be provided if the court had the facilities of a Betacam professional recorder. The FOCA men agreed to release a Beta version of the tape that was of immeasurably better quality.

Speaking to reporters outside the courtroom, Passarini said: "I am certain that the pictures supplied by FOCA are incomplete. Several details show this to be the case and I shall say so in the hearing." He implied that he was considering bringing other charges in connection with the videotape.

On 2nd June the court reconvened, ready to hear the much-anticipated evidence of reigning world champion Damon Hill, who had been Senna's team-mate that fateful day. The day started with a disagreement after Michael Breen, Hill's lawyer and manager, insisted that all television cameras be cleared from the courtroom. Peter Goodman organised it so the court complied and the cameras were removed so that Hill could begin his testimony.

Hill's day in court was marked by a poor translator who at times turned the proceedings into farce. Hill, usually the most eloquent of men, proved he had a very poor memory of such a momentous day in his life. He had also turned up too late to be briefed by Peter Goodman. Hill told the court that alterations were made to the steering column of both his and Senna's cars in the 1994 season. Passarini asked him exactly when the steering column had been modified. Hill said: "I don't know exactly. I think it was before we went to the first test, but I can't be sure." Passarini pushed him. Hill said: "I can't remember the exact date. I seem to remember it being done before we ran the car. In other words, before it went to a racetrack." Pushed further to confirm it was before the season started, Hill said: "Yes." There was a moment of high drama as the translator misinterpreted the 'yes' as a 'no'. Luckily there were enough bi-lingual people in court to correct his error.

Passarini asked him when he had known about the modifications. He answered: "I don't know when it was done, I can't tell you. I was made aware that it had been done." Passarini asked him who had informed him of the change and Hill said he couldn't remember. He said he could not remember whether Senna had complained about the handling of his car after the steering-column modification, although he could remember details of a meeting he attended with the Williams team.

Passarini then turned the subject to power steering and Hill confirmed the car had it. But amazingly, under oral testimony, he couldn't remember whether the car had had it the previous year when he debuted with the team. Passarini then reminded Hill of a statement he had given to the prosecutor in June 1994 that the system was new that year.

The power-steering question was important. It has long been the view of many that the cause of the accident was a power-steering malfunction that locked the steering at the Tamburello curve just before the accident, explaining why Senna went straight on and didn't take the corner. There had certainly been problems in-race with the power steering, as revealed by the telemetry from the Renault black box. The electronic system was only in its third race. There had been previous problems with it, as there would be with any new system. Steve Nichols, the former McLaren car designer, asked to comment on it by *The Guardian*'s investigative reporter Richard Williams in 1995, had revealed the pressure had risen suddenly and then fallen suddenly in the few seconds prior to the accident, for no apparent reason. Nichols said in 1995: "If the power steering broke you'd expect the hydraulic pressure to go straight to zero."

Passarini had no evidence to back this theory but pressed the point to an unconvincing Hill. He asked him: "In the two previous races in 1994, did you race with or without the power steering?" Hill replied: "I honestly don't remember."

Hill also said that Patrick Head had told him to switch off his power steering as he waited on the grid after Senna's accident for the restart of the race. The power steering was activated from the cockpit. He said: "It was obvious at the restart that they wanted to be sure things were all right in the car. I didn't ask for a reason. I just did what I was told."

Passarini then asked him whether he had talked to Senna about the car or if Senna had complained about it. Hill said: "I don't remember." Asked about the car, he said: "We found it very tight in the car – in my case the problem was that there was very little room between myself and the steering wheel."

He said he had viewed the video footage at a meeting with Williams engineers at the team's Didcot headquarters less than a week after the tragedy. In the courtroom more than an hour was spent viewing the film from Senna's on-board camera, and Hill was invited by Passarini to comment on it.

Hill took the view immediately after seeing the film at the Williams factory and in the courtroom that Senna was attempting to correct oversteer. He said: "There are two distinct times when the car looks to be oversteering and the steering wheel is exactly the way I would expect to see it to correct oversteer."

Asked whether the apparent oversteer in Senna's car was due to low tyre pressure or the state of the Imola track, Hill answered: "You cannot separate the two. My idea looking at it is that the car seems to oversteer when it crosses the place on the circuit where there are some marks." Hill said he had not experienced any problems with oversteer at the San Marino Grand Prix. His testimony tallied with Williams' defence lawyers, who in March had claimed Senna's death was due to anomalies in the asphalt track surface.

Hill also undermined another of the prosecution's claims – that FOCA TV had failed to supply the complete film shot by the on-board camera in Senna's car – stating that the footage he saw during the meeting at Williams also ended before Senna's car left the track.

Bombarded with questions by state prosecutor Maurizio Passarini, Hill repeatedly answered: "I cannot remember, it was too long ago."

However, he was clear about Passarini's assertions that a weld made to shorten the column snapped moments before impact: "I came away from the meeting with the opinion that there must have been some other reason for the accident other than the obvious one that there had been a failure in the steering," he said.

Some observers at the court that day said Hill was wholly unconvincing and afterwards critics said he had suffered from 'selective amnesia'. At times his continual answer of 'I don't remember' met with much hilarity. But others say he was just trying to tell as much as he could remember, truthfully.

The following day, 3rd June, there was a reconstruction by Michael Guttilla, director of vehicle simulation products at Mechanical Dynamics Motorsport Group, the company that developed a customised software package called ADAMS used by Formula One teams. Williams engineer Diego Milen claimed the reconstruction showed Senna's Williams had suffered from oversteer, forcing him to correct the trajectory on two occasions. This eventually led to the car leaving the track and impacting with the wall at the Tamburello curve.

Maurizio Passarini challenged the simulation and the validity of the data presented, saying that the Imola track surface is of diverse gradients whereas those used in the reconstruction were flat. Therefore these facts would influence the outcome of a car travelling at 310kph.

Passarini had all his wits about him that day, and dented Michael Guttilla's credibility. In the reconstruction, Senna was said to have achieved pole position in qualifying on the Saturday; in fact, he had achieved the best time on the Friday and had refused to continue qualifying on the Saturday after the death of Roland Ratzenberger. The blunder embarrassed the Williams lawyers. Guttilla was also challenged by Bendinelli's lawyers, acting for circuit operator Sagis, who challenged the validity of the circuit data used in the reconstruction, which they defined as arbitrary and unverified. They maintained Williams had obtained its data through unofficial sources.

At the end of the day the court saw the better quality Betacam tape of the Senna car footage, supplied by FOCA TV. The pictures were much clearer and revealed much more. Michele Alboreto had also seen the new tapes privately – he was reportedly shocked when he viewed the new images and, due to the improved quality, noticed the sideways movement of Senna's steering wheel.

The hearing resumed on 25th June and was preceded by a programme the previous night on Italian prime-time television that analysed the trial so far. The programme, called 'Senna Trial: The Black Hole', was broadcast on Italia 1.

The programme was full of speculation, including the downloading of the black boxes by mystery people and criticism of Hill's testimony. It claimed the Williams team had gone into cover-up mode after the accident and removed parts from Hill's car. The programme also stated that a mysterious Frenchman, a Renault employee, had downloaded the black boxes and left Italy secretly that night. It was clear that the defendants were also being tried on Italian television – clearly an intolerable situation, especially for the British defendants more used to the niceties of English justice.

On Wednesday 4th June, testimonies continued about the modifications made to Senna's steering column. Witnesses were called by the Williams defence lawyers, the first being Tony Pilcher, in charge of production at the Williams factory. Pilcher was asked by Williams lawyer Dominioni if he was involved with the manufacture of modified parts for the steering-column assembly. Pilcher replied that he was responsible for their production.

Stortoni, Newey's lawyer, objected – asking whether Pilcher was under investigation – and the judge immediately overruled him.

Dominioni continued, showing two drawings of the steering assembly to Pilcher, who explained them to the court. He said the original drawing was dated 3rd February 1994. It showed the steering column of the Williams Renault FW15 to be 905mm long. This was elaborated from the plans of Alan Young and was given to him on 10th March 1994 for production.

Pilcher explained that Senna had requested a modification – the new column measurement was to be 917.3mm and two new elements were to be introduced. The assembly consisted of nine components, manufactured simultaneously by different departments at Williams.

The assembly was manufactured and inspected to assure conformity between drawing and product. If the part failed inspection procedures, it would either be reworked or discarded. The same applied to quality – if satisfactory, the piece and its components, each carrying an ID label, would be placed in the store.

From there the piece would be drawn for fitting to the car by the mechanics. Williams produced three column assemblies and the modifications were executed immediately after 10th March, in time for the Brazilian Grand Prix.

Williams' lawyers showed that the steering-column modifications had been done properly and that Senna's steering column was the same as Hill's.

Maurizio Passarini then questioned Pilcher about the dates of the modifications and the materials used. Pilcher testified that at least two to three days were required for that type of modification. The parts were machined from two types of compatible steel, T45 and EN14.

Another Williams witness that day was Max Nightingale, who was responsible for aerodynamics and hydraulic steering. Williams had first used power steering in 1994.

Nightingale was asked about the tests done after the Senna accident with respect to the steering and suspension. He said: "Patrick Head asked for the tests to be performed. Our data was based on the high peaks of Senna's telemetry, which were probably due to bumps on the track. These are incompatible with a break otherwise they would have been reset." He confirmed that, as a precaution, the power steering on Hill's car was disabled after Senna's crash.

The next witness was Williams employee Simon Wells, responsible for hydraulic tests. He testified that he had not found any signs of stress on the steering of Damon Hill's car, but he had not carried out a test. In a strange outburst, Passarini accused Wells of being 'a technician who conducted an examination that he was unable to accomplish'.

Afterwards, reporters crowded round the lawyers as they left the courtroom, eager for their reaction to the TV programme the previous evening and in particular the suggestion that a mysterious 'Mr X', or presumably 'Monsieur X', knew the truth about the crash in which Ayrton Senna died. Maurizio Passarini said he had seen the programme but replied to all questions with a firm 'no comment'. Williams lawyers had not seen the programme. Roberto Causo, the FISA lawyer, was more forthcoming: he confirmed the existence of 'Mr X' but said he was a French engineer whose only role was to transport the black box from Imola to Paris.

On Thursday 3rd July Williams engineers Gary Woodward, Dickie Stanford, Simon Scoins and Brian O'Rourke testified for the defence. They said that the crash in which Ayrton Senna died was not caused by steering-column failure. Gary Woodward, who was responsible for the interior mechanics of Senna's car, testified that the column in his Williams Renault was carefully checked before the race. He said: "After each Grand Prix the cars are subjected to a crack test, using penetrating liquids to identify any fractures in the suspension or steering columns. The steering columns are replaced halfway through the season. The tests carried out after the Pacific Grand Prix in Aida, Japan, found no defects in Senna's car."

At that point Maurizio Passarini asked him if he was aware of the modifications made to Senna's steering column. Woodward replied: "Steering-column modifications, which complied with the rules, were made to Senna's car. All three cars had the same modifications prior to the race in Brazil."

Simon Scoins, a Williams electronics engineer responsible for downloading telemetry, admitted he had received the Williams black box from Senna's car after the crash. He said: "I was shocked when I lifted the material cover from Senna's car. The Williams data recorder was above the gearbox, 180cm from its natural position. Three of the four connectors were disconnected or damaged. I carried it to the garage where I attempted to connect it. It was useless. I tried inserting the RAM card but without success. I have no knowledge of the Renault data recorder."

Composite-materials specialist Brian O'Rourke said: "As the right front wheel of Senna's car hit the wall, the violent impact caused a torsion on the steering column, causing it to break."

The following day Maurizio Passarini again showed the enhanced Betacam video images. They were taken from Senna's in-car camera and, according to the prosecution, showed anomalies regarding Senna's steering column.

Two fixed points were shown located on Senna's steering wheel: a yellow button and a V mark, the first with a distant radius 83mm from the centre of the steering wheel, the second 55mm.

Relative arcs showed the shift of the points indicated with reference to two moments in the race, the period behind the safety car and the first lap of the restarted race.

Then Passarini produced a new video regarding the evidence. The circumference traced from the yellow button was relative to the movement of the chassis, whereas just before the crash the yellow button lowered to the level of the V, which represented a deflection of 28mm.

Dominioni introduced a video brought from the factory: the steering of Senna's car showed it had a flexibility of 15mm. Mauro Forghieri told the court angrily: "Any driver would have refused to drive with steering in that condition."

The following Wednesday, 9th July, was destined to be the last day in court before the summer recess: the hot courtroom proved explosive.

The witnesses called were Mr Nosetto and Professor Rafaele Dal Monte for the prosecution; and Mssrs Minelli, Marchionna, Saliti (general secretary of the Italian Motorsport Commission, or CSAI) and Muscioni (an FIA safety inspector) for the circuit.

Roberto Causo, defence lawyer for FIA delegate Roland Bruynseraede, who was in court for the first time, attacked the conditions with regard to the concrete run-off area and the escape route from the track at the time of the crash.

Roberto Nosetto was a director of Santerno, the company responsible for the circuit, between 1980 and 1989. He explained: "There were two rules, that of the CSAI of 1962 and an international one which had evolved with time. The wall at Tamburello into which Ayrton Senna crashed met the standard. It was constructed of resilient cement, made to absorb any impact at an angle not exceeding 30 degrees. Senna's impact was 22 degrees." Nosetto told the court that in 1989, when he finished his administration, to the rear of the grass border a course layer of wide cement was constructed measuring 9-13 metres. This area was to allow for emergency procedures.

Passarini asked Nosetto for his opinion on the way Senna's Williams Renault left the track. He told the court that the Williams flew, in the sense that the front wheels rose and fell, leaving visible tyre tracks. It then crossed over the grass/cement areas, with a braking distance of 38.5 metres, which happened in 0.6 seconds. On the track the deceleration was 4G, on the grass/cement it was 0.8G. Bendinelli's lawyer, Roberto Landi, objected: "The word 'flew' is misleading. Better to say 'a slight lifting'."

Professor Dal Monte told the court: "The Williams lost ground adhesion. The average gradient of the track then was plus 3.1 per cent, the average of the escape shoulder plus 2.1 per cent. At Tamburello there was not a way of escape as denoted by the regulations. There was not enough space to reduce the speed of the car."

Nosetto added: "The escape area should have had the same inclination as the track. There could be some undulations provided that the ideal line of track continuation was consistent, without gradients and with a maximum radius of 50 metres."

Then the defence lawyers for the Imola circuit produced a CD, based on the telemetry data, full of diagrams which gave the real and optimal braking times. According to this data, Senna hit the wall at 188kph (116.8mph) against the 216kph (134.2mph) calculated by the prosecution's experts. In ideal conditions Senna would have crashed at 167kph (103.7mph), against the 140kph (86.9mph) estimated by the prosecution. But in both cases the front right wheel of his car would have become detached, hitting his head at the same point and with enough force to kill. And there it stopped, while the lawyers went on holiday and Jacques Villeneuve and Michael Schumacher wrestled for the world championship.

After the long summer break, the trial resumed on 16th September in cooler weather. When it opened there was drama as David Coulthard failed to appear as a witness. The day had been planned to examine Coulthard's evidence and recall Michele Alboreto, whose earlier evidence conflicted directly with Coulthard's.

Williams' lawyer, Oreste Dominioni, maintained that as Coulthard would not be available until the end of the Formula One season, his written statement should be accepted. This did not go down well with prosecutor Maurizio Passarini, who clearly felt Coulthard had been nobbled. He stated that as Coulthard lived in nearby Monaco he shouldn't have a problem with travelling 400 kilometres to attend the trial. However, if his written deposition added nothing to that already offered by the defence, then it should not be admitted.

The no-show put Dominioni in a difficult spot: he required Coulthard to refute Alboreto's evidence as they were in direct conflict over the movement shown on Senna's steering wheel.

Passarini took the opportunity to make a speech but he was preaching to the converted. The judge was also unimpressed by Coulthard's no-show. He said: "People involved in Formula One don't want to be thought hostile towards the environment. No one will go to prison for this, and that is logical as the whole sport entails risks hardly avoidable. But this trial is obliged to at least defend the memory of two drivers, I talk also of Ratzenberger, as they cannot defend themselves. It bothers me that people are defending positions which are indefensible."

In the event Passarini recalled Michele Alboreto to the stand. On 17th March he had testified, after viewing a VHS video of the crash, that he felt mechanical failure made Senna unable to negotiate the Tamburello curve. Now he was recalled because he had had a chance to view the much-improved Betacam version of the tape, and had made public his views based on that. Passarini wanted them put into the court record. Alboreto was again adamant that there was a technical failure. "You don't go off on that bend unless there is a mechanical failure," he said. He also stated that on circuits like Imola the stresses and strains on the steering column would cause flexing 'in the order of two or three millimetres'.

Oreste Dominioni then read out the written statement that former Williams test driver David Coulthard had made, which stated that the amount of movement seen on the steering wheel of Senna's car was normal. The statement said that the steering wheel in the McLaren, which Coulthard drove in 1996, behaved similarly. Coulthard's statement directly countered Alboreto's evidence.

Alboreto, very direct and impassioned, replied that movement was allowed, considering the torsion inflicted by the arms of the driver and the composition of the material. Oscillation could depend on the distance from the support, but only by two or three millimetres.

Coulthard supported the Williams theory that the movement as seen on the Betacam video was perfectly normal. Judge Costanzo accepted his testimony, provided that he subsequently appeared in person.

During Alboreto's testimony, film was also shown of previous crashes at Tamburello involving Gerhard Berger, Nelson Piquet, Riccardo Patrese and Alboreto himself.

Outside the court, Alboreto said he was convinced Senna's crash was caused by mechanical failure, not driver error. Being semi-retired allowed him to speak freely, he said. This was in reference to Coulthard's statement, which Alboreto implied was obtained under duress.

He told reporters: "I'm even more convinced that it was a technical problem that caused Senna to crash, now I have seen the video. There is a tape which shows the flexing movement of the steering wheel was two to three centimetres. No steering wheel moves a few centimetres. Should the court accept this film as evidence it will prove that something was wrong with Senna's car." It was clear outside the court how close Alboreto and Senna were, as he declared: "I hope this trial will come to the defence of a man, a great driver, who is no longer with us. Shortly after his death I heard ridiculous stories – that the crash was caused by Ayrton fainting or because he was thinking about his fiancée. Senna deserves the recognition that he was not to blame for his own death. I don't want to see anyone go to prison, but his memory must be protected."

Alboreto refuted Coulthard's statement, claiming he was being told what to say to safeguard his future in Formula One. "Coulthard has the prospect of a long career in Formula One," he said.

Others felt at the time that Alboreto's testimony was so vehement because he had a long-standing past grudge against the Williams team over a drive that was promised but never materialised. Whatever the truth, Alboreto has taken it to his grave. In 2001 he was killed in a testing accident in Germany, driving an Audi R8 Le Mans car.

The debate over the Coulthard no-show set the scene for a spat between Passarini and Williams' defence lawyers, who produced experts to conduct a simulation to prove that the behaviour of Senna's car was similar to that of the simulator. This followed on from Mike Guttilla's testimony.

Passarini displayed the images from Senna's in-car camera to prove that he steered to the right. A Williams expert said the movements visible were not only circulatory as dictated by the force of the torsion.

Finally Williams' lawyers screened a lab video of a 1994 car taken from the team's museum. It featured a driver (David Coulthard) at the wheel simulating the movements made in a race. According to the defence, it reconstructed the oscillations of Senna's steering wheel before the accident, with the yellow button that moved in a springy compatible way conducive to the materials used and the imposed effort from the driver. In his written statement, Coulthard said the steering wheel in his 1996 McLaren behaved similarly.

Passarini was not impressed. "The film shown today has the same value as the defendant who says 'I wasn't in that place on that night'," he said. "It remains the comment of a defendant."

The court reconvened on Monday 22nd September to examine the Williams computer simulation shown on the 16th. Passarini called Professor Pietro Fanghella of the University of Genoa to question Williams engineer Diego Minen.

Professor Fanghella said: "My graphs showed that when superimposing the traces of the real telemetry onto those of the simulation there was a temporal difference of 1.5 seconds. Regarding Tamburello, the responses in the simulation do not relate to those of Senna. In comparing the two graphs there were discrepancies of 25 per cent, 50 per cent and in some cases 100 per cent. The simulation captures only the course of the vehicle, not the corrections made by the driver. The steering wheel is not in relationship with the angle of the steering wheel in the program."

Minen replied: "The relationship between the steering trajectory and the steering wheel is not comparable due to the unstable track surface – a phenomenon that happened only once but which, for Williams, is the reason Senna left the track. The temporal difference in the telemetry real-simulation is of 1.2 seconds and this is not relevant. It is impossible to quantify the angle of the steering applied by the driver by looking at the yellow button on the steering wheel."

The following day saw first questioning of two defendants, Federico Bendinelli and Roland Bruynseraede. Passarini reminded the court that Bendinelli was managing director of Sagis, the company that runs the Imola circuit, and that Bruynseraede was the FIA delegate present at Imola on Sunday 1st May 1994. Also due to attend was Giorgio Poggi, the circuit manager, but he was ill.

Passarini repeated his claim that Senna's accident was initially caused by steering-column failure, the secondary cause being his inability to brake sufficiently – a result of the raised edge of the track, which stopped the car's wheels from gripping the surface.

First to testify was Bruynseraede, who granted the FIA licence to the Imola circuit in 1994. He stated that he had inspected the track two months before the race, and that circuit officials had always observed any demands made to improve safety. He said the final track inspection was made on the Wednesday preceding the race and nothing was found to cause concern. He said: "The FIA had never required alterations to Tamburello and I had never received complaints from the drivers regarding that part of the track." He added that in any case, he had not been involved in the bureaucratic procedures through which the Imola circuit obtained its licence from the FIA.

Bendinelli stated that the Imola circuit had been modified but that all alterations were made with FIA approval. He said that the FIA had never found fault with the angle at the track's edge, before or after Senna's crash. Adding that Imola and many other circuits had modified their layouts after 1994, he explained why: "Critical situations were being created for the cars, most likely because of the abolition of active suspension. The FIA took remedial action with changes to the circuits, especially the faster ones, and also to the cars. The FIA felt that drivers were relying too much on computers and therefore the human element was being lost from the sport." He said Senna himself had welcomed the abolition of active suspension and was one of its most vocal opponents.

Bruynseraede told the court that in 14 years he had received only one request to alter the circuit. It came from Alain Prost, who in 1989 was acting as the drivers' representative. Prost requested that a grass verge at Tamburello be cemented over to allow drivers to brake more quickly and give more control should they exit the track at that point.

Bendinelli's lawyer, Roberto Landi, asked his client about the modifications to Tamburello after the 1994 fatal accident. He replied: "Tamburello is now different but the track gradient with the run-off area is the same as before the alteration."

The day ended with Passarini making presentations regarding David Coulthard's no-show and the Scot's previous protestations that he could not attend before the season ended on 26th October. He said that unless Coulthard attended the trial session on 28th October, his statement should not be admitted as evidence.

The judge said that the trial would resume on 3rd October, when Frank Williams, Patrick Head and Adrian Newey would attend.

When 3rd October dawned it took only five minutes for Judge Costanzo to adjourn the session after Frank Williams, Patrick Head and Adrian Newey failed to turn up. Lawyers told the court that due to a ceramics trade fair being held in Bologna, all hotels in the Imola area were booked up: their clients had found it impossible to secure accommodation. The lawyers told the court that they would attend on 29th October. To avoid a wasted day the judge and lawyers spent two hours finalising the trial's schedule as it neared its conclusion: on 7th November, Maurizio Passarini would begin his summing-up for the prosecution; then on 10th, 11th, 12th, 14th, 17th, 18th and 21st November, the defence could sum up its case.

As scheduled, on 28th October David Coulthard finally arrived to testify. Pressure had been put on a reluctant Coulthard to attend in person by the Williams' lawyers because his evidence was vital. Peter Goodman denies it was. But there is no doubt they breathed a sigh of relief when he appeared.

Coulthard said the movement shown by Senna's steering column/wheel was perfectly acceptable. Coulthard stated that in 1994 it was normal for the Williams' steering column to move both up and down and left and right by several milimetres, and for the driver's hands to rub against the cockpit. As the steering wheel was constructed of carbon fibre this would also flex. He said the regulations had since been changed, and the collapsible steering wheels were much stiffer.

Passarini asked Coulthard if he knew how much 'play' there was in the steering column, independently of the steering wheel. Coulthard retorted: "No, I have never done that test because I have never driven a car without a steering wheel." His remarks brought the house down – even the dourest of the Italian court officials found them amusing.

The court was shown the video of Coulthard sitting in a stationary Williams Formula One car, showing the movement in the steering wheel. After reading Coulthard's oral testimony, Alboreto told reporters that he had never before experienced that behaviour in a steering wheel.

On 29th October the trial resumed amid great anticipation: Frank Williams, Patrick Head and Adrian Newey were due to personally testify. In the event neither Newey nor Head turned up – they informed the court via their lawyers that they had exercised their rights not to answer questions, and opted to submit written statements at a later date. But Frank Williams had arrived in Italy the previous day in his own plane and apologised for being late arriving from his hotel. The trial was adjourned to await his arrival, expected by late morning.

When he finally arrived, Passarini asked him about the Williams team's own internal investigations. Williams said: "We were looking for as much fact as possible and were anxious to see as much television footage as we could. We as a company formed the opinion that the steering column did not break. This was decided after examining the telemetry readings and also a lot of simulations."

Williams went on to say that the team had considered various explanations, but he did not offer a theory for the cause of Ayrton Senna's crash. He did say he remembered that alterations were made to the steering column after 1st May. "I remember that all the remaining cars were checked and were OK. Even so, we decided to change the columns and manufacture different versions to remove any doubt about integrity."

Asked whether he had any doubts about Senna's steering column, Williams replied: "Absolutely. We had doubts, that's why we're here today, trying to find out what happened."

Passarini asked Williams why Senna's steering column was modified. Williams said: "Ayrton wanted more room in the cockpit and it was decided to change the steering column. When it was decided, I don't remember. There would have been communication with all the relevant people. I can't be accurate or specific because I do not follow, and never have done, every operation on a daily basis."

Williams said he didn't know who was responsible for making the changes, only that many people would have been involved. "Senna made three or four pages of recommendations to make the car go faster after every practice session. I remember that he was not happy about the amount of space, and there were many other things he wanted to change. He also wanted a very large steering wheel – it was one of his trademarks," he said.

Williams said that he was not aware changes had been made until after the race. Passarini offered a judgement on Senna's opinion of the car, which Williams rejected, saying: "The driver did not say he could not drive the car, rather that he would like more space so he would be less tired in the latter half of the race."

Passarini brought up the fact that the Williams team's own experts had discovered over 40 per cent metal fatigue in Senna's steering column. Williams said: "But I'm certain that the plane I arrived in yesterday had cracks in it."

Pushed further about any action he would have taken had he known the extent of the metal fatigue in Senna's column, Frank Williams restated that he was not responsible for technical issues.

Speaking to reporters later outside the court, Williams said: "We'll probably never know what happened. But I made it clear in court today that we think that the car probably left the road rather than suffered a steering column failure."

Williams was effectively the last witness for the trial. The summings-up were scheduled to begin on 7th November. On that day Maurizio Passarini, after nine months of legal action regarding Ayrton Senna's death, gave his closing statement to the court at Imola. The state prosecutor first recapped the events leading up to the fatal crash, again focusing on the steering-column modifications made by Williams. He referred to the events of that tragic Imola weekend, the death in qualifying of Roland Ratzenberger, the initial accident at the start of the race, the deployment of the safety car and the race restart.

Passarini said that driver error must be excluded. Two investigations by independent laboratories reached the same conclusion. The steering column had signs of fatigue over 75 per cent of the circumference and 40 per cent of the section. Reference was made to the testimony given by defence witness David Coulthard regarding the normality of the two centimetres of oscillations shown on a Williams steering column.

Almost certainly with a view to undermining comments made earlier by Frank Williams, Passarini made a point of highlighting the fact that after the race restart, Senna clocked what would prove to be the third-fastest lap of the race, discounting many theories – including Williams' – that a loss of tyre pressure, due to the cooling of the tyres whilst following the safety car, could have caused Senna's loss of control.

Passarini also introduced the multimedia evidence showing the behaviour of the car, telemetric information and Senna's last moments at the wheel. He made it clear that he was unhappy with some aspects of the defence, for example the data recorder installed in Senna's Williams-Renault. This box was said to have been smashed during the accident with vital information it contained thus lost.

Passarini said that Senna's data recorder contained 20 memory chips, but only two were damaged – those whose data would have been retained even when the power supply failed. "It must be a coincidence, but it makes you wonder if someone was very jealous regarding its contents," he said.

In a surprise move, the state prosecutor announced that certain officials from the Formula One Constructors' Association (FOCA) were to be investigated over alleged false testimonies. The probe was to be carried out by the Bologna attorney's office.

Passarini talked about the problems he had encountered in obtaining the final footage from Senna's in-car camera. He claimed that the responses given by the FOCA TV employees were 'disconcerting or downright comic, if not tragic'. He said that Bernie Ecclestone, at one time expected to be called as a witness, was not directly concerned with the investigation. He did indicate, however, that letters Ecclestone has sent to the legal authorities would be examined to see if there was a separate case to answer.

This could relate to the film taken from Senna's on-board camera. The Williams team was provided with the footage within a week of Senna's death, Passarini's office took over six months to obtain the tape. He said: "This is typical of the disdain with which the Formula One world has treated this enquiry."

Passarini also attacked Francesco Longanesi Cattani, the FIA's press supremo, and said he may face an investigation. He did not say what for.

Passarini always contended that the footage supplied from Senna's in-car camera was incomplete because it stopped 0.9 seconds before Senna's fatal impact. He said that nine minutes had been spent following Senna's Williams and therefore it was comical to believe that it was 'sheer coincidence' that FOCA TV staff decided to switch shots just before impact.

He did not believe the testimonies given by the FOCA TV employees, who maintained that the car camera was switched from Senna's vehicle to that of Gerhard Berger's by chance. "A moment later Ayrton Senna was dead," he said.

The state prosecutor maintained that the camera was still running at the time of the crash and said he believed the missing footage would have proved his case: that the steering column snapped whilst Senna was still on the track.

Then dramatically and without warning, Passarini recommended that all charges against Frank Williams, Roland Bruynseraede, Federico Bendinelli and Giorgio Poggi be dropped. He said that as both Frank Williams and Federico Bendinelli merely dealt with the administrative side of the business they could not be held directly responsible for the crash that claimed Ayrton Senna's life.

Passarini said that although safety standards at Tamburello were questionable, Poggi and Bruynseraede did not commit any crime. Senna was killed not by his car's impact with the Tamburello wall but because a piece of suspension pierced his helmet, causing fatal head injuries. He said that the question was whether, if his car had been travelling at a lower speed, Senna would still have died: as this issue was in doubt, charges should be dropped. It begged the question why Passarini had wasted the court's time and seriously complicated the trial by charging the men in the first place.

However, he then went on to say that both Patrick Head and Adrian Newey should be convicted as they were both ultimately responsible for the design changes made to Senna's car. The state prosecutor claimed that the fact that Senna asked for modifications didn't reduce the responsibility of the accused. He recommended that the court award one-year suspended sentences to both defendants. The maximum sentence is five years. "Newey and Head designed the steering column modifications badly, and especially, did not check how the plan was put into execution," he said.

There was no guarantee that the judge would take Passarini's advice to acquit four men, but from that point on it was deemed a formality.

Federico Bendinelli said afterwards: "I was convinced the circuit bore no responsibility for what happened, and neither did Frank Williams. His position was the same as mine. I was calm and confident from the start."

Friday 14th November saw Adrian Newey's lawyers Landi and Stortoni in action. They argued that Newey was not directly involved with the alterations to Senna's steering column. The prosecution, they maintained, should have taken account of the actions of the two technicians responsible for the steering modifications, namely Young and Fisher.

Stortoni said the prosecution felt that, although Newey had not worked on the modifications directly, he was ultimately responsible. But there was no proof that Newey ordered the job. In fact when Williams held an internal investigation into the cause of the accident, Newey wasn't even asked to attend.

The final session for the defence came on 18th November with closing statements from Patrick Head's lawyers, Dominioni and Gandossi. Dominioni's strategy was to try and dissect the prosecution's case. He launched a lengthy attack on the prosecution's technical advisers, saying that Passarini had never asked them whether a lack of stability in Senna's car, due to the track surface, could have caused the fatal crash.

Dominioni told the court: "Passarini's reconstruction of the incident which cost the life of Ayrton Senna has no basis in proof, it is unfounded and those accused must be cleared." He said that Senna's steering column was the same as Damon Hill's, both having been designed prior to the start of the 1994 racing season. Looking at the testimony of one of the prosecution's experts, Dominioni said it was not possible to say whether a part constructed with the safety equal to a coefficient of one could have broken.

The fatigue on the piece emphasised by the prosecution should have been revealed at 350,000 cycles (a cycle is any fit application that provokes wear on the part); but the steering column, inspected after the first two Grand Prix races of the season, had experienced 27,000 cycles, a value clearly lower than the safety limit. The question then was when and why, because up to the last control check with the penetrating liquids, this had not been highlighted. "Unfortunately, in life exists the unpredictable, the unforeseen event and the inexplicable," Dominioni said.

He asserted that there were contradictions within the prosecution's case, above all those of Forghieri concerning the tyre pressure. On the fundamental point of the tyre pressure, he said the prosecution's experts had relied on presumptive evaluations, not actual data. The Goodyear tyre company disagreed with Forghieri, claiming that the prosecution's reconstructions were wrong. The temporal logic and dynamics of the incident, which began at the time of 11.24 seconds as a consequence of a violent collision on the track, caused one swerve of the car, and resultant oversteer as Senna tried to correct.

Dominioni said the prosecution maintained that the steering column broke causing Senna's Williams to veer to the right, and in his 60 metres off the track Senna didn't try to steer. The defence maintained that this was not because the wheels didn't react to the steering, but because Senna with great clarity kept the wheels straight to achieve the best possible braking.

He said it was useless to compare the Friday session times with those of the accident because conditions were unequal. As Senna's on-board camera was not fixed rigidly, the film was not reliable due to optical illusions.

Dominioni recalled that Michele Alboreto had accused Coulthard of not speaking the truth about the oscillations of the Williams' steering wheel. He stated that Alboreto in turn was unreliable and prejudiced. He said: "I therefore ask for the acquittal of [Frank] Williams and Head for they have not committed any crime. The incident didn't occur through the breaking of the steering column."

Dominioni said that the cause of Senna's fatal loss of control was still unknown. He reiterated the theory given by Frank Williams, who had earlier stated that Ayrton Senna's crash could have been the result of a combination of cold tyres and the uneven track surface.

On 19th November the defence lawyers continued their summing-up speeches. Although the prosecutor had cleared Giorgio Poggi, his lawyer – and nephew – Manrico Bonetti still went ahead. He said that after a long career, which started in 1973 as a track inspector, Poggi was due to retire after the Imola race on 1st May 1994. He maintained that Poggi was a scrupulous executive and there was a limit to his responsibilities. He asked therefore for a full acquittal.

On Wednesday 12th November, Roland Bruynseraede's lawyer, Roberto Causo, said the personalities of the prosecution's team of experts had strongly conditioned the investigation. He argued that if the prosecution's case were to be believed, then the Imola track was in breach of the regulations and would have to be demolished and rebuilt.

Landi, for Sagis, concluded that Bendinelli and Poggi had had operational roles since 1980. Then the alterations to the circuit, requested and designed by Nosetto, were already approved and under construction. Their activities had always been subject to FIA scrutiny.

On 21st November, at the penultimate hearing of the trial, Maurizio Passarini replied to the defence's closing statements.

The state prosecutor told the court that the Tamburello curve, even though subjected to alterations in 1989, was still a very dangerous place, exposing cars to high mechanical stress. The modifications previously undertaken should have encompassed the elevating of the shoulder by 30-40cm to conform to the regulations.

Passarini disproved the objections raised by the Williams defence, saying that it was untrue that the prosecution's experts had not considered the theory of instability, which in one out of 50 cases could account for a car leaving the track. He said that all aspects of the track had been examined, and everyone was aware that the underside of the car had made violent contact with the ground.

The state prosecutor maintained that Williams' reconstruction of the incident must be discounted. He claimed that the team's data was disproved by the telemetry, which did not show that Senna, whilst trying to correct an oversteer problem, had understeered. He said it was in fact quite the opposite - what impressed about Senna's car was that, with the diminution of the lateral acceleration, the torsion applied to the steering column reached zero, which signified that Senna had abandoned using the steering.

Passarini said Senna did this not to achieve optimum braking but because, at this point, the steering column broke. Had the steering column been performing normally, the telemetry should have shown this.

He said it was permissible to have doubts about when and where Senna's steering column was modified, but that it was pointless to say that the steering column on Hill's car was of the same standard. He said: "It is not a valid defence to say that this breaking is considered an unpredictable phenomenon and that there is not a causal link between the incident and the death of the driver. The breaking of the steering column was the main cause – without this the car would not have left the track. Because of the senior positions held by Head and Newey at Williams, they cannot claim to be exempt from the responsibilities of quality control."

Adrian Newey's lawyer quickly concluded the day's proceedings: the defence's main argument was unassailable, he said. Williams and Head's lawyer had done most of his talking for him.

On 26th November 1997, the nine-month trial into Ayrton Senna's death drew to a close. State prosecutor Maurizio Passarini repeated his request for Adrian Newey and Patrick Head to be found guilty of manslaughter, having dropped the charges against Federico Bendinelli, Giorgio Poggi, Roland Bruynseraede and Frank Williams.

Asking for the acquittal of their respective clients, the various lawyers for the six accused gave their final statements. Judge Antonio Costanzo retired to consider the verdict, which he said he would announce at 1.30pm on 16th December 1997. Judge Costanzo proved remarkably accurate. At the appointed time he delivered the verdict everyone had expected, clearing all six defendants of manslaughter charges arising from Ayrton Senna's death. The defendants' legal teams punched the air in celebration.

The judge had ignored Maurizio Passarini's recommendations for one-year suspended sentences to be delivered to Patrick Head and Adrian Newey. He said he would publish his reasons within 90 days. None of the defendants was present to hear the verdicts.

Peter Goodman, the Williams team solicitor who had observed the whole proceedings at the front of the courtroom, said: "We had a good hearing, all the facts came out and I'm sure the right verdict was reached."

Roland Bruynseraede's lawyer, Roberto Causo, said: "By this verdict the judge has recognised that Formula One is an extremely dangerous sport." Giovanni Carcaterra, representing the Senna family, said: "The Senna family only wanted to discover what actually happened – they were not interested in sentences." Passarini said he looked forward to reading the judge's report:"I need to see whether the judge ruled that the incident was due to the breaking of Senna's steering column, although there was no criminal responsibility, or if he felt that the column did not break. In that case I would be even more disappointed." Few doubted the verdict was right. A guilty verdict may have ended top-line motor racing in Italy, perhaps for ever. The FIA issued a statement: "The FIA has noted today's decision of the Imola court, but will not comment until it has examined the full text of the decision and studied its implications."

Williams as a team said: "Williams Grand Prix Engineering is pleased to confirm that Frank Williams, Patrick Head and Adrian Newey have been acquitted of all charges which were the subject of the Imola trial. Our legal advisers inform us that the prosecution has an automatic right of appeal. Clearly we would hope that this matter will not be pursued any further."

Even Ferrari team principal Jean Todt got in on the act. "I haven't commented during the trial because I felt I should wait until the verdict – it has been rather laborious and lengthy, and is therefore a judgement of conscience which has to be accepted and respected. It is not easy to give an opinion on a motor race when you know of the dangers and risks involved. My comments are positive because the fact is there has been a very careful examination of all the events, and because of the outcome of the trial," he said.

Damon Hill said he believed the judge's decision would help Formula One's image after the recent controversies: "I know this trial has been hanging over Williams and this vindication expresses a feeling about the team's utter integrity and the standard of its engineering. I never had any doubts about either."

Veteran team-owner Ken Tyrrell expressed his pleasure on behalf of the other team-owners:"I, like other team bosses, am delighted that they brought in the correct verdict. The idea that Williams, the most successful team with probably the best engineered car in Formula One, would have made a mistake was unthinkable," he said. "I would have been apprehensive racing in

Italy if this decision had found Williams guilty of manslaughter. I realise that in Italy someone has to be held responsible in the event of a death, but it is a quirk of the law and the authorities need to look at that."

In the 381-page written report published on 15th June 1998, six months after the verdict, Antonio Costanzo cited the reason for Ayrton Senna's crash at the 1994 San Marino Grand Prix as the breaking of the 'modified' steering column fitted to his Williams-Renault FW16B. He stated that without that condition Ayrton Senna's car would not have left the track at the Tamburello bend.

With the publication of the official report the chief prosecutor, Maurizio Passarini, could appeal against the judge's decision to find the defendants 'not guilty'. No one thought he would seek an appeal after all that had happened and the dangers for Italian motorsport if he succeeded. But he did. For him it had become a vendetta. He wanted what he saw as the bad design and workmanship of the steering-column modifications carried out on Ayrton Senna's Williams-Renault to be punished. In response Williams also appealed against the factual finding.

The appeal proved a waste of time – Passarini was out of step with the public mood and that of his own colleagues in the Italian judiciary – it was heard in Bologna on 19th November 1999. Three days later the appeal court absolved Patrick Head and Adrian Newey of all charges related to the death of Ayrton Senna. The decision was based on paragraph two of Article 530 of the Italian penal code – 'when no more evidence is presented during an Appeal session, and when the first session has concluded with full absolution, the accusation has to be declared as non-existent'. The defence simply utilised the knowledge that the prosecution would have no chance of submitting new evidence. Williams's appeal was rather more successful on the findings of fact and it also reversed the original judge's view that the actual steering was broken, which meant the team and defendants were completely vindicated. Peter Goodman says: "We don't consider it to be a mystery any more. It was not a failure in the car."

But the matter of the death of Ayrton Senna was not finally concluded until 14th March 2002, when Peter Goodman arranged for the wreck of the Williams Renault FW16, in which he lost his life, to be recovered from Bologna police station and returned to the factory of Williams Grand Prix Engineering some eight years after he died. The car is believed to have been destroyed and the engine was returned to Renault.

CHAPTER 34

The Aftermath for Brazil

The consequences of Sunday 1st May 1994

Fifty miles away across the sprawling São Paulo skyline, on the 10th floor of an innocuous building on Rua Dr Olava Edigio, an eerie calm replaces the commotion of a Formula One weekend taking place in the nearby district of Interlagos. Looking out of her office window, Viviane Lalli can just make out the ant-like figures leaving the Interlagos circuit in their thousands. The weekend, as it does every year, brings back the awful memories of Imola in 1994. The tears will flow again for her and for so many ordinary Brazilians still moved by the death of Ayrton Senna.

For Viviane Lalli, one thought fills her head as she sheds those tears: "Yes, Brazil lost a hero. But I lost a brother." In the eight years that have passed, it is the champion's sister who has captured the hearts of a nation ravaged by poverty and desperate for heroes. For many Brazilians, Viviane Lalli has filled the vacuum created by her brother's death.

She says Brazil's love affair with her brother started in June 1986 when France knocked Brazil out of the World Cup. That same day, Ayrton Senna won the French Grand Prix and on the grid proudly held aloft a Brazilian flag. She says now: "Up to then most people only saw Ayrton as a racing driver, but there was something beyond that. There was a human being, with an extraordinary personality that went far beyond motor racing. Over the years since his death, other people have started to see more of what the real Ayrton was about. That is why, as time passes, the legend of Ayrton Senna grows. It means different things to different people, but it means something to everyone. Whether you have done something great with your life, or done nothing at all, Ayrton believed you could always do better."

The connection between Senna's Formula One racing and Brazil's footballing exploits remained until the end. When Brazil took its fourth World Cup at USA'94, goalkeeper Claudio Taffarel declared: "From the bottom of our hearts we dedicate this victory to our friend Ayrton Senna. He too was heading for his fourth title."

The people of Brazil refer to Viviane as a new 'Mother Theresa'. Since her brother's death she has completely devoted her life to improving the lives of others. Ayrton Senna earned more in death than he did alive, and everything made now goes back to the Senna Foundation in São Paulo – from where his sister distributes it back to the millions of Brazilian children without the hope of a future.

Licensing from the Senna trademark brings in $6 million a year and other products add around $47 million. From Senna sunglasses to pens and watches, and the cartoon character Senninha, the Senna Foundation is now a hugely successful non-profit organisation, growing at 25 per cent a year. Nearly 200,000 Brazilians have Senna credit cards.

The elegant 46-year-old mother of three is now arguably Brazil's most famous woman. The country's political leaders have wooed her to stand for high office, the beauty magazines to choose life in front of the lens and business bosses to lend her genial marketing skills to their companies.

For Viviane Lalli, however, seven days a week from 9am to 9pm, life has only one purpose: helping others. "Before Ayrton died we had a brief conversation in São Paulo about it," she says. "He said he wanted to put his fortune to good use, so he could give others a chance to make something of their lives – the people who don't get a chance. But that was it – just a conversation. I came with a couple of ideas that I was going to show him after the Imola race in Europe, but never got the chance. I think he would be proud though."

The Ayrton Senna Foundation is officially advised by Bernie Ecclestone, Frank Williams, Alain Prost and Gerhard Berger, and that is the only connection to modern-day Formula One. Viviane has been to only two Grand Prix races since her brother's death – two years ago in São Paulo and Australia – and has no plans to do it ever again. She rarely attended races when he was alive and does not enjoy it, although her whole life has seemingly revolved around it. She says: "It's too difficult, too painful to go. Not just when Interlagos comes round, but any Formula One weekend.

That was his world, not mine, and I don't want to be reminded of it.

"Everyone talks about the great Ayrton Senna, the legend, Brazil's hero – this international star. For me none of that mattered when he died. I lost a brother, my parents a son. Just because he was famous doesn't make the pain of his death any less, and it doesn't make it any less now."

Viviane and Ayrton Senna were very close for most of their lives together. They grew up in a wealthy family, looked after by servants and sheltered from the outside world by high walls and steel gates. When Ayrton married at 20, then divorced at 21, Viviane became a motherly figure to her younger brother at the same time as she started raising her own children.

She recalls those times: "The thing that I remember most about him was his determination, and he usually got what he wanted. He just couldn't sit still – even at school, he was always quarrelling with other boys. I used to intervene when we were kids, then one day I got knocked out in a fight so I never bothered again. I think the most important thing I ever taught him was that to be a winner you need self-control. He didn't always have that."

By 1994, the last year of Ayrton's life, Viviane was busy raising her three children, whilst keeping her full-time job as a child therapist. Despite having a famous brother, she had managed to completely stay out of the limelight until the Imola tragedy. "For 20 years I worked in the clinic as a children's therapist. It was just me and the receptionist. No one had ever heard of me and I liked it that way. But the image of Ayrton was very public and people demanded that someone from the family represented the name. I had to do it, as the rest of the family wouldn't come forward.

"As the days and weeks passed after he died, and the country went from mourning to being proud of the Ayrton Senna they knew, for me it was different. Suddenly there was a huge responsibility to carry his name. Nobody asked me if I was still mourning. I didn't have a choice," she says.

She may have had no choice, but few can argue with the results she has achieved. The foundation is run as a business with quarterly targets and sales forecasts like any other organisation – except all the profit goes to charity. The results are produced in an annual report like any other public company, and they make impressive reading: last year 288,000 children were helped in some direct way and $7 million of official investments made.

For Ayrton Senna, being based in Europe highlighted the problems suffered in Brazil. It made him realise there was a big difference between the rich and the poor in his home country. As he once said: "The rich cannot live on an island surrounded by a sea of poverty. We all breathe the same air.

We should give everyone a chance, at least a fundamental chance." In death Senna had that chance.

The potentially massive income stream he left behind has been his legacy. Deciding the exact mission was Viviane Senna's hardest task: "I had great difficulty deciding what to do in a country where there are so many necessities, so many difficulties. But by September 1994 I had decided on a mission to work with children and adolescents." By 1997 she had also made education a top priority. One of the driving forces was that she remembered something her brother once said: "If we really want to change something, we should start with the children through their education."

She herself has taken to the road, campaigning fiercely for changes in the law on controversial social issues. It's a dangerous business, particularly in Brazil. But for her, fate seems to have determined that she play this role for the rest of her life.

Seven years ago, after coming to terms with the loss of her brother, another tragedy struck. Her husband Flavio Lalli was killed in a motorcycle accident. Ironically he was trying out one of the new 'Ayrton Senna Motorcycles' that were being sold to charity. His death came only 10 months after her brother's. Their three children, now aged 24, 22 and 18, work for the foundation, living with the memory of their uncle and their father.

"I will go on with this forever, if life will let me," says Viviane. "Everyone wants me to run for mayor, run for this and run for that political party. Oh no, never. To change the world, by whatever small amount, you don't have to be a politician or a lawyer. Ayrton taught me that you should do what comes naturally – and if you do it well, it will make a difference. That's what I am trying to do here."

The odds are she will keep performing at an extraordinary rate – aided by her devotion to her job and, equally significant, to the legend of her brother, Ayrton Senna.

As she says: "I never look for sponsors, they always come to me." She does not accept every company – she has an image to maintain that is closely guarded. "The companies have to have an acceptable way of operating. They must have certain morals such as not encouraging traffic," she says. Computer company Compaq and Brazilian petrol company Petrobras were the first to donate to the charity. The following year a further three joined. By 1999, 10 companies were giving their support, including Audi, Mattel and Microsoft. Texaco has also recently signed up.

The most important project for Brazil is the education project known as

Acelera Brasil, which is designed to help children with their education and keep them off the streets. "In that way they can be better prepared for the workplace," says Viviane. "To date more than 100,000 children in public schools in 240 cities around Brazil have taken part in the Acelera programme. One of Brazil's greatest problems is the low quality of education. Every year 40 per cent of the children fail in their first year. Elementary school lasts eight years but only four per cent of children complete the eight years. This costs the country US$3 billion. But the cost is not just monetary – it is social. After failing several times, the adolescents grow ill-prepared for the labour market. If they are not prepared for the labour market they go into prostitution and crime. There is also a political cost. Without a good education they are unable to make wise voting decisions when the time comes. At best they might be able to make an uneducated decision. At worst they could be subjected to bribery – in exchange for food or money they might give up their voting rights. Cases of farm workers being collected in trucks and taken to polling stations to vote for a preferred candidate in exchange for as little as a plate of food are not unheard of."

Viviane Lalli is hoping her methods will be adopted by other schools and organisations across Brazil. "The idea is social technology, where the concept can be applied by others. Just like a tape that does not have to be used in one tape recorder, but all tape recorders all over the world."

She is convinced that the foundation has helped fuel change in the social consciousness of the Brazilian people. To prove her point, she cites an example of an architect who, on hearing her give a speech on the radio, decided to redesign the local orphanage and turn it from a run-down building into a modern and bright one.

She says: "People used to think these social matters were for the government. But now they feel co-responsible. The reason for the change in people's attitudes is because they have realised it is no good being critical about the lack of change – they have to make it themselves."

Senna admits that she helps encourage this change in mentality through the use of her brother's image: "I use it to encourage a feeling of co-responsibility. We have many examples of doing something, but the image makes people feel co-responsible." Partly because she can make such a difference to people's lives, Viviane Lalli is becoming a zealot herself and showing the same determination her father and brother did to rise to the top. She confesses that a feeling of underachievement helps push her forward. "I always feel like there is more to do. It is not an obligation, rather a consciousness that by doing more I can save more people," she says.

In another part of São Paulo a small plastic Brazilian flag waves over a neatly tended grave. Unlike other tragedies and loss of heroes, Senna's death is no easier for Brazilians to accept now than it was in 1994. Many more years have to pass before that happens.

CHAPTER 35

Senna's Legacy to the Drivers

More consequences of Sunday 1st May 1994

As practice begins for the 2002 San Marino Grand Prix, the modern generation of Formula One cars leave the pitlane on their grooved tyres with the drivers peeping over the edge of the high cockpit sides. With a splutter of legalised traction control, they take to the 3.064-mile anti-clockwise track, passing the distinctive Marlboro tower and flying past the lines of greenery at 190mph before slowing to just 85mph for the first corner, the Tamburello Chicane.

Behind the barrier on the inside of the corner stands a statue of Ayrton Senna. During the Grand Prix weekend it is fenced off from the public, but at other times of year visitors are free to leave flowers and sit on the adjacent bench to contemplate the past. At the other side of Tamburello, the wall still stands, edged as far away from the track as is possible before the ground inclines steeply to make way for the stream which runs beneath the corner and joins the Santerno River a few feet away, where the fans pitch their tents on its banks. Once the wall was decorated with paintings and graffiti of Formula One's lost hero, but that section has since been removed, out of the way of the elements.

Less than a fortnight after Imola in 1994, the Formula One circus moved on to Monaco. It was there, during Thursday's practice session, that Austrian Karl Wendlinger lost control of his Sauber Mercedes when exiting the tunnel and slammed heavily into the barriers at the chicane. The news was not good. Wendlinger suffered serious head injuries and remained in a coma for three weeks. To a paddock that was hoping to put the tragic events of the previous race behind it, it was a cruel blow. After the crashes of Ayrton Senna, Roland Ratzenberger and Rubens Barrichello at Imola and the testing smashes of Jean Alesi and JJ Lehto, it was clear that something had to be done immediately.

On the day after Wendlinger's crash, FIA president Max Mosley announced that an 'expert advisory group' would be instituted to decide on the best course of action. There would be five members: Professor Sid Watkins, FIA technical delegate Charlie Whiting, FIA safety delegate Roland Bruynseraede, a representative for the drivers and one for the designers. Gerhard Berger, elected head of a newly-reformed Grand Prix Drivers' Association, was chosen as the driver and Tyrrell's Dr Harvey Postlethwaite as the designer.

A plan was designed with the aim of cutting speeds, reducing downforce and improving track safety. Firstly, in Monaco, the pitlane would have a speed limit set of 50mph to prevent another accident like Alboreto's. For the Spanish Grand Prix two weeks after Monaco, downforce would be cut by about 15 per cent by reducing the size of the cars' rear underwing, removing all parts of the front wing behind the foremost part of the front wheel, and raising the front wing end plates by 10mm.

The teams were originally hostile to the changes – they claimed any alterations to the technical regulations should not be rushed through in a matter of weeks. Former racer Jacques Laffite told *Paris Match*: "We need to think, and not take hasty, stupid measures. Each time a problem crops up, like the skirts a few years ago, the federation takes a common-sense approach and bans them. We need to see the same thing next year. What difference does it make to a crowd if a Formula One car goes at 280kph or 310kph? No difference. The spectacle is the same. The drivers are impressive virtuosos facing off on an asphalt arena. The race for power needs to stop. That's the lesson to be learned from this black Sunday. Whatever regulations there are, drivers will always get killed. But don't forget that we're also test drivers, that our cars use new technologies which one day end up in Joe Bloggs' car. We assume responsibility for the risks we take. That's what we're paid for, and we enjoy it. It's a unique pleasure.

"We're reaching breaking-point. We might have practically indestructible vehicles, but the human body can no longer withstand the constraints being placed on it. Can you imagine that for a while now the engineers have been looking at fitting cars' instruments in helmet visors using a holographic system? The drivers are human beings, not robots. By pushing things further, we're ultimately signing drivers' death warrants each time they go on the road."

But the FIA was under immense pressure. Governments, the press, the fans, safety campaigners – all were calling for something to be done. Even the Vatican had got involved. The changes were rushed through. Teams like Williams, which had nervous cars, were worried that the reduction in downforce would only make the cars more twitchy (although in the event, the drivers actually found the cars easier to drive).

In fact there were only two more major accidents that year, and they came before all the new regulations were in place. The first was a few days after Monaco, when Pedro Lamy's Lotus suffered a rear wing failure in testing at Silverstone, left the track and cleared a safety fence, leaving him with serious leg injuries; the second was at the Spanish Grand Prix when Roland Ratzenberger's replacement Andrea Montermini crashed his Simtek into a tyre barrier at 135mph on Saturday morning. The Italian escaped with a broken foot.

On the Friday of Spain, things had come to a head between the teams and the FIA. Throughout the morning's free practice session, only five teams – Ferrari, Minardi, Tyrrell, Larrousse and Sauber – took to the track. The others were locked in urgent discussions with Max Mosley inside the Williams motorhome. As a result it was announced that the FIA technical committee would from then on include eight engineers and three drivers. The teams were, in effect, taking control of what would happen and when.

The other change at Barcelona was to the track. At the instigation of the GPDA, which had threatened to boycott the race if the situation was not improved, a temporary chicane of tyre bales had been placed on the ultra-fast Nissan kink. Combined with a self-imposed, no-passing rule at the spot, it served its purpose. The corner would be redeveloped entirely for the 1995 race.

Similar makeshift chicanes began to crop up at Grand Prix tracks around the world. Silverstone worked the hardest, managing to make permanent alterations to most of the track in just 19 days after consultation with the FIA and the GPDA. A temporary chicane was installed at Canada; Hockenheim's chicanes were reprofiled; Monza's Lesmos were adapted; Estoril's turn eight was circumvented with a slow hairpin which actually caused a couple of accidents; a chicane appeared on a fast stretch of track at Jerez. Ironically, many of the changes were named after Senna, who would probably have disliked the restrictions to racing they posed. In the end, the situation got out of hand. When kerbing was used to turn Spa's Eau Rouge into a ridiculous 50mph chicane, the authorities began to look at ways to improve run-off areas and crash barriers for 1995, so that the popular fast corners could be kept intact.

Since 1994, many of the old famous tracks have gone from the calendar and have been replaced with safer equivalents. Only Spa-Francorchamps genuinely harks back to the old days. As a result, safety has been greatly improved, although often at the cost of spectacle and tradition.

The second wave of safety revisions came into place at the 1994 Canadian Grand Prix, where the lower front wishbones were strengthened and the minimum car weight increased by 25kg. The German Grand Prix saw the first appearance of the plank. This constituted a skidblock made of hard jabroc wood bolted to the floor of the cars, which must not be worn down beyond a certain point. The move was intended to limit downforce by increasing ride height, thus preventing the cars from bottoming out. A loss equivalent to 60bhp was achieved by the middle of the season.

A programme of high-energy crash testing took place to decide what should be done. By the end of 1994 the number of high-risk corners in Formula One had been reduced from 27 to eight, through both the changes to the tracks and the reduced speeds.

For 1995 further restrictions were made to reduce engine power and downforce, which would result in stepped floors, three-litre engines and higher cockpit sides. In 1996, high cockpit sides became mandatory. In 1998, the FIA reduced speeds with the introduction of grooved tyres. A year later, the number of grooves was increased from three to four. From 2003, head and neck supports will be compulsory for all drivers.

When Mika Häkkinen hit a wall at 105mph in Friday's qualifying session at Adelaide in 1995, he was very lucky to survive. In the past eight years there have been several other lucky escapes at high-speed corners: Jos Verstappen at Stavelot at Spa in 1996; Olivier Panis at the Pont de la Concorde in Montreal in 1997; Mika Salo and Jacques Villeneuve at Spa's Eau Rouge in 1998; Michael Schumacher at Stowe at Silverstone in 1999; Heinz-Harald Frentzen at the Pont de la Concorde in 1999; Villeneuve and Ricardo Zonta at Eau Rouge in 1999; and Luciano Burti, perhaps the luckiest of all, at Blanchimont at Spa in 2001. There have also been a number of first-lap pile-ups when the drivers have emerged with only cuts and bruises, although two marshals have been killed in the past two years.

There is no doubt that the accidents could have been vastly more serious if not for the improvements in safety, but just how much more dangerous can only be hypothesised.

CHAPTER 36

The Consequences for F1

How Senna's death changed the sport

On a cold 2002 January morning at Silverstone, the new BMW Williams FW24 is unveiled to the public for the first time. It is an understated affair with nothing to entertain the gathered world media except the car itself and the key team figures and drivers. Williams has always seemed to prefer it that way.

The car's livery is substantially the same as the previous year – respectable navy striped with crisp clean white, although attention is drawn to the new FedEx decals that adorn the front wing. None of the attention is reserved for the small decal on the inside of the wing struts, which is barely visible in the shadow of the car's nose. There, in white and navy, sits a small Senna S.

Although he spent only three races with the team, Senna is not forgotten. His portrait is the only photograph of a driver that appears in Frank Williams' study and Juan Pablo Montoya is an avid fan. The Colombian was delighted to be presented with a replica yellow helmet by the Senna Foundation over the winter months and remarked: "Some of my earliest Formula One memories are of watching Ayrton Senna on the TV. I loved watching the way he dealt with Alain Prost. Ayrton was different to everyone else. He was my hero."

Senna's death left Williams in a state of chaos from which lesser teams would have struggled to recover – certainly Simtek never recovered from the death of Roland Ratzenberger. Williams left Imola in 1994 with just seven points to Benetton and Michael Schumacher's 30, only one driver and the prospect of a manslaughter trial looming. But even this paled under the weight of one overwhelming fact: Ayrton Senna was dead and he had died in a Williams car.

In the wake of Imola the team released a simple statement that both managed to capture the sadness of the moment and present a strong will to carry on. It read: 'Williams Renault will find a replacement driver: Formula One won't'.

Gerhard Berger seriously considered retirement after the deaths of Senna and Ratzenberger, telling Austrian television shortly after the race that he had 'absolutely no desire to get into a racing car'. On the Wednesday before Monaco he called an emotional press conference: "I earned good money. I was driving in good teams. I was winning races. I had pole positions. Basically not a lot to prove. So what is the point of still taking the risk? That was my question to myself last week. But the other side is, what is the rest of your life?"

In Monte Carlo, several people admitted that they expected to see the familiar yellow helmet appear at any moment. There was a solemn minute's silence on the grid and the front row was left empty in memory of Senna and Ratzenberger. There was little doubt that Senna would have taken pole, at this his best of tracks, had he lived. Hill went out after tangling with Mika Häkkinen on the first lap. Schumacher took a commanding win and the deficit in the championship was 40 points to seven.

Williams had not replaced Senna for Monaco but there was constant speculation over who would take the second Williams seat. Rumour had it that Williams did not think Hill capable of leading the team through such a crucial period and was looking out for a worthy veteran to lead it in the championship fight. This may have been no more than a psychological ploy to boost Hill's determination to succeed and if it was, it worked.

Williams first turned to German rookie Heinz-Harald Frentzen, but in the wake of Karl Wendlinger's accident he did not want to leave Sauber without a driver in such troubled times. It was eventually decided to draft in the team's test driver David Coulthard and pay him £5,000 a race. He knew the car and had worked well with the team so far, although his appointment would at first be only on a temporary basis.

In the wake of Senna's death and the retirements of Alain Prost and Nigel Mansell, Formula One was left without a star. Bernie Ecclestone was well aware of this and wanted Mansell back from the States to fill the vacant Williams seat. The 1992 champion was getting restless in IndyCars, where his second year had turned out to be a great deal less illustrious than the first. But Mansell's asking price was $1 million a race and a further £12 million would be needed as compensation for the Newman-Haas IndyCar team. Ecclestone reportedly told Mansell to give up that 'Mickey Mouse rent-a-car' and 'get back to the real stuff'. Encouraged by Ecclestone and Renault, Williams agreed that Mansell would race at the French Grand Prix in Magny-Cours in June – which did not clash with any IndyCar commitments – and the final three races of the season after the American championship had finished. Coulthard would deputise in-between.

But Mansell's arrival was not the only financial problem that was dogging Williams in the wake of Senna's death. Frank Williams had agreed to continue paying Senna's salary for the rest of his contract in the event of a tragedy – a full £8 million a year for two years – while Lloyds had to pay out some £20 million to those who had insured against his demise. Though the team and sponsors got some compensation, Senna's estate walked away with most of the loot. The trial itself cost Williams $4 million in legal and investigative fees, while Senna's relatives were richer to the tune of £36 million as a result of his death. He was literally worth more dead than alive.

Formula One also profited from Senna's death. After the events of Imola, television viewing figures rose by a massive 30 per cent across the world. Some blamed ghoulish viewers; others said the extra viewers had merely had their attention drawn to the sport and the championship battle. Whatever the reason, the figures rose – and were certainly helped by the growing rivalry between Michael Schumacher and Damon Hill.

The battle had grown so intense that Mansell's return to action in France was relegated to a sideshow. His appearance seemed barely needed to spice up the action any more – Hill and Schumacher, with only five seasons' Formula One experience between them, had caught the public imagination. The world was divided in its support. To his enemies, Schumacher was the arrogant, cheating German and Hill the noble saviour, trying to hold together his struggling team in the wake of Senna's death. To his fans, Schumacher was the heroic genius struggling against the authorities and Hill the inferior challenger who had the authorities on his side. It was pure theatre.

In Spain, Schumacher made the perfect getaway from pole and pulled out a second a lap from Hill until lap 18. Then his car got stuck in fifth gear and he was forced to drive like that for the remainder of the race. He finished second, a superb achievement, but one that was completely overshadowed as Hill took Williams' first victory of the year. Adrian Newey wept openly and Frank Williams permitted a rare smile.

It was a sorely needed victory. In Canada Schumacher won again with Hill second. In France Mansell returned and Hill beat him to pole by 0.07 seconds.

It was all in vain, however, as Schumacher got away from fourth with a start so brilliant it reminded people of days of traction control. Schumacher won again – making it six times out of seven – and Hill was again second. When he returned to the Williams motorhome after the race he found Patrick Head glued to a television screen, repeatedly replaying a tape of Schumacher's stunning start.

The drivers' championship stood 66 points to Schumacher, 29 to Hill and the constructors' 67 to Benetton, 36 to Ferrari and 31 to Williams. The frequent changes of second driver had resulted in a lack of consistent points scoring. At Benetton, JJ Lehto and Jos Verstappen were alternating rapidly as Lehto struggled to recover from the neck injury he had received in pre-season testing, but neither driver had managed to get close to Schumacher's pace. For that reason, with Williams able to boast Mansell and Coulthard in the second car, it looked as if the constructors' championship was still open even if the drivers seemed way beyond reach.

But Silverstone was the turning point. Hill took pole at his home track by just 0.003 seconds from Schumacher. Approaching the start, the Benetton driver seemed determined to gain a psychological advantage and he overtook Hill on the original warm-up lap, then twice on the second warm-up lap, which was called after Coulthard stalled on the grid. Schumacher then got the better start, but his pre-start behaviour was in contravention of the rules and he was shown the sign for a five-second stop-go penalty. For lap after lap as his team argued with the stewards he stayed out on the circuit, only to be forced in 10 laps later at the risk of a disqualification. The rules said that the penalty had to be taken within three laps of the driver being notified, but Schumacher still managed second behind a jubilant Hill and the team was fined $25,000.

Before the FIA World Council in Paris a few days later, that became $500,000, disqualification from Silverstone and a two-race ban for Schumacher. Defying the race stewards was heavily frowned upon, but all the same it seemed to be a hefty punishment for an originally small misde-meanour. In the midst of threats from irate German fans to torch the Hockenheim forests, blockade roads and harm other drivers, it was decided that the ban would be suspended until the Benetton team had had a chance to appeal, allowing Schumacher to compete in his home Grand Prix in Germany two weeks after Silverstone.

That was not the only punishment for Benetton. At San Marino, software analysis company Liverpool Data Research Associates had been called in to investigate the allegations that some of the teams were using illegal driver aids. The top three cars of Michael Schumacher, Nicola Larini and Mika Häkkinen were investigated and the teams asked to surrender their source codes to LDRA. Ferrari – aware that it had been the centre of cheating allegations earlier in the season – readily complied, but Benetton and McLaren refused, claiming intellectual copyright. Under pressure from the FIA and fined $100,000, both teams eventually complied. LDRA discovered McLaren was running a programme that permitted automatic gearshifts, but after much deliberation the FIA concluded it was just within the bounds of legality. The findings from Benetton's software, however, were dynamite.

The FIA's report into the findings read: "On race day [1st May 1994], each of the teams were requested to supply the source code for the software on board the car and schematic circuit diagrams of the electrical system.

"One team complied in full with this request and a demonstration of the complete electrical system was set up with entirely satisfactory results.

"Having received nothing from the other two teams, a fax was sent on 9th May asking for urgent action.

"An alternative suggestion was received from Benetton Formula Limited. In this letter dated 10th May, it stated the source code could not be made available for commercial reasons.

"In a fax to Benetton Formula dated 15th May, we accepted this proposal, on the condition that Article 2.6 of the technical regulations was satisfied.

"On 27th May we received a detailed programme for the demonstration at Cosworth Engineering.

"The tests which were scheduled to take place on 28th June were cancelled, by Benetton, after some discussion with Ford concerning non-disclosure agreements.

"In a fax dated 28th June, we again requested the tests take place as a matter of urgency.

"The demonstration and tests took place on 6th July. We received a report from LDRA on 11th July that left a number of unanswered questions, which we were advised could only be addressed by close examination of the source code.

"In a letter to Benetton dated 13th July we made it clear the demonstration had been unsatisfactory and we required the source code for the software.

"Following another exchange of letters on 13th and 14th July a meeting was set up at the Benetton factory on 19th July, an agenda for which was received on 18th July giving our advisers full access to the source code, but only on Benetton's premises and subject to the instructions set out in Appendix 11.

"Analysis of this software, which had been used at the San Marino Grand Prix, revealed that it included a facility called 'launch control'. This is a system which, when armed, allows the driver to initiate a start with a single action. The system will control the clutch, gearshift and engine speed fully automatically to a predetermined pattern.

"Benetton stated that this system is used only during testing. Benetton further stated that 'it [the system] can only be switched on by recompilation of the code'. This means recompilation of the source code. Detailed analysis by LDRA experts of this complex code revealed that this statement was untrue. 'Launch control' could in fact be switched on using a laptop personal computer connected to the gearbox control unit (GCU).

"When confronted with this information, the Benetton representatives conceded that it was possible to switch on the 'launch control' using a laptop PC but indicated that the availability of this feature of the software came as a surprise to them.

"In order to enable 'launch control', a particular menu with 10 options has to be selected on the PC screen. 'Launch control' is not visibly listed as an option. The menu was so arranged that, after 10 items, nothing further appeared. If however, the operator scrolled down the menu beyond the 10th listed option, to option 13, launch control could be enabled, even though this is not visible on the screen. No satisfactory explanation was offered for this apparent attempt to conceal the feature.

"Two conditions had to be satisfied before the computer would apply 'launch control': first, the software had to be enabled either by recompiling the code, which would take some minutes, or by connecting the laptop PC as outlined above, which could be done in a matter of seconds.

"Secondly, the driver had to work through a particular sequence of up-down gearshift paddle positions, a specific gear position had to be selected and the clutch and throttle pedals had to be in certain positions. Only if all these actions were carried out would the 'launch control' become available.

"Having thus initiated 'launch control', the driver would be able to make a fully automatic start. Such a start is clearly a driver aid as it operates the clutch, changes gear and uses traction control by modulating engine power (by changing ignition or fuel settings), in response to wheel speed.

"When asked why, if this system was only used in testing, such an elaborate procedure was necessary in order to switch it on, we were told it was to prevent it being switched on accidentally."

It seemed that Senna had been right about the traction control, although Schumacher was adamant that the launch control system had not been in use. He said: "I know we don't use any traction control. I know where these rumours are coming from and they had better watch themselves... I know that we don't have anything. We proved it to the FIA and there has been a statement from them that we don't have any traction control. What more can we do than proving, showing and being really willing to prove that we don't have anything? What more can we do? And there are still these rumours. The only thing I can think of is that they are jealous."

Accusations flew as Ross Brawn insisted that the systems were just defunct software from 1993, left on the system because they were too difficult to remove. Other teams' engineers retorted that they had been able to remove their driver aids in the space of two days over the winter.

The FIA was eventually forced to capitulate and Benetton escaped sanctions because the regulations only required that traction control must not be used, not that it must not be present in the software. Some people believed that the FIA had only been so harsh on Benetton after Silverstone because it was punishing the team for every small indiscretion having been unable to penalise it for the mere presence of traction control. The FIA then declared that all such software must be removed from the cars before the Italian Grand Prix and was forced to admit that: "The best evidence is that Benetton Formula Limited was not using 'launch control' at the 1994 San Marino Grand Prix. Had the evidence proved it was, the World Motor Sport Council would have been invited to exclude it from the world championship. Given the evidence available, such a course of action would obviously have been wrong."

The German Grand Prix was a disaster for Benetton. Schumacher's engine failed while Verstappen's car burst into flames during a pitstop, leaving the driver and crew lucky to escape with minor burns. Luckily for them, Hill was also unable to score. The team was initially blamed by the FIA for the fire but was absolved. Two weeks later in Hungary, Schumacher won and Hill was second. The gap in the drivers' championship was 76 points to Schumacher, 45 to Hill.

There was more controversy for Benetton at Spa. The weekend started badly for Williams when Renault announced that from 1995 it would be supplying engines to Benetton too. Renault wanted the biggest star in Formula One, and with Senna's death that was Schumacher. The German finished first in the race ahead of Hill, but was disqualified when his car was found to have an illegally worn plank and the team was fined $500,000. He blamed it on a spin earlier in the race.

Schumacher's delayed two-race ban kicked in for the following rounds in Italy and Portugal after Benetton's appeal predictably failed. Hill won both races. On Schumacher's return for the European Grand Prix at Jerez the pair were forced to shake hands after some bickering in the newspapers. Schumacher won and Hill was second, although the Williams driver could have won if not for a faulty fuel rig. In Japan, Hill produced the drive of his life to take a stunning aggregate win on a soaking wet track, just over three seconds ahead of Schumacher.

Going into the final round at Adelaide, Schumacher was leading the drivers' championship by a single point from Hill.

It was almost inevitable that there would be a further controversy at the Australian Grand Prix. It came on lap 36. Schumacher, leading but pushed hard by a quickening Hill, ran off the track and hit the wall. Hill came round the corner, saw Schumacher coming off the verge and went for the gap, not realising the Benetton had hit the wall and would soon be eliminated from the running anyway. Schumacher aggressively defended his line and the pair collided. Hill managed to drag his car back to the pits, but the suspension was bent and he could not continue. Harking back to the days of Prost and Senna at Suzuka, Michael Schumacher became perhaps the most controversial world champion in the history of the sport. A new winner was born.

As Hill and Patrick Head fumed in the pits and Schumacher was informed by trackside marshals of his new status, Mansell took victory. In compensation for the loss of the drivers' crown, Williams Renault had become constructors' champion.

Ironically Schumacher dedicated his victory to the last man to win the title by collision. "Winning the championship feels like a dream. I don't know how to explain it. The emotions are in me but I cannot really express them. Early in the season it had been clear to me that I was not going to win the championship, that it was going to be Ayrton. But he hasn't been here for these last races and so I would like to take this championship and give it to him. It was difficult at the time to show my feelings because I am not someone who likes to show his feelings on the outside, but I always thought about it. And now it is the right time to give something which I achieved, something which he should have achieved, to him."

It was not difficult to conclude that if Damon Hill had lost the title by just a single point then Senna would have been able to win it. Damon Hill might have been a race winner and future champion, but Senna was Senna. Victory in 1994 would have meant a fourth world title and perhaps another six or seven wins to add to his total of 41. He might also have beaten Schumacher to the title in 1995 and had he stayed at Williams the following year he would almost certainly have taken the 1996 crown.

Senna had always said that he wanted to end his career with Ferrari. Had he lived he would probably have joined the team in 1997 or 1998, just as its fortunes were on the upturn, although there is little doubt that Senna and Schumacher would not have run in the scarlet cars side by side. Schumacher might even have ended up in the blue and white of a Williams rather than the scarlet of a Ferrari, and then the 1997 battle would no doubt have been very close. Would Senna have succeeded in delivering Ferrari's longed for world championship three years earlier than Schumacher managed? Julian Jakobi confirms that this was Senna's plan. Jakobi says: "I had had preliminary negotiations with Luca di Montezemolo. Ayrton was offered the deal that Michael took in 1996."

Had that occurred and Senna had joined Ferrari in 1998 after four years with Williams, having scored three or even four world championships, he would likely have managed at least one world championship with Ferrari before retiring after three seasons with the Italian team, aged 40 at the end of 2000.

Had he lived it is probable that he could have set new records of around 75 victories, 100 poles and seven, or even eight world titles. Certainly Michael Schumacher's career would have been very different and not nearly so impressive as it is now.

As it is Ayrton Senna's record remains 65 poles, 41 wins and three world championships in 10 full seasons of competing. Plus the thoughts of what might have been.

1974 to 1982 Karting

Ayrton Senna raced go-karts with varying degrees of seriousness for nine years of which the last two overlapped with his car driving career. His first ever go-kart win was on the 1st July 1973 at the Interlagos kart track. He started in the junior category in 1974, going into the 100cc category in 1976. Between 1977 and 1989 he raced in the Inter category before finally moving up to the 135cc category in late 1980 and competing in the world championship for the first time. The early years were spent mainly in Brazilian local championships and the latter years outside Brazil.

1974   *Championship:* Sao Paulo Championship
Category: junior category
Classification: 1st

1975   *Championship:* Brazilian Championship
Category: junior category
Classification: 2nd

      Championship: "Nacional Italcolomy" tour
Category: junior category
Classification: 1st

1976   *Championship:* Sao Paulo Championship
Category: 100cc category
Classification: 2nd

      Championship: Brazilian Championship
Category: 100cc category
Classification: 3rd

      Championship: "Three hours of go-karting", Sao Paulo
Category: 100cc category
Classification: 1st

1977   *Championship:* South American Championship, Uruguay (San Jose)
Category: Inter category
Classification: 1st

Championship: Brazilian Championship
Category: Inter category
Classification: 2nd

Championship: Sao Paolo Championship
Category: Inter category
Classification: 2nd

Championship: "Three hours of go-karting", Sao Paulo
Category: Inter category
Classification: 1st

1978   *Championship:* World Championship, France (Le Mans)
Category: Inter category
Classification: 6th

Championship: Japanese Grand Prix, (Sugo)
Category: Inter category
Classification: 4th

Championship: Brazilian Championship
Category: Inter category
Classification: 1st

Championship: "Three hours of go-karting", Sao Paulo
Category: Inter category
Classification: 1st

Championship: Sao Paulo Championship
Category: Inter category
Classification: 2nd

1979   *Championship:* World Championship, Portugal (Estoril)
Category: Inter category
Classification: 2nd

Championship: South American Championship, Argentina (San Juan)
Category: Inter category
Classification: 2nd

Championship: San Marino Championship
Category: Inter category
Classification: 1st

Championship: Brazilian Championship, Oberlandia, (Mato Grosso)
Category: Inter category
Classification: 1st (1st round)

Championship: Swiss Grand Prix, (Wholen)
Category: Inter category
Classification: 2nd

Championship: Italian Grand Prix, (Parma)
Category: Inter category
Classification: 2nd

Championship: Champions Cup, Italy (Jesolo)
Category: Inter category
Classification: 10th

1980   *Championship:* South American Championship
Category: Inter category
Classification: 1st

Championship: Brazilian Championship
Category: Inter category
Classification: 1st

Championship: World Championship, Belgium (Nivelles)
Category: 135cc category
Classification: 2nd

1981   *Championship:* World Championship, Italy (Parma)
Category: 135cc category
Classification: 4th

Championship: Champions Cup, Italy (Jesolo)
Category: 135cc
Classification: retired, accident

Championship: Swiss Grand Prix (Wholen)
Category: 135cc category
Classification: 1st

1982   *Championship:* Porto Alegre Championship
Category: 135cc
Classification: 1st

Championship: World Championship, Sweden (Kalmar)
Category: 135cc category
Classification: 14th

1981 Formula Ford 1600

Ayrton Senna competed in three championships in Britain in the Formula Ford 1600 category in 1981, his first season in cars. Driving a Van Diemen RF80 he did one race in the P&O Ferries championship. In the RAC and Townsend Thoresen series he drove a Van Diemen RF81 and won both series. He did not compete in the end of season Formula Ford Festival at Brands Hatch.

Date: 1st March (P&O)
Circuit: Brands Hatch
Qualifying: 8th
Race: 5th

Date: 8th March (TT)
Circuit: Thruxton
Race: 3rd + 9.48s

Date: 15th March (TT)
Circuit: Brands Hatch
Race: 1st
Time: 15 laps in 15m07.02s

Date: 22nd March (TT)
Circuit: Mallory Park
Qualifying: pole
Race: 2nd + 1.25s

Date: 3rd May (TT)
Circuit: Snetterton
Qualifying: pole
Race: 2nd + 3.9s

Date: 5th April (TT)
Circuit: Mallory Park
Race: 2nd + 0.15s

Date: 24th May (RAC)
Circuit: Oulton Park
Race: 1st
Time: 15 laps in 16m48s
Fastest Lap: fastest lap

Date: 25th May (TT)
Circuit: Mallory Park
Race: 1st
Time: 15 laps in 12m43.09s

Date: 7th June (TT)
Circuit: Snetterton
Race: 1st
Time: 15 laps in 18m16.05s
Fastest Lap: 1m22.02s, fastest lap

Date: 21st June (RAC)
Circuit: Silverstone
Race: 2nd

Date: 27th June (TT)
Circuit: Oulton Park
Race: 1st
Time: 15 laps in 16m49.05s
Fastest Lap: 1m06.03s, fastest lap

Date: 4th July (RAC)
Circuit: Donington Park
Race: 1st
Fastest Lap: fastest lap

Date: 12th July (RAC)
Circuit: Brands Hatch
Qualifying: third row
Race: 4th
Fastest Lap: fastest lap

Date: 25th July (TT)
Circuit: Oulton Park
Race: 1st
Time: 15 laps in 16m59.7s
Fastest Lap: 1m06.04s, fastest lap

Date: 26th July (RAC)
Circuit: Mallory Park
Qualifying: pole
Race: 1st
Time: 15 laps in 12m44.04s
Fastest Lap: 50.01s, fastest lap

Date: 2nd August (TT)
Circuit: Brands Hatch
Race: 1st
Time: 15 laps in 12.58s

Date: 9th August (RAC)
Circuit: Snetterton
Race: 1st
Time: 15 laps in 19m19.89s
Fastest Lap: 1m11.06s, fastest lap

Date: 15th August (TT)
Circuit: Donington Park
Race: 1st
Time: 12 laps in 16m13.73s

Date: 31st August (TT)
Circuit: Thruxton
Qualifying: pole
Race: 1st
Time: 10 laps in 14m28.07s
Fastest Lap: 1m25.07s, fastest lap

Date: 29th September (TT)
Circuit: Brands Hatch
Race: 2nd + 6.4s
Fastest Lap: fastest lap

1982 Formula Ford 2000

Ayrton Senna competed in two championships in Formula Ford 2000 category in 1982. In the Pace Petroleum British championship and the EFDA European series. He drove exclusively for the works supported Rushen Green team in a Van Diemen Nelson RF82 and won both championships.

Date: 7th March
Circuit: Brands Hatch
Qualifying: pole
Race: 1st
Race Time: 11m57.45s
Fastest Lap: fastest lap

Date: 27th March
Circuit: Oulton Park
Qualifying: pole
Race: 1st
Race Time: 15m37.65s
Fastest Lap: fastest lap, new lap record

Date: 28th March
Circuit: Silverstone
Qualifying: pole
Race: 1st
Race Time: 14m30.85s
Fastest Lap: fastest lap, new lap record

Date: 4th April
Circuit: Donington Park
Qualifying: pole
Race: 1st
Race Time: 18m49.15s
Fastest Lap: fastest lap, new lap record

Date: 9th April
Circuit: Snetterton
Qualifying: pole
Race: 1st
Race Time: 17m07.1s
Fastest Lap: fastest lap

Date: 12th April
Circuit: Silverstone
Qualifying: pole
Race: 1st
Race Time: 14m31.5s
Fastest Lap: fastest lap

Date: 18th April (EFDA)
Country: Belgium
Circuit: Zolder
Qualifying: pole
Race: retired, lap 3, engine

Date: 2nd May (EFDA)
Country: Great Britain
Circuit: Donington Park
Qualifying: pole
Race: 1st
Time: 20 laps in 24m57.47s
Fastest Lap: new record, 1m14.28s

Date: 3rd May
Circuit: Mallory Park
Race: 1st
Race Time: 15m44.3s
Fastest Lap: fastest lap

Date: 9th May (EFDA)
Country: Belgium
Circuit: Zolder
Qualifying: pole
Race: retired, spin
Fastest Lap: fastest lap

Date: 30th May
Circuit: Oulton Park
Race: retired, lap 11, puncture

Date: 31st May
Circuit: Brands Hatch
Race: 1st
Race Time: 15m54.8s
Fastest Lap: fastest lap

Date: 6th June
Circuit: Mallory Park
Race: 1st
Race Time: 11m47.2s
Fastest Lap: fastest lap

Date: 13th June
Circuit: Brands Hatch
Qualifying: pole
Race: 1st
Race Time: 11m44.8s
Fastest Lap: fastest lap, new lap record

Date: 20th June (EFDA)
Country: Germany
Circuit: Hockenheim
Qualifying: pole
Race: retired, lap 1, accident

Date: 26th June
Circuit: Oulton Park
Qualifying: pole
Race: 1st
Race Time: 16m10.4s
Fastest Lap: fastest lap

Date: 3rd July (EFDA)
Country: Netherlands
Circuit: Zandvoort
Qualifying: pole
Race: 1st
Time: 12 laps, 20m08.03s

Date: 4th July
Circuit: Snetterton
Qualifying: pole
Race: 2nd + 3.65s

Date: 10th July
Circuit: Castle Combe
Qualifying: pole
Race: 1st
Race Time: 15m47.2s
Fastest Lap: new record, 1m02.6s

Date: 1st August
Circuit: Snetterton
Qualifying: 2nd
Race: 1st
Race Time: 16m52.0s
Fastest Lap: fastest lap, new lap record

Date: 8th August (EFDA)
Country: Germany
Circuit: Hockenheim
Qualifying: pole
Race: 1st
Time: 11 laps, 26m59.20s
Fastest Lap: fastest lap

Date: 15th August
Country: Austria
Circuit: Osterreichering
Qualifying: pole
Race: 1st
Time: 12 laps in 24m21.32s
Fastest Lap: fastest lap

Date: 22nd August (EFDA)
Country: Denmark
Circuit: Jyllandsring
Qualifying: pole
Race: 1st
Time: 8 laps in 19m34.96s
Fastest Lap: fastest lap

Date: 30th August
Circuit: Thruxton
Race: 1st
Race Time: 20m40.9s
Fastest Lap: fastest lap, new lap record

Date: 5th September
Circuit: Silverstone
Qualifying: pole
Race: 1st
Race Time: 14m33.65s
Fastest Lap: fastest lap (57.6s)

Date: 12th September (EFDA)
Country: Ireland
Circuit: Mondello Park
Qualifying: pole
Race: 1st
Time: 20 laps in 19m32.71s
Fastest Lap: fastest lap, new lap record,
57.92s

Date: 26th September
Circuit: Brands Hatch
Race: 2nd + 0.88s
Fastest Lap: fastest lap, new lap record

Returned to Brazil before the end of
the championship

1982-1983 Formula 3

In 1982 Ayrton Senna drove in Formula 3 for the West Surrey Racing team drivng a Ralt Toyota Nicholson RT3 D/82. Before that at the end of the 1982 season he drove a one off race at Thuxton in a West Surrey Ralt RT3 Nicholson D/81. At the end of the 1983 season he drove in the traditional Macao Grand Prix for Formula 3 cars for the Teddy Yip team in a Ralt Toyota Novamotor RT3E

Date: 13th November 1982
Circuit: Thruxton
Qualifying: pole
Qualifying Time: 1m13.4s (1) & 1m13.54s (1)
Race: 1st
Race Time: 18m37.4s
Time: 15 laps in 18m37.43s
Fastest Lap: fastest lap

Date: 6th March 1983
Circuit: Silverstone
Qualifying Time: 53.90s (2) & 53.77s (1)
Qualifying: 2nd
Race: 1st
Time: 20 laps in 18m07.14s
Average Speed: 106.50mph
Fastest Lap: fastest lap

Date: 13th March 1983
Circuit: Thruxton
Qualifying Time: 1m13.46s (1) & 1m19.22s (2)
Qualifying: pole
Race: 1st
Time: 20 laps in 26m36.31s
Average Speed: 106.27mph
Fastest Lap: fastest lap

Date: 20th March 1983
Circuit: Silverstone
Qualifying time: 1m34.74s (1) & 1m25.14s (1)
Qualifying: pole
Race: 1st
Time: 12 laps in 19m36.51s
Average Speed: 107.66mph
Fastest Lap: fastest lap

Date: 27th March 1983
Circuit: Donington Park
Qualifying time: 1m19.665s (1) & 1m18.06s (1)
Qualifying: pole
Race: 1st
Time: 20 laps in 23m23.35s
Average Speed: 100.42mph
Fastest Lap: fastest lap

Date: 4th April 1983
Circuit: Thruxton
Qualifying time: 1m13.07s (1) & 1m13.05s (3)
Qualifying: pole
Race: 1st
Time: 20 laps in 25m03.29s
Average Speed: 112.85mph

Date: 24th April 1983
Circuit: Silverstone
Qualifying time: 53.30s (1) & 53.38s (1)
Qualifying: pole
Race: 1st
Time: 25 laps in 22m33.59s
Average Speed: 106.9mph
Fastest Lap: fastest lap

Date: 2nd May 1983
Circuit: Thruxton
Qualifying time: 1m33.55s (1) & 1m1.08s (1)
Qualifying: pole
Race: 1st
Time: 20 laps in 24m51.88s
Average Speed: 113.70mph
Fastest Lap: fastest lap

Date: 8th May 1983
Circuit: Brands Hatch
Qualifying time: 43.35s (1) & 43.14s (1)
Qualifying: pole
Race: 1st
Time: 20 laps in 17m21.06s
Average Speed: 83.21mph
Fastest Lap: fastest lap

Date: 30th May 1983
Circuit: Silverstone
Qualifying time: 53.05s (1) & 53.29s (2)
Qualifying: pole
Race: 1st
Time: 30 laps in 27m00.98s
Average Speed: 107.14mph
Fastest Lap: fastest lap

Date: 11th June 1983
Circuit: Silverstone

Qualifying time: 1m32.27s (1) &
1m24.08s (2)
Qualifying: 2nd
Race: retired, lap 7, accident

Date: 19th June 1983
Circuit: Caldwell Park
Qualifying time: 1m22.57s (1) & did
not take part
Race: withdrawn (accident) DNQ

Date: 3rd July 1983
Circuit: Snetterton
Qualifying time: 61.89s (5) & 61.81s (2)
Qualifying: 4th
Race: retired, accident
Fastest Lap: fastest lap

Date: 16th July 1983
Circuit: Silverstone
Qualifying time: 1m26.57s (3) &
1m26.13s (1)
Qualifying: pole
Race: 1st
Time: 20 laps in 28m59.55s
Average Speed: 121.37mph
Fastest Lap: fastest lap

Date: 24th July 1983
Circuit: Donington Park
Qualifying time: 1m08.42s (1) &
1m10.41s (4)
Qualifying: pole
Race: 2nd
Average Speed: 100.23mph
Fastest Lap: fastest lap
Date: 6th August 1983
Circuit: Oulton Park

Qualifying time: 57.38s (2) & 57.43s (1)
Qualifying: 2nd
Race: retired, accident
Average Speed: 101.31mph
Fastest Lap: fastest lap

Date: 29th August 1983
Circuit: Silverstone
Qualifying time: 53.18s (1) & 53.43s (2)
Qualifying: pole
Race: 1st
Time: 30 laps in 27m02.45s
Average Speed: 107.04mph

Date: 11th September 1983
Circuit: Oulton Park
Qualifying time: 59.62 (1) & 57.24s (1)
Qualifying: pole
Race: Retired (accident)
Average Speed: 101.08mph

Date: 18th September 1983
Circuit: Thruxton
Qualifying time: 1m17.79s (1) &
1m14.01s (1)
Qualifying: pole
Race: retired, lap 2, engine

Date: 2nd October 1983
Circuit: Silverstone
Qualifying time: 1m30.62s (4) &
1m35.44s (1)
Qualifying: 4th
Race: 2nd
Average Speed: 121.66mph

Date: 23rd October 1983
Circuit: Thruxton
Qualifying time: 1m13.55s (1) &
1m13.36 (1)
Qualifying: pole
Race: 1st
Time: 15 laps in 18m39.78s
Average Speed: 113.62mph
Fastest Lap: fastest lap

*20th November: Macau Grand Prix, pole
position, winner – 30 laps in
1h11m34.96s
Heat 1: 1st – 15 laps in 35m44.65s –
Fastest lap and new record: 2m21.59s
Heat 2: 1st – 15 laps in 35m50.31s
Total time: 1h 11m 96s*

1984 to 1994 Formula One

Ayrton Senna competed in Formula One for 11 seasons before his death in the 11th. He drove for four teams, Toleman in 1984, Lotus between 1985 and 1987, McLaren between 1988 and 1993 and Williams in 1994. In 1984 he drove a turbocharged Toleman Hart TG183B and a Toleman Hart TG184. In 1985 he dorve a Lotus Renault 97T. In 1986 he drove a Lotus Renault 98T. In 1987 he drove a Lotus Honda 99T. In 1988 he drove a Mclaren Honda MP4/4. In 1989 he drove a McLaren Honda MP4/5. In 1990 he drove a McLaren Honda MP4/5B. In 1991 he drove a McLaren Honda MP4/6. In 1992 he drove a McLaren Honda MP4/7A. In 1993 he drove a McLaren Honda MP4/8. In 1994 he drove a Williams Renault FW16.

1984

Race: Brazilian Grand Prix
Circuit: Jacarepagua
Date: 25th March 1984
Qualifying Time: 1m33.525s
Qualifying Position: 16th
Race Position: retired, lap 8, turbo pressure
Fastest lap: 18th fastest: 1m42.286s

Race: South African Grand Prix
Circuit: Kyalami
Date: 7th April 1984
Qualifying Time: 1m06.981s
Qualifying Position: 13th
Race Position: 6th + 3 laps
Fastest lap: 15th fastest: 1m12.124s

Race: Belgian Grand Prix
Circuit: Zolder
Date: 29th April 1984
Qualifying Time: 1m18.876s
Qualifying Position: 19th
Race Position: 6th + 2 laps
Fastest lap: 15th fastest: 1m22.633s

Race: San Marino Grand Prix
Circuit: Imola
Date: 6th May 1984
Qualifying Time: 1m41.585s
Qualifying Position: DNQ

Race: French Grand Prix
Circuit: Dijon-Prenois
Date: 20th May 1984
Qualifying Time: 1m05.744s
Qualifying Position: 13th
Race Position: retired, lap 35, turbo
Fastest lap: 15th fastest: 1m10.100s

Race: Monaco Grand Prix
Circuit: Monte Carlo
Date: 3rd June 1984
Qualifying Time: 1m25.009s
Qualifying Position: 13th
Race Position: 2nd + 7.446s
Fastest lap: fastest: 1m54.334s

Race: Canadian Grand Prix
Circuit: Circuit Gilles Villeneuve
Date: 17th June 1984
Qualifying Time: 1m27.448s
Qualifying Position: 9th
Race Position: 7th + 2 laps
Fastest lap: 13th fastest: 1m31.882s

Race: U.S.A. East Grand Prix
Circuit: Detroit
Date: 24th June 1984
Qualifying Time: 1m42.651s
Qualifying Position: 7th
Race Position: retired, lap 21, accident
Fastest lap: 10th fastest: 1m47.444s

Race: U.S. Grand Prix
Circuit: Dallas
Date: 8th July 1984
Qualifying Time: 1m38.256s
Qualifying Position: 6th
Race Position: retired, lap 47, drive shaft
Fastest lap: 9th fastest: 1m46.419s

Race: British Grand Prix
Circuit: Brands Hatch
Date: 22nd July 1984
Qualifying Time: 1m11.890s
Qualifying Position: 7th
Race Position: 3rd + 1m03.328s
Fastest lap: 3rd fastest: 1m13.951s

Race: German Grand Prix
Circuit: Hockenheim
Date: 5th August 1984
Qualifying Time: 1m49.395s
Qualifying Position: 9th
Race Position: retired, lap 4,
accident, rear wing failure
Fastest lap: 11th fastest: 1m55.712s

Race: Austrian Grand Prix
Circuit: Osterreichring
Date: 19th August 1984
Qualifying Time: 1m29.200s
Qualifying Position: 10th
Race Position: retired, lap 35, oil pressure
Fastest lap: 7th fastest: 1m34.348s

Race: Dutch Grand Prix
Circuit: Zandvoort
Date: 26th August 1984
Qualifying Time: 1m15.960s
Qualifying Position: 13th
Race Position: retired, lap 19, engine
Fastest lap: 13th fastest: 1m21.683s

Race: European Grand Prix
Circuit: Nurburgring
Date: 7th October 1984
Qualifying Time: 1m22.439s
Qualifying Position: 12th
Race Position: retired, lap 1, accident

Race: Portuguese Grand Prix
Circuit: Estoril
Date: 21st October 1984
Qualifying Time: 1m21.936s
Qualifying Position: 3rd
Race Position: 3rd + 20.042s
Fastest lap: 7th fastest: 1m24.373s

1985
Race: Brazilian Grand Prix
Circuit: Jacarepagua
Date: 7th April 1985

Qualifying Time: 1m28.389s
Qualifying Position: 4th
Race Position: retired, lap 48, electrics
Fastest lap: 5th fastest: 1m38.440s

Race: Portuguese Grand Prix
Circuit: Estoril
Date: 21st April 1985
Qualifying Time: 1m21.007s
Qualifying Position: pole
Race Position: 1st
Race Time: 67 laps in 2h00m28.006s
Average Speed: 90.182mph
Fastest lap: fastest: 1m44.121s

Race: San Marino Grand Prix
Circuit: Imola
Date: 5th May 1985
Qualifying Time: 1m27.327s
Qualifying Position: pole
Race Position: 7th, lap 57,out of fuel
Fastest lap: 5th fastest: 1m31.549s

Race: Monaco Grand Prix
Circuit: Monte Carlo
Date: 19th May 1985
Qualifying Time: 1m20.450s
Qualifying Position: pole
Race Position: retired, lap 13, engine
Fastest lap: 8th fastest: 1m24.803s

Race: Canadian Grand Prix
Circuit: Circuit Gilles Villeneuve
Date: 16th June 1985
Qualifying Time: 1m24.816s
Qualifying Position: 2nd
Race Position: 16th + 5 laps
(turbo's collar loose)

Fastest lap: 1st fastest: 1m27.445s
(lap record)

Race: U.S. Grand Prix
Circuit: Detroit
Date: 23rd June 1985
Qualifying Time: 1m42.051s
Qualifying Position: pole
Race Position: retired, lap 51, accident
Fastest lap: fastest time: 1m45.612s
(lap record)

Race: French Grand Prix
Circuit: Paul Ricard
Date: 7th July 1985
Qualifying Time: 1m32.835s
Qualifying Position: 2nd
Race Position: retired, lap 26
engine /accident
Fastest lap: 3rd fastest: 1m41.552s

Race: British Grand Prix
Circuit: Silverstone
Date: 21st July 1985
Qualifying Time: 1m06.324s
Qualifying Position: 4th
Race Position: 10th + 5 laps
(fuel injection)
Fastest lap: 2nd fastest: 1m10.032s

Race: German Grand Prix
Circuit: Nurburgring
Date: 4th August 1985
Qualifying Time: 1m18.792s
Qualifying Position: 5th
Race Position: retired, lap 27, cv joint
Fastest lap: 7th fastest: 1m24.270s

Race: Austrian Grand Prix
Circuit: Osterreichring
Date: 18th August 1985
Qualifying Time: 1m28.123s
Qualifying Position: 14th
Race Position: 2nd + 30.002s
Fastest lap: 8th fastest: 1m31.666

Race: Dutch Grand Prix
Circuit: Zandvoort
Date: 25th August 1985
Qualifying Time: 1m11.837s
Qualifying Position: 4th
Race Position: 3rd + 48.491s
Fastest lap: 7th fastest: 1m17.835s

Race: Italian Grand Prix
Circuit: Monza
Date: 8th September 1985
Qualifying Time: 1m25.084s
Qualifying Position: pole
Race Position: 3rd + 1m00.390s
Fastest lap: 9th fastest: 1m31.703s

Race: Belgian Grand Prix
Circuit: Spa-Francorchamps
Date: 15th September 1985
Qualifying Time: 1m55.403s
Qualifying Position: 2nd
Race Position: 1st
Race Time: 43 laps in 1h34m19.893s
Average Speed: 117.943mph
Fastest lap: 5th fastest: 2m03.479s

Race: European Grand Prix
Circuit: Brands Hatch
Date: 6th October 1985
Qualifying Time: 1m07.482s

Qualifying Position: pole
Race Position: 2nd + 21.396s
Fastest lap: 5th fastest: 1m12.601s

Race: South African Grand Prix
Circuit: Kyalami
Date: 19th October 1985
Qualifying Time: 1m02.825s
Qualifying Position: 4th
Race Position: retired, lap 8, engine
Fastest lap: 7th fastest: 1m10.077s

Race: Australian Grand Prix
Circuit: Adelaide
Date: 3rd November 1985
Qualifying Time: 1m19.843s
Qualifying Position: pole
Race Position: retired, lap 62, engine
Fastest lap: 2nd fastest: 1m24.140s

1986
Race: Brazilian Grand Prix
Circuit: Jacarepagua
Date: 23rd March 1986
Qualifying Time: 1m25.501s
Qualifying Position: pole
Race Position: 2nd + 3.27s
Fastest lap: 3rd fastest: 1m34.785

Race: Spanish Grand Prix
Circuit: Jerez de la Frontera
Date: 13th April 1986
Qualifying Time: 1m21.605s
Qualifying Position: pole
Race Position: 1st
Race Time: 72 laps in 1h48m47.735s
Average Speed: 104.071mph
Fastest lap: 7th fastest: 1m28.801s

Race: San Marino Grand Prix
Circuit: Imola
Date: 27th April 1986
Qualifying Time: 1m25.050s
Qualifying Position: pole
Race Position: retired, lap 11,
wheel bearing
Fastest lap: 9th fastest: 1m31.999s

Race: Monaco Grand Prix
Circuit: Monte Carlo
Date: 11th May 1986
Qualifying Time: 1m23.175s
Qualifying Position: 3rd
Race Position: 3rd + 53.646s
Fastest lap: 2nd fastest: 1m26.843s

Race: Belgian Grand Prix
Circuit: Spa-Francorchamps
Date: 25th May 1986
Qualifying Time: 1m54.576s
Qualifying Position: 4th
Race Position: 2nd + 19.827s
Fastest lap: 2nd fastest: 1m59.867s

Race: Canadian Grand Prix
Circuit: Circuit Gilles Villeneuve
Date: 15th June 1986
Qualifying Time: 1m24.188s
Qualifying Position: 2nd
Race Position: 5th + 1 lap
Fastest lap: 5th fastest: 1m27.479s

Race: U.S. Grand Prix
Circuit: Detroit
Date: 22nd June 1986
Qualifying Time: 1m38.301s
Qualifying Position: pole

Race Position: 1st
Race Time: 63 laps in 1h51m12.847s
Average Speed: 84.971mph
Fastest lap: 2nd fastest: 1m41.233s

Race: French Grand Prix
Circuit: Paul Ricard
Date: 6th July 1986
Qualifying Time: 1m06.526s
Qualifying Position: pole
Race Position: retired, lap 3, accident
Fastest lap: 13th fastest: 1m12.882s

Race: British Grand Prix
Circuit: Brands Hatch
Date: 13th July 1986
Qualifying Time: 1m07.524s
Qualifying Position: 3rd
Race Position: retired, lap 27, gear box
Fastest lap: 14th fastest: 1m14.024s

Race: German Grand Prix
Circuit: Hockenheim
Date: 27th July 1986
Qualifying Time: 1m42.329s
Qualifying Position: 3rd
Race Position: 2nd + 15.437s
Fastest lap: 4th fastest: 1m49.424s

Race: Hungarian Grand Prix
Circuit: Hungaroring
Date: 10th August 1986
Qualifying Time: 1m29.450s
Qualifying Position: pole
Race Position: 2nd + 17.673s
Fastest lap: 2nd fastest: 1m31.261s

THE LIFE OF SENNA

Race: Austrian Grand Prix
Circuit: Osterreichring
Date: 17th August 1986
Qualifying Time: 1m25.249s
Qualifying Position: 8th
Race Position: retired, lap 13, engine
Fastest lap: 9th fastest: 1m33.437s

Race: Italian Grand Prix
Circuit: Monza
Date: 7th September 1986
Qualifying Time: 1m24.916s
Qualifying Position: 5th
Race Position: retired, lap 1, clutch

Race: Portuguese Grand Prix
Circuit: Estoril
Date: 21st September 1986
Qualifying Time: 1m16.673
Qualifying Position: pole
Race Position: 4th + 1 lap
Fastest lap: 4th fastest: 1m21.283s

Race: Mexican Grand Prix
Circuit: Hermanos Rodriguez
Date: 12th October 1986
Qualifying Time: 1m16.990s
Qualifying Position: pole
Race Position: 3rd + 52.513s
Fastest lap: 4th fastest: 1m20.237s

Race: Australian Grand Prix
Circuit: Adelaide
Date: 26th October 1986
Qualifying Time: 1m18.906s
Qualifying Position: 3rd
Race Position: retired, lap 43, engine
Fastest lap: 13th fastest: 1m24.149s

Race: Brazilian Grand Prix
Circuit: Jacarepagua
Date: 12th April 1987
Qualifying Time: 1m28.408s
Qualifying Position: 3rd
Race Position: retired, lap 50, engine
Fastest lap: 5th fastest: 1m35.312s

Race: San Marino Grand Prix
Circuit: Imola
Date: 3rd May 1987
Qualifying Time: 1m25.826s
Qualifying Position: pole
Race Position: 2nd + 27.545s
Fastest lap: 4th fastest: 1m30.851s

1987
Race: Belgian Grand Prix
Circuit: Spa-Francorchamps
Date: 17th May 1987
Qualifying Time: 1m52.426s
Qualifying Position: 3rd
Race Position: retired, lap 1, accident

Race: Monaco Grand Prix
Circuit: Monte Carlo
Date: 31st May 1987
Qualifying Time: 1m23.711s
Qualifying Position: 2nd
Race Position: 1st
Race Time: 78 laps in 1h57m54.085s
Average Speed: 82.0844mph
Fastest lap: fastest: 1m27.685s

Race: U.S. Grand Prix
Circuit: Detroit
Date: 21st June 1987
Qualifying Time: 1m40.607s

Qualifying Position: 2nd
Race Position: 1st
Race Time: 63 laps in 1h50m16.358s
Average Speed: 85.633mph
Fastest lap: fastest: 1m40.464s
(lap record)

Race: French Grand Prix
Circuit: Paul Ricard
Date: 5th July 1987
Qualifying Time: 1m07.024s
Qualifying Position: 3rd
Race Position: 4th + 55.255s
Fastest lap: 7th fastest: 1m12.231s

Race: British Grand Prix
Circuit: Silverstone
Date: 12th July 1987
Qualifying Time: 1m08.181s
Qualifying Position: 3rd
Race Position: 3rd + 1 lap
Fastest lap: 3rd fastest: 1m11.605s

Race: German Grand Prix
Circuit: Hockenheim
Date: 26th July 1987
Qualifying Time: 1m42.616s
Qualifying Position: 2nd
Race Position: 3rd + 1 lap
Fastest lap: 4th fastest: 1m49.187s

Race: Hungarian Grand Prix
Circuit: Hungaroring
Date: 9th August 1987
Qualifying Time: 1m30.387s
Qualifying Position: 6th
Race Position: 2nd + 37.727s
Fastest lap: 4th fastest: 1m32.426s

Race: Austrian Grand Prix
Circuit: Osterreichring
Date: 16th August 1987
Qualifying Time: 1m25.492
Qualifying Position: 7th
Race Position: 5th + 2 laps
Fastest lap: 3rd fastest: 1m28.449s

Race: Italian Grand Prix
Circuit: Monza
Date: 6th September 1987
Qualifying Time: 1m24.907s
Qualifying Position: 4th
Race Position: 2nd + 1.806s
Fastest lap: fastest: 1m26.796s (lap record)

Race: Portuguese Grand Prix
Circuit: Estoril
Date: 20th September 1687
Qualifying Time: 1m18.354s
Qualifying Position: 5th
Race Position: 7th + 2 laps
Fastest lap: 3rd fastest: 1m20.217s

Race: Spanish Grand Prix
Circuit: Jerez
Date: 27th September 1987
Qualifying Time: 1m24.320s
Qualifying Position: 5th
Race Position: 5th + 1m13.507s
Fastest lap: 11th fastest: 1m30.088s

Race: Mexican Grand Prix
Circuit: Hermanos Rodriguez
Date: 18th October 1987
Qualifying Time: 1m19.089s
Qualifying Position: 7th

Race Position: retired, lap 54, spin
Fastest lap: 3rd fastest: 1m20.586s

Race: Japanese Grand Prix
Circuit: Suzuka
Date: 1st November 1987
Qualifying Time: 1m42.723s
Qualifying Position: 7th
Race Position: 2nd + 17.384s
Fastest lap: 3rd fastest: 1m45.805s

Race: Australian Grand Prix
Circuit: Adelaide
Date: 15th November 1987
Qualifying Time: 1m18.488s
Qualifying Position: 4th
Race Position: disqualified, having
raced with irregular brake ducts (2nd,
34.845s behind)
Fastest lap: 2nd fastest: 1m20.456s

1988
Race: Brazilian Grand Prix
Circuit: Jacarepagua
Date: 3rd April 1988
Qualifying Time: 1m28.096s
Qualifying Position: pole
Race Position: disqualified, car change
after parade lap
Fastest lap: 9th fastest: 1m34.657s

Race: San Marino Grand Prix
Circuit: Imola
Date: 1st May 1988
Qualifying Time: 1m27.148s
Qualifying Position: pole
Race Position: 1st
Race Time: 60 laps in 1h32m41.264s

Average Speed: 121.636mph
Fastest lap: 2nd fastest: 1m29.815s

Race: Monaco Grand Prix
Circuit: Monte Carlo
Date: 15th May 1988
Qualifying Time: 1m23.998s
Qualifying Position: pole
Race Position: retired, lap 66, accident
Fastest lap: fastest: 1m26.321s

Race: Mexican Grand Prix
Circuit: Hermanos Rodriguez
Date: 29th May 1988
Qualifying Time: 1m17.468s
Qualifying Position: pole
Race Position: 2nd + 7.104s
Fastest lap: 2nd fastest: 1m18.776s

Race: Canadian Grand Prix
Circuit: Circuit Gilles Villeneuve
Date: 12th June 1988
Qualifying Time: 1m21.681s
Qualifying Position: pole
Race Position: 1st
Race Time: 69 laps in 1h39m46.618s
Average Speed: 113.805mph
Fastest lap: fastest: 1m24.973s (lap record)

Race: U.S.A East Grand Prix
Circuit: Detroit
Date: 19th June 1988
Qualifying Time: 1m40.606s
Qualifying Position: pole
Race Position: 1st
Race Time: 63 laps in 1h54m56.635s
Average Speed: 82.2012mph
Fastest lap: 2nd fastest: 1m44.992s

Race: French Grand Prix
Circuit: Paul Ricard
Date: 3rd July 1988
Qualifying Time: 1m08.067s
Qualifying Position: 2nd
Race Position: 2nd + 31.752s
Fastest lap: 2nd fastest: 1m11.856s

Race: British Grand Prix
Circuit: Silverstone
Date: 10th July 1988
Qualifying Time: 1m10.616s
Qualifying Position: 3rd
Race Position: 1st
Race Time: 65 laps in 1h33m16.367s
Average Speed: 124.115mph
Fastest lap: 4th fastest: 1m23.595s

Race: German Grand Prix
Circuit: Hockenheim
Date: 24th July 1988
Qualifying Time: 1m44.596s
Qualifying Position: pole
Race Position: 1st
Race Time: 44 laps in 1h32m54.188s
Average Speed: 120.017mph
Fastest lap: 3rd fastest: 2m05.001s

Race: Hungarian Grand Prix
Circuit: Hungaroring
Date: 7th August 1988
Qualifying Time: 1m27.635s
Qualifying Position: pole
Race Position: 1st
Race Time: 76 laps in 1h57m47.381s
Average Speed: 95.5617mph
Fastest lap: 2nd fastest: 1m30.964s

Race: Belgian Grand Prix
Circuit: Spa-Francorchamps
Date: 28th August 1988
Qualifying Time: 1m53.718s
Qualifying Position: pole
Race Position: 1st
Race Time: 43 laps in 1h28m00.549
Average Speed: 126.416mph
Fastest lap: 2nd fastest: 2m01.061s

Race: Italian Grand Prix
Circuit: Monza
Date: 11th September 1988
Qualifying Time: 1m25.974s
Qualifying Position: pole
Race Position: retired, lap 49, collision
with Schlesser
Fastest lap: 3rd fastest: 1m29.569s

Race: Portuguese Grand Prix
Circuit: Estoril
Date: 25th September 1988
Qualifying Time: 1m17.869s
Qualifying Position: 2nd
Race Position: 6th + 1m18.269s
Fastest lap: 8th fastest: 1m22.852s

Race: Spanish Grand Prix
Circuit: Jerez de la Frontera
Date: 2nd October 1988
Qualifying Time: 1m24.067s
Qualifying Position: pole
Race Position: 4th + 46.710s
Fastest lap: 3rd fastest: 1m28.273s

Race: Japanese Grand Prix
Circuit: Suzuka
Date: 30th October 1988

Qualifying Time: 1m41.853s
Qualifying Position: pole
Race Position: 1st
Race Time: 51 laps in 1h33m26.173s
Average Speed: 119.229mph
Fastest lap: fastest: 1m46.326s

Race: Australian Grand Prix
Circuit: Adelaide
Date: 13th November 1988
Qualifying Time: 1m17.748s
Qualifying Position: pole
Race Position: 2nd + 36.787s
Fastest lap: 4th fastest: 1m21.668s

1989
Race: Brazilian Grand Prix
Circuit: Jacarepagua
Date: 26th March 1989
Qualifying Time: 1m25.302s
Qualifying Position: pole
Race Position: 11th + 2 laps
Fastest lap: 3rd fastest: 1m33.685s

Race: San Marino Grand Prix
Circuit: Imola
Date: 23rd April 1989
Qualifying Time: 1m26.010s
Qualifying Position: pole
Race Position: 1st
Race Time: 58 laps in 1h26m51.245s
Average Speed: 125.479mph
Fastest lap: 2nd fastest: 1m27.272s

Race: Monaco Grand Prix
Circuit: Monte Carlo
Date: 7th May 1989
Qualifying Time: 1m22.308s

Qualifying Position: pole
Race Position: 1st
Race Time: 77 laps in 1h53m33.251s
Average Speed: 84.1343mph
Fastest lap: 3rd fastest lap time:
1m26.017s

Race: Mexican Grand Prix
Circuit: Hermanos Rodriguez
Date: 28th May 1989
Qualifying Time: 1m17.876s
Qualifying Position: pole
Race Position: 1st
Race Time: 69 laps in 1h35m21.431s
Average Speed: 119.3mph
Fastest lap: 3rd fastest: 1m20.585s

Race: U.S. Grand Prix
Circuit: Phoenix
Date: 4th June 1989
Qualifying Time: 1m30.108s
Qualifying Position: pole
Race Position: retired, lap 44,
electrical problem
Fastest lap: fastest time: 1m33.969s
(lap record)

Race: Canadian Grand Prix
Circuit: Circuit Gilles Villeneuve
Date: 18th June 1989
Qualifying Time: 1m21.049s
Qualifying Position: 2nd
Race Position: 7th + 3 laps
(engine failure)
Fastest lap: 2nd fastest: 1m32.143s

Race: French Grand Prix
Circuit: Paul Ricard

Date: 9th July 1989
Qualifying Time: 1m07.228s
Qualifying Position: 2nd
Race Position: retired, lap 1, (2nd start), differential

Race: British Grand Prix
Circuit: Silverstone
Date: 16th July 1989
Qualifying Time: 1m09.099s
Qualifying Position: pole
Race Position: retired, lap 11, accident
Fastest lap: 7th fastest: 1m13.737s

Race: German Grand Prix
Circuit: Hockenheim
Date: 30th July 1989
Qualifying Time: 1m42.300s
Qualifying Position: pole
Race Position: 1st
Race Time: 45 laps in 1h21m43.302s
Average Speed: 139.539mph
Fastest lap: fastest: 1m45.884s

Race: Hungarian Grand Prix
Circuit: Hungaroring
Date: 13th August 1989
Qualifying Time: 1m20.039s
Qualifying Position: 2nd
Race Position: 2nd + 25.967s
Fastest lap: 4th fastest: 1m23.313s

Race: Belgian Grand Prix
Circuit: Spa-Francorchamps
Date: 27th August 1989
Qualifying Time: 1m50.867s
Qualifying Position: pole
Race Position: 1st

Race Time: 44 laps in 1h40m54.196s
Average Speed: 112.826mph
Fastest lap: 4th fastest: 2m12.890s

Race: Italian Grand Prix
Circuit: Monza
Date: 11th September 1989
Qualifying Time: 1m23.720s
Qualifying Position: pole
Race Position: retired, lap 44, engine, oil pressure
Fastest lap: 2nd fastest: 1m28.179s

Race: Portuguese Grand Prix
Circuit: Estoril
Date: 24th September 1989
Qualifying Time: 1m15.468s
Qualifying Position: pole
Race Position: retired, lap 48, collision with Mansell
Fastest lap: 4th fastest: 1m19.490s

Race: Spanish Grand Prix
Circuit: Jerez de la Frontera
Date: 1st October 1989
Qualifying Time: 1m20.291s
Qualifying Position: pole
Race Position: 1st
Race Time: 73 laps in 1h48.264s
Average Speed: 106.5mph
Fastest lap: fastest: 1m25.779s (lap record)

Race: Japanese Grand Prix
Circuit: Suzuka
Date: 22nd October1989
Qualifying Time: 1m38.041
Qualifying Position: pole
Race Position: disqualified, dangerous

driving (1st, 53 laps in 1h35m03.980s)
Fastest lap: fastest: 1m43.025s
(unofficial lap record)

Race: Australian Grand Prix
Circuit: Adelaide
Date: 5th November 1989
Qualifying Time: 1m16.665s
Qualifying Position: pole
Race Position: Retired, lap 13, collision
with Brundle
Fastest lap: 5th fastest: 1m41.159s

1990
Race: U.S. Grand Prix
Circuit: Phoenix
Date: 11th March 1990
Qualifying Time: 1m29.431s
Qualifying Position: pole
Race Position: 1st
Race Time: 72 laps in 1h52m32.829s
Average Speed: 90.5649mph
Fastest lap: 3rd fastest: 1m32.178s

Race: Brazilian Grand Prix
Circuit: Interlagos
Date: 25th March 1990
Qualifying Time: 1m17.277s
Qualifying Position: pole
Race Position: 3rd + 37.722s
Fastest lap: 3rd fastest: 1m20.067s

Race: San Marino Grand Prix
Circuit: Imola
Date: 13th May 1990
Qualifying Time: 1m23.220s
Qualifying Position: pole
Race Position: retired, lap 4, right rear

wheel rim broken
Fastest lap: 14th fastest: 1m30.615s

Race: Monaco Grand Prix
Circuit: Monte Carlo
Date: 27th May 1990
Qualifying Time: 1m21.314s
Qualifying Position: pole
Race Position: 1st
Race Time: 78 laps in 1h52m46.982s
Average Speed: 85.81mph
Fastest lap: fastest: 1m24.245s
(lap record)

Race: Canadian Grand Prix
Circuit: Circuit Gilles Villeneuve
Date: 10th June 1990
Qualifying Time: 1m20.399s
Qualifying Position: pole
Race Position: 1st
Race Time: 70 laps in 1h42m56.400
Average Speed: 111.3mph
Fastest lap: 5th fastest lap: 1m23.375s

Race: Mexican Grand Prix
Circuit: Hermanos Rodriguez
Date: 24th June 1990
Qualifying Time: 1m17.670s
Qualifying Position: 3rd
Race Position: retired, lap 64, right
rear wheel
Fastest lap: 6th fastest: 1m19.062s

Race: French Grand Prix
Circuit: Paul Ricard
Date: 8th July 1990
Qualifying Time: 1m04.549s
Qualifying Position: 3rd

Race Position: 3rd + 11.606
Fastest lap: 6th fastest: 1m08.573s

Race: British Grand Prix
Circuit: Silverstone
Date: 15th July 1990
Qualifying Time: 1m08.071s
Qualifying Position: 2nd
Race Position: 3rd + 43.088s
Fastest lap: 5th fastest: 1m12.250s

Race: German Grand Prix
Circuit: Hockenheim
Date: 29th July 1990
Qualifying Time: 1m40.198s
Qualifying Position: pole
Race Position: 1st
Race Time: 45 laps in 1h20m47.164s
Average Speed: 141.259mph
Fastest lap: 2nd fastest: 1m45.771s

Race: Hungarian Grand Prix
Circuit: Hungaroring
Date: 12th August 1990
Qualifying Time: 1m18.162s
Qualifying Position: 4th
Race Position: 2nd + 0.288s
Fastest lap: 5th fastest: 1m22.577s

Race: Belgian Grand Prix
Circuit: Spa-Francorchamps
Date: 26th August 1990
Qualifying Time: 1m50.365s
Qualifying Position: pole
Race Position: 1st
Race Time: 44 laps in 1h26m31.997s
Average Speed: 131.562mph
Fastest lap: 2nd fastest: 1m55.531

Race: Italian Grand Prix
Circuit: Monza
Date: 9th September 1990
Qualifying Time: 1m22.533s
Qualifying Position: pole
Race Position: 1st
Race Time: 53 laps in 1h17m57. 878s
Average Speed: 146.997mph
Fastest lap: fastest: 1m26.254s (lap record)

Race: Portuguese Grand Prix
Circuit: Estoril
Date: 23rd September 1990
Qualifying Time: 1m13.601s
Qualifying Position: 3rd
Race Position: 2nd + 2.808s
Fastest lap: 6th fastest: 1m18.936s

Race: Spanish Grand Prix
Circuit: Jerez de la Frontera
Date: 30th September 1990
Qualifying Time: 1m18.387s
Qualifying Position: pole
Race Position: retired, lap 54, bored radiator
Fastest lap: 12th fastest: 1m27.430s

Race: Japanese Grand Prix
Circuit: Suzuka
Date: 21st October 1990
Qualifying Time: 1m36.996s
Qualifying Position: pole
Race Position: retired, 1st lap collision
with Prost

1991
Race: Australian Grand Prix
Circuit: Adelaide
Date: 4th November 1991

Qualifying Time: 1m15.671s
Qualifying Position: Pole
Race Position: retired, lap 62, spin
Fastest Lap: 3rd fastest: 1m19.302s

Race: U.S. Grand Prix
Circuit: Phoenix
Date: 10th March 1991
Qualifying Time: 1m21.434s
Qualifying Position: pole
Race Position: 1st
Race Time: 81 laps in 2h00m47.828s
Average Speed: 92.4886mph
Fastest lap: 4th fastest: 1m27.153s

Race: Brazilian Grand Prix
Circuit: Interlagos
Date: 24th March 1991
Qualifying Time: 1m16.392s
Qualifying Position: pole
Race Position: 1st
Race Time: 71 laps in 1h38m28.128s
Average Speed: 116.265mph
Fastest lap: 3rd fastest: 1m20.841s

Race: San Marino Grand Prix
Circuit: Imola
Date: 28th April 1991
Qualifying Time: 1m21.877s
Qualifying Position: pole
Race Position: 1st
Race Time: 61 laps in 1h35m14.750s
Average Speed: 120.342mph
Fastest lap: 2nd fastest: 1m27.168s

Race: Monaco Grand Prix
Circuit: Monte Carlo
Date: 12th May 1991

Qualifying Time: 1m20.344s
Qualifying Position: pole
Race Position: 1st
Race Time: 78 laps in 1h53m02.234s
Average Speed: 85.6156mph
Fastest lap: 5th fastest: 1m25.250s

Race: Canadian Grand Prix
Circuit: Circuit Gilles Villeneuve
Date: 2nd June 1991
Qualifying Time: 1m20.318s
Qualifying Position: 3rd
Race Position: retired, lap 26,
electrical problem
Fastest lap: 10th fastest lap time:
1m24.647s

Race: Mexican Grand Prix
Circuit: Hermanos Rodriguez
Date: 16th June 1991
Qualifying Time: 1m17.264s
Qualifying Position: 3rd
Race Position: 3rd + 57.356s
Fastest lap: 3rd fastest: 1m18.750s

Race: French Grand Prix
Circuit: Magny Cours
Date: 7th July 1991
Qualifying Time: 1m14.857s
Qualifying Position: 3rd
Race Position: 3rd + 34.934s
Fastest lap: 5th fastest: 1m20.570s

Race: British Grand Prix
Circuit: Silverstone
Date: 14th July 1991
Qualifying Time: 1m21.618s
Qualifying Position: 2nd

Race Position: 4th + 1 lap
Fastest lap: 4th fastest: 1m27.509s

Fastest lap: fastest: 1m26.061s
(lap record)

Race: German Grand Prix
Circuit: Hockenheim
Date: 28th July 1991
Qualifying Time: 1m37.274s
Qualifying Position: 2nd
Race Position: 7th, Retired, lap 44,
out of fuel
Fastest lap: 5th fastest: 1m44.213s

Race: Hungarian Grand Prix
Circuit: Hungaroring
Date: 11th August 1991
Qualifying Time: 1m16.147s
Qualifying Position: pole
Race Position: 1st
Race Time: 77 laps in 1h49m12.796s
Average Speed: 104.302mph
Fastest lap: 2nd fastest: 1m22.392s

Race: Belgian Grand Prix
Circuit: Spa-Francorchamps
Date: 25th August 1991
Qualifying Time: 1m47.811s
Qualifying Position: pole
Race Position: 1st
Race Time: 44 laps in 1h27m17.669s
Average Speed: 130.415mph
Fastest lap: 5th fastest: 1m56.471s

Race: Italian Grand Prix
Circuit: Monza
Date: 8th September 1991
Qualifying Time: 1m21.114s
Qualifying Position: pole
Race Position: 2nd + 16.262s

Race: Portuguese Grand Prix
Circuit: Estoril
Date: 22nd September 1991
Qualifying Time: 1m13.444s
Qualifying Position: 3rd
Race Position: 2nd + 20.941s
Fastest lap: 4th fastest: 1m18.856s

Race: Spanish Grand Prix
Circuit: Circuit de Catalunya
Date: 29th September 1991
Qualifying Time: 1m19.064s
Qualifying Position: 3rd
Race Position: 5th + 1m02.402s
Fastest lap: 7th fastest: 1m24.771s

Race: Japanese Grand Prix
Circuit: Suzuka
Date: 20th October 1991
Qualifying Time: 1m34.700s
Qualifying Position: 2nd
Race Position: 2nd + 0.344s
Fastest lap: fastest: 1m41.532s
(lap record)

Race: Australian Grand Prix
Circuit: Adelaide
Date: 3rd November 1991
Qualifying Time: 1m14.041s
Qualifying Position: pole
Race Position: 1st
Race Time: 14 laps in 24m34.899s
Average Speed: 80.2625mph
Fastest lap: 2nd fastest: 1m42.545s

1992

Race: South-African Grand Prix
Circuit: Kyalami
Date: 1st March 1992
Qualifying Time: 1m16.277s
Qualifying Position: 2nd
Race Position: 3rd + 34.675s
Fastest lap: 2nd fastest: 1m18.140s

Race: Mexican Grand Prix
Circuit: Hermanos Rodriguez
Date: 22nd March 1992
Qualifying Time: 1m18.79s
Qualifying Position: 15th
Race Position: retired, lap 11, transmission
Fastest lap: 13th fastest: 1m20.721s

Race: Brazilian Grand Prix
Circuit: Interlagos
Date: 5th April 1992
Qualifying Time: 1m17.902s
Qualifying Position: 3rd
Race Position: retired, lap 18, electrics
Fastest lap: 21st fastest: 1m23.101s

Race: Spanish Grand Prix
Circuit: Circuit de Catalunya
Date: 3rd May 1992
Qualifying Time: 1m21.209s
Qualifying Position: 3rd
Race Position: 9th + 3 laps, spin
Fastest lap: 5th fastest: 1m43.176s

Race: San Marino Grand Prix
Circuit: Imola
Date: 17th May 1992
Qualifying Time: 1m23.086s
Qualifying Position: 3rd

Race Position: 3rd + 48.984s
Fastest lap: 5th fastest: 1m27.615s

Race: Monaco Grand Prix
Circuit: Monte Carlo
Date: 31st May 1992
Qualifying Time: 1m20.608s
Qualifying Position: 3rd
Race Position: 1st
Race Time: 78 laps in 1h50m59.372s
Average Speed: 87.1964mph
Fastest lap: 3rd fastest: 1m23.470s

Race: Canadian Grand Prix
Circuit: Circuit Gilles Villeneuve
Date: 14th June 1992
Qualifying Time: 1m19.775s
Qualifying Position: pole
Race Position: retired, lap 37, electronics
Fastest lap: 6th fastest: 1m23.728s

Race: French Grand Prix
Circuit: Magny Cours
Date: 5th July 1992
Qualifying Time: 1m15.199s
Qualifying Position: 3rd
Race Position: retired, 1st lap collision
with Schumacher

Race: British Grand Prix
Circuit: Silverstone
Date: 12th July 1992
Qualifying Time: 1m21.706s
Qualifying Position: 3rd
Race Position: retired, lap 52, gearbox
Fastest lap: 5th fastest: 1m25.625s

Race: German Grand Prix

Circuit: Hockenheim
Date: 26th July 1992
Qualifying Time: 1m39.106s
Qualifying Position: 3rd
Race Position: 2nd + 4.500s
Fastest lap: 2nd fastest: 1m42.272s

Race: Hungarian Grand Prix
Circuit: Hungaroring
Date: 16th August 1992
Qualifying Time: 1m16.267s
Qualifying Position: 3rd
Race Position: 1st
Race Time: 77 laps in 1h46m19.216s
Average Speed: 107.139mph
Fastest lap: 3rd fastest: 1m19.588s

Race: Belgian Grand Prix
Circuit: Spa-Francorchamps
Date: 30th August 1992
Qualifying Time: 1m52.743s
Qualifying Position: 2nd
Race Position: 5th + 1m08.369s
Fastest lap: 2nd fastest: 1m54.088s

Race: Italian Grand Prix
Circuit: Monza
Date: 13th September 1992
Qualifying Time: 1m22.822s
Qualifying Position: 2nd
Race Position: 1st
Race Time: 53 laps in 1h18m15.349s
Average Speed: 146.45mph
Fastest lap: 5th fastest: 1m27.190s

Race: Portuguese Grand Prix
Circuit: Estoril
Date: 27th September 1992

Qualifying Time: 1m14.258s
Qualifying Position: 3rd
Race Position: 3rd + 1 lap
Fastest lap: fastest: 1m16.272s (lap record)

Race: Japanese Grand Prix
Circuit: Suzuka
Date: 25th October 1992
Qualifying Time: 1m38.375s
Qualifying Position: 3rd
Race Position: retired, lap 2, engine
Fastest lap: 21st fastest: 1m46.229s

Race: Australian Grand Prix
Circuit: Adelaide
Date: 8th November 1992
Qualifying Time: 1m14.202s
Qualifying Position: 2nd
Race Position: retired, lap 18, collision
with Mansell
Fastest lap: 3rd fastest: 1m17.818s

1993
Race: South-African Grand Prix
Circuit: Kyalami
Date: 14th March 1993
Qualifying Time: 1m15.784s
Qualifying Position: 2nd
Race Position: 2nd + 1m19.824s
Fastest lap: 6th fastest: 1m20.755s

Race: Brazilian Grand Prix
Circuit: Interlagos
Date: 28th March 1993
Qualifying Time: 1m17.697s
Qualifying Position: 3rd
Race Position: 1st
Race Time: 71 laps in 1h51m15.485s

Average Speed: 102.9mph
Fastest lap: 2nd fastest: 1m20.187s

Race: European Grand Prix
Circuit: Donington Park
Date: 11th April 1993
Qualifying Time: 1m12.107s
Qualifying Position: 4th
Race Position: 1st
Race Time: 76 laps in 1h50m46.570s
Average Speed: 102.901mph
Fastest lap: fastest: 1m18.029s
(lap record)

Race: San Marino Grand Prix
Circuit: Imola
Date: 25th April 1993
Qualifying Time: 1m24.007s
Qualifying Position: 4th
Race Position: retired, lap 42,
hydraulics
Fastest lap: 3rd fastest: 1m27.490s

Race: Spanish Grand Prix
Circuit: Circuit de Catalunya
Date: 9th May 1993
Qualifying Time: 1m19.722s
Qualifying Position: 3rd
Race Position: 2nd + 16.873s
Fastest lap: 2nd fastest: 1m21.717s

Race: Monaco Grand Prix
Circuit: Monte Carlo
Date: 23rd May 1993
Qualifying Time: 1m21.552s
Qualifying Position: 3rd
Race Position: 1st
Race Time: 78 laps in 1h52m10.947

Average Speed: 86.2693mph
Fastest lap: 3rd fastest: 1m23.737s

Race: Canadian Grand Prix
Circuit: Circuit Gilles Villeneuve
Date: 13th June 1993
Qualifying Time: 1m21.706s
Qualifying Position: 8th
Race Position: retired, lap 63, alternator
Fastest lap: 3rd fastest: 1m22.015s

Race: French Grand Prix
Circuit: Magny-Cours
Date: 4th July 1993
Qualifying Time: 1m16.264s
Qualifying Position: 5th
Race Position: 4th + 32.405s
Fastest lap: 3rd fastest: 1m20.521s

Race: British Grand Prix
Circuit: Silverstone
Date: 11th July 1993
Qualifying Time: 1m21.986s
Qualifying Position: 4th
Race Position: 5th + 1 lap
(out of fuel, lap 58)
Fastest lap: 5th fastest: 1m24.886s

Race: German Grand Prix
Circuit: Hockenheim
Date: 25th July 1993
Qualifying Time: 1m39.616s
Qualifying Position: 4th
Race Position: 4th + 1m08.229s
Fastest lap: 2nd fastest: 1m42.162s

Race: Hungarian Grand Prix
Circuit: Hungaroring

Date: 15th August 1993
Qualifying Time: 1m16.451s
Qualifying Position: 4th
Race Position: retired, lap 17, throttle
Fastest lap: 13th fastest: 1m22.838s

Race: Belgian Grand Prix
Circuit: Spa Francorchamps
Date: 29th August 1993
Qualifying Time: 1m49.934s
Qualifying Position: 5th
Race Position: 4th + 1m39.763s
Fastest lap: 5th fastest: 1m54.185s

Race: Italian Grand Prix
Circuit: Monza
Date: 12th September 1993
Qualifying Time: 1m22.633s
Qualifying Position: 4th
Race Position: retired, lap 8, collision
with Brundle
Fastest lap: 9th fastest: 1m27.939s

Race: Portuguese Grand Prix
Circuit: Estoril
Date: 26th September 1993
Qualifying Time: 1m12.491s
Qualifying Position: 4th
Race Position: retired, lap 19, engine
Fastest lap: 15th fastest: 1m18.365s

Race: Japanese Grand Prix
Circuit: Suzuka
Date: 24th October 1993
Qualifying Time: 1m37.284s
Qualifying Position: 2nd
Race Position: 1st
Race Time: 53 laps in 1h40m27.912s

Average Speed: 115.334mph
Fastest lap: 4th fastest: 1m43.217s

Race: Australian Grand Prix
Circuit: Adelaide
Date: 7th November 1993
Qualifying Time: 1m13.371s
Qualifying Position: pole
Race Position: 1st
Race Time: 79 laps in 1h43m27.476s
Average Speed: 107.611mph
Fastest lap: 3rd fastest: 1m16.128s

1994
Race: Brazilian Grand Prix
Circuit: Interlagos
Date: 27th March 1994
Qualifying Time: 1m15.962s
Qualifying Position: pole
Race Position: retired, 55th lap, spin
Fastest lap: 2nd fastest: 1m18.764s

Race: Pacific Grand Prix
Circuit: TI Aida
Date: 17th April 1994
Qualifying Time: 1m10.218s
Qualifying Position: pole
Race Position: retired, 1st lap, collision

Race: San Marino Grand Prix
Circuit: Imola
Date: 1st May 1994
Qualifying Time: 1m21.548s
Qualifying Position: pole
Race Position: retired, 7th lap accident★
Fastest lap: 22nd fastest: 1m44.068s
★Fatal crash

1982 to 1984 Other Races

Ayrton Senna had five main careers in karting, Formula Ford 1600, Formula Ford 2000, Formula 3 and Formula One. But between 1982 and 1984 he alo had one-off races in saloon and sports cars. In 1982 he drove his one and only celebrity race at Oulton Park in the north of England. In May 1984 he competed in a race for Formula One drivers current and retired in identical Mercedes 190s which he won. Later that year he had one off run in a world championship saloon car race in a Porsche 956.

30th May 1982
Oulton Park
"Shell Super Sunbeam for Celebrities"
Sunbeam Talbot T1
Result: 1st (9m50.2s)

12th May 1984
Nurburgring
inaugural SCR race
Mercedes Benz 190E
Result: 1st

15th July 1984
Nurburgring 1000kms
Porsche 956
Result: 8th

1981-1983 Championship Tables

Ayrton Senna won eight series championships in his 13 years of driving cars. It is an unmatched record that will never likely be beaten. Only Mika Hakkinen comes close in this battle and Nelson Piquet also won many championships. Alain Prost was also a multiple series winner.

1981 RAC Formula Ford 1600 championship

1	**Ayrton Senna**	**105 points**
2	Rick Morris	95 points
3	Enrique Mansilla	75 points

Scoring system: 1st: 20; 2nd: 15; 3rd: 12; 4th: 10; 5th: 8; 6th: 6; 7th: 4; 8th: 3; 9th: 2; 10th: 1. Best 11 finishes only to count.

1981 Townsend Thoresen Formula Ford 1600 championship

1	**Ayrton Senna**	**210 points (222 overall)**
2	Rick Morris	156 points
3	Alfonso Toledano	155 points

Scoring system: 1st: 20; 2nd: 15; 3rd: 12; 4th: 10; 5th: 8; 6th: 6; 7th: 4; 8th: 3; 9th: 2; 10th: 1; fastest lap: 2. Best 11 finishes only to count.

1982 Pace British Formula Ford 2000 championship

1	**Ayrton Senna**	**378 points**
2	Calvin Fish	297 points
3	Kenny Andrews	203 points
4	Russell Spence	192 points
5	Frank Bradley	163 points
6	Tim Davies	152 points

Scoring system: 1st: 20; 2nd: 15; 3rd: 12; 4th: 10; 5th: 8; 6th: 6; 7th: 4; 8th: 3; 9th: 2; 10th: 1; pole position: 1; fastest lap: 1.

1982 EFDA Formula Ford 2000 Euroseries

1	**Ayrton Senna**	**132 points**
2	Calvin Fish	87 points
3	Cor Euser	66 points
4	Kristian Nissen	62 points
5	Jesper Villumsen	58 points
6	Henrik Larsen	32 points

Scoring system: 1st: 20; 2nd: 15; 3rd: 12; 4th: 10; 5th: 8; 6th: 6; 7th: 4; 8th: 3; 9th: 2; 10th: 1; pole position: 2.

1983 British Formula Three championship

1	**Ayrton Senna**	**132 points**
2	Martin Brundle	123 points
3	Davy Jones	77 points
4	Calvin Fish	67 points
5	Allen Berg	32 points
6	Mario Hytten	23 points

Scoring system: 1st: 9; 2nd: 6; 3rd: 4; 4th: 3; 5th: 2; 6th: 1; fastest lap: 1. Best 17 finishes only to count.

1984 Formula One World Championship

1	Niki Lauda	McLaren TAG	72 points
2	Alain Prost	McLaren TAG	71.5 points
3	Elio de Angelis	Lotus Renault	34 points
4	Michele Alboreto	Ferrari	30.5 points
5	Nelson Piquet	Brabham BMW	29 points
6	Rene Arnoux	Ferrari	27 points
7	Derek Warwick	Renault	23 points
8	Keke Rosberg	Williams Honda	20.5 points
9	**Ayrton Senna**	**Toleman Hart**	**13 points**
10	Nigel Mansell	Lotus Renault	13 points
11	Patrick Tambay	Renault	11 points
12	Teo Fabi	Brabham BMW	9 points
13	Riccardo Patrese	Alfa Romeo	8 points
14	Jacques Laffite	Williams Honda	5 points
15	Thierry Boutsen	Arrows Ford/BMW	5 points
16	Eddie Cheever	Alfa Romeo	3 points
17	Stefan Johansson	Tyrrell Ford, Toleman Hart	3 points
18	Andrea de Cesaris	Ligier Renault	3 points
19	Piercarlo Ghinzani	Osella Alfa Romeo	2 points
20	Marc Surer	Arrows Ford/BMW	1 point

Scoring system: 1st: 9; 2nd: 6; 3rd: 4; 4th: 3; 5th: 2; 6th: 1.
Best 11 scores only to count. Half points awarded for races stopped before half distance.

1985 Formula One World Championship

1	Alain Prost	McLaren TAG	73 points (76)
2	Michele Alboreto	Ferrari	53 points
3	Keke Rosberg	Williams Honda	40 points
4	**Ayrton Senna**	**Lotus Renault**	**38 points**
5	Elio de Angelis	Lotus Renault	33 points
6	Nigel Mansell	Williams Honda	31 points
7	Stefan Johansson	Tyrrell Ford, Ferrari	26 points
8	Nelson Piquet	Brabham BMW	21 points
9	Jacques Laffite	Ligier Renault	16 points
10	Niki Lauda	McLaren TAG	14 points
11	Thierry Boutsen	Arrows BMW	11 points
12	Patrick Tambay	Renault	11 points
13	Marc Surer	Brabham BMW	5 points
14	Derek Warwick	Renault	5 points
15	Philippe Streiff	Ligier Renault, Tyrrell Renault	4 points
16	Stefan Bellof	Tyrrell Ford	4 points
17	Andrea de Cesaris	Ligier Renault	3 points
18	Rene Arnoux	Ferrari	3 points
=	Ivan Capelli	Tyrrell Renault	3 points
20	Gerhard Berger	Arrows BMW	3 points

Scoring system: 1st: 9; 2nd: 6; 3rd: 4; 4th: 3; 5th: 2; 6th: 1.
Best 11 scores only to count.

1986 Formula One World Championship

1	Alain Prost	McLaren TAG	72 points (74)
2	Nigel Mansell	Williams Honda	70 points (72)
3	Nelson Piquet	Williams Honda	69 points
4	**Ayrton Senna**	**Lotus Renault**	**55 points**
5	Stefan Johansson	Ferrari	23 points
6	Keke Rosberg	McLaren TAG	22 points
7	Gerhard Berger	Benetton BMW	17 points
8	Jacques Laffite	Ligier Renault	14 points
9	Michele Alboreto	Ferrari	14 points
10	Rene Arnoux	Ligier Renault	14 points
11	Martin Brundle	Tyrrell Renault	8 points
12	Alan Jones	Beatrice Hart	4 points
13	Johnny Dumfries	Lotus Renault	3 points
14	Philippe Streiff	Tyrrell Renault	3 points
15	Patrick Tambay	Beatrice Hart	2 points
16	Teo Fabi	Benetton BMW	2 points
17	Riccardo Patrese	Brabham BMW	2 points
18	Christian Danner	Osella Alfa Romeo, Arrows BMW	1 point
19	Philippe Alliot	Ligier Renault	1 point

Scoring system: 1st: 9; 2nd: 6; 3rd: 4; 4th: 3; 5th: 2; 6th: 1.
Best 11 scores only to count.

1987 Formula One World Championship

1	Nelson Piquet	Williams Honda	73 points (76)
2	Nigel Mansell	Williams Honda	61 points
3	**Ayrton Senna**	**Lotus Honda**	**57 points**
4	Alain Prost	McLaren TAG	46 points
5	Gerhard Berger	Ferrari	36 points
6	Stefan Johansson	McLaren TAG	30 points
7	Michele Alboreto	Ferrari	17 points
8	Thierry Boutsen	Benetton Ford	16 points
9	Teo Fabi	Benetton Ford	12 points
10	Eddie Cheever	Arrows Megatron	8 points
11	Jonathan Palmer	Tyrrell Ford	7 points
12	Satoru Nakajima	Lotus Honda	7 points
13	Riccardo Patrese	Brabham BMW, Williams Honda	6 points
14	Andrea de Cesaris	Brabham BMW	4 points
15	Philippe Streiff	Tyrrell Ford	4 points
16	Derek Warwick	Arrows Megatron	3 points
17	Philippe Alliot	Lola Ford	3 points
18	Martin Brundle	Zakspeed	2 points
19	Ivan Capelli	March Ford	1 point
20	Rene Arnoux	Ligier Megatron	1 point
21	Roberto Moreno	AGS Ford	1 point

Scoring system: 1st: 9; 2nd: 6; 3rd: 4; 4th: 3; 5th: 2; 6th: 1.
Best 11 scores only to count.

1988 Formula One World Championship

1	**Ayrton Senna**	**McLaren Honda**	**90 points (94)**
2	Alain Prost	McLaren Honda	87 points (105)
3	Gerhard Berger	Ferrari	41 points
4	Thierry Boutsen	Benetton Ford	27 points
5	Michele Alboreto	Ferrari	24 points
6	Nelson Piquet	Lotus Honda	22 points
7	Ivan Capelli	March Judd	17 points
8	Derek Warwick	Arrows Megatron	17 points
9	Nigel Mansell	Williams Judd	12 points
10	Alessandro Nannini	Benetton Ford	12 points
11	Riccardo Patrese	Williams Judd	8 points
12	Eddie Cheever	Arrows Megatron	6 points
13	Mauricio Gugelmin	March Judd	5 points
14	Jonathan Palmer	Tyrrell Ford	5 points
15	Andrea de Cesaris	Rial Ford	3 points
16	Satoru Nakajima	Lotus Honda	1 point
17	Pierluigi Martini	Minardi Ford	1 point

Scoring system: 1st: 9; 2nd: 6; 3rd: 4; 4th: 3; 5th: 2; 6th: 1.
Best 11 scores only to count.

1989 Formula One World Championship

1	Alain Prost	McLaren Honda	76 points (81)
2	**Ayrton Senna**	**McLaren Honda**	**60 points**
3	Riccardo Patrese	Williams Renault	40 points
4	Nigel Mansell	Ferrari	38 points
5	Thierry Boutsen	Williams Renault	37 points
6	Alessandro Nannini	Benetton Ford	32 points
7	Gerhard Berger	Ferrari	21 points
8	Nelson Piquet	Lotus Judd	12 points
9	Jean Alesi	Tyrrell Ford	8 points
10	Derek Warwick	Arrows Judd	7 points
11	Eddie Cheever	Arrows Judd	6 points
12	Michele Alboreto	Tyrrell Ford, Lola Lamborghini	6 points
13	Stefan Johansson	Onyx Ford	6 points
14	Johnny Herbert	Benetton Ford, Tyrrell Ford	5 points
15	Pierluigi Martini	Minardi Ford	5 points
16	Mauricio Gugelmin	March Judd	4 points
17	Andrea de Cesaris	Dallara Ford	4 points
18	Stefano Modena	Brabham Judd	4 points
19	Alex Caffi	Dallara Ford	4 points
20	Martin Brundle	Brabham Judd	4 points
21	Satoru Nakajima	Lotus Judd	3 points
22	Christian Danner	Rial Ford	3 points
23	Emanuele Pirro	Benetton Ford	2 points
24	Rene Arnoux	Ligier Ford	2 points
25	Jonathan Palmer	Tyrrell Ford	2 points
26	Olivier Grouillard	Ligier Ford	1 point
27	Gabriele Tarquini	AGS Ford	1 point
28	Luis Perez-Sala	Minardi Ford	1 point
29	Philippe Alliot	Lola Lamborghini	1 point

Scoring system: 1st: 9; 2nd: 6; 3rd: 4; 4th: 3; 5th: 2; 6th: 1.
Best 11 scores only to count.

1990 Formula One World Championship

1	**Ayrton Senna**	McLaren Honda	**78 points**
2	Alain Prost	Ferrari	71 points (73)
3	Nelson Piquet	Benetton Ford	43 points (44)
4	Gerhard Berger	McLaren Honda	43 points
5	Nigel Mansell	Ferrari	37 points
6	Thierry Boutsen	Williams Renault	34 points
7	Riccardo Patrese	Williams Renault	23 points
8	Alessandro Nannini	Benetton Ford	21 points
9	Jean Alesi	Tyrrell Ford	13 points
10	Ivan Capelli	Leyton House Judd	6 points
11	Roberto Moreno	EuroBrun Judd, Benetton Ford	6 points
12	Aguri Suzuki	Lola Lamborghini	6 points
13	Eric Bernard	Lola Lamborghini	5 points
14	Derek Warwick	Lotus Lamborghini	3 points
15	Satoru Nakajima	Tyrrell Ford	3 points
16	Alex Caffi	Arrows Ford	2 points
17	Stefano Modena	Brabham Judd	2 points
18	Mauricio Gugelmin	Leyton House Judd	1 point

Scoring system: 1st: 9; 2nd: 6; 3rd: 4; 4th: 3; 5th: 2; 6th: 1.
Best 11 scores only to count.

1991 Formula One World Championship

1	Ayrton Senna	McLaren Honda	96 points
2	Nigel Mansell	Williams Renault	72 points
3	Riccardo Patrese	Williams Renault	53 points
4	Gerhard Berger	McLaren Honda	43 points
5	Alain Prost	Ferrari	34 points
6	Nelson Piquet	Benetton Ford	26.5 points
7	Jean Alesi	Ferrari	21 points
8	Stefano Modena	Tyrrell Honda	10 points
9	Andrea de Cesaris	Jordan Ford	9 points
10	Roberto Moreno	Benetton Ford, Jordan Ford, Minardi Ferrari	8 points
11	Pierluigi Martini	Minardi Ferrari	6 points
12	JJ Lehto	Dallara Judd	4 points
13	Bertrand Gachot	Jordan Ford, Lola Ford	4 points
14	Michael Schumacher	Jordan Ford, Benetton Ford	4 points
15	Satoru Nakajima	Tyrrell Honda	2 points
16	Mika Häkkinen	Lotus Judd	2 points
17	Martin Brundle	Brabham Yamaha	2 points
18	Emanuele Pirro	Dallara Judd	1 point
19	Mark Blundell	Brabham Yamaha	1 point
20	Ivan Capelli	Leyton House Ilmor	1 point
21	Eric Bernard	Lola Ford	1 point
22	Aguri Suzuki	Lola Ford	1 point
=	Julian Bailey	Lotus Judd	1 point
24	Gianni Morbidelli	Minardi Ferrari	0.5 points

Scoring system: 1st: 10; 2nd: 6; 3rd: 4; 4th: 3; 5th: 2; 6th: 1.
Half points for races stopped before half distance.

1992 Formula One World Championship

1	Nigel Mansell	Williams Renault	108 points
2	Riccardo Patrese	Williams Renault	56 points
3	Michael Schumacher	Benetton Ford	53 points
4	**Ayrton Senna**	**McLaren Honda**	**50 points**
5	Gerhard Berger	McLaren Honda	49 points
6	Martin Brundle	Benetton Ford	38 points
7	Jean Alesi	Ferrari	18 points
8	Mika Häkkinen	Lotus Ford	11 points
9	Andrea de Cesaris	Tyrrell Ilmor	8 points
10	Michele Alboreto	Footwork Mugen-Honda	6 points
11	Erik Comas	Ligier Renault	4 points
12	Karl Wendlinger	March Ilmor	3 points
13	Ivan Capelli	Ferrari	3 points
14	Thierry Boutsen	Ligier Renault	2 points
15	Johnny Herbert	Lotus Ford	2 points
16	Pierluigi Martini	Dallara Ferrari	2 points
17	Stefano Modena	Jordan Yamaha	1 point
18	Christian Fittipaldi	Minardi Lamborghini	1 point
19	Bertrand Gachot	Larrousse Lamborghini	1 point

Scoring system: 1st: 10; 2nd: 6; 3rd: 4; 4th: 3; 5th: 2; 6th: 1.

1993 Formula One World Championship

1	Alain Prost	Williams Renault	99 points
2	**Ayrton Senna**	**McLaren Ford**	**73 points**
3	Damon Hill	Williams Renault	69 points
4	Michael Schumacher	Benetton Ford	52 points
5	Riccardo Patrese	Benetton Ford	20 points
6	Jean Alesi	Ferrari	16 points
7	Martin Brundle	Ligier Renault	13 points
8	Gerhard Berger	Ferrari	12 points
9	Johnny Herbert	Lotus Ford	11 points
10	Mark Blundell	Ligier Renault	10 points
11	Michael Andretti	McLaren Ford	7 points
12	Karl Wendlinger	Sauber Ilmor	7 points
13	JJ Lehto	Sauber Ilmor	5 points
14	Christian Fittipaldi	Minardi Ford	5 points
15	Mika Häkkinen	McLaren Ford	4 points
16	Derek Warwick	Footwork Mugen-Honda	4 points
17	Philippe Alliot	Larrousse Lamborghini	2 points
18	Rubens Barrichello	Jordan Hart	2 points
19	Fabrizio Barbazza	Minardi Ford	2 points
20	Alessandro Zanardi	Lotus Ford	1 point
21	Erik Comas	Larrousse Lamborghini	1 point
22	Eddie Irvine	Jordan Hart	1 point

Scoring system: 1st: 10; 2nd: 6; 3rd: 4; 4th: 3; 5th: 2; 6th: 1.

1985-1993 Formula One wins by season

Ayrton Senna spent 11 years racing Formula One cars and scored victories in every year except the first and the last. In 1985 he had an uncompetitive car and in 1994 he was killed in the third race of the season but not before he had taken pole in each and led each before retiring.

1985 Lotus Renault 97T: two wins

In only Senna's second year he got a car capable of taking him to victory. He took two wins at a time when his experienced and highly-rated team-mate Elio de Angelis took just one, and the Brazilian newcomer also took another four podium places. His performance was good enough to net him fourth place in the championship and he could have done better had he not been hampered by unreliability – he led nine of the 16 rounds and 26 per cent of the total distance, the record for a driver that year. Both victories came in the wet.

1986 Lotus Renault 98T: two wins

In 1986 Ayrton Senna took another two victories to add to his tally. He led half of the 16 rounds and finished a close fourth in a championship in which he was for the first time a genuine championship contender until the final races.

1987 Lotus Honda 99T: two wins

The 1987 season saw Senna take his by then customary two victories, including Monaco. He led seven races and finished third in the championship behind the dominant Williams Hondas of Nelson Piquet and Nigel Mansell.

1988 McLaren Honda MP4/4: eight wins

In 1988, with the mighty MP4/4 underneath him, Senna became the first driver to take eight wins in a season. He retired from the lead on another two occasions and led over half the total race distance. This amazing success pushed him to his first world title despite stiff opposition from team-mate Alain Prost, who himself took a hefty total of seven victories.

THE LIFE OF SENNA

1989 McLaren Honda MP4/5: six wins

Alongside the six victories he officially took in the MP4/5, Senna was also disqualified from a hard-fought first place at Suzuka and retired from the lead four times. He led 13 of the races and nearly half of the laps, almost double the distance of the eventual champion, his team-mate Alain Prost. He took five victories where he led every lap, equalling his tally of 1988. Each one of the six wins was accompanied by a pole position at the same race.

1990 McLaren Honda MP4/5B: six wins

It was another six wins for Senna in his second championship-winning year. The Brazilian again led almost half of the available distance. He became the first ever driver to lead 14 rounds in a single season, only missing out on Hungary, where he sat close behind Thierry Boutsen's Williams Renault for the entire race but could not overtake on the tricky track, and Suzuka where he crashed out at the first corner. Each victory was coupled with a pole position.

1991 McLaren Honda MP4/6: seven wins

This year saw Senna take his second greatest tally of wins after 1988 as he scooped his third world title. The Brazilian led all but nine of the first 282 laps of the season, winning at his home race and at Monte Carlo in the process. He led every lap on five occasions that year. In all he led nearly half the laps and 10 of the races.

1992 McLaren Honda MP4/7A: three wins

Just three wins may have seemed like a meagre total compared to his performances in the previous four seasons, but against the mighty Williams Renault FW14Bs it was a magnificent achievement. Unreliability meant the Brazilian could take only fourth in the championship, but he and team-mate Gerhard Berger put in some stunning performances to ensure Williams did not enjoy quite the dominance that McLaren had in 1988.

1993 McLaren Ford MP4/8: five wins

Once again faced with dominant Newey-designed Williams Renaults Senna managed to take an impressive five wins, a record sixth Monaco victory and perhaps his greatest race ever – the European Grand Prix at Donington – among them. Once in the lead he was almost unstoppable. He led six races.

1985 to 1993
41 Formula One wins

Ayrton Senna won 41 races in nine seasons out of 161 he started a win rate of 25 per cent which is on the par with the very best. His most most succesful year was in 1988 when he won eight races in a year and shared virtually all the honours with his team mate in 1988. His worst winning season was his Lotus years whn he won two race in each of the three seasons.

1. 1985 Portuguese Grand Prix: Estoril, *67 laps in 2h00m28.006s*
Second: Michele Alboreto, Ferrari, +1m 02.978s
Third: Patrick Tambay, Renault, +1 lap
Senna's first victory was also one of his best. In the Portuguese downpour he took a clean sweep: he won, took pole position, fastest lap and fastest practice time of the weekend and led every lap. He never looked beatable. It was a drive more than worthy of a veteran as opposed to a young driver with only 15 Formula One races behind him.

2. 1985 Belgian Grand Prix: Spa-Francorchamps, *43 laps in 1h34m19.893s*
Second: Nigel Mansell, Williams Honda, +28.422s
Third: Alain Prost, McLaren TAG, +55.109s
Once again in the wet Senna was magnificent. At the ultimate driver's circuit he proved himself against the rest of the field. Even by the end of the first lap his lead looked secure. He led every lap but the ninth, when during a dry spell his team-mate Elio de Angelis briefly moved into first as Senna pitted to change tyres.

3. 1986 Spanish Grand Prix: Jerez de la Frontera, *72 laps in 1h48m47.735s*
Second: Nigel Mansell, Williams Honda, +0.014s
Third: Alain Prost, McLaren TAG, +21.552s
This remains the second closest victory in history. A race-long battle between Senna, Mansell and Prost that became all the more thrilling in the closing laps. Mansell on fresh rubber was catching Senna by four seconds a lap and whoever got the better kick from the final corner would be victor. Senna won courtesy of a misplaced finish line.

4. 1986 USA East Grand Prix: Detroit, *63 laps in 1h51m12.847s*
Second: Jacques Laffite, Ligier Renault, +31.017s
Third: Alain Prost, McLaren TAG, +31.824s
This was Senna's first victory at one of his best tracks. It was a hard-fought win for the Brazilian around the slow and twisting street circuit. He twice lost the lead and picked up a puncture along the way but in the end he outpaced and outdrove his rivals to take his first of many street circuit victories.

5. 1987 Monaco Grand Prix: Monte Carlo, *78 laps in 1h57m54.085s*
Second: Nelson Piquet, Williams Honda, +33.212s
Third: Michele Alboreto, Ferrari, +1m12.839s
In 1987 Senna took his first victory at what is considered to be his best circuit. He started in second and got away from the grid still in that position behind poleman Nigel Mansell. He inherited the lead when the Englishman's turbo gave up on lap 30. It was his first of a record six victories in the principality.

6. 1987 USA East Grand Prix: Detroit, *63 laps in 1h50m16.358s*
Second: Nelson Piquet, Williams Honda, +33.819s
Third: Alain Prost, McLaren TAG, +45.327s
In Detroit, Senna took his second victory in a row in 1987. It was almost a replay of his Monte Carlo triumph. Mansell again started from pole with Senna beside him, once again took the lead at the start, and again suffered a problem – this time a sticking wheelnut at a tyre stop – to hand the lead and the victory to his Brazilian rival.

7. 1988 San Marino Grand Prix: Imola, *60 laps in 1h32m41.264s*
Second: Alain Prost, McLaren Honda, +2.334s
Third: Nelson Piquet, Lotus Honda, +1 lap
The mighty McLaren MP4/4s were particularly impressive at Imola. They were three seconds better than anyone else in qualifying and after Prost had problems getting off the startline, Senna knew he could not be touched. It was a lights-to-flag victory for the Brazilian with only his new team-mate, Alain Prost, still on the same lap.

8. 1988 Canadian Grand Prix: Montreal, *69 laps in 1h39m46.618s*
Second: Alain Prost, McLaren Honda, +5.934s
Third: Thierry Boutsen, Benetton Ford, +51.409s
Alain Prost took the lead at the start but Senna was determined and executed a brilliant overtaking manoeuvre on lap 19 to wrest the lead away from the

Frenchman. He completed the hat-trick of win, pole position and fastest lap in Canada to boost the championship challenge to his team-mate and rival Prost.

9. 1988 USA East Grand Prix: Detroit, *63 laps in 1h54m56.635s*
Second: Alain Prost, McLaren Honda, +38.713s
Third: Thierry Boutsen, Benetton Ford, +1 lap
Another win in Detroit for the Brazilian confirmed Senna's street circuit dominance. It was another lights-to-flag victory for him to savour but it was not won without great effort. At the end of the race Senna emerged exhausted from the car in the 34 degree searing heat, from a race in which only seven other cars made it to the finish.

10. 1988 British Grand Prix: Silverstone, *65 laps in 1h33m16.367s*
Second: Nigel Mansell, Williams Judd, +23.344s
Third: Alessandro Nannini, Benetton Ford, +51.214s
Silverstone was not without problems for Senna – torrential rain on one of the fastest tracks of all time, fuel consumption worries, a Ferrari resurgence in form – but he battled through to win the race all the same. It gained McLaren its eighth consecutive victory that season – the first time ever that a team had achieved the feat.

11. 1988 German Grand Prix: Hockenheim, *44 laps in 1h32m54.188s*
Second: Alain Prost, McLaren Honda, +13.609s
Third: Gerhard Berger, Ferrari, +52.095s
Senna took advantage of Prost's lack of confidence in the wet to blast easily into the lead at the start. He was the master in the changeable weather conditions that Hockenheim produced and made the tricky decision of using wet tyres throughout. It paid off. He kept hold of his early lead unchallenged until the chequered flag.

12. 1988 Hungarian Grand Prix: Hungaroring, *76 laps in 1h57m47.381s*
Second: Alain Prost, McLaren Honda, +0.529s
Third: Thierry Boutsen, Benetton Ford, +31.410s
At the Hungarian Grand Prix, Senna produced yet another fantastic performance. He led every lap, with Prost technically taking the lead for just a fraction of a second at the start, but it was one of the closest contests between the McLaren pairing all season. The clash fittingly made the drivers equal leaders of the championship on 66 points.

13. 1988 Belgian Grand Prix: Spa-Francorchamps, *43 laps in 1h28m00.549*
Second: Alain Prost, McLaren Honda, +30.470s
Third: Ivan Capelli, March Judd, +1m15.768s
Spa-Francorchamps was one of Senna's favourite circuits. Although Prost went into first at the start, by the time they surged into Les Combes on the initial lap, Senna had taken a lead that he would not lose. There was celebration for the team when McLaren took the constructor's championship, although it had never really been in doubt.

14. 1988 Japanese Grand Prix: Suzuka, *51 laps in 1h33m26.173s*
Second: Alain Prost, McLaren Honda, +13.363s
Third: Thierry Boutsen, Benetton Ford, +36.109s
Senna took one of his greatest victories and his first world title. When he stalled on the grid it looked as if the championship was over. He
managed to get the car going but found himself 14th. By the end of the first lap he was in eighth, and he progressed through the field to finally take the lead from Ivan Capelli's March Judd on lap 28.

15. 1989 San Marino Grand Prix: Imola, *58 laps in 1h26m51.245s*
Second: Alain Prost, McLaren Honda, +40.225s
Third: Alessandro Nannini, Benetton Ford, +1 lap
Senna's most controversial win. He made an agreement with Prost that whoever was in the lead at the first corner would be unchallenged. Senna was in front and Prost did not overtake. Then Gerhard Berger had a fiery crash and the race was restarted. Prost made the better getaway, but Senna overtook and led until the chequered flag.

16. 1989 Monaco Grand Prix: Monte Carlo, *77 laps in 1h53m33.251s*
Second: Alain Prost, McLaren Honda, +52.529s
Third: Stefano Modena, Brabham Judd, +1 lap
Senna's second Monaco victory was a lights-to-flag affair and he never looked in danger. In fact he hardly seemed to be trying, despite building up almost a minute's lead before the end of the race. He lost first and second gears in the later stages, but kept pushing to the maximum so those behind would not realise he had a problem.

17. 1989 Mexican Grand Prix: Mexico City, *69 laps in 1h35m21.431s*
Second: Riccardo Patrese, Williams +15.560s
Third: Michele Alboreto, Tyrrell Ford, +31.254s

Senna started from pole position and sped away from the pack at the start until a midfield pile-up at the end of lap one meant the race was red-flagged. This made little difference and Senna took the lead again at the second start and led all the way to the flag while the rest of the field shuffled in from behind.

18. 1989 German Grand Prix: Hockenheim, *45 laps in 1h21m43.302s*
Second: Alain Prost, McLaren Honda, +18.151s
Third: Nigel Mansell, Ferrari, +1m23.254s
After a four-race lean period mid-season, Senna was back on winning form at Hockenheim. Admittedly it was a lucky win – Prost led most of the race but in the later stages the Frenchman suffered gearbox problems and Senna flew past with just three laps to go to bring himself back into championship contention.

19. 1989 Belgian Grand Prix: Spa-Francorchamps, *44 laps in 1h40m54.196s*
Second: Alain Prost, McLaren Honda, +1.304s
Third: Nigel Mansell, Ferrari, +1.824s
When the rain came down it seemed inevitable who would emerge as the winner. Senna took the lead at the start and, taking care to avoid aquaplaning, led right until the end. The small gap to second and third places was due to a cautious spell late in the race where he slowed down considerably due to safety concerns.

20. 1989 Spanish Grand Prix: Jerez de la Frontera, *73 laps in 1h48.264s*
Second: Gerhard Berger, Ferrari, +27.051s
Third: Alain Prost, McLaren Honda, +53.788s
This was far from Senna's most exciting victory – certainly not compared to his other win at Jerez in 1986 – but it was a useful and important triumph because it kept his championship challenge alive. The Brazilian was in dominant form – he started from pole, led every lap and clocked the fastest lap by 0.432 seconds along the way.

21. 1990 US Grand Prix: Phoenix, *72 laps in 1h52m32.829s*
Second: Jean Alesi, Tyrrell Ford, +8.685s
Third: Thierry Boutsen, Williams Renault, +54.080s
Unusually Senna was outshone. A young Jean Alesi took the lead at the start and continued until lap 33, when inevitably Senna caught and passed him. But Alesi was having none of it. The Tyrrell driver overtook him again immediately and managed to hold the lead for another two laps. It was the sort of battle Senna enjoyed.

22. 1990 Monaco Grand Prix: Monte Carlo, *78 laps in 1h52m46.982s*
Second: Jean Alesi, Tyrrell Ford, +1.087s
Third: Gerhard Berger, McLaren Honda, +2.073s
By 1990 Senna had started to prove himself invincible at Monte Carlo. Taking pole, the win and the fastest lap he was dominant throughout the weekend. In the race he led every one of the 78 laps. His only loss all weekend was when he took second in the first timed practice session to Alesi, who was once again making his mark.

23. 1990 Canadian Grand Prix: Montreal, *70 laps in 1h42m56.400*
Second: Nelson Piquet, Benetton Ford, +10.497s
Third: Nigel Mansell, Ferrari, +13.385s
The track started off damp, but rather than the rain it was more a series of bizarre incidents that helped Senna to race victory, including a minute's penalty for Gerhard Berger, a groundhog that was run over by Alessandro Nannini's Benetton Ford and a series of collisions. Senna rose above it all to retain a healthy championship lead.

24. 1990 German Grand Prix: Hockenheim, *45 laps in 1h20m47.164s*
Second: Alessandro Nannini, Benetton +6.520s
Third: Gerhard Berger, McLaren Honda, +8.553s
Senna took the lead at the start, but dropped back through the field during pit-stops. When the race order settled down, only Nannini's Benetton lay ahead of the Brazilian, struggling on worn tyres after taking the gamble not to pit. Senna caught and passed the Italian with 12 laps to go and powered on to victory.

25. 1990 Belgian Grand Prix: Spa-Francorchamps, *44 laps in 1h26m31.997s*
Second: Alain Prost, Ferrari, +3.550s
Third: Gerhard Berger, McLaren Honda, +28.462s
The 1990 Belgian Grand Prix was another classic performance from Ayrton Senna in which he took pole position, clocked the fastest lap and led every lap on the way to a totally commanding victory. The win significantly increased his championship chances. This was the 25th race victory of his career and took him above Jackie Stewart's tally.

26. 1990 Italian Grand Prix: Monza, *53 laps in 1h17m57. 878s*
Second: Alain Prost, Ferrari, +6.054s
Third: Gerhard Berger, McLaren Honda, +7.404s

Monza produced yet another race where Senna led every single lap, took pole position and recorded the fastest lap in the race. It had to be started twice as Derek Warwick's Lotus Lamborghini ended up upside down at the Parabolica first time around. But Senna was unperturbed and easily kept his lead on both occasions.

27. 1991 US Grand Prix: Phoenix, *81 laps in 2h00m47.828s*
Second: Alain Prost, Ferrari, +16.322s
Third: Nelson Piquet, Benetton Ford, +17.376s
Senna began his third championship-winning season in style with victory at another American street circuit. He started from pole and led every lap of the race. In winning he became the first driver ever to score 10 points for a victory and made it to the magical tidemark of 27 wins, a total only ever exceeded by five other drivers.

28. 1991 Brazilian Grand Prix: Interlagos, *71 laps in 1h38m28.128s*
Second: Riccardo Patrese, Williams +2.991s
Third: Gerhard Berger, McLaren Honda, +5.416s
After years of trying, Senna finally took his first win at home. He led every lap, despite a number of problems. Towards the end of the race his gearbox started to play up and he had to drive the final laps in sixth gear. Then it began to rain and the conditions were treacherous. He took the flag so exhausted that he had to be helped from the car.

29. 1991 San Marino Grand Prix: Imola, *61 laps in 1h35m14.750s*
Second: Gerhard Berger, McLaren +1.675s
Third: JJ Lehto, Dallara Judd, +1 lap
When the rain poured down shortly before the start at Imola, it seemed inevitable that Senna would emerge the victor. He did not have it all his own way, however. Although the Brazilian started from pole, Riccardo Patrese had the better start and led the first nine laps for Williams Renault before a misfire put paid to his chances.

30. 1991 Monaco Grand Prix: Monte Carlo, *78 laps in 1h53m02.234s*
Second: Nigel Mansell, Williams +18.348s
Third: Jean Alesi, Ferrari, +47.455s
Senna was back at his best track to make it four wins from the first four races of the 1991 season. He put in another seemingly effortless

performance: grabbing pole position, taking the lead at the start and building up the gap to the rest of the field to take the race. It was his 30th overall career victory and his fourth in Monte Carlo.

31. 1991 Hungarian Grand Prix: Hungaroring, *77 laps in 1h49m12.796s*
Second: Nigel Mansell, Williams Renault, +4.599s
Third: Riccardo Patrese, Williams, +15.594s
After his early dominance, Senna was back on form at the Hungarian Grand Prix. The records state that he led all 77 laps, but this does not show how tough a battle he faced against the Williams Renaults. Patrese harried him early on and in the closing stages let Mansell through, who hassled him all the way to the end.

32. 1991 Belgian Grand Prix: Spa-Francorchamps, *44 laps in 1h27m17.669s*
Second: Gerhard Berger, McLaren +1.901s
Third: Nelson Piquet, Benetton Ford, +32.176s
It was a magnificent fifth victory for Senna in Spa-Francorchamps, although it was far from easy. He led until the first round of pitstops, when Nigel Mansell and Jean Alesi got ahead of him. Both their cars suffered later and Senna went back into the lead. Despite problems with his gearbox, he found some gears and kept going.

33. 1991 Australian Grand Prix: Adelaide, *14 laps in 24m34.899s*
Second: Nigel Mansell, Williams Renault, +1.259s
Third: Gerhard Berger, McLaren Honda, +5.120s
It began to rain before the race and the start was delayed. When the cars eventually did get off it was predictably chaotic and six cars had crashed by lap eight. Two marshals were injured and following gestures from Senna and other drivers concerned for safety, the race was stopped after only 14 laps and half points were awarded.

34. 1992 Monaco Grand Prix: Monte Carlo, *78 laps in 1h50m59.372s*
Second: Nigel Mansell, Williams Renault, +0.215s
Third: Riccardo Patrese, Williams +31.843s
Nigel Mansell, in the all-conquering Adrian Newey-designed FW14B, had won the first five races of the season. It seemed as if Monaco would be his, then with eight laps to go he was forced to pit with a loose wheelnut. He emerged behind Senna, and despite running close the Brazilian somehow held him off to the end of the race.

35. 1992 Hungarian Grand Prix: Hungaroring, 77 *laps in 1h46m19.216s*
Second: Nigel Mansell, Williams +40.139s
Third: Gerhard Berger, McLaren Honda +50.782s
The Hungaroring produced a chaotic race that saw the placings chop and change right until the final stages. Senna leapt into second at the start but found himself harried by Mansell. Mansell dropped away and when Riccardo Patrese in the other Williams spun off, Senna inherited the lead and collected yet another victory.

36. 1992 Italian Grand Prix: Monza, 53 *laps in 1h18m15.349s*
Second: Martin Brundle, Benetton Ford +17.050s
Third: Michael Schumacher, Benetton +24.373s
A surprise 1992 win for Senna at one of the faster circuits on the calendar. He led just six of the laps and was never a match for the Williams Renaults of Nigel Mansell and Riccardo Patrese in terms of speed. However, a double hydraulic failure for the Williams pairing meant he snatched the lead in the closing stages and went on to victory.

37. 1993 Brazilian Grand Prix: Interlagos, 71 *laps in 1h51m15.485s*
Second: Damon Hill, Williams Renault +16.625s
Third: Michael Schumacher, Benetton +45.436s
This race did not start well. He got off in second, was overtaken by Damon Hill and then received a 10-second penalty for overtaking under a yellow flag. He emerged from the pits in fourth just as a storm brewed up. Senna took the lead in the confusion that ensued as the cars switched to wets and then back to slicks again as the track dried.

38. 1993 European Grand Prix: Donington Park, 76 *laps in 1h50m46.570s*
Second: Damon Hill, Williams +1m23.199s
Third: Alain Prost, Williams Renault +1 lap
Senna's greatest victory. He suffered a poor start and was in fifth as the cars moved off the sodden grid, struggling to hold on to even that place. But by the end of the first lap he had overtaken the four cars in front, no lesser drivers than Michael Schumacher, Karl Wendlinger, Alain Prost and Damon Hill. The rest of the race was irrelevant.

39. 1993 Monaco Grand Prix: Monte Carlo, 78 *laps in 1h52m10.947*
Second: Damon Hill, Williams Renault +52.118s
Third: Jean Alesi, Ferrari, +1m03.362s

THE LIFE OF SENNA

Senna had crashed heavily in Thursday qualifying and was suffering from a sore thumb. He managed to race and gained places not from star driving but from Alain Prost stalling during a penalty stop and Michael Schumacher suffering hydraulic failure. It was his record sixth Monaco crown and his fifth in a row.

40. 1993 Japanese Grand Prix: Suzuka; *53 laps in 1h40m27.912s*
Second: Alain Prost, Williams Renault, +11.435s
Third: Mika Häkkinen, McLaren Ford, +26.129s
Suzuka saw a race-long challenge between Senna and Prost, first one and then the other taking the upper hand. However, the occasion was more famous for the Brazilian punching Eddie Irvine for getting in his way than the victory. It was the 103rd win for his McLaren team, which took it equal with Ferrari at the top of the all-time tally.

41. 1993 Australian Grand Prix: Adelaide; *79 laps in 1h43m27.476s*
Second: Alain Prost, Williams Renault, +9.259s
Third: Damon Hill, Williams Renault, +33.902s
Senna led for the full distance, barring pitstops, on what was an emotional occasion. It was old rival Alain Prost's last race before retirement and it was a touching moment when they met on the podium for the last time. Few would have guessed that the race would also mark Senna's final victory and that he would be dead three races later.

Ayrton Senna's nearly wins
As memorable as some of the victories are the races that Ayrton Senna should have won. He could have taken his first ever Formula One victory for Toleman Hart at Monte Carlo back in 1984. He was catching race leader Alain Prost at an unbelievable speed but the race was stopped on lap 31 due to heavy rain. In 1988 two silly accidents lost him races in McLaren's best ever year. After receiving a pit signal to slow down, he crashed into the barriers at Monte Carlo from a huge lead in the later stages of the race. Then at Monza he collided with backmarker Jean Louis Schlesser's Williams with just two laps to go. At Suzuka, in 1989, he fought hard to take back the lead from Alessandro Nannini after controversially crashing with Alain Prost at the chicane but was excluded after the chequered flag for 'dangerous driving'. On that occasion the loss of the race cost him his championship chances.

1985 to 1994 Formula One Pole Positions by Season

Ayrton Senna scored 65 pole positions from 162 attempts to start a race.(He failed to qual-
ify once in 1984). No one has ever come close to exceeding this record and it reflected his
ability to drive race cars fast on the limit continualy. Michael Schumacher is the nearest
with 37 poles and there is some doubt whether he will ever beat Senna's record.

1985 Lotus Renault 7 poles

At the first Grand Prix of the season, Ayrton Senna's home race in Brazil, his talented team-mate Elio de Angelis out-qualified him by 0.308secs. Senna put his
Lotus on pole in the next three races. His seven-pole tally was remarkable, the
stuff usually expected from serious championship challengers rather than
drivers in a good car in only their second year. His top spots at Monte Carlo and
Detroit illustrated his street circuit mastery.

1986 Lotus Renault 8 poles

Johnny Dumfries was never intended to be in the same class as Senna, but ended
up a huge average of 11.5 grid positions behind him throughout the season, his
best attempt a 10th place to Senna's third at his home race at Brands Hatch. The
same circuits brought success, Imola and Detroit in particular.

1987 Lotus Honda 1 pole

Only one pole for Senna in a lean year for Lotus that saw the Brazilian win only
two races. Against his Japanese team-mate Satoru Nakajima he was on a different
level. His single pole was his worst tally for the next four seasons.

1988 McLaren Honda 13 poles

The year of the McLaren MP4/4 that took 15 wins out of a total of 16 – and 15
poles, Senna taking a record 13 of them. Even Alain Prost could not fare much
better in qualifying than the Brazilian's other team-mates, out-qualifying him
twice only, once at his home Grand Prix in France. He was an average of
0.583secs behind across the season.

1989 McLaren Honda 13 poles

The 1989 season was almost a complete re-run of 1988 for Senna in qualifying terms. He took 13 poles, usually from team-mate Prost, who again only out-qualified him twice. In conjunction with his 1988 pole tally he notched up a record of eight poles in a row that still stands today.

1990 McLaren Honda 10 poles

Senna had performed so well in the previous two years that his 10 poles in this season must have seemed almost disappointing. Gerhard Berger became Senna's new team-mate at McLaren and managed a better job than Prost had in qualifying, although not in the actual race. However, he still only outpaced the Brazilian four times.

1991 McLaren Honda 8 poles

Taking half the season's poles was below par for Senna in the year that saw him take his third world championship title. Despite taking the first four poles of the season to give him seven in succession, the growing speed of the Williams Renault unsettled his mid-season charge. Three margins back to second of over a second was an impressive tally.

1992 McLaren Honda 1 pole

Only a single pole for Senna in a year that saw even him struggle against the mighty Williams Renault FW14Bs. His record against team-mate Berger improved to the stage where the Austrian could only manage to out-qualify the Brazilian once, surprisingly in the second race of the season in Mexico, a track where Senna had always been on form.

1993 McLaren Ford 1 pole

Once again faced with a magnificent display by Williams, Senna had very little chance to shine. His sole pole came right at the end of the season. After Michael Andretti was dropped from McLaren, having been further off Senna's pace than his other team-mates had been, he was replaced by the young Mika Häkkinen, who promptly out-qualified Senna in their first race together at Estoril. Senna was rattled and maybe this new challenge was what drove him to pole two races later.

1994 Williams Renault 3 poles

Ayrton Senna only competed in three races in his final year, but he scored pole in each comfortably from Michael Schumacher in a Benetton Ford. Had he lived he may have been able to draw near his previous best total of 13, as his trouncing of the other major pole contenders, Schumacher and Senna's team-mate Damon Hill, indicates.

1985 to 1994
65 Formula One Pole Positions

Ayrton Senna is the all times master of the pole position and his record of 65 poles will probably never be beaten. He had that unique ability that no diver had or had since to drive the one of perfect lap. Often he was on pole by huge margins.

1. 1985 Portuguese Grand Prix; Estoril　　　　　　　**Gap: 0.413s**
In the wet Friday session Senna was fastest with 1m 21.708s, almost matching Nelson Piquet's 1984 record. In the dry on Saturday he clocked a time of 1m 21.007s. His Friday time was beaten on Saturday only by the McLaren of Prost.

2. 1985 San Marino Grand Prix; Imola　　　　　　　**Gap: 0.027s**
Senna's first pole at a circuit where he would clock up a record eight was taken by the narrowest of all his margins from the Williams Honda of Keke Rosberg. He was to make Imola his own over the next 10 years.

3. 1985 Monaco Grand Prix; Monte Carlo　　　　　　　**Gap: 0.086s**
Senna's first pole of five at the street circuit that he would become synonymous with. He qualified over a second ahead of his illustrious team-mate Elio de Angelis in ninth, in only his second season of racing.

4. 1985 USA Detroit Grand Prix; Detroit　　　　　　　**Gap: 1.198s**
Senna took pole by over a second from Nigel Mansell's Williams, which was impressive in itself, but the gap back to Michele Alboreto's Ferrari in third was 1.697s and to Alain Prost's McLaren in fourth a stunning 2.037s.

5. 1985 Italian Grand Prix; Monza　　　　　　　**Gap: 0.146s**
A big disappointment for the tifosi as Senna was 1.384s and 2.389s faster than the Ferraris of Michele Alboreto and Stefan Johansson respectively. Senna specialised in rubbing Ferrari's nose in it in Italy particularly.

6. 1985 European Grand Prix; Brands Hatch　　　　　　　**Gap: 0.313s**
A lap that impressed many of the Formula One fraternity with its maturity and

style. Only Nelson Piquet's Brabham BMW and Nigel Mansell's Williams were within a second of the Brazilian. His team-mate Elio de Angelis was left 2.845s behind in ninth.

7. 1985 Australian Grand Prix; Adelaide Gap: 0.694s

The seven-10ths gap to Nigel Mansell's Williams in second was large but paled into insignificance compared to the margin between Senna and the rest of the field – Mansell's team-mate Keke Rosberg in third was 2.044s behind.

8. 1986 Brazilian Grand Prix; Jacarepagua Gap: 0.765s

Senna's determination to beat his compatriot Nelson Piquet at their home race saw him emerge exhausted from the cockpit after setting his fastest lap in the closing minutes of qualifying. Predictably he stuffed Piquet.

9. 1986 Spanish Grand Prix; Jerez de la Frontera Gap: 0.826s

An impressive gap over second placed compatriot Nelson Piquet's Williams Honda at a usually close circuit with a short lap-time. Senna's pole time was 1m 21.605s in a season where the Williams Honda was clearly the fastest car.

10. 1986 San Marino Grand Prix; Imola Gap: 0.519s

Senna makes it three out of three for the first trio of races of the 1986 season. It was impressively his fourth pole in a row, overlapping from 1985. Made even more extraordinary by the fact that the Williams Honda was easily the best car.

11. 1986 USA Detroit Grand Prix; Detroit Gap: 0.538s

Senna dominated the American street circuit as usual. He shone in qualifying and then topped his performance off with a win. He was particularly dominant at the tight tricky street circuits where driving skill was at a premium.

12. 1986 French Grand Prix; Paul Ricard Gap: 0.229s

Senna took pole from the Williams Honda of Nigel Mansell with a car that was far off the pace. He struggled in the latter half of the season as Lotus concentrated all development on making the new Honda car ready for 1987.

13. 1986 Hungarian Grand Prix; Hungaroring Gap: 0.335s

Senna took pole from Nelson Piquet's Williams Honda in his Lotus 98T with the Renault engine despite the lack of grip he continually complained of to his Lotus mechanics – who struggled to solve problems that Senna simply drove around.

14. 1986 Portuguese Grand Prix; Estoril   **Gap: 0.816s**
An impressive lap at one of Senna's best circuits, with only Nigel Mansell's
Williams staying within a second of the Brazilian. Despite the short lap time, 20
of the 27-strong grid could not get within two-and-a-half seconds of pole.

15. 1986 Mexican Grand Prix; Mexico City   **Gap: 0.289s**
A good pole in which Ayrton Senna put his Lotus Renault 98T 1.431s between
himself and the sixth-placed man, eventual champion Alain Prost in his TAG
McLaren. Only the car stopped Senna winning the 1986 world championship.

16. 1987 San Marino Grand Prix; Imola   **Gap: 0.120s**
Senna's only pole of the year, at the track where he later scored a record eight.
Only Nigel Mansell's Williams Honda and Alain Prost's McLaren were within a
second of Senna. The active suspension Lotus Honda 99T was hopeless in qualifying.

17. 1988 Brazilian Grand Prix; Jacarepagua   **Gap: 0.536s**
Pole for Senna at his home race and the beginning of a six-race run. Only five
cars were within two seconds of his time but this became completely irrelevant
when he was forced to start from the pitlane after trouble selecting gears.

18. 1988 San Marino Grand Prix; Imola   **Gap: 0.771s**
The gap of 0.771s to team-mate Alain Prost in second was impressive, but the gap
of 3.352s to Nelson Piquet's Lotus Honda in third was amazing. It was a true testament to the combined skills of Senna and McLaren Honda.

19. 1988 Monaco Grand Prix; Monte Carlo   **Gap: 1.427s**
Considered by many to be the greatest qualifying lap of all time. Senna was in a
trance-like situation on his fastest lap, driving his car round the narrow streets on
another plane. No one came remotely close to him that weekend.

20. 1988 Mexican Grand Prix; Mexico City   **Gap: 0.629s**
A modest time gap to the next best by Senna's 1988 standards but substantial by
anybody else's. Team-mate Alain Prost was never any threat in second. The
McLaren Honda MP4 car was the class of the field that year.

21. 1988 Canadian Grand Prix; Montreal   **Gap: 0.182s**
Alain Prost gave Senna a run for his money at the Montreal track where he was

THE LIFE OF SENNA

usually the star. The Frenchman still could not wrestle away pole from his team-mate driving an identical car, the McLaren Honda MP4/4 which took 15 poles from 16 races.

22. 1988 USA Detroit Grand Prix; Detroit   Gap: 0.858s
A magnificent performacne on a rough track that suited the Ferraris rather than the McLarens. Senna's sixth pole in a row equalled the record set by Stirling Moss in 1959-60 and Niki Lauda in 1974. He couldn't quite get the record.

23. 1988 German Grand Prix; Hockenheim   Gap: 0.277s
After losing out twice in a row to Alain Prost and Gerhard Berger's Ferrari, Senna was back in form at Hockenheim setting his fastest lap on Friday, before the weekend's share of rain nullified the last qualifying session.

24. 1988 Hungarian Grand Prix; Hungaroring   Gap: 0.108s
A rougher than usual qualifying session for the McLarens. Senna just managed to edge pole from Nigel Mansell's Williams but Alain Prost could only manage seventh spot on the grid in his identical McLaren Honda MP4/4.

25. 1988 Belgian Grand Prix; Spa-Francorchamps   Gap: 0.410s
Times were set in the dry Friday session. Senna believed he could have gone quicker after Gabrielle Tarquini's Coloni Ford crashed impairing his fast lap. Then he didn't get a quick run on the rainy Saturday but he was still miles ahead.

26. 1988 Italian Grand Prix; Monza   Gap: 0.303s
Senna complained of traffic but still took pole from Alain Prost. It was his 10th pole of the season, beating the record of nine set by Ronnie Peterson in 1973, Niki Lauda in 1974 and 1975, and Nelson Piquet in 1984.

27. 1988 Spanish Grand Prix; Jerez de la Frontera   Gap: 0.067s
Senna snatched pole away from Alain Prost by the smallest margin of the year at this circuit famous for its tight finishes at a very difficult track to lap well. The circuit has very short straights where the Honda engine could not stretch itself.

28. 1988 Japanese Grand Prix; Suzuka   Gap: 0.324s
Senna took pole only to discover that the grid layout gave an advantage to the second-placed man, Alain Prost, something that was to rankle with him for years to come. Third-placed Gerhard Berger's Ferrari was 1.5s behind.

29. 1988 Australian Grand Prix; Adelaide   Gap: 0.132s

Senna once again pipped Alain Prost at the last minute, taking his 13th pole of the season. Nobody else was within a second-and-a-half of the brilliant Brazilian on the challenging and demanding street circuit where he excelled as usual.

30. 1989 Brazilian Grand Prix; Jacarepagua   Gap: 0.870s

Senna once again showed a considerable pace at his home event and never looked to be in any danger of losing pole position. His second fastest time would have also blown the field away, by 0.602s. It was staggering.

31 1989 San Marino Grand Prix; Imola   Gap: 0.225s

Senna's fifth consecutive pole in San Marino broke the record of four consecutive poles at a single circuit set by Juan Manuel Fangio at Monte Carlo. Apart from Prost only Mansell's Ferrari and Patrese's Williams Renault were within two seconds.

32. 1989 Monaco Grand Prix; Monte Carlo   Gap: 1.148s

Senna was once again devastating, with over a second back to Prost and 2.024s to Thierry Boutsen's Williams in third. Some thought the timing system had a glitch. Senna was a staggering 1.690s faster than his 1988 time.

33. 1989 Mexican Grand Prix; Mexico City   Gap: 0.897s

A substantial gap to team-mate Alain Prost in second meant that no one on the grid, close as they were to each other, could come near Senna's time. His normally aspirated McLaren Honda MP4/5 was far faster than the turbo of the previous year.

34. 1989 USA Grand Prix; Phoenix   Gap: 1.409s

Senna's record eighth pole in a row, a tally that Michael Schumacher came close to but could not surpass earlier this year. It was also Senna's 34th pole, taking him past Jim Clark's record 33. On the Arizona street circuit no one else stood a chance.

35. 1989 British Grand Prix; Silverstone   Gap: 0.167s

Despite gearbox trouble Senna still took pole from team-mate Alain Prost, for what was his only time on top at Silverstone. He was generally succesful on all types of circuit but Silverstone remained a qualifying enigma to him.

36. 1989 German Grand Prix; Hockenheim   **Gap: 1.006s**
On the last corner of his pole lap, Ayrton Senna ran over a kerb and ruptured one of the McLaren Honda's radiators. But his time was still over a second better than team-mate Alain Prost's closest grab in his identical car.

37. 1989 Belgian Grand Prix; Spa-Francorchamps   **Gap: 0.596s**
Senna's gap to Alain Prost in second was a small one for a long circuit, in an over two minute lap. Spa remains the most challenging fast circuit in the beautiful Ardennes region famous for sweeping corners. And Prost always excelled there.

38. 1989 Italian Grand Prix; Monza   **Gap: 1.014s**
A second's gap on this fast circuit and relatively short lap time to Gerhard Berger's Ferrari was a sensational performance. Only the top six were within three seconds of him and he was over three seconds better than his pole time in 1988.

39. 1989 Portuguese Grand Prix; Estoril   **Gap: 0.591s**
Senna managed to beat Gerhard Berger's Ferrari by over half a second, putting up a challenge to the rapidly improving Ferraris that the McLaren Honda MP4/5 of Alain Prost was unable to muster in an identical car and engine.

40. 1989 Spanish Grand Prix; Jerez de la Frontera   **Gap: 0.274s**
A smaller than usual gap to Gerhard Berger's Ferrari in second, but the 1.077s to Alain Prost in the other McLaren Honda in third was a true sign of Senna's qualifying strength in an absolutely identical car.

41. 1989 Japanese Grand Prix; Suzuka   **Gap: 1.730s**
Statistically Senna's best pole ever. The gap of 1.730s to Alain Prost remains the fifth largest gap of three decimal places and the biggest percentage he recorded back to second. But not compensation for starting on the dirty side of the track.

42. 1989 Australian Grand Prix; Adelaide   **Gap: 0.738s**
Senna convincingly out-qualified Prost, despite complaining that his now bitter enemy had blocked him on his fast lap. It was the last head-to-head between the two great drivers in identical equipment. The score was 26-4 in poles.

43. 1990 Brazilian Grand Prix; Interlagos   **Gap: 0.611s**
The first ever Grand Prix in Senna's home city of São Paulo. Coming off the back of an opening round qualifying defeat – to new team-mate Gerhard Berger

– no one offered him any real resistance when he put in a stunning lap in the dying minutes.

44. 1990 San Marino Grand Prix; Imola   Gap: 0.561s

The 44th pole for Senna at Imola. Only Gerhard Berger was within a second of his Brazilian team-mate. Senna was to absolutely dominate pole position at Imola for many years until he lost his life there on 1st May 1994 – from pole.

45. 1990 Monaco Grand Prix; Monte Carlo   Gap: 0.462s

Still streets ahead of the rest, but it was even better than it looked as Senna's really fast lap was ruined by Gregor Foitek's Onyx Ford blocking his path at the Nouvelle Chicane. It was his fourth pole at Monte Carlo out of seven starts.

46. 1990 Canadian Grand Prix; Montreal   Gap: 0.066s

Breathtakingly close, but still a Senna triumph over new team-mate Gerhard Berger in the new McLaren Honda MP4/6. Berger was fresh to McLaren and had yet to see the true brilliance of his new partner. That was to come.

47. 1990 German Grand Prix; Hockenheim   Gap: 0.236s

Although Gerhard Berger in second managed to stay reasonably close to Senna's time, the third-placed Ferrari of Alain Prost was a second-and-a-half behind. It ended a dry spell of three missed poles, his longest since 1987.

48. 1990 Belgian Grand Prix; Spa-Francorchamps   Gap: 0.583s

Senna was untouchable again at the Belgian track by half a second from team-mate Gerhard Berger on a grid that was close for such a long circuit with a plus two minute lap time. Berger was in a similar position to Prost the year before.

49. 1990 Italian Grand Prix; Monza   Gap: 0.402s

After a lot of problems Senna didn't get a proper run on Saturday until the very last minutes when he snatched pole from the grasp of rival, and local Ferrari favourite, Alain Prost. It fuelled and continued the feud begun the year before.

50. 1990 Spanish Grand Prix; Jerez de la Frontera   Gap: 0.437s

Martin Donnelly crashed his Lotus Lamborghini heavily into a barrier and Senna rushed to the scene where Donnelly lay close to death in the middle of the track. The next day, he went over a second faster than he had before for his 50th pole.

51. 1990 Japanese Grand Prix; Suzuka   **Gap: 0.232s**
Another hard-fought Suzuka pole for Senna and still the same old problems of finding that pole was still on the dirty side of the track. His race didn't last long as he
won the 1990 championship by running Prost off the road at the very first corner.

52. 1990 Australian Grand Prix; Adelaide   **Gap: 0.573s**
With the world championship won Senna once again excelled around the
Adelaide Park circuit, taking pole from team-mate Gerhard Berger by over half a
second. He retired from the race but by then it didn't matter.

53. 1991 USA Grand Prix; Phoenix   **Gap: 1.121s**
A stunning street circuit pole from Alain Prost's Ferrari got Senna's year off to a
flier. The new McLaren Honda MP4/5B car had been finished very late and
Senna had taken three months off over the winter and done little testing.

54. 1991 Brazilian Grand Prix; Interlagos   **Gap: 0.383s**
Senna himself described this as an 'incredible lap'. Only the Williams Renaults of
Riccardo Patrese and Nigel Mansell were within a second of the Brazilian and
they were the class of the field. This was a driver wringing the best from a car
that wasn't.

55. 1991 San Marino Grand Prix; Imola   **Gap: 0.080s**
Senna's seventh consecutive pole at the Italian circuit which set an all-time
record. The gap back to Riccardo Patrese's Williams Renault is testament more to
the Italian hero's desire to do well at his home track than any fault of Senna's.

56. 1991 Monaco Grand Prix; Monte Carlo   **Gap: 0.465s**
Senna's fifth and final Monaco pole position, beating a surprising contender in
the guise of Tyrrell Honda's young rising star Stefano Modena. He went on to
win the race after Nigel Mansell's dominant Williams Renault had a puncture.

57. 1991 Hungarian Grand Prix; Hungaroring   **Gap: 1.232s**
After a lean mid-season, Senna returned to the top spot in style, with well over a
second to the second quickest Williams of Riccardo Patrese. Only the other
Williams of Nigel Mansell was within two seconds of the brillliant Brazilian.

58. 1991 Belgian Grand Prix; Spa-Francorchamps   **Gap: 1.010s**
Another pole-grabbing margin of over a second for Senna at a circuit he loved. Second

spot went to old rival Alain Prost in a Ferrari with the Williams Renaults of Nigel
Mansell and Riccardo Patrese well off the pace. Senna won the race from both.

59. 1991 Italian Grand Prix; Monza   Gap: 0.133s
There was only a narrow margin over the Williams of Nigel Mansell as the
competition from the Renault engined team grew stronger and stronger. Senna
was then in no doubt that he was in the second best car on the grid.

60. 1991 Australian Grand Prix; Adelaide   Gap: 0.344s
Senna's 60th pole position, taken over his McLaren team-mate Gerhard Berger by
only 0.344s at one of his most competitive circuits. After two years as team-mate
Gerhard Berger had pushed Senna closer than Alain Prost.

61. 1991 Canadian Grand Prix; Montreal   Gap: 0.097s
Senna's only pole of 1992. An inspired performance as he knocked Nigel Mansell
off pole for the first time that year. The Williams Renaults were vastly superior to
Senna's Honda engined McLaren MP4/7. No other team took a pole.

62. 1993 Australian Grand Prix; Adelaide   Gap: 0.436s
Senna's sixth pole at the Australian track, a tally beaten only by his eight at Imola.
Yet again it was the only pole of the season not to go to the Williams Renaults of
Alain Prost and Damon Hill. He broke a run of 24 consecutive top spots for that
team.

63. 1994 Brazilian Grand Prix; Interlagos   Gap: 0.328s
A final home pole for Senna and his first for Williams Renault. The gap of three-
10ths to Michael Schumacher in second was not as revealing about the quality of
Senna's performance as the gap of 1.423s back to Jean Alesi's Ferrari in third.

64. 1994 Pacific Grand Prix; Aida   Gap: 0.222s
Senna took pole without much of a challenge when Michael Schumacher failed
to emerge for the Saturday session in an effort to conserve his tyres. The Williams
Renault FW16 was recognised as a difficult car saved by Senna's brilliance.

65. 1994 San Marino Grand Prix; Imola   Gap: 0.337s
Senna's final pole position at the circuit where he scored an amazing record of eight.
Despite not running on Saturday due to Roland Ratzenberger's fatal accident, his
exceptional Friday time remained unbeaten to take pole for the very last time.

Formula One Career Statistics

Ayrton Senna sits at the top of many of the tables of Formula One records although, as the years go by, Michael Schumacher is seizing many of the records he set. Had he lived and driven a normal career there is no doubt he would have broken every record that there is such was his dominance. Perhaps his greatest achievement was to lead no less than one third of all the laps he competed.

Grands Prix entered	162
Grand prix's Started	161
Not Qualified	1
Wins	41
Pole Positions	65
Podiums	80
Fastest Laps	19
Points	614
Laps	8,219
Miles driven	23,575.18
Grand Prix's led	86
Laps led	2,986
Miles led	8,395.48

Top 20 Pole Scorers of all Time

Ayrton Senna really excelled at winning pole position. As at the Japanese Grand Prix in 2003, Michael Schumacher still needed 11 poles to take his record. As he has managed to score an average of four a season he will probably just manage to beat Senna's record in the years of driving in Formula One he has left.

1	**Ayrton Senna**	**65**
2	Michael Schumacher	55★
3	Jim Clark	33
4	Alain Prost	33
5	Nigel Mansell	32
6	Juan Manuel Fangio	29
7	Mika Häkkinen	26
8	Niki Lauda	24
=	Nelson Piquet	24
10	Damon Hill	20
11	Mario Andretti	18
=	Rene Arnoux	18
13	Jackie Stewart	17
14	Stirling Moss	16
15	Alberto Ascari	14
=	Ronnie Peterson	14
=	James Hunt	14
18	Jack Brabham	13
=	Graham Hill	13
=	Jacky Ickx	13
=	Jacques Villeneuve	13

★ *As of 2003 Japanese Grand Prix*

Top 20 Race Winners of all Time

Ayrton Senna may have scored 65 poles but he only managed to convert them into 41 race wins a poor score by his achievements. Alain Prost, not a great qualifier was clearly his better at race craft. But if Senna had lived he would have made his score seem irrelevant and even Michael Schumacher would not have got near him.

1	Michael Schumacher	70★
2	Alain Prost	51
3	**Ayrton Senna**	**41**
4	Nigel Mansell	31
5	Jackie Stewart	27
6	Jim Clark	25
=	Niki Lauda	25
8	Juan Manuel Fangio	24
9	Nelson Piquet	23
10	Damon Hill	22
11	Mika Häkkinen	20
12	Stirling Moss	16
13	Jack Brabham	14
=	Graham Hill	14
=	Emerson Fittipaldi	14
16	Alberto Ascari	13
17	Mario Andretti	12
=	Carlos Reutemann	12
=	Alan Jones	12
20	David Coulthard	13★
=	Jacques Villeneuve	11★

★ *Up to and including the 2003 Japanese Grand Prix*

Top 20 Point Scorers of All Time

Ayrton Senna's outright lack of race wins against the performances of Michael Schumacher and Alain Prost reflect the fact that he only holds third place in the all time points scorers tables. And he was never a man who settled for second or third. It was always win or bust with him and this affected his final points tally.

1	Michael Schumacher	1,038*
2	Alain Prost	798.5
3	**Ayrton Senna**	**614**
4	Nelson Piquet	485.5
5	Nigel Mansell	482
6	David Coulthard	451*
7	Niki Lauda	420.5
8	Mika Häkkinen	420
9	Gerhard Berger	385
10	Jackie Stewart	360
=	Damon Hill	360
12	Carlos Reutemann	310
13	Graham Hill	289
14	Emerson Fittipaldi	281
=	Riccardo Patrese	281
16	Juan Manuel Fangio	277.64
17	Jim Clark	274
18	Jack Brabham	261
19	Jody Scheckter	255
20	Denny Hulme	248

* Up to an including the 2003 Japanese Grand Prix

Top 20 All Time Races Led

Ayrton Senna has only recently been taken over by Michael Schumacher in the all time races led table. But Senna's astonishing record of leading a third of the laps he raced is an outstanding one. Had Senna lived, Michael Schumacher would never have got close.

1	Michael Schumacher	110★
2	**Ayrton Senna**	**86**
3	Alain Prost	84
4	David Coulthard	58★
=	Nelson Piquet	58
6	Nigel Mansell	55
7	Jackie Stewart	51
8	Damon Hill	45
=	Mika Häkkinen	45
10	Jim Clark	43
11	Niki Lauda	41
12	Juan Manuel Fangio	39
13	Stirling Moss	32
=	Graham Hill	32
=	Gerhard Berger	32
16	Riccardo Patrese	29
17	Jack Brabham	28
18	Ronnie Peterson	27
19	Rene Arnoux	25
20	Alan Jones	24

★ *Up to an including the 2003 Brazilian Grand Prix*

Senna's Formula One Cars 1984 to 1994

Ayrton Senna drove 11 different types of car in his Formula One career stretching over 10 seasons. He also tested a Williams, a Brabham and McLaren in 1983. He only failed to win in a Toleman, a Brabham and a Williams.. His most success was in a McLaren with 35 win and six in a Lotus.

Toleman TG183B

Engine:	Hart 415T, 1.5 litre, 4 cylinder turbo
Tyres:	Pirelli
Principal designer:	Rory Byrne
Chassis:	Carbon-fibre monocoque
Gearbox:	Hewland FGB (5 speed)
Fuel:	Agip
Wheelbase:	2692mm
Track:	Front: 1848mm
	Rear: 1683mm
Dry weight:	540kg
Raced:	1984 (4 races)

Toleman TG184

Engine:	Hart 415T, 1.5 litre, 4 cylinder turbo
Tyres:	Michelin
Principal designers:	Rory Byrne, John Gentry
Chassis:	Carbon-fibre monocoque
Gearbox:	Hewland (5 speed)
Fuel:	Agip
Wheelbase:	2800mm
Track:	Front: 1765mm
	Rear: 1676mm
Dry weight:	540kg
Raced:	1984 (11 races)

Lotus 97T

Engine:	Renault EF4B (EF 15), 1.5 litre, V6 turbo
Tyres:	Goodyear
Principal designer:	Gerard Ducarouge
Chassis:	Kevlar carbon-fibre monocoque
Gearbox:	Lotus-Hewland (5 speed)
Fuel:	Elf
Wheelbase:	2720mm
Track:	Front: 1816mm
	Rear: 1620mm
Dry weight:	540kg
Raced:	1985

Lotus 98T

Engine:	Renault EF4B (EF 15), 1.5 litre, V6 turbo
Tyres:	Goodyear
Principal designer:	Gerard Ducarouge
Chassis:	Kevlar carbon-fibre monocoque
Gearbox:	Lotus-Hewland (5 speed)
Fuel:	Elf
Wheelbase:	2600mm
Track:	Front: 1816mm
	Rear: 1620mm
Dry weight:	540kg
Raced:	1986

Lotus 99T

Engine:	Honda RA167E, 1.5 litre, V6 turbo
Tyres:	Goodyear
Principal designer:	Gerard Ducarouge
Chassis:	Carbon-fibre monocoque
Gearbox:	Lotus (6 speed)
Fuel:	Elf
Wheelbase:	2720mm
Track:	Front: 1800mm
	Rear: 1650mm
Dry weight:	540kg
Raced:	1987

McLaren MP4/4

Engine:	Honda RA168E, 1.5 litre, V6 turbo
Tyres:	Goodyear
Principal designers:	Gordon Murray, Steve Nichols
Chassis:	Carbon-fibre monocoque
Gearbox:	McLaren/Weismann (6 speed)
Fuel:	Shell
Wheelbase:	2875mm
Track:	Front: 1824mm
	Rear: 1670mm
Dry weight:	540kg
Raced:	1988

McLaren MP4/5

Engine:	Honda RA109E, 3.5 litre, 72° V10
Tyres:	Goodyear
Principal designers:	Gordon Murray, Steve Nichols, Neil Oatley
Chassis:	Carbon-fibre monocoque
Gearbox:	McLaren (6 speed, transverse)
Fuel:	Shell
Wheelbase:	2896mm
Track:	Front: 1820mm
	Rear: 1670mm
Dry weight:	500kg
Raced:	1989

McLaren MP4/5B

Engine:	Honda RA100E, 3.5 litre, 72° V10
Tyres:	Goodyear
Principal designers:	Neil Oatley, Tim Wright, Gordon Kimball
Chassis:	Carbon-fibre monocoque
Gearbox:	McLaren (6 speed)
Fuel:	Shell
Wheelbase:	2940mm
Track:	Front: 1820mm
	Rear: 1670mm
Dry weight:	505kg
Raced:	1990

McLaren MP4/6

Engine:	Honda RA121E, 3.5litre, 60° V12
Tyres:	Goodyear
Principal designers:	Neil Oatley, Henri Durand
Chassis:	Carbon-fibre monocoque
Gearbox:	McLaren (6 speed, transverse)
Fuel:	Shell
Wheelbase:	2832mm
Track:	Front: 1824mm
	Rear: 1670mm
Dry weight:	505kg
Raced:	1991

McLaren MP4/7A

Engine:	Honda RA 122E/B, 3.5 litre, 75° V12
Tyres:	Goodyear
Principal designers:	Neil Oatley, Henri Durand
Chassis:	Carbon-fibre monocoque
Gearbox:	McLaren (6 speed, transverse, semi-automatic)
Fuel:	Shell
Wheelbase:	2960mm
Track:	Front: 1803mm
	Rear: 1676mm
Dry weight:	505kg
Raced:	1992

McLaren MP4/8

Engine:	Ford HB Series VII, 3.5 litre, 75° V8
Tyres:	Goodyear
Principal designers:	Neil Oatley, Henri Durand
Chassis:	Carbon-fibre monocoque
Gearbox:	McLaren (6 speed, transverse, semi-automatic)
Fuel:	Shell
Wheelbase:	2845mm
Track:	Front: 1690mm
	Rear: 1615mm
Dry weight:	505kg
Raced:	1993

Williams FW16

Engine:	Renault RS6, 3.5 litre, 67° V10
Tyres:	Goodyear
Principal designer:	Adrian Newey
Chassis:	Carbon-fibre monocoque
Gearbox:	Williams/XTrac (6 speed, transverse, semi-automatic)
Fuel:	Elf
Wheelbase:	2990mm
Track:	Front: 1670mm
	Rear: 1600mm
Dry weight:	515kg
Raced:	1994

Bibliography

Hilton, Christopher, *Ayrton Senna – His full car racing record*
(Patrick Stephens Limited) 1995 Hardback 192 pages ISBN 1 85260 543X

Sutton, Keith, *Ayrton Senna - A Personal Tribute* (Osprey Automotive)
1994 Hardback   214 pages ISBN 1 85532 507 1

Henry, Alan, *Remembering Ayrton Senna* (Weidenfeld and Nicholson Ltd)
1994 Hardback 95 pages ISBN 297 83450 9

Rendall, Ivan, *Ayrton Senna – A Tribute* (Pavilion Books Ltd)
1994 Hardback 174 pages ISBN 1 85793 517 9

Sutton, Keith, *Everlasting Hero – Ayrton Senna* (Sony Magazines Inc)
1994 Hardback 198 pages ISBN 4 7897 0922 1

Galeron, Jean-François, *Magic Senna* (Editions La Sirène)
1994 Hardback 95 pages ISBN 2 84045 095 X

Senna, Ayrton, *Ayrton Senna's Principles of Racing Driving* (Hazelton Publishing)
1991 Hardback 208 pages ISBN 0 1874557 40 3

Noble, A, *They Died Too Young – Ayrton Senna* (Parragon Books)
1995 Hardback 76 pages ISBN 075250 699 4

Hilton, Christopher, *Senna's 50 Poles* (CBS/Sony Publishing)
1990 Paperback 96 pages ISBN 4 7897 0608 7

Bobby, Paolo, *Ayrton Senna Da Silva – A Worldwide Myth*
(Bobby Paolo, Club Ayrton Senna) Paperback 128 pages

Henry, Alan, *Ayrton Senna – Portrait of a Champion* (Hazelton Publishing)
1988 Hardback 94 pages ISBN 0 905138 60

Giaccon, Mauro, *L'ultimo Ayrton* (Giorgio Nada Editore)
1996 Hardback 96 pages ISBN 88 7911 164 7

Koike, Norio, *Ayrton Senna – Official Photobook* (Forme)
1995 Hardback 160 pages ISBN 88 86682 00X

Galisteu, Adriane, *Adriane – My Life With Ayrton* (APA Publishing)
1995 Hardback 96 pages ISBN 0 646 214 209

Hilton, Christopher, *Ayrton Senna – The Hard Edge of Genius* (Corgi Books)
1991 Paperback 282 pages ISBN 0 552 13754 5

Williams, Richard, *The Death of Ayrton Senna* (Bloomsbury Publishing)
1999 Paperback 216 pages ISBN 0 7475 4495 6

D'Alessio, Paolo, *Obrigado Ayrton Simply The Best* (Giorgio Nada Editore)
1995 Hardback 116 pages ISBN 88 7911 141 8

Cavicchi, Carlo & Orsi, Angelo, *Senna Veri* (CL Conti Editore)
1994 Hardback 168 pages

Hawkins, Richard & Hugh Gollner, *Senna – Portrait of A Racing Legend*
(Oxford International Publications Ltd) 1994 Hardback 94 pages ISBN 0 952867 0 9

Mansell, Nigel, *Nigel Mansell – My Autobiography* (Collins Willow)
1995 Hardback 352 pages ISBN 0 00 218947 4

Hilton, Christopher, *Gerhard Berger – The Human Face of Formula 1*
(Patrick Stephens Ltd) 1995 Hardback 288 pages ISBN 1 85260 515 4

Watkins, Sid, *Beyond The Limit* (Macmillan)
2001 Hardback 224 pages ISBN 0 333 901188 6

Nye, Doug, *McLaren – The Grand Prix, Can-Am and Indy Cars*
(Hazelton Publishing) 1988 Hardback 324 pages ISBN 0 905138 54 6

Walker, Murray, *1994 Grand Prix Year* (Hazelton Publishing)
1994 Paperback 144 pages ISBN 1 874557 01 2

Hamilton, Maurice, *Frank Williams* (Macmillan)
1998 Hardback 290 pages ISBN 0 333717163

Tremayne, David, *Echoes of Imola* (Motor Racing Publications)
1996 Hardback 160 pages ISBN 1 899870 05 9

Collings, Timothy, *Schumacher* (Bloomsbury Publishing Plc)
1994 Hardback 200 pages ISBN 0 7475 1965 X

Watkins, Sid, *Life at the Limit* (Macmillan)
1996 Hardback 258 pages ISBN 0 333 65774 8

Mansell, Nigel, *2001 Formula 1 Annual* (European Press Ltd)
2001 Hardback 672 pages ISBN 0 9541368 0 2

Higham, Peter & Jones, Bruce, *World Motor Racing Circuits – A Spectators Guide*
(Andre Deutsch) 1999 Hardback 192 pages ISBN 0233 99619 2

Henry, Alan, *50 Years of World Championship Motor Racing* (Hazelton Publishing)
2000 Hardback 336 pages ISBN 1 874557 78 0

Sturm, Karin, *Ayrton Senna – Goodbye Champion, Farewell Friend*
(Motor Racing Publications) 1994 Hardback 160 Pages ISBN 0 947986 1

Santos, Francisco, *Ayrton Senna* (Libros Cupula)
1994 Paperback 224 pages ISBN 84 3291347 2

Hilton, Christopher, *Ayrton Senna* (Haynes Publishing)
1999 Hardback 304 pages ISBN 1 85960611 3

Hayhoe, David & Holland David, *Grand Prix Data Book 1997*
(Duke Marketing Ltd) 1996 Hardback 567 pages ISBN 0 9529325 0 4

Index

The Life of
SENNA
The biography of Ayrton Senna

TOM RUBYTHON

Tom Rubython is editor-in-chief of *BusinessF1* magazine, the monthly publication for Formula One's business community. He is the founder and former publisher of *Formula 1 Magazine* and ex-editor of *EuroBusiness* magazine. A specialist business writer and well-known Formula One columnist, he led a team of writers and researchers who spent three years investigating the 34 years of the life of Ayrton Senna. The book started out as a series of individual articles and by the time the project reached completion, Rubython and his collaborators Gerald Donaldson, David Tremayne and Caroline Reid were all convinced Senna was the greatest racing driver of all time.

KEITH SUTTON

Keith Sutton began his career photographing motor racing in 1980 but got his first big break when he met Ayrton Senna in 1981. Sutton was the same age as Senna and the two men clicked. He became Senna's first official photographer and unofficial PR man. And it was Senna who invited Sutton to his first Grand Prix in Brazil in 1984. A few years later the two men split up after Sutton formed his own agency called Sutton Motorsport Images. But they remained friends up to Senna's death in 1994. Keith Sutton is now widely regarded as Formula One's top photographer.

GERHARD BERGER

Gerhard Berger started his racing career driving AlfaSuds and rose through the ranks of Formula Ford and Formula Three before joining Formula One in 1984. In 1986, he won his first Grand Prix in Mexico for Benetton. He then drove for Ferrari and McLaren and won eight races. He finished his career with the Benetton team, winning his final race at the German Grand Prix in 1996, retiring at the end of that year. He soon returned to the tracks in a non-driving capacity as BMW's motorsport director before retiring again at the end of 2003.